D0204547

OUR "REG
READERS RAVE

I love *Uncle John's Bathroom Readers*! Never stop!

—Liam T.

I've been a huge fan of *Bathroom Readers* ever since I was a kid.
Just wanted to let you know how much I love them!

—Carrie S.

Do you have a readers' Hall of Fame? I started reading the series after I joined
the Army and I now have 74 *Bathroom Readers* and that has to be a record.
Thank you for all the great books over the years.

—Michael M.

As a big fan of Uncle John's, I look forward to the newest edition every year.

—John S.

One whole bookshelf in my home is dedicated to *Bathroom Readers*, though I
(and now my entire family, including grandchildren) read them EVERYWHERE.

—William M.

I have enjoyed your books for many years,
and have given them as gifts countless times.

—Doug M.

On page iii of your *Old Faithful Bathroom Reader*, Carl S. says that he has 25 of your
books. While this is impressive, it does not match my collection of 75. The knowledge
I gain from reading your books is unbelievable. Thanks for producing these books!

—Steve A.

Love your books. Keep up the good work.

—Michelle S.

I now enjoy going to the restroom, for I know I will get to read one of your books.

—Willie P.

CONTENTS

Because the BRI understands your reading needs, we've
divided the contents by length as well as subject.
Short—a quick read
Medium—2 to 3 pages
Long—for those extended visits, when something a little more involved is required
*Extended—for those leg-numbing experiences

*   *   *

"Truth is like the sun. You can shut it out for a time, but it ain't goin' away."

—Elvis Presley

INTRODUCTION

One score and twelve years ago (translation: the late 1980s), I had an uncanny idea to create a book full of facts and trivia for people—like us—who read in the bathroom. It was supposed to be a one-time shot, but there was something about that 228-page tome that really struck a chord with readers of all ages and backgrounds. So we did another volume, and then another, and another…and here we are, 30 years later, putting the finishing touches on the 32nd annual edition:

Uncle John's Truth, Trivia, and the Pursuit of Factiness Bathroom Reader.

This book is a whole lot bigger than that first one was, but it retains the same tried-and-true ingredients that have led to more than 20 million *Bathroom Readers* being sold: a host of absorbing articles covering a wide array of topics ranging from silly to serious.

People always ask us where we come up with new topics to write about, so here's an interesting story: I was visiting the great city of Boston recently, and decided to call my cousin Jonathan for dinner. When he came into my hotel lobby a few hours later, he had a wide-eyed look on his face and said, "Paul's across the street!" I had no idea what he was talking about, but he said it again, this time pointing toward the door, "Paul's across the street!" I looked out the window and saw a Revolutionary War–era cemetery with a plaque saying Paul Revere was buried there. My first thought: I wonder where America's other Founding Fathers are buried. My second thought: That would make a great article for this year's book. And that's pretty much the essence of *Uncle John's Bathroom Reader*—hundreds of Bostonians walk past that cemetery every day, but we trivia hounds see it…and we want to know more. (By the way, that cemetery is called the Granary, and you can read about it on page 332.) Here's some more of what's in store for you:

- *Origins:* hashtags, infomercials, the MRI, strip malls, and how pizza got to America
- *Speaking of food…* the biology of hot sauce, candy bar trivia, bloody foods, and fast-food chains that died out
- *Speaking of dying…* a website that tells you if someone croaked in your house, "dead" people who showed up at their own funerals, and dares that went very, very wrong
- *Speaking of blunders…* a rogue's gallery of dumb crooks (like the bank robber who stopped to give a TV interview), messy truck spills, gun goofs, and some of the worst business decisions in history

- *Speaking of history...* the story of the Great Seal, Civil War surgery techniques, the real "Grizzly" Adams (and the man who played him on TV)
- *Speaking of pop culture...* *Simpsons* guest stars, ridiculous TLC shows, the demise of Saturday morning cartoons, and bitter sports feuds
- *Speaking of sports...* surfer slang, plays that changed the rules, baseball's only switch-pitcher, and some unfortunate sports nicknames like "Big Donkey" and "Doo Doo"
- *Speaking of doo-doo...* poop-themed toys, the prisoner who refused to poop for a month, and that time Bill Gates left a "present" on the podium. (Don't worry, it's not as gross as it sounds.)

And that's just the tip of the iceberg.

Once again, I have to hand it to the dedicated trivia hounds here at the Bathroom Readers' Institute who work their tails off all year long to bring you these books. Thank you, folks:

Gordon Javna	**Lidija Tomas**	**Bo, Lou, and Ivy,** *B.R.I.T.*
Jay Newman	**Thom Little**	**Jonathan Small**
Brian Boone	**J. Carroll**	**Glenn Cunningham**
John Dollison	**Derek Fairbridge**	**Sue Newman**
Pablo Goldstein	**Megan Boone**	**John Javna**
Kim Griswell	**Maggie Javna**	**Thomas Crapper**

We're what you might call info-nerds. No matter where we are, our radars are constantly tracking the world for new material—whether in an old graveyard or in the day's headlines...like this head-scratcher that just appeared on my screen: "Feral Pig Steals Beer, Gets Drunk and Starts Fight With a Cow." When I see something like that, it makes me happy to be alive.

And because you've made it this far into the introduction, you're probably an info-nerd as well. Wear the badge proudly! Whether you've been a *Bathroom Reader* fan for years, or you're just now discovering us, we're honored to have you along for the ride. So strap yourself in, because this behemoth of a book is going to move you.

As always, go with the Flow...

—Uncle John and the BRI staff

Hi, Mom!

YOU'RE MY INSPIRATION

*It's always interesting to find out where the architects of pop
culture get their ideas. Some of these may surprise you.*

CAESAR THE APE: Andy Serkis's motion-capture character from the *Planet of the Apes* prequels goes from wise leader to vengeful revolutionary. To portray the leader, Serkis (who also played Gollum and King Kong) asked himself, "Who is an example of a really intelligent, powerful but egalitarian leader?" His answer: Nelson Mandela. When it came time for him to portray the vengeful Caesar, Serkis took inspiration from Clint Eastwood's character in *The Outlaw Josey Wales*.

LANA DEL REY: When the soulful singer-songwriter ("Video Games," "Summertime Sadness") was 11 years old, "I saw Kurt Cobain singing 'Heart-Shaped Box' on MTV and it really stopped me dead in my tracks. I thought he was the most beautiful person I had ever seen. Even at a young age, I really related to his sadness." The Nirvana front man remains an influence on Del Ray, especially "in terms of not wanting to compromise lyrically or sonically."

DONALD DUCK: It's obvious where his surname came from (he's a duck), but what about "Donald"? The most likely theory: When Walt Disney was creating Mickey's best friend in 1932, he read about Donald Bradman in the papers. The Australian cricketing legend, while on a North American goodwill tour in 1932, scored what's called a duck (similar to a strikeout in baseball). A popular editorial cartoon featured a somewhat familiar-looking duck wearing a shirt that says "Donald's Duck." Not long after, Disney's Donald Duck debuted.

"JUST DO IT": In 1988 an ad man named Dan Wieden read about the 1977 execution of convicted murderer Gary Gilmore, whose last words were "Let's do it." Wieden really liked the directness of the statement and pitched "Just Do It" to Phil Knight, whose Nike shoe company was struggling. Knight was apprehensive, in part because of the grisly inspiration. According to Wieden, "I said, 'Just trust me on this one.' So they trusted me and it went big pretty quickly."

CHUCKIE FINSTER: In the 1990s Nickelodeon cartoon *Rugrats,* the character of Chuckie was based in part on the man who wrote the show's music, Mark Mothersbaugh (who fronted Devo and later scored such films as *The Royal Tenenbaums, The Lego Movie,* and *Thor: Ragnarok*). "We both had thick glasses," said Mothersbaugh. "We're both nearsighted. And I had pretty wild hair back then. I didn't have kids yet, so it still had color in it."

F. Scott Fitzgerald was the first writer to use the word "wicked" to mean "wonderful."

I SHOULD BE SOUVLAKI

If you're going to go to the trouble of opening an eatery, why not give it a funny name, like these real restaurants, bars, and cafés?

Lettuce Souprise You

What the Pho

Pho Ever Yum

UnPhoGettable

Wasabi Lobby

Like No Udder Vegan Ice Cream

Lebaneser Scrooge

Bun of Brothers

Planet of the Grapes

I Should Be Souvlaki

Abra Kebabra

Basic Kneads Pizza

Party Fowl

Lox Stock & Bagels

Life of Pie

Brew'd Awakening

Eggspectation

My Big Fat Greek Restaurant

Between Buns

The Crabby Oyster

Chez What?

Poo Ping Palace

The Bar F Saloon

Miso Hapi

The Wurst Shop in Dickinson

Club Foot

Jonathan Livingston Seafood

Lawrence of Oregano

A Salt & Battery Fish and Chips

It's About Thyme

Debbie Does Donuts

Seoul Man

The Elbow Room

What Ales You

Barca Lounge

Nacho Daddy

Nacho Mama's

Aesop's Tables

Half Fast Subs

Cluck U

Sacred Chow

Taco Bill

Lard Have Mercy

Nincomsoup

Turnip the Beet

Vincent Van Doughnut

The Chocolate Log

Frying Nemo

New Cod on the Block

Wish You Were Beer

Lord of the Fries

Lord of the Wings

Just Falafs

Fleetwood Macchiato

The Middle Feast

Massive Wieners

Frank & Stein (hot dogs and beer)

Bread Zeppelin

Fishcotheque

Pita Pan

Baguettaboutit

Burgatory

The Dairy Godmother

Squat and Gobble Cafe

Open Sesame

Moon Wok

Drink Wisconsinbly Pub

Bean Me Up

Pour Judgment

I Dream of Weenie

Pastabilities

Kale Me Crazy

Only country where both lions and tigers still live in the wild: India.

OBSCURE GEOGRAPHY

You can probably point out a canyon (a deep gorge, often with a river running through it) or a peninsula (land surrounded by water on all sides but one). But who knew that every kind of waterway, bunch of trees, or open field had its own definition? Here are some esoteric geographical features that you can use to annoy family and friends. (You're welcome.)

Backwater. A section of river where the water is seemingly still, or where there's almost no current.

Butte. A medium-height hill with very steep sides and a flat top, that stands on its own, meaning it's not part of another series of hills.

Stack. Found along ocean coasts, stacks are steep columns of vertical rock formed by waves knocking into them and eroding them over the centuries.

Arroyo. Also known as a dry gulch, it's a stream-formed gully located in a desert area where water flows through for only part of the year.

Steppe. A large, sweeping grassland free of trees (except for ones by a river or lake).

Guyot. Also called a tablemount, a guyot is an isolated, underwater hill with a flat top that ascends to no more than 660 feet below the surface of the water.

Interfluve. A long, narrow, elevated piece of land (like a plateau) that develops between two parallel rivers or streams.

Palisades. Tall, strong, steep cliffs made of basalt.

Spur. The term for a flat ridge that juts out of the side of a mountain or hill.

Shoal. Also called a sandbar or sandbank, a shoal is a small hill of sand in that, at high tide, becomes submerged in a body of water, creating a shallows.

Syrt. A highland or plateau—flat land at a higher elevation than the surrounding area—split in two by water erosion, most commonly found in Russia and Central Asia.

Taiga. The thick forest of conifers (spruce, fir, and pine) with low levels of rainfall, found just south of Arctic regions.

Chaparral. A small forest, or a thicket of thorny shrubs or small trees that's so dense you can't walk through it.

Kettle. A sediment-filled pool of water left behind in a hollow as floodwaters drain, or a glacier melts or moves away.

Piedmont. The hilly area at the base of a mountain. Also known as foothills.

Seamount. A submerged volcano or mountain that rises from the ocean floor, but whose summit is below the water surface.

The fidget spinner was invented in 1993...but didn't catch on until 2017.

NAME THAT SPORT

The origins of the names of baseball, basketball, and football are pretty obvious…but what about some of the less obvious sports?

TENNIS As early as the 12th century, the French played a game called *tenez*, which means "take" or "receive." But linguists say that in the colloquial French of the time, the word meant something more like "be aware" or "look alive"…which is what you might want to hear if a small ball was barreling toward your head. Indeed, players of tenez would shout out that very word at the beginning of a round when serving. It made its way into English (as te'netz) around the year 1400 or so. But the game of tennis wouldn't evolve into something close to the game we know today until the late 1500s, which is when French and English players started using nets and racquets. Before that, tenez (or te'netz) was played with just a ball and the players' hands.

POLO Games similar to polo—a simple stick-and-ball game, made more exciting and dangerous with the addition of having to do it on horseback—date back hundreds of years in South Asia. It was so entrenched in Asian culture that in the Tibetan Balti language, *pulu* means "ball." That's what players in India called the sport in the late 19th century when British colonists got a taste for it (and brought it back to England), altering the spelling from pulu to polo.

GOLF The first time anybody wrote down the word "golf" was in 1457 when Scottish ruler King James II banned "ye golf." Reason: the sport was so popular that soldiers were skipping out on their compulsory archery practice to play it. The word referred to an early form of the sport, not played on individual holes on a plot of land set aside for the purpose, but more of a target-based, short-range game played in fields or in neighborhoods. As the sport caught on in Scotland (despite royal edicts from James II and his successors), it was spelled several ways, including "goff," "gowf," "goif," "gowfe," "golve," and, especially, "gouff." Whatever its spelling, historians now believe it comes from the Scottish Gaelic word *golf*, which means "to strike." (Makes sense.)

HOCKEY Ice hockey is a sport most associated with Canada, but the game we call field hockey is probably much older, dating back to the early 1500s (at least) in Ireland, where documents refer to a pastime played with a ball and "hockie stickes." What's a hockie sticke? A stick with a hook or a curve at the end, like a shepherd's staff; the word *hockie* comes from the Old French word *hoc*, which means "hook."

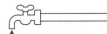

Jerry Lewis never wore the same pair of socks twice.

OOPS!

Everyone makes outrageous blunders. So go ahead and feel superior for a few minutes.

FORGET THE HOLE THING

In 2018 an installation at a Portuguese art gallery called "Descent Into Limbo" created the illusion of a black circle painted onto a white floor. But it was an actual hole—eight feet in diameter and eight feet deep. The artist, Anish Kapoor, set up the lighting so there were no shadows, making it really look like a black circle painted onto a floor. Despite several signs warning patrons not to approach the hole, one of them did and fell in, and had to be hospitalized.

GONE TO POT

Someone donated a cooler to a Goodwill store in Monroe, Washington, in 2017. Whoever it was obviously didn't check its contents beforehand. When Goodwill workers opened it, there were five bags of marijuana stashed inside, totaling 3.75 pounds. It's illegal to own more than one ounce of cannabis in Washington, and this stash had a street value of several thousand dollars. Debbie Willis of the Monroe Police Department said that they were unable to track down the mysterious benefactor. "There are many people on social media claiming it's theirs, but we have yet to have one walk through the door."

OH, NUTS!

In September 2018, an Ohio University freshman named Zoey Oxley was writing one of the first papers of her college career. She typed her own name in the header but couldn't remember the instructor's name, so she put "Professor whats his nuts" as a placeholder. "I made a mental note to change it," Oxley later told reporters. But she forgot… until shortly after she uploaded the paper—which could not be un-uploaded. And then she sent a frantic email to John Hendel (aka Professor whats his nuts) informing him that she got his name wrong and begging him not to hold it against her. The next day, after Hendel read the paper, he wrote back to her: "Well, the university would likely want me to tell you about professionalism and to make sure you proofread your paper before you submit it." But he decided not to hold it against her because, as he told her, "It's funny."

> **She put "Professor whats his nuts" as a placeholder.**

GRAND THEFT OOPS

In 2018 a woman rented a Nissan Something-or-other (she had no idea what model it was) and began her vacation in Cornwall, Ontario. Her first stop: a Walmart to pick up some groceries. When she finished shopping, she got back into the black Something-or-other and drove away (the key fob had been left in the car). And boy, did she have some nasty words for the rental company when she returned the car two weeks later. For one thing, the car was dirty. And for another, someone had left a set of golf clubs in the trunk. A bewildered clerk went out to look at the car and then informed the lady, "That's not our car." They'd rented her a Sentra; this was an Infiniti. Happy ending: the owner of the Infiniti, who'd reported it stolen from the Walmart parking lot, got back his car…and his golf clubs.

A BRIDGE TOO FAR

Turkish people take their historic stone bridges very seriously. So when a particularly treasured arch footbridge near the mountain village of Arslanca went missing in 2018, angry villagers launched an investigation, speculating that archaeological treasure hunters had dismantled the 300-year-old bridge rock by rock and stolen it. Some villagers said they'd seen the bridge as recently as a week before it was reported missing (it was located outside of town). Others weren't so sure, but they were all angry…until the results of the investigation came in. The police concluded that "the bridge was destroyed by a flood three months ago." No one had even noticed.

PART MAN, PART SPOON

One night in 2017, a 25-year-old Chinese man, identified in news reports as Zhang, made a drunken bet that he could tie a string to a metal spoon, swallow the spoon, and then retrieve it. The first two parts of the bet went fine, the third part—the retrieval—not so fine. The string came off and the spoon remained in Zhang's esophagus. But it didn't really hurt, and he could still eat, so he didn't go to the doctor and went on with his life. A year later, Zhang got punched in the chest (it's unclear why), and then felt a stabbing pain so intense that he immediately went to the hospital. An X-ray and endoscopy revealed the eight-inch spoon was still there, and that his esophagus was infected. During a two-hour surgery, doctors got the spoon out the same way it went in, through his mouth. Zhang was expected to make a full recovery.

THE OLD MAN AND THE SWAMP

If you're a duck hunter, it's a good idea to bring along a dog that can retrieve the duck you just shot. Otherwise, you have to go get it yourself. That's the predicament faced by a 79-year-old hunter from New Hampshire (name not released). His dead duck landed in a swamp, so the man trudged through the mud to get the duck…and before he knew it, he was neck-deep and couldn't move. That's where he spent the next 33 hours until game wardens finally found him. The man was suffering from hypothermia but was otherwise okay.

"THE HIKING SUCKS"

Proving you can't please everybody, here are some one-star Yelp reviews of some of America's most treasured national parks and monuments.

Hawai'i Volcanoes National Park: "Paid $20 to get in. Didn't even get to touch lava."

Crater Lake: "Ok yes the water is very blue. And then also the water is quite blue, not to mention that the water is very blue. Other than that, mosquitoes ate the whole family alive, we left after one hour."

Haleakala: "Do yourself a favor and just google 'pretty sunrise' and save yourself the disappointment."

Yellowstone: "If you've seen one geyser, you've seen them all."

Badlands: "I didn't see what the big deal was. We drove a million years to see some semi impressive rock formations? And there were RATTLESNAKES everywhere? Dumb. You lose cell service because you're in Nowhere USA. The only thing bad about these lands is entire experience. Waste of time. Thank god I was drunk in the backseat for the majority of the trip."

Yosemite: "How about you cut down the surrounding burned trees and make another parking lot or five."

Zion: "Picture a bunch of fraternity and sorority folks at Six Flags or Disney World and you will get an idea of what Zion is truly like in the summer."

Big Bend: "I visited last year around Labor Day weekend. I thought there'd be lot of visitors and tourists but I was wrong. The park was empty. I found it lonely."

Grand Canyon: "Every 500 feet a new vantage point of the same thing: a really big hole in the ground."

Petrified Forest: "Literally more petrified wood at the gift shop than in this entire 'forest.' "

Sequoia: "There are bugs and stuff, and they will bite you on your face."

Denali: "DON'T TAKE THE BUS… drive the 19 miles in with your car. You'll see just as much and you don't have to listen to stupid tourists run their mouths all day."

Death Valley: "This is the ugliest place I've ever seen."

Devil's Tower: "Just a large elevated rock in the middle of nowhere."

Carlsbad Caverns: "A walk along dimly lit paths with rocks and pits and pools illuminated BFD. If you have never been inside a cave or seen a picture of a cave this might interest you, otherwise don't waste your time, energy nor money."

Joshua Tree: "Ugly and the hiking sucks."

Itchy fact: It would take 1.1 million mosquitoes to drink all of a full-grown adult's blood.

SUPERHERO FIRSTS

It's a bird…it's a plane…it's…a page of superhero trivia!

★ **FIRST FEMALE SUPERHERO**

It wasn't Wonder Woman. She and her "lasso of truth" debuted in an October 1941
issue of *All Star Comics*. But more than a year earlier, in February 1940, readers
of *Jungle Comics* were introduced to a superhero named Fantomah—an immortal
woman from ancient Egypt who fought evil in the present day when she turned into
a skull-faced monster. After that appearance, the character was never seen again.

★ **FIRST SUPERHERO MOVIE**

While numerous film serials that centered on superheroes like Mandrake the
Magician, Batman, Captain America, and Captain Marvel played in movie
theaters in the 1940s, the first full-length film in the genre was 1951's *Superman
and the Mole Men*. It also happened to be the pilot for the 1952–58 TV series
Adventures of Superman.

★ **FIRST SUPERHERO KILLED IN THE LINE OF DUTY**

The January 1940 publication *Pep Comics* #1 unveiled a character named the
Comet, the alter ego of scientist John Dickering, who discovers a lighter-than-air
gas that, when injected, allows him to leap into the stratosphere and melt things
with his eyes. Then in *Pep Comics* #17…he croaks.

★ **FIRST SUPERHERO WEDDING**

After bumming around the fringes of DC Comics titles for years, underwater
warrior Aquaman did something truly remarkable in *Aquaman* #18 in 1964: He got
married. The king of Atlantis made a queen out of his lady love, Mera, which was
the first time superheroes got hitched on the page.

★ **FIRST SUPERHERO MOVIE TO WIN AN OSCAR**

At the 1990 Academy Awards, *Batman* took home the Oscar for Best Art
Direction. Nineteen years later, Heath Ledger became the first actor to win an
Oscar for playing a comic book villain, portraying the Joker in *The Dark Knight*.
(It was presented posthumously, because Ledger died of a drug overdose in 2008,
shortly after completing his work on *The Dark Knight*, and a year before the
Oscar was awarded.)

Goats that listen to Mariah Carey's "All I Want for Christmas Is You" produce more milk.

LOGO ORIGINS

*You see these corporate logos everywhere, but did you ever
wonder how they came to be? Wonder no more.*

Company: Audi

Logo: Four interlocking rings

Meaning: The company—and its logo—are based on carmakers that had been
around since the early 20th century. In 1932 two German car companies, DKW
and Wanderer, merged with two others, Horch and Audi, to form the Auto Union.
Both Horch and Audi were founded by engineer August Horch. ("Audi" is the Latin
equivalent of the word *horch*, which is German for "listen.") The rings in Audi's logo
represent those four car companies.

Company: Mercedes-Benz

Logo: A three-pointed star, with its points touching the inner rim of a circle

Meaning: Carmaker Gottlieb Daimler's company, Daimler-Motoren-Gesellschaft,
released a model called the Mercedes in 1901. In 1926 DMG merged with Karl Benz's
company to create Daimler-Benz, later Mercedes-Benz. The three points of the star
represent the three things Daimler wanted to create machines to traverse: land, water,
and air.

Company: Arby's

Logo: A cowboy hat

Meaning: When Arby's opened in the early 1960s, Westerns were all the rage on
TV and at movie theaters. And what do we associate with cowpokes? Beef cattle.
So when Arby's opened in 1964, it marketed its hamburger alternative—roast beef
sandwiches—with a giant cowboy hat atop all its restaurants. The extra-tall hat
allowed room for a lot of copy, and in big letters the signs proclaimed, "Arby's Roast
Beef Sandwich is Delicious." In 1975 the logo was reduced to a simple outline of a
cowboy hat, and all the text was dropped except for "Arby's."

Company: Starbucks

Logo: A mermaid (from the neck up)

Meaning: When Starbucks Coffee Tea and Spices opened in Seattle in 1971, the
founders named the company after a character from the novel *Moby-Dick* and wanted
something associated with the sea for its logo. They found a 16th-century wood
carving of a two-tailed mermaid, and hired graphic designer Terry Heckler to build
on that. His design was a crowned, naked mermaid...still with the two tails. In 1987,

The phrase "kid gloves" comes from boxing gloves made from goat, or "kid," leather.

after Starbucks was acquired by Howard Schultz and began a national expansion, the decision was made to lose the mermaid's lower half (and her navel), cut out most of the tail (the rest is off to the sides and looks like arms now), and to focus on her smiling face.

Company: Microsoft

Logo: A square made up of four other squares, each a different color: red, green, yellow, and blue

Meaning: Microsoft's main competitor, Apple, had an obvious logo, thanks to its name (it's an apple). So Microsoft had to be a bit more clever. The company assigned a different color to the branding of each of its main four divisions, and those are represented in the corporate logo. The blue is for its flagship Windows operating system, the red is for its Office suite of productivity software, the green is for its Xbox video game sector, and the yellow is for its hardware line of Surface tablets.

Company: NBC

Logo: A peacock with rainbow-colored wings

Meaning: NBC, once a radio network and then a black-and-white television broadcaster, started airing color programs in 1954 and needed a logo that would strikingly announce that fact. Inspired by the phrase "proud as a peacock" (because they were proud of the color changeover), the marketing department chose the image of a peacock for their logo, and made its wings six different colors. Why six? That's how many divisions NBC had at the time.

* * *

A RANDOM BIT OF FACTINESS

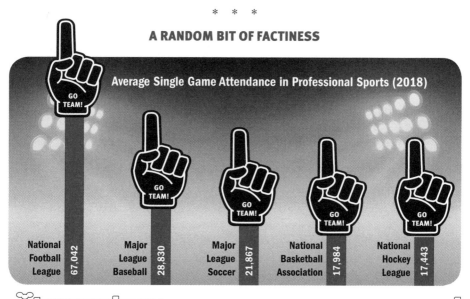

Average Single Game Attendance in Professional Sports (2018)

National Football League	Major League Baseball	Major League Soccer	National Basketball Association	National Hockey League
67,042	28,830	21,867	17,984	17,443

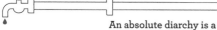

An absolute diarchy is a country ruled by two people.
Example: Swaziland, which is ruled by the king and his mother.

GHOST SHIPS

We're used to thinking of "ghost ships"—ships adrift on the high seas—as relics of the distant past. But every once in a while, ships are still found adrift, sometimes with no clue as to what happened to their crews.

THE *RYOU-UN MARU*

Background: This 164-foot-long Japanese fishing vessel was tied up at its dock in Aomori Prefecture when the most powerful earthquake ever recorded in Japan struck off its eastern coast in March 2011. The earthquake was followed by a giant tsunami, which swept the unoccupied *Ryou-Un Maru* from its mooring and carried it far out to sea.

Ghost Ship: Japanese authorities and the owner of the *Ryou-Un Maru* assumed that the ship sank, as did countless others carried off by the tsunami. But a year later the ship was spotted drifting more than 4,700 miles away off the coast of British Columbia. The owner of a Canadian fishing vessel tried to tow the ship back to port in order to claim it as salvage, but the attempt failed. Because the ship was unlit at night and her fuel tanks were filled with diesel fuel, it was deemed a navigation hazard and a potential ecological hazard if it ran aground. So when it drifted into the Gulf of Alaska that April, the U.S. Coast Guard fired on it and sank it. (They also filmed the sinking, and you can watch it on YouTube.)

THE *BAYCHIMO*

Background: In October 1931, this 230-foot Hudson's Bay Company cargo steamer got trapped in the sea ice near Barrow, on the northern coast of Alaska. A skeleton crew set up camp on the ice and planned to remain with the ship through the winter, but when a powerful blizzard freed the ship from the ice and blew it out to sea, it was abandoned to its fate.

Ghost Ship: Few people thought the ship would survive the winter without being crushed by the ice, but it did, beginning a pattern of floating free in the summer months, and getting trapped in the ice again in winter months, that lasted nearly 40 years. The last person to board the ship was apparently a sea captain named Hugh Polson, who tried to salvage it in 1939. That attempt failed, and the ship continued to drift for another 30 years. The last confirmed sighting of the *Baychimo* was in 1969, stuck in the ice between Point Barrow and Icy Cape in the Chukchi Sea. What happened to the ship after that—and whether it is still afloat—is unknown.

THE *LYUBOV ORLOVA*

Background: In January 2013, this derelict, 295-foot-long Russian cruise ship was being towed from St. John's, Newfoundland, to a wrecking yard in the Dominican Republic. But the towline broke, leaving the *Lyubov Orlova* adrift in the North Atlantic off the Newfoundland coast. Because the ship posed a threat to offshore oil installations in the area, the Canadian government arranged for the ship to be towed away. The weather did not cooperate. Stormy seas, including 20-foot waves and 35-knot winds, led the towing ship to cut the *Lyubov Orlova* loose rather than risk further danger by towing it all the way back to a Canadian port. By then, the ship was in international waters, which made it the owner's responsibility, not the Canadian government's, which washed its hands of the matter. "It is very unlikely that the vessel will re-enter waters under Canadian jurisdiction," the government said in a statement.

The abandoned cruise ship drifted eastward across the Atlantic for two months.

Ghost Ship: The abandoned cruise ship drifted eastward across the Atlantic for two months. As it moved closer to the UK and Ireland, it was the subject of lurid tabloid stories speculating that it was filled with thousands of "cannibalistic rats" with nothing to eat but each other, and who would wreak havoc on land wherever the ship ran aground. Then in late February 2013, the ship's emergency radio beacons, or EPIRBs, activated when the ship was 700 miles off the Irish coast. The EPIRBs are designed to activate when they are immersed in water, such as when a ship is sinking. This, and the lack of any further sightings of the ship since then, led international authorities to conclude that the *Lyubov Orlova* had finally sunk.

THE *ITALIA*

Background: Who says a ghost ship can't be an *airship*? The *Italia* was a dirigible similar in appearance to the Goodyear Blimp. In 1928 it embarked on a mission to visit the North Pole by air. The expedition ran into trouble on the morning of May 25, 1928, when it lost altitude and crashed onto the ice with such force that much of the gondola and crew cabin broke off. With this weight removed, the airship was suddenly much lighter, and as it rose into the air, it began drifting away with six members of the crew still aboard.

Ghost Ship: Thinking fast, the crew started tossing essential equipment and supplies out of the airship, in the process giving the crewmembers on the ice a better chance of surviving until help arrived days or weeks later. (The survivors were spotted by a search plane on June 20 and rescued.) But this may have doomed the airborne crew's

Lime juice can cause chemical burns if it reacts with sunlight on your skin.

chances of survival, because tossing out all those supplies made the *Italia* hundreds of pounds lighter, causing it to rise even higher in the sky—too high to jump from the crippled airship to safety below. The *Italia* slowly drifted away; how far and for how long it drifted and where it finally landed is unknown; it and the six crewmembers still aboard were never seen again.

THE *MV JOYITA*

Background: Dubbed the "*Mary Celeste* of the South Pacific," the MV *Joyita* was a 69-foot charter cabin cruiser that departed Apia, Samoa, at 5:00 a.m. on October 3, 1955, with 25 passengers and crew, bound for the Tokelau Islands, some 320 miles to the north. The trip was supposed to take between 41 and 48 hours, but the *Jovita* never arrived.

Ghost Ship: Five weeks later, the ship was found abandoned and adrift, 600 miles west of its intended course; the passengers and crew were nowhere to be seen. At the time of its discovery, the *Jovita* was flooded and listing heavily to the port (left) side. The ship's clocks, which ran off the ship's electrical power, were all stopped at 10:25 p.m. The interior lights were switched to the on position, as were the running and navigation lights, which are used at night. The life rafts were missing, and the ship's log and other items that would be useful in life rafts were not on the ship. This evidence led investigators to suspect that the ship began taking on water late one night, sparking a panic that caused the passengers and crew to take to the life rafts sooner than was necessary…or wise. If the emergency had happened during daylight hours, cooler heads might have prevailed, and the passengers and crew might have stayed with the ship and been rescued. But that's not what happened. An extensive search that covered 100,000 square miles of open water (conducted in the days after the *Jovita* went missing) yielded nothing. No trace of the missing passengers and crew has ever been found.

* * *

FIVE FAMOUS FOODIES AND THE FOODS THEY HATE
1. Guy Fieri: eggs
2. Ina Garten: cilantro
3. Rachael Ray: store-bought mayonnaise
4. Ree Drummond: bananas
5. Giada De Laurentiis: coconut

If you peel off a Post-It from the side, it won't curl like when you pull from the bottom.

HOORAY FOR HARRY!

It's time we heard what the Harrys have to say.

"It is amazing what you can accomplish if you don't care who gets the credit."
—Harry S. Truman

"When in doubt, do something."
—Harry Chapin

"It's something my mother believed in: If you are in a position of privilege, if you can put your name to something that you genuinely believe in, you can smash any stigma you want, and you can encourage anybody to do anything."
—Prince Harry

"I'm sure there are more people capable than I, better looking than me, better educated than me, smarter than me. But I've got the job."
—Sen. Harry Reid

"A real girl isn't perfect. A perfect girl isn't real."
—Harry Styles

"I DON'T MIND IF MY SKULL ENDS UP ON A SHELF AS LONG AS IT'S GOT MY NAME ON IT."
—Debbie Harry

"The two are unrelated. I'm not into turtles or space stuff."
—Harry Connick Jr., on his album *Star Turtle*

"Neckties satisfy modern man's desire to dress in art."
—Harry Anderson

"The greatest escape I ever made was when I left Appleton, Wisconsin."
—Harry Houdini

YOU STOLE *WHAT?*

You might be able to steal someone's heart, or a glance, or a base—but could you steal a vineyard? Here are some odd things that people have taken without asking.

TOED AWAY

Joshua Williams, 28, of Upper Hunt, New Zealand, attended the traveling Body Worlds exhibition in Auckland in May 2018. As he was viewing the various corpses and dissected body parts (preserved through a process called plastination), a sudden urge came over him, and before he knew it, he'd stolen two toes from an unguarded foot. Not replicas—actual *human toes*. Later, Williams had another urge: he posted a photo of his ill-gotten gains on Instagram, along with the caption: "I stole a toe from an uncovered display lol." The cops didn't lol. They arrested Williams, who apologized profusely. He claimed he didn't realize the toes were worth thousands of dollars, and he was mortified to be facing a seven-year prison term for theft and "interfering with a dead body." But Judge Bill Hastings took pity on him. "Excuse the pun," he said, "but you have been toe-tally overcharged." A conviction, said Judge Hastings, would leave Williams with the reputation of a "grave-robber with a shovel" for the rest of his life. He let the toe thief go.

HAMMER TIME

Police in Healdsburg, California, are on the lookout for a big ball-peen hammer. How big? It's 21 feet long and weighs 800 pounds. Made out of steel and redwood, the enormous tool had spent the previous year as an art installation on the lawn of a community center, until it went missing in October 2018. The artist, Doug Unkrey, offered a $1,000 reward for the hammer's return. He figures that it took at least eight people and a flatbed truck to steal it, but he doesn't understand the motive: "Why would you take this thing? Where are you going to put it?"

AMBULANCE CHASERS

In 2018 a 37-year-old Oregon woman named Christy Lynn Woods, who has a "lengthy and colorful rap sheet," was walking past a Roseburg apartment building where paramedics were trying to revive an unconscious woman. But Woods was more interested in their ambulance; it was unlocked, and the keys were in the ignition. So she jumped in and sped away. Then she led cops on a 30-mile chase over city streets and the interstate highway. The joy ride nearly turned deadly when—while traveling at 85 miles per hour with sirens blaring—Woods rear-ended a police car that was trying to divert traffic. She managed to keep going (the officer maintained control of his car and was unhurt), but a few minutes later, spike strips slashed all four of the ambulance's tires. Woods pulled into a gas station and gave up. Then she tried to play nice. "I didn't try to hurt anyone," she claimed from the back of a squad car. Then she blamed the paramedics: "Why did they leave it unlocked?" According to the *Daily Mail,* it was the 39th time Woods had been arrested since 2011, but this time she hit the jackpot, being charged with "first-degree attempted assault, second-degree assault, unauthorized use of a motor vehicle, attempting to elude police in a vehicle, failure to perform the duties of a driver, two counts of first-degree criminal mischief, reckless endangering, reckless driving, interfering with a medical services provider, and driving while suspended." It's a good bet Woods won't be going on any more joy rides for a long time.

STOLEN COLON

Want to make a thousand bucks? That's the reward being offered for a 10-foot-long inflatable colon that went missing from the back of a pickup truck at the University of Kansas in October 2018. The replica human colon, which weighs 150 pounds and is valued at more than $4,000, is part of the Cancer Coalition's "Get Your Rear in Gear" campaign, and they really want it back.

THE GRAPES OF WRATH

In October 2018, a vineyard went missing from a hillside in southern Germany. Not the vines, just the grapes—but *all* of the grapes. The sophisticated thieves made away with more than 3,500 pounds of grapes that were going to be made into Riesling wine. According to BBC News, local vintners blame rival winemakers because the thieves "unerringly select the choicest grapes, steal them just as they ripen, and have access to specialized harvesting equipment." The BBC also pointed out that this vineyard wasn't on a remote hillside; it's right next to a busy supermarket near the village of Deidesheim, and the theft occurred on a weekday afternoon.

THE GRATED CHEESE ROBBERY

A tractor-trailer carrying 41,000 pounds of parmesan cheese went missing from Marshfield, Wisconsin, in 2016. That was one of three incidents that year in which $90,000 worth of Wisconsin cheese was stolen. In another incident, a truck driver left a trailer full of cheddar in a supposedly secure lot in the Milwaukee suburb of Oak Creek (to get his truck serviced). When he returned a few hours later, the trailer and its 20,000-pound $46,000 payload were gone. Who was behind these robberies? As of last report, authorities have yet to apprehend anyone, and they weren't even sure of the thieves' end game. It's not like you can just sell giant blocks of cheese door to door.

Update: Two of the cheesy trailers were recovered a few weeks later—one turned up at a grocery store, the other in a warehouse (both shipments had to be thrown out). But the location of the third truck of cheese—and the identity of the Wisconsin cheese pirates—remains a mystery. (You could call it a…cold queso.)

Brazil is home to the world's largest cashew tree—it sprawls over 80,000 square feet of land.

I DARE YOU!

We've all felt the overwhelming call to do something silly or stupid because a friend or older sibling dared us to. These people did…and paid a terrible price.

DON'T GET WITH *THE PROGRAM*

In 1993 the James Caan college football drama *The Program* hit movie theaters. It featured a lot of scenes of older players hazing younger ones, including a sequence where players lay down on the dividing line in the middle of a road while cars zoom past them on either side. Not long after the film came out, 24-year-old Marco Birkhimer decided he wanted to try the stunt…because a friend dared him to do it. (Both men had been drinking heavily.) So Birkhimer took a rest in the middle of Route 206 in Bordentown, New Jersey. He was struck by two cars and died instantly.

FORE!

While many rock musicians like to smash up hotel rooms, Ed Sheeran decided to smash up fellow superstar Justin Bieber. "We'd been out to a dive bar. He just drank water and I got hammered. Then we went to a golf course, and he lay on the floor and put a golf ball in his mouth and told me to hit it out of his mouth," Sheeran told the *Guardian.* Sheeran accepted the challenge. Then he heard a sickening "dull thud" sound. He'd missed the ball, and had instead "cracked Justin Bieber right in the cheek with a golf club."

SLUG BUG

One day in 2010, 19-year-old Sam Ballard was hanging out on the patio outside his home in Sydney, Australia, drinking wine with some fellow rugby players. Then Ballard saw a slug crawling on the ground, and jokingly wondered if he should eat it. His friends enthusiastically dared him to do it, so Ballard popped it into his mouth, and it slithered down his throat. Some time later, Ballard complained of weakness and severe leg pain. His mother, Katie, thought it could be multiple sclerosis, because her husband had that condition. Then Ballard mentioned the slug he'd consumed. That *was* the source of the pain and weakness. Doctors diagnosed him with rat lungworm disease. Some slugs eat the feces of rats or frogs, which contain a parasitic worm. That infects the slug, and Ballard ate one such infected slug. Soon after his diagnosis, he fell into a coma that lasted for more than a year, and then woke up paralyzed and requiring a feeding tube and 24-hour care. After eight years of living like that, Ballard died in 2018.

When T. S. Eliot worked for a publishing house, he rejected George Orwell's *Animal Farm.*

POWERFULLY STUPID

In 2010, 18-year-old New Hampshire high-schooler Kyle DuBois finished his project in his industrial education class and had some time to kill, so he decided to mess around with some of the classroom's electrical equipment. Someone—it's unclear exactly who—dared DuBois to attach some wired alligator clamps to his own nipples. The incentive: one of his pals said he'd give him…a can of Mountain Dew. DuBois accepted the challenge (hey, a can of soda was on the line), attached the clamps, and turned on the battery they were attached to. It delivered a strong jolt of electricity, sending DuBois into cardiac arrest. An ambulance took him to a local hospital, where he was treated for severe burns and respiratory failure. (His family sued the teacher for negligence. No word on the outcome.)

A TIP FROM UNCLE JOHN

If you ever find yourself stranded in the middle of the ocean, treading water, you can survive (or at least not die right away) by using a technique called "downproofing." 1. Take off your pants and tie the legs together in a tight knot. 2. Lift the pants by the waistband above your head and whip them through the air to "inflate" them. 3. Stick your head through the knot and keep the waistband underwater. The whole thing will act as a makeshift flotation device.

WHAT FUN!

A bunch of guys in their 20s were hanging around a playground in the Niederviehbach area of southern Germany in 2012, when somebody challenged somebody else (names not included in news reports) to a dare. The young man agreed to let his friends use packing tape to secure him to a push-style merry-go-round (also called a roundabout), and then spin him around as fast as they could. They couldn't get him going around fast enough to their liking, so they attached a car to the merry-go-round and stepped on the gas. That sent the device spinning at a tremendous speed, so fast that the man broke loose from the playground equipment and flew into the air. He was pronounced dead at the scene due to severe head injuries.

* * *

WHAT THE DUCK?

At some point in Donald Duck's long history, Disney animators worked out an extensive family tree for the character. Among Donald's relatives: his sister Delia (mother of Huey, Dewey, and Louie), Gladstone Gander, Abner "Whitewater" Duck, Gus Goose, Downy O'Drake (Scrooge McDuck's father), Fanny Coot, Molly Mallard, "Dirty" Dingus McDuck, Gretchen Grebe, and Gertrude Gadwall.

If you ever see a face in an inanimate object, that's called *pareidolia*.

ANIMALS UNDER THE INFLUENCE

Drugs—they're not just for people anymore.

STONED SHEEP

Nellie Budd had a farm, and on that farm she had some sheep, and those sheep got really high one day in 2014 after they ate seven large bags of marijuana (yes sir, yes sir, seven bags full). Budd had no idea how the buds ended up on her farm; the police suspect that a dealer stashed them in what probably seemed like a good hiding place under a hedgerow. Budd's sheep were later seen "stumbling on their feet," as she described it, adding, "they probably had the munchies." Estimated street value of the flock's supper: $5,000. (Budd says they suffered no lasting effects.)

MAGIC MUSSELS

In 2018 the Washington Department of Fish and Wildlife tested mussels and other filter-feeders in Puget Sound for controlled substances. Result: they tested positive for oxycodone. How'd it get there? Trace amounts of the pain-relieving opioids ended up at wastewater treatment plants, which are unable to filter out all the drugs. In the past, this wasn't a huge problem, but the opioid epidemic of the 2010s saw a dramatic spike in the amount of drugs that have been making their way into waterways. And not only oxycodone. "We found antibiotics, we found antidepressants, chemotherapy drugs, and heart medications," said project biologist Jennifer Lanksbury.

ZONED-OUT ZEBRAFISH

In an effort to better understand the science of addiction, researchers at University of Utah Health say they've "devised a system that allowed zebrafish, a small tropical fish, to self-administer doses of hydrocodone, an opioid commonly prescribed to people for pain." Zebrafish, it turns out, "share similar biological pathways [with people] that lead to addiction." So it shouldn't be surprising that the results were very…humanlike: Within a few days, the zebrafish were increasing their drug intake, even when doing so meant putting themselves at risk. (The researchers placed the mechanism that delivers the drug into shallower and shallower water.) After a couple of days off the drugs, the zebrafish displayed typical signs of withdrawal, most notably increased anxiety. Lead researcher Randall T. Peterson called the discovery "exciting," in that it could provide a "useful and powerful model" to follow when treating humans for addiction.

The skyscraper at 20 Fenchurch in London reflects sunlight to the ground so intensely that it has melted parts of cars that park in front of it.

E-CTOPUS

As if octopuses weren't weird enough already, it appears that they really dig "rolling" on ecstasy. The discovery came about during a 2018 study of the antisocial behavior of octopuses, which only cohabitate while mating—otherwise they kill each other. But not on MDMA, the drug also known as ecstasy. Although the brains of humans and octopuses have little in common, they have nearly identical genes "for a protein that binds the signaling molecule serotonin to brain cells," according to NPR. "This protein is also the target of MDMA." That's why scientists decided to give ecstasy to the invertebrates. The first dosage was probably a bit too much: "They looked like they were freaked out," said lead reseacher Gul Dolen of Johns Hopkins University. "They would sit in the corner of the tank and stare at everything." So after a few tweaks, the scientists found the right dose, and the otherwise solitary animals not only preferred to be around each other, but they actually "hugged"—as in, they wrapped their tentacles around each other and gently stroked each other.

BOOZY BIRDS

Have you noticed an increase in the number of birds flying into your windows? Is it October? Do you live in Gilbert, Minnesota? If you answered yes to these questions, there's a perfectly logical explanation for it: the birds are drunk. It happens every October, and 2018 was such a bad year that the Gilbert Police Department issued a statement telling people not to panic. The odd behavior, they warned, would last only while there were still berries on bushes. An early frost caused the berries to ferment before most of the birds flew south for the winter, so the birds got drunk and started flying into people's windows and cars. The public was assured that "there is no need to call law enforcement about these birds as they should sober up within a short period of time." The cops concluded their post with the following list of bird behaviors that, if you see, you should definitely call them:

The birds got drunk and started flying into windows and cars.

- Heckle and Jeckle walking around being boisterous or playing practical jokes
- Woodstock pushing Snoopy off the doghouse for no apparent reason
- The Roadrunner jumping in and out of traffic on Main Street
- Big Bird operating a motor vehicle in an unsafe manner
- Angry Birds laughing and giggling uncontrollably and appearing to be happy
- Tweety acting as if he is 10 feet tall and getting in confrontations with cats
- Any other birds after midnight with Taco Bell items

About a third of Americans have their fingerprints on file with law enforcement.

ALTERED ARACHNIDS

"The more toxic the chemical, the more deformed a web looks in comparison with a normal web." That's the conclusion of a 1995 NASA study in which scientists gave common spiders doses of caffeine, amphetamines, marijuana, and chloral hydrate. They were re-creating a 1948 study conducted by German zoologist H. M. Peters and pharmacologist Peter Witt. Peters simply wanted the orb weavers to spin their webs at a time other than pre-dawn (so he didn't have to wake up so early to study them). Witt fed various spiders sugar water laced with "caffeine, mescaline, amphetamine, LSD, or strychnine" in the hopes of throwing off their sense of time. It threw off a lot more than that, as evidenced in their wonky webs: some got big, some got small, some didn't do anything at all. (Interestingly, the caffeinated spider spun the weirdest web.) So what have all these doped-up arachnids taught us about drugs over the years? Not much, according to a 2015 article in *Vice:* "It turns out, giving a spider drugs is just one possible interruption to a process within a brain that is, like all nonhuman brains, alien to us. We can't plausibly look at the handiwork of that arachnid and assume we know anything more about the drug that made it that way."

Still, it's fun to look at their drug-induced handiwork. Here are what the webs from the 1995 NASA study look like:

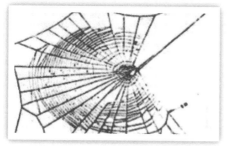

This spider was given mescaline.

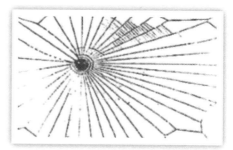

This spider was tripping on LSD.

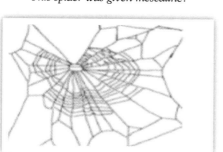

This spider was high on marijuana.

This spider was crazed by caffeine.

HEADLINES, FLORIDA STYLE

The phrase "Florida Man" actually has its own Wikipedia entry. It is defined as a meme that "calls attention to Florida's supposed notoriety for strange and unusual activity." These actual news headlines help define it a little more.

"Florida Man Arrested for Calling 911 After His Cat Was Denied Entry Into Strip Club"

"Another Person Seen Clinging to Car Hood on I-95 in Miami"

"Florida Man on Drugs Kills Imaginary Friend and Turns Himself In"

"Hardware Store Discards 15 Feet of Carpet After Florida Man Rolls Himself Up in It and Pees"

"8-HOUR STANDOFF ENDS AFTER PALM HARBOR MAN TELLS POLICE HE WAS SHOOTING AT RATS IN HIS BACKYARD"

"Florida Man Charged With Assault With a Deadly Weapon After Throwing Alligator Through Wendy's Drive-Thru Window"

"Florida Man Calls 911 During Police Chase, Asks for Donald Trump"

"THOUSANDS OF GUN OWNERS IN FLORIDA PLANNING TO 'SHOOT DOWN' HURRICANE IRMA"

"Florida Man Wrecks Liquor Shop, Blames 'Hookah-Smoking Caterpillar' from *Alice in Wonderland*"

"Florida Man Stuffing Fish down Pants in Pet Store Theft Caught on Camera"

"Tampa Teacher Arrested for Drunkenly Letting a 14-year-old Boy Drive Her to Waffle House"

"Cape Coral 'Off-the-Grid' Woman Thought George Michael's Song 'Faith' Would Heal Dog"

Toothpaste can be made from oranges.

I SPY...AT THE MOVIES

You probably remember the kids' game "I Spy, with My Little Eye..."
Filmmakers have been playing it for years. Here are some in-jokes and
gags you can look for the next time you see these movies.

Hook (1991)

I Spy... George Lucas and Carrie Fisher

Where to Find Them: Steven Spielberg's take on the classic Peter Pan story featured a cameo from the *Star Wars* creator and the woman who played Princess Leia. Lucas and Fisher are the kissing couple on the bridge that begins to float away when fairy dust lands on them. (They're so small on the screen it's tough to make out who they are.)

The Matrix (1999)

I Spy... Sushi recipes

Where to Find Them: The green computer code that opens the movie (and is seen several more times throughout the trilogy) was created by visual effects guru Simon Whiteley. He scanned the characters into a computer from his Japanese wife's sushi cookbook and then digitally manipulated them. "Without that code," says Whiteley, "there is no Matrix."

Independence Day (1996)

I Spy... A line from *Jurassic Park*

Where to Find It: David (Jeff Goldblum) is a passenger in a spaceship trying to escape aliens when he says, "Must go faster!" It sounds nearly identical to the "Must go faster!" line reading Goldblum gave as Dr. Ian Malcolm in 1993's *Jurassic Park* when he's a passenger in a Jeep trying to escape the T. rex. It sounds identical because it is. *Independence Day* director Roland Emmerich liked that line so much he looped in a recording of it. *Jurassic Park* director Steven Spielberg was reportedly upset at having a line he'd written and directed reused in another film only three years later.

Django Unchained (2012)

I Spy... Franco Nero, star of *Django*, the 1966 Italian "spaghetti Western" that this movie is based on

Where to Find Him: Django (Jamie Foxx) is sitting at a bar when a stranger with a white hat sits down next to him. That's Nero, who asks: "What's your name?" Foxx:

Twitter started out as a podcasting search tool. (It flopped.)

"Django." Nero: "Can you spell it?" Foxx: "D-j-a-n-g-o. The 'D' is silent." Nero: "I know." Nero later said that he wanted a bigger part in the movie that was inspired by his cult character, and suggested to Tarantino that he play a "horseman in black" who haunts young Django and is later revealed to be his father. Tarantino said no, and cast him as the stranger at the bar instead.

Cold Feet (1989), The Fisher King (1991), and The Big Lebowski (1998)

I Spy... A white baseball shirt with black sleeves that features an illustration of Japanese sporting hero Kaoru "the Gentleman of Baseball" Betto

Where to Find It: On Jeff Bridges. That's one of his favorite shirts. And because he's Jeff Bridges, he got to wear it in all those movies. (Watch all three films in order and you can see how the shirt ages over the decade.)

Alice in Wonderland (2010)

I Spy... A famous sound effect

Where to Find It: When Tweedledee and Tweedledum (both played by Matt Lucas) are captured by a JubJub bird, the creature lets out an otherworldly shriek. The sound designers must have been Trekkies—they used the same shriek emitted by the massive alien space probe in *Star Trek IV: The Voyage Home* (the one with the whales).

Ralph Breaks the Internet (2018) and Shark Tale (2004)

I Spy... An indestructible license plate

Where to Find It: When Ralph (voiced by John C. Reilly) is inside the violent racing game *Slaughter Race*, he comes across a shark that opens its mouth to reveal a Louisiana "Sportsman's Paradise" license plate. In *Shark Tale*, Lenny the shark (Jack Black) throws up the very same license plate, which was first seen by movie audiences at the beginning of *Jaws* (1975). It was pulled from the stomach of a dead tiger shark.

Bonus: *Jaws* director Steven Spielberg put a message on that Louisiana license plate—the number "007-981." It happened that, at the time, Spielberg *really* wanted to direct the next James Bond movie. So he decided to place several references to *Live and Let Die*—the then most recent Bond film—on the license plate. (One example: in the Bond film, a Louisiana cop hides behind a billboard with the "Sportsman's Paradise" slogan, a reference to the license plate in *Jaws*.) When Spielberg asked Bond producer Albert Broccoli outright if he could direct the next Bond movie, Broccoli told him no, saying Spielberg wasn't "good enough" of a director. Interestingly, in the next Bond movie—*The Spy Who Loved Me*—Broccoli introduced a new henchman character named Jaws (Richard Kiel)...who nearly gets eaten by a shark.

Most popular singer in Iraq: Lionel Richie.

BEST-SELLERS OF THE 19TH CENTURY

Take a look at this week's best-selling books list in your local newspaper.
Perhaps you've read and enjoyed one or two of them…but will they be
considered "classic" 100 years from now? Probably not. How do we
know? Check out these examples of what most Americans were reading
in the 1800s. Hint: It wasn't Moby-Dick or Huckleberry Finn.

★ ***The Spanish Brothers: A Tale of the 16th Century* by Deborah Alcock**
This historical novel from 1871 takes place about 300 years before that, during the
Spanish Inquisition of the early 1500s. After two brothers of Seville secretly convert
to Protestantism, they're rounded up by the Catholic Church and tortured, never
losing their convictions. Alcock reportedly earned so much from the sales of this
salacious story with religious overtones that she was able to buy two carriages. (That's
a lot of money.)

★ ***She: A History of Adventure* by H. Rider Haggard**
First serialized in *The Graphic* in 1886 and 1887, this influential early work of
fantasy literature is the first-person account of a daring explorer named Horace
Holly. Along with his loyal ward, Leo, he ventures deep into "darkest Africa," and
stumbles upon a lost kingdom. It's ruled by the all-powerful She, a white-skinned
queen named Ayesha. (And all of her subjects have dark skin.) Similar works by
later authors—such as *The Jungle Book* by Rudyard Kipling and *The Lost World* by
Arthur Conan Doyle—endured into the 21st century; *She* did not.

★ ***Guy Mannering* by Sir Walter Scott**
Sir Walter Scott only wrote poetry under his own name. Slightly embarrassed of
his less artistic and more blatantly commercial historical fiction, he published
those novels anonymously. He eventually claimed credit, of course, and his
most famous novel today is *Ivanhoe.* During his creative heights in the 1810s,
however, his most popular work was *Guy Mannering,* a thrilling tale of smugglers,
kidnapping, and grand adventure. In this story set in the 1760s, Harry Bertram,
five-year-old son of a Scottish lord, witnesses some smugglers kill a customs officer,
so they kidnap him and bring him along on their criminal exploits. Released just
a few months after Scott's previous hit novel, *Waverly,* fans lined up at bookstores
to buy copies of *Guy Mannering.* It sold 2,000 copies on its first day, and 50,000 in
the next few months. It had such influence that the Prince Regent (later crowned

King George IV) requested an audience with the author. It was so popular that a dog breeder named a new kind of Scottish terrier after a character in the book—the Dandy Dinmont Terrier.

★ *Looking Backward: 2000–1887* by Edward Bellamy

In this 1888 work of science fiction, a Boston man named Julian West falls into a hypnosis-induced sleep in the late 19th century…and wakes up in the year 2000. By then, the United States is a socialist (or, as the book calls it, "Nationalist") utopia. A guide named Dr. Leete shows Julian all the advancements in society, such as how the government owns everything and redistributes wealth equally, and the government provides free food for all. *Looking Backward* was so popular—the only novels that sold more copies in the United States in the 1800s were *Uncle Tom's Cabin* and *Ben-Hur*—that more than 150 "Bellamy Clubs" were formed. Club members sat around and discussed ways to enact the reforms of the book.

★ *The Soldier's Wife* by George W. M. Reynolds

If staying power is any indication, Reynolds wasn't nearly as accomplished a writer as his English contemporary Charles Dickens. But in the 1850s, his work greatly outsold that of the *Great Expectations* writer. Reynolds's serialized *Mysteries of London* sold 40,000 copies a week (at a penny a pop), and he also wrote the first werewolf novel, *Wagner the Wehr-Wolf,* and one of the first romance novels, *Rosa Lambert.* But *The Soldier's Wife* was his biggest blockbuster, selling 60,000 copies on the day it hit stores in 1852. It has a little something for everyone. It's about an innocent young man who joins the British Army but who rubs his superiors the wrong way, and frequently gets whipped (500 lashes on more than one occasion). Along the way he manages to carry on a swoon-worthy love affair, but is ultimately executed by a firing squad.

★ *Trilby* by George du Maurier

Who hasn't dreamed of leaving their mundane life and moving to Paris to live a bohemian lifestyle, hanging around in cafés reading poetry all day, and drinking wine all night? A lot of that romantic imagery first became embedded in the American consciousness from the 1894 novel *Trilby.* The story is about Trilby O'Ferrall, a half-Irish girl working in Paris as both a laundress and a model for painters. Every man she meets in this idealized 1850s Paris falls madly in love with her, among them an older cad named Svengali. (*Trilby* introduced that word into the English language.) After being serialized in *Harper's Monthly* in 1894, it was published as a novel in September 1895 and quickly sold a whopping 200,000 copies. (If the sales figure doesn't wow you, keep in mind that at that time there were no big-box retail stores, no bookstore chains, and no internet.)

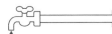

Does yours? Lots of microwaves have a mute function. Try holding down the "2" button.

AND NOW...FOR SOMETHING COMPLETELY QUOTABLE

The influential British comedy troupe Monty Python formed in 1969. Here's what its six members had to say off-screen.

"I don't do drugs. I've got enough bizarre chemicals floating around in my head."
—Terry Gilliam

"We don't deliberately set out to offend. Unless we feel it's justified."
—Graham Chapman

"John Cleese once told me he'd do anything for money. So I offered him a pound to shut up, and he took it."
—Eric Idle

"LIFE DOESN'T MAKE ANY SENSE, AND WE ALL PRETEND IT DOES."
—Eric Idle

"If God did not intend for us to eat animals, then why did he make them out of meat?"
—John Cleese

"If you want to create comedy, try to make people laugh. If you can make people laugh, head in that direction. If nobody laughs, well, that's not good news."
—Terry Jones

"I always wanted to be an explorer, but it seemed I was doomed to be nothing more than a very silly person."
—Michael Palin

"Creativity is not a talent. It is a way of operating."
—John Cleese

THE FIRST SHOW ON...

*Every TV channel or service has to start somewhere. Here's
the first original show for a bunch of them.*

CARTOON NETWORK

The Ted Turner-owned service was initially a repository for old cartoons like *The Flintstones* and *The Yogi Bear Show*. In December 1993, it aired its first brand-new program, *The Moxy Show*. It consisted of more old cartoons, but intercut them with brand-new 3-D animation segments starring a dog named Moxy and a flea named Flea.

HBO

The network known for its adult-oriented, hard-hitting dramas like *The Sopranos* and *Game of Thrones* first branched out from Hollywood movies and boxing matches (HBO stands for "Home Box Office," after all) in 1983, with the kids' show *Fraggle Rock*, produced by Muppet master Jim Henson.

SHOWTIME

HBO's biggest competitor has always been Showtime, but that network had original shows first. The premium cable service set itself apart from other nascent cable channels in 1982 with *A New Day in Eden*, a salacious soap opera in the vein of *Dallas* or *Falcon Crest*...except that it offered frequent full-frontal nudity.

AMAZON PRIME VIDEO

To think that Amazon used to just sell books, which it would *mail* to customers. Now it sells everything, and offers customers a trove of streaming movies and TV shows. It's earned critical acclaim for its original shows like *Transparent* and *The Marvelous Mrs. Maisel*. The first Amazon Video original series was a 2013 sitcom called *Alpha House*, co-created by *Doonesbury* cartoonist Garry Trudeau, about four Republican congressmen who live together in a Washington, D.C., townhouse.

THE CW

In 2006 mini networks UPN and The WB merged to become The CW. Several shows from each channel made the jump to the new network, and the first week of programming consisted almost entirely of those shows' season finales from the previous spring. On September 18, 2006, The CW debuted with a special episode of *Entertainment Tonight* and a rerun of the 2005–06 season finale of family drama *7th Heaven*.

Watermelon rind is edible (and full of vitamins).

MTV

Today, MTV airs mostly reality shows, and very few music videos, which comprised all of the network's content when it debuted in August 1981. By the late 1980s, MTV started moving into regularly scheduled shows. First musical show: *Dial MTV*, a viewer-request program. First non-musical show: the game show *Remote Control* in 1987.

ABC

Following CBS and NBC's jump from radio to television, the American Broadcasting Corporation became the third major TV network with its launch in April 1948. The first show broadcast on its affiliates in Philadelphia, Baltimore, New York, and Washington, DC: *On the Corner*, a talk show starring comedian Henry Morgan.

FOX

Before the "fourth network" launched its first prime-time lineup in April 1987 (which included *Married…With Children* and *The Tracey Ullman Show*), Fox programmed a late-night talk show called *The Late Show*, hosted by longtime *The Tonight Show* guest host Joan Rivers.

NETFLIX

More than five years after the online service introduced streaming movies and TV shows, it started making its own exclusive shows. The very first, in 2013: *House of Cards*. It was an American remake of a British show, starring Kevin Spacey as the ruthless, cutthroat, and murderous politician Frank Underwood.

HULU

The online service was the first internet-based network to win a Best Drama Series Emmy (for *The Handmaid's Tale*, in 2017). The first time the network programmed something that wasn't TV episodes that had previously aired on other, traditional networks was the comedy-laced entertainment/news show *The Morning After* in 2011.

NICKELODEON

Beginning in the late 1970s as a Columbus, Ohio, area station called QUBE, Nickelodeon went national on early cable systems in April 1979. Into the 1980s, it filled its schedule with kids' programs and made-for-TV movies imported from Canada. The first original, made-for-Nickelodeon show was a 1980 talk show for kids called *Livewire*. Host Mark Cordray led discussions of current events issues with kids, and then usually brought on a band. R.E.M. made its American TV debut on *Livewire*.

What's the difference between whiskey and bourbon? Bourbon is made in the U.S.

LUNKERS, LOGS, AND MACK ATTACKS

Learn all this deep-sea fishing lingo and you might be able to get a job on one of those Deadliest Catch boats. Okay, not really, but at least you'll know what they're talking about.

- **Candy:** Fish used as bait; more often than not, it's live squid.

- **Barney:** A know-it-all fisherman who also seems unable to actually catch anything (as in the similar talks-a-big-game Barney Fife from *The Andy Griffith Show*).

- **Fresh dead:** In lieu of live squid, a fisherman's next choice is just-killed, or "fresh dead," squid.

- **Green stuff:** cold or dirty water.

- **Boil:** A disturbance on the surface level of the water when a big fish chases after a smaller fish.

- **Soaking bait:** Throwing candy out into the ocean…and waiting until it gets a bite.

- **Chummer:** A seasick fisherman.

- **Dogs:** Seals (because they bark).

- **Bucketmouth:** A massive sea bass.

- **Alby:** An albacore tuna.

- **Longfin:** An albacore tuna.

- **Log:** A large barracuda.

- **Lunker:** A massive trout or sea bass.

- **Bounce:** To haul a fish up and into a boat without any help.

- **Condo:** A huge float of kelp moving its way across the sea.

- **Steel kelp:** An offshore oil rig.

- **Come unbuttoned:** When a fish wriggles its way off of a hook.

- **Coffee grinder:** When a line gets a bite and the reel spins wildly.

- **Mack attack:** Fishermen have to throw bait at mackerel to get them to go away, so that they can catch more desirable fish. A "mack attack" occurs when the mackerel eat up everything tossed their way…and they still won't scram.

- **Breezers:** Unwanted fish swimming through a prime fishing spot.

- **Hitchhiker:** A ling cod that's attached itself to a rockfish.

- **Chickens:** Seagulls.

- **Cocktail:** When fishermen use two or more baits on the same hooks at the same time.

- **Bird's nest:** A pile of unwound, overrun fishing line falling off a spool.

Makes sense: During the Cold War, missile manufacturer Raytheon made refrigerators.

TERRRIBLE TYPOS

It's a 9ood thing we never make any mistooks, or this pgae would be really ironic.

The player's name is Carter Hart—but here's how an ESPN headline writer spelled it: "Philadelphia Flyers recall goalie Carter Harter."

A 155-year-old bottle of Allsopp's Arctic Ale was auctioned on eBay in 2007 as "Allsop's." Because the second "p" was missing, only three people saw the listing, and one of them bought it for $304. He then relisted it—with the *correct* spelling—and made over $500,000.

Did the biggest blowout in NBA history take place on January 29, 2017? Here's how a California newspaper reported Golden State's 2-point win over Portland: "Warriors 1113, Blazers 111."

North Carolina's *Yancey County News* asks a tough question: "So What's Is the President's Gun Policy?"

A doozy from the *Post-Journal* in Jamestown, New York. They meant "Roles" (we hope): "Julia Roberts Finds Life and Her Holes Get Better with Age"

Some sweet advice from an electronic traffic alert sign: "Winter Conditions Drive with Cake."

This sign would have benefited from some punctuation: "HUNTERS PLEASE USE CAUTION WHEN HUNTING PEDESTRIANS USING TRAILS"

The *New York Times* had to apologize for putting the city of Stockton out to sea: "An obituary on Wednesday about Alex Spanos, the owner of the Chargers, misstated the location of Stockton, Calif… It is about 80 miles east of San Francisco, not west."

A sign for a fund-raising event outside the Royal Canada Legion in Etobicoke, Ontario: "Christmas Bazaar & Craft Show / Fight Children with Diabetes"

Reporting the death of Marvel Comics legend Stan Lee in 2018, New Zealand's *Gisborne Herald* got him confused with another celebrity: "Spike Lee Dies at 95."

At a doughnut shop: "Mini Dognuts $2.25"

In 2010 the *Irish Times* reported on a medical publication that accidentally described a renowned therapist as "the rapist." (Luckily, it was changed before it went to press.)

Try it: Soaking shrunken clothes in warm water and hair conditioner will unshrink them. After soaking, stretch them back to their normal size.

THE PRESIDENT'S DESK

Eighteen presidents have used the Oval Office since William Howard Taft moved in in 1909. In all that time, only six desks have served as the "First Desk."

OPEN FOR BUSINESS

It wasn't long after Theodore Roosevelt moved into the White House in 1901 that he realized the building would not be big enough to accommodate both his large family and his presidential staff. So he ordered the construction of a West Wing that would serve as office space for himself and his administration, freeing up some second-floor offices in the Executive Mansion to be converted into more living space for the First Family. But TR's West Wing office was rectangular. It wasn't until his successor, William Howard Taft, doubled the size of the West Wing in 1909, that a new, oval-shaped office was added to serve as the president's office. It was the first Oval Office.

The (Theodore) Roosevelt Desk

Though Teddy Roosevelt never occupied the Oval Office, his desk did. When Taft moved into the newly completed office in October 1909, he continued to use the desk he'd inherited from Roosevelt: a sturdy but plain mahogany desk built in the Federalist style that he set in front of the large windows that faced south.

The Hoover Desk

Roosevelt's desk served as the presidential desk through the administrations of Taft, Woodrow Wilson, Warren G. Harding, Calvin Coolidge, and into Herbert Hoover's term. But after a Christmas Eve fire caused extensive damage to the West Wing in 1929, Hoover accepted the gift of a 17-piece set of art deco office furniture, including a desk (made entirely of American woods and faced with maple burl veneer) that was donated by an association of furniture makers in Grand Rapids, Michigan. The Roosevelt desk, which suffered little damage from the fire, was put in storage.

When Franklin D. Roosevelt defeated Hoover and became president in 1933, he kept Hoover's desk—rather than his fifth cousin Theodore Roosevelt's desk—and used it for the entire 12-plus years of his presidency. (During extensive renovations, he also moved the Oval Office to its present location in the southeast corner of the West Wing, a location that permitted him to come and go quietly, without attracting the attention of his aides.) Then, after FDR died in office in April 1945, his successor, Harry Truman, had the Hoover desk and other personal items sent to Roosevelt's home in Hyde Park, New York. The Hoover desk remains on display in a re-creation of

Marlon Brando liked to stay up all night watching ants walk around his kitchen.

FDR's Oval Office at the site, which is now the Franklin Roosevelt Presidential Library and Museum. To replace it, Truman had the (Theodore) Roosevelt desk pulled out of storage. It remained the president's desk through both the Truman and the Eisenhower years (1945–1961).

The *Resolute* Desk

Of all six desks to serve as the president's desk in the Oval Office, the *Resolute* desk has the longest history in the White House, though it wasn't moved into the Oval Office until after John F. Kennedy became president in 1961. It was made from timbers taken from the HMS *Resolute*, a British Royal Navy ship that became trapped in ice in the Canadian arctic in 1853 and had to be abandoned. By the summer of 1855, the *Resolute* had floated free of the melting ice, and it was found adrift on the open sea by an American whaling ship and sailed to Connecticut. There, the U.S. government paid to have the ship repaired, and returned it to England in 1856 as a gesture of "national courtesy." The ship remained in service until 1879. After it was scrapped, Queen Victoria had some of the salvaged English oak timbers made into an ornate desk that she presented as a gift to President Rutherford B. Hayes in 1880, in thanks for returning the HMS *Resolute* in 1856.

President Hayes used the *Resolute* desk in his private study in the White House residence, where it remained in use for the next 80 years. Originally the "kneehole" was open, and visitors to the White House could see a president's legs when he was seated at the desk. But President Franklin D. Roosevelt was sensitive about being seen with the steel leg braces he'd worn since being crippled by polio in the early 1920s, so he commissioned the desk's most prominent feature: a wood "modesty panel" in front that featured a carved presidential seal. The modesty panel covered the kneehole and would have concealed FDR's legs from view had he lived long enough to use it, but he died before work on the modesty panel was completed.

By 1961 the *Resolute* desk had been relegated to the White House's ground-floor Broadcast Room; that was where First Lady Jacqueline Kennedy found it while working on an ambitious project to redecorate the White House and restore its historic character. She thought the desk's unique maritime history would appeal to JFK, so she had it moved to the Oval Office in February 1961. (In one famous picture taken of the desk in 1962, a young John F. Kennedy Jr. can be seen peeking out through the open modesty panel while his father sits at the desk.)

The Johnson Desk

After JFK was assassinated in 1963, his successor, Lyndon B. Johnson, removed the *Resolute* desk from the Oval Office and replaced it with the mahogany desk that he had used as U.S. senator and vice president. Johnson later had four buttons installed in his desk. If he pushed the first button, an aide brought him coffee; pushing the second button meant he wanted tea; the third button would bring him a Coke; and the fourth meant that LBJ wanted his favorite soft drink, Fresca.

The "Wilson" Desk

LBJ only *loaned* his desk to the White House; when he left office in 1969, he took it with him back to Texas. Today it is on display in the replica Oval Office at his presidential library in Austin. That left his successor, Richard Nixon, without a desk, so Nixon picked a large mahogany desk that he had used when serving as Dwight D. Eisenhower's vice president. He liked the desk because he believed that it had been used by President Woodrow Wilson, whom he admired. But that was untrue, and the name is a misnomer: no one named Wilson ever used the desk.

Rather than settle for buttons that brought beverages, Nixon had the Secret Service install five hidden microphones in the desk, which Nixon used to secretly record Oval Office conversations. When the existence of the recordings became known during the Watergate scandal, they helped seal Nixon's fate and forced him to resign the presidency in 1974.

The C&O Desk

Nixon's successor, Gerald R. Ford, continued to use the Wilson desk. But when Ford left office in 1977, *his* successor, Jimmy Carter, opted to bring the *Resolute* desk back into the Oval Office. Ronald Reagan also used the desk, but when his term ended in 1989, his successor, George H. W. Bush, wanted the desk he'd used while serving as Reagan's vice president: a walnut desk built in 1920 for one of the owners of the Chesapeake & Ohio Railway. To date, Bush is the only president to use the C&O desk in the Oval Office; after he left office in 1993, Bill Clinton went back to using the *Resolute* desk. It has remained in use in the Oval Office by every president since then. (One "improvement" made by Donald Trump: a red LBJ-esque button in a small box decorated with the presidential seal. The box sits on the desktop and whenever Trump pushes the button, an aide brings him a Diet Coke.)

* * *

"Is running for president just 'starting a podcast' for rich people?"

—Patton Oswalt

No buts about it: When shown photos of other chimpanzees' rear ends, chimps can recognize the chimps that they know.

SPORTS CONTRACT DISASTERS

*The worst of the worst, awarded to players and coaches
who were supposed to be the best of the best.*

CHARLIE WEIS

In 2005, after offensive coordinator Charlie Weis
helped lead the New England Patriots to three Super
Bowl wins in four years, he was hired as the head
coach of his alma mater, the University of Notre
Dame. After signing a six-year, $12 million contract,
Weis's NFL-style play had an immediate impact,
making Notre Dame one of the best teams in college
football. Halfway through that first season, the team's
executive tore up the first contract and signed Weis
to an unprecedented 10-year deal worth a reported
$30 to $40 million. The team was ranked ninth in
the nation that year, which is commendable, but
was not the championship season they were hoping
for. After that, Weis wasn't able to re-create the
magic, and he was fired after season five, resulting in
a $19-million buyout for the remaining years on his
contract. Starting in 2012, Weis coached the University of Kansas for three years of
a five-year contract before being let go, leading to another buyout, this time for $5.6
million. That's nearly $25 million that Weiss was paid to *not* coach football (and $25
million more than all of his student-athletes were paid to play it).

ALBERT HAYNESWORTH

From 2002 to 2008, Tennessee Titans defensive tackle Albert Haynesworth racked
up an impressive 24 quarterback sacks. A bidding war ensued when he became a free
agent, and was won by the Washington Redskins, who agreed to pay Haynesworth
$100 million over seven years. Much of that was guaranteed to the player, a rarity
in the owner-friendly NFL. After Haynesworth received his massive payday, he
showed up to camp out of shape, criticized his coaches' defensive schemes, and
his performance on the field was far from stellar. Two mediocre seasons later, the
Redskins traded him, and were out $50 million.

First literary reference to French fries: in Charles Dickens's *A Tale of Two Cities.*

ALLAN HOUSTON

In the 1999 NBA playoffs, New York Knick Allan Houston hit a running jump shot that sealed the Knicks' first-round victory, so when his contract was up for renegotiation in 2001, Houston's agent used that heroic moment to leverage the team into an incredible six-year, $100 million contract. Houston was a pretty good player when he was healthy, but nowhere near good enough for such an exorbitant contract, which limited the team's buying power for other talent. He missed most of the next two seasons due to bad knees. That, along with his monster salary, made it impossible for the Knicks to trade him. Houston retired in 2005, but he was still one of the league's highest-paid players for the next two seasons. His contract caused such a kerfuffle that the NBA later created the Allan Houston rule—an amnesty clause allowing teams to waive players without the player's salary counting toward their salary cap.

GILBERT ARENAS

In 2008 Washington Wizards star Gilbert Arenas signed a six-year, $111 million contract to continue playing basketball in the nation's capital. He had missed most of the previous season due to a knee injury, but before that, Arenas was a promising all-star who some thought would mature into Washington's version of Kobe Bryant. So Wizards executives felt it was crucial to the team's success that they keep him in town. In the first year of his new contract, Arenas played only two games due to nagging injuries. The following season was even worse. In December 2009, Arenas got into a heated argument with teammate Javaris Crittenton over unpaid gambling debts. Both men brandished weapons from their lockers. Arenas pled guilty to felony gun charges and was suspended by the NBA for the rest of the season. The Wizards traded him, and he played his last game in 2012 after being put on waivers, using the Allan Houston rule. Arenas still collected every dollar of that contract, though. (It could have been worse: Crittenton is currently serving 23 years in prison for manslaughter.)

> Arenas was a promising all-star who some thought would mature into Washington's version of Kobe Bryant.

ALBERT PUJOLS

Albert Pujols shocked the baseball world when he announced his decision to leave the St. Louis Cardinals for the Los Angeles Angels after the 2011 season. One of the best hitters in baseball, Pujols had been a three-time MVP in St. Louis and led his team to two World Series titles. Angels owner Arte Moreno offered the veteran a 10-year, $254 million contract, but Pujols was already 32 years old, and had already been in the majors for a grueling 11 seasons. He was able to extend his career as a designated hitter (meaning he didn't have to play defense), but his batting average, on-base percentage,

A 2009 search of Loch Ness for its monster found no monster...and 100,000 golf balls.

and walks all dropped significantly. The Angels have made the playoffs only once during his tenure (and were swept). At last report, Pujols, who is eight years into the deal, said he has every intention of fulfilling his contract.

PHIL JACKSON

Nicknamed the "Zen Master" for his ability to turn volatile, disparate players into winning teams, Jackson coached the Chicago Bulls and Los Angeles Lakers to a combined 11 championships. In 2014 he was hired to turn around the struggling New York Knicks, but not as head coach. Taking the title of president, Jackson signed a five-year, $60 million contract. His first move: he hired the untested Derek Fisher, his "floor general" with the Lakers, as the Knicks' head coach. Fisher signed a five-year, $25 million contract...and led the Knicks to a franchise-worst 17–65 record. He was fired midway through his second season. Jackson followed up the Fisher debacle with a series of puzzling free agency signings, ill-conceived draft picks, and an unnecessarily public feud with his only superstar player, Carmelo Anthony. The only thing Jackson did right was drafting Kristaps Porzingis, an unknown Latvian seven-footer who quickly endeared himself to NBA fans across the nation. But by the end of Jackson's third season, damaging reports emerged that he fell asleep during a scouting trip and that he was thinking about trading Porzingis. After a disappointing 80–166 record, Jackson and the Knicks agreed to part ways. He received the full $24 million remaining on his contract.

RICK DiPIETRO

In 2000 the New York Islanders selected Rick DiPietro first overall in the NHL Draft, only the second time a goalie has been a number-one draft pick. Six years later, he signed a whopping 15-year, $67.5 million contract, locking him in until he was 39 years old. Any player would have a hard time living up to that contract, but "Rickety" Rick DiPietro wasn't even that good when healthy. He suffered a litany of injuries that allowed him to play only 50 games in a five-season span. With eight years left on his contract, in 2013 the Islanders cut DiPietro by coming to terms on a deferred payout on most of his remaining salary: $1.5 million per year over 16 years. (Not a bad retirement fund, if you can get it.)

* * *

BOY, OH BOY

How did authors Susan Eloise Hinton and Joanne Rowling become known as S. E. Hinton and J. K. Rowling? Their publishers figured their books would sell better if boys didn't know the authors were women.

Ouch! About 750 Americans lose a finger in snowblower accidents each year.

LOONY LOTTO WINNERS

What would you do if you won the lottery? Here's what not to do.

THERE IS NO "WE" IN "LOTTERY" In 2007 airplane mechanic Arnim Ramdass began acting strangely around his Florida home. According to his wife, Donna Campbell, he suddenly disconnected their phone and refused to let anyone turn on a TV. Why was he behaving so oddly? Campbell didn't know, but she got her first clue when she got a piece of mail about Ramdass's purchase of a new house. Rather than confront her husband, she went to her computer, Googled her husband's name, and found several news stories about how he and 16 coworkers had won a $19 million jackpot in the Florida Lottery. Ramdass's share came to about $600,000, with which he'd planned to steal away to his new home, leaving his wife in the process. Shocked, Campbell sued her husband for a piece of the windfall, but a judge sided with Ramdass. (Soon after, Campbell filed for divorce.)

BAD MATH Somehow, winning the lottery put Suzanne Mullins in a financial hole she couldn't crawl out of. After nabbing a $4.2 million payout from the Virginia Lottery in 1993, Mullins had to split the winnings with two other players, and then opted for yearly payments instead of a lump sum. That left her with around a $48,000 annuity… which wasn't enough to cover the loan she'd taken out to pay off her son-in-law's $1 million in medical bills. Result: Mullins had to file for bankruptcy.

IT HAD A NICE RING TO IT Most 19-year-olds don't have enough life experience or training to understand day-to-day money management, let alone how to handle millions of dollars. So you almost can't blame Jonathan Vargas of Gaston, South Carolina, for how he decided to spend most of the $35.3 million he won playing Powerball in 2008. Sure, he bought his mother a house, but he invested most of his winnings in a wrestling TV production company called Wrestilicious. Meant to compete with the WWE and the WCW, this one featured women in lingerie wrestling in a pink ring. Wrestilicious was bankrupt within a year.

BAD LUCK, GOOD LUCK, BAD LUCK Winning the lottery couldn't have come at a better time for David Lee Edwards. In 2001 the Kentucky ex-con—unemployed and living in his mother's basement—won $27 million in the Powerball jackpot. Almost immediately, he bought a $600,000 house, $1 million worth of cars, a $78,000 watch, a private jet, hundreds of swords and medieval weapons, and a fiber-optics installation company. Within a year, he'd spent $12 million…but neglected to pay his taxes. The bank foreclosed on the house, the woman he'd married after he struck it rich got arrested for stabbing her boyfriend, and Edwards died in 2013.

Technical term for opening a bottle of champagne with a sword: sabrage.

ASK THE EXPERTS

Questions about the world we live in, with answers from the world's top trivia experts.

DON'T SAY CHEESE

Q: *Do English people really have bad teeth?*

A: "There is nothing wrong with British smiles. According to dozens of jokes, one spy-spoof movie series and even some Britons themselves, the British and bad teeth go as hand-in-hand as tea and crumpets. You can even tell when a British film star has been to Hollywood, the story goes, because they suddenly procure a bright white, perfectly aligned smile. And, as BBC *Magazine* discovered when they reviewed the state of British teeth, some UK-based dentists say that their customers prefer a more 'natural look' than their American counterparts.

"Yet what does the data say? First, it depends on what you mean by 'bad.' Whether you choose to whiten or straighten your teeth is a matter of fashion. In terms of dental health, what really matters is decay. On that measure, Britain does better than many other countries around the world—including the United States. In a recent World Health Organization report of the dental status of children, British youths had fewer decayed, missing, or filled teeth than those in France, Spain, and Sweden; Britain's rates were comparable with Germany, the Netherlands, and Finland. The United States, on the other hand, did quite a bit worse. At the age of 12, children in the United Kingdom have on average better teeth than their American counterparts." (From "Do Brits Really Have Bad Teeth?" by Claudia Hammond, BBC Future)

TAKING STOCK

Q: *Why are there no publicly traded law firms?*

A: "Actually, there is one. In May 2007, an Australian personal injury firm, Slater & Gordon, went public in a move that stirred debate among lawyers worldwide. (Arguing attorneys—what fun!) Traditionally, a lawyer's first responsibility is to the courts; the client's needs are considered secondary. If a law firm were a public corporation, the reasoning goes, lawyers would also need to provide value to shareholders. This could potentially create sticky situations: Shareholders might not be thrilled about a firm defending a controversial client, for example.

"But with Australia jumping over the line, the U.S. likely will follow suit and move to publicly traded law firms. Proponents point out that even when a law firm is owned by lawyers, financial concerns can potentially interfere with serving a client. They also argue that public capital would give some law firms the financial leeway

In some Alaskan kindergartens, children are taught how to butcher moose.

to accept more low-income clients and risky cases. Finally, of course, lawyers could make a lot of money on initial public offerings—not that such a prospect matters to a lawyer." (From *Why Do Guys Like Duct Tape?* from Apandisis Publishing)

JUST TO BE SURE

Q: *Why are autopsies performed on criminals who have just been executed?*

A: "A convicted murderer is brought into a chamber. He is strapped to an electric chair. The executioner flips the switch. The prisoner dies. One wouldn't think Quincy would be required to diagnose the cause of death. Yet, as far we know, every state that has capital punishment requires an autopsy to be performed on the executed prisoner. Three reasons:

1. "Ascertaining the cause of death can still be contested, even if it seems obvious. For legal reasons, states find it prudent to protect themselves.

2. "'An autopsy will reveal the presence or absence of any preexisting diseases, injuries, or potential toxic substances (alcohol, drugs, poisons),' says Michael Graham, Chief Medical Examiner of St. Louis, Missouri. Dr. Bill Hamilton of Gainesville, Florida, recalls that when a body of a prisoner executed in Florida was shipped to California for burial, a cemetery official found what he thought were signs of torture. Eventually, the body was exhumed and the 'abuse' turned out to be electrical burns associated with electrocutions. Routine autopsies would forestall such accusations.

3. "Most states have laws specifying that *any* person who dies in custody of prison systems must be autopsied. In this litigious age, the last thing state penal systems need are lawsuits or investigative journalists hounding them years after an execution." (From *What Are Hyenas Laughing at, Anyway?* by David Feldman)

HOUSTON, WE HAVE A PBBLLBBBTLL!

Q: *Can a fart propel an astronaut through the space station?*

A: "You'd think it should work, at least a little bit—farts are an outgassing of flatus from the body, and you'd think the basic Newtonian law of action/reaction should mean that the farter is pushed away from the fart material, resulting in some sort of propulsive motion. There's no documented NASA study of FARTS (Fast Acting Rectal Transportation System) or anything like that, but there is an admission that informal tests were attempted from retired Canadian ISS astronaut Chris Hadfield when the topic of getting 'stuck' (floating in a module, and finding oneself unable to reach anything to push against) in the middle of a large space station module came up. His answer: 'We all tried it - too muffled, not the right type of propulsive nozzle :)'" (From "Can You Use Your Farts to Propel Yourself in Zero Gravity?" by Jason Torchinsky for *Jalopnik*)

The first song Prince wrote was called "Funk Machine." He was seven years old.

MOUTHING OFF

MOLLY'S MUSINGS

Texas-born journalist and essayist Molly Ivins (1944–2007) wrote about politics…but at least she was funny about it.

"BEING SLIGHTLY PARANOID IS LIKE BEING SLIGHTLY PREGNANT—IT TENDS TO GET WORSE."

"Be outrageous, ridicule the fraidy-cats, rejoice in all the oddities that freedom can produce."

"The thing about democracy is that it is not neat, orderly, or quiet. It requires a certain relish for confusion."

"I believe that ignorance is the root of all evil. And that no one knows the truth."

"I've always found it easier to be funny than to be serious."

"We should all laugh more at our elected officials—it's good for us and good for them."

"You could probably prove, by judicious use of logarithms and congruent triangles, that real life is a lot more like soap opera than most people will admit."

"You can't ignore politics, no matter how much you'd like to."

"Some days, I'd feel better with Punxsutawney Phil in the Oval Office. At least he doesn't lie about the weather."

WHEN ATHLETES FART

*When you watch a sporting match, do you wonder how much
the athletes fart? We do. Here's what we found out.*

THUNDEROUS BOLT

Tommy Bolt was an excellent golfer (he won the 1958 U.S. Open), and he had a
pretty cool name. But he also had a nickname, "Terrible Tommy," which he got
because of his bad behavior. If a shot didn't go his way, he'd routinely break out
into a temper tantrum or throw a club. At the 1959 Memphis Invitational Open,
he approached the tee and made an outburst…from his rear end. Bolt broke wind
in full view (and earshot) of other golfers, spectators, and PGA officials. After he
finished his round, the PGA fined Bolt $250. (They called it "conduct unbecoming a
professional golfer.")

POOL FARTS

Snooker, a variant of billiards, is technically a sport, combining strategy and
physical exertion to get the right balls into the right holes. It's also one of the
most-watched live competitive events on TV in the UK. At the 2013 Snooker
World Championship semifinals, featuring Judd Trump against Ronnie O'Sullivan,
Trump was setting up for a crucial shot late in the game. Suddenly, the silence in the
hall (not to mention Trump's concentration) was broken by the loud, unmistakable
sound of flatulence. The fart came from someone in the spectator gallery, who
understandably didn't take credit for their work, even though Trump laughed.
Interruption over, Trump set up for the shot again…and once more the rogue farter
let loose. This time Trump was irritated. The disturbance got so in his head that he
missed his big shot…and lost the match.

GRAND SLAM OF FARTS

Darts is extremely popular in Europe, and to win the Grand Slam of Darts is the sport's
greatest achievement. Gary Anderson of Scotland has won the whole thing twice, but
to get into the 2018 finals he first had to defeat
Wesley Harms of the Netherlands. Harms
claims that Anderson stooped very low during
their face-off to secure the win. Several times

> **He was bombarded by a "fragrant
> smell" of "rotten eggs."**

when he walked past Anderson, he was bombarded by a "fragrant smell" of "rotten eggs," Harms told a Dutch TV station. "It'll take me two nights to lose this smell from my nose." Anderson agreed that there was a gas leak but claimed that it came from someone in the audience. "If the boy thinks I've farted he's 110 percent wrong," Anderson told the BBC. "I had a bad stomach once on stage before and admitted it. So I'm not going to lie about farting on stage." Despite Harms's protests, Anderson's win stood. Said Barry Hearn, head of the sport's overseeing body, the Professional Darts Corporation, "Something doesn't smell right."

A TIP FROM UNCLE JOHN

While flatulence is normal and healthy, there are some steps you can take to cut down on excessive farting. 1. Slow down at meals and eat smaller portions. That helps the body digest food easier, thus reducing gas production. 2. Drink more water. That can aid the body in processing food, which in turn leads to fewer gas leaks.

A CAVALIER ATTITUDE

LeBron James can do it all on the basketball court: dunk, drive, make three-pointers, rebound, block, steal...and fart and get away with it. During a nationally televised game in 2009, James emerged from the locker room and nonchalantly took a seat on the Cleveland Cavaliers' bench in an open spot next to teammate Anderson Varejao. James kept a perfectly straight face as he let out a stinker...only breaking his stoicism after Varejao started wildly overreacting when he got a whiff of the broken wind.

* * *

EXTREMELY TOUGH MOVIE QUOTE QUIZ

Can you guess what films spawned these memorable lines? (Answers on page 527)

1. "Forget it, Jake. It's Chinatown."
2. "Welcome...to Jurassic Park!"
3. "Sincerely yours, the Breakfast Club."
4. "They tell me you're a man with true grit."
5. "The first rule of Fight Club is: You do not talk about Fight Club."
6. "My name's Forrest, Forrest Gump."
7. "Gooooooood morning, Vietnam!"
8. "We're sending you back...to the future!"
9. "I wish I was big!"
10. "Dude, where's my car?"
11. "I'm Batman!"

...There are Lego versions of his characters from *The Lego Movie*, *Guardians of the Galaxy*, and *Jurassic World*.

LEFT BEHIND

Ever slapped yourself in the forehead for leaving something behind? But it's unlikely that any of your forgotten stuff compares to these 32 items left in taxis, hotel rooms, Ubers, subways, and on planes.

1. A goat dressed like Abraham Lincoln
2. A bathtub full of potatoes
3. A full set of 18k-gold teeth
4. A case of cheerleaders' pompoms
5. A live chicken
6. A birth certificate and Social Security card
7. Multiple cats, a $100 tip, and a note that said "Thanks for taking care of these guys."
8. A breast pump with breast milk
9. A baseball signed by Babe Ruth
10. A replica of Meghan Markle's wedding dress
11. A black-and-white tuxedo for a small dog
12. An army rucksack filled with false teeth
13. A Harry Potter magic wand
14. A Bible filled with cat photos
15. A bag of haggis
16. A mannequin
17. A fish tank complete with fish and water
18. A blue-eyed cockatoo called Brexit
19. A giant stuffed Spider-Man toy
20. A *Joseph's Amazing Technicolor Dream Coat* costume
21. A journal kept by a man who thought his wife was trying to kill him
22. A pair of yet-to-be-implanted breast implants
23. A bag containing two dead mice
24. A *Star Wars* skateboard
25. "Why I Love Salad": a notebook filled with 40-plus handwritten pages
26. A dead alligator
27. Deer antlers and a welding helmet
28. A full rabbi costume, including the beard
29. A Swarovski-encrusted 5-foot wedding cake
30. A glass eye in a glass of water
31. A liter of fake blood
32. A bag of snails

Scientists say the first cold virus was transferred to humans from camels.

FORGOTTEN FAST-FOOD CHAINS

Do you remember eating at any of these chain restaurants years ago? Apparently you didn't eat there often enough, because they all went out of business.

PUP 'N' TACO (1956–1984). A chain of just over 100 stores, primarily in California. They specialized in a few items: pups (hot dogs), tacos (Mexican food)…and pastrami sandwiches. Pup 'N' Taco was a fast-food pioneer but lost out in a crowded market it helped invent. Taco Bell bought the chain for its real estate in 1984, and closed them all down.

KENNY ROGERS ROASTERS (1991–2011). Kentucky governor John Y. Brown turned Kentucky Fried Chicken into an international conglomerate, and he tried again with roasted chicken, licensing the name and image of country music star Rogers as his angle. KRR closed its last North American store in 2011, but remains a popular chain in Southeast Asia.

WETSON'S (1959–1975). Wetson's did in New York what McDonald's had done for the Midwest—serve up 15-cent burgers and 10-cent fries by the millions. They even had a couple of clown mascots—Wetty and Sonny. But when McDonald's expanded into the New York metro area, Wetson's couldn't compete and its 70 locations slowly closed until none were left.

HEAP BIG BEEF (1967–1972). This chain sold "He-Man sized roast beef sandwiches" (a Heap Big Beef sandwich cost 59¢; Great Big Beef cost 99¢) in hundreds of A-frame restaurants decorated with a Native American theme. Also on the menu: Shawnee Shakes and Pawnee Pies.

GINO'S (1957–1982). A few retired Baltimore Colts football players, including namesake and spokesman Gino Marchetti, opened this East Coast chain in 1957. It set itself apart from other fast-food joints by offering higher-quality products: from ground sirloin "banquet on a bun" burgers, and fries cut fresh daily at each location. In the end, the Marriott Corporation bought all 350 Gino's stores and converted them into Roy Rogers restaurants.

RED BARN (1961–1988). The first fast-food restaurant with a double-patty burger (the Big Barney) and a salad bar, more than 400 Red Barns dotted 19 states. That's a lot of restaurants, but only a small percentage of what competitors like McDonald's, Burger King, and Wendy's had, and those big chains saturated Red Barn right out of business.

LUM'S (1956–1983). A Miami hot dog stand turned into a chain of family-style fast-food joints with a menu focused on beer-steamed hot dogs. It grew to 400 restaurants by 1971, which is when Kentucky Fried Chicken chairman John Y. Brown bought the company. He sold it to the German fast-food chain Wienerwald in 1978. That purchase, along with some other ill-advised business decisions, forced Wienerwald into bankruptcy in 1982, leading to the closure of Lum's.

MACHEEZMO MOUSE (1981–2003). This Portland, Oregon, chain served Mexican-style fast food, but with a "healthy" twist: they used Monterey Jack cheese instead of fattier cheddar, and higher-fiber black beans instead of pinto beans. Company founder Tiger Warren died in a plane crash in 1999, and his successors' poor management led to a mountain of debt so insurmountable that in 2003 the company suddenly shut down all its locations.

LA PETITE BOULANGERIE (1977–2000). *Boulangerie* is French for "little bakery." This mall-based chain sold muffins, bagels, and other bakery goods at more than 68 locations across the country. A series of lawsuits cut into profits in the 1980s, and in 1987 what was left was absorbed by its chief competitor—Mrs. Fields Original Cookies.

SANDY'S (1958–1979). An early McDonald's franchisee wanted to expand into new territory, but CEO Ray Kroc wouldn't let them and then demanded a bigger piece of the profits for the McDonald's they already owned. Solution: they started this burger-and-fries McDonald's competitor. Using checkered patterns and a Scottish theme, the chain grew to more than 120 locations all over the Midwest… until the early 1970s, when McDonald's and Hardee's put them out of business. (Hardee's actually bought them out.)

FORGOTTEN SODAS TO WASH DOWN THAT FORGOTTEN FOOD

> **Josta (1995–1999).** Pepsi's fruity, chocolatey energy drink enhanced with a stimulant called guarana.

> **Chime (1964–1972).** Coca-Cola's Dr Pepper ripoff before it introduced its next Dr Pepper ripoff, Peppo (later renamed Mr. Pibb).

> **Sunbolt (1994).** Carbonated, caffeinated Gatorade.

> **Orbitz (1997).** A clear beverage with little balls of gelatin suspended in it.

> **Hubba Bubba (1988–1989).** Bubble gum–flavored soda.

> **Evervess (1966–1973).** Pepsi's attempt to market club soda as a soda option, rather than as a mixer.

> **dnL (2002–2005).** The name is "7 Up" upside-down, reflecting how this was a caffeinated version of the famous noncaffeinated 7 Up.

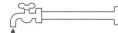

Mama Cass Elliot and Keith Moon of The Who died in the same London apartment (four years apart).

STRANGE CRIME

Some true crime stories are tough to categorize. They're just…strange. (Shameless plug: For more bizarre crime stories like these, check out Portable Press's Strange Crime.)

WRONG HOUSE, JERKS

One morning in July 2018, a Manchester, England, man awoke to an alarming discovery: someone had let the air out of his van's tires and spray-painted this message on his house: "PAY YOUR BILL YOU B*ST*RD." The man (who wished to remain anonymous in news reports) was frightened but also perplexed…because he had no unpaid bills. A few days later, he awoke to find a second spray-painted message: "PAY YOUR BILL DONNA!" He didn't know anyone named Donna. And this time, the perpetrator cut the van's brake line and even set fire to his neighbor's van. The police said they'd try to look into the matter, but there wasn't much for them to go on. The homeowner painted his own message ("DONNA DOES NOT LIVE HERE"), but he's still so scared that neither he nor his wife can sleep through the night. "Someone has obviously upset someone," he told the *Manchester Evening News*, "and I am stuck in the middle of it."

TREAD LIGHTLY

It was a scary scenario for an FBI agent and three members of the Oregon State Police Bomb Squad in September 2018. They were investigating a rural property belonging to 67-year-old Gregory Lee Rodvelt. Acting on a tip that the 15-acre compound was protected by "improvised devices," the officers proceeded to enter the grounds. First obstacle: a gate blocked by a minivan, surrounded by metal-toothed animal traps. They disabled the traps and then walked through the gate. Second obstacle: another gate, this one with a wire attached to it. The wire went up a hill and was attached to a shim, which was holding up a large cylindrical hot tub. If the gate was opened, the wire would dislodge the shim, and the hot tub would roll down the hill, *Raiders of the Lost Ark*–style. They disabled that trap too. Next obstacle: the house itself, which had a metal door, and metal bars on all the windows. The bomb squad used a small explosive charge to open the door, and the FBI agent went in first. Blocking his way was a wheelchair, which he carefully rolled aside and…BANG! "I'm hit!" he yelled, as blood gushed from his leg. The wheelchair, it turned out, had been rigged with a shotgun. The FBI agent survived, but it took several days to clear the property of traps (there were many). Rodvelt, who wasn't there (he was already in custody in Arizona on separate charges), was charged with a felony count of assaulting a federal officer.

A QUICK STORE RUN

Contraband is hard to come by in prison, so four inmates in Mississippi's Holmes-Humphreys County Correctional Facility came up with a novel idea: go out and get

---

A spider's blood is pale blue. It gets that color from copper.

some. Late one night in 2017, they escaped from their cells, snuck outside, climbed over the fence, and then walked to a nearby Dollar General Store. They broke in, stole cigarettes, lighters, and other items, and then *returned* to the prison, where they climbed the fence, snuck back in, and made it back to their cells, undetected. Only problem: the store's security cameras led authorities right to them. The local police chief, Robert Kirklin, was perplexed as to why the escaped prisoners would break out, only to break right back in. "That is just something," he told *Mississippi News Now.* "Now I've heard it all."

THE IMPERFECT CRIME

One night in the summer of 2018, a Blackpool, England, woman named Zoe Doyle received a frantic call from her boyfriend. The 45-year-old man, Leigh Ford, said he'd been kidnapped, and that if she didn't transfer all of their money to the kidnappers' bank account, they threatened to cut off his legs (and another part of his body). Doyle, who was 35 weeks pregnant, thought Ford was kidding and told him to come home. A few minutes later, he called back, even more upset, and she could hear people yelling terrible things in the background. So Doyle did as she was told: she transferred everything they had—a whopping £80—and then called police, who sent over a hostage negotiator and put an entire team (including a helicopter) on the case. Then they all waited for Ford to call back. They waited all night. The next day, police found Ford limping on a sidewalk. He said the kidnappers had let him go. Suspicious investigators did a little digging and soon found surveillance footage of Ford and his friends buying a bunch of booze from a local shop…at the same time he was supposedly being kidnapped. He was arrested for wasting police resources and sentenced to 16 weeks behind bars, causing him to miss the birth of his child. "The silly thing was," said a dumbfounded Doyle, "it was his own money. He could have spent it if he had wanted." Instead, she said, "He put me through hell." At last report, the couple had reconciled and were raising their baby together.

BAD MARE DAY

Canadian Mounties mounted an investigation after a farmer reported that someone had trespassed onto his land and had given his 18-year-old horse, Yoshi, a haircut. "She came running into the shelter in a bit of a panic," said Frank Dourte of Prince Edward Island. "And when I looked at her, she was missing a bit of mane, both on her tail and from her bangs, way down to her wither." Dourte was especially troubled by the crime because it occurred during daylight while the horse was outside. So someone had to "enter the property, cross the electric fence and barbed wire, go into the field, and start trimming the mane of my horse." As of last report, there are no suspects, but the Mounties are on the case. "It didn't appear to be anything malicious," said RCMP Constable Robert Honkoop, "but certainly peculiar."

In 1640 Pope Urban VIII forbade all Spanish priests from smoking tobacco.

RANDOM ORIGINS

Once again, the BRI asks—and answers—the question:
Where does all this stuff come from?

UMBRELLA DRINKS

The little umbrella (or parasol) that traditionally garnishes rum-based faux-tropical cocktails has become so common that the term "umbrella drink" is now synonymous with them. The drinks got popular in the 1930s and '40s as part of a "tiki bar" fad. But neither of the big tiki bar chains, Don the Beachcomber and Trader Vic's, were the first to put small umbrellas into drinks—Harry Yee, a bartender at the Hilton Waikiki, was. His personal touch up to that point was placing a stick of sugarcane in drinks, but he found that patrons would chew on them and leave them behind in ashtrays for him to clean up. Looking for something a little less work-intensive, he used small orchids to garnish his drinks for a few years, and then really struck gold in the late 1950s when he switched to the tiny umbrellas the Hilton had around for patrons to use as toothpicks.

HAWAIIAN PIZZA

Most standard pizza toppings are savory and salty—cheese, pepperoni, olives, and even anchovies. What kind of mind, then, would come up with the idea of putting a sweet (and cold) ingredient like pineapple on a (hot) 'za? This innovation on the classic Italian dish was invented not in Italy but by a Greek man in Canada. Sam Panopoulos left his native Greece and emigrated to Canada in 1954 at age 20, and worked in the uranium mines in southern Ontario. A few years later, he and his two brothers opened a few diners. It happened at their Satellite Restaurant in Chatham, Ontario: Panopoulos was in the kitchen, making a pizza one day in 1962, when he spotted a can of chunked pineapple on the shelf, and thought it might be a good topping.

CROWDFUNDING

The internet has created a whole new kind of economy in which friends, fans, and supporters can prepay for a product or service that's still on the drawing board. Through "crowdfunding" sites like Kickstarter and Patreon, artists can solicit the entire world for donations, which they can then use to fund their album, movie, or other endeavor, in exchange for some kind of token prize or the patron's name in the credits. (Crowdfunding sites can actually be used for anything—thousands of people have used them, for example, to pay off huge medical bills.) The first time anybody made a significant amount of money through what is essentially electronic panhandling was when the English rock band Marillion used the nascent internet

25% of women say they've "ghosted" someone by not responding to
their calls, texts, or social media posts.

to get fans to pre-fund its 1997 concert tour of the United States. (They raised a respectable £39,000, or $60,000.)

STRIP MALLS

Los Angeles is famous for its car culture (and its clogged highways and long commutes). It started in the 1920s, when the price of automobiles dropped enough to allow widespread ownership. People wanted to do everything in their cars, and in 1924 the first "drive-in market" opened in Glendale, near Los Angeles. It wasn't a fast-food place or a drive-in movie—it was a convenience store. These stores are usually located at busy intersections, so patrons could park right in front, quickly grab a couple of items inside, and be on their way in a few minutes. Those stores became the anchors of small shopping centers. There were 250 drive-in markets in Southern California by the end of the 1920s, just as supermarkets started becoming popular...and started replacing drive-ins. Strip malls (or mini-malls) re-emerged in 1973, again in Los Angeles, and again because of cars. Gas shortages led to hundreds of gas stations going out of business, and real-estate developers started replacing them with a row (or an L-shape) of retail stores, housing nail salons, massage parlors, restaurants, dry cleaners, doughnut shops, and laundromats. (And just like in the earlier fad of the 1920s, the parking was free, plentiful, and close.) The first modern strip mall was built on the corner of Osborne Street and Woodman Avenue in the Panorama City neighborhood of Los Angeles; by the mid-1980s, Southern California was home to 3,000 mini-malls. (By 2010 there were more than 60,000 of them across the United States.)

LOW-CARB DIETS

There's always another fad diet people go nuts over for a few weeks—often a "low-carb" regimen that calls for eliminating starches like pasta, potatoes, and rice in favor of lots of protein (and fat). Some of the more popular low-carb diets: Atkins, ketogenic, Paleo, Whole30, and South Beach. But the first weight-loss craze that had people pushing away the bread and reaching for the bun-less bacon cheeseburgers was *The Drinking Man's Diet*. In 1962, former salesman and cosmetics executive Robert Cameron self-published a book by that title. A friend had told him that if he ate nothing but carbohydrate-free meat (and drank nothing but low-carbohydrate gin and red wine), he'd lose weight. He did. "I was never hungry and never missed a martini," Cameron boasted in this book that went on to sell 2.4 million copies. Cameron's diet offered an alternative to the other diets of the 1960s, like the cabbage soup diet. He wasn't a doctor or a nutritionist—he geared the book toward men like him: hard-drinking, steak-eating guys of the *Mad Men* era. The book faded from popular consciousness by the time the similar Atkins diet hit it big in the 1970s. As for Cameron, he died a lean man at age 98.

A gallon of water weighs 8.34 pounds. A cubic foot of the stuff weighs 62.4 pounds.

CELEBRITY GOOD DEEDS

We see a lot of news reports about famous people doing nice stuff for us "normals"—and in a lot of cases, we can't help but wonder if it's out of the goodness of their heart…or just a PR stunt. These stories, we're pretty sure, are not PR stunts.

"I GOT THIS."

Therra Gwyn Jaramillo was down on her luck. It was August of 2018, and she was still reeling from having lost her husband to brain cancer a few years earlier. The British-born freelance writer was living in Atlanta, Georgia, and due to unpaid writing work and a broken water heater, she was nearly broke. "It's just me who is responsible for taking care of everything now," she explained in a long Facebook post, "the house, the property, four rescued dogs, two rescued cats, an elderly, blind chicken named Dixie Licklighter, my disabled brother…and myself." On the verge of a nervous breakdown, Jaramillo got a lifeline from a friend in the form of a $250 gift certificate to the upscale grocery store Whole Foods—a place she can't usually afford to shop.

Grateful but exhausted, Jaramillo drove herself to the store and did her shopping, but "my head hasn't worked all month," and only after she had put all of her groceries on the conveyer belt did she realize that the tab was going over the allotted $250. Then she panicked when she saw that her bags of dog food got mixed up with the groceries of the young man in line in front of her. She tried to tell the cashier not to ring those up, and as she was trying to remove some of the overage items, the man spoke up, "I might as well get it."

> On the verge of a nervous breakdown, Jaramillo got a lifeline from a friend.

Jaramillo politely declined, but the man insisted. "I said I got this." Then she realized he was talking about buying *all* of her groceries, not just the dog food. And he insisted. "I stared wide-eyed at this handsome young African-American man, this stranger, as if he'd just dropped through the ceiling like a black James Bond, like a Batman, like the Black Panther." (Did we mention she's a writer?) "Then I started to cry."

The man told Jaramillo that his name was Chris, and she hugged him and thanked him for footing the $375 bill. Only later did she find out from the cashier that the man was actually Ludacris—the Grammy-winning hip-hop artist known for such hits as "Rollout (My Business)" and "Southern Hospitality," as well as for his role as Tej in the *Fast and the Furious* films. Jaramillo described the rapper as "awesome run amok" and promised to pay it forward by telling her story. "What Ludacris had no way of knowing," she wrote, "is that his quiet kindness and generous gesture came at a moment when my candle was out."

If March begins on a Friday, so will November.

"I SAW THAT LOOK OF PANIC."

Steve John, an executive with a car company in northern California, nearly choked to death in 2006. Some food got lodged in his throat, but a friend saved him with the Heimlich maneuver. Eight years later, John was serving as tournament director for the AT&T Pebble Beach National Pro-Am. While attending a PGA party with professional golfers and celebrities, the same thing happened again: "I was drinking water and eating these little appetizers. I threw down a piece of cheese and [suddenly] it just didn't work." By "didn't work," he meant it got caught in his windpipe and he couldn't breathe—*at all*—and the man he was talking to at the time, Clint Eastwood, could see it on his face that something was seriously wrong.

Before John knew it, the 83-year-old living legend was behind him and was thrusting both fists upward into John's abdomen until that hunk of cheese popped out. "Clint saved my life," said John, who is barely half Eastwood's age. "I can't believe I'm 202 pounds and he threw me up in the air three times." Afterward, the octogenarian made the young man "drink a big glass of water with a bunch of lemon squeezed in it." Eastwood later said that he'd never given anyone the Heimlich maneuver before, but he'd practiced it just in case. He's just glad he recognized what was happening in time: "I looked into his eyes," he told his hometown paper, the *Carmel Pine Cone*, "and I saw that look of panic people have when they see their life passing before their eyes. It looked bad."

"LET'S DEAL HIM SOME GOOD ONES."

Michael Beatty was in a bad mood. You'd be too, if this happened to you: "Two weeks in hospital with Sepsis/DKA [diabetes] and coded twice. Long recovery along with massive medical costs." Those were the first two lines of the heartbreaking GoFundMe page that was set up in December 2018 for the Vietnam veteran from Huntsville, Alabama. Beatty's low point came when he went into cardiac arrest: "I was not aware that I ripped everything out…and I was totally wild and crying to Beth Ann [his wife] to 'please help me.' That got to her so badly she had to step out. So they gave me most everything up to Morphine with no effect. Finally they tried Ativan and I went limp and silent."

A month or so later, with only a small monthly retirement check to sustain him, Beatty was recovering at home, faced with a mountain of bills and a GoFundMe page that was still far short of meeting its $5,000 goal (which wouldn't even be enough to cover his bills). Then, while scrolling through his Twitter feed, he saw a tweet by Patton Oswalt in which the comedian made up a vulgar rhyme insulting President Trump. Beatty replied, "@pattonoswalt I just realized why I was so happy you died in *Blade Trinity*."

Nearly half of all cream of mushroom soup sold is used to make green bean casserole.

Oswalt, who enjoys engaging clever trolls, engaged with this one, and the two men had a bit of a tit-for-tat over their political differences. Then Oswalt decided to have a look at Beatty's feed (to amass more ammo, no doubt). A few minutes later, the comedian disengaged and posted a new tweet to his 4.6 million followers:

> Aw, man. This dude just attacked me on Twitter and I joked back but then I looked at his timeline and he's in a LOT of trouble health-wise. I'd be pissed off too. He's been dealt some s*** cards—let's deal him some good ones. Click and donate—just like I am about to.

Within a half hour, Beatty's GoFundMe goal of $5,000 was fully met; by the end of that day, the account had topped $35,000. "Patton," Beatty wrote back, "you have humbled me to the point where I can barely compose my words. You have caused me to take pause and reflect on how harmful words from my mouth could resolve in such an outpouring. Thank you for this."

* * *

SILLY UNITS OF MEASUREMENTS

Mother Cow Index. In the late 1800s, this was used in the American Southwest as a way to measure the size and quality of a plot of land—the more pregnant cows an acre of land could handle, the better it was…and the more it was worth.

FLOPS. It's a loose acronym for FLoating point Operations Per Second—a measure of computing power.

Nibble. Another computer metric, it's a tiny bit of memory. Eight bits equals one byte; four bits equals one nibble. (So one byte is two nibbles)

Furman. Named for mathematician Alan T. Furman, it's used to measure an angle of a round object. One Furman is equivalent to 1/65,336 of a circle.

Shake. Two shakes = one lamb's tail. Just kidding. In nuclear engineering, a shake equates to 10 nanoseconds. (That's a hundred-billionth of a second.)

Morgen. A measurement used by Dutch colonists in South Africa until the 1970s, a morgen (Dutch for "morning") was the amount of land that one man with one ox could till before lunch.

Butt. The quantity of wine that can fit into a barrel.

Air-conditioning a football stadium can cost more than $500,000 a month.

A SWITCH *PITCHER?*

Just for fun, try throwing a wad of paper into the wastebasket with your opposite hand. Tough, isn't it? Now try striking out a big-league hitter with your opposite hand. Here's the story of an unconventional pitcher and the bizarre at bat that changed the rules of baseball.

MATCH GAME

In baseball, one of the key elements of pitcher/batter matchup strategy comes down to what hand they use. Typically, right-handed batters don't perform as well against right-handed pitchers, and the same is even truer for lefties against lefties. Most batters, lefty or righty, don't like to face southpaws, who have an uncanny ability to "paint the outside corner" of the strike zone, where it's tough for righties to hit it. Lefties dominate lefties by taking away their main advantage of hitting well against right-handed pitchers. As a result, the left-handed specialist has become a key part of a team's late-inning strategy. It also leads to longer games due to frequent instances of a left-handed pinch-hitter being brought in to face a righty, and then the righty is replaced by a lefty, and so on, and so forth. In the case of a switch-hitter, he can simply choose to bat from whichever side of the plate gives him the best advantage.

So why aren't there any "switch-pitchers"?

BRANCHING OUT

There were a few ambidextrous pitchers in the 19th century, including Tony Mullane, who won 284 games while pitching with both arms. The practice died out after that... mostly. There was an ambidextrous pitcher named Greg Harris who played from 1981 to 1995, but none of the eight teams he played for let him pitch as a lefty until the second-to-last game of his career, when he got to pitch with both arms. A nine-year-old boy from Omaha, Nebraska, named Pat Venditte was watching that game and said to himself, "I can't wait to do that too one day."

Like Harris, Venditte is a natural right-hander. At the age of three, Pat's father taught him to throw with his left arm as well, thinking it would give him an advantage. And it did. Venditte debuted his ambidextrous pitching style in Little League. (Some people mistook him for twins.) When he got to college, his coach wouldn't let him use his specially made, symmetrical glove with two thumbholes. Reason: the coach didn't want a "circus." Even so, Venditte got drafted by the New York Yankees. He made his minor-league debut in 2008, where he was allowed to use his special glove...and the circus that his former coach had feared commenced.

Venditte made his debut as a relief pitcher for the Staten Island Yankees. The fourth batter he faced was switch-hitter Ralph Henriquez of the Brooklyn Cyclones,

Sacré bleu! French women weren't allowed to vote until 1944.

who walked up to the right side of home plate. It was the bottom of the ninth with two outs; Venditte was trying to preserve the lead. Venditte, who'd been pitching righty, switched his glove to pitch as a lefty. Henriquez asked the umpire if he was allowed to switch hands like that, only to be told there was no rule against it. So Henriquez walked around to the left side of the plate and squared up as a lefty. Venditte removed his glove and switched back to a lefty. Henriquez broke his stance and returned to the other side of the plate. "This is becoming a comedy show here," remarked one of the announcers. This back-and-forth went on for seven minutes before the umpires finally had enough. They told Henriquez to stay on the right side. Venditte, pitching right-handed, struck him out to end the game.

STAY IN YOUR LANE

You can thank that strange at bat for what's known as the Pat Venditte rule, which took effect later that season. It limits how many times a pitcher and batter can change their stance during a single at bat. The rule states that "a pitcher must indicate visually to the umpire-in-chief, the batter, and any runners the hand with which he intends to pitch, which may be done by wearing his glove on the other hand while touching the pitcher's plate." In addition, the pitcher can't switch hands unless he is injured during the at bat. One switch is allowed by both the pitcher and hitter during the at bat, but it can only happen once a pitch has been thrown. And the pitcher isn't allowed any warm-up throws when he switches (so he'd better have loosened that arm in the bullpen, or he could injure it if he tries to pitch at full strength).

A CALL TO ARMS

After spending seven years in the minors, Venditte was called up by the Oakland A's in 2015, and has pitched for a few other teams since then. He says he's fully aware that many see him as a novelty. "Any time you're different," he remarked in 2018, after signing with the Los Angeles Dodgers, "you have to convince people, and the only way to do that is with results, and that's what I found myself doing with every outing." Venditte has performed well thus far in his career, mostly throwing curveballs and fastballs, with the occasional changeup. His velocity is much harder throwing from his right side, because that's his normal throwing arm. But he gets more curve from his left arm. As far as which arm he'll use against any particular hitter, he leaves that up to the coaches. "To watch Venditte, it's a remarkable thing to see what one person's body is capable of doing," said Boston Red Sox manager John Farrell after Venditte's impressive major league debut. "Even guys in the dugout were kind of marveling."

As of this writing, he is still the only ambidextrous pitcher in the big leagues. Perhaps there's a both-armed up-and-comer who got inspired by Pat Venditte the same way Greg Harris inspired him all those years ago.

In 1930 Addis Housewares made the first artificial Christmas trees using the same brush bristle machinery it used to make toilet brushes.

INNER SPACE

Today, MRIs and other imaging technologies are so commonplace that it's easy to forget how miraculous they were when it first became possible to see inside the human body.

LOOK BUT DON'T TOUCH

In 1969 Dr. Raymond Damadian, an assistant professor at the State University of New York, visited the lab of a U.S. Navy physicist named Freeman Cope and got a demonstration of an unusual method Cope used to study materials in test tubes. Instead of working with the materials directly, Cope inserted the test tubes into an electromagnet and bombarded them with energy. When the electromagnet was turned on, the sample in the test tube absorbed energy. Then, when the magnet was turned off, the sample released the energy in the form of electromagnetic waves. An antenna built around the test tube received these signals, and by studying the signals, Cope was able to analyze the molecular structure of his samples in great detail, without ever touching the samples physically.

The technique had been used by physicists in labs since the 1940s, but it was new to Damadian. He had been trained as a physician, and he thought the technique might be useful in medicine as well. What if the test tube and the electromagnet surrounding it were large enough to hold an entire person? "I said, 'Cope, I can't believe what you just did. You took a sample with an antenna around the outside of the test tube and got all this detailed chemical information.' I said, 'Do you realize, that if we could ever do that on a human body, we could get chemistry from anywhere in the body, we could spark an unprecedented revolution in human medicine.' Well," Damadian told the BBC in 2018, "he thought that was crazy."

But Damadian was convinced the idea had merit. So he and two of his SUNY graduate students, Larry Minkoff and Mike Goldsmith, spent the next several years building a device large enough to scan an entire human being. They wrapped the outside of a large cylinder with 30 miles of niobium-titanium wire to create the electromagnet, then they added a liquid helium cooling system to keep the wire cool, which made the magnet even more powerful. Because the machine could only focus on one particular point in space, Damadian and his students also built a sliding wooden frame for the person being scanned to lie on. Adjusting the frame while the patient was on it made it possible to scan different parts of the body, by moving each part into the focus point. Mike Goldsmith designed the receiving antenna: instead of building it into the machine, which is how modern MRI scanners work, Goldsmith's antenna wrapped around the patient and was worn like a corset.

You thought lions were bad? Hippos kill more people than any other wild animal in Africa.

THROUGH THICK AND THIN

By 1977 the machine, which they named "Indomitable" because of all the technological and other obstacles they'd overcome to build it, was complete and ready to be tested. There was just one problem: nobody wanted to get in it. As far as Damadian and his grad students could tell, there was no risk associated with exposure to large electromagnetic fields. But no one had ever stuffed themselves inside such a powerful electromagnetic field before, so who really knew? Damadian finally decided that since the machine was his idea, he would have to be the one to climb inside it. He strapped on the antenna and got inside the machine; then his grad students turned it on and tried to scan him. No luck—the machine did not produce any readings. They weren't sure what the problem was…until someone suggested, diplomatically, that maybe Dr. Damadian was too fat for the antenna, which wasn't sensitive enough to pick up the signals after they passed through his body fat.

The only way to test this theory was to scan someone who was skinnier than Damadian. Larry Minkoff was a lot skinnier, but he refused to do it. Finally, after seven weeks of watching Damadian closely and observing no apparent ill effects from the scan, on July 3, 1977, Minkoff worked up the nerve to put on the antenna and climb into the machine. "We put Larry in, we got a signal immediately from his heart, and I said, 'Holy smokes! It's actually going to work,' " Damadian told the BBC.

When the wooden frame was positioned to scan Minkoff's heart, it detected large amounts of water, which is present in large quantities in the blood that is pumped through the heart. When Damadian moved the frame so that Minkoff's lungs were in position to be scanned, the signal indicating the presence of water faded to almost nothing—exactly what he expected it to do, because the lungs contain much less blood than the heart. Over the next five hours, Damadian collected data from 106 different points on Minkoff's body, including his liver and spinal cord, which the computer then used to construct into a crude image.

SEEING THINGS DIFFERENTLY

Damadian's machine was the first MRI machine large enough to scan an entire person, and the image the Indomitable's computer created from the 106 different data points it scanned that day was the first MRI scan of a human being. But the technology that it used, analyzing the signals from hydrogen cells, turned out to be a dead end. Damadian assumed that the signals given off from cancerous tissues would be different enough from the signals given off by healthy tissue to enable his scanner to be used to detect cancer. He was wrong—signals given off by different parts of the body varied so much that it was difficult to tell which cells were cancerous. But Damadian's work inspired another scientist, a chemistry professor at Stony Brook University named Paul Lauterbur, to develop his own MRI scanning technique, which used two magnetic fields—a strong one and a weak one—to create two-dimensional images of the tissue being scanned.

BLIND SPOT

That method of scanning proved to be a much more effective diagnostic tool. Then an English scientist named Peter Mansfield improved upon Lauterbur's technique, coming up with a way to scan patients in minutes instead of hours. Their machines were so far superior to Damadian's first machine that when Damadian started his own company to build MRI machines in the 1980s, he abandoned his own designs in favor of Lauterbur's and Mansfield's. Their contributions to the development of the MRI were so significant that when the Nobel Committee decided to award the inventors of the MRI scanner with the 2003 Nobel Prize for Medicine, they awarded it to Lauterbur and Mansfield, but *not* to Damadian.

The slight was controversial, and it made Damadian so angry that he took out full-page ads in the *New York Times* and other papers protesting the decision. But there's no way to appeal a Nobel Prize decision, and though there's nothing to stop the Nobel Committee from honoring Damadian in a subsequent year, as of 2018 they have not done so, and he still hasn't received the Nobel Prize that he feels he deserves. "I made the original contribution and made the first patent," he told the *New York Times* in 2004. "If people want to reconsider history apart from the facts, there's not much I can do about that."

A TIP FROM UNCLE JOHN

Claustrophobia, a fear of small spaces, can strike during an MRI session, not only because you're in such a small space, but also because you're worried about a possible major medical problem. Here are some ways to reduce the panic:

1. Try focused breathing—breathe in for five seconds, then out, then repeat.

2. Just simply count. Monotony can be soothing.

3. Even covering your face with a towel or washcloth can make you feel like you're someplace else... anyplace else.

*   *   *

WHY DO AUCTIONEERS SPEAK SO QUICKLY?

"They talk like that to hypnotize the bidders. Auctioneers don't just talk fast—they chant in a rhythmic monotone to lull onlookers into a conditioned pattern of call and response, as if they were playing a game of 'Simon Says.' The speed is also intended to give the buyers a sense of urgency: Bid now or lose out. And it doesn't hurt the bottom line, either. Auctioneers typically take home from 10 to 20 percent of the sale price. Selling more items in less time means they make more money."

—Slate

In 1969 Jefferson Airplane performed "We Can Be Together" on *The Dick Cavett Show*...

1960s MOVIE TRIVIA

Here are a few behind-the-scenes facts about some 1960s Hollywood classics.

It's a Mad, Mad, Mad, Mad World (1963)

The all-star cast of this madcap comedy includes dozens of cameos from old movie stars such as Leo Gorcey of the Bowery Boys, the Three Stooges, Buster Keaton, and Jack Benny. But Benny, it turns out, wasn't the producers' first choice for his small role. It had been offered to Stan Laurel (of Laurel and Hardy fame), but he turned it down. Reason: when his partner, Oliver Hardy, died in 1957, Laurel said he'd never perform again. And he never did.

Cleopatra (1963)

This epic movie was over *four hours long*. But director Joseph L. Mankiewicz wanted it to be even longer. His original plan (nixed by Twentieth Century Fox) was to release it in two parts—*Caesar and Cleopatra* and *Antony and Cleopatra*, with a combined running time of *six* hours.

The Graduate (1967)

It's got one of the most famous (and frequently parodied) endings in movie history. Benjamin (Dustin Hoffman) interrupts the wedding of his former girlfriend Elaine (Katharine Ross), and they run off and hop onto a bus to escape her enraged friends and family. Then, they just sit there silently…not really sure how to start their lives together. That final scene was an accident. Director Mike Nichols wasn't around that day, so film editor Sam O'Steen was in charge. Only problem: he was a novice director, and didn't know when he was supposed to say "Cut." Result: the film kept rolling… and captured something magical.

The Sound of Music (1965)

Julie Andrews started shooting this movie right after she'd finished filming *Mary Poppins*. To entertain the kids playing the Von Trapp children between takes, Andrews sang them "Supercalifragilisticexpialidocious." *Mary Poppins* hadn't been released yet, so the kids thought Andrews had written the song on the spot, just for them.

....and singer Grace Slick became the first person to say the F-word on American TV.

101 Dalmatians (1961)

Disney's previous animated feature, *Sleeping Beauty*, was a box office flop and left the company in debt. If *101 Dalmatians* hadn't been a hit, the company had plans in place to cease making cartoons altogether, and instead focus on live-action movies and theme parks. But *101 Dalmatians* wound up being a smash, so it was business as usual for Disney.

Doctor Zhivago (1965)

It went on to become one of the top-grossing movies of the year (and all time), but for its first few weeks of release, theaters playing the epic Russian love story were mostly empty. Then Maurice Jarre's theme song from the film, "Lara's Theme," became an unlikely radio hit—so much so that it made people want to go see the movie.

Romeo and Juliet (1968)

Franco Zeffirelli's blockbuster take on the classic Shakespeare play cast unknowns Leonard Whiting and Olivia Henry in the title roles. The movie's biggest star, however, appeared anonymously. Sir Laurence Olivier, who won a Best Actor Oscar for *Hamlet* in 1948, loved Zeffirelli's work at England's National Theatre, and agreed to appear in his film purely out of his love for Shakespeare. Olivier served as the film's narrator, provided the voices for several background characters, and dubbed in the voice of Lord Montague because actor Antonio Pierfederici's thick Italian accent made his lines (in English) too difficult for audiences to understand.

Easy Rider (1969)

While the cocaine and LSD used by the drug-taking bikers in this movie weren't real, all the marijuana that Jack Nicholson, Dennis Hopper, and Peter Fonda smoked on-screen was. During the pivotal campfire scene, which took several days to film, the trio reportedly went through more than 100 joints.

Butch Cassidy and the Sundance Kid (1969)

One memorable part of the classic buddy Western is when Butch Cassidy (Paul Newman) showboats on his bicycle to impress Etta Place (Katharine Ross). Newman did the stunts himself. Reason: the stuntman hired to do the scenes kept falling off the bike.

American Express started in 1850 as a delivery service.

IT'S A WEIRD, WEIRD WORLD

Here's proof that truth is stranger than fiction.

LETTUCE MEAT IN PEAS

In 2018 the quiet town of Calais, in northern France, nearly saw an all-out war between those who sell meat and those whose goal is to get the French to stop eating meat, referred to in the press as "militant vegans" (which sounds like an oxymoron). Some of the town's butchers, fishmongers, and cheese shops claimed the vegans vandalized their shops, and asked for police protection; others vowed revenge. The mayor's response: he called off a "Vegan Festival" that was going to be held that September. He wouldn't reveal the exact reason for the abrupt cancellation, saying only that he'd been made aware of "a series of operations aimed at stirring up trouble." How were the butchers planning to disrupt the vegan festival? According to one of them, "We were ready to organize a big barbecue."

FOOL'S GOLD

Tran Ngoc Phuc, a 36-year-old Vietnamese businessman, isn't afraid to flaunt his wealth. (Although he does travel with five bodyguards.) He became "news" in December 2018 after a series of YouTube videos showed him wearing gold jewelry that's so enormous that it doesn't even look real. But it

is. He wears a gold chain around his neck—and it's an actual chain, like the kind you'd use to lock a gate. Hanging from the chain is a gold plaque about the size of a *Bathroom Reader*. He also wears an enormous gold bracelet and four gold rings the size of Rubik's Cubes. Combined worth of all this bling: $550,000. Phuc—or, as he prefers to be called, Phux XO (the name of a karaoke bar he owns)—made his millions in his 20s by trading oil. And he insists that there's more to his jewelry than just showing everyone how obscenely rich he is. A feng shui consultant once told him that gold brings good luck. Phuc now wears so much good luck that he had to go to a chiropractor for a sore neck—the result of wearing nearly 30 pounds of gold. According to news reports, Phuc is planning to buy a gold shirt and a gold hat to complete his ensemble.

NAILED IT

Doug Bergeson could see the nail beating with his heart. It was *in* his heart. And he was standing there with a nail gun in his hand, wondering what to do next. With no one else around, the Wisconsin farmer decided leave the nail sticking out of his heart and drive himself to the hospital, figuring that he'd get there sooner than if he waited for an ambulance. "At about eight miles in," he later said, "it started to hurt quite a bit." Bergeson made it to the hospital, and was admitted immediately. When his wife arrived, her jaw dropped at the sight of the 3½-inch nail protruding from her husband's chest. He shrugged and said, "Oops." Here's how it happened: Bergeson was installing a fireplace in a home he was building for his family when he had to get a nail into an awkward spot. "I was on my tip-toes and I just didn't quite have enough room, and it fired before I was really ready for it, and then it dropped down and it fired again." It was that second nail that pierced his heart…at 90 mph. After a successful surgery, the surgeon gave the nail to Bergeson and told him that it had penetrated "the thickness of a piece of paper" away from a main artery. Had he been in a slightly different position, or if he was breathing in instead of out, he would have been dead within a few minutes. But the nail missed the artery, and he didn't even bleed.

THE WRONG STUFF

Dozens of concerned citizens—including one NASA engineer—alerted the authorities in February 2017 about a crashed space capsule sitting in a field about 100 feet from Interstate 10 near Casa Grande, Arizona. The silver, egg-shaped object was about the size of a cement truck mixer. It had rivets and burn scars, and its hull had an American flag printed on it, along with the stenciled words "United States" and "Capt. J.

Millard." A parachute was splayed out behind it. Police arrived and told curious onlookers to keep back while they inspected the object. It didn't take long to realize there was no danger. That's because it *was* a cement truck mixer. It had been sitting there in that exact spot for 30 years, but no one took much notice of it until a local artist named Jack Millard decided to give it a spacey makeover. When the *Arizona Republic* tracked him down, Millard seemed amused by the reaction to what he called a "glorified yard ornament." Why'd he do it? "I just get these impulses to create."

LAWYER, LAWYER, PANTS ON FIRE

In March 2007, Stephen Gutierrez, a 28-year-old Miami defense attorney, was giving the closing arguments in an arson case in which the defendant, Claudy Charles, was accused of burning his own car to collect insurance money. Gutierrez was trying to convince the jury that cars can spontaneously catch fire. Then his pants caught on fire. Literally. Smoke started rising from his pocket and the lawyer ran out of the courtroom in a panic. When he returned a few minutes later—with wet, singed pants—he insisted that it was an accident. He told the judge that he'd been fiddling with an e-cigarette in his pocket when it somehow caught fire…proving his point that accidental fires *really do happen!* The judge was skeptical, and so was Mr. Charles, who said, "I want another lawyer." He got one. And he was found guilty anyway.

45% of Americans have brown eyes. 27% have blue, and 9% have green.

STALLED CARS

Here are some forgotten automobiles that came and went—and fast.

CHEVROLET SERIES M COPPER COOLED (1923)
Chevy thought that this car would give them an upper hand over the dominant car of the day—the Ford Model T. It offered a sophisticated air-cooled engine (rather than water-cooled), made possible with copper wiring. Clever idea. It didn't work. Chevy canceled a 50,000-model order after the first few hundred cars they'd sold suffered from low-speed overheating, engine failure…and engine fires.

HYUNDAI EQUUS (2016)
Hyundai is known for making reliable, affordable cars. Unlike its competitors, it didn't have a separate luxury line (Toyota has Lexus; Nissan has Infiniti). So this fancy car (auto magazines compared the Equus to a Rolls-Royce) didn't make much noise in 2016. People thought it was just another Hyundai, not a luxury car. However, it *did* cost $70,000, another thing people didn't associate with Hyundai. Only a few hundred sold.

AMC AMX 400 (1968)
The American Motors Corporation was formed out of a merger between Hudson Motor Car Company and the Nash-Kelvinator Corporation. In business as AMC since 1954, the company's cars became iconic of the 1960s and 1970s—cheap, ugly cars like the Pacer and the Gremlin. Those were nothing compared to the AMX 400, a customizable car. Bolt-on kits designed by George Barris (designer of the Batmobile from the campy 1960s *Batman* TV series) were sold at AMC dealers. The kit allowed drivers to make their car "unique" with some very specific options. For example: the headlights were hidden behind a louvered grille. It also added dozens of cross bars from the roof down to the back bumper, it featured a two-tone paint job (colors: cream and orange), and it had light strips across the tail end that glowed based on what the driver was doing—green when revving, yellow when coasting, and red when stopped.

FACEL FACELLIA (1960)
After building its reputation in the 1940s and 1950s as one of France's leading manufacturers of large, expensive cars outfitted with powerful engines shipped in from American companies like Chrysler and DeSoto, Facel started building compact cars for the common man in 1960. One problem: the Facellia's small, cheap engines (made by Facel) had a tendency to fall

> The Facellia's small, cheap engines had a tendency to fall apart, or even shatter.

apart, or even shatter. Within four years Facellia was off the market…and its failure led to the demise of Facel itself.

YUGO GV (1985)

Marketed as the latest and greatest compact car in the tradition of the Volkswagen Beetle, Yugo—a brand of automobiles built in communist Yugoslavia just 15 years earlier—cost just $3,990. American production of the GV (it stood for "good value") ceased in 1992, but in Europe—where it was called the Zastava Koral—it remained in production until 2008. Why didn't it work in America? The Yugo broke down a lot, and its tiny engine didn't have the "oomph" to take it much past 60 mph, so it couldn't quite keep up on American highways.

LINCOLN BLACKWOOD (2002)

Luxurious SUVs became a mainstay for the auto industry in the 2000s. Ford tried to push the idea of luxury *trucks* in 2002 with the Blackwood, a truck based on the successful Lincoln Navigator. The debut model cost $52,000 (a lot for a truck), but failed to provide what consumers expected. It only came in black, for example, and the cabin (where the driver sits) wasn't as fancy as the bed (where the cargo sits), which was stainless steel and carpeted.

ALFA ROMEO ARNA (1983)

The legendary Italian sports car company teamed up with Nissan, best known for making reliable, no-frills compact cars. (Arna is an acronym for Alfa Romeo Nissan Autoveioli.) Nissan's team of engineers building a car designed by Alfa Romeo? That combo should have yielded great results. Instead, they went the other way and produced a nondescript car: a hatchback built by Alfa Romeo, based on Nissan's standard design.

BRICKLIN SV-1 (1974)

After he founded Subaru of America in the late 1960s, Malcolm Bricklin started his own car company specifically to manufacture one car, which he designed and then named after himself, the Bricklin SV-1. It had a lot of cool features, such as gull-wing doors and a body made of durable acrylic resin and fiberglass. But its main selling point: it was extra safe. ("SV" stands for "safety vehicle.") Bricklin designed it to withstand rollovers (it had a steel safety cage), and gave it bumpers that absorbed impact. It also sported a powerful V-8 engine…which could never run at full capability because a lack of air vents made it overheat. And it had too many special features to be built using assembly-line production. Result: only about 3,000 were ever produced.

World's first "unwillingly independent" nation: Singapore, tossed out of Malaysia in 1965.

TALK OF THE '10s

Every age has its slanguage. In the groovy 1960s, some people were trendsetters, which was A-OK. Others had hang-ups, which was pretty heavy, and The Man was a downer. The 1980s were righteous and totally tubular, and in the 1990s, anyone who didn't like their McJob had to take a chill pill—otherwise they could end up going postal. Get the idea? The 2010s were no exception. The decade had its own share of unique words and phrases. But because of the instant nature of 21st-century internet culture, a lot of them became overused almost as soon as they appeared, generating intense criticism and ending up on year-end "Most Annoying" lists (which didn't seem to hurt their popularity). Here are some of our favorite words of the '10s, and how we got them.

SELFIE

Meaning: A self-portrait taken of one or more people on a digital camera

Story: Here are two important photography milestones:

1. In 1839 Robert Cornelius produced a daguerreotype image of himself, which was the first known photographic self-portrait ever taken.
2. In 2002 Nathan Hope posted a blurry close-up photo of his cut lip, followed by this description: *"Um, drunk at a mates 21st, I tripped ofer and landed lip first (with front teeth coming a very close second) on a set of steps. I had a hole about 1cm long right through my bottom lip. And sorry about the focus, it was a selfie."*

That's the first known appearance of the word "selfie." Hope later said that he didn't coin it; it was common slang at the time in his home country. Based on the word structure of "selfie," can you guess which country? That's right—*selfie* is Australian for "self-portrait." A common "slanguage" practice Down Under is to take the first syllable of a word and add an "ie" ending—as in *barbie* (barbecue), *firie* (firefighter), and *Aussie* (Australian).

The word caught on internationally a few years later when the first front-facing camera phones hit the market, ushering in the age of the selfie. It was the *Oxford English Dictionary's* 2013 Word of the Year (and in 2015, the term "selfie stick" was added to the dictionary).

Backlash: Both the word (and the practice) have been blamed for everything from enabling a culture of narcissists to ruining photography, but the fad, which hit its peak in the 2010s thanks to a billion or so social network users on Facebook, Twitter, and Instagram, is proving to be critic-proof. As far back as 2014, Google was estimating that 93 million selfies were taken *every day*. "What [George] Orwell failed to predict,"

According to *Guinness World Records*, the most difficult tongue twister is "The sixth sick sheik's sixth sheep's sick."

noted comedian Keith Lowell Jensen, "is that we'd buy the cameras ourselves, and that our biggest fear would be that nobody was watching."

MANSPLAIN

Meaning: When a man attempts to explain something to a woman in a patronizing manner, assuming she doesn't know as much as he does

Story: This portmanteau of "man" and "explain" was borne out of a 2008 essay called "Men Explain Things to Me: Facts Didn't Get in Their Way" by Rebecca Solnit. She tells a story about an older, distinguished man at a party who'd heard she was an author, and asked, "So, what are your books about?" When Solnit mentioned that one of them was about influential English photographer Eadweard Muybridge, the man interrupted and asked her if she'd read the "very important book" about Muybridge that had been published that year. Solnit's friend tried to tell the man that he was actually talking *about Solnit's book,* "but," she writes, "he just continued on his way. She had to say that it was her book three or four times before he finally took it in. And then, as if in a 19th-century novel, he went ashen. That I was indeed the author of the very important book it turned out he hadn't read, just read about in the New York Times Book Review a few months earlier, so confused the neat categories into which his world was sorted that he was stunned speechless—for a moment, before he began holding forth again. Being women, we were politely out of earshot before we started laughing."

Solnit didn't actually use the word "mansplain" in her story; it first appeared about a month later in a comment thread under a repost of the essay, where other women shared their own mansplaining tales. Then it became a trending hashtag on Twitter, and two years later in 2010, "mansplain" was the New York Times Word of the Year.

Backlash: Even though Solnit didn't coin the verb, she often gets the credit for it. And at first, she tried to distance herself from *mansplain* "because it seems a little bit more condemnatory of the male of the species than I ever wanted it to be." In fact, that was the main beef people had against the word—that it pigeonholed men in the same manner that they were accused of pigeonholing women. But then, Solnit recalled, "A PhD candidate [a young woman] said to me, 'No, you need to look at how much we needed this word, how this word let us describe an experience every woman has but we didn't have language for.'" So now Solnit is proud of it. (At the BRI, we call it "Unclejohnsplain"…and he does it to *everybody.*)

SAFE SPACE

Meaning: A place—either real of figurative—where one can go to escape from a hostile or traumatic environment

Story: The roots of this term can be traced to Los Angeles in the 1960s, where a "safe space" was any place LGBTQ people could go to avoid being harassed or arrested for

being gay (which was considered a crime). From there, it was adopted by the Women's Liberation Movement of the 1970s and '80s to describe, not so much a physical place, but a community where women felt they could safely speak about their experiences.

Backlash: The actual "safe spaces" that have spurned such heated debates first showed up on U.S. college campuses in the early 2000s as places for students (usually female) to go if they felt threatened. The *Telegraph* noted in 2015 that the word has been co-opted: "The notion of the 'safe space' first emerged to describe a place of refuge for people exposed to racial prejudice or sexism. But the phrase has changed meaning to the point where now it often implies protection from 'exposure to ideas that make one uncomfortable,' according to Nadine Strossen, a prominent law professor and former head of the American Civil Liberties Union." That echoes a common sentiment—mostly among conservatives—that colleges are becoming too "politically correct" and a threat to free speech.

BAE

Meaning: An affectionate nickname for a significant other

Story: "Bae" was added to the *Oxford Dictionary* in 2015—a year after the Pharrell Williams/Miley Cyrus duet "Come Get It Bae" hit #23 on the Billboard Hot 100. But when it comes to tracking the word's origins, etymologists are stumped. The most commonly cited origin—that it's an acronym for "before anyone else"—is false. It's also not a shortened version of Beyoncé, a popular assumption that came about due to the simultaneous ascensions of the word and the pop star. Katherine Connor Martin, head of *Oxford*'s U.S. dictionary, explained to *Esquire* why finding the origin of slang words can be tough to do, even in the internet age: "Slang is often very transient, first appearing in subcultures, and then tends to be proliferated online. It's usually difficult to predict which words will break through." The earliest verifiable appearance of "bae" is from 2003, when an internet user named "Trong" submitted the word to *The Urban Dictionary*, defining it as "bastardization of the term 'babe'."

Backlash: "Bae" is one of those words you can put into two distinct categories: people who use it unabashedly, and people who hate it. The most common criticism of "bae," as the *Independent UK* pointed out in 2015 after naming it "one of the most annoying words in the world right now," is that it's a pointless abbreviation, writing, "Yeah, cos 'babe' takes way too long to say. Yuck." Echoing that sentiment, the definition of "bae" as "significant other" has been demoted to only the second entry of the word in *The Urban Dictionary*. That's based on the number of "upvotes" it has amassed (about 800). The number-one definition, which has amassed nearly 70,000 upvotes, is "a Danish word for poop."

For more of the decade's most controversial words and phrases, twerk your way on over to page 205.

You sound different on a recording than you do in your head because when you speak, your ears pick up vibrations from your throat.

CLOWN QUOTES

Freaked out by clowns? Too bad! Honk-honk!

"A clown is like aspirin, only he works twice as fast."
—Groucho Marx

"A good clown caricatures his fellow men; a great one parodies himself."
—Pierre Mariel

"It is meat and drink to me to see a clown."
—William Shakespeare

"A clown is an angel with a red nose."
—J. T. "Bubba" Sikes

"Every human being is a clown but only few have the courage to show it."
—Charlie Rivel

"The arrival of a good clown exercises a more beneficial influence upon the health of a town than the arrival of twenty asses laden with drugs."
—Thomas Sydenham

"The comic spirit masquerades in all things we say and do. We are each a clown and do not need to put on a white face."
—James Hillman

"I had a friend who was a clown. When he died, all his friends went to the funeral in one car."
—Steven Wright

"Jesters do oft prove prophets."
—William Shakespeare

"A clown is a poet in action."
—Henry Miller

"The art of the clown is more profound than we think...It is the comic mirror of tragedy and the tragic mirror of comedy."
—André Suarès

"I REMAIN JUST ONE THING, AND ONE THING ONLY—AND THAT IS A CLOWN. IT PLACES ME ON A FAR HIGHER PLANE THAN ANY POLITICIAN."
—Charlie Chaplin

"Wearing underwear on the outside of your clothes can turn a tedious trip to the store for a forgotten carton of milk into an amusement park romp."
—Dr. Hunter "Patch" Adams

"The cleverest character in comedy is the clown, for he who would make people take him for a fool, must not be one."
—Miguel de Cervantes

"The fact that some geniuses were laughed at does not imply that all who are laughed at are geniuses. They laughed at Columbus, they laughed at Fulton, they laughed at the Wright brothers. But they also laughed at Bozo the Clown."
—Carl Sagan

"CLOWN AND GURU ARE A SINGLE IDENTITY: THE SATIRIC AND SUBLIME SIDE OF THE SAME HIGHER VISION OF LIFE."
—Theodore Rozak

"By laughing at me, the audience really laughs at themselves and realizing they have done this, gives them sort of a spiritual second wind for going back into the battles of life."
—Emmett "Weary Willie" Kelly

THE ZSA ZSA WORKOUT

The 1980s saw the advent of these two unrelated cultural phenomena: personal fitness and home video. Unrelated? Not really. After Jane Fonda's Workout (adapted from her 1981 book) and Richard Simmons's Sweatin' to the Oldies sold millions of copies, dozens of other celebrities tried to cash in on the fad. Did you (or your parents) ever exercise to…

Arnold Schwarzenegger:
Shape Up with Arnold
(1982)

Marie Osmond: Exercise
for Mothers-to-Be (1983)

The Raquel Welch Total
Beauty and Fitness
Program (1984)

Bruce Jenner: Winning
Workout (1984)

David Carradine's Tai Chi
Workouts for Beginners
(1987)

Alyssa Milano: Teen Steam
(1988)

Angela Lansbury's Positive
Moves (1988)

Fitness Walking with Sally
Struthers (1990)

Heather Locklear Presents:
Your Personal Workout
(1990)

Sandy Duncan:
The 5-Minute
Workout (1990)

Warm Up with
Traci Lords (1990)

CherFitness:
A New Attitude
(1991)

Jennie Garth's Body
in Progress (1992)

Dixie Carter's
Unworkout (1992)

Cindy Crawford:
Shape Your Body
Workout (1992)

Zsa Zsa Gabor: "It's
Simple, Darling" (1993)

Fabio Fitness (1993)

Young at Heart:
Body Conditioning
with Estelle Getty
(1993)

La Toya Jackson:
Step Up Workout
(1993)

The Marky Mark
Workout: Form…Focus…
Fitness (1993)

Mary Tyler Moore:
Everywoman's Workout
Aerobics (1994)

Regis Philbin: My
Personal Workout
(1994)

Claudia Schiffer: Perfectly
Fit Buns (1995)

Your Personal Best
Workout: Elle Macpherson
(1995)

Paula Abdul's Get Up
and Dance (1995)

Milton Berle's Low
Impact / High Comedy
Workout for Seniors
(1994)

Makes sense: A citizen of the Ivory Coast (western Africa) is called an Ivorian.

WHO'S "THE BOSS"?

As if being adored by millions and being paid millions of dollars to make music for a living, pop and rock stars also get to have really cool nicknames. Here's where they came from.

THE CHAIRMAN OF THE BOARD: In the early 1950s, William B. Williams, a disc jockey at WNEW, a New York radio station, mused on air that Frank Sinatra, who also had a show at the station, should have a title, like Benny Goodman (the "King of Swing") and Duke Ellington. So he started calling Sinatra the Chairman of the Board. The nickname caught on and Sinatra actually credited Williams with reviving his career. By 1960, Sinatra wanted more creative control. He left his longtime label, Capitol Records, and formed his own company, Reprise Records. Sinatra not only became Reprise's biggest star, but also its president and CEO. In other words, he literally was the "chairman of the board."

THE VELVET FOG: Like Frank Sinatra and Dean Martin, Mel Tormé was one of the great crooners, a polished singer who performed standards and the most romantic entries in the Great American Songbook in the 1940s, '50s, and '60s. (He also had a big comeback in the 1980s with a number of appearances as himself on the TV sitcom *Night Court*.) Despite having one of the most colorful nicknames out there, Tormé didn't much like being known as "the Velvet Fog"—he jokingly referred to himself as "the Velvet Frog." But the moniker alludes to Tormé's impossibly smooth and gentle singing voice, like a fog made of velvet. New York DJ Fred Robbins came up with it in 1947, and popularized it on the air.

THE FAB FOUR: Early in their career, the Beatles were famously rejected by Decca Records because an executive thought guitar groups were "on their way out." But a Decca Records press agent named Tony Barrow, who had helped arrange the audition, wasn't giving up on them. Barrow's friend, Beatles manager Brian Epstein, hired him to write press releases to tout the band to concert promoters and record labels (including EMI, which signed them). Barrow came up with the term "fabulous foursome" to describe the group, but in one of his press releases, he casually referred to them as the "Fab Four"…and it stuck.

SLOWHAND: In 1964 Eric Clapton was beginning to build a name for himself as a talented blues-rock guitarist as a member of the Yardbirds. In order to play faster and bend notes, he used light-gauge guitar strings, and he'd break at least one per show. The concert would have to come to a halt while Clapton changed his string, during which the crowd would fill time with a slow, rhythmic clapping. The British term for that: slow handclap. Yardbirds manager Giorgio Gomelsky shortened the term and saddled Clapton with it as a nickname.

THE KING (OF ROCK 'N' ROLL): It's probably the most famous nickname in music, but before Elvis Presley became known as "the King," or alternately "the King of Rock 'n' Roll," promoters billed him as "the Atomic Powered Singer." The latter name came—and stuck—in 1956, the same year Elvis scored his first hit single. Elvis came of age and broke out in Memphis, and in May 1956, *Memphis Press-Scimitar* entertainment reporter Robert Johnson labeled Elvis "the fledgling king of rock n' roll." Some disc jockeys picked up on it, dropped the "fledgling" as the singer got more and more popular, and influential gossip columnist Hedda Hopper started using it too. Before long, Elvis's manager, Colonel Tom Parker, began demanding his client be referred to as "the King."

THE BOSS: It's more than a little ironic that Bruce Springsteen, whose songs about regular people from small towns made him the unofficial voice of the working class, was saddled with a nickname of a hated, spirit-crushing authority figure. The name actually predates his fame. While fronting one of his first bands, Earth, in the late 1960s, it was his job to negotiate payment with club owners, and make sure his fellow musicians got their cut. He was, in other words, the Boss.

THE KING OF POP: In the early 1990s, Michael Jackson was one of the biggest musical stars in the world, but he didn't have what other superstars like Elvis Presley or Bruce Springsteen did: a superlative nickname like "the King" or "the Boss." So, he hired a publicist named Bob Jones, who issued a press release to every major media outlet proclaiming that Jackson would henceforth be known as "the King of Pop." Jones and Jackson even required MTV to refer to Jackson on the air as the King of Pop at least twice a week…or else they'd withhold access to his latest music video.

THE RED ROCKER: When singer David Lee Roth left his band, Van Halen, at the height of its popularity in 1985, the remaining members recruited Sammy Hagar to replace him. Hagar was already well known for his solo career, which included big hits like "I Can't Drive 55" and "There's Only One Way to Rock." Hagar is also obsessed with the color red, which he says makes him "act different" and that it "gives [him] comfort." While promoting his self-titled second solo record—often referred to as The Red Album—with a concert in Seattle in 1977, he took the stage wearing all red. A kid approached him for his autograph and asked Hagar to sign it "the Red Rocker." Hagar adopted it as his nickname.

Weird law: It's illegal to sleep in a cheese factory in South Dakota.

TOILET TECH

Better living through bathroom technology.

HIYA, SQUIRT

Product: Loogun

How It Works: The toilet is a remarkable feat of technology, but toilet design hasn't really changed much over the past 150 years. Most traditional commodes are outfitted with a hard-to-reach lip, which is where refill water comes into the bowl. That's also where gunk can collect, and where most toilet brushes can't reach. Enter the Loogun. It's a high-powered squirt gun with an angled tip. Simply fill with water, hold it inside the toilet, aim at the underside of the bowl, and voilà…the dirty deposits are gone.

NO LOOGUN NECESSARY

Product: VorMax

How It Works: Bathroom fixture manufacturer American Standard has created a toilet that doesn't need a deep, manual cleaning with extra tools. The VorMax toilet is shaped unlike any other—it has a specially curved rim that leaves few places for solid waste to collect. Moreover, the entire bowl is treated with a chemical coating that prevents sticking. That, along with powerful water jets, makes the VorMax, according to American Standard, "the cleanest flush ever engineered."

BATHROOM BUTLER

Product: U by Moen

How It Works: Do you hate fiddling with the shower faucet, nudging it a little bit to the hot side, and a little bit to the cold, in pursuit of the perfect temperature day after day? Well, U by Moen allows you to set your water temperature digitally. The system can remember several different settings for multiple users (say, "John's morning shower"). But wait, there's more. Using Amazon's voice-activated Alexa software, users can just walk into the bathroom and say, "Alexa, start John's morning shower," and the U by Moen will get it going.

THE FAIREST ONE OF ALL

Product: Mirror Clearer

How It Works: Besides waste elimination, the modern bathroom has two purposes: bathing and getting ready. But ironically, if you take a shower, you can't immediately use the bathroom to shave, do your hair, or put on makeup because the steam from the hot shower fogs up the mirror. Sure, you can wipe the mirror off with your hand or a towel, but that just leaves streaks or smudges…and it quickly fogs up again. Somebody finally invented the perfect combination of bathroom and automotive technology: the Mirror Clearer. It's basically a windshield wiper attached to a suction cup. Simply stick it on the mirror and manually run it across the mirror until it's clear.

YOU CAN GO YOUR OWN BIDET

Product: GoBidet Handheld Bidet

How It Works: More popular in Europe than in the United States, bidets are bathroom appliances that assist in cleaning you up…uh…after you use the facilities, sending a high-powered stream of water to your bottom. Some bidets are standalone, others are built into high-tech toilets. The GoBidet is an external, add-on bidet that works with any toilet. Resembling a shower head or Waterpik (and operating in much the same way), this wand connects to the toilet's water supply, and users are supposed to reach behind themselves when they use it, and hopefully catch all the water (and waste) in the toilet bowl.

URINE FOR A TREAT

Product: The Main Drain

How It Works: It's a problem as old as the toilet: men and women living together grappling over the state of the toilet seat. Women want it down (because that's how they use the facilities), while most men tend to leave it up. The makers of the Main Drain market their product as a solution for that…because it's a urinal for men that attaches to a toilet without having to change the state of the seat at all. Consisting of a small plastic urine catcher (a funnel, really) attached to a tube, it clips onto the toilet and the tube empties into the bowl. The seat remains down; the Main Drain just swivels to the side when the guy is done.

HAVE A SEAT

Product: Kohler Purefresh Toilet Seat

How It Works: There's an old saying that some people are so arrogant that they think their poop doesn't stink. But in reality, *everybody's* stinks. Toilet maker Kohler has come up with a way to eliminate bathroom odors at the source with its Purefresh seat. The seat has a carbon deodorizing system that automatically neutralizes foul odors, *and* a built-in air freshener that provides another, more pleasant scent to help conceal them. As soon as the user sits down, a battery-powered fan goes to work, directing the air trapped in the toilet bowl between ceramic and fanny into the carbon filter. As that air circulates out, a "scent pack" recirculates the smell of "Garden Waterfall," "Soft and Fresh Laundry," or "Avocado Spa."

Until the 16th century, wedding rings were worn on the thumb.

DRAWING FROM LIFE

*It's hard to create a character out of nowhere, so sometimes the
people who make cartoons go to the movies, or turn on the TV…
and make an animated version of what they see on the screen.*

TROY McCLURE

You might remember him from such shows as *The Simpsons*, where he appeared
frequently (voiced by the late Phil Hartman) as a washed-up B-movie actor. With his
glory days long behind him, McClure was forced to star in school educational films
and host infomercials. He's an amalgam of lots of briefly popular and forgotten actors,
especially the two that are his namesakes: Troy Donahue and Doug McClure.

YOGI BEAR

Art Carney created the voice he used to play good-natured but dimwitted Ed Norton
on *The Honeymooners* by imitating old Borscht Belt and vaudeville comedians. And
Daws Butler created the voice *he* used to play good-natured but picnic-basket-thieving
Yogi Bear in the 1960s Hanna-Barbera cartoon series by imitating Carney's portrayal
of Ed Norton. (It seemed that Hanna-Barbera "borrowed" the name from New York
Yankees catcher Yogi Berra, but the cartoon studio claimed it was just a coincidence…
when Berra brought a lawsuit against them. Berra later withdrew the suit.)

TOP CAT

One of the most popular (and edgiest) sitcoms of the late 1950s: *The Phil Silvers Show*,
also known as *You'll Never Get Rich* and *Sergeant Bilko*. Bilko was a con man, always
trying to run scams out of his sleepy military base with the assistance of his troops,
including Private Doberman, played by Maurice Gosfield. The Hanna-Barbera cartoon
Top Cat, which hit the air in 1961, just two years after *Sergeant Bilko* went off the air,
is more or less an animated remake of that show. Arnold Stang portrayed Top Cat,
a con man always trying to make a buck, and he just imitated Phil Silvers. Another
character, Benny the Ball, is based on Private Doberman, and Gosfield stepped in to
voice the part.

Lesser-known names for Area 51: Dreamland, Paradise Ranch, Groom Lake, and Watertown.

BETTY BOOP

Before the scantily clad, flapper-based cartoon character Betty Boop—with her round face, cropped hair, and "boop-oop-a-doop" catchphrase—became a sensation in the 1930s, Paramount Pictures had a popular contract player named Helen Kane. Her calling cards: a round face, cropped hair, and the catchphrase "boop-oop-a-doop." Kane sued Betty Boop's animator, Fleisher Studios, but a judge ruled that her persona wasn't distinctive enough to have been illegally lifted.

BUZZIE, FLAPS, ZIGGY, AND DIZZY

With their moptop haircuts, playful attitudes, and Liverpudlian accents, the singing vultures that Mowgli encounters in Disney's 1967 animated adaptation of Rudyard Kipling's *The Jungle Book* were pretty blatantly based on the Beatles. Animators came up with the birds, and the film's chief songwriters, Robert and Richard Sherman, suggested that producers hire the actual Beatles to voice their cartoon counterparts. On behalf of his bandmates, John Lennon said no.

A TIP FROM UNCLE JOHN

How to draw from life: cartoonists say start by figuring out a person's basic face shape—round, thin and narrow, pear-shaped, etc. Then draw a center line, from top to bottom, to use as a reference point for placing the nose, eyes, and mouth. Once you've got them in a good spot, work on exaggerating them. (You're making a cartoon, not a portrait.)

FOGHORN LEGHORN

Audiences who saw Looney Tunes cartoons in movie theaters during the 1940s probably would've recognized that the loud, Southern-drawling, know-it-all, extra-large rooster was a takeoff of the name and character of Senator Beauregard Claghorn, a blowhard of a politician from the South voiced by Kenny Delmar on *The Fred Allen Show*, an extremely popular radio show of the era. (Animators and writers even lifted one of Claghorn's signature lines—"That's a joke, son!"—directly, and used it for the cartoon character.)

* * *

FOOD NEWS

Chocolate bars are vegetables! Well, sort of. Chocolate derives from the cacao bean, which is technically classified as a vegetable. White chocolate has a similar consistency to chocolate and uses similar ingredients, except for a major one: cocoa powder (also known as chocolate solids). So technically, it's not chocolate.

First captioned TV show: Julia Child's *The French Chef.*

AS THE TURNTABLE TURNS

Turntables have made a big comeback. Music companies are releasing new and old albums on vinyl again, so it's time to find your old record player, dust it off, and give it a spin. Well, unless your player is one of these weird ones that disappeared into gadget history.

MISTER DISC (1983)
Manufacturer Audio-Technica oddly boasted that this portable record player was "no bigger than a man's shoe." It also looked like a man's shoe, with the slab containing a battery compartment, a headphone jack for its included foldable headphones, and a tiny tone arm that could play both LPs and 45s (which had pretty much disappeared by the early 1980s). While Mr. Disc was touted as portable, it couldn't actually play music on the go—the user had to keep it on a flat, even surface, and it wouldn't work if it was moved. Also marketed as the Sound Burger in Japan, Mister Disc was an awkward piece of technology, but what really killed its chances of success was that it hit stores right around the same time as the much more portable, cassette-playing Sony Walkman.

THE SOUNDWAGON (1976)
It looks like a toy car—a Volkswagen Bus that fits in your hand—but it's actually "the world's smallest portable vinyl record player." Users simply turned it on, placed it on a record, and the little thing would race around an LP, using a stylus on its underside to play the music through its tiny embedded speaker. (Talk about a car stereo.) The Soundwagon was primarily sold by manufacturer Stokyo as a toy to kids in Japan. Real music fans stayed away because the Soundwagon tended to ruin vinyl records.

LASER TURNTABLE 9 (2015)
What if somebody took the technology that made compact discs possible, and applied it to vinyl records, an older and more primitive form of music storage and playback? A company called ELP Japan did just that. Instead of a stylus on the end of a tone arm, the Laser Turntable uses a precise laser to read a record's groove. Cost: $15,000.

GABRIEL (2013)
For the hardcore audiophile, there aren't just "records." There are stereo records, mono records, 45s, 78s, and other, even more obscure types of vinyl. DaVinciAudio aimed to please audiophiles with its Gabriel player. The device is equipped with four separate tone arms, which can be equipped with different styluses and cartridges. Base cost: $79,000.

The tiny nation of San Marino is defended by a Crossbow Corps that dates back to 1295.

MOUTHING OFF

POLI-TALKS

*Actual quotations from real politicians that make us wonder
if literally anyone can go into government.*

"The number one job facing the middle class, and it happens to be a three-letter word: J-O-B-S."
—Vice President Joe Biden

"For seven and a half years I've worked alongside President Reagan. We've had triumphs. Made some mistakes. We've had some sex…uh…setbacks."
—Vice President George H. W. Bush

"Obviously, we've got to stand with our North Korean allies."
—Governor Sarah Palin

"We lose 93 million Americans a day to gun violence."
—Governor Terry McAuliffe

"The interior of the earth is extremely hot—several million degrees."
—Vice President Al Gore
(It's actually around 10,000°F.)

" I do not support a livable wage. "
—Congresswoman Karen Handel

"I AM ACTUALLY HUMBLE. I THINK I'M MUCH MORE HUMBLE THAN YOU WOULD UNDERSTAND."
—President Donald Trump

"The pyramids were made in a way that they had hermetically sealed compartments… to preserve grain for a long period of time."
—Secretary of Housing and Urban Development Ben Carson

"I'm not familiar precisely with what I said, but I'll stand by what I said, whatever it was."
—Governor Mitt Romney

THE RISE OF THE INFOMERCIAL

Don't wait! As a bonus, we'll throw in this page of trivia about those 30-minute-long commercials that air on late-night TV! Act now! Operators are standing by!

BACKGROUND

Those program-length ads that run on TV during non-prime-time hours to sell hair tonics, miracle diets, mops, bottle tops, juicers, psychic connections, kitchen gadgets, snuggies, wearable towels, and dozens of other items that promise to change your life are most commonly called "infomercials." That's a combination of "information" and "commercial"…except that the only information they provide is how to buy the product they're advertising. So really, they're just commercials…except that in TV and advertising lingo, they're called "direct response television." This refers to the fact that in order to buy the product being pitched for $29.97—or three easy payments of $9.99 (plus shipping and handling)—you've got to call the toll-free number at the bottom of the screen and deal *directly* with the company, rather than buying it from a store.

Infomercials are also called "long-form advertising," because they're so much longer than the usual 30- or 60-second TV commercials. These programs are up to 30 minutes long, and local stations and cable networks use them to fill in little-watched time slots, such as late night, early morning, or anytime over the weekend. But unlike actual TV shows, infomercials cost broadcasters nothing—the company shilling their wares pays to produce the show and then pays the broadcaster because, after all, it's advertising.

Here's how these annoying programs became even more ubiquitous than reality shows.

1949	In the experimental wild west of TV's infancy, networks are willing to try anything. In 1949 a TV station in New York City airs a show entirely paid for by a sponsor: a 30-minute-long advertisement for the Vitamix blender. It's the first example of an infomercial, but the format won't really take off for more than three decades.
Early 1950s	In the 21st-century TV landscape, advertisers buy pre-measured ad time slots during shows. But in the early days of television, companies sponsored entire shows, and interrupted them with live ads by studio pitchmen. Paying for a show also gives them the right to insert their name into the show's title. Among the most popular shows of the 1950–51 TV season:

Texaco Star Theater, The Colgate Comedy Hour, and *Gillette Cavalcade of Sports.* But all that changes in the 1950s and 1960s, when the Federal Communications Commission (FCC) creates rules limiting commercial time to as little as 12 minutes per hour...while also doing away with sponsors' names in TV show titles.

Late 1960s and early 1970s

Direct-response TV hits mainstream television, but the ads aren't 30-minute shows—it's a saturation airing of short commercials (anywhere from 30 seconds to two minutes long) for kitchen gadgets (such as Popeil's Veg-O-Matic) and other home goods. One famous example: K-Tel. TV viewers are bombarded by the company's commercials for music compilation LPs, such as *20 Power Hits, Disco Fire, Super Bad,* and *24 Great Truck Drivin' Songs.*

1976

Direct-response TV ads are now so well known that they get the *Saturday Night Live* parody treatment. In a faux commercial for the "Bass-o-Matic," Dan Aykroyd plays a sleazy pitchman who puts a fish in a blender to create a new way to consume bass: drink them.

1977

XETV, a TV station licensed by the Mexican government in the city of Tijuana, caters to the English-speaking market in Southern California. Because it isn't under the jurisdiction of U.S. federal law, it can skirt the FCC's limit of 18 minutes of advertising per hour. On Sunday mornings, the Mexican station airs half-hour shows produced by San Diego realtors, showcasing Southern California homes for sale.

1979

Don Lewis, head of the Don Lewis Agency in Burbank, California, coins the term "infomercial" to describe direct-response long-form advertising to clients. One of his first clients: fitness enthusiast and entrepreneur Kurt Wolfe, who uses the infomercial format (at the government-mandated length of 18 minutes) to sell his $395 home gym.

1982

Another major proponent of the infomercial, Frank Cannella, forms a company called Cannella Response Television and buys network air time to sell New Generation, a baldness remedy developed by a Sacramento, California, inventor named Robert E. Murphy Jr. (The U.S. Postal Service later charges Murphy with mail fraud because the product's main ingredient—polysorbate 60, an emulsifier commonly used to cut grease—does nothing to stimulate hair growth.)

Ex-heavyweight champ Mike Tyson keeps hundreds of pigeons and attends pigeon "beauty pageants."

1984	Ronald Reagan, a free-market capitalist who believes that government regulation stifles business and hurts the economy, is elected president. Under his direction, the FCC lifts all regulations that impose time limits on advertising. Not only do broadcasters no longer have to limit advertising to 18 minutes per hour, they can sell air time in chunks as large as they want. Thirty minutes seems to be the sweet spot. Infomercials become increasingly prominent at this point, especially because there are so many brand-new channels with time to fill due to the rise of cable television. There is a lot of competition and relatively little viewership, and the cable outlets need money to survive. So they turn to infomercials to stay afloat.
1992	Third-party presidential candidate—and independently wealthy billionaire—H. Ross Perot finds his way into the political mainstream with direct-response TV, directly addressing viewers (and voters) by buying up 30-minute chunks of air time on hundreds of TV stations to explain his economic plan for the future.
1993	Access Television Network launches the first 24-hour infomercial cable network.
2000 to present	No longer consigned to late-night time slots—where stations can get paid to air infomercials, instead of programming they have to pay for—infomercials seep into all the day parts of a TV schedule. They take over afternoon TV most of all. In lieu of game shows and soap operas, it now becomes common for TV stations to fill little-watched hours between their highly rated noon newscasts and profitable late-afternoon talk shows with half-hour commercials for kitchen gadgets and miracle mops.

Now you know how infomercials came about, but wait…there's more. To get a new look at some of TV's greatest products you'll never need, turn to page 212. Operators are standing by, so act now!

* * *

THE DUDE ADVISES

"Wake up in the morning, go to the bathroom, pee, brush your teeth, look in the mirror, and laugh at yourself. Do it every morning to start off the day, as a practice."

—Jeff Bridges

Small world: There are more bacteria in your mouth than there are people on the planet.

TRUCK SPILLED *WHAT?*

Ever heard the saying, "If you bought it, a truck brought it"?
That's all fine and good unless the truck failed to bring it.

BACKGROUND

Anecdotally, a cargo truck spilling its payload all over the road is pretty funny. (It definitely makes for good bathroom reading.) In reality, however, these accidents are much messier than they might seem on the surface—and costly, too. The trucking company loses a lot of money, as do those on the supplying and receiving ends. These accidents can also be very wasteful and in some cases cause damage to the environment. Then there's the human cost—everything from traffic closures to injuries and deaths. But as much press as truck spills get (which is quite a lot), you can take solace in the fact that, out of the millions of cargo trucks navigating the world's roadways every day, only a tiny fraction of them will ever crash. When they do, you can count on us to tell you all about it. Here are some spills involving trucks carrying food and beverages.

ENTREES

✗ In November 2017, a Swedish truck carrying a load of meatballs on its way to pick up a load of potatoes (seriously) lost control on an icy patch and ended up on its side in a ditch. Part of the truck was blocking the road, and it couldn't be moved until all 20 tons of meatballs were removed from the overturned trailer…by hand. It took all night.

✗ In 2017 on I-30 in Arkansas, a semi hauling 30,000 frozen DiGiorno and Tombstone pizzas "split open" after the truck hit a bridge overpass. Frozen pizzas cascaded out, covering a huge swath of highway. Because the truck wasn't blocking the road, motorists kept going, driving right over the spill area. Result: hundreds of flattened pizzas. Traffic was closed in both directions for four hours while workers picked up the thin-crust pizzas.

✗ The press called it the "Ham Jam," and it ruined a lot of Christmas dinners. The December 2013 crash occurred on a Georgia interstate when a truck driver rolled his rig while driving too fast up a curving on-ramp. When the truck tipped over, all 20 tons of Christmas hams—an estimated 12,000 servings' worth— rolled out on the highway, causing a massive holiday backup.

A Hollywood-based "Christmas tree stylist" can earn as much as
$80,000 decorating a single celebrity Christmas tree.

SEAFOOD

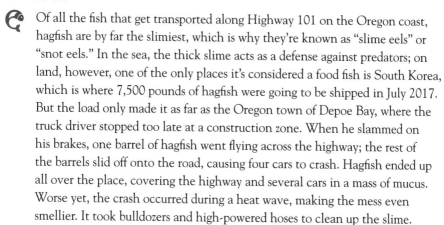

Of all the fish that get transported along Highway 101 on the Oregon coast, hagfish are by far the slimiest, which is why they're known as "slime eels" or "snot eels." In the sea, the thick slime acts as a defense against predators; on land, however, one of the only places it's considered a food fish is South Korea, which is where 7,500 pounds of hagfish were going to be shipped in July 2017. But the load only made it as far as the Oregon town of Depoe Bay, where the truck driver stopped too late at a construction zone. When he slammed on his brakes, one barrel of hagfish went flying across the highway; the rest of the barrels slid off onto the road, causing four cars to crash. Hagfish ended up all over the place, covering the highway and several cars in a mass of mucus. Worse yet, the crash occurred during a heat wave, making the mess even smellier. It took bulldozers and high-powered hoses to clean up the slime.

One afternoon in March 2018, a cargo truck near Mellerud, Sweden, somehow lost its load of more than one hundred barrels of pickled herring. The barrels remained intact…until a car smashed through them, splattering the fish all over. When emergency crews arrived, they were perplexed. "I'm not really sure about the best way to clean herring," Jonas Gustafsson told reporters. "Right now it's very slippy." Six months later, another Swedish truck driver lost a load of herring—this one caused by an elk that ran onto a busy highway. The driver managed to avoid hitting the animal, but in doing so, he tipped over the truck. "There's herring on a 100-meter stretch of the road, and herring fillets in the ditch," said an official. Workers had to remove all of the herring by hand while the elk grazed nearby.

VEGGIES

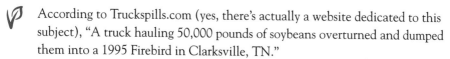

According to Truckspills.com (yes, there's actually a website dedicated to this subject), "A truck hauling 50,000 pounds of soybeans overturned and dumped them into a 1995 Firebird in Clarksville, TN."

Hordes of flaming avocados attacked motorists on a Texas highway in December 2017 after a cargo truck caught fire. Firefighters arrived, closed the road, and put out the avocados—all 20 tons of them. According to the Department of Agriculture, the avocados were worth around $50,000.

For more truck spills, drive (carefully!) over to page 280.

The first Earth Day was also the 100th birthday of Communist leader Vladimir Lenin.

BLOODY GOOD FOOD

When people order their steak "bloody," that juice isn't blood—the blood has already been drained. The juice is mostly water tinted red by proteins in the muscle tissue. But for all you wannabe vampires out there, here are some foods and drinks that are made with real blood.

Black Pudding: This is an example of a *blood sausage*, a food item that's been made all over the world, in a variety of styles, since ancient times. Like most of the dishes on this page, blood sausage came from the need to use every part of an animal, so that nothing went to waste. Still popular in the UK and Ireland today, black pudding is pig's blood, suet, oats, and spices stuffed into casings (animal intestines) and boiled. When sliced, it looks a bit like pepperoni slices. Eat as is, or fry it up. Black pudding can also be crumbled and served with scrambled eggs.

Blodplättar: Swedish for "small blood pancakes," they're made with flour, a pinch of salt, and equal parts milk and blood. (Make sure the blood is strained so there are no clots.) Recipes often call for a sweetener, such as molasses, to cut the metallic taste of the blood. Blood pancakes can be served with meats, or as a dessert with berries, jams, or syrup.

Boat Noodles: From Thailand, this rich, meaty noodle-soup was traditionally made and sold from small boats traveling Bangkok's canals, although today it's more commonly found in restaurants near the canals. Ingredients include noodles, pork, pig's liver, beef, bean curd, bean sprouts, green onions, sugar, and many different spices. When it's nearly cooked, pig's blood is added as a thickener and to add (bloody good!) flavor.

Pig's Blood Cake: This Taiwanese street food consists of sticky rice and pig's blood formed into rectangular cakes, into which wooden sticks are inserted—like popsicles. Then they're soaked in a warm pork and soy broth. When you order this delicacy, the vendor will roll it in finely chopped peanuts, then in chopped cilantro. Result: a chewy, savory, nutty, semisweet snack.

Czarnina: Also spelled *czernina*, this traditional Polish sweet-and-sour soup is found in hundreds of varieties around Poland and neighboring countries. Basic ingredients: duck blood mixed with vinegar (the vinegar prevents the blood from clotting). Other ingredients may include duck meat (including the gizzard, liver, heart, feet, and neck), flour, noodles, potatoes, dumplings, spices, and dried fruit such as raisins, prunes, and pears. (If duck blood is not available, goose, chicken, pig, or rabbit blood can be used as a substitute.)

Good news? Bad? The average person forms 33 lasting friendships across their lifetime.

Ratham Poriyal: This is stir-fried lamb's blood, seasoned with chopped onion and spices. It's a popular breakfast dish in the southern Indian state of Tamil Nadu. (Note: As is the case with a couple of these recipes, the blood for *ratham poriyal* comes in coagulated form, and resembles a dark red, moist cake.)

Pepitoria: Popular in the northern-central Santander region of Colombia, this warm dish is made from the blood of a goat, along with chopped goat innards—kidneys, heart, liver, stomach, and intestines—mixed with seasoned rice, eggs, peas, bread crumbs, and spices. It's most commonly served as a side dish.

Goose Blood Tart: This sweet pastry was served as a traditional Christmas dessert in parts of Wales, and while it appears to be largely a thing of the past, it's still prepared by Welsh foodies. In case you want to give it a go, you'll need short-crust pastry, a pound or so of currants, a half pound of suet, brown sugar, golden syrup, a little salt...and the blood from two (or more) geese. (A tip from the National Museum of Wales: "The blood of about three geese would be put in a greased basin and boiled in a saucepan half full of water. Then the blood would be allowed to cool and set solid before it was rubbed between the fingers to make fine crumbs.") After preparation, the mixture is baked in a pastry, like a pie. Result: a pielike tart with a smooth, dense, dark, custardy filling that tastes a bit like plum pudding. (And blood.)

*   *   *

A RANDOM BIT OF FACTINESS

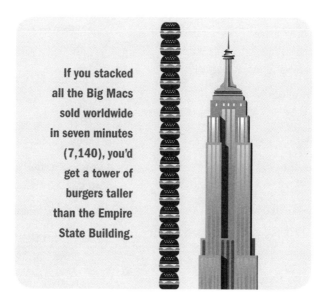

If you stacked all the Big Macs sold worldwide in seven minutes (7,140), you'd get a tower of burgers taller than the Empire State Building.

Scientists say humans are born with just two innate fears: falling and loud noises. The rest you learn later.

EVERYBODY FARTS

These real T-shirts adorned with slogans about farting could be the lowest form of comedy…but hey, they make Uncle John laugh.

Who just farted? This guy!

Does this smell infected?

I don't fart, I giggle with my a******

While you were reading this…I farted

Proud farter (I mean father)

Fart loading: Please wait

When I fart, you'll be the second to know

Warning: Do not pull this guy's fingers

Beware: My protein comes from beans

I think I might have over-trusted that last fart

Life lesson: If you fart while talking to a girl outside, the smell does not dissipate, it just lingers around mocking you

Fart Wars

I didn't fart…my butt likes you so much that it blew you a kiss

That moment when you realize it wasn't a fart

I'm a fart smella, no wait, I mean smart fella

Hug me! I fart!

MILF: Man, I like to fart!

How come it didn't smell like farts before you showed up?

If you're not farting, you're dead

May your day be more beautiful than a unicorn farting rainbows

I fart. What's your superpower?

Warning: This human may emit toxic gas in public spaces

Farts don't show up in an MRI do they? Asking for a friend.

Home is where the fart is

Danger: Explosive gas in rear

Eat. Sleep. Fart. Repeat.

It wasn't me, it was the dog!

Beware of taco fart

Fart is my second favorite F-word

Did you just fart, or do you always smell that way?

Just as I started to enjoy the sweet smell of success, somebody farted

If you can't smell my fart, you can't have my heart

If a clown farts, does it smell funny?

Farted from the bottom, now I'm here

My farts smell like freedom!

Gum chewers fart more than non-chewers. (They swallow lots of air.)

WHEN WORLDS COLLIDE

Humans and animals occupying the same space at the same time…
with memorable results.

WATCH FOR FALLING SHEEP

It was a baaad day for an Irish teenager when a clumsy sheep tumbled down a cliff and landed right on top of him. The animal was trying to jump over a crag when it slipped and fell. It injured the teen's "head, neck, back, abdomen, and leg," according to the *Irish Times*. A team of 17 rescuers arrived and transported the teen to a hospital, where he was expected to make a full recovery. The sheep "was uninjured and left the area unaided."

KEEP YOUR FLIPPER TO YOURSELF

In August 2018, an amorous dolphin prompted French officials to close several beaches on France's northwest coast. The BBC reported that, for several weeks prior to the ban, the bottlenose dolphin, nicknamed Zafar, had been "entertaining and delighting" beachgoers. Then his behavior changed—biologists explained that he was *rutting*—and some disturbing reports claimed he had confronted a Spanish woman and was "anxious to interact." Zafar "rubbed up against boats and swimmers," and "wouldn't allow a woman swimmer back to shore." (She had to be rescued by a boat.) The final straw: Zafar tossed a woman into the air. Luckily, she escaped before he was able to…do whatever he was trying to do. But after that, beachgoers were told to stay out of the water until Zafar calmed down.

THE GRAZER AND THE TASER

"Recently there has been a lot of weird cow activity in Navajo County," said Sheriff Kelly Clark of Arizona in September 2018. For example, a woman called 911 to complain that a cow had her pinned in a field and wouldn't let her go. Deputy Vincent Palozzolo responded to the scene. First, he yelled at the cow. It didn't move. Then he tried to push the cow. It didn't move. Then he shot his Taser into the air, hoping it would scare the cow, but it still didn't move. So the cop tased the cow. Then it moved. It charged Palozzolo, knocking him over and pinning him to the ground. The cop freed an arm…and tased and tased until the animal finally got up and ran away. Neither human nor cow was seriously injured. It's still unclear why the cow pinned the woman in the first place.

What's the difference between a castle and a palace? A castle can be used as a place of military defense.

MONKEYING AROUND

In June 2018, in Okeechobee, Florida, a Home Depot cashier was on her break when she spotted a spider monkey—wearing a diaper and dragging a leash—running amok in the parking lot. The cashier tried to catch the monkey (named Spanky), but when she grabbed Spanky's leash, he attacked her, biting her several times and scratching her face. Then he darted off into the store and found his owner, 56-year-old Tina Ballard, who *thought* she had secured him in her SUV. Both the monkey and its owner were told never to return to the Okeechobee Home Depot. Ballard was later arrested for trying to smuggle the illegal pet out of the state. At last report, Spanky was going to live at a monkey sanctuary.

> **Both the monkey and its owner were told never to return to the Okeechobee Home Depot.**

THE BELLY AND THE BULL

On Independence Day 2018, a heavyset Tracy, California, man named Dean King went to a rural property to look at a car that had been advertised for sale. No one was around. He started walking around the car when, all of a sudden, a large bull charged and gored him right in the gut. King landed hard on the ground, but was able to crawl under a bush before the bull did any more damage. The bull kept him trapped there, snorting and poking at his legs, for 20 minutes. King finally heard a car horn honking and called out for help. He was rushed to the hospital and underwent emergency surgery. Doctors told King that he was lucky: his enormous gut kept the bull's horns from puncturing anything important. "If I was skinny, I wouldn't have survived," he said.

OH, BEEHIVE

During a bus trip through rural Vietnam, several male passengers asked the driver to make a pit stop. The bus pulled over, and the men got out and started urinating. There happened to be a large beehive nearby, and the bees would have left the men alone… had one of them not decided to pee on it. By the time the stinging and screaming and running was over, 22 people had to be treated for bee stings. The bees even chased the men back onto the bus where, according to news reports, "Several of the men complained about being stung on the private parts."

GOOD SAMARITAN

In 2018 a bus driver named Billy Willox of Canberra, Australia, spotted a dead kangaroo on the side of the road. He slowed down and saw some movement in the

Before he discovered spinach, Popeye got his strength by rubbing a magic chicken.

brush nearby. Suspecting it might be a stranded joey (a baby kangaroo), Willox pulled over to investigate, only to discover that 1) there was no joey, and 2) the kangaroo wasn't dead. "It was fast, really fast," he later told the *Canberra Times*. "I didn't even get that close to it and it suddenly just got up. It scratched at my eyes and my face and started clawing at my back." By the time Willox got back into his car, he was covered in blood. He managed to get himself to the hospital, where doctors performed emergency surgery to his eyes. Thankfully, Willox made a full recovery. He hopes his experience will keep others from approaching seemingly dead kangaroos on the side of the road. "We tend to think they're quite friendly," he said, "but that was one angry kangaroo."

INSULT, MEET INJURY

Late one night in April 2018, a call came in to the St. Catharines, Ontario, police department about two suspicious men prowling in a backyard. When officers arrived with a canine unit, one of the would-be thieves—Richard Pickering—ran to another backyard and hid inside a large bush. But Pickering wasn't alone—there was a skunk in there, and it sprayed him. Unable to run because the cops were getting closer, he had no choice but to stay in there with the skunk and the stench. A few minutes later, the police dog smelled the skunk and led the cops right to Pickering. Not only did he get sprayed by the skunk, he also got bitten by the police dog.

* * *

THREE FAILED VIDEO STREAMING SERVICES

AEREO. This service allowed subscribers to record over-the-air, broadcast TV onto their computer, so they could watch it anytime. (Sort of like TiVo…or a VCR.) Broadcast networks sued it out of existence, arguing that Aereo didn't do what cable companies did—pay for the right to rebroadcast those channels.

VIDANGEL. This service offered "filtered" content—mainstream Hollywood movies, with all the non-family friendly content (profanity, nudity, sex, and violence) edited out. VidAngel declared bankruptcy in 2016 to avoid being sued for flagrantly ignoring copyright laws.

SEESO. For just $4 a month, subscribers could view comedy content, including every episode of *Saturday Night Live*, *Monty Python's Flying Circus*, and *The Office*, plus Canadian sitcoms, and some original series. After less than two years, and fewer than a million subscribers, it closed down.

Every time Khloé Kardashian plugs a product on Instagram, she makes as much as $13,000.

HONEY, WE'RE KILLING THE KIDS

The cable channel TLC (The Learning Channel) used to air educational programs and kids' shows. But over the past decade it seems to have expanded the definition of "learning," with some of the weirdest reality shows on TV. Here's a sampling. All of these are real!

Best Funeral Ever

Dr. Pimple Popper

My 600-lb Life

The 685-lb. Teen

Secretly Pregnant

Freaky Eaters

The Boy with a Tumor for a Face

Hoarding: Buried Alive

Extreme Couponing

Extreme Cheapskates

Extreme Cougar Wives

Mall Cops: Mall of America

Livin' for the Apocalypse

Little Chocolatiers

Little Parents, Big Pregnancy

Big Hair Alaska

Alaskan Women Looking for Love

My Strange Addiction

Sex Sent Me to the ER

Strange Sex

My Teen Is Pregnant and So Am I

I Didn't Know I Was Pregnant

Quints by Surprise

Virgin Diaries

Dancing Tweens

Sister Wives

Seeking Sister Wife

Brother Husbands

Breaking Amish

90 Day Fiancé

Honey, We're Killing the Kids

Fast Food Babies

Little Shop of Gypsies

Pete Rose: Hits & Mrs.

Former Smokers

I Eat 33,000 Calories a Day

My Five Wives

Potty Power

Sextuplets Take New York

My Feet Are Killing Me

Our Twinsane Wedding

The Spouse House

Suddenly Rich

America's Worst Tattoos

Police Women of Cincinnati

Thanks, Mom! Baby koalas eat their mother's poop.

DUMB CROOKS

Here's proof that crime doesn't pay.

CAUGHT BROWN-HANDED

On a hot summer day in 2018, Matthew Bloomquist, 29, and a friend drove a pickup truck onto a rural Minnesota farm and stole some lumber. On their way off the property, Bloomquist drove through a big pile of manure…and got stuck. It had been raining that week, making the ground muddier and the manure even smellier. And the more Bloomquist spun the wheels, the deeper his truck sank. The two crooks spent over an hour trying to get unstuck, even using some of the lumber for traction, but the truck wouldn't budge. Then the farmer showed up. Bloomquist gave up. (The buddy ran away.) When the cops arrived a few minutes later, Bloomquist was standing there— covered in dung—smoking a cigarette. According to the police report, "He was wearing jean shorts over long underwear and no shoes, which the deputies assumed were somewhere in the manure pile." The report, which was titled "Something Doesn't Smell Right," also mentioned that "the trip to the jail was made with the windows open."

SHEAR HORROR

In August 2018, a middle-aged man (unidentified in press reports) burst into a Tokyo convenience store, brandished a pair of nose hair scissors, and demanded all the money in the register. Apparently intimidated by the shears (even though they were less than an inch long), the clerk ran away, leaving the robber in the store alone. But without the clerk, the robber couldn't get into the register or the safe, so he stood there deliberating his next move. While he was doing that, a police officer walked into the store and arrested the nose hair trimmer bandit.

INFAMOUS FOR 15 MINUTES

Here's a helpful tip from the Lawrenceville (Georgia) Police Department: "When after having robbed several banks and you are at another bank casing the place for an additional robbery and are approached by a news crew in the parking lot…DO NOT stop and agree to an interview with said news crew." They were referring to Eric Rivers, 24. He had just robbed a Chase Bank (his third robbery of the day) and was walking over to a nearby Fidelity Bank, when a WGCL-TV reporter stopped him in the parking lot and asked if he would answer some questions about public transit. Rivers agreed, then gave his real name and did the interview. Afterward, he went into the bank to case it out. Meanwhile, the police had been told by the Chase Bank manager that the suspect was last seen approaching a news van, so the cops got Rivers's name from the news crew. When they showed up later at the robber's house, they said Rivers was "surprised" they'd found him.

FRIED

We love stories of dumb crooks who leave behind a trail of whatever they stole. Here's a new one: In 2015 a woman in Chickasha, Oklahoma, called police after $4,000 worth of items were stolen from her house—including electronics, golf clubs, and a Fry Daddy deep fryer. By the time police arrived, the woman's neighbor, Matthew Kennedy, had already cracked the case. "I noticed a trail of oil leading from that backdoor to my other neighbor's backdoor," he told reporters. The neighbor, Steven McCarthey, 29, had been drinking with his friend, William Bitsche, 40, when they decided to burgle the woman's house. But as Kennedy noted, "If you're going to steal a Fry Daddy, you should probably pour out the oil before you drag it across the street." Police followed the trail of fryer grease (which is probably still there today) and found all the stolen items in McCarthey's house. Both men were arrested; the woman who lived across the street reportedly moved away.

KEEP YOUR PANTS ON

It was a typical burglary…until the burglar took his clothes off. Baltimore County (Maryland) police had to blur out the man's naughty bits when they released the surveillance footage to the media in 2016. It shows him rummaging through a Slice Pizza restaurant completely nude. It's unclear why he's nude. The owner, Yani Riza, thinks that the criminal may have torn his pants in the small air vent that he'd squeezed through to get in. (That still doesn't explain why he disrobed completely.) Finding no cash on the premises, the naked thief took a company checkbook. And a water bottle. "Seeing the footage was weird," Riza told WBAL TV. "Knowing that somebody was naked running around the store, it's funny." That aside, Riza wanted justice, so he offered a "lifetime pizza reward" to anyone who turned the nude dude in.

Update: A few days later, the naked thief, 23-year-old Jonathan Newman, was apprehended—not because someone turned him in, but because he tried to cash one of the stolen checks at a local bank. And his tattoos made it pretty easy for the cops to positively ID him. (His clothes were found in a nearby Dumpster.)

Switzerland has enough fallout shelters to house its entire population.

ONE-ISSUE WONDERS

This is the 32nd edition of Uncle John's Bathroom Reader. *That's 31 more issues than these short-lived magazines managed to produce.*

❭ ***Infobahn.*** This 1995 magazine carried the subtitle "The Magazine of Internet Culture" and contained articles about how the online world was rapidly changing the face of media. One victim of the internet: print media…like *Infobahn*, which didn't make it to issue number two.

❭ ***Publick Occurrences Both Forreign and Domestick.*** This Boston-based news publication went on sale in 1690 when Massachusetts was still a British colony. In fact, that's why it lasted only one issue: The publisher didn't get permission to print and distribute it from the local crown-appointed authorities, so the British crown shut it down.

❭ ***Possibilities.*** Avant-garde composer John Cage experimented with noise, weird instruments, and even nothing at all (his piece "4'33" consists of four minutes and 33 seconds of silence). In 1947 he got into publishing and, with painter Robert Motherwell, founded a literary magazine called *Possibilities*. The premiere issue featured interviews with painter Joan Miró and composer Edgard Varèse, and writings by poet David Smith, and by artists Mark Rothko and Jackson Pollock. *Possibilities* was subtitled "An Occasional Review," which wasn't quite accurate because Cage published just the one issue.

❭ ***Plus Voice.*** In 1994, after the hysteria of the AIDS crisis calmed down and new medical treatments allowed people with AIDS or HIV to live longer, relatively normal lives, this magazine was introduced to serve the community of HIV victims. Featuring articles with titles like "Teen Trouble," "Mothers with HIV," "Black, Gay, and Positive," and "When Condoms Fail," the audience for *Plus Voice* wasn't large enough to warrant a second issue.

❭ ***Unbelievable.*** Publishers intended for this to be a quarterly magazine that dug deep into important matters of the day. In its first issue in the winter of 1940–41, it included a thorough takedown of newspaper tycoon William Randolph Hearst, and it tied him to the growing fascist movement in Europe. Weeks after *Unbelievable* #1 hit newsstands, Hearst's King Features Syndicate sued the magazine's parent company, Friday, Inc., and drove it out of business.

MOUTHING OFF

iJERK

The late Apple guru Steve Jobs had a well-deserved reputation for being a tech and business genius…but also for being sharp-tongued, arrogant, and mean.

"This company is in shambles, and I don't have time to wet-nurse the board. So I need all of you to resign. Or else I'm going to resign and not come back on Monday."

—to the Apple board of directors when he returned to the company after a long absence in 1997

"You make some of the best products in the world—but you also make a lot of crap. Get rid of the crappy stuff."

—to a Nike executive

"Do you want to spend the rest of your life selling sugared water or do you want a chance to change the world?"

—in trying to lure Pepsi executive John Sculley to Apple

"That's the kind of Porsche that dentists drive."

—pointing out a low-end sports car to a reporter

"YOU'VE BAKED A REALLY LOVELY CAKE, BUT THEN YOU'VE USED DOG S*** FOR FROSTING."

—to a programmer who worked for him

"Look, I don't know who you are, but no one around here is too important to fire besides me. And you're fired!"

—to a man in an elevator at Apple headquarters (the man wasn't an Apple employee)

"My job is to say when something sucks."

—in his book, *Motivating Thoughts of Steve Jobs*

"EVERYTHING YOU HAVE DONE IN YOUR LIFE IS S***! SO WHY DON'T YOU COME WORK FOR ME?"

—in trying to recruit an engineer

NOT DEAD YET

Those awkward times when the Grim Reaper shows up early.

Restless Leg: In 2013 mourners were attending the funeral of a 34-year-old Zimbabwe man named Brighton Dama Zanthe. As they passed by his coffin to pay their respects, Zanthe's boss, Lot Gaka, announced, "His legs are moving." All of a sudden, there was a mad dash for the exit, but Gaka kept his cool and called an ambulance. The "dead man" was rushed to the hospital, where he spent two days in intensive care before making a full recovery. Zanthe had been ill for several months before he appeared to slip away and was pronounced dead. "It's a miracle," said Gaka, "and people are still in disbelief." "I feel okay now," said Zanthe.

Beyond Recognition: When Juan Penayo left his house in June 2018, the 20-year-old Paraguayan man didn't tell his mother where he was going. When he didn't come home the next day, the family put out a missing person's report. A few hours later they were told by police that the charred remains of a body had been found in a nearby city (an all-too-common occurrence in a region plagued by violent drug traffickers). Penayo's family couldn't be certain that the remains were him, but no one else had been reported missing…so they assumed it was him. Two days later, while family members were gathered around his casket, he walked in the front door and asked what was going on. (No word on where he was for those three days…or the identity of that other body.)

Sleepy Time: Ninety-five-year-old Budh Ram had been declared dead by a doctor after fainting at his home in India in 2018. As family members were giving him a bath ahead of his funeral, he started shaking. They quickly carried him to a bed, where he came to a few minutes later and said, "I was just having a nap."

Two More Weeks: In 2014 a 78-year-old farmer named Walter Williams "died peacefully" in his Mississippi home… and then woke up in a body bag two days later. The two morgue workers who were about to embalm him were shocked, as was his family when they received the call that Williams was still alive. He was taken to the hospital, where it was determined that a combination of medicines had rendered his vital signs unresponsive. He was sent home, where his family was overjoyed to have him back…for two more weeks. Then he really died. "I think he's gone this time," said his nephew, Eddie Hester, who later told reporters, "The same coroner and the same funeral home director came, and I said, 'I thought y'all were going to send somebody else,' and everybody laughed about it."

What do you and 63,000 other species of vertebrates have in common? Backbones.

WHO'S AFRAID OF FRANZ KAFKA?

When a book is translated into another language, or just offered for sale in other countries, publishers may give it a new title to appeal to local tastes. Sometimes they're weird, sometimes they're silly, and sometimes they're completely baffling.

US: *Where's Waldo* (Martin Hanford)	☞	**UK:** *Where's Wally*
Sweden: *Men Who Hate Women* (Stieg Larsson)	☞	**US:** *The Girl with the Dragon Tattoo*
US: *Diary of a Wimpy Kid* (Jeff Kinney)	☞	**Mexico:** *Diary of Greg the Toad*
US: *The Great Gatsby* (F. Scott Fitzgerald)	☞	**Sweden:** *A Man without Scruples*
US: *The Fault in Our Stars* (John Green)	☞	**Macedonia:** *The World Is Not a Factory for Fulfilling Wishes*
US: *The Grapes of Wrath* (John Steinbeck)	☞	**Japan:** *The Angry Raisins*
US: *The Hobbit* (J. R. R. Tolkien)	☞	**Sweden:** *Hompen*
US: *Twilight* (Stephenie Meyer)	☞	**France:** *Fascination*
UK: *Animal Farm* (George Orwell)	☞	**France:** *Animals Everywhere!*
US: *Catch-22* (Joseph Heller)	☞	**Italy:** *Subsection 22*
US: *The Catcher in the Rye* (J. D. Salinger)	☞	**Russia:** *Over the Abyss in Rye*

In 2014 McDonald's test-marketed bubble gum–flavored broccoli. (It McFlopped.)

US: *Outlander* (Diana Gabaldon)	☞	**UK:** *Cross Stitch*
US: *To Kill a Mockingbird* (Harper Lee)	☞	**Germany:** *Who Disturbs a Nightingale*
US: *The Horse Whisperer* (Nicholas Evans)	☞	**France:** *The Man Who Murmured Into Horses' Ears*
US: *Brave New World* (Aldous Huxley)	☞	**France:** *The Best of All Worlds*
UK: *Northern Lights* (Philip Pullman)	☞	**US:** *The Golden Compass*
US: *Who's Afraid of Virginia Woolf?* (Edward Albee)	☞	**Czechoslovakia:** *Who's Afraid of Franz Kafka?*
US: *A Heartbreaking Work of Staggering Genius* (Dave Eggers)	☞	**Croatia:** *A Heartbreaking Work of Insecure Genius*
US: *The Hunger Games, Catching Fire,* and *Mockingjay* (Suzanne Collins)	☞	**Germany:** *Deadly Games, Dangerous Love,* and *Flaming Fury*
US: *Harry Potter and the Deathly Hallows* (J. K. Rowling)	☞	**Spain:** *Harry Potter and the Relics of the Dead*
US: *Little Women, Part II* (Louisa May Alcott)	☞	**UK:** *Good Wives*
UK: *Murder on the Orient Express* (Agatha Christie)	☞	**US:** *Murder on the Calais Coach*
US: *The Man in the High Castle* (Philip K. Dick)	☞	**Germany:** *The Oracle from the Mountain*

*   *   *

"If you think this Universe is bad, you should see some of the others."

—Philip K. Dick

In 1995 a bust of Frank Zappa was erected in Vilnius, Lithuania's capital, "to mark the end of communism."

IRONIC, ISN'T IT?

*There's nothing like a good dose of irony to put the problems
of day-to-day life into proper perspective.*

HANDS-OFF IRONY

Amir Hussain Lone is one of the most remarkable cricket players on the Indian subcontinent, even though he has no arms. As captain of Jammu and Kashmir's para-cricket team, Lone uses his toes to bowl, and he's able to swing by holding the cricket bat between his chin and shoulder—like a violin. Lone lost his limbs in an accident at age eight while visiting his father's sawmill, which, ironically, made cricket bats.

DON'T EAT THE IRONY

One definition of irony: a situation that's the exact opposite of what is expected. In November 2016, a video of a wild polar bear petting a Siberian husky went viral. The feel-good video of the two predators having an inter-species personal moment topped seven million views on YouTube, garnering comments like "omg so cute!" and "sometimes animals are more human than humans." The reality: The video was filmed at a sled-dog training site in northern Manitoba, and the polar bear isn't petting the dog—it's "feeling" the dog to determine whether it would make a good meal. The training site's owner reported that, a few weeks prior, another husky had been killed on "the only day we didn't feed the (censored) bears."

> **The feel-good video of the two predators having an inter-species personal moment topped seven million views.**

CONSERVING IRONY

In 2018 the U.S. Fish and Wildlife Service conducted a survey that revealed only 5 percent of Americans—about 11.5 million people—are hunters. That's a sharp decline from previous years. You'd think that would be good news for wildlife conservation efforts, but it's actually having the opposite effect. Reason: Most of the funds that go to conservation comes from the sale of hunting permits. Fewer hunters means less revenue, and less revenue means fewer resources for conservation. So in order to start saving animals, more Americans need to start killing them.

IRONY IN THE SLOW LANE

Buried in a rather obvious news story that lowering speed limits does in fact cause people to drive slower, the Insurance Institute for Highway Safety also reported this ironic tidbit:

Before the Korean War, Korean electronics giant Samsung sold dried fish and noodles.

"The number of deaths related to speeding were actually higher on roads where the speed limit is 35 mph or lower, than it is on roadways where cars are going much faster."

THE IRONY HEATS UP

- In 2018 the U.S. Marine Corps had a problem with a fleet of F-35 fighter jets that were parked on a runway in Japan: They kept getting struck by lightning, requiring the Marines to install lightning rods on each jet. "If nothing else," reported *The Drive*, "it's another good reason for pilots to call the jets by their new nickname, Panther, instead of their official moniker, Lightning II."

- In September 2018, the fire department in Vancouver, British Columbia, responded to a call about a van that was engulfed in flames. Firefighters were able to contain the blaze, but the van was totaled. The vehicle was owned by Vancouver Fire, a company that specializes in fire safety.

IRONIC PLACEMENT

In 2018 a new solar farm was constructed in Ukraine. Local leaders heralded it as the beginning of a new era of energy independence for the country. "It's really hard to underestimate the symbolism of this project," said Evhen Variagin, the chief executive of Solar Chernobyl LLC. That's right, the solar farm is located right across the street from the shuttered Chernobyl nuclear power plant, site of the worst nuclear accident of the 20th century.

IRONIC

Nigel Richards of New Zealand has an uncanny ability: he can read a dictionary from cover to cover and remember how to spell every single word. He's used this skill to become one of the world's best Scrabble players, winning dozens of English-language Scrabble championships. In 2015 he decided to enter a French-language tournament. He got a French dictionary and read it cover to cover...and won the French tournament, despite the fact that he couldn't speak a word of French.

INVENTIVE IRONY

You can thank William Phelps Eno (1858–1945) for the stop sign, the crosswalk, traffic circles, and one-way streets. These innovations made driving much less hazardous, earning Eno the title "Father of Traffic Safety." Ironically, Eno never learned to drive.

IRONIC DESCENT

In 1996, mountain climber Charlotte Fox nearly died when she took part in a doomed trip up Mount Everest. Eight climbers perished when a blizzard interrupted their descent.

Fox not only survived, but she went on to summit several more of the world's highest peaks. Then she died at her Colorado home in 2018 after falling down a flight of stairs.

IRONY UNDER THE INFLUENCE

- On Halloween night in 2009, an Ohio college student named James Miller dressed up as a Breathalyzer device. After having too much to drink, he drove the wrong way on a one-way street and got pulled over. He subsequently failed a Breathalyzer test and was arrested for DUI.

- By 1992 Sam Kinison was one of the most popular stand-up comedians in the world, thanks to his bombastic routines and controversial views, including this defense of drunk driving: "We don't *want* to drink and drive, but there's no other way to get the (censored) car back to the house!" Not long after he said this, Kinison was killed by a drunk driver.

TRAPPED BY IRONY

A snake got stuck in a mousetrap. The incident happened in East London in September 2018. The RSPCA was called out to free the corn snake (most likely an escaped pet), which was injured but not seriously. This story was strange enough to make the news, but is it *really* ironic—a predator getting trapped in a trap designed for its prey—or just a bit odd? Which leads us to our final entry…

IRONIC, IT ISN'T

In an ironic twist, in 2018 the editors of Dictionary.com labeled "ironic" as the most misused word in the English language. Is that ironic? Or just a strange twist of fate for a word that has come to mean a lot of things to different people? Therein lies the problem—few people can agree what irony is. In fact, the most common occurrence of the word probably comes in the phrase "That's not ironic." The problem, say the dictionary's editors, is that when speaking of situational irony, defined as "the opposite of what is expected is what happens," it's often misused to describe a mere coincidence or an odd-but-not-ironic occurrence.

Perhaps it's merely a case of a word changing its meaning. Just like "literally" is now being used to mean "figuratively" (because, literally everyone uses "literally" wrong), "ironic" is undergoing a similar transformation; it can now describe situations that aren't technically ironic, but still suck in a "universe has it in for you" way. It's kind of like that Alanis Morissette song that everyone says isn't ironic—maybe one day soon, it will be.

To find out more about what irony is—and isn't—turn to page 398.

More good news: You can die by overdosing on laxatives.

BEATLES FACTS

Even though they broke up nearly 50 years ago, it's amazing that there are still little-known interesting tidbits out there to discover about the Fab Four.

During Beatlemania, Beatles fans routinely broke into Paul McCartney's house. How? They discovered where he hid a spare key. He didn't mind; he left the key there. Reason: once inside, the fans would do things like wash his dishes and iron his clothes.

Early Beatles concerts were such a frenzied collection of excited (mostly female) young fans that the venues reportedly smelled strongly of urine. Yep—fans were so excited that they couldn't control their bladders. Rock star Bob Geldof attended one such concert and years later told a reporter that there were "rivulets of p*** in the aisles."

John Lennon had a small role in the forgettable 1967 film *How I Won the War*, but two things happened on that set. A picture of Lennon in costume became the cover image for the first issue of *Rolling Stone*, and during a break in filming, he wrote "Strawberry Fields Forever."

In 1987 George Harrison scored a #1 hit with "Got My Mind Set on You," a cover of an old soul song that he'd unsuccessfully lobbied his fellow Beatles to record in the late 1960s.

Movie executives in charge of the 1964 film *A Hard Day's Night* thought the Fab Four's Liverpudlian accents were too difficult to understand, and considered dubbing over them. Paul McCartney protested, and their real voices stayed. However, the band's voices for the 1968 animated movie *Yellow Submarine* were all performed by impersonators.

In 2009 Pope Benedict XVI officially forgave the late John Lennon for his misunderstood 1966 comment that the Beatles were "more popular than Jesus."

Before the band took off, Ringo Starr worked as a waiter on a ferryboat, and Paul McCartney was a delivery man.

The official origin of the band's name is that it's a play on Crickets, the name of Buddy Holly's backing band, as well as a musical pun—"Beat" instead of "Beet," thus "Beatles." (And it was the suggestion of original band member Stuart Sutcliffe.) John Lennon, however, claimed that it came to him in a dream, in which a man riding a "flaming pie" told him to call his band "Beatles with an 'a.'" *Flaming Pie* also happens to be the name of a 1997 Paul McCartney album.

Tallest Beatle: it's a tie between John Lennon, Paul McCartney, and George Harrison. They were all 5'11". (Ringo was 5'8".)

The working title of *Abbey Road* was *Everest*. The name was cribbed from the name of a cigarette brand smoked by recording engineer Geoff Emerick, but when management suggested the band go shoot an album cover near Mount Everest, the Beatles changed their minds and named it after the studio where they recorded.

The "last" Beatles song, which means all four were present in a studio at the same time, was "I Want You (She's So Heavy)." All Beatles were present and accounted for on August 20, 1969.

The Beatles appear on the cover of their album *Help!* doing semaphore gestures with flags. It's assumed they spelled out "H-E-L-P," but it actually spells out N-U-J-V.

The Beatles announced their split in April 1970, but the papers dissolving all of the group's business dealings weren't ready to be signed until 1974. On December 29, 1974, John Lennon became the fourth and final band member to sign them—which he did at the Polynesian Village Hotel, adjacent to Disney World, where he was vacationing with his son Julian and girlfriend, May Pang.

In French-speaking countries, *A Hard Day's Night* was titled *Quatre Garcons Dans Le Vent,* or "Four Boys in the Wind."

As a teenager, Paul McCartney tried to pick up girls by pretending to be a brooding French art student. He'd go to parties dressed in black and sit in a corner with a guitar and sing "French" songs, which were total nonsense. That inspired the French sequence in the Beatles' song "Michelle."

The Beatles' famous "mop top" haircuts were the suggestion of Astrid Kirchherr, girlfriend of Stuart Sutcliffe (the Beatles' original bass player until he quit the band in 1961).

Possibly the only non-Beatle to know what it felt like to be a Beatle: Jimmy Nicol. In June 1964, Ringo Starr developed tonsillitis and was too sick to perform on several concert dates. Nicol, a session drummer that Beatles producer George Martin liked (and he'd played in a Beatles cover band, so he knew the arrangements), was Ringo's stand-in for eight concerts.

John Lennon wrote "Good Morning Good Morning" as both a parody of obnoxious TV commercials for cereal, and as a sarcastic response to Paul McCartney's sunny "Good Day Sunshine."

UNCLE JOHN'S PAGE OF LISTS

Top random tidbits from our bottomless files.

5 Foods That Relieve Constipation

1. Apples
2. Oats
3. Citrus fruits
4. Berries
5. Leafy greens

7 Bands Banned in the USSR in the 1980s

1. Tina Turner
2. Julio Iglesias
3. Donna Summer
4. Alice Cooper
5. Van Halen
6. Talking Heads
7. Pink Floyd

6 Types of Fire Extinguishers

1. Water
2. Spray
3. Foam
4. Dry powder
5. Carbon dioxide
6. Wet chemical

8 National Birds

1. Germany: Golden eagle
2. Indonesia: Javan hawk-eagle
3. Panama: Harpy eagle
4. Philippines: Philippine eagle
5. Poland: White-tailed eagle
6. Scotland: Golden eagle
7. United States: Bald eagle
8. Zimbabwe: African fish eagle

7 Types of Dementia

1. Alzheimer's disease
2. Vascular dementia
3. Lewy body dementia
4. Frontotemporal dementia
5. Parkinson's disease
6. Huntington's disease
7. Creutzfeldt-Jakob disease

9 Nations with Nukes

1. China
2. India
3. Israel
4. France
5. North Korea
6. Pakistan
7. Russia
8. United Kingdom
9. United States

7 Songs That Inspired Band Names

1. "Death Cab for Cutie" (Bonzo Dog Doo-Dah Band)
2. "Deep Purple" (Peter DeRose)
3. "Cocteau Twins" (Simple Minds)
4. "Jet" (Wings)
5. "Boys to Men" (New Edition)
6. "Radio Head" (Talking Heads)
7. "Nickel Creek" (Byron Berline)

There's only one instance on record of an elephant having triplets.

WEIRD SCIENCE NEWS

*This year's edition of scientific oddities features toenails,
toilet paper, hot dogs, sick llamas, and zombie deer.*

NAILED IT

In 2018 the medical journal *JAMA Dermatology* published a study about a woman
experiencing *onychomadesis*—the slow separation of a nail from a toe or finger, before
it eventually falls off altogether. The patient's case baffled doctors because in the
months leading up to the toenail loss, she'd suffered no infection or skin problem,
hadn't taken any medications with onychomadesis as a known side effect, and suffered
from no autoimmune or hereditary medical conditions. Then the woman remembered
something she did six months earlier that *might* have caused her nail to fall off: she'd
had a "fish pedicure"—a novelty procedure in beauty parlors and health spas in which
the customer rests their feet in a tub of water inhabited by many small *Garra rufa* fish.
The fish normally eat plankton, but they'll also nibble on dead human skin. They eat
away the bad skin, providing a unique foot treatment. Scientists aren't sure how the
procedure could spread infections, although it's likely microbes that remain in a fish's
mouth after it chomps on one customer's feet could get transferred onto the feet of the
next customer.

IMPLICATED BY HOT DOG

In February 2019, police in Minneapolis arrested 52-year-old businessman Jerry
Westrom at his office. The charge: murder. They'd scientifically linked him to the
death of 35-year-old Jeanne Ann Childs…whose body was found at her apartment
more than 25 years earlier, in June 1993. The investigation had long ago gone
cold. Detectives had been unable to identify a viable suspect, even after recovering
DNA from a bedspread, towel, and washcloth in Childs's home. But then in 2018,
as home genealogy and DNA kits were becoming a popular fad, police decided to
enter the DNA from the Childs murder into an online database. It resulted in two
matches, and one was for a man with a criminal record who lived in Minneapolis in
1993—Westrom. Detectives located Westrom and followed him to a hockey game,
where they observed him as he ate a hot dog, wiped his mouth with a napkin, and
then threw away that napkin. After he walked away, the detectives dug through the
trash to retrieve the napkin, tested it for DNA…and it was a match with the stuff
found in 1993.

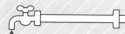

DR. ROBOT

Hundreds of large hospitals around the world these days are equipped with surgical robots. Matching the hand movements and directions of a surgeon in control, robotic arms and fingers can make finer cuts and perform procedures with greater precision than even the most delicate of doctors. Freeman Hospital in Newcastle, England, has a surgical robot, which operated without incident until November 2018. The incident: robots are machines, and machines malfunction. Freeman's surgical robot, programmed to repair patient Stephen Pettitt's damaged heart valve, instead went haywire, flailing every which way with its sharp surgical tools. In the melee, it "attacked" a nurse and inserted stitches "in an unorganized fashion" into Pettitt's heart. But robots only do what they're programmed to do, so the fault ultimately rests with the physician in charge, which in this case was lead surgeon Sukumaran Nair. In a hearing addressing the incident, he admitted that he missed multiple mandatory training sessions in which he would've learned to properly operate the robot. Even worse, during the procedure, the overseeing surgeons assigned to assist Nair should anything go wrong had left the operating room to go on a coffee run. It's not like it would've mattered anyway, because at one point the robot punctured Pettitt's aortic septum, which splattered so much blood on the camera that those doctors wouldn't have been able to see anything on their monitors. Pettitt, who already had a weak heart, then had to endure more surgery— stitch removal, followed by the procedure that the robot was supposed to do, but this time with human surgeons. He did not survive.

A TIP FROM UNCLE JOHN

If you want job security in the age of robots, experts say these are some of the jobs least likely to be usurped by an automaton:

1. Emergency management director
2. Substance abuse social worker
3. Occupational therapist
4. Lodging manager
5. Dietitian
6. Choreographer
7. Physician or Surgeon
8. Psychologist
9. Elementary school teacher
10. Police supervisor

YOU LLOSE, FLU

The reason you should get an annual flu shot is because each year brings a few new strains of influenza. The flu virus is adept at mutating itself, which means neither last year's flu shots nor the body's built-up immunities will fight off next year's flu. But scientists at the Scripps Institute in California have created synthetic, flu-fighting, tough-to-trick antibodies…out of stuff they extracted from llamas. They infected llamas with 60 different flu strains (those poor llamas) to provoke an immune response and ramp up antibody production. Then they observed which antibodies attacked the most kinds of flu, and took elements from the four best to genetically craft a synthetic super-antibody. Once they had their secret weapon, the scientists gave mice fatal doses of flu, and treated them with the super-antibody. Result: it neutralized all the flu strains but one…and that one doesn't infect humans.

OH DEER

Chronic wasting disease (CWD) is also called "zombie deer disease," but it also affects elk and moose, not just deer. The "zombie" part is accurate, though. Turning its victims into creatures resembling the ambling undead from a horror movie, CWD deteriorates an animal's brain and spinal cord, leading to sudden weight loss, a lack of coordination, drooling, and violent behavior. Scientists first identified the disease in the 1960s, but infection rates are on the rise…and so are venison consumption rates among humans. In 2019 scientists identified CWD in at least 24 U.S. states and two Canadian provinces. They estimated that 15,000 infected animals are eaten every year. While there are no reported cases of humans contracting it (yet), the virus has jumped to primates.

GO FOR ONE-PLY

Also called the *taiga* or "snow forest," the coniferous boreal forest covers nearly two-thirds of Canada, the second-largest nation (by area) on Earth. That's enough forest to absorb the carbon dioxide emissions of 24 million cars annually. The wood in that forest is a precious, nonsustainable natural resource, and it's what's used to make that extra-soft and cushiony toilet paper that's become the TP of choice over the last two decades. According to a study by the Natural Resources Defense Council, more than 28 million acres of Canadian forest—an area about as large as Pennsylvania—has been cut down since 1996; most of that provided the raw materials to make luxury toilet paper. The biggest market for that soft stuff: the United States, which buys 20 percent of all TP worldwide, despite making up just 4 percent of the population. The NRDC cites Americans' desire for thick toilet paper to be "worse than Hummers" as far as environmental damage is concerned.

* * *

RANDOM FACT

When Google went down one afternoon in 2013 for one to five minutes (depending on where the user lived), worldwide internet usage dropped 40%.

Typically, the fingernail that grows fastest is the one on the middle finger of your dominant hand.

PLAYS THAT CHANGED THE RULES

As veteran football coach Herm Edwards likes to say, "You play to win the game." But these players ended up playing to change the rules.

THE SLAPPY SACKER

THE SETUP: One of the greatest defensive ends in NFL history, Hall of Famer Deacon Jones played for several teams from 1961 to 1974. Jones revolutionized his position—and the game—with his prowess for tackling quarterbacks in the backfield before they could throw the ball. That's known as a "sack," a term that Deacon himself helped popularize in the 1960s.

THE PLAY: Jones made his 173 career sacks with the help of a secret weapon: right after the ball was snapped, he would slap the opposing offensive lineman on the side of his head, distracting him long enough for Jones to get a jump start.

NEW RULE: Three years after Jones retired, the NFL banned slapping. "The head slap was not my invention," Jones remarked, "but Rembrandt, of course, did not invent painting. The quickness of my hands and the length of my arms, it was perfect for me. It was the greatest thing I ever did, and when I left the game, they outlawed it."

THE HOLY ROLLER

THE SETUP: Completing the trifecta of biblical football plays—after a "hail Mary" (a last-second throw down the field) and "the Immaculate Reception" (Terry Bradshaw's touchdown pass that bounced off one player and was caught by another)—the "Holy Roller" was also attributed to divine intervention. Or, as the TV sportscaster excitedly described it: "the most zany, unbelievable, absolutely impossible dream of a play!"

THE PLAY: With 10 seconds left in a 1978 game, the Oakland Raiders were down by six points against the San Diego Chargers, and they were on the Chargers' 14-yard line. They had time for one more play to try to score a touchdown and win the game. Right after the ball was snapped, the Chargers' defense broke through. Just as they were about to tackle Raiders quarterback Ken Stabler,

> **"The most zany, unbelievable, absolutely impossible dream of a play!"**

he tossed the ball forward, underhand-style, and it bounced to Raiders running back Pete Banaszak on the 10-yard-line. Unable to grab the ball, Banaszak clumsily kicked it forward and it bounced and rolled to tight end Dave Casper, who rolled it and then kicked it into the end zone, where he fell on top of it for the game-winning touchdown.

Blue blood, green thumb: England's Prince Charles talks to plants.

NEW RULE: Because the referees had ruled Stabler's underhanded toss a fumble, the touchdown stood. If he'd tossed it on purpose, it would be an incomplete pass. Either way, it's up to the referee's discretion as to the player's intention. But that off-season, the NFL changed its fumble rules to prevent any future last-minute trickery. Now, if a player fumbles during the final two minutes of play, only the fumbling player is allowed to advance the ball.

THE TOM DEMPSEY RULE

THE SETUP: New Orleans Saints kicker Tom Dempsey was born with a stub for a right hand and no toes on his right foot, so he wore a specially modified shoe with a flat toe.

THE PLAY: It was while wearing this flat-toed shoe that Dempsey kicked a record 63-yard field goal to give the Saints a 19–17 win against the Detroit Lions in 1970.

NEW RULE: The front offices of several other teams complained to the NFL about Dempsey's "advantage." Then rumors spread that Dempsey had a steel plate hidden in his shoe. He denied it. Near the end of his career in 1977, the NFL rule book was changed to state that "any shoe that is worn by a player with an artificial limb on his kicking leg must have a kicking surface that conforms to that of a normal kicking shoe." Dempsey was grandfathered in and allowed to use his shoe for his final years, and he maintained that it never gave him an unfair advantage. "Unfair, eh? How about you try kicking a 63-yard field goal to win it with two seconds left and you're wearing a square shoe, oh yeah, and no toes either!" Did Dempsey's shoe give him an advantage? No other kicker was able to make a longer field goal for 43 years.

THE ROB RAY RULE

THE SETUP: During a fight in a National Hockey League game, it can be hard for a player to throw a punch because of the whole "standing on slippery ice" problem. So to keep from falling down, the two fighters will use one hand to throw punches, and the other hand to hold on to their opponent's jersey. But what happens if you don't have a jersey for them to hold on to?

THE FIGHT: In the late 1990s, Buffalo Sabres enforcer Rob Ray used this disadvantage to his advantage in fights by taking off his jersey, elbow pads, and shoulder pads. Then, looking like an old-time boxer with big pants and no shirt, he would use both fists to devastate his opponents.

NEW RULE: That is, until the NHL instituted the Rob Ray rule. Now, if a player intentionally removes his clothing during a fight, he is ejected. Following the rule change, Ray continued his long career of beating people up, but with his jersey on.

In the 1970s, Playskool made *Gilligan's Island* bath toys for toddlers.

INTERNATIONAL SHAME CLAIM TO FAME

Every country is famous for something…it just might not be for something they're proud of.

HIGHEST MURDER RATE

The Central American nation of Honduras experiences 90.4 (reported) murders per 100,000 people each year. (In the United States, it's just below five per 100,000.)

HIGHEST INCOME TAX

Belgium has a progressive tax, meaning people who earn more pay more. Its top rate is 50 percent, plus all employees pay a 13 percent social security tax. That works out to an average of about 42 percent of a paycheck going to the government. However, housing and groceries in Belgium are among the least expensive in the developed world, and the government pays for many social services, including health care. Belgians have the lowest out-of-pocket health care costs in western Europe.

MOST POLLUTED AIR

India's sky is the dirtiest in the world. According to a study by the environmental crusaders at Greenpeace, seven of the ten cities with the world's worst air quality (and 22 of the 30 most polluted cities) are in India.

POOREST COUNTRY

The Central African Republic. It's got the lowest GDP in the world, with a per capita income of $700 per person.

WORST INFLATION

After political turmoil destabilized the country in 2018, Venezuela's rate of inflation passed 1 million percent by the end of the year. The International Monetary Fund forecast that the nation could reach as high as 10 million percent by the end of 2019.

HIGHEST POPULATION DENSITY

Europe's tiny (and wealthy) Principality of Monaco has the most people in the smallest space. Covering about three-quarters of a square mile, it's home to just over 39,000 people, giving it a population density of about 49,000 people per square mile.

HEAVIEST DRINKERS

When you add up the alcohol in all of the beer, wine, and spirits consumed in the small European country of Moldova each year, the average person consumes 17.4 liters of pure alcohol each year.

Animal most likely to injure zookeepers: zebras.

LEAST LITERATE

One of the newest countries on earth, South Sudan (established in 2011), has the fewest literate adults. Only about 27 percent of men and women there can read.

MOST CANCEROUS

Australia, a land of much sunshine, leads the world in cancer rates. Each year, 468 out of 100,000 residents are diagnosed with cancer (primarily skin cancer). The United States is 5th highest with 352, Canada is 11th with 334, and Israel ranks 50th with 233 per 100,000. The lowest cancer rates can be found in Syria, Bhutan, and Nepal, at approximately 90 cases per 100,000 residents.

MOST SMOKERS

Per capita, the tiny mountainous nation of Andorra, which sits between Spain and France, smokes the most. Each year, the average Andorran purchases and smokes 6,398 cigarettes. That's just under a pack a day for every man, woman, and child.

MOST STRESSED

According to a Bloomberg study that factored in murder rates, GDP, income inequality, unemployment, and life expectancy, the most beleaguered country in the world is Nigeria, with a score of 70.1. (Number 2: South Africa, with a score of 70.)

HIGHEST OBESITY RATE

The Pacific Ocean island nation of Nauru is small, but its people are large. Just over 60 percent of the population is considered obese. (According to the Centers for Disease Control, nearly 40 percent of Americans are classified as obese.)

LOWEST LIFE EXPECTANCY

Due to a poor health care system and infrastructure that allows for the spread of disease, the people in Chad live, on average, to the age of 49 years and 9 months. (In the tiny, wealthy European nation of Monaco, the average lifespan is 89.)

* * *

REALITY TV STARS WHO BECAME POLITICIANS

LAURA MORETT (*Survivor*) ran unsuccessfully for a seat in the Oregon legislature in 2016.

KEVIN POWELL (*The Real World*) ran for Congress in New York three times…and lost.

CLAY AIKEN (*American Idol*) ran for a House seat representing North Carolina in 2014.

SEAN DUFFY (*The Real World*) is currently a U.S. representative from Wisconsin.

DONALD TRUMP (*The Apprentice*) was elected president of the United States in 2016.

Paper trail: More than 27,000 trees a day are made into toilet paper.

THEY LIED ABOUT THEIR AGE

Uncle John has been working on this piece about famous people who publicly fibbed about how old they were since 2012, when he was 19 years old.

★ **MILA KUNIS** When filming on Fox's retro sitcom *That '70s Show* began in 1998, the least experienced member of the show's cast was Mila Kunis, who played spoiled rich girl Jackie Burkhart. Producers wanted everyone who even auditioned to be at least 18 years old. Reason: to avoid child labor restrictions and allow for long shooting days, if necessary. When Kunis auditioned in 1998, she was under 18, but told casting directors not to worry if they picked her for the part because she "would be 18," implying that she'd hit that milestone soon. Kunis was intentionally vague…but not technically lying. She was actually just 14 at the time.

★ **GABRIELLE CARTERIS** This actor was also cast on a 1990s Fox show about teenagers, but unlike Kunis, she had to pretend she was much *younger* that she was. In 1990 Carteris landed the role of Andrea Zuckerman, the brainy high school newspaper editor on *Beverly Hills, 90210*. One problem: Carteris was 29 years old, more than a decade older than her character. Afraid she'd lose the part if producers found out her true age, she was also afraid she'd get sued for providing false information on her contract. She consulted an attorney, who told her that she didn't have to give her exact age if she didn't want to—only that she was "over 21." It worked.

★ **EVA PERON** Americans probably best know Eva Peron by the affectionate nickname the people of her native Argentina bestowed on her after her rise to power: Evita. (That's also the name of the Andrew Lloyd Webber musical that immortalized her.) "Evita" literally translates to "Little Eva," and Evita had to alter her birth records so that nickname would be more accurate. When Peron, who was born in 1919, assumed her role as first lady (and vice president) of Argentina in 1946, she had officials change her birth certificate so that it said she was born in 1922. Reason: so she'd seem more youthful…and also so it looked like her parents were married at the time of her birth, which they were not.

★ **TOM SHAW** Shaw led the University of Oregon to a conference title in golf in 1959, graduated in 1962, and joined the PGA Tour the following year. He was never a superstar, but he won four tournaments and finished in the top 10 more than 20 times. His best season was 1965, when he was 26. "I had a good year at 26, and I thought I'd just stay there for a while," he told a reporter in 1989. "I didn't see anything wrong with it. When I first started out on the tour everyone lied about their ages." So when he turned in his official PGA biography each year, he changed his birthdate so the math always added up to 26. Nobody noticed…until 1977, when golfers Jack Nicklaus and Tom Weiskopf exposed the ruse. "Nicklaus turned me in. He knew he was younger than me—or at least he thought he was." The PGA still didn't care…until Shaw tried to sign up for the Senior PGA Tour in 1989. It admits golfers age 50 and older, and according to its records, Shaw was only 46. In order to play on the Senior Tour, Shaw had to admit that he'd been lying to the PGA for all those years.

★ **DANNY ALMONTE** The breakout stars of the Little League World Series are always the most precocious kids—the ones who play at a level beyond their age, which is supposed to be between 10 and 12. In 2001 pitcher Danny Almonte stunned fans (and opposing teams) with his 76 mph fastballs. His team from the Bronx finished in third place in the Little League World Series, but the only reason they made it to the playoffs at all was because Almonte had thrown a no-hitter earlier in the season. He was so good—and, at 5'8", so tall—that rumors spread that he *couldn't* be 12. He wasn't. Shortly after the season ended, *Sports Illustrated* found Almonte's birth records, proving he was actually 14 at the time of the Little League World Series. The young pitcher later claimed the team's adult organizers had fudged the details to keep him on the mound. Almonte continued to pitch—in high school and college—until 2009, when he was forced to give it up because of a sore arm.

★ **DAN NAINAN** Nainan bills himself as the definitive "millennial" comedian, and it got him noticed. In November 2016, the then-35-year-old comedian was quoted in an AP story about undecided voters. He's also been quoted about millennial issues in *Forbes*, *Cosmopolitan*, the *Chicago Tribune*, the *New York Times*, and on Fox, CNN, and NPR. The reason he landed so much media attention: he hired Help a Reporter Out, a service that gets exposure for their "experts" by allowing deadline-facing journalists to quote them as a source. Still, Nainan's life story *was* compelling: After watching the Twin Towers collapse on 9/11 from his office at Intel, he decided to pursue comedy full-time. Nainan's profile claims he was a senior engineer at Intel, and for years did product demonstrations at trade shows. But the math didn't quite check out. If Nainan was 35 in 2016, he would've been a veteran engineer at Intel with years of experience under his belt…at age 20. Internet reporters noticed these discrepancies, started investigating, and found a traffic court case citation in which Nainan's date of birth was listed as May 1961. As it turned out, the young "millennial" comic was actually pushing 60. The exposure of his lies pretty much ended his career.

A quart of soy sauce contains enough salt to kill a person if they drink it all at once.

A ROYAL PAIN-ENBAUM

One of our favorite movies is The Royal Tenenbaums. *Gene Hackman plays the title character, an abrasive patriarch who tries to win back his family's love by telling them he's dying. Critics called it one of Hackman's greatest performances. But for years, the actor would rarely discuss making the film. A decade later, we found out why.*

JUICY GOSSIP

Despite rumors of friction on the set of 2001's *The Royal Tenenbaums*, Gene Hackman's costars avoided talking about him, preferring to stick with the "it was an honor to work with him" line. Then, at a tenth-anniversary screening attended by some of the stars (but not Hackman), director Wes Anderson and Gwyneth Paltrow (who played Royal's adopted daughter Rachel) both confessed: "We were scared of him." Angelica Huston (who played Royal's wife Ethelene) revealed that during one tense exchange, Hackman told Anderson to "pull up your pants and act like a man." Huston said she actually feared for Anderson's safety.

Then Bill Murray (who played Raleigh St. Clair) chimed in: "I'll stick up for Gene. I'd hear these stories, like, 'Gene threatened to kill me today!' He can't kill you, you're in a union. 'Gene threatened to take all of us and set fire to us.' It's a union shoot, it's New York, he can't set fire to you!"

AMATEUR HOUR

The problem, said Murray, was that Hackman is an Oscar winner, and most of the actors he had to work with...weren't. "He does his thing and it takes about 50–60 seconds, and Luke [pointing to Luke Wilson, who played Royal's son Richie] blew his line 13 or 14 times. I thought Luke was good. He's not good. Because at the time, he was in love with this girl over here." (He pointed to Paltrow, who blushed.) "So that's the problem with Gene. He had to work with Luke who was dizzy in love and Kumar Pallana [who played Pagoda, Royal's Indian servant]." Then Murray got really worked up. "How many of you have worked with Kumar? None of you! You wouldn't be here if you had. Kumar makes Luke Wilson look like [British actor John] Gielgud! If I had to work with Kumar and Luke Wilson, I would have set fire to this whole building."

Paltrow was a little more diplomatic: "To be in his presence and watch him do his thing. It's like—you know, you're Gene Hackman, you can be in a bad (censored) mood."

7 percent of Italy's GDP can be attributed to organized crime.

TAKING THE HIGH ROAD

Anderson thanked his actors for sticking up for him, and then he stuck up for Hackman: "Even though he was very challenging with me, it was very exciting seeing him launch into his scenes." To put Hackman's experience into perspective, Anderson added that the veteran actor didn't really want to be in a "quirky indie film" in the first place, didn't want to work for scale, and didn't want to play a part that was specifically written for him (a rule Hackman always had), but his agent talked him into it. So Hackman struggled his way through the shoot, repeatedly saying that this would be his last movie.

> **Hackman didn't really want to be in a "quirky indie film" in the first place.**

Nevertheless, he ended up winning the Golden Globe for Best Actor in a Motion Picture – Musical or Comedy. (Despite being nominated, Hackman was a no-show at that year's awards ceremony. Presenter Renée Zellweger explained to the audience that "Gene missed his connection in the Caribbean and sends his regrets.")

The Royal Tenenbaums wasn't quite Hackman's last movie—he did three more before retiring, giving him an even 100 for his career. When an interviewer asked him in 2011 if he'd ever consider taking on one more film role, Hackman answered, "If I could do it in my own house, maybe, without them disturbing anything, and just one or two people."

* * *

OBSCURE (AND REAL) COFFEE DRINKS

Ristretto. An espresso shot brewed quickly, before the machine is done making it, which means there's less water in the brew. Result: a less-bitter but more highly concentrated caffeine kick.

Cortado. Unlike a latte, which combines espresso with steamed milk, a cortado is espresso with steamed half and half (and not frothy).

Affogato. Vanilla ice cream with a shot of espresso poured on top.

Caffé con panna. Espresso topped with a dollop of whipped cream.

Shakerato. A cold drink (that looks like a dark beer with a foamy head) made by combining espresso, sugar, and ice, and shaking it until it's frothy.

Marocchino. Espresso, cocoa powder, and foamed milk are mixed, and then dusted with more cocoa powder. Then a layer of Nutella is spread around the rim of the glass.

Corretto. Espresso served with a few drops of rum or coffee liqueur.

Top-scoring brothers in NHL history: The Gretzkys. (Wayne scored 2,857 points; Brent scored 4.)

INCORRECTLY CORRECTED

Does the following sentence make you want to bang your head against a wall? "I literally died because I could of cared less." It contains three of the most controversial words and phrases in English today. Which are right, and which are wrong? The answers may surprise you.

LITERALLY

The primary definition of "literally" is "actually." Both words can be used to add emphasis to a point: "There are literally thousands of fans on Uncle John's Facebook page." There really are thousands, so that sentence is accurate. But a lot of grammar nerds would tell you this sentence is wrong: "He literally glowed." He glowed? Like a light bulb? That's impossible.

Is it? Tell that to F. Scott Fitzgerald, who wrote the line in *The Great Gatsby* a century ago. And he's not alone: Mark Twain, Charles Dickens, James Joyce, and other literary greats also used *literally* in a figurative sense. The editors at *Merriam-Webster* are quick to point this out when critics complain that the dictionary is killing the word by including this secondary definition: "in effect, virtually."

According to *Merriam-Webster*, "There is…a strong impulse among lexicographers to catalog the language as it is used, and there is a considerable body of evidence indicating that *literally* has been used in this fashion for a very long time." Literalists (a term we just made up) may then ask, "Without *literally*, what word do we use?" Answer: in addition to *actually*, there's *really*, *truly*, *completely*, *precisely*, *genuinely*, *legitimately*, and many more.

End note: The meanings of words change more often than you might think. Take "fantastic" (from the French *fantastique*), which originally meant "something conceived via imagination" (like a fantasy), but for whatever reason, people kept using the word incorrectly, and now it means…fantastic.

I COULD CARE LESS

Grammar nerds who foam at the mouth upon hearing "could care less" may be forgetting a few key points about common colloquial expressions, or *idioms*. First, these expressions aren't necessarily coined; they come about organically and can be in use for many years before someone writes them down. Second, idioms don't have to be logical. For example, "head over heels" *should* mean upright, not upside down…but upside down is what you picture when you hear "head over heels." Or how about the idiom "meteoric rise"? Do meteors rise? Don't they fall?

The phrase "I could care less" means you don't care much at all. The original version—"I couldn't care less"—came from Great Britain around 1900. Taken literally, it means that you care so little about something that there's no smaller amount of caring possible. "Could care less," however, implies that you *do* care—at least a little bit. The American version, a variant that dates back to the 1960s, is meant to express sarcasm, like the Yiddish expression "I should be so lucky." For example: "Uncle Joe wants to visit for two weeks? I should be so lucky. And he's bringing his bottle cap collection? I could care less."

So both *could* and *couldn't* are acceptable; it's up to you to decide which one works best for your particular situation. But if you go with "could" and someone screams "couldn't," tell them you could care less, and then they will probably care even more.

COULD'VE, WOULD'VE, SHOULD'VE

These are contractions of "could have," "would have," and "should have," so when speaking, there's nothing incorrect about pronouncing it "could've." Some people believe that's incorrect, though, because they think it's a verbalization of a common misspelling of the phrase as "could of." It's not. When speaking, "could've" is acceptable, but spelling it out as "could of" is simply wrong.

BONUS: TWO MORE "INCORRECTIONS"

- **Don't start a sentence with a conjunction:** Though some may scoff at starting a sentence with "and," "but," or "so," there's no rule against this. But there is a rule against adding a comma after the preposition. This is incorrect: "But, I told him not to go in there after John." You would only keep that comma if there was a dependent clause, as in "But, and I shouldn't have to say this, I told him not to go in there after John."

- **Don't end a sentence with a preposition:** This was a common complaint of stodgy editors in the 19th century, who would rather we all talk like Shakespeare, but this has never, ever been a rule of grammar. Sometimes you need that ending preposition. Otherwise, how would you be able to ask John what he has to go on?

Yoda was going to be named Minch Yoda, until George Lucas decided that Yoda sounded better without the Minch.

THE REST OF THE (FAKE) STORY

All these stories are part of the fabric of American culture…even though none of them have ever been verified as having actually happened. But that hasn't stopped countless news outlets and books from sharing them as true. Interestingly, there's one factor that links them all together: ABC Radio broadcaster Paul Harvey shared them on his popular syndicated radio show The Rest of the Story, *which ran from the 1950s to 2008. So enjoy these urban legends, courtesy of Paul Harvey.*

THE STORY: Some airport baggage handlers are removing the luggage and cargo from the bowels of a plane when they come across a pet crate with a dog inside. Bad news: The dog is deceased. Fearing they'll be blamed for the pet's death (and get fired), the handlers chip in some money and set out to a pet store to buy a lookalike dog as a replacement. They find one and get it in the crate just in time for the dog's owner to claim it. The dog immediately bursts out of the container and licks the woman's face. That causes her to faint; when she comes to, she explains that the dog had died while she was on her trip, and she'd been bringing the animal back home for burial.

THE REST OF THE STORY: As far back as the 1950s, airline employees shared this tale as if it had actually happened. It got retold so often that in 1987, Paul Harvey reported it as a quirky-but-true news item on his radio show *The Rest of the Story*. It was quirky…but it wasn't true.

THE STORY: A state trooper spots a driver weaving between lanes, and, suspecting that the driver is drunk, pulls the car over to administer a Breathalyzer test. The driver fails the test, and the trooper is about to read him his rights and take him in when, a few dozen yards in front of them, two cars collide in a nasty accident. The trooper orders the drunk driver to stay put so he can go assist with the collision, but the suspect does nothing of the sort. Instead, he hops behind the wheel and speeds off, driving himself home. He parks the car in his garage and instructs his wife to tell law enforcement, should they come calling, that he'd been home all night. The next morning, police do arrive, and the wife tells them her husband was home all night, with his car parked in the garage. When they ask to see the car, she takes them to the garage…where they discover not the guy's car but the state trooper's vehicle. And it's still running. With the red-and-blue-lights still flashing.

According to scientists, the ozone layer smells like geraniums.

THE REST OF THE STORY: Paul Harvey shared this fake story as an actual piece of news on *The Rest of the Story* in 1986.

THE STORY: Paul Newman was a legendary movie star, but he was still a human being, and human beings get hot and eat ice cream in the summer. So one hot day in 1986, Newman goes into an ice-cream parlor in New England, and gets in line behind an older woman. She immediately recognizes him, can't stop staring at him, and is so flummoxed she can't speak. Somehow, she still manages to order an ice-cream cone, barely breaking her loving gaze at the blue-eyed screen idol. A few moments later, witnesses later report, they see the dazed woman standing outside the shop, staring at the change in her hand. Out walks Newman, licking an ice-cream cone. He says to the woman, "If you're looking for your cone, it's in your purse, right where you put it."

THE REST OF THE STORY: A number of gossip columnists and radio hosts published this tall tale as fact, although the subject wasn't always Newman— sometimes it was Jack Nicholson, sometimes it was Robert Redford. Paul Harvey attributed the story to Newman.

> **A TIP FROM UNCLE JOHN**
>
> Even though we all do it, lying isn't natural. Your body involuntarily does certain things when your brain and your mouth conspire to lie. Watch for these signs in others, because they might be signs that the person you're talking to is being less than honest:
>
> 1. Their face turns slightly pink
> 2. Their nostrils flare a little
> 3. They blink more than usual
> 4. Their shoulders slump

THE STORY: A highway patrolman in rural Oklahoma is driving down a farm road one morning when he comes across a farmer shouting and waving his arms. He slows down, rolls down his window, and hears the man shouting, "Pig! Pig!" Insulted and shocked by this derogatory name for a police officer, the trooper shouts back, "Redneck! Redneck!" and speeds away. He drives on for another 50 yards or so, and after cresting a hill…runs right into a 300-pound pig taking a nap on the road.

THE REST OF THE STORY: Yep, Paul Harvey related this amazing tale on a January 1988 episode of *The Rest of the Story*. While it's very similar to urban legends dating back to the early 1970s, Harvey's exposure spread the story so far and wide that reporters at the Associated Press were inspired to track down its origins. Turns out the trooper was a man named Bill Runyan. So was it a true story? No. Runyan told the AP that long ago, his cousin worked as the editor of a small newspaper, and he routinely spun Runyan's anecdotes and work stories into wacky news items. "Were the story true, I would have had to file an accident report," Runyan told reporters.

Chance you'll find Boardwalk and win McDonald's Monopoly: 1 in 651 million.

"129 WAYS TO GET A HUSBAND"

This 1958 McCall's magazine article was compiled by "sixteen experts," including a marriage counselor, an airline stewardess, a psychologist, and a bachelor. We couldn't fit all 129 entries, so we only included the really dated, eye-rolling ones…which turned out to be most of them.

WHERE TO FIND HIM

2. Have your car break down at strategic places.

6. Read the obituaries to find eligible widowers.

9. Sit on a park bench and feed the pigeons.

12. Become a nurse or an airline stewardess—they have very high marriage rates.

14. Be nice to everybody—they may have an eligible brother or son.

17. Be friendly to ugly men—handsome is as handsome does.

19. Get lost at football games.

20. Don't take a job in a company run largely by women.

21. Get a job demonstrating fishing tackle in a sporting goods store.

22. On a plane, train, or bus, don't sit next to a woman—sit next to a man.

24. Don't be afraid to associate with more attractive girls; they may have some leftovers.

26. Don't room with a girl who is a sad sack and let her pull you down to her level.

29. When traveling, stay at small hotels where it is easier to meet strangers.

30. Learn to paint. Set up an easel outside an engineering school.

HOW TO LET HIM KNOW YOU'RE THERE

31. Stumble when you walk into a room that he's in.

32. Forget discretion every once in a while and call him up.

34. Wear a Band-Aid. People always ask what happened.

35. Make a lot of money.

38. Dropping the handkerchief still works.

39. Have your father buy some theater tickets that have to be gotten rid of.

40. Stand in a corner and cry softly. Chances are good that he'll come over to find out what's wrong.

41. Don't let him fish for your name the next time you meet. None of this "guess who" stuff.

The World Testicle Cooking Championship is held in Gornji Milanovac, Serbia, each year.

43. Buy a convertible. Men like to ride in them.

44. Learn how to bake tasty apple pies. Bring one into the office and let the eligible bachelors taste it.

45. Laugh at his jokes.

47. "Accidentally" have your purse fly open, scattering its contents all over the street.

HOW TO LOOK GOOD TO HIM

48. Men like to think they're authorities on perfume. Ask his advice on what kind you should wear.

49. Get better-looking glasses—men still make passes at girls who wear glasses—or try contact lenses.

50. Practice your drinking with your women friends first.

51. If you dye your hair, pick a shade and stick to it.

52. Wear high heels most of the time—they're sexier!

53. Unless he happens to be shorter than you are!

54. Tell him he's handsome.

55. Take good care of your health. Men don't like girls who are ill.

56. If you look good in sweaters, wear one on every third date.

58. Get a sunburn.

60. Go on a diet if you need to.

61. When you are with him, order your steak rare.

62. Don't tell him about your allergies.

63. European women use their eyes to good advantage. Practice in front of a mirror.

64. Buy a full-length mirror and take a good look before you go to greet him.

66. Get that fresh-scrubbed look by scrubbing!

68. Use the ashtray; don't crush out cigarettes in coffee cups!

70. Don't be too fussy.

72. Don't whine—girls who whine stay on the vine!

HOW TO LAND HIM

73. Show him you can have fun on a cheap date—but don't overdo it!

74. Don't let your parents treat him like a potential husband.

76. Double-date with a gay, happily married couple—let him see what it's like!

78. Send his mother a birthday card.

80. Talk to his father about business and agree that taxes are too high!

82. On the first date tell him you aren't thinking of getting married!

83. Don't talk about how many children you want.

84. If he's a fisherman, learn to scale and clean fish.

A sudden rush of adrenaline is what causes blushing.

86. When you're out strolling with him, don't insist on stopping at every shop window.

87. Don't tell him how much your clothes cost.

88. Learn to sew, and wear something that you made yourself.

93. Find out about the girls he hasn't married. Don't repeat the mistakes they made.

96. Be flexible. If he decides to skip the dance and go rowing on the lake, *go*—even if you are wearing your best evening gown.

98. Turn wolves into husband material by assuming they have honor.

102. Make your home comfortable when he calls—large ashtrays, comfortable chairs.

103. Learn to play poker.

104. If he's rich, tell him you like his money—the honesty will intrigue him!

105. Never let him believe your career is more important than your marriage.

108. Don't tell dirty stories.

109. Stop being a mama's girl—don't let him think he'll have in-law trouble, even if you know he will!

110. Point out to him that the death rate of single men is twice that of married men.

WILD IDEAS—ANYTHING GOES

111. Go to Yale.

112. Get a hunting license.

113. If your mother is fat, tell him you take after your father. If he's fat too, tell him you're adopted!

114. Stow away on a battleship.

115. Rent a billboard and post your picture and telephone number on it.

116. Paint your name and number on your roof and say, "Give me a buzz, pilots."

117. Start a whispering campaign on how sought-after you are.

119. Ride the airport bus back and forth from the airport.

122. Carry a camera and ask strange, handsome men if they would mind snapping your picture.

124. Make and sell toupees—bald men are easy catches!

128. Let it be known in your office that you have a button box and will sew on bachelors' loose buttons.

129. Don't marry him if he has too many loose buttons!

EPILOGUE

A few entries we left out actually do hold up today, like #4, "Join a hiking club" or #101, "Remain innocent but not ignorant." However, as the article concludes, "Even a quick glance at the list will show you that the day has passed when a reasonably pretty girl can sit, hands folded, on her front veranda waiting for Mr. Right to come along. As our brainstorming panel sees it, getting married today is a problem in social engineering."

Canadian with the most #1 hits in the U.S.: Drake (6).

FROM THE BRAIN OF BOURDAIN

Chef, writer, and TV travel show host Anthony Bourdain died in 2018 at the age of 61. Here are some of the best things he ever said about three of the best things in life: food, travel, and philosophy.

"Without experimentation, a willingness to ask questions and try new things, we shall surely become static, repetitive, and moribund."

"As you move through this life and this world you change things slightly, you leave marks behind, however small."

"PEOPLE CONFUSE ME. FOOD DOESN'T."

"What nicer thing can you do for somebody than make them breakfast?"

"If I'm an advocate for anything, it's to move. As far as you can, as much as you can. Walk in someone else's shoes...or at least eat their food."

"Your body is not a temple. It's an amusement park. Enjoy the ride."

"Skills can be taught. Character you either have or you don't."

"Plans should be ephemeral, so be prepared to move away from them."

"I became successful in my forties. I became a dad in my fifties. I feel like I've stolen a car—a really nice car—and I keep looking in the rearview mirror for flashing lights. But there's been nothing yet."

"You're never going to find perfect city travel experience or the perfect meal without a constant willingness to experience a bad one. Letting the happy accident happen is what a lot of vacation itineraries miss."

"Perhaps wisdom is realizing how small I am, and unwise, and how far I have yet to go."

"If I believe in anything, it is doubt. The root cause of all life's problems is looking for a simple answer."

"Travel is about the gorgeous feeling of teetering in the unknown."

"AN OUNCE OF SAUCE COVERS A MULTITUDE OF SINS."

"UNDER 'REASONS FOR LEAVING LAST JOB,' NEVER GIVE THE REAL REASON, UNLESS IT'S MONEY OR AMBITION."

"Context and memory play powerful roles in all the truly great meals in one's life."

"I don't have an agenda, but I do have a point of view...and it might change from minute to minute."

CELEBRITY NEAR-MISSES

Being famous didn't save these folks from just-a-little-too-close brushes with death.

MILTON HERSHEY

Claim to Fame: Founder of the Hershey Chocolate Company and inventor of the Hershey Bar, the first mass-produced milk chocolate bar that ordinary people could afford (Price: 2¢)

> The check was a deposit on a first-class cabin aboard the *Titanic* for Hershey and his wife Kitty.

Near Miss: If you visit the Hershey Story museum in Hershey, Pennsylvania, one of the items you'll see on display there is a canceled check for $300 from Milton Hershey to the White Star Line, owners of the *Titanic*. The check was a deposit on a first-class cabin aboard the *Titanic* for Hershey and his wife Kitty. They had spent the winter in Nice, France. But some business issue arose and Hershey was eager to return home early to deal with it. So rather than wait until the *Titanic* sailed on April 10, 1912, Hershey booked passage on the German liner *Amerika*, which departed on April 6. (The *Amerika* was one of the ships that transmitted ice advisories to the *Titanic* in the hours before it sank.)

EDWARD G. ROBINSON

Claim to Fame: Hollywood actor best known for his gangster roles in films such as *Little Caesar* and *Key Largo* in the 1930s and '40s

Near Miss: Robinson was traveling in Europe with his family in August 1939. These were the last days of peace before Adolf Hitler's invasion of Poland on September 1 sparked the beginning of World War II. As the international situation deteriorated in the last days of August, Robinson decided to cut short his trip and bring his family back to the United States. He tried to buy tickets on the passenger liner *Athenia*, but there had been an error in booking, so the Robinsons had to settle for a single cramped cabin on an American liner called the *Washington*. That inconvenience turned out to be a lucky break: On September 3, 1939, the *Athenia* was torpedoed by a German submarine off the west coast of Ireland and sunk, killing 117 passengers and crew.

THE FOUR TOPS

Claim to Fame: Motown vocal group best known for their hits "Baby I Need Your

Loving," "I Can't Help Myself (Sugar Pie Honey Bunch)," and "Reach Out I'll Be There" in the 1960s

Near Miss: In December 1988, the group was in London taping two performances for the BBC television show *Top of the Pops*. The group wanted to record both performances in a single session, and had already booked their flight home to Detroit on Pan Am Flight 103 on December 21. But a BBC producer insisted that they record the performances in separate sessions, forcing them to take a later flight home. Shortly after 7:00 p.m. on the evening of December 21, a bomb planted aboard Flight 103 by Libyan agents exploded, causing the airplane to disintegrate in the skies over Lockerbie, Scotland, killing everyone aboard. "The producer on *Top of the Pops* was the reason we didn't get on that plane," Duke Fakir, the last surviving original member of the Four Tops, told the BBC in 2016. "I was so glad, so, so glad we didn't do it in one session."

SETH MacFARLANE

Claim to Fame: Voice actor and creator of the animated series *Family Guy* and *American Dad*, and creator and star of the live-action sci-fi series *The Orville*

Near Miss: MacFarlane, a graduate of the Rhode Island School of Design, delivered a speech at his alma mater on September 10, 2001, and had a ticket for the following morning's American Airlines Flight 11 from Boston to Los Angeles. Two things caused him to miss his flight: 1) he was up late celebrating with old friends, and 2) his travel agent had given him the wrong departure time—8:15 a.m. instead of 7:45 a.m. Hung over, MacFarlane arrived at the airport 10 minutes too late to board the plane...which was hijacked by the 9/11 terrorists 15 minutes into the flight and flown into the North Tower of the World Trade Center. (Actor Mark Wahlberg also had a ticket on Flight 11, but he changed his plans and caught a flight to Canada instead, because a friend invited him to view a film at the Toronto Film Festival.)

GUGLIELMO MARCONI

Claim to Fame: Inventor of the radio

Near Miss: As you might expect with the first person to transmit "wireless" telegraph messages across the Atlantic, Marconi made regular transatlantic crossings as he set up a business to capitalize on what would soon be a boom in communication between Europe and the United States. By the time he was offered free passage on the maiden voyage of the *Titanic* in early 1912, he already had 40 transatlantic trips under his belt and was familiar with the services offered aboard various passenger liners. At that time, he was preparing for a patent-infringement lawsuit against an American

Fastest-growing tissue in the human body: bone marrow.

telegraph company, and he had a lot of work that he wanted to do during the trip. But Marconi's secretary, Giovanni Magrini, "was hopeless on board ship, he was seasick from shore to shore," Marconi's daughter Degna Marconi recounted in her 1962 book, *My Father, Marconi*. "Father switched his passage to the *Lusitania*, which departed three days earlier, because he had a mountain of paperwork to clear away and knew that the public stenographer [on the *Lusitania*] was quick and competent."

DAN QUAYLE

Claim to Fame: Vice president of the United States under President George H. W. Bush

Near Miss: In November 1978, Quayle was a freshman congressman from Indiana when another member of Congress, Leo Ryan, invited him to participate in a fact-finding mission to the Peoples Temple cult compound in Guyana, South America. The purpose of the trip was to find out whether members of the cult were being held there against their will. But Quayle's wife Marilyn was expecting their third child and needed help with the other two, so Quayle begged off the trip so that he could stay home with his wife. Congressman Ryan went without him, and was murdered along with four other members of his party during the Jonestown massacre, in which more than 900 cult members committed suicide or were murdered on the orders of Jim Jones, the founder and leader of the cult.

MICHAEL JACKSON

Claim to Fame: Singer, songwriter, presumptive "King of Pop," and the third best-selling music artist of all time after the Beatles and Elvis Presley

Near Miss: Jackson's brother Jermaine writes in his 2011 book *You Are Not Alone: Michael, Through a Brother's Eyes* that Jackson had meetings in the World Trade Center on the morning of 9/11. But on the night of September 10, he stayed up so late visiting with his mother, his sister Rebbie, and others that he never made it to his first appointment of the day. "None of us had a clue that Michael was due at a meeting that morning at the top of one of the Twin Towers," Jermaine Jackson writes. "We only discovered this when Mother phoned his hotel to make sure he was okay. She, Rebbie, and a few others had left him there around 3:00 a.m. 'Mother, I'm okay, thanks to you,' he told her. 'You kept me up talking so late that I overslept and missed my appointment.'"

* * *

"I'd kill for a Nobel Peace Prize."

—Steven Wright

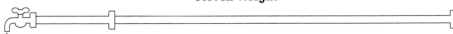

Carnauba wax is used in car wax and as a food additive, to give gummy candies their shine.

BATHROOM NEWS

*Here are a few fascinating bits of bathroom trivia that
we've flushed out from around the world.*

BRUSH WITH THE LAW

In December 2013, violent clashes broke out on the streets of Hamburg between German police and protestors. Among the protestors' beefs: a stop-and-search law that allows cops to confiscate anything they want. The protests took a silly turn after a 23-second video surfaced on YouTube that showed a hooded man being detained by riot police: They pinned him up against a wall, lifted his shirt, and confiscated a toilet brush. (Then they arrested him.) It's unclear why the man was carrying a toilet brush, but his arrest really inspired the protestors. The next night, dozens of angry Hamburgers (people who live in Hamburg) hit the streets with their own toilet brushes. Some in the press were calling it the "Toilet Brush Revolution" (a phrase that sadly never caught on). According to the *World Bulletin,* in addition to "flashing their toilet brushes at police officers," some of the Hamburgers "adopted a new way to protest these stop-and-search measures by carrying ridiculous items in their bags such as cucumbers and dirty underwear."

MESSAGE FROM THE PAST

In July 2018, Alex and Jess Monney were remodeling their bathroom in San Jose, California, when they discovered a note hidden behind a wall that read: *"We remodeled this bathroom summer 1995. If you're reading this, that means you're remodeling the bathroom again. What's wrong with the way we did it?!?!?"*

Accompanying the note was a photograph of the previous owners. Beneath that was a photo of the owners' pet rabbit. Amused, the Monneys tweeted a photo of the note (and the rabbit), and the tweet went viral, amassing tens of thousands of shares (even one from comedian Sarah Silverman). The Monneys were interviewed by NBC (it must have been a slow news day) and Alex had a message for the former owners: "Thank you for the note. It gave us a lot of smiles. Your bathroom was great. Sorry for messing with it."

> **A TIP FROM UNCLE JOHN**
>
> Here are two simple, natural ways to mask or eliminate unwanted throne room odors: put a bowl of white vinegar and baking soda on the tank or a container of activated carbon on the bowl, just behind the toilet seat.

BATH & BREAKFAST

Proving that the "tiny home" craze is getting a bit out of hand, a 200-square-foot apartment for rent in St. Louis,

Missouri, made the news in 2018 for its odd floor layout: The bathroom and kitchen comprise the same tiny room. The stove is next to the kitchen sink, which is next to the toilet, which is next to the bathtub, which is right across from the stove. The good news: if you have long arms, you can flip your burgers while you're taking a shower. The bad news: you'll need to space out your cooking and going times. The ad for the tiny apartment, which passed all city inspections and rents for a low $525 per month, drew dozens of queries. And according to the landlord, the new tenant is very happy.

TOILET SNAKE

"It's one of those things where you think, 'it can't actually happen,'" said Animal Control supervisor Rebecca Franklin, "but now it has." What happened? In July 2018, a ball python poked its head out of James Hopper's toilet in Virginia Beach, Virginia. At first, Hopper wasn't even sure the snake was real. "When I saw the tongue," he told WTKR-TV, "I was like, 'Wow.'" Although pythons aren't venomous (they kill their prey by squeezing all the air out of it), Hopper was lucky that he didn't find out about the toilet snake the hard way. Hopper and his roommate carefully used a fishing pole and some string to lasso the 2.5-foot snake and pull it out of there. Then they called Animal Control to help track down the python's owners, who hadn't seen their pet for two weeks.

THE UNFLUSHABLES

They called it the "fatberg." It was 23 feet long and weighed a ton. It looked like a giant, black monster from the underworld. What was it made of? Thousands of used wet wipes, held together by fat and sewage. Workers used a crane to extract half of the fatberg from a clogged sewer line; the other half had to be removed by hand. This particular fatberg came from the bowels of a neighborhood in New South Wales, Australia, in 2016. But there are more of them growing out there, perhaps even one below you. NSW utility spokesperson Nick Kaiser blames these blockages on a recent fad of adults who habitually use wet wipes: "They're being advertised as basically an extra way to freshen yourself up after the bathroom." But despite what it says on the label, wet wipes are not "flushable." Kaiser offers a friendly reminder: "The safest way to think about what you can put down your toilet is the three Ps: pee, paper, and poo."

* * *

A FART JOKE

Q: Why is it against the rules to fart at Apple headquarters?

A: Because they don't have Windows.

Ew! The day after Thanksgiving is so busy for plumbers that they call it "Brown Friday."

THE DEADLIEST ROLLER COASTERS

The memory of a roller coaster ride stays with you—especially the screams of the riders (and you) as the car reaches the top and starts to drop, and everyone wonders if they're going to make it to the end intact. In a few rare cases, the thrill-seeking passengers didn't.

THE BIG DIPPER (1930)

Krug Park in Omaha, Nebraska, was one of the nation's premier amusement parks. Until July 24, 1930. On that fateful day, the Big Dipper's four cars were packed full of riders. The coaster was clicking its way up the first incline when a bolt holding the front brake shoe came loose and got caught under the rear part of the leading car. That caused the car to jump the track and plummet 35 feet down to the ground. The three trailing cars were pulled down after it and landed in a mangled mess of coaster parts and people. Four riders died and 19 more sustained critical injuries—still the deadliest roller coaster accident in American history. After that, Krug Park's attendance steadily dropped until it closed in 1940.

THE BIG DIPPER (1972)

This Big Dipper was located at London's Battersea Park Fun Fair, and it's responsible for the deadliest coaster accident in world history...and one of the most gruesome. On May 30, 1972, the Dipper was climbing up the first incline when the chain suddenly snapped and sent all 31 passengers hurtling backward. Five people were crushed to death and 13 more were severely injured. The park's general manager and the ride's engineer were both charged with manslaughter, but both were acquitted. Nevertheless, the wooden coaster was torn down and the park limped along for two more years before closing for good.

WILD WONDER

In 1997 the State of New Jersey came down hard on the owners and operators at Gillian's Wonderland Pier for failing to follow regulations after a series of accidents on the Wild Wonder coaster. But it wasn't enough to prevent a tragedy that claimed the lives of two people in 1999. The ride suffered a rare double mechanical failure when the drag train that towed the car up the ride's first ascent released too early. Then the rollback feature malfunctioned and the coaster started rolling backward down the track into a sharp curve. A 38-year-old mother and her daughter were flung out of the car after the safety bar failed to restrain them. They hit the coaster's walls hard

A nectarine is a peach with a recessive gene that prevents peach fuzz from forming.

and were hurled 10 feet to the ground. Neither survived. Meanwhile, the car kept rolling backward until it hit another car, injuring two more people. The park was fined $55,000 for the accident, and the Wild Wonder was torn down.

DERBY RACER

The Derby Racer was a pre–World War II wooden roller coaster at Revere Beach, Massachusetts, (seven miles north of Boston) that featured two cars "racing" each other on parallel tracks. The first fatality occurred in June 1911, a few months after the ride opened, when an executive from the roller coaster company fell out while speaking to his fellow riders about proper safety. Six years later, a man was crushed and broke every bone in his body when his hat flew out and he fell out after it. A severely injured rider who was thrown from the roller coaster in 1929 sued the company that operated it and had his case reach the Supreme Court. (He won.) The Derby Racer was demolished in 1936.

ROUGH RIDERS

Part of the thrill of riding a rickety "old-school" wooden roller coaster is the feeling that it could fly off the track at any second. And that was known to happen in the early days of amusement parks. Take Rough Riders, a Coney Island roller coaster that had several serious accidents from 1907 to 1916. The worst occurred in the year before they tore it down. The rough ride started at the top of a hill, rolled past scenes depicting Teddy Roosevelt's cavalry in the Spanish-American War, and then climbed an incline—powered with the aid of an electric third rail—before falling again and twisting and turning its way to the end. A driver was supposed to turn the power off after the coaster made its big climb. On a July day in 1915, with six people on the coaster, the driver didn't slow down and the coaster went way too fast into a sharp curve. The car jumped the track and flipped on its side, hurling three people 30 feet to their death. A mother was able to save herself and her four-year-old son by clinging onto the car's handrail until police arrived to rescue them.

THE MINDBENDER

The Mindbender at Galaxyland Amusement Park in Edmonton, Alberta, is billed as "the largest indoor triple-looping roller coaster on Earth." Only three months after opening in 1986, and one day after an inspector declared the Mindbender safe, it earned a new description: world's most dangerous indoor coaster. Just before reaching the third and final loop, a loose bolt on the rear car's wheel assembly prevented the car from clearing the loop. The car went out of control and slammed into a concrete pillar, killing three people and injuring 19, one critically. The coaster was given a year-long refit, was returned to service, and—fortunately—has been accident-free since then.

Big picture: The human eye has 67 times higher resolution than a fancy 4K television.

WHAT A CARD!

The subject matter for trading cards in the United States used to be limited to sports. Over the decades, companies like Topps and Fleer started adding themes such as movies, history, TV shows, science fiction, cartoon characters, superheroes…and pretty much everything else imaginable. Here are a few unusual series of trading cards. Maybe you remember…

Desert Storm (1991). The first Gulf War lasted six months—that's how long it took the American military and Coalition Forces to dislodge Iraqi dictator Saddam Hussein from Kuwait. And that was plenty of time for Topps to make Gulf War merchandise. This set treats an actual war—which resulted in the loss of property and life—like it was a sport or movie, with 264 cards featuring locations, events, weapons, and notable individuals involved in the war. (The President George H. W. Bush card is titled "THE COMMANDER IN CHIEF.")

***Warriors of Plasm* (1993).** This was an attempt to combine the "Collect 'em all!" nature of both comic books and trading cards. Veteran DC and Marvel writer Jim Shooter created a new science-fiction comic book called *Warriors of Plasm*, but rather than publishing it as a printed issue, a card maker put each individual panel drawing onto a card, and released it to the public that way. To read the entire story, kids had to collect every card and then order them in a binder.

Rad Dudes (1990). Garbage Pail Kids were a big fad in the mid-1980s. Parodying Cabbage Patch Kids dolls, these cards graphically depicted revolting characters like Barfin' Barbara (she's vomiting into a saucepan) and Bony Tony (he's unzipping his skin to reveal his skeleton). Rad Dudes were clearly a much less nauseating knockoff of the Garbage Pail Kids, but were still trying to be cool by showing teens doing "rad" things. Check out volleyball-playing Spikin' Spencer, cheerleading Rah Rah Rachael, and basketball-playing Awesome B'Ball Blake.

***Titanic* (1998).** These cards were an attempt to mine the success of the 1997 movie *Titanic*, which played into theaters well into 1998 and won the Academy Award for Best Picture. But these aren't cards showing scenes from the movie, or pictures of Leonardo DiCaprio and Kate Winslet. These *Titanic* cards are about the horrific real-life event of 1912 that inspired the movie. Cards ghoulishly and hauntingly show photos of the doomed ship, its deceased passengers, and newspaper headlines reporting on the boat's sinking.

First YouTube video to reach one billion views: "Gangnam Style" in 2012.
(It now has over three billion views.)

The Soaps of ABC, Featuring *All My Children* (1991). If there's one thing baseball card-collecting kids love, it's daytime soap operas! Okay, not really, which is why this effort by ABC to test the trading card waters failed. A set featuring characters and scenes from the long-running soap *All My Children* sold so poorly that plans for sets based on *One Life to Live* and *General Hospital* were scrapped.

The Andy Griffith Show (1990). Pacific Cards released a 110-card set of stills and promotional images from *The Andy Griffith Show*...more than 20 years after the black-and-white TV series had been canceled. Was this set for kids, who would be unfamiliar with the show, or geared at middle-aged adults...who don't really spend their money on trading cards? (Answer: neither.)

Supersisters (1979). Most trading cards of the day depicted male athletes or male superheroes, so it was refreshing for there to be a feminist movement–inspired line of trading cards depicting notable women of the past and (then) present, such as Rosa Parks, Gloria Steinem, and Jane Pauley.

The Original Hot Aire Trading Cards (1991). A couple of hot-air balloon enthusiasts got the idea to make a series of trading cards about the world's most impressive hot-air balloons while they attended the 1991 Albuquerque International Balloon Fiesta. Interest was limited, to say the least.

True Crime (1992). Who wouldn't want cards of some of the most horrifying and despicable serial killers in history? All the classics are here: David "Son of Sam" Berkowitz, John Wayne Gacy, Ted Bundy, Jeffrey Dahmer...

*   *   *

HELP WANTED: DRAGONSLAYER

This strange classified ad appeared in an Oklahoma City newspaper in January 2019.
"I am quite sure most of you have seen the rather large green dragon that has been flying over the northeast OKC for the better part of a week. I am looking for someone to:

- Lure said dragon away from OKC to a more rural area.
- Force said dragon to land in rural area.
- Slay said dragon in whatever way you see fit.

No pay, dragon slaying is its own reward. *Please note that I am not talking about the red dragon that frequents the area from time to time. He and I have an agreement.*"

Prince Harry and Meghan Markle's secret security code names: Danny Collins and Daphne Clark (which stand for the Duke and Duchess of Cambridge).

THE MARK TWAIN SYNDROME

Having a successful career just isn't enough for some authors. Some are so prolific that they adopt a pen name just to write even more books.

Author: Daniel Handler
Also Known As: Lemony Snicket

Details: Handler writes novels for adults under his own name, but writes children's books under his pen name…and they're tremendously more successful than the novels. As Lemony Snicket, he published the *A Series of Unfortunate Events* books, a mock-gothic, darkly humorous collection about the hard-luck Baudelaire orphans, pursued by the wicked Count Olaf, who is after their supposed inheritance. (Lemony Snicket is also a character in the series, serving as an omniscient, lovelorn narrator.) More than 65 million Snicket books have sold, which is about 64 million more than Handler's six books, which includes a collection of short stories called *Adverbs*; a violent novel about a withdrawn teenage girl who becomes a pirate, called *We Are Pirates*; and the experimental *Watch Your Mouth*, which is about incest and takes the form of an opera.

Authors: The Brontë sisters—Charlotte, Emily, and Anne
Also Known As: Currer, Ellis, and Acton Bell

Details: In 1846 Charlotte Brontë sent a batch of her best poetry to Robert Southey, the poet laureate of England, for his review. Remarkably, he read them and responded. Less remarkably, he didn't like them…because the author was a woman. "Literature cannot be the business of a woman's life," Southey wrote, "and it ought not to be. The more she is engaged in her proper duties, the less leisure she will have for it, even as an accomplishment and a recreation." Brontë got so mad that she took some of those same poems, along with those written by her equally literary-minded sisters, Emily and Anne, and submitted them to a London publisher called Aylott and Jones. The company had no problem with female writers, but that could be because Brontë left that information out. She submitted the manuscript as *Poems by Currer, Ellis, and Acton Bell*, deriving male pseudonyms that shared the first initial of the names of each sister. The book sold only two copies (really), but all three sisters continued to publish under their pseudonyms, including the classic novels *Jane Eyre* (Charlotte), *Wuthering Heights* (Emily), and *Agnes Grey* (Anne).

> He didn't like the poems… because the author was a woman.

Author: Stephen King
Also Known As: Richard Bachman

Details: King is almost as well-known for the number of books he publishes (and which often push 1,000 pages) as he is for his classic tales of horrors and frights, such as *It*, *The Stand*, *The Shining*, *Misery*, and *Carrie*. He wrote so many books when his career took off in the 1970s that his publishers refused to print more than one King novel a year, fearing that so much material would cannibalize sales. So King started writing novels under the name of Richard Bachman. That way he could double his output without putting too many "Stephen King" novels into bookstores. Among the most popular works of "Richard Bachman": *The Running Man* and *Thinner*.

Author: Agatha Christie
Also Known As: Mary Westmacott

Details: Christie is probably the greatest crime and mystery writer ever, ushering in the concept of the "popular novel" as we know it with such page-turners as *Murder on the Orient Express* (1934) and *Death on the Nile* (1937), both featuring the genius Belgian detective Hercule Poirot. (She also wrote the stage play *The Mousetrap*, which has been continuously running in London since 1952.) She wrote 66 novels (most of them best-sellers) and 14 short story collections as Agatha Christie. But she also wrote six romance novels under the name of Mary Westmacott; she used the pseudonym so as to not confuse audiences into thinking they were about to buy a salacious crime story. The works of "Westmacott" include *Giant's Bread* (1930) and *Absent in the Spring* (1944).

Author: Isaac Asimov
Also Known As: Paul French

Details: Asimov could be the most prolific major author of all time, having penned more than 40 novels (among them such science-fiction classics as *I, Robot*), and nearly 300 nonfiction books about science and the world around us. He was also a professor, on staff at the Boston University School of Medicine. In 1951 Asimov reluctantly agreed to Doubleday & Co.'s request that he write a sci-fi novel for kids, which would also be adapted into a TV show. Television in the early 1950s wasn't exactly art. In fact, Asimov thought the TV offerings of the day were "uniformly awful" and he didn't want to be associated with it. But he loved to write…and he loved to get paid, so he agreed to write the book (*David Starr: Space Ranger*) under the name of Paul French. The TV series never happened, but "Paul French" wrote a total of six David Starr books.

"I would rather have written *Cheers* rather than anything I've written." —Kurt Vonnegut

Author: J. K. Rowling

Also Known As: Robert Galbraith

Details: By 2013 there probably wasn't a more famous author in the world than J. K. Rowling. As the author of the staggeringly successful *Harry Potter* books—all seven volumes rank in the top 20 best-selling novels of all time—Rowling became the first billionaire writer. The release of the latter *Potter* books became cultural events in the English-speaking world, with details of their plots carefully guarded, leading up to bookstores around the globe opening at midnight for parties and celebrations to get the book to fans as quickly as possible. That put a lot of pressure and attention on Rowling, who, at the end of the day, was still just a person trying to write a decent novel. After the last *Potter* book hit the stores in 2007, she wrote and quietly published a mystery novel for adults under the name Robert Galbraith, which Rowling later said was "a liberating experience. It has been wonderful to publish without hype or expectation, and pure pleasure to get feedback under a different name." The novel, *The Cuckoo's Calling*, was a flop before the secret of its author was out…and a best-seller after.

* * *

A RANDOM BIT OF FACTINESS

Convicted Offenses in the U.S. (2018)

Drug-related crimes:	45.4%
Weapons and explosives:	18.5%
Sexual offenses:	9.9%
Immigration-related crimes:	6.5%
Extortion, bribery, fraud:	6.3%
Burglary:	4.9%
Robbery:	3.6%
Murder, assault, kidnapping:	3.3%
Other:	1.2%
White-collar crimes:	0.3%
Threatening national security:	0.1%

(Source: Prison Policy Initiative)

First packaged mix sold: Aunt Jemima Pancake Flour (1889).

HERE LIES GEORGE WASHINGTON

Uncle John was in Boston for business (picking up his baked beans, no doubt) and just so happened to be staying in a hotel across the street from the graveyard where Paul Revere and John Hancock are buried. That got him wondering—where are the others? That simple question led to an entire section in the book we're calling "Finding the Founding Fathers." Here's the first of six articles.

ELDER STATESMEN

America's Founding Fathers were colonial soldiers and politicians who, at great risk to their lives and livelihoods, banded together to protest English rule and the unfair taxes imposed by King George III. They drafted the Declaration of Independence in 1776, then fought and won the Revolutionary War, and wrote the U.S. Constitution in 1787, literally "founding" the United States of America. (During the 19th century, they were simply called the Fathers. In 1916 future president Warren G. Harding added "Founding.") Among the most notable are George Washington, John Adams, John Hancock, Benjamin Franklin, Alexander Hamilton, and Thomas Jefferson.

We've written a lot about these men before, but never with the focus on where they were buried, why they were buried there, and what's transpired at their grave sites since then. During our research, we rediscovered an important fact about history: If you were famous when you were alive—as George Washington was—then a lot will be known about your life. But if you weren't famous, or never wrote anything down, then your entire existence may be reduced to nothing more than a name in the county records, if that. And even if you *were* famous, if your enemies end up writing the history books—as was the case with Alexander Hamilton—then what is known about you will probably be less than if your friends had gotten to tell your story.

In fact, most of the Founding Fathers' contributions weren't widely known until long after they were gone. And if certain details were lacking in the historical records, those details were invented decades later by biographers and tourism bureaus, who were often more concerned with their own agendas than they were with telling the truth. And if darker parts of the Founding Fathers' lives—like the fact that most of them were slave owners—didn't mesh with modern sensibilities, then those parts of their lives were often sanitized.

The main reason we know as much as we do about the Founding Fathers today is because of the heroes—from then and now—who made it their mission to preserve these men's legacies, often in the face of powerful adversaries.

Slick: Every morning while President Calvin Coolidge ate boiled wheat for breakfast, an assistant rubbed Vaseline into his scalp.

GEORGE AND MARTHA

One of the most difficult tasks in Martha Washington's life was deciding where her late husband would be laid to rest. She was torn between interring him at their Mount Vernon estate, which is what he wanted, or handing his body over to the U.S. Congress to put it on permanent display in the city named after him, which is what they wanted.

It was a far cry from 40 years earlier, when Martha Custis, a widowed twentysomething who had inherited her late husband's considerable fortune, married a dashing military captain named George Washington, which suddenly made him one of the richest young men in the colony of Virginia. In 1759 George and Martha (and her two children, Jacky and Patsy) moved into a small house that George's late father had built in the 1730s; it was named Mount Vernon by George's older half-brother Lawrence. George spent four decades expanding the house into a sprawling 21-room mansion just south of Washington, D.C., overlooking the Potomac River (which for most of Washington's life was little more than swampland).

Everything changed in the late 1760s when Washington, who originally wanted to be a farmer, drafted a resolution opposing taxation without representation and took it to George Mason at the Virginia House of Burgesses. There were many factors that led to the American Revolution, but Washington's resolution was one of the catalysts, and it put him on the "national" stage. When the Revolutionary War began in 1775, General Washington was appointed commander-in-chief of the Continental Army. With Martha at his side for much of the war, he helped lead the colonists to victory in 1783. That December, Washington moved back to Mount Vernon, which had barely survived the war. Then he was pulled right back into politics. (When Washington reluctantly decided to run for president, he resigned from the army, to underscore his belief that a nation should be ruled not by the military but by civilians.)

THE OLD CRYPT

"I can truly say I would rather be at Mount Vernon with a friend or two about me, than to be attended at the Seat of Government by the Officers of State and the Representatives of every Power in Europe." Washington wrote that in a letter dated June 15, 1790, but he wasn't able to retire to his beloved estate until he declined the offer to run for a third term as U.S. president in 1797. Washington had been a sickly man for most of his life, and his health deteriorated after he left office. So did the family crypt at Mount Vernon.

A few hundred feet from the house, near the banks of the Potomac River, the Old Crypt consists of a small wooden door set in a brick wall at the base of the hill, which opens to a small vault. The first known burial there was in 1745 (George's infant cousin, Jane Washington). By the end of the century, the tomb held about 20 members

Fast food: Lobsters can swim up to 5 feet per second.

of Washington's extended family. And the president wanted nothing more upon his death than to join them…but not there. Here's an excerpt from his will:

> The family Vault at Mount Vernon requiring repairs, and being improperly situated besides, I desire that a new one of Brick, and upon a larger Scale, may be built at the foot of what is commonly called the Vineyard Inclosure, on the ground which is marked out. In which my remains, with those of my deceased relatives (now in the old Vault) and such others of my family as may chuse to be entombed there, may be deposited. And it is my express desire that my Corpse may be Interred in a private manner, without parade, or funeral Oration.

DOWN AND OUT

> In a futile attempt to ease the old man's constant coughing, doctors drained 80 ounces of his blood (nearly half his total volume).

Washington's will included plans for the new tomb, and he put aside the money for it, but work hadn't even started in December 1799 when the former president came down with a fatal case of…it's uncertain what actually did him in—the most likely culprits are one or more of the following: "croup, quinsy, Ludwig's angina, Vincent's angina, diphtheria, and streptococcal throat infection due to acute pneumonia."

One thing's for certain: it was an excruciating end. In a futile attempt to ease the old man's constant coughing, doctors drained 80 ounces of his blood (nearly half his total volume). Martha was at his bedside the entire time, as were their friends, doctors, and their grandchildren (from Martha's first marriage—George himself never procreated). Among Washington's last recorded words on that day, December 14, was a request that he be "decently buried…in less than three days after I am dead." It took four.

MOSTLY DEAD

The next morning, Dr. William Thornton arrived to treat the ailing president, only to find out that he was too late. But Thornton had a plan: Because Washington had died "by the loss of blood and the want of air" on a frigid December night, and his body was cold, all Thornton had to do was warm the president's body and give him some blood and some air. He'd seen frozen frogs brought back to life, so why not George Washington? He told the other doctors present he would slowly warm Washington's body in a bath of cold water, perform a tracheotomy so that air could refill his lungs, and then give him a transfusion with the blood of a lamb. The barbaric procedure never took place, and it's unknown if Martha was even part of the discussion.

The president's funeral took place four days after he died. Only a few close friends and family were in attendance, but not Martha. She watched from the third floor of

Mount Vernon as her late husband's lead casket was entombed into the dilapidated crypt, where he joined nearly two dozen other bodies, whose wooden coffins were in various stages of rot and decay.

MARTHA'S CHOICE

The 68-year-old widow was quickly besieged by throngs of well-wishers, though she had neither the inclination nor the energy to entertain them, and certainly didn't have it in her to start work on the new tomb. She was also receiving thousands of condolence letters, including one from her successor as First Lady, Abigail Adams: "I intreat, Madam, that you would permit a Heart deeply penetrated with your Loss, and sharing personally in your Grief to mingle with you the Tears which flow for the much Loved partner of all your joys and Sorrow's."

Another letter—one that Martha was dreading—came from Abigail's husband, President John Adams: "I entreat your assent to the interment of the remains of the General under the marble monument to be erected in the capital, at the city of Washington, to commemorate the great events of his military and political life." Congress had to have Martha's permission to move George's body because he had stated explicitly in his will that he was to be buried at Mount Vernon. Martha, as an executor of the will, could go against her husband's wishes if she chose to. But would she?

To find out where the father of his country was laid to rest, turn to page 227.

* * *

FOR THE BIRDS

PETA (People for the Ethical Treatment of Animals) is a controversial animal rights group that advocates against animal cruelty and for pro-animal behavior, such as adopting a vegan diet. In 2018 it released a statement entitled "Stop Using Anti-Animal Language," designed to make people rethink the use of some everyday clichés. The statement gave a few examples, and offered these replacement suggestions:

"Kill two birds with one stone" ➡	"Feed two birds with one scone"
"I'll be the guinea pig" ➡	"I'll be the test tube"
"Beat a dead horse" ➡	"Feed a fed horse"
"Bring home the bacon" ➡	"Bring home the bagels"
"Take the bull by the horns" ➡	"Take the flower by the thorns"

Popular 18th-century drink: saloop, a hot beverage made from ground orchid roots.

ROBOTS IN THE NEWS

Be aware of what's going on in the world of robots...before they rise up and kill us all.

NEWS BOT

One of the reasons that people who don't like robots don't like robots is the fear of automation—that robots and other machines will take away jobs from human beings. That's a legitimate fear. Most U.S. auto production, for example, is now performed by robots...but who would've thought that news anchors would also fear being replaced by machines? It could happen. Created by Hiroshi Ishiguro and a team at the Intelligent Robotics Laboratory at Osaka University in Japan, "Erica" is an android designed to look like a 23-year-old human woman. (She really does look like that, if you ignore her hollow, lifeless eyes.) She's been programmed to do the two things real news anchors need to be able to do: 1) sit still in a chair, and 2) recite a script at a medium pace. She can even banter with a human co-anchor. Ishiguro says he initially designed Erica to be a receptionist, but then figured news anchor was a better fit.

FEAR BOT

There are certain things that humans almost universally find unsettling—haunted houses, monsters, and death, to name a few. A team of researchers from the MIT Media Lab in Massachusetts and CSIRO's Data61 in Australia teamed up to build an algorithm that they fed to a robot. The machine, outfitted with artificial intelligence that allows the robot to learn, uses the algorithm to figure out what humans find frightening, and then applies the knowledge to digitally manipulate innocuous photos so they look scarier. The robot makes gleaming towers look like decrepit haunted houses, turns landscapes into polluted and smoldering wastelands, and beloved characters like Kermit the Frog into zombie corpses. Why would anybody build a robot that can push humanity's buttons? Ironically, the researchers created a robot that makes scary things to explore why people find robots so scary.

CHECK-IN BOT

In Japanese, *henn na* means "weird," and that's also the name of a small and quirky chain of hotels in Asia that wants to be the first in the hospitality industry to be entirely staffed by robots. Its latest entry: a hotel in east Tokyo where a couple of robot

The warty comb jellyfish creates a "temporary anus" every time it needs to poop.

dinosaurs work the lobby, checking in arriving guests. Perched behind a desk (and in front of a jungle scene backdrop), the human-sized, velociraptor-like robots snap into motion when they detect an approaching guest. Then they scream "Welcome" (in one of four languages: Japanese, Korean, Chinese, or English) and wave their long, claw-topped arms. With the aid of a tablet computer, the dinosaurs will check in guests and help them get settled, but they will not take bags to the guest's room…even though they're wearing cute little bellhop hats.

DELIVERY BOT

In some larger cities, delivery robots are already a thing. Wheeled, trash can–sized (and shaped) robots are dispatched by restaurants and stores to deliver goods to customers who live within walking (or rolling) distance. In May 2018, Arizona governor Doug Ducey signed a law to allow the emerging army of delivery robots to legally traverse the state's sidewalks—as opposed to the streets, where they might get run over. The catch: the robots must be programmed to be respectful of human pedestrians and to use crosswalks properly. "It causes them to have to obey the laws," said state representative Kelly Townsend, who sponsored the bill. "So they can't just whiz out into the street, they can't run into somebody, they have to go by our current laws." While the law requires robot manufacturers to build those safety precautions into the robot's artificial intelligence, Arizona residents aren't all on board. "The robots on the sidewalk? They could be running into us, or I could be running into one with the stroller," said Arizona mother Caitlin Erickson.

REEF BOT

Coral reefs look like rocks, but they're actually massive living things, and like a lot of other sea creatures, they're endangered. But here comes some weird robot science to the rescue. A team led by Dr. Erik Engeberg of Florida Atlantic University has built "jellybots," or underwater robots that look like jellyfish. Propelled by hydraulic rubber tentacles and a pump in its main body that uses centrifugal force to create propulsion, the jellybots can softly and safely squeeze through narrow gaps in coral without leaving any destruction in their wake. Scientists will direct them to travel over coral reefs and use them to scan and record any damage. "Studying and monitoring fragile environments, such as coral reefs, has always been challenging for marine researchers," Dr. Engeberg told reporters. "Soft robots have great potential to help with this." Making this high-tech, futuristic-sounding notion sound ever more high-tech and futuristic: the prototypes were created with the use of a 3-D printer.

Nazi rocket scientist Wernher von Braun helped design Disneyland's Rocket to the Moon attraction.

PENCIL POPPERS AND ZONKERS

Fly fishing isn't just a sport—it's an obsession. And part of the obsession is figuring out which lures work best for which fish on which day in which stream. What's a fly fisherman to do? Make ("tie") your own lures ("flies"). It's considered an art and a science (although many experts say all lures work the same). We consider it an opportunity to chuckle at the funny names these artists give to their hand-tied flies.

Woolly Bugger	Swedish Pimple	Bunny Leech
Trout Frog	Phoebe	Disco Midge
Irish Sleech	Uncle Josh Pork Frog	Thunder Chicken
Zonker	Scooter Popper	Grease Stain
Black Ghost	Tangless Sally	Gravel Gertie
Red Eyed Damsel	Lil' Barky	Quill Gordon
Rusty Spinner	Hula Popper	Chernobyl Ant
Orange Death	Badonkadonk	The Good Wife
Mrs. Simpson	Grizzly Klinkhammer	Rat Face McDougal
Booby Nymph	Crystal Thorax	Blender Nun
Parachute Hopper	Atomic Worm	Monkey Puke
Humpy	Copper John	Moose Turd
Musky Duckinglin	Goofus Bug	Meat Whistle
Blinky Bumblebee	Sofa Pillow	Dave
Power Worm	Bacon and Eggs	Pencil Popper

The measles are nine times as contagious as Ebola.

TIMELINE: THE OLD WEST

*Howdy, pardner. Hop into Uncle John's patented Wayback Machine, and we'll embark
on a chronological journey through that not-so-long-ago time period called the Old West.*

BACKGROUND

The loosely defined time period alternately referred to as the American West, the
Old West, and the Wild West ranges from the early 1800s to the 1890s. But the story
started long before that. The first humans to inhabit western North America came
down the coast via a land bridge between Asia and North America (now known as
the Bering Strait) around 20,000 years ago, or maybe more. And there's archaeological
evidence of advanced civilizations, complete with big cities and well-established trade
routes, going as far back as 11,000 years ago.

The first Europeans to arrive were the Spanish Conquistadors in the early 16th
century, who made it as far north as Kansas. (In doing so, they introduced the horse
to North America.) A few decades later, in 1579, British explorer Francis Drake sailed
to what is now San Francisco. In the 1670s, the French colonized the Americas from
New Orleans all the way north to Canada, calling their colony Louisiana (after the
French king Louis XIV). As more Eurasians claimed various regions as their own,
skirmishes between them and with the Indians escalated into all-out wars.

In 1776, when the United States declared its independence from England, the
western boundary of the new nation was located only a few hundred miles inland at
the Appalachian Mountains. Americans didn't know much about what was on the
other side of the mountains, and few dared to venture to those wild and lawless lands.
But that would soon change.

1803	President Thomas Jefferson makes the Louisiana Purchase (Napoleon needed the money to fight his wars in Europe), more than doubling the size of the new nation. The purchase proves worthwhile due to a population explosion: there were approximately five million Americans in 1800; by 1850 there were 23 million.
1804	Jefferson sends Meriwether Lewis and William Clark on an expedition to the Pacific Ocean. Over the next two and a half years, Lewis and Clark travel more than 7,000 miles, make contact with 70 Indian tribes, and catalog 200 plant and animal species. Most important, the explorers mark out the beginning and end portions of the Oregon Trail.
1810	New York business magnate John Jacob Astor founds the Pacific Fur Company, opening up trade with the Indians of the Pacific Northwest. The British, French,

Spanish, and Russians will lay claim to this region, but Astor's company gives the Americans the foothold they'll need to keep it. Meanwhile, to the south, Mexico declares its independence from Spain.

1811 The steamboat *New Orleans* begins carrying passengers up and down the Mississippi River. A few years later, steamboats will also take to the Missouri River. This opens up travel and trade to even more people, and helps turn New Orleans, Memphis, St. Louis, and Minneapolis into big cities.

1823 Most Americans are still wary of moving west due to a lack of law enforcement. This starts to change with the formation of the Texas Rangers. In addition to protecting homesteaders and aiding the U.S. military in battles, the Rangers (who are still active today) will foil an assassination attempt on President William Howard Taft in 1909, and gun down notorious fugitives Bonnie and Clyde in 1934.

1827 The city of Independence, Missouri, is established, marking the beginning of the Oregon Trail. The Concord Stagecoach also debuts this year. Over the next three decades, these horse-drawn covered wagons will transport approximately 400,000 people out west via the Oregon Trail to become farmers, ranchers, miners, and business owners. Though arduous and uncomfortable, these "wagon trains" prove to be much safer than traveling alone. Other trails will soon be established in California and the Southwest. Today's Interstate Highway System follows many of these wagon routes.

1829 A Mexican caravan traveling west along the Spanish Trail trade route from Colorado rests in a desert oasis before making the final leg over the mountains to Los Angeles. The travelers name the area Las Vegas ("The Meadows").

1830 In order to remove several Native American tribes from territory in the southeast, President Andrew Jackson signs the Indian Removal Act, which allows the U.S. government to forcibly move Indians to reservations. This escalates the ongoing Indian Wars and begins the Trail of Tears, the collective name for numerous forced Indian relocations from their fertile lands in the South to the harsher environments west of the Mississippi.

1836 The Battle of the Alamo takes place. This former Franciscan mission in San Antonio is occupied by about 200 Texans (including Davy Crockett) who are fighting for independence from Mexico. The small militia holds off thousands of troops for 13 days before Mexico takes back the mission. "Remember the Alamo!" becomes a rallying cry for Texans. A few weeks later, they win the Battle of San Jacinto (near the Gulf Coast), and Texas declares itself a republic.

1842 American explorer John C. Frémont earns his nickname as "the Pathfinder"

The inventor of the lollipop, Connecticut confectioner George Smith, named it after Lolly Pop, a racehorse.

when Congress sends him to retrace the footsteps of previous explorers. Frémont's maps of California and, later, the Oregon Territory further open the West to expansion...but not for everyone.

1844	Oregon City becomes the first incorporated city in the West, but the provisional government passes the "Lash Law," making it illegal for any black people to settle in the Oregon Territory (offenders will be whipped). The reason: fear that freed slaves could incite Indian uprisings. This and similar laws that follow won't be fully repealed until 1926.
1845	The phrase "Manifest Destiny" is coined (by whom exactly is disputed). This philosophy says that Americans are destined by God to control the lands all the way to the Pacific Ocean. A popular newspaper column commands, "Go West, young man," and hundreds of thousands of young men do just that.
1845	Texas ceases to be a republic and joins the United States. Mexico's leaders refuse to acknowledge this, sparking the Mexican-American War. President James Polk dispatches troops to drive the Mexicans back. The war ends in 1848 with the Treaty of Guadalupe Hidalgo, which gives California and New Mexico to the United States.
1846	The United States obtains the Oregon Territory (which includes what will later be called Washington) from England via a treaty, completing the border between the United States and southern Canada.
1847	The Mormons settle Salt Lake City in the Utah Territory.
1848	Gold is discovered at Sutter's Mill, near Coloma, California, beginning the California gold rush. In the months that follow, hundreds of thousands of "Forty-niners" will head west to strike it rich. The population of San Francisco grows from about 1,000 to more than 25,000 within a few years.
1850	California becomes a state. Back east in Chicago, Allan Pinkerton establishes the first national detective agency. Pinkerton's detectives thwart several train robberies and bring many of these robbers to justice, making the West even safer.
1856	John "Grizzly" Adams opens the first zoo in the West in San Francisco.
1859	Oregon becomes a state. (Washington, to the north, won't win statehood until 1889.)
1860	The Pony Express drastically speeds up mail service between the coasts (but it will only last 18 months before going out of business due to high operating costs).
1861	While the Civil War rages back East, the first transcontinental telegraph is completed, bringing the country even closer together.

Highest paid actor for a debut leading role: Dwayne "the Rock" Johnson, $5.5 million for *The Scorpion King*.

1862	The first of several "Homestead Acts" passed by Congress allows any American man (including freed slaves) who has never taken up arms against the government to claim up to 160 acres of cheap land on the frontier. Over the next few decades, more than 1.6 million claims will be approved, establishing the Plains as a major hub of agriculture. (The Homestead Act lasted until 1988; the final approved claim was for 80 acres in Alaska.)
1864	Nevada becomes a state.
1865	The first true cowboy hat, known as the "Boss of the Plains," debuts. Designed by John B. Stetson, this flat-brimmed, sun-blocking waterproof hat also works as a bucket and a stash for the wearer's valuables.
1866	The "Long Drive" begins, in which Texas cowboys drive tens of thousands of head of cattle from the Plains to the railroad in Missouri. Along the way, the riders lose a lot of their animals to cattle rustlers. This becomes a major problem throughout the West, which leads to cries for more law enforcement. Over the next four decades, more than 27 million cattle will be driven from states in the West to train stations to be transported to the East.
1869	The ceremonial "Golden Spike" is nailed into the train tracks at Promontory Point in the Utah Territory, completing the Transcontinental Railroad. Built mostly by migrant Chinese workers, rail replaces the stagecoach and steamboat as the main means of cross-country travel, and will remain so until well into the 20th century.
1872	A large swath of land called Yellowstone, which straddles the Montana and Wyoming Territories, is found to contain the most geysers on earth. President Ulysses S. Grant signs the bill that establishes it as the country's first national park.
1874	An improved version of barbed wire (invented a few years earlier) is patented by Joseph F. Glidden in Illinois. Wooden fences are expensive, and simple wire fences fail to keep cattle enclosed, but barbed wire is inexpensive and provides ranchers with a much more effective way to cordon off their land, drastically altering the "open range" feel of the Wild West, and leading to more disputes with the Indians.
1876	General William Custer makes his last stand in a battle against the Sioux, Cheyenne, and Arapaho Nations along the Little Bighorn River in the Montana Territory, where gold had recently been discovered in the Black Hills. The Indians win the battle, but lose the Plains Indians War. The survivors are moved to reservations.

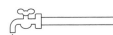

Why does hot coffee taste so much better than lukewarm? Because...

1881 **and** **1882**	Some of the most enduring tales of the Old West come about in these two years. At the Maxwell Ranch in New Mexico, outlaw Billy the Kid (Henry McCarty, aka William H. Bonney) fails to reach middle age after he's shot dead by Sheriff Pat Garrett. In Tombstone, Arizona, the gunfight at the O.K. Corral lasts all of 30 seconds when the Earp brothers, with the help of temporary deputy Doc Holliday, defeat outlaws Billy Clairborne and the Clanton and McLaury brothers. And in 1882 in St. Joseph, Missouri, (the outlaw) Jesse James is assassinated by (the coward) Robert Ford.
1883	Buffalo Bill Cody's "Wild West" show opens in North Platte, Nebraska. The traveling show becomes one of America's most popular forms of entertainment (pre-vaudeville), lasting until 1913. Featuring reenactments of famous battles, sharpshooting demonstrations, and a chance to meet celebrities like Wild Bill Hickcok and Sitting Bull, Cody's shows help solidify the mythos of the Old West, which will continue in movies with stars like Tom Mix, John Wayne, and Clint Eastwood, and on TV with shows like *Wagon Train, Gunsmoke, Bonanza, Lonesome Dove,* and *Deadwood.*
1886	The surrender of Geronimo puts an end to major conflicts in the Apache Wars, which saw the Indians fighting for their lands in the Southwest. Geronimo goes on to become a celebrity, but he's never allowed to return to his birthplace.
1889	North and South Dakota become states. A year later, Wyoming and Idaho win statehood, followed in 1896 by Utah.
1890	After several clashes with American soldiers, the Plains Indians' efforts to protect their homeland ends at Wounded Knee in South Dakota. Between 250 and 300 Indians are killed in the massacre. The major newspapers report the military's version of events—that the soldiers had put down a Sioux insurrection—further vilifying the Indian in American culture.

THE "NEW" WEST

When did the Old West come to an official end? Some sources say as early as the 1890s, when the mass migration out west had slowed to a trickle, while others put it at 1912, when the additions of Arizona and New Mexico completed the contiguous United States as we know it today. But even as recently as a century ago, much of the western United States still had that wild frontier feeling. The last stagecoach robbery occurred in Jarbidge, Nevada, in 1916, and the last train robbery occurred in Oregon in 1923. But it was in 1924, after several Apache were arrested for stealing some horses in Arizona, that the Indian Wars were declared over. With that, the West was won.

...bitter taste receptors are dulled on food hotter than 95 degrees.

GROOVY TRIVIA FROM '70s MOVIES

Behind-the-scenes facts you didn't know about movies you've seen a hundred times.

American Graffiti (1973)

Ever wonder why there are so many names in the credits at the end of a movie? Blame *American Graffiti*. George Lucas's nostalgic film about 1960s car culture had a relatively tiny budget of $777,000. He couldn't afford to pay crew members, so he offered them an on-screen credit at the end of the movie instead. That ended the tradition of only department heads making it into the credits, and began the current practice of *everyone* getting their name on screen.

Grease (1978)

The 1950s-set movie was based on a popular stage musical, and some changes were made. For example, the song "Look at Me, I'm Sandra Dee," originally had the lyric "No, no, no, Sal Mineo / I would never stoop so low!" It was changed to "Elvis, Elvis, let me be / keep that pelvis far from me!" Reason for the new lyrics: Mineo, best known for his role in the movie *Rebel Without a Cause*, had been murdered just before the film began production. Nice touch, but it turned out to be pointless because Presley died a year later, on the very day Stockard Channing was filmed singing those lines about him.

Animal House (1978)

John Belushi—as frat boy slob John "Bluto" Blutarski—actually improvised one of the movie's most famous scenes. In the cafeteria line sequence, Belushi was supposed to load up a tray with specific food items and be on his way. Instead, he grabbed objects at random and worked with them. For example, he took a sandwich and squeezed it until it burst out of the cellophane, and then shoved it in his mouth…and he nailed the scene in a single take.

Young Frankenstein (1974)

The film's star, Gene Wilder, co-wrote the script with director Mel Brooks, who, unlike in most of his other movies, never appears on screen. Reason: Wilder thought Brooks's

Ironic fact: According to experts, duct tape should never be used to seal air ducts.

manic comic presence would be too distracting in the black-and-white monster movie parody. However, Brooks's *voice* made it into the movie. He made the off-screen sounds of a howling wolf and a cat getting hit with a dart.

Rocky (1976)

Sylvester Stallone couldn't get any acting work, so he wrote a movie for himself: *Rocky.* (It took him three and a half days.) One studio offered him $350,000 for the screenplay, but they didn't want him to be in it. (They wanted Burt Reynolds.) Even though he had only $100 in his bank account and his wife was pregnant, Stallone refused and cut a different deal: $20,000 for the script…and a $350 per-week acting fee. *Rocky* went on to win Best Picture and made Stallone into a movie star.

Jaws (1975)

Steven Spielberg hired an old friend, a TV writer named Carl Gottlieb, to play a major role in *Jaws*—the role of newspaper reporter Harry Meadows. Then, just before filming began, Spielberg also asked Gottlieb to help rewrite the film's messy shooting script. By the time Gottlieb finished, he'd almost entirely eliminated one role—the role of Harry Meadows.

The Towering Inferno (1974)

Paul Newman and Steve McQueen were both huge movie stars of the 1960s and '70s—and rivals, too. McQueen turned down a role in *Butch Cassidy and the Sundance Kid* simply because Newman was in it. But they both wound up in the ensemble cast of the 1974 disaster movie *The Towering Inferno.* McQueen took the part on the condition that he'd get equal billing to Newman. He also asked for (and received) the same salary as Newman, as well as the *exact* same number of lines.

Blazing Saddles (1974)

Movies are usually written by one or two people, but for his zany Western parody, Mel Brooks employed six writers, including Andrew Bergman, who wrote *Tex X,* the novella upon which the movie was based, and Richard Pryor. But all those cooks made for a sloppy stew: the film's first draft ran 412 pages, which would have been a seven-hour film. Among the bits that were eventually cut: a free-verse "street poem" for Sheriff Bart, a vaudeville comedian character who opened for singer Lili Von Shtupp (Madeline Kahn), and a little person named Ash Tray who wore an ashtray on his head.

According to a 2018 study, 1/3 of American teens didn't read a single book in 2017.

YOUR CHEATIN' HEART

"The time will come," sang Hank Williams, "When you'll be blue / Your cheatin' heart / Will tell on you." These are some pretty big tells.

PONCHOS AND PUNCHES: A real-life telenovela broke out in Mexico City one steamy summer night in 2018. A man wanting to propose to his girlfriend hired a mariachi band to serenade her at her house. As they were playing the song "Si nos Dejan" ("If They Let Us"), the woman emerged onto her balcony in what would have been a very romantic moment…if one of the mariachi singers hadn't been her husband. She'd been secretly living in this house while carrying on with a man who had no idea she was already married. "The music came to an abrupt end," wrote the *Daily Mail*, "as the singer traded blows and insults with the woman's lover."

BENCHED: A man in Peru was mapping out a driving route using Google Street View when he clicked onto the *Puente de los Suspiros de Barranco* ("Bridge of Sighs of the Ravine"). On that bridge he saw a bench. And on that bench he saw a woman (with her face blurred out). And lying back on her lap he saw a man (face also blurred out). It was a tender moment that stopped the Google mapper in his virtual tracks. Blurred or not, he could recognize his own wife. And that wasn't him lying on her lap. The dejected husband posted pictures of his grim discovery on Facebook, along with the news that he was filing for divorce.

ACCOUNT-ABILITY: A man thought he'd found the perfect way to fool around on his girlfriend: create a second Facebook account with a fake name, and use it to flirt with other women. His plan might have worked if not for Facebook's "suggested friends" feature. His profile picture, along with a different name, popped up in his girlfriend's sidebar. She clicked on the account, and there he was in all his cheatin' glory. (She "unfriended" him.)

WATCHING TELLY: In 2018 a 51-year-old English woman and her 15-year-old daughter sat down to watch a live variety show on TV. That week's episode featured a wedding party that was led through a corridor and—surprise!—onto a stage in front of a live audience. Everyone had a big laugh…until Mom and the daughter saw Dad on TV holding another woman's hand. He probably hadn't expected to be on television in England, because he'd told his wife and daughter he'd be in Dubai on business. Oops. It turned out that the husband was actually married to that other woman. He'd forged divorce documents to do so, which landed him a bigamy conviction and six months in prison. The two women became friends.

SPORTS BEEFS

There are friendly sports rivalries and then there are these…which turned downright nasty.

MIKE SHANAHAN vs. AL DAVIS

In 1988 Los Angeles Raiders owner Al Davis hired the Denver Broncos' wunderkind offensive coordinator Mike Shanahan as head coach. This was the first time the notoriously paranoid Davis had hired outside the organization, and Shanahan quickly learned why. From the beginning, Shanahan complained that Davis was micromanaging him. After a losing season, both men fired (and rehired) members of the coaching staff who were deemed either Davis or Shanahan loyalists. Four games into his second season, Shanahan was fired, setting off a complicated and messy battle over severance pay, and leading Shanahan to take the matter to NFL commissioner Paul Tagliabue. The Raiders were ultimately ordered to pay up, but their attorneys refused, claiming that Shanahan had committed perjury in the arbitration hearing.

> Shanahan ordered his quarterback to throw a football at Davis's head.

The beef boiled over (again) during a 1994 pregame warm-up when Shanahan, who was a coach for the visiting San Francisco 49ers, ordered his quarterback to throw a football at Davis's head. The ball hit the 65-year-old owner in the leg. In 1995, after Shanahan became the Broncos' head coach, Davis mocked him in the press, calling him "overwhelmed" and "insecure." Shanahan had the last laugh, though, as his Broncos dominated the Raiders and won two Super Bowls. He even said he would drop his years-long fight for the severance pay if Davis donated the money to Oakland's public school system. Al Davis died in 2011, having never won another Super Bowl since the Raiders' 1983 championship season. (But he never paid Shanahan, either.)

KOBE vs. SHAQ

The high-profile feud between Los Angeles Lakers stars Kobe Bryant and Shaquille O'Neal is one of the greatest "What if?"s in sports. What if the confident, withdrawn, all-business Kobe and the good-natured, fun-loving Shaq had gotten along? Despite reaching four NBA Finals and winning three of them in a row, they played together for eight tension-filled seasons. During a team practice in 2003, the 7-foot, 1-inch Shaq and the 6-foot, 6-inch Kobe nearly got into a fight over an interview in which Bryant had described O'Neal as "childlike."

Their relationship soured even further after O'Neal's 2004 trade to the Miami Heat. Bryant said (in a leaked police report about a sexual assault investigation) that Shaq had paid $1 million to a mistress as "hush money." O'Neal called the notion "ridiculous," and retorted, "I'm not the one buying love." And then there's the viral video of O'Neal "freestyle rapping" vulgar insults about Bryant and making fun of him for his divorce. Whenever their teams faced off, they'd downplay the feud to reporters, but they rarely shook hands.

Update: In February 2018, the duo sat down for an NBA TV documentary about their rivalry. They're not necessarily friends, but they do seem to have buried the hatchet. That same month, a statue of O'Neal was unveiled at the Staples Center in Los Angeles. At the ceremony, Kobe said to Shaq, "I just want to say thank you. I've learned so much from you as a player."

JOSÉ MESA vs. OMAR VIZQUEL

In game seven of the 1997 World Series, Cleveland Indians closing pitcher José Mesa came to the mound in the bottom of the ninth with a 2–1 lead and a chance to give the Indians their first championship in half a century. He blew the save, and the Florida Marlins won in extra innings. But was the defeat all Mesa's fault? From an early age, players are taught that baseball is a team sport, and you shouldn't blame any one player for a loss. Indians shortstop Omar Vizquel, who was friends with Mesa, broke that cardinal rule in his 2003 autobiography, writing, "Jose's own eyes were vacant. Completely empty. Nobody home. You could almost see right through him. Not long after I looked into his vacant eyes, he blew the save and the Marlins tied the game."

Vizquel probably should have waited until after he retired to write that. Both men were still playing…on different teams. Mesa vowed that whenever he faced Vizquel at the plate, he would intentionally throw the ball at him. He kept his word. After the first plunking, the league fined Mesa to send a warning. But the reliever refused to budge: "I won't try to hit him in the head, but I'll hit him. And if he charges me, I'll kill him. If I face him 10 more times, I'll hit him 10 times. Every time." He then added, "Even my little boy told me to get him." Mesa hit Vizquel three times over a five-year period. Both players are now retired, and there have been no reports of any hatchets being buried.

GEORGE STEINBRENNER AND REGGIE JACKSON vs. BILLY MARTIN

In 1975 New York Yankees owner George Steinbrenner hired former Yankees player Billy Martin as manager. They clashed from the very beginning. Despite winning the 1977 World Series, Martin was steadily gaining a reputation as a stubborn alcoholic who couldn't avoid trouble in or out of the dugout. "Sometimes I would do just the

20 plant species are responsible for 90 percent of human food products.

opposite of what George wanted me to do," Martin later revealed, "because I won't let anyone tell me how to manage. If I'm going down the tube, I'm going to do it my way." Martin also clashed with future Hall of Fame slugger Reggie Jackson. The two nearly got into a fistfight in the Yankees' dugout on national television. "People think I hate Billy," Jackson told reporters. "I don't. I just hate some of the things he did...He's not an intellectual, but there is a cunningness to him that is something to behold."

Midway through the 1978 season, the first of Martin's five dismissals came after he dished on Jackson and Steinbrenner in an interview: "One's a born liar, and the other's convicted." (Several years earlier, Steinbrenner had pleaded guilty of making illegal contributions to Richard Nixon's reelection campaign.) After the Yankees had a slow start in 1979, Steinbrenner decided to give Martin a second chance. Then an off-season bar fight with a marshmallow salesman (even 40 years later, that's still funny) led to Martin's second dismissal. Steinbrenner gave him his job back in 1983. The following season, Martin got into yet another bar fight, and got fired. Steinbrenner hired Martin yet again in 1985, and then the hothead manager got into a bar fight with one of his own pitchers. Martin received a broken arm and another pink slip. "The only real way to know you've been fired," he quipped, "is when you arrive at the ballpark and find your name has been scratched from the parking list." His fifth and final tenure as the Yankees' manager lasted just one season in 1988. When Martin's replacement didn't work out, Steinbrenner offered the 61-year-old a sixth chance to manage the Yankees. Martin took the job, but he died on Christmas night in 1989 in a drunk-driving accident.

In between his stints with the Yankees, Martin also managed the Minnesota Twins, Detroit Tigers, Texas Rangers, and Oakland A's, but his only World Series victory came in 1977. That was the series that earned Reggie Jackson the title of "Mr. October" for hitting three home runs on three swings in game six. "I felt vindicated," Jackson said recently. "All that stuff I'd been through with Billy, none of it mattered anymore at the moment. I can't imagine ever feeling as good as I felt, taking that turn around the bases the third time."

* * *

"One day you're a signature. The next day you're an autograph." —**Billy Wilder**

A TIP FROM UNCLE JOHN

Psychologists say that these are some of the best ways to de-escalate a verbal fight already in process. First, instead of responding to what the other person just said, ignore it and slowly count to three. That will give you time to calm down and collect your thoughts. Then, even if you're just a *little* more chill, you can reply rationally and return to the core issue that started the argument...and evaluate whether your position is even worth fighting for.

TROUBLE ON THE BUS

Have you taken a bus lately? Most bus drivers are serious and safety-conscious. But we'll let you decide whether the drivers in these stories belong behind the wheel of a 30,000-pound vehicle. (And if you're reading this book on a bus, you might want to turn the page. Now.)

BREAKDOWN

On March 1, 2019, a group of Northampton, Pennsylvania, middle- and high-schoolers boarded the bus for home. Students said the bus driver, 44-year-old Lori Ann Mankos, had been fun at first, but after just two weeks on the job, she'd gone from frazzled to furious. On that fateful Friday, she didn't follow her route. She missed stops. She drove through potholes hard enough to bounce students out of their seats. When she took a right-hand turn too fast, the bus ended up halfway into the oncoming lane of traffic. The kids freaked. "Pull over!" they shouted. Mankos's response: she gave her young riders "the finger" and told them to "go f***" themselves. But then she did pull over—into a Sunoco gas station, where she tossed the keys to the station attendant and hit the road on foot. Like the students she abandoned, Mankos had to call her parents for a ride. "I can't take it anymore!" she wailed. Mankos's mom believes her daughter had a nervous breakdown caused by the kids' bad behavior. Stephen Scholler—father of one of the passengers—has some advice for future drivers: "If the kids are giving you a hard time, you don't just abandon them. You're the adult. You call for another bus and wait there until that bus arrives."

MUTINY ON THE GREYHOUND

Even the best drivers veer over the white line now and again, so when a Greyhound driver on a 20-hour haul from Phoenix to Dallas did it the first time, riders probably weren't too concerned. Concern grew, however, as she did it again…and again…and again. "We politely asked her four times to pull over," said passenger Jasmine McLellan. The driver seemed to be sleepy and started pinching her cheeks with tweezers to stay awake. "It was awful," said McLellan. When the bus started leaning, one fed-up passenger went ballistic. He stood up and clapped his hands over the driver's head while shouting, "You should have stopped it when you were swerving!" Other passengers joined his cry for the driver to stop and call for a replacement. She wouldn't. In fact, with the bus still moving, the driver stood up to argue. What finally stopped the peril? One of the passengers called Border Patrol agents. They "escorted" the bus off the road to wait for a fresh driver. In a statement about the terrifying trip, Greyhound said, "We take driver fatigue very seriously." Let's hope so. A government study credits "driver fatigue" in more than a third of passenger-bus crashes.

Dogs have over three times as many taste buds as cats.

FATAL DISTRACTION

In December 2018, a Washington, D.C., tour-bus driver managed to kill both Skagway, Alaska, mayor Monica Carlson *and* her 85-year-old mother in a pedestrian crosswalk on Pennsylvania Avenue. The mother–daughter pair were in town to visit the White House for Christmas and to visit Arlington National Cemetery, where Carlson's son, a Marine who died in Afghanistan, is buried. Though the accident happened at 9:40 p.m., the crosswalk was well-lit. The driver, 45-year-old Gerard James of Baltimore, had passed required drug and alcohol screenings. He had a clean record and a valid commercial driver's license. So what went wrong? Video from inside the bus showed James picking up his cell to take a call just as he was making the fatal turn. When he learned what caused the tragedy, Carlson's brother-in-law, Steven Hites, said, "God almighty, that says it all."

SAVED BY THE BANK

When Jason Rhodes, program director of the Above the Rim AAU basketball team in Gary, Indiana, received free tickets for a Chicago Bulls game, it must have seemed like a godsend. To get to the game, the team chartered a bus from the Jesus Saves Missionary Baptist Church. Kids, coaches, and chaperones had a blast at the game, and they hit the road home in high spirits. Apparently, their 82-year-old driver, Wilton B. Carr, did, too. As exhausted kids snoozed in their seats, Carr suddenly veered off the Indiana Toll Road and crashed through two barriers while traveling at 30–40 mph. The bus hit a gravel embankment; kids and coaches went flying. Rhodes believes that embankment was the team's salvation. "Without it," he said, "there might have been multiple fatalities." Four players, ages 10 to 14, and a 49-year-old man had to be taken to area hospitals. As for the intoxicated octogenarian, Indiana State Police were not inclined toward forgiveness. Noting his watery eyes, slurred speech, and a strong odor of alcohol, officials charged Carr with five counts of driving while intoxicated and two counts of endangerment.

BLAME THE BIRD

On February 12, 2019, at around 7:30 a.m., a pigeon managed to fly aboard an M14 bus at 14th Street and 8th Avenue in New York City. After flapping around a bit, the bird headed for the windshield. The startled driver immediately ran the bus off the street, careening onto the sidewalk and crashing into the metal scaffolding around a construction site. Steel beams rained down, barely missing a pedestrian, but no one was injured. (Fortunately, there was only one passenger on the bus.) What was the pigeon doing? One observer probably hit the bird's-eye, telling reporters, "He was probably cold and said, 'Let me go inside. It's raining.'"

NICE STORIES

Every now and then we like to lock our inner cynics
in a box and share some good news.

EGGNOG AND GINGERSNAPS

In December 2017, a troubled 17-year-old girl (unnamed in press reports) snuck out of her Winnipeg foster home and broke into the house where Leah Ross, a former lawyer, lived alone. The teenager ransacked the basement, taking anything she could find, and then left. Later that day, she realized that she'd left her phone and keys in the basement, so she had no choice but to go back and try to retrieve them. When the girl showed up at the back door—wearing Ross's sweater, coat, and watch—Ross was standing there. She quickly took a photo of the girl and then asked, "Are you going to hurt me?" The girl immediately broke down and started crying, and the two shared a long hug. Then Ross invited her inside. They sat together at the kitchen table and had eggnog and gingersnaps. Not long after, the pastor from across the street showed up, followed by the police. Ross refused to press charges, and is still in contact with the teenager and her foster parents. According to the CBC, the two have formed a "special bond."

WHEELS OF FORTUNE

In February 2018, in Queensland, Australia, a young woman named Tegan Langley was sitting in her car in a McDonald's parking lot when a strange man walked up and asked her if she "knew the state of her tires." Langley knew they were bald, but she didn't have enough money to replace them. "This complete stranger," who she later learned was named Tony, "explained he couldn't live with himself if he walked away from the situation knowing they were about to blow at any time." So Tony convinced Langley to follow him to a nearby tire shop. "$535, a lot of tears on my behalf, a few hugs, three brand new tires, and a wheel alignment later, he left." All Tony asked for in return was that "one day when I'm in the position where I'm able to help someone, I pay it forward." Langley's first step: tell her story on Facebook. After the *Mirror* reported on it, her post has amassed over 50,000 Likes. That's 50,000 more people (plus everyone who reads this book) who will know about Tony's generosity.

PEN PALS

In 2009 Brian Greenley and Alison Hitchcock met at a yoga retreat in Berkshire, England, and became friends. A year later, Greenley divulged that he'd just been diagnosed with stage 3 bowel cancer. Hitchcock wanted to do something for her

Snickers salad (chopped Snickers bars, green apples, Cool Whip) is an Iowa "party staple."

friend, so she said she'd write him a letter. "I asked if she was a great letter writer," Greenley told *Huffpost* in 2019, "and she said no." Hitchcock, who actually teaches creative writing at a university, gave herself the simple challenge of writing something to cheer him up. The first letter came a few weeks later. "It was very funny," Greenley said, "a massive distraction." Hitchcock sent dozens more over the next few years as Greenley underwent surgeries and chemotherapy. The two friends eventually realized that other cancer patients might appreciate receiving a real letter in an envelope, so they started a charity called From Me To You. Through their "Donate a Letter" campaign, people from all over the world can send an anonymous letter to a cancer patient in Great Britain. One of thousands of such recipients is Veronica Farley, 69, of East Sussex. While she was undergoing treatment for thyroid cancer and feeling isolated, she received a letter from a New Zealand woman named Christine who "wrote about the wallabies in her garden who were eating her eucalyptus trees." Farley said the letter really helped her. "I was overwhelmed that a complete stranger had taken the time to write to me. It was such a kind thought."

THE SHOEBOX

In 2000 a seven-year-old Idaho boy named Tyrel Wolfe packed a shoebox full of Christmas gifts, which included toiletries, school supplies, a toy, and a photo of himself on his Idaho farm. As part of a church program called Operation Christmas Child, the shoebox was mailed to the Philippines, where it ended up with a nine-year-old girl named Joana Marchan. She really liked the presents—especially the photo, which had Tyrel's name on it—and sent a thank-you note in return. It never got to him. Nearly a decade later, Joana, by that time in college, decided to see what that little boy was up to, so she looked him up on Facebook and sent him a friend request. Tyrel, 18, didn't know who this strange young woman was, so he did the responsible thing and ignored the request. Two years later, Joana decided to try again. Hesitantly, he responded, "How do you know me?" She told him about the shoebox and the photo of the "cute cowboy with the wooded background." The two hit it off immediately and began a correspondence. (They really bonded over their mutual love of Christian music.) One year later—and twelve years after sending the Christmas present—Tyrel traveled to the Philippines and met Joana in person. Two years later, they were married. At last report, the Wolfe family—Tyrel, Joana, and their son Harlann Jun—is living happily ever after in Idaho.

* * *

"It is impossible to persuade a man who does not disagree, but smiles."

—Muriel Spark

Michael Bolton was Paula Abdul's babysitter.

WEIRD PODCASTS

Over the last decade, podcasts have emerged as a new medium for news and entertainment. Every week, millions of listeners download popular podcasts like Serial, WTF, Stuff You Should Know, *and thousands more, including some really strange ones…like these.*

The Worst Idea of All Time. New Zealand comedians Tim Batt and Guy Montgomery discuss movies…but it's always *the same movie.* For the first year, the hosts watched Adam Sandler's *Grown Ups 2* once a week, and then talked about it every podcast as it slowly drove them mad. They repeated the yearlong experiment with *Sex and the City 2,* and then the Zac Efron electronic musical comedy *We Are Your Friends.*

My Dad Wrote a Porno. A man named "Rocky Flintstone" published six erotic novels about the sexy adventures of Belinda Blumenthal as she travels the world selling pots and pans. This podcast breaks down each and every chapter, with commentary from British comedian Jamie Morton, who claims to be the son of "Rocky Flintstone."

Beautiful / Anonymous. Comedian Chris Gethard calls up random phone numbers and tries to engage whoever answers in a conversation. His goal: to persuade them to tell their life stories.

Pod Godz. Two guys talk about—and criticize—other podcasts.

Talking a Number 2: Forrest Gump 2. Host Dakota Martin spends each episode discussing the ins and outs of *Forrest Gump 2*…a movie that doesn't exist.

Never Seen It. Each week, host Kyle Ayers assembles a group of friends (fellow Los Angeles comedians) who have never seen a famous movie (*Dirty Dancing,* Harry Potter, *Fight Club, The Exorcist,* etc.). And then they write and perform a new script approximating what they think the movie would be like.

Mike and Tom Eat Snacks. Remember the charming 2000s NBC dramedy *Ed,* about a guy who opens a law office in a bowling alley in a small town? It starred Tom Cavanaugh and Michael Ian Black, and on this podcast, the duo reunites to eat junk food and describe it to listeners.

Blastropodcast. In this parody of "interesting stuff" podcasts, comedian Mark Soloff portrays a time-traveling guy from the Italian Renaissance named Dottore Balordo who teaches listeners all about science…except that all of it is woefully incorrect.

8-Bit Book Club. Years ago, a cheap and easy-to-read "novelization" was part of every major movie's marketing plan. Apparently, video game novelizations were also a thing, and on this podcast, the hosts read through "novels" such as *Mega Man 2: The Novel* and *Sonic the Hedgehog: Fortress of Fear,* cracking jokes as they do.

The technical name for a cardboard coffee sleeve is a *zarf.*

IT'S A POP STAR CONSPIRACY

Here's a rundown of what's going on in the world of music—what the singers, rappers, bands, and their managers don't want you to know! Okay, not really. These are just some silly, far-fetched conspiracy theories that recently floated around about some of the biggest names in rock and pop.

★ ***Justin Bieber is a shapeshifting monster.*** At a concert in 2017, hundreds of Australian fans claimed to have witnessed the teen idol transform into a lizard before their very eyes. Amazingly, in this age of camera-enabled smartphones, there's no footage of this shocking moment, but there is video of Bieber in which some conspiracy buffs insist they can see his eyes turn a lizardlike black. (Other celebs who've been tagged by conspiracists as reptilian include Mark Zuckerberg, Bob Hope, and Queen Elizabeth.)

★ ***Kanye West promised to get young African Americans to vote Republican if President Donald Trump advanced the political agenda of West's wife, TV personality Kim Kardashian.*** West upset a lot of his liberal-leaning fans by publicly supporting Republican president Donald Trump. By wearing a "Make America Great Again" hat, West was able to get his wife, Kim Kardashian, an audience with the president. As a result of that meeting, President Trump granted clemency to Alice Marie Johnson, a convicted drug trafficker who Kardashian (and others) felt had been unfairly sentenced to life imprisonment for a first-time offense. That's all true. The conspiracy theory: Trump freed Johnson in return for West becoming a mouthpiece for the GOP. What was in it for West? He wanted people to take his wife seriously.

★ ***Kris Kristofferson is a secret, high-level government agent.*** Kristofferson has lived a varied and fascinating life. He's a country music singer, a successful songwriter (he wrote "Help Me Make It Through the Night," "Me and Bobby McGee," and "Sunday Morning Coming Down"), and a movie star. He also attended Oxford University as a Rhodes Scholar, and served in the military in the 1960s as a fighter pilot and helicopter pilot. But according to some conspiracy theorists, the military experience was just a cover: He was *actually* working as a brainwasher for MK-ULTRA, the U.S. government's secret mind-control experiment.

★ ***Child beauty queen and murder victim JonBenét Ramsey didn't die in 1996...she grew up to be pop superstar Katy Perry.*** According to theorists, the proof is obvious: they look alike.

Lactobacillus delbrueckii bulgaricus, used to make yogurt, is the national microbe of India.

★ ***Courtney Love and a teen idol stole one of Kurt Cobain's guitars from her own daughter.*** Cobain, the lead singer of Nirvana, committed suicide in 1994, and ever since then, there's been wild speculation that he was actually murdered by his wife, Courtney Love. In 2018 a musician named Isaiah Silva claimed that Love had conspired to steal a guitar from him. Silva was previously married to Cobain and Love's daughter, Frances Bean Cobain, and he claims that Love and actor Ross Butler (star of the hit teen shows *Riverdale* and *13 Reasons Why*) got together to break into Silva's house and swipe a guitar his ex-wife had left there, the one that Kurt Cobain had used on Nirvana's famous 1993 appearance on *MTV Unplugged*. Silva says it was all orchestrated by talent manager Sam Lufti, whose clients include…Love and Butler.

★ ***Tupac Shakur faked his death.*** Shakur died in a Las Vegas drive-by shooting in 1996. Or did he? At the time of his death, the rapper was signed to Death Row Records, a label founded by Marion "Suge" Knight, who as of 2019 is serving a 28-year prison sentence for vehicular manslaughter. He has a long rap sheet of other violent crimes, and Shakur so feared being murdered by Knight that he faked his death and fled to Malaysia. (All of this is according to Suge Knight Jr.)

★ ***Taylor Swift died and was replaced with a body double.*** In 2017 Swift released the hit single "Look What You Made Me Do." In the video for the song, there's a part where the singer says, "Sorry, the old Taylor can't come to the phone right now. Why? 'Cause she's dead." The song is supposed to be about personal rebirth and leaving the past behind, but some fans believe this line is a tacit admission that Swift is *literally* dead, and the woman walking around performing as Taylor Swift is an impostor, hired to keep raking in millions for Swift's record company.

★ ***Britney Spears and Justin Timberlake are clones.*** The story goes that back when they first got famous in 1999, the teen sensations and boyfriend/girlfriend couple got into a serious car accident in which Spears was instantly decapitated. Not wanting to let go of its cash cow, Jive Records replaced her with a clone (and they trot out a new one every few years). As for Timberlake, the current incarnation is also a clone, while the real one is still in a coma after that fateful car accident.

★ ***The Beatles aren't real.*** They weren't four guys from Liverpool named John, Paul, George, and Ringo who got together to form a band, write songs, and rock the world. It would be physically impossible, say proponents of this conspiracy theory, for four individuals to have produced so many hit albums in such a short period of time, while maintaining a vigorous touring schedule. So how was the deception pulled off? By the use of "multiples"—a revolving door of lookalike actors who played the roles of the "Fab Four," singing and performing songs written by teams of record label employees. (So they were like the Monkees?)

At least 4 people have been killed by thrown or swung golf clubs that broke and bounced back.

TRIVIA NIGHT

You could do trivia night at a bar, or in the comfort of your own home.
Gather some friends, pick a trivia master, and have fun! Answers
are on page 501, but each question contains a hint.

1. What do these five words have in common: panther, purple, wolf, twelfth, toilet?
   Hint: The thing they share is a thing they lack.

2. Which candy was taken to the South Pole in the 1930s?
   Hint: It was discontinued in 2018.

3. Which branch of the U.S. Armed Forces was a part of another military branch until 1947?
   Hint: Its name ended in "Corps" before it split off on its own.

4. What's unique about the hyoid bone?
   Hint: If it's broken, it helps forensic investigators determine the cause of death.

5. In what two recent decades were the most popular baby names Michael and Jessica?
   Hint: The names that took over the top spots next were Jacob and Emily.

6. Singer Bruno Mars was named after Bruno Sammartino, a legend of what sport?
   Hint: The sport's abbreviation was changed by one letter in 2002.

7. Farriers put what things on what animals?
   Hint: They probably have good fortune.

8. What famous action movie prop is a depiction of a woman giving birth?
   Hint: The prop is discovered at the beginning of the movie, then it's lost, and it's never spoken of again.

9. Which U.S. state has the most pickup trucks?
   Hint: It's not Texas.

10. India is the world's largest democracy, and the U.S. is #2. Which country has the third largest democracy?
    Hint: Waterfront property is plentiful there.

What's the difference between a puma, mountain lion, panther, and cougar? Nothing.

11. If an animal has albinism, what color are its eyes?
Hint: They're neither red nor white.

12. Recorded in 1966 and '67, what two #1 songs by the Monkees have the same word in their titles?
Hint: Faithful fans will know.
(Shrek *fans might also know.*)

13. Which two pop divas famously feuded when they were both *American Idol* judges in 2013?
Hint: In 2010 the singers collaborated on the hit single "Up Out My Face."

14. Who invented champagne?
Hint: His name should be familiar, even if you don't drink champagne.

15. Puck, Miranda, Ariel, Umbriel, Titania, and Oberon are some of the moons of what planet?
Hint: The planet is blue.

16. Though technically not its capital, what city is the seat of government of the Netherlands?
Hint: It also begins with "The."

17. What food name comes from the Arabic word for "chickpea"?
Hint: It's what you eat when you don't know the words.

18. How many teaspoons are in a tablespoon?
Hint: It would be difficult to accurately measure out half a tablespoon using a teaspoon.

* * *

11 REAL HOW-TO BOOKS

- *How to Raise Your I.Q. by Eating Gifted Children*, by Lewis B. Frumkes
- *How to Become a Schizophrenic*, by John Modrow
- *How to Survive Robot Uprising*, by Daniel H. Wilson
- *Ducks: How to Make Them Pay*, by William Cook
- *Knitting with Dog Hair*, by Kendall Crolius
- *How to Talk to Your Cat About Gun Safety*, by Zachary Auburn
- *Bombproof Your Horse*, by Rick Pelicano and Lauren Tjaden
- *Drink as Much as You Want and Live Longer*, by Frederick M. Beyerlein
- *Fancy Coffins to Make Yourself*, by Dale L. Power
- *The Beginners Guide to Sex in the Afterlife*, by David Staume
- *How to Write a How-to-Write Book*, by Brian Piddock

Rarest blood type: Rh-null, also called golden because it's so rare.
Only about 40 people worldwide have it.

THE MANDELA EFFECT

Uncle John could've sworn he wrote this article years ago.

BACKGROUND

In 2009 a writer and researcher named Fiona Broome attended DragonCon, a science-fiction and fantasy fan convention in Atlanta. She was talking with friends when somebody brought up Nelson Mandela, the South African civil rights leader who died in prison in the 1980s. Several other people in the group expressed similar feelings—the dismay they'd felt when they'd learned of Mandela's death. Broome, however, was confused: Mandela didn't die in his cell in the 1980s—he was released in the early 1990s and became the president of South Africa. So how could her friends have gotten it so wrong? To get answers, Broome started a website to discuss this phenomenon, which she called the "Mandela effect." She received hundreds more accounts from people who were convinced that Mandela died in prison in the 1980s. In fact, they remembered hearing about it on the news; some even remembered seeing the funeral on TV.

Psychologists refer to this as *confabulation*—a fake memory that results from misinterpreted, flawed, or overlapping memories, or simply absorbed and processed misinformation. The reason for the false memories about Mandela: likely a combination of other publicly televised funerals and footage of Mandela's release, all misremembered by people who were very young and very impressionable when the events "occurred."

When someone realizes that they, along with thousands of others, remembered an event like this incorrectly—something for which there's incontrovertible proof that they were wrong—it creates such a deep feeling of confusion and mental dissonance that they start to look for explanations. Some such "explanations" include conspiracy theories, cover-ups, and even "split/alternate universes." But it's not caused by any of those—it's just a flaw in the human brain. Here are some other examples of the Mandela effect.

Mandela Effect: In 2016 hundreds of people on the internet claimed to have remembered watching a family movie in the mid-1990s called *Shazam*. A comedy adventure about a sassy genie, the film starred stand-up comedian Sinbad as the title character. One problem: This movie *doesn't exist*. There are no tapes, posters, or records of it ever being released or airing on TV.

Reality: There was a widely released movie about an African American genie that hit movie theaters in 1996, but it wasn't *Shazam* starring Sinbad—it was the

First snack advertised on TV: Lay's potato chips.

similarly titled *Kazaam* starring professional basketball player Shaquille O'Neal. When a reporter asked about the *Shazam/Kazaam* phenomenon in 2016, Sinbad quipped, "It was Shaq, but we all [meaning all African Americans] look alike."

Mandela Effect: For more than 30 years, kids have grown up with the Berenstein Bears; the book series has provided important life lessons via stories about a family of bears. Oh, except they aren't called the Berenstein Bears—they're the *Berenstain* Bears, after authors Stan and Jan Berenstain. When millions of millennials realized they'd gotten that vowel wrong for their entire lives, it became an internet phenomenon. Some people weren't even able to admit (on the internet) that their brains had remembered the name wrong, insisting that they actually *were* the Berenstein Bears back in the 1970s or '80s and that the world split into an alternate universe where it's spelled differently. Some even provided proof in the form of Berenstain Bears merchandise, such as stuffed animals, labeled "Berenstein." (There you go! Artifacts from the other universe!)

Reality: So many people's brains remembered it as "Berenstein" and not "Berenstain" because names that end in "stein" are much more common than ones that end in "stain," and memories are distorted by "filling in the blanks" or associations. (As for those stuffed animals, apparently toy manufacturers can suffer from confabulation, too.)

More examples of the Mandela Effect in action

- Budweiser's signature low-calorie beer isn't Bud Lite, as many people think. It's actually Bud Light. Those who think otherwise are conflating it with its competitor, Miller Lite.

- Despite you being in the theater in 1980 watching *The Empire Strikes Back* and hearing Darth Vader say, "Luke, I am your father," the character didn't actually say that. He says, "No! *I* am your father."

- Auguste Rodin's famous sculpture *The Thinker* doesn't rest his head on his fist. His head sets on limp fingers turned inward.

- Those old Bugs Bunny and Daffy Duck cartoons were presented under the "Looney Tunes" banner, not Looney Toons. The use of "toons" as a short version of "cartoons" was popularized by the 1988 film *Who Framed Roger Rabbit*. Warner Bros. started calling its cartoons *Looney Tunes* (and *Merrie Melodies*) in the 1930s. Reason: the series was designed to compete with cartoons from Disney called *Silly Symphonies*.

A third of Americans are a different religion now than when they were kids.

GROANERS

A wise man once said, "When fighting clowns, always go for the juggler." Please don't come after us for these.

Windmill #1: "What kind of music do you like?"
Windmill #2: "I'm a big metal fan."

Did you hear about the mom who told a dad joke? It was a faux pa.

Q: Why did Beethoven get rid of his chickens?
A: All they would say is, "BACH! BACH! BACH!"

Did you hear about the illustrator who ran out of ideas? She drew a blank.

Q: Why do gorillas have big nostrils?
A: Because gorillas have big fingers.

Did you hear about the bachelor who sold his vacuum cleaner? It was just collecting dust.

Q: What do you call a dog that does magic tricks?
A: A labracadabrador.

Q: What do you call a dead magician?
A: An abracadaver.

Q: What do *Titanic* and *The Sixth Sense* have in common?
A: Icy dead people.

The inventor of Velcro died. RIP.

Buffalo Jr.: "Well, Dad, I'm off to college."
Buffalo Sr.: "Bison."

That guy just hit me with a bunch of milk and cheese products! How dairy!

Q: What do you call an arrogant prisoner going downstairs?
A: A condescending con descending.

Q: What do you call a broken can opener?
A: A can't opener.

"I stand corrected," said the man in his new orthopedic shoes.

Q: What's red and bad for your teeth?
A: A brick.

We were going to make this an entire page of ceiling jokes, but they'd just go over your head.

Q: What's the difference between a blackbird and a bluebird?
A: They're both black except for the bluebird.

Did you hear about the guy who fell into the upholstery machine? He's fully recovered.

Q: What do you call a herd of sheep tumbling down a hill?
A: A lambslide.

A widow is mourning at her husband's grave. A man approaches and asks, "Mind if I say a word?"
    "Okay," she says.
    "Plethora."
    "Thanks. That means a lot."

Did you hear about the husband who accidentally gave his wife a glue stick when she asked for her lipstick? She still isn't talking to him.

Q: Can you help me round up these 18 sheep?
A: Twenty.

I want a rubber band sandwich, and make it snappy! (That last pun really is a stretch.)

Q: Why are all your sheep purple?
A: I herded them through the grapevine.

Q: What was the last thing Grandpa said before he kicked the bucket?
A: "I'm going to kick this bucket."

The African antelope called the dik-dik marks its territory with its tears.

EVEL WAYS

Evel Knievel, the canyon-jumping, rocket-powered-motorcycle-riding daredevil, was one of the most famous people on earth back in the 1970s. And he had a unique perspective on life.

"I'm not a stunt man. I'm not a daredevil. I'm an explorer."

"I learned one thing from jumping motorcycles that was of great value on the golf course. Whatever you do, don't come up short."

"Anybody can jump a motorcycle. The trouble begins when you try to land it."

"If you fall during your life, it doesn't matter. You're never a failure as long as you try to get up."

"I guess I thought I was Elvis Presley, but I'll tell you something. All Elvis did was stand on a stage and play a guitar. He never fell off on that pavement at no 80 m.p.h."

"I don't have any problems in life, just situations."

"You come to a point in your life when you really don't care what people think about you, you just care what you think about yourself."

"Women are the root of all evil. I ought to know. I'm Evel."

CONSTITUTIONAL WRONGS

The framers of the U.S. Constitution didn't make it easy to amend America's founding document. Out of 11,000 proposed amendments, only 27 have made it through the ratification process to become the supreme law of the land. From odd to annoying, here are a few fails.

TITLES OF NOBILITY AMENDMENT (1810)

"If any citizen of the United States shall accept, claim, receive or retain, any title of nobility or honor, or shall, without the consent of Congress, accept and retain any present, pension, office or emolument of any kind whatever, from any emperor, king, prince or foreign power, such person shall cease to be a citizen of the United States, and shall be incapable of holding any office of trust or profit under them, or either of them."

The above amendment was actually *approved* by Congress. Some historians say that lawmakers wanted to keep Napoleon's American-born sister-in-law from being proclaimed "Duchess of Baltimore." Others say Congress feared foreign titles made far-too-tempting bribes. Though technically still active, the nobility amendment fell short of the 13 states (three-fourths of the total at that time) needed for ratification, and never became law. American citizens who might be grateful: honorary British knights Steven Spielberg, George H. W. Bush, and Kevin Spacey, as well as Meghan Markle, the Duchess of Sussex.

SELF-DENIAL (1876)

Residents of Potter County, Pennsylvania, must have really hated the Senate back in 1876. According to records in the National Archive, they complained to Congress that the Senate "always advanced the interest of the money, railroad, and manufacturing speculators to the prejudice of the common welfare." Their proposal: pass a constitutional amendment eliminating the Senate. (The proposal never made it to the Senate.)

THE U.S.E. (1893)

Wisconsin representative Lucas Miller thought the United States would grow…and grow…and grow. He envisioned a republic that added state after state until "every Nation on Earth" had become part of the country. His proposed amendment: rename the nation "the United States of the Earth" in preparation for that future. Miller was not nominated for a second term.

April Fool's Day tradition in Italy: placing paper fish on friends' backs.

EQUAL RIGHTS FOR WOMEN (1923)

In 21st-century America, every citizen has equal rights under the law. Except some citizens. The idea of the Equal Rights Amendment was to guarantee equal legal rights for all American citizens regardless of gender, thus ending the legal distinctions between men and women in terms of divorce, property, employment, and other matters. The amendment (proposed in 1923) passed out of Congress in 1972 and was allowed seven years for ratification. Didn't happen. Congress then extended the deadline to 1982. It was ratified by 35 states, three short of the required 38. Since then, two more states signed on…but the 1982 deadline expired. In 2019 California representative Jackie Speier introduced a resolution that would eliminate the deadline, allowing the amendment to become part of the Constitution whenever it is ratified by the legislatures of three-fourths of the states. Stay tuned…

NO MILLIONAIRES (1933)

Washington state representative Wesley Lloyd wanted a constitutional amendment outlawing millionaires. He wanted income in excess of $1 million applied to the national debt. Congress did not agree.

YOU'RE FIRED! (1974)

As the nation digested the resignation of President Richard M. Nixon in 1974, Wisconsin representative Henry Reuss was looking toward the future. At the time, people seemed persuaded that the impeachment process had done its job. Reuss did not agree. The country had endured a two-year slog of an investigation, complete with constant haggling over the definition of "impeachable offenses." Had it not been for the "Saturday Night Massacre"—when President Nixon fired Special Prosecutor Archibald Cox and accepted the resignations of Attorney General Elliot Richardson and Deputy Attorney General William Ruckelshaus—Congress might never have acted. There had to be a smoother way to remove someone from the Oval Office. In the aftermath of Watergate, Reuss proposed a new amendment to allow "a Resolution of No Confidence in the President." Such a resolution would require a three-fifths majority of both the House and Senate. If the vote succeeded, the amendment called for a special presidential election on the first Tuesday in November of the next even-numbered year. The amendment went nowhere.

> The country had endured a two-year slog of an investigation, complete with constant haggling over the definition of "impeachable offenses."

JAIL BARRED (2001)

It might seem strange that the Constitution needed an amendment to prohibit excessive bail, excessive fines, and cruel and unusual punishments. Apparently, it did. The Eighth Amendment, passed into law in 1791, took care of that. But that wasn't enough for Indiana representative Julia Carson. She wanted a new amendment that would retain the prior prohibitions and also prohibit incarceration (both before and after trial) for minor traffic offenses. Wait…the Constitution doesn't already prohibit that? No. Nevertheless, Carson's bill never made it out of committee.

CONTINUITY OF CONGRESS (2003)

Article I of the Constitution requires that a quorum of the majority of its members be present in order for Congress to conduct business. On September 11, 2001, both houses of Congress were in session. Had United Airlines Flight 93 hit its likely intended target (Capitol Hill), only a handful of those elected officials would have been left to handle legislation in the aftermath of the attack. The Senate would have been okay because state governors can appoint interim senators as needed. But if a member of the House dies, a replacement must be chosen by special election, even though it can take up to four months to hold a special election. This amendment would have given Congress the power to make temporary appointments, by legislation, to both houses of Congress in the event a large number of members were unable to perform their duties. The amendment failed. The House reaffirmed its commitment to the one thing every member has in common: being duly elected by the people.

NO BUDGET, NO PAY (2012)

Most people understand that if they want to get paid, they have to do the work they've been hired to do. That's why Tennessee representative Jim Cooper introduced the "No Budget, No Pay" Act in 2012. Cooper's amendment prohibited paying any member of Congress (excluding the vice president) if both houses of Congress didn't pass the federal budget by October 1. Not only that, they couldn't receive retroactive pay for the period between October 1 and when they ultimately did pass the budget. It wasn't the first time Congress proposed punitive measures related to passing the budget. The 107th Congress (2001–2002) rejected an amendment that would have forced Congress members *and* the president to forfeit their salaries, on a per diem basis, for every day past the end of the fiscal year that a budget for that year remained unpassed. "Any other job in the world, you don't do your job, you don't get paid," Cooper said in 2012. "Congress shouldn't be any different."

* * *

"Forgive your enemies, but never forget their names." —**John Kennedy**

THE TV DETECTIVE WITH SOMETHING EXTRA

Who doesn't love a good police procedural TV show? Out of the hundreds of cops and detectives that have graced screens over the last few decades, the ones who stood out have a unique skill or character trait that helps them catch the bad guy. Can you match the detective show with the special skill? Answers are on page 501.

1. They solved crimes... with math.

2. They solved crimes... with forensics.

3. They solved crimes... with forensic anthropology.

4. They solved crimes... with computers.

5. They solved crimes... with a supercomputer.

6. She solved crimes... because she can talk to ghosts.

7. He solved crimes... because he could wake murder victims for one minute and ask them who killed them.

8. He solved crimes...by asking people on the internet for help.

9. She solved crimes... because her partner was a mystery novelist.

10. He solved crimes... with the aid of his obsessive-compulsive disorder.

11. He solved crimes... because he was psychic.

12. He solved crimes... by pretending to be psychic.

13. He solved crimes... because he could mentally empathize with murderers.

14. He solved crimes... because he was a time-traveling secret agent from the 1780s.

15. They solved crimes... with the help of a reformed con artist.

16. She solved crimes... because she never forgets a single detail.

17. He solved crimes... because he can fight off the supernatural creatures causing them.

18. He solved crimes... because he's Sherlock Holmes.

19. He solved crimes... with the aid of a brain-enhancing drug.

20. He solved crimes... with his brain.

a) *Castle*
b) *Bones*
c) *Person of Interest*
d) *Psych*
e) *NUMB3RS*
f) *CSI: Crime Scene Investigation*
g) *Wisdom of the Crowd*
h) *Elementary*
i) *CSI: Cyber*
j) *Unforgettable*
k) *Limitless*
l) *Medium*
m) *Hannibal*
n) *Monk*
o) *Grimm*
p) *The Mentalist*
q) *Pushing Daisies*
r) *Sleepy Hollow*
s) *The Dead Zone*
t) *White Collar*

Rarest diamonds in the world: red diamonds.

THE OLD LADY WHO WASN'T

We've written about Jeanne Calment a few times over the years. She's a Frenchwoman who died in 1997 at the ripe old age of 122, after earning a hallowed place in Guinness World Records *as the world's oldest person. "God must have forgotten me," she often joked. That's one theory for how Calment got her record. Here's another.*

THE RUSSIAN REPORT

In January 2019, a report was published that accused Jeanne Calment—whom Guinness verified was 122 when she died—of only living for 99 years. The controversial findings were put forth by a Russian mathematician named Nikola Zak, with the help of a gerontologist (someone who studies aging) named Valery Novoselov. Zak didn't set out to disprove a world record. His initial aim was to create a "mathematical model of the lifespan of supercentenarians" (people over 110). But everything changed when he started noticing problems with Calment's story. "The more I searched, the more contradictions I found," he told *Agence France-Presse*.

After analyzing all of her interviews, biographies, witness testimony, and surviving photographs—and comparing them with public records from her French birth town—Zak came to the startling conclusion that Calment's daughter, Yvonne, had assumed her mother's identity. Likely reason: Tax evasion. In 1934, says Zak, it wasn't Yvonne who died—as has long been thought—but Jeanne herself. Yvonne was a young woman, and she stood to inherit her mother's money…but she would have to pay taxes on it. If, on the other hand, she simply told people that she *was* her reclusive mother, the money would all be hers, tax-free. All of a sudden, Zak's theory goes, Yvonne became Jeanne, and she gained 22 years just like that.

AGE OF REASON

The Russian mathematician offered some compelling evidence, including, according to *Agence France-Presse*, "discrepancies between physical characteristics listed on Calment's identity card from the 1930s and her appearance in later years." Among the discrepancies: different eye colors and different heights. Novoselov, the gerontologist, studied footage of Calment in her later years, and she looked *very* healthy for someone who was over 110. "The state

> **A TIP FROM UNCLE JOHN**
>
> Eating vegetables and not smoking will help you live longer, but here's one unexpected life-lengthener: flossing. Studies show that cleaning between your teeth can add as much as six years to your life. Reason: It removes infectious bacteria and other germs before they can enter your bloodstream.

of her muscle system was different from that of her contemporaries," he said. "She could sit up without any support. She had no signs of dementia." Most damning of all: When Calment became a famous supercentenarian, she reportedly had all of her old photographs burned to hide the evidence. But she couldn't hide it all.

REWRITING HISTORY

Jeanne Calment is considered a national hero in France, and it was a big deal when Guinness verified her age, so it's no surprise that the Russian report was met with a lot of blowback. Guinness stood by its initial assessment, saying there was "never any doubt" to the authenticity of the documents they were provided with. They accuse Zak of attempting to defame Calment (although it's unclear what he would gain from doing that). The former mayor of Arles, the town she lived in, called the theory "completely impossible" and "ridiculous."

Zak and Novoselov stand by their findings. They maintain that Calment's age could have been verified in 1997 if an autopsy had been performed, but her family wouldn't allow it at the time. And it's unlikely they'll ever agree to letting anyone exhume the body for a DNA test. At the very least, says Zak, the age-verification methods need to be more vigorous, and Calment's case "should be used as an example of the vulnerability of seemingly well-established facts."

OLD NEWS

If it is true that Jeanne Clement was 22 years younger than she claimed to be, it could put a whole new spin on an article we wrote about her in *Uncle John's Uncanny Bathroom Reader* called "The Real Estate Deal of a Lifetime." Back in 1965, Calment was living in a fancy apartment that was coveted by a lawyer named Andre-François Raffray. He offered to buy it from her by way of an *en viager* transaction, wherein he would pay her a monthly stipend of 2,500 francs ($500) until she died, and then the apartment would become his. As we wrote in *Uncanny*, "One of the risks associated with *en viager* transactions is that the seller can lie about their age or pretend to be sicker than they really are, in order to extract larger monthly payments from a buyer who believes the seller might die at any minute." Raffray, 47, was under the impression that Jeanne was 90, and that she'd been a heavy smoker and drinker for 70 years, and she was already two decades beyond her life expectancy, so it seemed like a really good deal. She even said she ate two pounds of chocolate *per week!*

However, if Nikolai Zak's theory is correct, Raffray actually made the deal with a 68-year-old woman who was in much better health than she let on. Thirty years later, Raffray died after having paid nearly $180,000 for an apartment that he never got to live in. "It happens in life that we make bad deals," Calment joked at the time. She died two years later at the age of…?

Makes sense: "Himalayas" translates to "houses of snow."

RESTAURANT CONFIDENTIAL

If you're like us, you've probably eaten in a chain restaurant once or twice. And if that's the case, you'll probably enjoy reading these gossipy facts about your favorite (or least favorite) dining establishment.

OUTBACK STEAKHOUSE

Outback is an American restaurant chain. So why is it Australia-themed, displaying boomerangs and other "Down Under" memorabilia on the walls, and offering "Aussie-Tizers" on the menu? Because it was founded in 1988. That was right around the time when all things Australian became hot in the United States, thanks to media exposure, such as Paul Hogan's TV ads for Australian tourism ("I'll slip an extra shrimp on the barbie for you"), his 1986 blockbuster movie *Crocodile Dundee*, and Australian football player Jacko's popular battery commercials ("Energizer! Oi!"). Some Florida restaurateurs looking to open a steakhouse needed an angle... and they found one.

OLIVE GARDEN

In 2014 Olive Garden received a hefty cash infusion from an investment company called Starboard Value. Representatives of that firm tried to change the way the restaurant did business because it was losing a lot of money, particularly because of its all-you-can-eat garlic breadsticks (probably the most popular thing Olive Garden offers). At the time, the chain produced about 675 million breadsticks annually, but the vast majority got thrown away because they tend to turn stale if they go uneaten for more than five minutes. Starboard suggested that Olive Garden serve just one breadstick per person, but executives figured that would drive business away. So, Starboard and Olive Garden compromised: the breadstick policy would remain in place, but they'd save money other ways...like cleaning the carpets of each of its hundreds of locations only once a month.

CHI-CHI'S

Chi-Chi's was one of the first major Mexican-inspired restaurant chains in the United States, and exposed millions to their first-ever tacos, burritos, and enchiladas. It also exposed people to hepatitis. In 2003 the biggest outbreak of hepatitis A in American history was the result of tainted green onions served in dishes at a Chi-Chi's in Pennsylvania. More than 650 people fell ill, and four people died. Also tainted: Chi-Chi's. It never recovered after the hepatitis outbreak, and the chain's entire American operation went out of business in 2004.

There are about 750 individual tiny flowers called florets on the head of a sunflower.

TGI FRIDAYS

The Briad Group is a consortium that owns more than two dozen TGI Fridays in New Jersey. In 2013, thirteen of those restaurants were raided by the state's Alcoholic Beverage Control office. Reason: bait and switch. Fridays was putting cheap booze into high-end brand bottles, and charging customers premium prices for it. One TGI Fridays even sold "scotch" that consisted of rubbing alcohol and brown food coloring. The company pleaded no contest to the criminal charges and paid a $500,000 fine.

RED LOBSTER

How much snow crab can people *really* eat? That's what executives at Red Lobster wondered in 2003, completely underestimating how much shellfish people will consume during an all-you-can-eat promotion. The seafood chain offered its "Endless Snow Crab" just as wholesale crab prices started to skyrocket, severely cutting into profit margins. The company wound up making no money at all on the deal. In fact, Red Lobster actually lost $3 million, forcing the company's president to resign.

CRACKER BARREL

In 1991 a dozen employees at various locations were fired under mysterious circumstances…and then the news emerged that the corporate office had just sent out a memo to managers ordering them to terminate any wait staff that didn't present "normal heterosexual values." In other words, they fired gay people, and they had to backpedal and eliminate the policy after protests erupted. In 2002 the company updated its nondiscrimination policy, officially adding sexual orientation to the list, a policy it now puts on display in every location.

APPLEBEE'S

In 1971 Julia Stewart got her first job: as a server at IHOP, or as it was known at the time, International House of Pancakes. As her work life progressed, she remained in the restaurant industry, working her way up the corporate ladder at Applebee's, eventually becoming president, the second most powerful person in the restaurant chain. But when she was passed over for the biggest job, CEO, she quit and returned to IHOP in 2001 as its new CEO. Six years later, she led IHOP's takeover…of Applebee's.

THE CHEESECAKE FACTORY

Three things that this restaurant is known for: It has an insanely long and varied menu, it's a common setting on *The Big Bang Theory*, and its dining rooms are extremely dimly lit. There's a reason for that last one. Multiple psychology and marketing studies show that eating in low light leads people to eat (and thus order) more food than they usually would.

There's enough concrete in the Hoover Dam for a two-lane road stretching from Seattle to Miami.

LIFE BEFORE X-RAYS

Ever wonder whether exposure to the small amount of radiation in an X-ray was worth the risk to your health? Here's an article published by the medical journal Dental Items of Interest *in 1891, decades before X-ray imaging became a common diagnostic tool.*

TOUGH TO SWALLOW

Nearly two years ago, Mrs. Mary Green, a domestic, then living on State street in [Bangor, Maine] declared that her false teeth had slipped down her throat, and that she suffered great distress and pain in consequence of the obstruction. Physicians who examined her, however, concluded that she was the victim of her imagination, but she insisted so strongly to the contrary, and appeared to experience so much suffering, that the doctors at the Bridgeport Hospital finally consented to perform a surgical operation, and extract the missing teeth if they should be found. The operation failed to reveal the existence of any teeth in Mrs. Green's interior, and the doctors then felt assured that she had been the victim of only a false fright.

Believing the woman to be the victim of a mental hallucination, and to allay her fright, the doctors performed a second operation, and assured her that they had found the teeth. Mrs. Green was better for a while, but again declared that she felt the teeth lacerating her vitals, and she was sent to the Homeopathic Hospital in New York, her previous Bridgeport experience being communicated to the hospital physicians by the Bridgeport doctors, together with their belief that she was a victim of imagination only. To satisfy her, another operation was performed at the New York hospital, but the surgeons found nothing.

SEEING IS BELIEVING

When Mrs. Green recovered from the effects of the anesthetic, however, a set of teeth were shown her, and she was assured that they were the teeth which she had swallowed. The patient thereafter got well rapidly, and professed to have no more trouble. The case was freely reported in medical journals and in the press throughout the country as a striking incident of the powers of the human imagination.

Mrs. Green died here of consumption [tuberculosis] yesterday, and an autopsy by Dr. Blodget revealed the fact that the doctors, and not the woman, had been victims of imagination. The doctor and his assistants found the plate and the teeth in the woman's esophagus, about two inches above the stomach. The curved plate fitted the pipe so well that "there was no obstruction to the food as it passed down the throat, and the plate was already partly encysted by a growth of flesh over the edge of the metal.

The physicians believe it to be the only case of the kind on record.

Experts say: The smaller the animal, the slower they perceive time.

THE BIG DUCK

Maybe, like us, you've seen one of these buildings on an old postcard and asked yourself, "What do they sell in that place?" Answer: exactly what it looks like.

Bondurant's Pharmacy (Lexington, Kentucky)

Shaped like a giant mortar and pestle, like the kind that compound pharmacies once used. (The mortar is the building; the pestle is a sign with an "RX" on top.) From 1974 to 2011, it was a drugstore. Now it's a liquor store.

Torre Telefónica (Santiago, Chile)

With the arrival of thin, rectangular smartphones, this telecom company's HQ building looks a little outdated. But when the 470-foot building went up in 1993, it looked just like the cell phones of the era. A portion of windows form a "screen," while part of the tower's side juts out like a small antenna.

Giant Artichoke (Castroville, California)

A must-see in the town that holds an annual Artichoke Festival is this massive 20-foot-tall artichoke, which houses an artichoke-themed restaurant called the Giant Artichoke.

National Fisheries Development Board Building (Hyderabad, India)

This council deals with fish and fishing issues, and it does that from inside of a five-story blue fish. (The fish's gills are actually windows.)

Eli's Florida Orange World (Kissimmee, Florida)

This 60-foot-tall half-orange sells grapefruit, tangerines…and oranges.

Pysanka Museum (Kolomyia, Ukraine)

A *pysanka* is an elaborately painted and decorated Ukrainian Easter egg. This museum, which is oblong like an egg and painted like a *pysanka*, houses one of the world's finest collections of that very thing.

Coney Island Hot Dog Stand (Bailey, Colorado)

You cannot eat this giant hot dog made of concrete and metal. You can eat the Coney Island–style hot dogs sold inside.

The Big Duck (Flanders, New York)

Built by a duck farmer in 1931 as a place to sell ducks and duck eggs. The duck-shaped building now sells duck-themed souvenirs.

The Doughnut Hole (La Puente, California)

Technically, the building looks like a doughnut, not a doughnut hole. But it's a drive-through doughnut shop, and the part that customers drive through is the doughnut hole, hence the name. (The doughnut portion of the building is where the employees make the doughnuts.)

The Longaberger Company Building (Newark, Ohio)

Longaberger made and sold handcrafted maple wood picnic baskets, and the company was headquartered in a 180,000-square-foot building shaped like a picnic basket. (The company went out of business in 2018 and the building is now vacant.)

First person in history to get a driver's license: Karl Benz, inventor of the first practical motor car (1888).

AMAZING ANAGRAMS

We're not saying these famous name anagrams—words or phrases that result when you rearrange the letters—reveal any hidden truths about the subject...but they are kind of fun.

DANIEL DAY-LEWIS	IDEAL SINEWY LAD
WARREN BEATTY	BEWARE TYRANT
JOE BIDEN	I NEED JOB
ROBIN WILLIAMS	I WARM BILLIONS
BILL MURRAY	RUMBLY LIAR
LEONARDO DICAPRIO	OCEAN IDOL OR A DRIP
JULIA ROBERTS	I RULE STAR JOB
CALISTA FLOCKHART	L.A. CHICK FARTS A LOT
THERESA MAY	TEARY SHAME
RUSSELL CROWE	SCOWLER RULES
MICHAEL JACKSON	SO CHECK JAIL MAN
LOUIS ARMSTRONG	ROUSING MORTALS
DONALD TRUMP	ADULT PORN M.D.
FIDEL CASTRO	COILED FARTS
BILLY JOEL	JOLLY BILE
CYNDI LAUPER	LUNACY PRIDE
QUEEN ELIZABETH THE SECOND	I SQUEEZE THE NOBLE HAND, ETC.
ELVIS COSTELLO	VOICE SELLS LOT
DUKE ELLINGTON	LIKED LONG TUNE
BRITNEY SPEARS	PRESBYTERIANS
LUCIANO PAVAROTTI	PUT ON A RAVIOLI ACT
PAUL MCCARTNEY	PAY MR CLEAN CUT
PRINCESS DIANA	ASCEND IN PARIS
WILLIAM SHAKESPEARE	I AM A WEAKISH SPELLER
NANCY REAGAN	AN ACE GRANNY
ALBERT EINSTEIN	ELITE BRAIN NEST
WOODY ALLEN	A LEWD LOONY
SERENA WILLIAMS	LEAN WAR MISSILE
WALT DISNEY	SADLY I WENT

Even when it's scared, a narwhal's heart only beats about four times per minute.

MUSIC TO OUR EARS

Without music, there'd be no Bathroom Readers. (It's hard to write in silence.)

"Music is the shorthand of emotion."
—Leo Tolstoy

"Music is one of the most powerful things the world has to offer. No matter what race or religion or nationality or sexual orientation or gender you are, it has the power to unite us."
—Lady Gaga

"Nothing pleases me more than to go into a room and come out with a piece of music."
—Paul McCartney

"Is there a meaning to music? My answer would be yes. Can you state in so many words what that meaning is? My answer would be no."
—Aaron Copland

"I NEED TO LISTEN TO CHILL MUSIC WHEN I'M DRIVING. IT PREVENTS ROAD RAGE."
—Aaron Paul

"MUSIC IS THE SILENCE BETWEEN THE NOTES."
—Claude Debussy

"Making music is like shopping for me. Every song is like a new pair of shoes."
—Rihanna

"MUSIC EXPRESSES THAT WHICH CANNOT BE SAID AND ON WHICH IT IS IMPOSSIBLE TO BE SILENT."
—Victor Hugo

"When I hear music, I fear no danger. I am invulnerable. I see no foe. I am related to the earliest times, and to the latest."
—Henry David Thoreau

"That's the amazing thing about music: there's a song for every emotion. Can you imagine a world with no music? It would suck."
—Harry Styles

"The music is in the air. Take as much as you want."
—Sir Edward Elgar

"We do not sing because we are happy, we are happy because we sing."
—William James

"When we wrote this song 25 years ago, we had no idea we'd have to play it...every...f*cking...night...for the rest of our lives."
—Huey Lewis, before playing "The Power of Love"

"If you are a chef, no matter how good a chef you are, it's not good cooking for yourself; the joy is in cooking for others—it's the same with music. "
—will.i.am

"People haven't always been there for me, but music always has."
—Taylor Swift

"A lot of music is mathematics. It's balance."
—Mel Brooks

"IT'S NOT THE NOTE YOU PLAY THAT'S THE WRONG NOTE—IT'S THE NOTE YOU PLAY AFTERWARDS THAT MAKES IT RIGHT OR WRONG."
—Miles Davis

OYSTER FACTS

Whether you eat them raw or fried—or not at all, because they're slimy and strange—oysters are a curious little monster from the depths of the sea.

- Oysters are *bivalve mollusks*. All that means is that they have soft flesh and gills, and live inside a hinged shell.

- What's a "spat"? A baby oyster that attaches itself to a hard surface—generally another oyster's shell—to grow.

- The life span of an oyster (if nobody catches it and eats it) tops out at 20 years.

- Humans have four-chambered hearts, red blood, and two kidneys. Oysters have three-chambered hearts, clear blood…and two kidneys.

- An oyster's gender can change at any time, based on its environment. Most begin life as males and wind up as female.

- Oysters were such big business in late 19th-century Baltimore (the "golden age of oystering") that a local company produced trading cards depicting major local packers, including Louis Grebb and H. W. Hitchcock. The cards were handed out to restaurants, grocery stores, and oyster bars as a form of promotion.

- An oyster shell doesn't always contain *just* an oyster. Sometimes they contain oyster crabs (also called pea crabs)—tiny crabs, about the size of a penny, that hide inside the oysters' gills and steal their food. (They're considered a delicacy on the East Coast.)

- You're more likely to find crabs inside of an oyster than a pearl. Only one out of 10,000 oysters contain that treasure, and even then it's not going to be a gleaming white, jewelry-quality pearl.

- Just by getting food, an adult oyster filters 20 to 50 gallons of water every day. That means an acre-sized reef full of oysters filters up to 24 million gallons each day. Oysters are prominent in Chesapeake Bay, where they can filter the entire bay in about three days.

- In restaurants and grocery stores, oysters are generally labeled according to their point of origin—Quonset Bay or Gulf Oysters, for example. And while there are over 200 varieties of oysters out there in the sea, only five are grown commercially for consumption in the United States.

In Ethiopia, the day officially starts at 6:00 a.m., not midnight.

THE NAME'S FAMILIAR

You know the names. Here's a look at the people behind them.

POP WARNER

In early 1929, a factory in a seedy section of Philadelphia enlisted Joseph J. Tomlin to do something about the teen vandalism it was experiencing. Within its first month of operation, 100 of its windows had been broken by juvenile delinquents who hung out in an adjacent lot and threw rocks for fun. Other factories in Philadelphia had the same problem, so Tomlin decided to get the owners together to fund a youth football league, hoping to keep those kids occupied (as well as provide them a place to channel all that aggressive energy). It worked. By fall 1929, the four-team Junior Football Conference hit the gridiron, and by 1933 it had expanded to 16 teams. That same year, veteran college football coach Glenn "Pop" Warner moved to Philadelphia to take a job as head coach at Temple University. Tomlin met Warner and asked him to speak at a JFC training clinic. On the day of the clinic, in April 1934, a nasty storm hit Philadelphia, and out of the dozen or so coaches that Tomlin had asked to speak, only Warner showed up. He lectured the 800 young football players who attended (and answered all their questions) for two hours. At the end of the night, Tomlin—following a vote by the players—renamed the league, changing it from the Junior Football Conference to the Pop Warner Conference. By the end of the decade, more than 150 teams were competing in the Pop Warner league, and it soon spread across the country as the "Little League" of football.

THOMAS AND NORMAN HALL

Brothers Thomas and Norman Hall were born in the 1870s to a Lancashire, England, milling family, but they went into business for themselves in 1893, manufacturing and selling jam under the name State Confectionery Works, and later just "Hall Brothers." They were cooking so much of the fruit and sticky-sweet concoctions that by the turn of the century they'd added a line of "boiled sweets"—fruit-and-spice flavored candies made from slow-cooking sugary syrups in copper pots and letting them cool until they hardened. By 1924 those had became profitable, and they dropped jam altogether to focus on hard candies. Two years later, Thomas Hall retired, leaving Norman Hall in charge of the company, and almost immediately he developed a "medicated sweet" to soothe dry and sore throats and coughs, a hard candy flavored with a blend he called "Mentho-lyptus," which combined menthol and eucalyptus extract. These "cough drops," as they were called, remained a regional favorite in Lancashire until the

Must have taken forever: J. R. R. Tolkien typed *The Lord of the Rings* with two fingers.

mid-1960s, when pharmaceutical company Warner-Lambert acquired Hall Brothers solely to set up a medicated sweets division. By 1975 about half of all cough drops sold worldwide were Halls Cough Drops. Today, the Halls line of products accounts for 20 percent of the worldwide medicated sweets market, which technically makes it the biggest candy manufacturer in the world.

J. D. POWER

After graduating from the prestigious Wharton Business School in the 1950s, James David Power worked for the Ford Motor Company and various advertising agencies before he decided to strike out on his own. And in 1968, he formed a market research company called J.D. Power and Associates at his kitchen table. (The only other "associates" at the time: his wife, Julie, and their three kids.) Power had important connections from his previous careers, and within two years, had signed on Toyota and Carnation as clients. What did he do? He conducted surveys about brand recognition, company perception, and customer satisfaction. He provided those services for all kinds of companies, but found a niche in 1981 with his exhaustive U.S. Automotive Customer Satisfaction Index Study. Car companies signed up (and paid) to be a part of it, both to learn about how consumers felt about their products...and because they could boast about it if they got high marks. In 1984 Subaru ran a Super Bowl commercial that highlighted its stellar performance in the J.D. Power rankings...the first of more than 300,000 car ads to do so.

FRANCESCO BERTOLLI

In 1865 Francesco Bertolli and his wife, Caterina, noticed a storefront open on the ground floor of their apartment building in the Tuscan city of Lucca, Italy. They opened a little grocery shop (today it would be called a "gourmet foods store") selling local staples, mostly cheese, wine, olives, and, most of all, extra virgin olive oil, which Bertolli acquired from local farmers and bottled himself. Bertolli's operation grew to be very successful, even as scores of Tuscans moved away in the explosive boom of emigration to the United States in the late 19th century. In the predominantly Italian neighborhoods that developed in major East Coast cities, particularly New York, Tuscans asked the operators of local Italian markets and delis to see if they could import Bertolli's oil...because they couldn't find any decent stuff (vital to traditional Italian cooking) in America. Bertolli soon shifted his business from retail olive oil sales in Italy to exporting olive oil to the United States. Bertolli's children took over the family business in the 1890s, and "Bertolli" became synonymous with olive oil, because for decades, it was the only major brand available in the United States.

The venom from a Japanese giant hornet can dissolve human flesh.

BUTT PLAY

What happens when pro athletes don't use their heads? Crazy plays like these.

THE BUTT FUMBLE

During a nationally televised prime-time football game against the New England Patriots on Thanksgiving 2012, the New York Jets' Mark Sanchez lined up for a first and 10 play, with his team down 14–0. He called for a fullback handoff in the huddle, but after taking the snap, Sanchez went left while his fullback went (correctly) to the right. Quickly realizing he had to salvage the broken play, Sanchez scrambled toward the line of scrimmage and ran face-first into the butt of his offensive lineman Brandon Moore. The collision was so powerful that Sanchez fumbled the ball, leading to a 32-yard touchdown return by the Patriots. The Jets would go on to lose 49–19, and this fumble became a symbol of the rapid end of the Jets' Mark Sanchez era. After his first two seasons resulted in appearances in the AFC Championship Game, the player once known as "the Sanchize" was released in 2013.

THE BUTT SLIDE

With his team already down by four runs in the first inning, Houston Astros shortstop Jonathan Villar tried stretching a single into a double during a 2013 game. Bad decision. Cincinnati Reds second baseman Brandon Phillips caught the throw from the outfield with plenty of time to spare, allowing him to coolly do a through-the-legs tag to get Villar out. For whatever reason—perhaps realizing how dumb his decision was—Villar pulled up from his headfirst slide at the last moment. But with the full force of his body heading toward second base, Villar's face collided straight into Phillips's rear end. The Astros were one of the worst teams in baseball that year and Villar's slide, looking less like a baseball play than an audition for a reboot of *The Human Centipede*, was widely considered one of the worst plays of the season.

THE BUTT INTERCEPTION

During a December 2017 game between the Atlanta Falcons and the New Orleans Saints, Falcons quarterback Matt Ryan threw a pass to receiver Marvin Hall as he crossed the middle of the field. Saints cornerback Marshon Lattimore was a step behind Hall and dove helplessly at him. But his miss wound up being a key play, because while Lattimore was lying facedown on the field, Hall bobbled the pass in the

The average American uses twice as much toilet paper (and water) per day than the average European.

air and it ended up landing in the crook of Lattimore's butt and legs. And because it never touched the ground, it was considered a live ball. Two of Lattimore's teammates immediately dove at his butt in an attempt to intercept the ball, but somehow it was Lattimore who rolled over and made the interception, which turned out to be the pivotal play in the Saints' victory. Lattimore went on to win the NFL's Defensive Rookie of the Year award.

THE BUTT PASS

During a 2016 basketball game, the Atlanta Hawks' big man, Josh Smith, got poked in the eye while defending a made basket. With no foul called by the refs and no time-out called by his unsympathetic coach, most of Smith's teammates ran down the court while Smith was under the basket, doubled over in pain. With nobody else there to take the inbound pass and the clock counting down, inbounder Andrew Goudelock bounced the ball off Smith's butt and scooped it up in order to avoid a five-second violation turnover. (Nice play.)

THE BUTT GOAL

In one of the weirdest NHL goals ever, Phoenix Coyotes goalie Mike Smith's butt crossed the plane of his goal line with the puck stuck in his pants. Here's what happened in this 2013 game. During overtime, the Buffalo Sabres' Mark Pysyk took a shot on goal. Smith blocked it, sending the puck flying into the air. When it came down, the puck somehow landed just where Smith tucked his jersey into his pants, and remained there as he backed up into his own goal. Pysyk saw the whole thing and pointed it out to the referee, who gave the Sabres the victory.

* * *

EIGHT CELEBRITIES WITH THE MIDDLE NAME "LYNN"

Jennifer Lynn Lopez
Stevie Lynn Nicks
Teri Lynn Hatcher
Jennifer Lynn Connelly
Bonnie Lynn Raitt
Vanessa Lynn Williams
Debra Lynn Messing
Jeff Lynn Goldblum

A peach is a *natiform*—it resembles the human buttocks.

THE SINISTER WORLD OF CYBERCRIME

With all the headlines about hackers who spread viruses or steal data, everyone is now aware of the existence of cybercrime—crimes perpetrated by use of computer or the internet. But have you heard of these shocking cyber invasions? They sound like they're straight out of a science fiction or crime thriller…but unfortunately, they're real.

NO ONE IS SAFE

As computer and internet use becomes more common across the globe (the number of internet users has now exceeded four billion), the cybercrime rate is accelerating, too. Any computer in the world can be hacked, even if it's offline, and everyone is at risk, even if you don't use a computer. Any database that stores your customer records can be infiltrated by hackers, putting you at risk of identity theft. Criminals have purchased sports cars, obtained drivers' licenses, and undergone expensive surgeries in someone else's name. One teenager in Kentucky discovered that he'd "owned" a $604,000 house in California for years. Cybercrime is so rampant, according to Norton Cybersecurity, that it claimed 978 million victims in 20 countries and netted $172 billion in 2017 alone.

A HACKER HAS NO NAME

For most cybercriminals, it's all about making money, usually by scamming people or ripping off companies. Some—mostly "amateur programmers"—try to make a name for themselves in hacker circles, some prey on people through cyberbullying or blackmail, and in rare cases, cybercriminals terrorize victims in person by stalking or assaulting them.

One of the first, and most chilling, examples of cyberstalking-turned-deadly involved two people from Nashua, New Hampshire, named Amy Boyer and Liam Youens. They went to high school together, but she didn't know him and had no interaction with him after that, as they attended different colleges. But unbeknownst to Boyer, Youens was obsessed with her and had been since middle school. He published two public websites dedicated to Boyer…and his hatred of her. On his main site, he wrote about wanting to murder her: "Looks like it's suicide for me. Car accident? Wrists? A few days later I think, 'hey, why don't I kill her too?'" Then he detailed exactly how he'd do it. It's not known whether anyone read the site; if so, they didn't report it. Youens bought information about Boyer—her birth date, Social Security number, and home and work addresses. On October 15, 1999, he went to her workplace and followed through with his savage plan, shooting her and then himself.

The fact that Boyer's cyberstalker went undiscovered isn't unusual. Most

The site of Julius Caesar's assassination in 44 BC is now a no-kill animal shelter for cats.

cybercriminals are evasive. "Hackers tend to be faceless, nameless, indeed, anonymous," writes tech journalist Amanda Schupak. It's difficult for authorities to track them down, and because they may reside anywhere in the world, bringing them to justice is nearly impossible. Of the estimated 2.5 million U.S. cyberstalking incidents from 2010 to 2013, the Department of Justice prosecuted only ten cases.

"YES, I'M OPRAH"

A more common cybercrime is identity fraud, which claimed nearly 17 million U.S. victims in 2017. One of the most outrageous cases, involving a Brooklyn busboy named Abraham Abdallah, occurred in 2000. Although identity theft has been around for centuries, it surged around that time with the rise of computers. That's because electronic databases store a wealth of personal data, and for the first time, access to those databases through the anonymity of the internet made it possible for any hacker to pose as someone else.

Abdallah didn't pose as random people, though; he impersonated famous ones. In an operation that the NYPD called the biggest identity theft in internet history, Abdallah used public library computers (and his own ingenuity) to hijack the accounts of America's richest people. Choosing his victims from a dog-eared copy of the *Forbes* issue listing the 400 richest Americans, Abdallah was able to find their Social Security numbers, phone numbers, mothers' maiden names, and other bits of personal data, which he jotted down in the magazine, next to each celebrity he targeted. Among his victims were Warren Buffett, Steven Spielberg, Martha Stewart, Michael Bloomberg, and Oprah Winfrey.

Here's how the scam worked:

- Sometimes pretending to be the millionaires, other times posing as their financial advisers, Abdallah called his victims' banks to gather information about them.
- Using forged corporate letterheads with official-looking stamps from Wall Street companies, he convinced credit bureaus that he worked for Merrill Lynch and Goldman Sachs. Credit agencies sent him celebrities' credit reports with account info.
- This was key: Using a high-tech phone with internet access, Abdallah set up virtual voicemail and e-fax accounts in his victims' names. Each account had a different area code, depending on where the victim lived. He then created a greeting, pretending to be the celebrity. (Before remote-access voicemail, the scammer would have needed separate mobile phones for every victim.)
- Through anonymous e-mail accounts, Abdallah requested that funds in the millionaires' bank accounts be transferred to new accounts that he'd set up. And he left a callback number. If banks called to verify the transactions, Abdallah

Porpoise comes from a French word that means "pig fish."

intercepted the message remotely and returned the call. In almost all cases, he was able to convince banks that he was the account owner.

- In addition to trying to steal their money, Abdallah used victims' credit cards to rent P.O. boxes and buy goods that were later shipped to those boxes.
- To further help evade authorities, he hired couriers to pick up and deliver packages to him.

Thanks to his meticulous planning, Abdallah was able to steal the identities of 217 wealthy people, from whom he attempted to snatch $80 million. "He's the best I've ever faced," said NYPD detective Michael Fabozzi, who specializes in computer crimes. "You rarely run into someone this good." But Abdallah got greedy. A request for a single transfer of $10 million set investigators on his trail, and the hunt ended when Detective Fabozzi nabbed him in 2001. The arrest was like a scene from an action movie. Abdallah jumped in his car and tried to drive away, but Fabozzi leaped on top of the car and dove headfirst through the open sunroof. He wrangled and handcuffed Abdallah while still upside down with his feet poking through the roof. Result: the scammer got 11 years in the slammer.

INFORMATION AT YOUR FINGERTIPS

As technology has evolved, so has cybercrime. Consider biometric identification, which sounded like science fiction not that long ago. Biometrics are physical characteristics that are uniquely yours, such as fingerprints, facial or iris structure, or the configuration of veins in your palm. Someone can create a biometric identity by, for example, scanning their fingerprint into a computer system, which stores the data. Each time they need access to a secure device or area, they provide a fingerprint that the computer system then compares to one in its database and allows (or prevents) entry. Biometric identification is convenient and easy to use. Perhaps you already swipe your finger to make PayPal payments on your phone. Or you place your palm on a reader to give high-tech hospitals instant access to your health history. In Europe, some ATMs now use fingerprints instead of PIN numbers, and some banks are inviting customers to submit a selfie photo that can be used to authorize digital transactions. Of course, these developments also create opportunities for hackers.

WHAT COULD POSSIBLY GO WRONG?

Biometric authentication is supposed to improve security and reduce cybercrime. Yet it may actually have the opposite effect by establishing biometrics databases…some of which have already been hacked. In 2015 hackers (with possible ties to China) penetrated the U.S. Office of Personnel Management (OPM) and stole files containing fingerprints of 5.6 million federal employees and job applicants. If you're wondering why the U.S. government, which spent $28 billion on cybersecurity in 2016, can't keep pace with hackers, the answer is simple: It isn't a fair fight. To fully protect a

Roald Dahl almost called his book *James and the Giant Cherry*.

network, IT teams must constantly find and patch every new vulnerability that arises. But it takes only one cyber invader exploiting a single hole to jeopardize an entire organization. The worst part about the OPM data leak? Some of the victims were probably U.S. intelligence officers, and the thieves (China) may be able to identify American spies overseas by comparing their prints to the stolen records. And unlike passwords, stolen fingerprints and other biometric data can never be changed, which means they'll never be safe to use for security purposes. Even if thieves don't have the ability to replicate a fingerprint yet, they'll simply hang on to the data until they do.

SCAMMERS GET SKIMMERS

In addition to hacking into databases, cybercriminals steal credit card data using devices called skimmers. You've probably heard about card skimmers that copy information from a card's magnetic stripe. Criminals install them over the card slots at ATMs and gas pumps, and customers use them unwittingly. Now fraudsters are working on next-generation skimmers to capture people's biometric data.

Fingerprint readers, like the ones on Apple devices, encrypt the data to protect it in case the machine is stolen. Theoretically, cybercriminals could trick people into using a skimmer that saves the raw data, perhaps by installing the skimmer over the fingerprint sensor at an ATM. In 2016 cybersecurity experts at Kaspersky Lab were surprised to discover that criminals were further ahead in this con than they expected. Twelve sellers already offer fingerprint skimmers, and three manufacturers are attempting to make fake palm and iris scanners. Using your biometric data, criminals could produce a high-quality model of your finger to unlock your device or provide digital access to your company's assets. Researchers have already re-created fingerprints using molded gelatin or Play-Doh, and have produced a 3-D replica of a face…all of which has fooled biometric readers.

Right now, there's no proof that criminals are reproducing people's biometrics. It's too time-consuming and expensive for the common crook to manage. However, it's no problem for security researchers, people who figure out how to hack devices and then inform their manufacturers. German computer scientist Jan Krissler, for example, demonstrated in 2013 how to fool the fingerprint sensor of the new iPhone 5S without much equipment. He captured the phone owner's fingerprint from the phone's surface, but he could've easily gotten it from a drinking glass or a doorknob. Using sprayable graphene and wood glue, Krissler created a model of the print and used it to unlock the phone. He figured out how to do this in less than two days. Even more astounding, the next year, Krissler duplicated someone's fingerprints using *photos* of her hands, (taken at different angles with a standard camera), plus some commercially available software. And the fingerprints weren't just anyone's—they belonged to Ursula von der Leyen, Germany's minister of defense.

For more ways that the Web enables cybercriminals, surf over to page 348.

Tulips come from Turkey.

SURFER SLANG

Hang ten, moondoggie, and catch a wave of some surfer slang.

Humpback. When a big wave is followed by a smaller wave, and they form into one very big wave.

Goofy foot. Most surfers ride with their left foot in front, and right in the back. Goofy foot is when they ride with the right in front.

Dawn patrol. Going surfing at sunrise.

Barney. An uncool or just plain bad surfer.

Frube. A surfer having such a bad time that he doesn't manage to catch a single wave all day.

Junkyard dog. A surfer with an awkward or unattractive surfing style.

Benny. A non-local, or tourist surfer.

Hodad. Somebody who hangs out on the beach all day but never surfs.

Paddlepuss. A surfer too nervous to swim too far out, and who just paddles themselves around near the shore.

Mushburger. Flat, boring, impossible-to-surf waves that completely lack juice.

A man in a gray suit. A shark. Also called Noah, and the Landlord.

Quiver. A surfer's personal board collection.

Rail bang. When a male surfer wipes out and the surfboard hits him hard… between the legs.

Beach leech. A surfer who doesn't have their own board, and asks to borrow one from another surfer's quiver.

Reef tax. Cuts and bruises endured from surfing into rocks or a reef.

Grommet. A kid surfer.

Grubbing. Wiping out (or falling off a surfboard).

Baggies. Surf shorts.

Sponger. A derisive term for a bodyboarder, or somebody who surfs by lying down on their board instead of standing up.

Gray belly. An old surfer.

Party wave. A tasty wave big enough that it can be surfed by multiple people at the same time.

"Akaw!" "Cool!"

Bomb. A gigantic wave.

Clucked. A surfer who fears bombs.

Juice. A wave's power.

The soup. The ocean.

Ankle buster. A wave that's too small to surf.

Glass job. The fiberglass sheen on a surfboard.

Uh-oh: Nostradamus didn't predict anything beyond the year 3797.

DO YOUR RESEARCH!

We at the BRI take pride in being researchers. Immersing yourself in a subject is essential if you want to accurately convey it to an audience. That counts with acting, too. Here are four odd stories about actors and how they prepared for their roles…to varying degrees of success.

WOLFERINE

When Hugh Jackman showed up on the set of X-Men in 1999, the 31-year-old Aussie was so excited to be playing Wolverine that he decided to show off how much he knew about wolves. He started slinking around with his head down, sniffing everything and everyone in a very menacing manner.

> *"What are you doing?" asked the director.*
> *"Yeah, man, I've been studying wolves and I think we can bring that to the screen!"*
> *"What? You're not a wolf, man. You're a wolverine!"*
> *Jackman laughed. "Yeah, but obviously there's no such thing as a wolverine."*

And then, in front of everyone, the actor got a quick biology lesson: wolverines are real animals (native to North America), and they are not "little wolves." Even worse: Jackman didn't need to study any mammal. The only things that Wolverine and a wolverine have in common are sharp claws and a reputation for being fierce. Otherwise, the adamantium-clawed, mutton-chopped mutant shares no traits with the largest member of the Mustelid family, which also includes weasels and ferrets. In Jackman's defense, as he later explained on promotional press junkets, "I'd never read an X-men comic, I'd never seen an actual wolverine. We don't have them in our zoos." (But he did spend three weeks studying everything there is to know about wolves, so there's that.)

ON A DIFFERENT PLANE

If you were going to play a fighter jet pilot in a movie, it might be a good idea to study up on piloting—unless it's an animated movie and you're a voice actor. Then you simply read the lines they wrote for you and act like you know what you're talking about. That would be enough for most actors, but not Holly Hunter. When she was voicing Helen "Elastigirl" Parr in 2004's The Incredibles, her character had to fly a fighter jet. Only this wasn't in the script. (Spoilers ahead.) Originally, another character—Helen's old friend, Snug—was going to fly the plane and then die when it crashes into the ocean. When Helen and the kids land safely in the water, she would see her old friend perish, creating a very sad moment, and propelling the plot forward.

George Washington owned dogs named Madame Moose, Drunkard, and Sweetlips.

One problem: the animators were running behind, so they asked director Brad Bird if maybe Helen could fly the plane instead…and not die. They explained that it would take them too long to design and cast a major character who was only going to get a few minutes of screen time. Bird agreed, and all of a sudden, Snug was out and Helen was a fighter pilot.

Hunter, who played an air-traffic controller in *Always* (1989), and whose uncle was a commander in the U.S. Air Force, was determined to get it right. She read flight manuals and met with fighter pilots and learned what all the terms meant, even down to the correct inflections.

So next time you're watching that scene in *The Incredibles* when Helen is desperately trying to outfly the cruise missiles, take a moment to marvel at how realistic she sounds when says into the radio, "Friendlies at two-zero miles south-southwest of your position. Angels 10. Track east. Disengage!" Then check out the next scene, where Helen would have watched her friend die. It had already been completed when they edited Snug out of the script—which is why in the final film, she seems really, really upset at the sight of an empty plane sinking into the sea.

Bonus Trivia: Brad Bird paid homage to his 1999 directorial debut *Iron Giant* by making Helen's pilot call sign IG-99 (India Golf Niner-Niner).

WHAT'S A PENGWING?

How does a top-tier nature program get a top-tier actor to narrate and then botch something as simple as the pronunciation of penguin? The show was an episode of the BBC's *South Pacific*, which aired in 2009, and the narrator was Benedict Cumberbatch. Everything about the documentary is normal until the renowned British actor gets to a line like, "A freshwater stream through the forest makes a handy highway for a parent pengwing on its way home." What's a pengwing? That was the number-one question from Cumberbatch's fans when he appeared on the *Graham Norton Show* in 2014. An embarrassed Cumberbatch was quick to point out that he didn't do the show alone: "There was a team of natural history experts funded by you, the tax-paying public." But seriously, how did they botch it? Apparently, the filmmakers did ask Cumberbatch to say the word again several times, but he just couldn't get it right, "so they just gave up," he said. (No word of explanation for the goof from the BBC.) Good news, though: Cumberbatch knows how to say the word now (he had to learn it for his role in the animated movie…*Penguins*). And even though he can say it, he prefers not to. "Now I'm completely terrified of the word. I don't go near it."

> Apparently, the filmmakers did ask Cumberbatch to say the word again several times, but he just couldn't get it right.

Dragons in Mesoamerican legends have feathers.

HEART TO HEART

Chalk this one up to odd luck. A major plot point of writer/director Adam McKay's 2018 dark comedy *Vice* is the numerous heart attacks suffered by Vice President Dick Cheney. But McKay didn't do a whole lot of research, basically just writing "Dick has a heart attack" wherever necessary in the script. While filming one of those heart attack scenes, Christian Bale, who was portraying Cheney, asked McKay how he wanted him to play it. "What do you mean?" asked McKay. "It's a heart attack. Your arm hurts, right?"

Bale, who *had* done his research, told McKay, "No, no—one of the more common ways is that you get really queasy and your stomach hurts." So that's how they did the scene.

Ironically, while making *Vice*, McKay had his own vices, overeating and smoking too much. So, several pounds overweight, he hit the home gym hard after filming wrapped. On his third workout, "I get tingly hands and my stomach starts going queasy," he told *Deadline Hollywood*. At first, he dismissed it, but then he remembered that scene with Bale. "I ran upstairs and downed a bunch of baby aspirin, and I called my wife who immediately called 911. Got to the hospital really fast, and the doctor said, 'Because you did that, no damage was done, your heart is still really strong.' That's because I remembered Christian Bale telling me that."

* * *

A RANDOM BIT OF FACTINESS

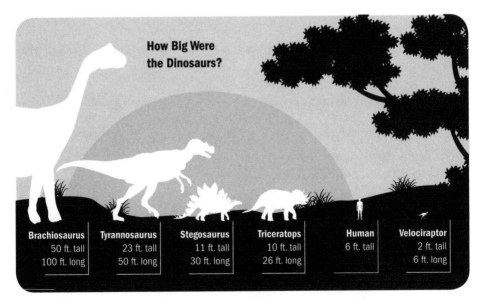

How Big Were the Dinosaurs?

Brachiosaurus	Tyrannosaurus	Stegosaurus	Triceratops	Human	Velociraptor
50 ft. tall	23 ft. tall	11 ft. tall	10 ft. tall	6 ft. tall	2 ft. tall
100 ft. long	50 ft. long	30 ft. long	26 ft. long		6 ft. long

Sour-sensing taste buds also detect the fizz in soda.

LOST AWARD SHOWS

Every year, dozens of awards shows hit the air—the Grammys, Emmys, Oscars, Golden Globes, American Music Awards, ad infinitum. While it's a crowded field, it used to be even more crowded. Here are some awards shows that got the prize for "best disappearing act."

CABLEACE AWARDS (1978–1997)

Today, cable TV shows dominate the Emmy Awards—the last network TV show that won the prize Emmy for Best Drama Series was *24*, in 2006. But up until 1988, cable shows weren't eligible for an Emmy, so a cable TV trade group made up its own awards show, the CableACE Awards. Airing on as many as 12 different channels all at once, they honored the best performances on cable-only shows at the time. CNN generally won in the news and public affairs categories, while premium services such as HBO and Showtime dominated the entertainment fields. Still, there wasn't enough good stuff on HBO and Showtime to fill out all the categories. In 1987, for example, Stuart Pankin won Best Actor in a Comedy Series for his work in HBO's news parody *Not Necessarily the News*, Anthony Hopkins won Best Actor in a Movie or Miniseries for HBO's *Mussolini and I*,… and Gary Busey won Best Actor in a Dramatic Series for his work on the USA late-night horror series *The Hitchhiker*.

FOOD NETWORK AWARDS (2007)

Seeing the success that MTV had enjoyed with its annual MTV Video Music Awards, the Food Network began its own ceremony in 2007. That was also the *last* year the network handed out awards for "Favorite Comfort Food Combo" and inducted someone into the nonexistent "Food Hall of Fame." (The winners were macaroni and cheese, and Julia Child, respectively.)

SCREAM AWARDS (2005–2012)

Film genres like horror, fantasy, and science fiction tend to get ignored by the Oscars, so the cable channel Spike TV (now called the Paramount Network) took it upon themselves to come up with a ceremony to honor those kinds of movies. Over the years, it also gave awards to TV shows and comic books. Some of the bigger categories included "Most Vile Villain" and "Scene of the Year," for the scariest film moment, which was called the "Holy Sh!t" award.

AMERICAN TELEVISION AWARDS (1993)

While TV industry professionals voted on the Emmys, this awards ceremony's voting base was TV critics. The 1993 nominations were almost identical to that year's Emmys. (For example, *Seinfeld* beat *Cheers* and *Murphy Brown* for Best Situation Comedy Series.) That redundancy is probably what killed the ATAs; the awards were canceled after the first year.

VH1 / *VOGUE* FASHION AWARDS (1995–2002)

In the 1990s, "supermodels" were a cultural phenomenon. No longer anonymous human billboards for chic and expensive clothes, they were celebrated like rock stars. That visibility also increased the celebrity of the fashion designers, such as Alexander McQueen, Todd Oldham, and Isaac Mizrahi. Because MTV had a successful award show in its annual Video Music Awards, network execs wanted its sister network, VH1, to have one too. So, in 1995, it teamed up with *Vogue* magazine to create the VH1/*Vogue* Fashion Awards. Categories included Designer of the Year, Model of the Year, Avant Garde Designer of the Year, and awards for fashionable celebrities and musicians. Oddly enough, the most enduring aspect of these awards was something that made fun of the world they celebrated: Ben Stiller's beyond-dumb male model character Derek Zoolander, who debuted in a sketch produced for the 1996 iteration of the show.

* * *

MAR-A-LAGO

When the Post Cereal heiress Marjorie Merriweather Post died in 1973, she bequeathed Mar-a-Lago (Spanish for "Sea-to-lake"), her Florida estate, to the federal government for use as a site for state visits by foreign dignitaries or a winter White House for U.S. presidents. She also left a sum of money to provide for the upkeep of the estate, but it wasn't enough to cover the actual costs of running the place. President Richard Nixon helicoptered in to look at it about a week before he resigned from office in August 1974, but neither he nor President Jimmy Carter were interested in using it. In 1981 the U.S. Congress passed legislation to return Mar-a-Lago to the Post estate. Donald Trump bought it from the Post estate in 1985…and turned it into his winter White House after he was elected president in 2016.

HERE COMES FERRY McFERRYFACE!

What happens when a gung-ho politician secretly ignores the will of the people and then his secret gets out? Let's go Down Under and find out.

BACKGROUND

In our 31st edition—*Uncle John's Actual and Factual Bathroom Reader*—we wrote about a public naming competition that nearly led to a British Royal Research Ship being called *Boaty McBoatface*. Despite widespread support for the silly name, the ship was rechristened the more dignified RRS *Sir David Attenborough*. (A submarine on the ship was named *Boaty McBoatface* to placate complainers.) The story made lots of press and inspired several copycats from all over the world (examples: Horsey McHorseface, Vloggy McVlogface, Trainy McTrainface, and Salty McSaltface).

That brings us to this particular "Facey McFaceface" tale, and it's the oddest of them all.

CONSTANCE McCONSTANCEFACE

In November 2017, New South Wales transport minister Andrew Constance held a naming competition for a new ferry coming to Sydney Harbour. A few weeks later he announced that, after receiving 15,000 suggestions, the winner was…*Ferry McFerryface*. "This one is for the kids," he beamed.

If Constance thought that Aussies would love the name, just as the Brits loved *Boaty McBoatface*, he was sorely mistaken. A representative from the Maritime Union of Australia called it "disrespectful" and "insulting." The union even threatened to not work on the ferry until the name was changed. The public reaction wasn't much better; whereas *Boaty McBoatface* had been a fresh and amusing distraction, by this point the joke had been played out. As one Tweeter put it: "*Ferry McFerryface* is so typically Australian. Take something that the UK did well and make it lame."

Constance stuck to his guns, and the words *Ferry McFerryface* were printed on the ship (in a really tacky typeface, too). He admitted that the name might not be "everyone's cup of tea, but the people voted for it so we listened." They held a welcoming ceremony to launch *Ferry McFerryface* with kids and balloons (and probably some grumbling dock workers).

Then came the rumors that the ship was cursed.

Veterinarians are three times more likely than the general public to have contemplated suicide.

MEET WHARFY McWHARFFACE

> Luckily, neither wharf nor ferry suffered serious damage, but everyone agreed: that name had to change.

It's uncertain whether *Ferry McFerryface* was actually cursed, but the ship did slam into a wharf in early 2018. Luckily, neither wharf nor ferry suffered serious damage, but everyone agreed: that name had to change. Luckily, the process was already underway. Constance decided to rechristen the ferry *May Gibbs*. Gibbs, who died in 1969, was a beloved Australian children's author, best known for her 1918 book *Snugglepot and Cuddlepie* (so it's a good bet she would have approved of *Ferry McFerryface*). But the story doesn't end there.

LIAR McLIARFACE

This whole story seemed a bit fishy, so Sydney's *9News* conducted an investigation. After they obtained documents from the transport minister's office (thanks to Australia's Freedom of Information Act), the shocking truth came out: *Ferry McFerryface* wasn't really the winner of the naming contest. It wasn't even close, *McFerryface* having received only 182 votes compared to the 2,205 votes for the actual winner: *Ian Kiernan*, the name of a renowned environmentalist who founded Clean Up Australia. You know who was really upset? Ian Kiernan. "I was greatly honored to have been considered to have my name on it," he said, "but then to turn it to something like *Ferry McFerryface* was a big disappointment." (It turned out that *Ferry McFerryface* didn't even get as many votes in Constance's rigged vote as *Boaty McBoatface*.)

McFACE THE MUSIC...FACE

When confronted, Constance confessed to making a "captain's choice" and picking *Ferry McFerryface* himself. Why? He was hoping the silly name would make the ferry a tourist attraction. He also defended choosing *May Gibbs* over *Ian Kiernan* because naming it for a kids' author will "retain the vessel's appeal to our youngest customers while also recognizing an Australian icon with a long connection to Sydney."

"He flat out lied about the competition, repeatedly saying *Ferry McFerryface* was the popular choice when he knew it was anything but," argued opposition lawmaker Jodi McKay, who called on the embattled transportation minister to resign. He didn't.

After the boat was officially rechristened, Constance explained that *Ferry McFerryface* had merely been a "summer name," and that *May Gibbs* would be its "forever name." Still not happy: Ian Kiernan.

What's petrichor? The name for the pleasant smells outside after a fresh rain.

THE MYSTERY OF THE CRYSTAL SKULL

A strange fad emerged in the early 20th century: Life-size facsimiles of human skulls carved from clear quartz crystal began showing up in the collections of museums and wealthy treasure hunters. Purported to have magical powers, these crystal skulls came with action-packed accounts of their discoveries and otherworldly tales of their origins. But who made them? When, where, and how were they made? And for what purpose? That's the mystery. Here's the story of the most fascinating of them all—the Mitchell-Hedges skull.

THE PLACE OF THE FALLEN STONES

British Honduras, 1924: Intrepid British adventurer F. A. Mitchell-Hedges is exploring the ruins of the lost Mayan city of Lubaantun, which means "Place of Fallen Stones." Joining him on the expedition is his adopted daughter Anna. It's her 17th birthday. While the rest of Mitchell-Hedges's team is taking a siesta, Anna climbs to the top of a pyramid to get a view of the ocean. But something at her feet catches her eye—there's a light emanating from a hole in the stones. She crouches down and peers into the dark room, and there, under a crumbled altar, is a glowing human skull made of clear quartz crystal. Anna runs back down the pyramid as fast as she can, yelling for her father to come see what she found. Later, they lower Anna—the smallest member of the team—via a rope into the room. She picks up the heavy artifact and can immediately feel its power.

The local Mayans later tell Mitchell-Hedges that if the government finds out about their discovery, the crystal skull will be confiscated, so they give the father and daughter permission to take it out of the country.

THE SKULL OF DOOM

That's one story of where this particular crystal skull came from. There are other stories, and other skulls: one is on display in the Musée du Quai Branly in Paris; another lives in the archives of the Smithsonian Museum in Washington, D.C. Since the late 19th century, the true nature of these Mesoamerican artifacts has been a source of heated debate—and the most controversial is the Mitchell-Hedges skull. The first big question: Who made it? Theories range from the ancient Mayans to cultures that predate them (such as people who traveled to Central America from the lost city of Atlantis). There are even claims that the crystal skulls were deposited on Earth by aliens.

F. A. Mitchell-Hedges first referred to his as the "Skull of Doom," the power of which he said could "kill a man." And even though he said he wanted to be buried with

English king Edward I hated air pollution so much that in 1285 he banned coal.

it, when he died in 1959 it became the property of his daughter, Anna, and she wasn't sure what to do with it. "It is a thing of evil in the wrong hands," she said at the time.

AXIS OF POWER

In 1964 Anna Mitchell-Hedges lent the crystal skull to a San Francisco art conservator named Frank Dorland in the hopes of finding out where it came from. "The first time I kept the skull in my home overnight," Dorland told author Richard Garvin in his book *The Crystal Skull,* "I was awakened by unusual noises. It sounded like a large jungle cat was prowling through the house, accompanied by the sound of chimes and bells. When we got up the next morning, our possessions were strewn all about the house. Yet, all the doors and windows were still closed and locked from the inside."

The skull spent six years in the care of Dorland, who, like others who have owned it, became obsessed with it. After studying the artifact in his lab, Dorland theorized that it was carved not from one but from three crystals. But he needed better equipment to prove it, so he took the skull to Hewlett-Packard's crystal labs in Santa Clara, California. Initial tests determined that it is comprised of a *single* crystal, but that's about the only conclusive thing they were able to find.

- It appeared that whoever made the thing did it in "total disregard to the natural crystal axis," said Dorland. If you carve against the axis, the crystal should shatter, or, as one crystallographer put it, "The damn thing shouldn't even be."
- The HP techs could find no microscopic indications of cut marks made by metal instruments, so exactly how it was made remained a mystery.
- Further tests determined that the skull was probably polished by hand with sand over a period of time using "300 man-years of effort."

By that point (around 1970), Anna Mitchell-Hedges had had enough of scientific studies. She took a Greyhound bus to California, retrieved her crystal skull from Dorland, and never let scientists near it for the rest of her life.

GOOD VIBRATIONS

Mitchell-Hedges settled in Kitchener, Ontario, where she opened a motel and made the crystal skull available for viewing—for a nominal fee—to curiosity-seekers and spiritualists. She'd tell her visitors that the skull was once the property of the High Priest of the Maya, that it had the power to "cause visions and cure cancer," and could even "be used to transfer the knowledge of an elder to a younger person." Right before President John F. Kennedy was assassinated, she said, the skull turned cloudy. She would invite her customers to touch the object, explaining that it always has a surface temperature of 70° Fahrenheit, no matter how cold or warm the room was. A visiting reporter once wrote that the skull is "strangely luminous, reflecting a piercing blue-white light from its eye sockets."

"Bergy bits" and "growlers" are scientific slang terms for small icebergs.

And it wasn't the "Skull of Doom" anymore. "That was one of my father's jokes," said Mitchell-Hedges. He'd said it was evil in the hopes of deterring would-be robbers. She called it the "Skull of Love." And it got a whole new lease on life thanks to the burgeoning New Age movement in the 1970s and '80s. "Peter O'Toole once sat with it for four hours," she told a reporter in 1996, "right over there on the carpet—he wanted to lie down." Mitchell-Hedges also bragged that Shirley MacLaine and William Shatner had made the trek to her motel to bask in its power. Science-fiction author Arthur C. Clarke called the Mitchell-Hedges crystal skull "the weirdest gem in the world."

RETURN TO LUBAANTUN

In 1981, when Mitchell-Hedges was 74 years old, she received a call from Bill Homann, a fellow adventurer and a huge admirer of her father. She and Homann became friends, and she later moved in with him in Indiana. In 1989 and again in 1996, they went back to British Honduras (now called Belize) to retrace the footsteps of the 1924 expedition. And in 2002, they were married. (She was 40 years older than him; he explained that they did it so she could be added to his health insurance plan.) For the last eight years of Anna's life, Homann was her primary caregiver and, as he told the *Illinois Times*, "She is my mentor and spiritual leader."

Anna died in 2007 at 100 years old. She attributed her long life to the skull, often telling people, "I take care of it, and it takes care of me." After a brief but contentious custody battle with the Mitchell-Hedges family, the skull was put in Homann's care.

SCREEN GEM

In 2008 Homann was the subject of the Sci-Fi Channel documentary *Mysteries of the Crystal Skull*. Here's how *TV Guide* described it: *Glimmers of ancient civilizations and lost worlds have forever intrigued and tantalized but few ancient mysteries generate quite the fervor of the Crystal Skulls: 13 quartz crystal human skulls, now scattered to the four winds, discovered amid ruins of Mayan and Aztec societies. Legend tells us that should they ever be united, they may unleash untold energy, revealing secrets vital to the survival of humankind.*

The documentary, presented by NBC newsman Lester Holt, followed Homann through dense jungles to Mayan ruins, scuba diving and spelunking, searching for another crystal skull (to no avail). That was only one of several documentaries that aired that year, all trying to cash in on *Indiana Jones and the Kingdom of the Crystal Skull*. The movie follows Indiana Jones to the Amazon jungle in Peru as he looks for a crystal skull, described as "a mind weapon, a new frontier of psychic warfare." Despite lukewarm reviews, the movie grossed nearly $800 million worldwide. All of a sudden, crystal skulls were all over the news. And then, a few months later when the hype died down, they were gone again.

Until December 2012—that was the month that the world was supposed to end, at least according to the ancient Mayan "Long Count" calendar. The only thing that would keep planet Earth from "falling off its axis," claimed the true believers, was for all 13 crystal skulls to be reunited at a sacred Mayan site.

HEAD CASE

Of all the weird news stories related to that "prophecy" in 2012, one of the weirdest was the report of a lawsuit filed on behalf of Dr. Jaime Awe, director of the Institute of Archaeology of Belize. Awe was suing the Mitchell-Hedges estate, demanding they "return the artifact to the people of Belize." Also being sued were Lucasfilm, Walt Disney Pictures, and Paramount for a cut of the "illegal profits" generated by the stolen skull. "Lucasfilm never sought, nor was given permission to utilize the Mitchell-Hedges Skull or its likeness in the Film," wrote Adam Tracy, the lawyer who filed the suit. When asked by *LiveScience* if the skull is genuine, Tracy answered, "The government of Belize does not believe the skull is fake. As such, I do not foresee any further testing of the artifact."

There were a few problems with this lawsuit from the outset. For one, the crystal skull in the movie doesn't have that much in common with the Mitchell-Hedges skull—it's larger, milkier in color, and it was found in South America, not Central America. Indiana Jones himself even backs this up in this line of dialogue from the movie: "It isn't anything like the Mitchell-Hedges skull. Look at the cranium—how it's elongated at the back." Another problem: the government of Belize was never in possession of the artifact in the first place, so it didn't have much legal footing.

But the biggest problem with Dr. Awe's lawsuit was that Dr. Awe himself didn't know anything about it! After it was reported in nearly every major news outlet worldwide (that's what first drew us to this story), Awe said he was approached by some people who told him they could get the skull back, but he told them he wasn't interested. It turned out that the lawsuit wasn't even filed in Belize, but in Chicago by Eyezzon Productions. It was a publicity stunt. The organizers—including Awe's supposed lawyer—were planning to hold a concert on December 21, 2012, in Xunantunich, another Maya site in Belize. The newly returned Mitchell-Hedges crystal skull would be revealed at the end of the concert, and the world would be saved…or something like that. The event never happened. There was very little chance that Belize's government would ever issue permits for a huge concert to be held at one of their most sensitive and culturally significant sites. As for Dr. Awe—he's a respected archaeologist with a reputation to maintain. He said he wished to "disassociate" himself from the lawsuit. Besides, he said, he doesn't even think the crystal skull comes from Belize.

The crystal skull mystery continues on page 329.

An acre of peanuts yields enough peanut butter for 30,000 peanut butter sandwiches.

YOUR FAVORITE MALL IS NOW...

There aren't as many shopping malls as there used to be. Hundreds of malls have completely gone out of business, but their gigantic concrete husks remain standing. What's to be done with these "dead malls"? Plenty.

...A COMMUNITY COLLEGE

When it opened in 1971, the 1.2-million-square-foot Highland Mall was the first big shopping center in suburban Austin, Texas. By 2010 its major tenant was the administrative offices of Austin Community College. The following year, the school bought the rest of the mall and surrounding land it didn't already occupy. Then, with the help of an architecture firm, it remodeled stores to suit its needs. Today the former JCPenney is home to a library, several classrooms, and a computer center with more than 600 terminals, and the site of a Dillard's department store is now a data hosting center where ACC students can earn internship credit.

...A PARK

Columbus City Center, located in the downtown district of Ohio's capital city, was a monster: 1.25 million square feet and three floors of shopping. As many as 144 tenants opened shop in the mall between 1989 and 2009, by which time only eight stores remained in operation. As of 2011, the City Center is now Columbus Commons. Most of the retail space was razed to make way for a multiuse, open-air park with an old-fashioned carousel, gardens, green spaces, a playground, and a stage for free concerts and exercise classes. It sits on top of the last vestige of the mall: an underground parking garage.

...A PUBLIC SERVICES COMPLEX

Jackson Mall, a 900,000-square-foot behemoth, was the first (and largest) shopping center in Mississippi's capital city. But when other malls started opening up nearby, anchor stores moved out, and by 1995, the Jackson Mall was nearly dead. That's when a local pediatrician, Dr. Aaron Shirley, got the inspiration to turn it into the Jackson Medical Mall, a medical complex for low-income members of the community. The complex opened in 1997, and today is home to numerous specialty clinics, a college of public service, a community meeting hall, and Mississippi's first African American–owned bank.

The human brain can read as many as 1,000 words a minute. Most people top out at 200.

...A BUNCH OF CHURCHES

The Euclid Square Mall opened in suburban Cleveland in 1977, home to a Higbee's, May Co., Toys "R" Us, Red Lobster, and hundreds of other tenants over the years. By 2013 so many stores had closed or moved out that the mall was almost empty. So 24 local Christian churches that weren't large enough or financially stable enough to afford a standalone building moved in. (Unfortunately, they all had to find other options when the City of Euclid, citing safety concerns over the rotten mall, closed the center down in 2016 and demolished it the following year.)

...AN APARTMENT COMPLEX

When the Westminster Arcade opened in Providence, Rhode Island, in 1828 (yes, 1828), it was America's first indoor shopping mall. The Greek Revival building sported three floors of high-end clothing boutiques for the New England elite of the era. It was also America's longest-lived mall, closing for good in 2008. If you stroll through the former mall's main open areas today, instead of stores, you'll find apartments. Construction companies renovated the mall's stores into 48 fully furnished "micro-apartments," which range in size from 225 to 775 square feet. (Cost: as much as $1,800 per month.) The building is also a self-contained town, with a handful of restaurants, a coffee shop, and a hair salon.

...GOOGLE

Big retail hubs provide a lot of jobs...most of which disappear when those malls decline and close. Fortunately for the city of Mountain View, soon after the 1984 closure of Mayfield Mall—the first enclosed mall in northern California when it opened in 1966—the city became a major pillar of Silicon Valley, the area where dozens of computer and tech companies are headquartered. A few months after the last store moved out, Hewlett-Packard came in and remodeled the Mayfield Mall into its main office building. Years later HP moved out, and in 2013, Google made the former mall the headquarters for its Google Glass project. In 2016, after Google Glass died, the company bought the building outright for $225 million and renamed it "Building RLS1."

*   *   *

THE OLD MAN OF THE SEA

Earth's longest-living mammal species is the bowhead whale, which can live more than 200 years. How old is that? The oldest bowheads living today were born before Herman Melville's book *Moby-Dick* was published in 1850. In 2007 a whale in Alaska was found to have a fragment of a harpoon in its neck that dated back to the 1880s.

Eew-lery: If you wear a ring and never take it off, there may be as many as 730 million germs under there.

TALK OF THE '10s

Here are some more word and phrase origins from the 2010s. Try not to get triggered, snowflake. (The first part is on page 67.)

BINGE-WATCH

Meaning: "Streaming" several episodes of a TV show in one sitting

Story: In rural England in the 1850s, the act of soaking a wooden vessel until it becomes watertight was known as "bingeing." From that came a description of anyone who drank too much liquor as being "on a binge." In the 1910s, the term "binge-drinker" appeared, followed in the 1950s by "binge-eater," and in the 1990s by "binge-reader." The term "binge-watcher" showed up around 2003, though who coined it is unknown. The first "binge-watching parties" came about after entire seasons of shows like *The X-Files* and *Sex and the City* were released on DVD sets.

But it was in the early 2010s—when Netflix transitioned from renting DVDs by mail to streaming TV shows—that the golden age of binge-watching began. In 2013 the term was voted the word "most likely to succeed" by the American Dialect Society, and two years later, the editors of *Collins English Dictionary* named it the 2015 Word of the Year, declaring binge-watching "the biggest sea change in our viewing habits since the advent of the video recorder nearly 40 years ago."

Backlash: Hard to believe, but some people view binge-watching as an unhealthy activity. Indeed, studies have shown that it can negatively affect sleep patterns. But immersing oneself in a story for hours on end is an ancient tradition. "I imagine binge-watching is only a technologically enhanced version of a behavior that has been around, at least in rudimentary form, for at least 50,000 years," Joseph Carroll, a literature professor at the University of Missouri–St. Louis, told *Mashable* in 2019.

Binge-watching is also changing the way TV is being written. *Mad Men* creator Matthew Weiner isn't a fan—he prefers the weekly episode experience. "I love the waiting," he said in 2015. "I love the marination. I think when you watch an entire season of a show in a day, you will definitely dream about it, but it's not the same as walking around the whole week saying, 'God, Pete really pissed me off!'"

SNOWFLAKE

Meaning: Someone who is easily offended

Story: As we reported in *Uncle John's Actual & Factual Bathroom Reader*, Chuck Palahniuk popularized this epithet in his 1996 novel (and subsequent film) *Fight Club*. While preparing for a terror attack, the main character, Tyler Durden, tells his minions, "You are not special. You are not a beautiful and unique snowflake." But

Skunks are immune to yellow jacket venom (but they can die from bee stings).

using "snowflake" as an insult goes back much further than *Fight Club*. According to Merriam-Webster, in the 1860s, Southerners who were pro-slavery were called "snowflakes." The barb resurfaced in the 1970s to describe Caucasians in general, or African Americans who were accused of acting "too white."

The positive meaning of "special little snowflake" goes back to the 1960s, but it really came to the fore in the '80s when the phrase started appearing in self-help, meditation, and teaching manuals—such as this passage from 1983's *Inside America's Christian Schools* by Paul F. Parsons about a teacher who "pointed out that God not only made every snowflake different but that every person is unique, too."

The 1990s is when savvy social commentators like Palahniuk began using it to mean "overly sensitive," and "snowflake" was lumped in with phrases like "helicopter parent" and "soccer mom." The word's popularity peaked in 2016, when the *Guardian* called it that year's "defining insult." They tracked down Palanhiuk to ask him if he thought "snowflake" is still as relevant 20 years later, and he said it was even more so. "There is a kind of new Victorianism," he explained. "The modern Left is always reacting to things. Once they get their show on the road culturally, they'll stop being so offended." Then he quickly added, "But that's just my bullsh*t opinion."

Backlash: In the late teens, the use of "snowflake" expanded from being a political snub thrown at liberals by conservatives to describing anyone—including President Donald Trump—who was accused of being easily "triggered." One popular meme that made the rounds on Facebook after the 2016 U.S. presidential election: "Liberal Snowflake? Winter is Coming." (That's a reference to *Game of Thrones*.) But British humorist John Cleese had a different take: "I think sociopaths use snowflake in an attempt to discredit the notion of empathy."

BREXIT

Meaning: The withdrawal of the United Kingdom from the European Union, a referendum that a majority of Brits voted in favor of in 2016

Story: This portmanteau of "Britain" and "exit" first showed up in early 2012—albeit in a slightly different form—in a prophetic article in the *Economist* magazine, entitled "A Brixit Looms." "Brixit" was inspired by "Grexit," which was coined that same year by economist Ebrahim Rahbari, about the notion that Greece might leave the EU. The first documented appearance of "Brexit" came from Peter Wilding, founder of the think tank British Influence. His May 15, 2012, blog post was titled "Stumbling towards the Brexit." But after the Greek crisis quieted down, the word fell into relative obscurity until the Brexit vote approached in 2016. Then it "blew up," as one linguist described, to become Google's number-one "What is…?" search of the year.

Backlash: "Brexit" had a competitor: "Bremain," a combination of "Britain" and "remain." Unfortunately for the Bremainers (one of whom was Brexit coiner Peter

Wilding), that word didn't quite roll off the tongue as well as "Brexit," and they became known instead as "anti-Brexiters"…and they lost the vote.

Bonus: The "-exit" suffix isn't going anywhere. Like "-gate" before it (from the 1970s Watergate scandal), these are two rare suffixes that have been added to modern English. So be on the lookout for "Calexit," "Texit," and "Italexit."

GHOSTING

Meaning: Abruptly ending a relationship with someone by breaking off all contact, especially on social media and dating sites

Story: Whoever gave life to "ghosting" is lost to history, but this truly is a 21st-century term, first appearing in *The Urban Dictionary* in 2006 as "the act of disappearing on your friends without notice." The word's popularity peaked in the mid-teens when news site after news site ran alarmist articles such as "And Then I Never Heard from Him Again: The Awful Rise of Ghosting," "Are Dating Apps to Blame for 'Ghosting'?" and "Ghosting: What to Do if You've Been a Victim." Though the word is modern, as *L.A. Magazine* wrote in 2019, "Ghosting isn't a revolutionary concept, it's just a newish name for something humans have done forever: choosing the path of least resistance out of selfishness or maybe self-preservation."

Proving there really is more than one way to leave your lover:

- The "slow fade" is incremental ghosting, wherein you try to ease your way out of their life, hoping they don't notice until you're gone.
- "Caspering" (named for Casper, the Friendly Ghost) is when you let your partner know you'll be eliminating them from your life, but in a friendly way.
- "Ghostbusting" is turning the tables on the ghoster by tracking them down and forcing them to acknowledge you.
- And for literature lovers, there's "Marleying," when an ex contacts you from out of nowhere during the holidays, just like the recently deceased Jacob Marley did to Ebenezer Scrooge in Charles Dickens's 1843 ghost story *A Christmas Carol*.

Bonus: This is one of several modern alternate meanings of "ghost," which spent most of its thousand-year existence as a noun meaning "spirit of a deceased person" (it comes from the Old English *gast*). A few examples: There's *ghosting* in comment threads (making comments invisible to everyone but the poster), *ghosting* in digital photography (when a moving object in bracketed exposures shows up blurry), *ghosting* in identity theft (pretending to be a dead person), *ghosting* in online gaming ("collaborating with an accomplice in observer mode to view opponents' positions in order to gain a competitive edge"), and *ghost-writing* (what you could be reading right now).

For more of the tumultuous teens' most talked-about terms,
stream your way over to page 317.

If you straightened out a French horn, it would be about 20 feet long.

MYTH-CONCEPTIONS

"Common knowledge" is frequently wrong. Here are some examples of things that many people believe…but according to our sources, they just aren't true.

Myth: George Washington was offered the title of king but chose to be president instead.

Fact: In 1782, near the end of the Revolutionary War, Colonel Lewis Nicola floated this idea in a letter he wrote to General Washington, explaining, "Some people have so connected the ideas of tyranny & monarchy as to find it very difficult to separate them," but "King George Washington," he said, "would be most likely to conduct & direct us in the smoother paths of peace." It's likely that Nicola, 65, was worried that after the war ended, he wouldn't receive his pension (a concern shared by many), and he didn't trust the new Congress to pay up. But Nicola never had the power to "offer" Washington anything, and none of the other Founding Fathers had even considered making him king. What the general did do was resign his commission before running for president, ensuring that the military would never run the government. Washington's response to Nicola: "You could not have found a person to whom your schemes are more disagreeable."

Myth: William Shakespeare was first and foremost a writer.

Fact: The Bard's first true passion was acting—and he made sure to give himself a part in most of his plays. In the mid to late 16th century, acting wasn't a respected profession. In fact, it was outlawed in London because it went against Puritan values. The Globe Theatre was located just outside of the city next to the brothels and pubs. That's why Shakespeare himself, as well as several biographers, played down this important part of his life.

Myth: Pineapples come from Hawaii, and they're so popular there that they became a pizza topping.

Fact: Massachusetts-born James Dole opened a pineapple canning factory in Honolulu in 1903. His innovative canning techniques, coupled with savvy marketing skills, put cans of Dole pineapples on supermarket shelves all over the United States. Few mainlanders had any clue that this "Hawaiian fruit" is native to South America and didn't even get to Hawaii until the late 17th century. For Hawaiians, pineapples are no more popular than any other fruit, and it's not a popular pizza topping. Hawaiian-style pizza was invented in Canada. Yet even though less than 2 percent of the world's pineapples are grown there today, Hawaii's travel and hospitality industries keep the pineapple front and center because that's what tourists expect.

What's "tipcat"? An ancient Egyptian sport that's similar to baseball.

Myth: The Stetson was the most popular cowboy hat in the Old West.
Fact: The wide-brimmed Stetson hat—first sold in 1865—might be what you picture when you think of a cowboy, but the hat most men wore back then was a bowler (also called a derby), invented in London in 1849. Smaller than a cowboy hat, bowlers are usually black with a rounded top and narrower brim. Most cowboys preferred them because they were less likely to blow off. They were also a lot cheaper than a $5 Stetson ($100 today). (That's why Charlie Chaplain's "Little Tramp" character wore a bowler and not a Stetson.)

Myth: The Declaration of Independence declared to England that the United States was forming its own country.
Fact: The Continental Congress knew that King George III would eventually see the declaration, but its main purpose was to inform the citizens of the 13 colonies what was going on, and to explain why, writing that Great Britain "has a history of repeated injuries and usurpations, all having in direct object the establishment of an absolute Tyranny over these States."

Myth: Presidents' Day is a federal holiday.
Fact: Despite what mattress retailers breathlessly try to tell you, there's no federal holiday called "Presidents' Day." According to the U.S. Office of Personnel Management's list of federal days off, "This holiday is designated as 'Washington's Birthday' in section 6103(a) of title 5 of the United States Code, which is the law that specifies holidays for Federal employees." In the 1960s, some Illinois lawmakers proposed changing the name to "Presidents' Day" to include Abraham Lincoln, whose birthday is also in February, but the measure failed. Some states and smaller municipalities have opted to call this holiday "Presidents' Day," and retailers tend to use it because it's easier to say than "Washington's Birthday Sale!"

Myth: Chicago is called the Windy City because of the "lake effect" winds that blow in from Lake Michigan.
Fact: The nickname goes back to 1858, when a scathing *Chicago Daily Tribune* article criticized Chicago's elites—often referred to as "windbags"—for "airing their vanity… in this windy city."

Myth: There's such a thing as stomach flu.
Fact: There is no medical condition called "stomach flu." Though the symptoms can feel flu-like—nausea, diarrhea, and general malaise—this condition is called *acute gastroenteritis*. It affects the GI tract, whereas the influenza virus is a viral infection that affects the respiratory system (your lungs). Neither of these conditions can be caused by the other, and only one can be accurately referred to as the flu.

Spider monkeys eat dirt. It apparently helps them digest their food.

OLD-TIME TIPS FOR WEDDED BLISS

What makes a marriage last? No one knows…but that doesn't stop "experts" from supplying advice. Here are a few such bits of advice from centuries past that tell us more about how society has changed than they do about matrimony.

"A sensible woman, to preserve the peace and secure the affections of her husband, will often sacrifice her own inclinations to his."

    —*The Young Wife, or Duties of Woman in the Marriage Relation*
      by WILLIAM ALCOTT (1837)

"She who weds with one of an inferior rank in life has no right to expect that her friends will associate with her husband, or treat him with that respect which she may think his due."

    —*Letters to Young Ladies on Their Entrance Into the World*
      by MRS. LANFEAR (1824)

"Conjugal life is the salvation of many women. Every specialist in the nervous and psychic disorders of women is aware that a healthy vita sexualis is the remedy for many troubles of the brain."

    —*The Psychology of Marriage* by WALTER M. GALLICHAN (1918)

"Don't marry a clown. Fun will grow stale and threadbare; one cannot live by it. Life is a trip that costs carfare, wash bills, board bills, trinkets, notions, and actual outlays. Real providers are never clowns."

    —*Don't Marry, or Advice As to How, When, and Who to Marry*
      by JAMES W. DONOVAN (1891)

"Wives generally have much more sense than their husbands, especially if the husbands are clever men. The wife's advices are like the ballast that keeps the ship steady. They are like the wholesome, though painful shears snipping off the little growth of self-conceit and folly."

    —*Manners, Culture, and Dress of the Best American Society*
      by RICHARD A. WELLS (1894)

U.S. city with the lowest rate of marriage: Washington, D.C.

"Appear always flattered by the little he does for you, which will excite him to perform more."

—*Marriage Tips for Married Ladies* (1838)

"Don't bother your husband with petty troubles and complaints when he comes home from work. Be a good listener. Let him tell you his troubles; yours will seem trivial in comparison. Remember your most important job is to build up and maintain his ego (which gets bruised plenty in business)."

—*Sex Today in Wedded Life* by EDWARD PODOLSKY (1943)

"Housekeeping accomplishments and cooking ability are, of course, positive essentials in any true home, and every wife should take a reasonable pride in her skill. Happiness does not flourish in an atmosphere of indigestion."

—*Sex Satisfaction and Happy Marriage* by REV. ALFRED HENRY TYRER (1938)

"That the underwear should be spotlessly clean goes without saying, but every woman should wear the best quality underwear that she can afford. And the color should be preferably pink."

—*Married Life and Happiness* by DR. WILLIAM JOSEPHUS ROBINSON (1922)

"The average man marries a woman who is slightly less intelligent than he is. That's why many brilliant women never marry. They do not come in contact with sufficiently brilliant men, or fail to disguise their brilliance in order to win a man of somewhat less intelligence. College males tell us that they want a girl for a wife who is intelligent but makes them feel they are still more intelligent!"

—*Modern Bride* (1952)

* * *

BETTER LATE THAN NEVER

In 1934 an 11-year-old girl checked out a book called *Spoon River Anthology* from a library in Shreveport, Louisiana. In October 2018, that girl's grandson was going through boxes in his attic when he found the tattered, old book. (He said it was a bit spooky to find it right before Halloween, because the book, written by Edgar Lee Masters, is full of poems written from the points of view of dead people.) Noticing the library stamp, the man returned it…84 years late. The maximum late fee at the library is $3. It was waived.

Quintessential comes from a Latin word that means "the fifth element."

BUT WAIT, THERE'S MORE

*Hundreds of strange products have been marketed through infomercials.
Most fail, but some make millions for the sellers…and that's why they
keep introducing more. Here are a few you might remember.*

MR. DENTIST. A cheap electric toothbrush marketed as a "fabulous tooth polisher that removes unsightly coffee and tobacco stains." It's suitable for men, women, kids *and*, the manufacturer assures viewers, man's best friend: "Buy a second Mr. Dentist for your dog, and his teeth will sparkle too!" (Also available: the Brush Buddies Justin Bieber Singing Toothbrush, which plays a selection of Bieber's hit songs for the dentist-recommended two minutes of tooth-brushing time. "Includes 4 of his hit singles! Get your Bieber smile today!")

SNUGGIE. A blanket with sleeves. Much tackier than a bathrobe, and not nearly as practical.

> This spray was marketed as a deodorant tough enough to tackle butt-crack odor.

DOC BOTTOMS ASPRAY ALL-OVER DEODORANT. Pronounced "A-Spray" in the infomercial, but only because you're not supposed to say "ass" on TV. This spray was marketed as a deodorant tough enough to tackle butt-crack odor. "I work hard for a living and I sweat a lot," says Lanny F., the customer featured in the infomercial. "I got odors in special places. And with Aspray I don't have to worry about that anymore…[long pause]…M-m-m-my butt." For $14.99 you got a bottle of butt crack spray, plus a bonus pen-sized portable "pocket shot." "Perfect for on the go, or give it to your smelly friend!" (MSNBC aired this infomercial only once, in the middle of the night, then promised that it "will never air it again." Today it lives on YouTube.)

COMFORT WIPE. Basically an 18-inch plastic extension wand for people who have trouble wiping themselves after going to the bathroom. "Being a big guy certainly has its advantages. And its disadvantages. This is a great product!" says the big guy in the commercial. (No word on whether he also uses Doc Bottoms Aspray All-Over Deodorant.)

SHAKE WEIGHT. A fitness dumbbell whose weights are attached to the handle with springs, allowing them to slide back and forth, and giving the user what the company describes as a "dynamic inertia" workout. To use, hold the Shake Weight in your hand and jerk it repeatedly up and down. What's wrong with that? The weights aren't as effective as ordinary dumbbells, and people look ridiculous using them. Videos of people

Donnie Dunagan voiced Bambi in *Bambi* as a boy and grew up to become the
U.S. Marines' youngest-ever drill instructor.

using the Shake Weight routinely go viral "as a result of the perceived sexually suggestive nature of the product." Even so, more than $40 million worth have been sold.

PED EGG. An egg-shaped device similar to a cheese grater, but used to grate gross dead skin off of feet. "An amazing new foot grooming miracle! Don't put sexy shoes on ugly feet! Now treat your feet to a foot makeover, with Ped Egg!"

Bonus: "The nasty foot shavings…stay inside the egg, so you can use it anywhere without the mess! Then just toss it in the trash."

GINSU KNIVES. Remember these classics? If you were alive in the 1970s and '80s, how could you not? Ginsu knives were cheap kitchen knives made by the Scott Fetzer Company in Ohio, but sold to the public under the made-up name Ginsu to give the impression they were made in Japan. (Also, marketers Barry Becher and Ed Valenti didn't think anyone "would buy a knife named Fetzer.") "In Japan, the hand can be used like a knife. But this method doesn't work with a tomato." *Splat!* Broadcast from 1978 to 1984, the ads sold more than 3 million sets of knives. "Barry had a great saying," Ed Valenti told the *New York Times* in 2012. "Whenever someone would ask, 'What does Ginsu mean in English?' he would answer, 'It means I never have to work again.'"

SAUNA PANTS. An electric heating pad shaped like a pair of snug-fitting boxer shorts. The pad wrapped around the wearer and was secured in place with Velcro. "Who has the time to spend at a spa? Plus the sauna experience can be expensive. Not anymore! Introducing the revolutionary Sauna Pants!"

SLOBSTOPPER. A polyurethane bib for go-getters who *must* eat and drink in the car, but lack the dexterity to avoid spilling food and hot coffee all over themselves. "Just slip it on and enjoy your busy lifestyle. It's waterproof on one side, and absorbent on the other. Bibs aren't just for babies!"

SHOEDINI. A shoehorn with a telescoping handle, so you can get your shoes off without bending over—that's it. But the commercials were narrated by comedian Gilbert Gottfried. "Just slide 'em in and slip 'em off. ShoeDini works with all your shoes!"

MUSIC VEST. Before there were Bluetooth earbuds, there was the Music Vest—a vest with small waterproof stereo speakers attached to the chest at shoulder level, one on the left and one on the right. It was available in shiny metallic silver or jet black. The silver vest looked like something a tacky alien would wear; the black version looked like it was made from a Hefty bag. No matter—the company marketed it as "the only fashion and personal sound system currently sweeping the country!"

JUMP SNAP ROPELESS JUMP ROPE SYSTEM. Why take unnecessary risks with a deadly *real* jump rope when you don't have to? The Jump Snap replaces the rope with

In zero gravity, candle flames are round and burn blue.

swinging weights attached to jump rope handles that make it feel like an actual jump rope. "Without the rope to trip you up, now you too can train like a pro!"

HAWAII CHAIR. A desk chair with a foam seat cushion attached to a 2,800 revolution-per-minute "hula motor" that moves the seat in a circular/orbital motion, supposedly allowing the user to exercise without getting out of the chair. "Take the 'work' out of your workout with the Hawaii chair!" Supports people weighing up to 300 pounds.

TIDDY BEAR. A small stuffed bear that a woman can strategically attach to a seat belt to prevent the seat belt from cutting into her, um, chest. (Get it? Tiddy Bear!)

CHEERS TO YOU CD. Do you hate yourself for spending all your hard-earned money on crap like the products listed above? No problem—there's a CD just for you: The Cheers to You CD contains eight, count 'em, *eight* audio recordings of "cheering and encouraging applause," overlaid with inspiring voice-over messages like "The finish line is closer than you think!" and "We're here for you, we believe in you!" And, promises the Good Cheer Company, "We guarantee you'll be feeling better about yourself and your life, or we'll give you your money back!"

But wait! There's *still* more!

- **Miracle Broom.** A handheld, battery-powered vacuum marketed for three years before Black & Decker introduced the Dustbuster and sucked up all their business.

- **Nad's.** An Australian hair removal product for women.

- **Million Dollar Smile.** One-size-fits-all fake teeth. (For cosmetic purposes only—they're not for chewing.)

- **Silver Sonic XL.** It looks like a set of headphones, but it's actually a snooping device to eavesdrop on conversations from across the room.

- **Flowbee.** An electric razor that attaches to a vacuum, it delivers simple haircuts and the trimmings get sucked up immediately.

- **Moon Shoes.** "Kid-powered trampolines…for your feet!"

- **Bruce Jenner PowerWalk Plus.** It's a treadmill.

- **Glass Froster.** Glasses are placed on top, and cold, compressed air immediately makes them cold and frosty.

- **Record Vacuum.** Place your LP vinyl record in the vertical slot. The record spins as the device removes dust and static electricity.

- **WaxVac.** A handheld vacuum cleaner…for sucking the wax out of your ears.

Literally bloodcurdling: Watching horror movies increases the amount of a clotting protein in your bloodstream.

A DAY AT THE RACES

*They're neck and neck down the stretch! Harness yourself in for
a quick rundown of the major types of horse racing.*

HORSING AROUND...AND AROUND... AND AROUND

Archaeological records suggest that the horse was first domesticated about 5,500 years ago in the grasslands of Central Asia; by about 2,500 years ago, horse racing was widely practiced throughout Asia and Europe. Thanks to the movies, we know a lot about one of the earliest forms: chariot racing, which debuted in 680 BC at the Olympic games in ancient Greece. Over the millennia, many different styles of horse racing have developed around the world, some you probably know well, and some not so well. Here are the most popular.

FLAT RACING

This is the version of horse racing most of us are familiar with, and the most common one in the world today. In flat racing, jockeys ride around an oval dirt or grass track. Individual tracks vary in length, from about half a mile to almost two miles in circumference. The races themselves range from about half a mile to two and a half miles—using either a portion of a track or several laps to complete. Some well-known flat racing events include the Kentucky Derby (Louisville, Kentucky), the Preakness Stakes (Baltimore, Maryland), the Epsom Derby (Surrey, England), and Australia's Melbourne Cup.

JUMP RACING

In jump racing, the horses and their riders compete on long courses dotted with several obstacles that must be jumped over. There are two main types:

- Hurdles: The courses are at least two miles long and include at least eight hurdles—which are a minimum of three and a half feet high.

- Steeplechase: The courses run between two miles and four and a half miles long, with varying numbers of fences at least four and a half feet high. There are also ditches—some empty, some filled with water. (Steeplechase originated in 18th-century Ireland. They used distant church steeples for finish lines, hence the name.)

Jump racing is the most dangerous style of horse racing—it takes considerable coordination and timing on both the horse's and the rider's part to jump a high hurdle at full gallop while shoulder to shoulder with other riders. Of the two, however, steeplechase is the most dangerous.

ENDURANCE RIDING

Endurance riding sees the horse and rider cover great distances over open country. The 2004 movie *Hidalgo* tells the partly true story of an Old West cowboy named Frank Hopkins, who must prove he is "the

World's Greatest Endurance Rider" by entering his mustang Hidalgo in a 3,000-mile race across the Saudi Arabian desert. Modern endurance races cover between 50 and 100 miles in a single day—with regular rest stops for veterinarians to check on the animals' health and well-being. And the winner is not simply the first one to cross the finish line: the fastest horses to finish the race are checked by a vet, and the horse in the best physical condition is declared the winner. One of the most popular endurance races is the 100-mile Tevis Cup, held every summer since 1955 in the mountains near Truckee, California. Roughly 150 horses compete each year… and only half finish the race. Record time: 10 hours and 46 minutes, set in 1981.

HARNESS RACING

Horses race around a flat track, each pulling a two-wheeled cart called a *sulky*, which carries the jockey. Unlike pretty much every other footrace in the world, the horses aren't allowed to run at full speed. They're limited to one of two gaits: a *trot* or a *pace*, both of which are kind of like jogging. If a horse breaks into a gallop during a trot or pace race, it's penalized or disqualified. That doesn't mean these races are slow: the specially bred horses that compete in harness racing can trot or pace at speeds exceeding 30 mph. (Canter on over to page 313 to learn more about the different horse gaits.)

QUARTER HORSE RACING

In the American colonies in the 17th century, British horse breeders started crossing English thoroughbred horses with horses that had arrived with Spanish explorers a century earlier. Result: the American quarter horse, a strong, quick breed that can run very fast over short distances—perfect for all-out sprints on short, straight tracks. They're called quarter horses because the original races were a quarter-mile long. Modern tracks range from 220 to 870 yards (about a half of a mile), and can be found throughout the United States and Canada.

MONGOL DERBY

If you're a history buff and a thrill-seeker, and you happen to have an extra $13,000, this is the horse race for you. Established in 2009, the Mongol Derby follows a 621-mile-long course that was developed by Mongolian mail carriers in the year 1224 when the region was ruled by Gengis Khan. Race organizers supply you with 27 small, stocky—and half-wild—Mongolian horses. You start the race on one horse, and the next horse will be waiting for you at a station along the route, and then another, and then an other, until you've ridden all 27 horses. (Your entrance fee will also provide you with training, lodging, food, and medical and veterinary care for you and your horses.) You and your horses will traverse grassy steppes, sandy dunes, steep forests, soggy wetlands, and several rivers. You'll face fog, rain, blazing heat, and bitter cold. And you must ride up to 14 hours a day if you want to finish the race in the allotted time of 10 days. The 2018 winners were Melbourne, Australia, workmates Adrian Corboy and Annabel Neasham, who completed the Mongol Derby in a record time of six days.

Monkeyade? There's a variety of lemon called the baboon.

🗣 MOUTHING OFF 🗣

—U. J. QUOTEPAGE

At the BRI, we're always looking for new and interesting ways to group quotations. Quotemaster Jay Newman came up with a double score with this collection: each of these quotations imparts a succinct bit of wisdom AND…well, just check out the attributions.

"Freedom of the press is guaranteed only to those who own one."
—A. J. Liebling

"A bore is simply a nonentity who resents his humble lot in life, and seeks satisfaction for his wounded ego by forcing himself on his betters."
—H. L. Mencken

"Genius is more often found in a cracked pot than in a whole one."
—E. B. White

"NOTHING CAN WEAR YOU OUT LIKE CARING ABOUT PEOPLE."
—S. E. Hinton

"DON'T WORRY ABOUT YOUR HEART, IT WILL LAST YOU AS LONG AS YOU LIVE."
—W. C. Fields

"Nothing is really work unless you would rather be doing something else."
—J. M. Barrie

"ADVERTISING IS LEGALIZED LYING."
—H. G. Wells

"You can't turn a thing upside down if there's no theory about it being the right way up."
—G. K. Chesterton

"WAR WILL EXIST AS LONG AS THERE'S A FOOD CHAIN."
—P. J. O'Rourke

CLASSIC HOLLYWOOD PUBLICITY STUNTS

Today, Hollywood promotes new movies with an onslaught of TV advertising, billboards, bus ads, and online "viral marketing." But before those things were invented, movie studios hired impresarios to stage elaborate publicity stunts. These outlandish events would then get covered by newspapers…generating a lot of attention for a film. Here are some of the weirdest from the golden age of Hollywood.

MOVIE: *Gone With the Wind* (1939)

STUNT: Margaret Mitchell's epic 1936 Civil War novel *Gone With the Wind* was a best-seller, Pulitzer Prize–winner, and landmark book in American literature. The film version was highly anticipated, and filmmakers drummed up publicity for it for a full three years before it hit theaters in 1939. The biggest publicity stunt for the movie had to do with *making* the movie. Producers held widely publicized auditions across the entire United States, searching for the perfect actress to play lead character Scarlett O'Hara. And as every city's newspapers wrote about this traveling road show, they were building up anticipation for a movie that hadn't even started *filming* yet. Producers interviewed more than 1,400 women for the role, but all of that was for show. In the end, they didn't even pick an American for the part—they chose British stage actress Vivien Leigh.

MOVIE: *Teacher's Pet* (1958)

STUNT: Clark Gable plays a hotshot newspaper reporter forced by his editor to take a newswriting class, only to end up falling in love with his instructor, played by Doris Day. It's set in newspaper offices, and to play the dozens of extras in newsroom scenes—reporters typing away at typewriters—Paramount hired about 50 actual reporters. (A few of them even got a line or two.) When the film came out, those same reporters happily gave the film nice write-ups in their newspapers.

MOVIE: *Down Missouri Way* (1946)

STUNT: This musical is about an agricultural professor (Martha O'Driscoll), who falls in love with a movie producer (John Carradine), who gives a film role to the professor's ultra-intelligent mule. The animal is the real star of *Down Missouri Way*, and so a publicity agent for Producers Releasing Corporation took that mule—Shirley—and marched her down Fifth Avenue in New York City (with a sign bearing

The pointy tip of your elbow is called an *olecranon*.

the movie's title on her back) and into a high-class restaurant that looked out onto the ice rink at Rockefeller Center. The agent demanded a table for the mule and himself, and staff would not oblige. So he lodged a complaint and alerted the media... which dutifully reported on Shirley the Mule, star of *Down Missouri Way*.

MOVIE: *The Outlaw* (1943)

STUNT: Legendary (and legendarily quirky) tycoon and movie mogul Howard Hughes directed this Western about Billy the Kid, but he knew exactly what the film's biggest, um, assets were: Jane Russell and her prodigious chest, which Hughes emphasized with tight, low-cut costumes. He also made Russell's figure the focus of the film's ad campaign. Posters depicted Russell lying on a hay bale with a skimpy shirt with the caption "What are the two greatest reasons for Jane Russell's rise to stardom?" Pretty salacious stuff for 1943, but that was only part of the stunt. When the film was released, he hired a skywriter to spell "THE OUTLAW" in the skies over Hollywood. After the words, the pilot was instructed to draw two giant circles...with little dots in the center. (Get it?)

MOVIE: *The Revenge of Tarzan* (1920)

STUNT: Veteran Hollywood publicist Harry Reichenbach rented a room at the Hotel Belleclaire in New York, not under his own name, but as "T. R. Zann." Reichenbach worked up a character for this T. R. Zann, claiming to be a world-renowned concert pianist who insisted on traveling with his own piano. That piano, he explained to the hotel (and reporters), would have to be hoisted up to his room, from the outside of the building and into his room window. The Belleclaire staff actually did use a system of ropes and pulleys to get a giant, piano-sized wooden crate into his room. But there wasn't a piano in that box...there was a lion, which staff found out about when Reichenbach called for room service to deliver a special breakfast: ten pounds of raw steak. They were startled, and a few bellhops called a number of New York newspapers, which all reported the story of this man called T. R. Zann...or "Tarzan."

MOVIE: *The Egg and I* (1947)

STUNT: To generate interest in the film version of Betty MacDonald's best-selling memoir about her move from the city to life on a chicken farm, publicity man Jim Moran sat on an egg. And he continued to do so for 19 days. He went to the Los Angeles Ostrich Farm and, with the help of a special wheelchair he could sit in without having to squat for most of three weeks, remained above an egg in a basket. For 40 cents, visitors could look at Moran up close, a sight to see when he'd put on a feathered headband and a matching pair of pants covered in feathers. When the ostrich egg hatched, Moran was on his way.

Each second, your fingernails grow about one nanometer longer.

THE ENDURANCE OF AUDREY HEPBURN

Audrey Hepburn was one of the most beloved movie stars of the 20th century, thanks to memorable performances in Breakfast at Tiffany's, Roman Holiday, Sabrina, My Fair Lady, *and many others. Sofia Loren once described her as "meek, gentle, and ethereal, understated both in her life and in her work." Another adjective to describe Hepburn: strong.*

THE WINTER OF 1944 When Audrey Hepburn (born Audrey Ruston in 1929) was a teenager, World War II broke out. Fearing a Nazi invasion, her British mother moved them from their home in Belgium to the Netherlands, hoping the Nazis wouldn't invade. But the Nazis did invade, and they occupied the Netherlands for five years, cutting off all food supplies in the fifth year. By that point it was just Audrey and her mother; her father had long since abandoned the family to become active in the British Fascist movement.

The mother and daughter nearly starved to death during the long winter of 1944. At one point their only sustenance was boiled grass and tulip bulbs. The frail teenager lost so much weight that she developed acute anemia, edema, and respiratory problems. Even so, Audrey was a gifted ballerina. Dancing under the stage name Edda van Heemstra (her mother's maiden name, which she used so she wouldn't sound too English), she took part in "silent performances" in which the audience would hold its applause, so that they wouldn't alert the Nazis patrolling outside. The proceeds from these performances went to the Dutch resistance effort.

Hepburn never fully recovered from that lean winter. At 5'7" and only 88 pounds, she tried to return to ballet dancing after the war, but the effects of malnourishment had dashed her dream of ever becoming a prima ballerina. So she got work as a dental assistant and took up modeling and acting.

A STAR IS BORN Everything changed when Hepburn landed a part in a movie being shot in Monte Carlo. The French novelist Colette happened to be vacationing there. She took one look at the bright-eyed young actress and offered her the lead role in the Broadway play *Gigi*. Hepburn had never acted on stage before, but after surviving starvation and the Nazis, she was up for anything. *Gigi* ran for 219 performances on Broadway, launching a legendary career that saw Hepburn become one of only 15 entertainers to win an Emmy, Grammy, Oscar, and Tony (the coveted EGOT).

Audrey Hepburn retired from acting in 1967 and, through her work as a UNICEF Goodwill ambassador, she dedicated the rest of her life to feeding starving children. She died in 1993 at the age of 63.

Uncle John's favorite word for "drunk": crapulent.

INITIALLY MYSTERIOUS

Some companies use initials in their names. It creates mystery and intrigue, as millions ask, "What do those letters stand for?" Well, here's what they stand for.

CVS. Consumer Value Stores.

H&M. The discount clothing chain started in 1940s Sweden as a women's store called Hennes—Swedish for "hers." The company then acquired a *men's* clothing store called Mauritz Widforss, and rebranded as Hennes and Mauritz, which was then abbreviated to just H&M.

LG. The South Korean electronics giant was originally named Goldstar Co., but merged with Lak Hai (pronounced "lucky") Chemical Co. in 1983, and became Lucky-Goldstar. In 1995 the company renamed itself LG.

TCBY. Frozen yogurt became a national sensation in the 1980s, when people thought it was healthier than ice cream. (It may have less fat, but it's still loaded with sugar.) One of the first chains selling it was I Can't Believe It's Yogurt. In 1984 it sued upstart rival This Can't Be Yogurt for attempting to mislead customers. The newer company rebranded itself (without changing its initials) as The Country's Best Yogurt, and then just went down to TCBY.

F.A.O. Schwarz. The late high-end toy store was the creation of Frederick August Otto (F.A.O.) Schwartz.

FIAT. It's actually an acronym, not somebody's name. The letters in the car maker's name stand for "Fabbrica Italiana di Automobil Torino," or "Italian automobile factory of Turin."

BVD. The names emblazoned on men's underwear belong to businessmen Bradley, Voorhees, and Day, who started the company in 1876. Their original product: bustles for women.

H&R Block. The tax preparation service was the brainchild of brothers Henry and Richard Bloch…who changed the spelling to avoid mispronunciation.

DHL. The shipping company was founded in San Francisco as a courier service in the 1960s by Adrian Dalsey, Larry Hillblom, and Robert Lynn.

K-Mart. The "K" is for Kresge, after founder Sebastian Kresge.

BJ's Wholesale Club. Founder Mervyn Weich named the company after his daughter Beverly Jean.

P.F. Chang. There's no such person. "P.F." comes from Paul Fleming, the guy who started the business, and "Chang" is a simplified version of the name of the original head chef, Philip Chiang.

After the military, what's America's largest buyer of explosives?
Disneyland (for its nightly fireworks shows).

SEMORDNILAP!

A palindrome is a word or phrase that's spelled the same forward and backward. A semordnilap is a word or phrase that forms a different word when spelled backward. (It's also "palindromes" backward.) In this quiz, can you guess the word that fills the first blank...and that word in reverse to fill in the second? (Answers are on page 501.)

1. You could argue that when _____ the Menace terrorized Mr. Wilson, he _____.

2. If you can find the earring I dropped in my bureau _____, I'll give you a nice _____.

3. Some might say that the love of a good _____ is proof that there's a _____ up there that loves us.

4. He _____ the day, even though the coffee was _____? Brave.

5. If you want to be happy, _____ a life of good, instead of one of _____.

6. If you need to buy some _____ of twine, check out the hardware store down at the docks, near the _____.

7. You can injure yourself when walking in your _____, like if you slip on a bunch of banana _____.

8. _____ and June Cleaver encouraged their kids to try art, which is why the Beaver loved to _____.

9. Want to go on a trip up to the bogs with us? There's plenty of _____ in this _____- bound van!

10. I took several short _____ in a ____of only two hours, so now I'm well-rested and ready to figure out the rest of these questions!

11. Those two were the best of friends, real solid _____, until the fight...and the _____.

12. Don't _____ your head on that door-_____!

13. If you're feeling _____, you could certainly try to comfort yourself by eating several _____.

14. Two clichés about witches: their faces are covered in _____, and they ride brooms made from _____.

15. He _____ for coal all day, wearing his trusty _____ jeans.

16. Whenever she _____ through her grandma's china hutch, she hopes to find some silver _____.

17. When the _____ swooped down into his face, the cave explorer tried to _____ them with a stick.

18. As _____ goes by, a chunk of uranium will _____ more radiation.

19. Every political _____ in Washington thinks they _____ everything about the government.

20. "Take a bath?" the toddler asked. "_____ I don't want to get into the _____!"

21. His pants didn't quite fit, so he gave them a _____ so they'd cover his _____."

22. A lid goes on _____ of a sauce _____.

The bookstore chain Borders started a dating site for book lovers in the UK called Happily Ever After. Both businesses are now defunct.

A SLICE OF HISTORY

Pizza just might be the definitive "American" food, despite its Italian origins. Here's the story of how pizza came from the Old World…to every strip mall, street corner, and grocery store freezer in the United States.

1500s Flatbreads covered in oil and various toppings, from figs and apricots to herbs, olives, and lamb, have been around for thousands of years. But the first recognizable pizzas likely appeared in 16th-century Naples, where local street vendors offer flat cakes they call *pizza* (which means "pie"). It is specifically a street food, and is seldom cooked in homes or restaurants.

1750s Between 1700 and 1750, Naples's population doubles to 400,000. *Lazzaroni*, the working poor, make up a huge portion of that number, and these workers—mostly porters, messengers, and laborers—need cheap food to eat. They buy pizzas from street vendors, who carry whole pies in large boxes and will cut off slices to order. The most common toppings: garlic, lard, and salt. Some vendors also offer horse milk cheese, whitebait (small fish, usually fried), basil, and a new ingredient just introduced from the New World, tomatoes.

1831 As pizza is still considered a cheap food for peasants and workers only, gourmets don't think much of it. While traveling through Italy, Samuel Morse (the inventor of the telegraph) writes about the dish in his diary. He calls it a "species of the most nauseating cake, covered over with slices of tomatoes, and sprinkled with little fish and black pepper and I know not what other ingredients, it altogether looks like a piece of bread that has been taken reeking out of the sewer."

1889 Various kingdoms and states united to become the Kingdom of Italy in 1871, and in 1889 King Umberto I and Queen Consort Margherita of Savoy tour the country and stop in Naples. Tired of the French-style banquets served in their honor, they call for local food to be cooked for them. The king's staff seeks out Raffaele Esposito, the owner of a popular tavern in Naples, to prepare the local delicacy, pizza. The *pizzaiolo* (pizza maker) obliges, preparing three pies for the royal couple: one with cheese and basil, one with whitebait, and one he invented for the occasion— the Margherita, with tomatoes, mozzarella, and basil representing the red, white, and green of the Italian flag. (This also marks the first ever pizza delivery.)

Front man: Ryan Gosling turned down a chance to audition for the Backstreet Boys.

1880s–1920s	In a 40-year period, more than four million Italian immigrants settle in New York, primarily in the New York/New Jersey area. Émigrés from Naples bring pizza with them to America.
Late 1800s	Italian-American peddlers in New York City, Trenton, Chicago, and Philadelphia imitate the street vendors who roamed Naples more than a century earlier, carrying around freshly baked pizzas and charging by the slice. The cost: about 2¢ each. (Instead of boxes, they carried their wares in metal washtubs.) Around this same time, cafés and restaurants in Italian neighborhoods in big cities start selling pizzas.
1904	An article in the *Boston Journal* marks the first time pizza is mentioned in an American publication.
1905	An Italian grocery store in Manhattan called Lombardi's opened in 1897, and in 1905 an employee named Filippo Milone converts it into a restaurant; pizza is the only item on the menu. In other words, it's the first pizzeria in the United States, selling individual-sized "tomato pies" at lunchtime to men who worked in nearby factories.
1910	Pizzerias continue to spring up around Manhattan and Brooklyn. The first pizza parlor outside of the city, Joe's Tomato Pies, opens in Trenton, New Jersey.
1925	Frank Pepe opens the first pizzeria outside of the New York/New Jersey area. After working as a street vendor for 20 years, he opens Frank Pepe Pizzeria Napoletana on Wooster Street in New Haven, Connecticut. (It's still there.)
1939	Pizza hits the West Coast when Casa D'Amore opens its first location in Los Angeles.
1943	Restaurateurs Ike Sewell and Ric Riccardo, along with chef Rudy Malnati, develop a new kind of pizza—Chicago-style deep-dish pizza. They introduce it at their restaurant, Pizzeria Uno in Chicago.
1945–1950	U.S. servicemen returning from being stationed in Italy during World War II bring home a taste for the Italian dish called pizza. Expanding its popularity beyond Italian neighborhoods, hundreds of pizzerias begin to spring up across America.
1947	In writing about the pizzeria boom, the *New York Times* says that pizza "could be as popular a snack as the hamburger if Americans only knew more about it."

It takes more than 2,500 gallons of water to make a single pair of blue jeans.

1950	Until now, the most popular pizza toppings in America have been sausage, bacon, and salami. In 1950 a New Haven, Connecticut, pizzeria called The Spot becomes the first to offer pepperoni.
1950	Celentano Brothers markets the first commercially available frozen, bake-at-home pizzas.
1950s– early 1960s	Small mom-and-pop pizza places start to feel the squeeze when major regional and national chains are founded…and quickly expand. Among them: Sacramento's Shakey's Pizza (1954), Wichita's Pizza Hut (1958), Detroit's Little Caesars (1959), and Michigan-based Domino's (1960).
1961	Chef Boyardee markets a product called Complete Pizza, a make-your-own pizza kit that includes crust mix, sauce, and no-refrigeration-needed cheese and sausage. The company advertises it with a TV commercial, making it the first television ad for pizza.
1962	Sam Panopoulos, proprietor of the Satellite Restaurant in Chatham, Ontario, introduces "Hawaiian pizza"—a cheese-and-sauce pie topped with pineapple and ham. It quickly spreads across North America.
1977	Chuck E. Cheese's Pizza Time Theatre opens its first location in San Jose, California, providing the unique combination of pizza with kid-entertaining animatronic characters.
1994	Pizza Hut launches PizzaNet, marking the first time customers can order pizza online.
1995	Pizza Hut figures out how to get more cheese into a pizza, unveiling the Stuffed Crust Pizza, in which a ring of mozzarella is baked into the outer crust. The chain spends $45 million on an ad campaign centered on a commercial featuring some guy named Donald Trump.
2001	Pizza Hut arranges to deliver to outer space. As part of a supply load to the International Space Station, the chain sends a six-inch salami-and-cheese pie. Why so small? So it can fit into the ISS's tiny oven.
2016	Thanks to a $125,000 grant from NASA to develop food preparation technology for astronauts on future Mars missions, pizza enters the 21st century. The robotics company BeeHex uses the grant money to develop Chef 3D, a robot that can "3-D print" a pizza. Special "ink tanks" full of ingredients lay out dough, sauce, and cheese, then it gets popped into an oven to cook for just five minutes.

There are about 13 million more cats in the U.S. than there are dogs.

YOU'RE MY INSPIRATION

Here are some more surprising inspirations behind pop culture icons.

THE *GAME OF THRONES* DRAGONS: The HBO show's visual effects team wanted to base the baby dragons on some kind of bird, but which one? After looking at bats and eagles, they ended up buying a chicken from Trader Joe's and cutting it up "to see how it works." When the dragons got big, the artists took inspiration from elephants, especially the way "their skin stretches and rolls over the bones."

***1984*:** A big inspiration for George Orwell's 1948 dystopian novel was Halford Mackinder's 1919 geopolitics book, *Democratic Ideals and Reality: A Study in the Politics of Reconstruction*. One passage in particular caught Orwell's eye: "Who rules East Europe commands the Heartland; who rules the Heartland commands the World-Island; who rules the World-Island commands the world." In this oft-quoted line from *1984*, Orwell kept Mackinder's structure but altered the nouns: "Who controls the past controls the future. Who controls the present controls the past."

WIND TURBINES: One problem with wind turbines: they're loud. Another problem: if winds come from different directions, the turbines can stall. Solution to both problems: add little bumps to the blades, which distributes the air in such a way that makes the blades quieter and less likely to stall. The inspiration: humpback whales. Unlike most whales that feed on krill, humpbacks must maneuver to catch prey. They can do this in part because of little bumps on their flippers called *tubercles*. And now wind turbines have tubercles, too. (But they still can't catch fish.)

DANIEL RADCLIFFE: After finishing up *Harry Potter*, Radcliffe bucked expectations by taking on one quirky role after another—including a talking corpse and the beat poet Allen Ginsberg. He didn't want to be "just another leading man," he said, so he modeled his career path after quirky character actor Steve Buscemi: "He's been in everything from *Fargo* to almost every movie Adam Sandler has ever made, and big action movies like *Armageddon* and *Con Air*." (In 2018 Radcliffe and Buscemi finally got to work with each other on the TBS sitcom *Miracle Workers*.)

"MAKE AMERICA GREAT AGAIN": This political campaign slogan was in use long before Donald Trump adopted it in 2016. In 1980 Ronald Reagan's slogan was "Let's Make America Great Again." And in 1991, in Bill Clinton's presidential announcement speech, he said, "I believe that together we can make America great again." (When Senator Ted Cruz uttered the phrase in one of his own campaign speeches, Trump accused Cruz of "ripping me off.")

The write stuff: A. A. Milne (*Winnie-the-Pooh*) had H. G. Wells (*War of the Worlds*) for a teacher,...

HERE LIES GEORGE WASHINGTON, PART II

Would Washington end up being buried in Washington? It all depended on Mrs. Washington. Here's the second part of the story.
(Part one is on page 138.)

MARTHA'S DECISION

As she had done so many times during her husband's military and political careers, Martha weighed her love for George Washington against the public's love for him. She also considered his wish that the two of them spend eternity together. She wrote back to President Adams and informed him that, after a "severe struggle," she would allow her husband's body to be moved to Washington, on one condition: that she be interred alongside him when her time came. "In doing this, I need not, I cannot, say what a sacrifice of individual feeling I make to a sense of public duty."

It took a few days for the news of the former president's death to reach Philadelphia, where the federal government was still housed. A national funeral was held there on December 26, where Congressman Henry Lee, in front of 4,000 mourners, famously eulogized Washington as "first in war, first in peace, and first in the hearts of his countrymen." Shortly thereafter, President Adams signed a joint resolution by Congress to have Washington's body moved from Mount Vernon and "deposited under…the United States Capitol."

One problem: Washington, D.C., wasn't quite there yet. The location, about 10 miles upriver from Mount Vernon, had only been chosen a decade earlier by George Washington, who wanted to call it Federal City. The U.S. Capitol Building (designed by Dr. William Thornton, who was an architect as well as a wannabe Frankenstein) was still under construction. It wouldn't get its famous dome until the 1820s, but two stories beneath where the floor of the Rotunda is now, work on an elaborate presidential tomb in a circular room with forty columns was begun. Into that tomb would go the remains of George and Martha Washington. A 10-foot circular opening was cut into the Rotunda floor so visitors could view their sarcophagi from above. The Crypt, as it's called today, is still there (it was used to store bicycles a century ago), but there are no Washingtons, or anyone else, interred in the U.S. Capitol. The hole in the floor was covered up long ago, and if you visit the Crypt, you'll see a famous bust of Abraham Lincoln and paintings of the Founding Fathers, including two of George Washington.

So why weren't George and Martha moved there?

…and played on a cricket team with J. M. Barrie (Peter Pan) and Arthur Conan Doyle (Sherlock Holmes).

POLITICS AS USUAL

After Washington's funeral, his already considerable fame skyrocketed. He had only left the presidency two years earlier and, with his passing, even those who had criticized him—including King George III—laid praise on him. But in an all-too-familiar scenario, partisan bickering kept Congress from making any progress on the tomb. George Washington, like his successor, John Adams, had been a Federalist. The Federalists favored a strong federal government, while the Republicans, led by Thomas Jefferson, favored a smaller government that didn't spend taxpayers' money on unnecessary body reburials.

But what really angered Jefferson was that during Washington's second term, the president chose to remain neutral in the Anglo-French War between France and Great Britain. Jefferson, who was then secretary of state, wanted the U.S. military to aid France (where he'd been an ambassador). When Washington refused to interfere, Jefferson resigned in protest.

> **Had the Federalists retained control of the White House, it's likely that the Washingtons would be interred in the Capitol Crypt today.**

Had the Federalists retained control of the White House, it's likely that the Washingtons would be in the Capitol Crypt today. But after Jefferson defeated Adams and took office in 1801, he moved on to other matters (such as the Louisiana Purchase). Even if President Jefferson *had* been in favor of the project, Congress couldn't come to a consensus on what type of monument to erect or how the funds should be allocated. Result: the bill stalled.

MEANWHILE...

Back at Mount Vernon, Martha Washington had a potential slave revolt to deal with, not to mention her own failing health. Her husband's 29-page will had stipulated that all of his slaves be freed upon Martha's death. But of the 317 slaves at Mount Vernon, only 123 of them belonged to George Washington; the rest had belonged to Martha's first husband, Daniel Parke Custis, and ownership of those slaves was to revert to his family after her death. What happened next isn't clear, but there were rumors that many of Washington's slaves didn't want to wait for Martha to die. After accusations arose that one of them had started a fire on the property, Martha's nephew, Judge Bushrod Washington, told her that if she feared for her safety, then she should let all of her husband's slaves free at once. So she did.

Martha Washington died on a spring day in May 1802. Her death made national news. She was placed in a lead casket alongside her husband in the Old Crypt.

The Ayam cemani chicken is completely black—including feathers, beak, meat, and internal organs.

IF AT FIRST YOU DON'T SUCCEED...

None of George and Martha's heirs were in a hurry to build the new tomb at Mount Vernon, so in 1816, Congress passed a new resolution to move the bodies to D.C., but again, nothing happened. In 1824, as the 100th anniversary of Washington's birth was approaching, another congressman, future President James Buchanan of Pennsylvania, said of Washington, "The man who was emphatically first in war, first in peace, and first in the hearts of his countrymen, has been sleeping with his fathers for almost a quarter of a century, and his mortal remains have yet been unhonored by that people, who, with justice, call him the father of their country." Buchanan, even more than most of his peers, idolized George Washington, and saw it as his mission to move the bodies. Another resolution was passed, and work on the Capitol Crypt (which had been interrupted due to the War of 1812) was completed.

Though Washington had no direct descendants, there were a lot of his nephews out there with the last name Washington, and they became Mount Vernon's new caretakers, starting with Judge Bushrod Washington. As it was (and still is) with many of the Founding Fathers' grave sites, there was disagreement among members of the Washington family. Some were eager for him to be moved to the Capitol; others were against it. But the decision belonged solely to whoever owned the estate.

MAKING THE PILGRIMAGE

There was another pressing matter. Mount Vernon was a working plantation, and its new owner—John Augustine Washington II—was tiring of all the "pilgrims" helping themselves to "artifacts" from Washington's dilapidated tomb. They stole bricks, dirt, flora, and whatever else they could take. A Russian ambassador removed a tree branch that he later presented to Tsar Alexander I. But the bulk of the visitors—most of them uninvited—came simply to bask in the presence of the father of the country. Some wept, some prayed. And it was all having a detrimental effect on the grave site. When reports of the aging tomb made their way to Congress, more pressure was put on Washington's heirs to let George and Martha go.

The final straw came in 1830 when a disgruntled gardener (he'd been fired) decided to exact his revenge by breaking into the tomb and stealing George Washington's skull. When he got into the dark tomb with the low ceiling, most of the coffins had rotted away, and there were bones everywhere...so he grabbed a skull and left. When John Washington II later investigated, he was relieved to find the lead caskets of George and Martha still sealed shut. (The story goes that the stolen skull belonged to a man named Blackburn, one of Bushrod Washington's in-laws.)

LAID TO REST

News of the grave robbing led to yet another resolution by Congress to move the Washingtons to Washington. They could still get him there by his 100th birthday in 1832, if only John Washington II would let them, but he wasn't the only one resisting. Virginia lawmakers didn't want their most beloved son taken out of the state, or out of the South. (A love for George Washington was one of the few things Northerners and Southerners had in common in those times.) They urged John Washington II to grant the president's dying wish to remain at his home…and Washington agreed, telling Congress no, he didn't want to upset his uncle's "perfect tranquility, surrounded by those of other endeared members of the family." That would be the last time the government tried to get their hands on George Washington.

In 1831 the Washington family finally got around to building the new tomb, and not a moment too soon. New coffins were built to replace the old ones, and more than 20 members of the family were relocated to their new home—a brick building with an arched entrance, and two large, white Egyptian-style obelisks out front. The project took so long to complete that George and Martha's coffins spent their first six years there in the back of the tomb. In 1837 two marble sarcophagi were donated by an architect from Philadelphia and placed in a vestibule (entrance room), so the coffins could be seen from outside. An iron gate protects the vault. An inscription on a tablet above the arch simply says:

> Within this Enclosure Rest the remains of Genl. George Washington.

LARGER THAN LIFE

When the Washingtons' lead caskets were placed inside the sarcophagi, John Washington II decided to have one last look at the president (either to make sure all of him was there, or to satisfy his own curiosity). According to a *Harper's* magazine account of the viewing, they opened the lid, "exposing to a view a head and breast of large dimensions, which appeared, by the dim light of the candles, to have suffered but little from the effects of time." The first thing they were surprised by was how large the president was. He stood over six feet tall; that's about a half a foot taller than most other men of the time. They also noted that the president had "tremendously" large hands.

FOR SALE

George and Martha Washington haven't been disturbed since they were sealed inside their marble sarcophagi (as far as we know), but Mount Vernon around them hasn't been so fortunate. The next owner, John Washington III, tired of swarms of

Surprised? The most littered item in the world is cigarette butts.

well-wishers disturbing his working plantation, which wasn't making a profit. He had little desire to become a tour guide and tell visitors all about his great-granduncle, but he knew there was money in it, so he started charging visitors a nominal fee to tour the estate and helped build new roads to make it easier to get there.

It still wasn't enough. In 1848 he tried to sell Mount Vernon to the State of Virginia or to the federal government, but as tensions were mounting between the North and the South, neither faction was interested. The property began to fall into disrepair.

THE MVLA

In 1853 a passenger on a steamer floated past the estate and couldn't believe what she saw. She wrote in a letter to her daughter, a South Carolina socialite named Ann Pamela Cunningham, that she was "painfully distressed at the ruin and desolation of the home of Washington. It does seem such a blot on our country!" There were even "No Trespassing" signs all over the place.

Four years later, Cunningham founded the Mount Vernon Ladies' Association (MVLA). Enlisting women from all 30 states, they raised sufficient funds to purchase Mount Vernon and the 200 acres surrounding it for $200,000 (over $5 million in today's money). John Washington III jumped at the offer, and the MVLA took over in 1860. Fortunately for them, Mount Vernon was considered neutral ground during the Civil War, so it was one of the few plantations in the area that didn't get ransacked. And with the end of the war and the Emancipation Proclamation of 1863, the hundred-year history of slaves living at Mount Vernon had ended.

> Mount Vernon was considered neutral ground during the Civil War, so it was one of the few plantations that didn't get ransacked.

Cunningham left these instructions when she retired in 1874: "Ladies, the Home of Washington is in your charge; see to it that you keep it the Home of Washington. Let no irreverent hand change it; no vandal hands desecrate it with the fingers of progress!" (In the 1950s, the MVLA had to raise money to buy land across the river before an oil company was able to install massive tanks and spoil the view from Washington's porch.)

CHANGING OF THE GUARD

In the late 1870s, while the MVLA was undertaking the arduous task of restoring the property, a former slave at Mount Vernon, Edmund Parker, was hired to stand guard at Washington's tomb. Most visitors thought he lived there. He didn't, of course. He had a wife and children at his home in Washington. But for 15 years he and several other

Nap rap: The healthiest time for a nap is 8 hours after waking up and 8 hours before bedtime.

African Americans, many of them former slaves, worked at Mount Vernon, and Parker was one of the best known of the former plantation's inhabitants. After Parker died, several more African American guards stood in front of Washington's tomb until the practice was ended in 1965.

Parker is one of the few "enslaved individuals" (so described on the Mount Vernon website) that we know anything about. At least 150 other slaves are buried in an unmarked graveyard on a hill in the woods just a short walk from Washington's tomb. In 1929 the MVLA placed a stone marker at the site that reads: "In memory of the many faithful coloured servants of the Washington family buried at Mount Vernon from 1760 to 1860. Their unidentified graves surround this spot." It is believed to be the first historical marker of its kind on a Southern plantation.

After that, however, the area became overgrown and was mostly forgotten until 1982, when Dorothy Gilliam, the first African American reporter at the *Washington Post*, went looking for the slave graveyard and uncovered the old marker. She wrote about her discovery: "The long walk from the stately tomb of George Washington to this abandoned memorial seemed drenched with the tears of the slaves." Gilliam's article sparked a renewed push to uncover the stories of Mount Vernon's slaves. Within a year, the MVLA had built a footpath to the cemetery and installed benches and a large stone memorial there. In 2014 the once-forgotten graveyard was cordoned off as an archaeological site. At last report, researchers were creating a map of the cemetery. One thing they've decided not to do, out of respect, is excavate the graves.

MOUNT VERNON TODAY

"There's a certain magic here at Mount Vernon," narrates Jeff Goldblum in a tourism video on the estate's website. "The rest of the world doesn't really exist." Goldblum's right. There are few places in the United States where more care has been put into showing visitors what life was like 250 years ago. And because Mount Vernon is far from a main road, nestled among trees and rolling hills, it's easy to forget you're less than 20 miles from the U.S. Capitol. The site is part of the National Park Service, but the MVLA is still in charge. Their mission remains to "preserve, restore, and manage" Mount Vernon.

Visiting Washington's tomb is still a somber undertaking, much as it was when the "pilgrims" came to pay their respects at the Old Crypt two centuries ago (although there's a lot less grave robbing today).

Our next Founding Father, John Adams, was much less controversial, so the story of his final resting place is much shorter. It can be found on page 274.

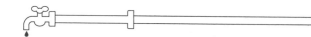

Iroquois nickname given to George Washington in 1753: "Town Destroyer."

AUDIO TREASURES

How many times have you found yourself scrolling through Spotify or Apple Music, wondering what's even worth checking out? It happens to us all the time—so we decided to offer a few recommendations. They're not necessarily weird or obscure...just good.

THE ZOMBIES *Odessey and Oracle* (1968), Psychedelic pop
Review: "One of the most enduring long-players to come out of the entire British psychedelic boom, mixing tripping melodies, ornate choruses, and lush Mellotron sounds with a solid hard rock base. The results are consistently pleasing, surprising, and challenging, some of the most powerful psychedelic pop/rock ever heard." (*All Music Guide Required Listening: Classic Rock*)

TEENAGE FANCLUB *Bandwagonesque* (1991), Rock
Review: "Equal parts Neil Young, Big Star, Rolling Stones, Lindsay Buckingham, and Eddie Money, plus a bunch of bands you never heard of, *Bandwagonesque* pulls the kinds of moves you'd expect from a much smarter, more ambitious group of guys. The lyrics are, for the most part, complex and intriguing, in that half-cynical manner that only really innocent twentysomething kids can convincingly pull off. *Bandwagonesque* is a moveable feast." (*Spin*)

A TRIBE CALLED QUEST *The Low End Theory* (1991), Hip-hop
Review: "If ever an album understood the direction in which music was heading, it is this classic work. Short, eloquent, and mature, *The Low End Theory* was a consummate link between generations, taking the essence of jazz and the essence of hip-hop and showing they originated from the same black center. Tribe incorporated jazz's spirit into their being and came up with gems." (*Classic Material: The Hip-Hop Album Guide*)

NICK DRAKE *Pink Moon* (1972), Folk
Review: "Drake accompanies himself only on acoustic guitar, except for the title track, on which he overdubs a brief, lovely piano part. His lyrics are so compressed as to be kind of folkloric haikus, simple in their structure and elemental in their imagery. His voice conveys, in its moans and breathy whispers, an alluring sensuality, but he sings as if he were viewing his life from a great, unbridgeable distance. That element of detachment is chilling." (*Rolling Stone*)

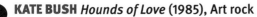

KATE BUSH *Hounds of Love* (1985), Art rock

Review: "*Hounds of Love* is actually a two-part album, consisting of the suites 'Hounds of Love' and 'The Ninth Wave.' The former is steeped in lyrical and sonic sensuality that tends to wash over the listener, while the latter is about the experiences of birth and rebirth. If this sounds like heady stuff, it could be, but Bush never lets the material get too far from its pop trappings and purpose. That vastly divergent grasp, from the minutiae of each song to the broad sweeping arc of the two suites, all heavily ornamented with layered instrumentation, makes this record wonderfully overpowering as a piece of pop music." (*All Music Guide*)

LCD SOUNDSYSTEM *LCD Soundsystem* (2005), Rock/Electronic

Review: "James Murphy of LCD Soundsystem specializes in fusing dance groove and punk attack. Several of the best tunes are inspired by Murphy's love-hate relationship with music: his struggle between wanting to be cool and feeling the impulse is loathsome, between his attachment to rock's heritage and his urge to rip it up and start again. Murphy weaves together sounds from the last 25 years of dance music, with a slant towards early-'80s mutant disco and recent house and hip-hop. He pushes the near-immaculate music into the realm of genius with witty lyrics and wonderfully tetchy vocals." (*Blender*)

LINDI ORTEGA *Little Red Boots* (2011), Country

Review: "Ortega, from Toronto, is as trad-country as they come, a rootin', tootin' chorus-slinger in the Dolly mold (musically at least). Like prime Parton, the 12 songs here remain unfailingly upbeat while Lindi warbles about often woefully downbeat subjects, usually involving her love-life. There's even a touch of the trademark vocal Dolly-wobble 'Black Fly,' which is all about a woman who just can't give up her no-good liar of a fellah. Then there's 'Dying of Another Broken Heart.' The tone? Still fairly cheery." (*BBC Music*)

> **A TIP FROM UNCLE JOHN**
>
> Another way to find new music: watch TV shows, which often feature great songs by up-and-coming artists. When you hear a song you like, use an app like Shazam to find out what it is.

LEON BRIDGES *Coming Home* (2015), R&B

Review: "Bridges sounds like the 21st-century reincarnation of Sam Cooke, with his smooth, soulful croon directly out the turbulent times of the early 1960s. And so with the obvious time-stamping and subtle musical odes to decades long past, it's easy to feel transported back to that bygone era. Bridges pays homage to an era so judiciously and so personally that it's hard to fault him as derivative. The horns throughout *Coming Home* augment the bass and the swing of the record." (*Paste Magazine*)

Number of Americans who still use an iron lung in 2019: three.

WEIRD WIKIPEDIA LISTS

When Uncle John saw this page, he cracked up laughing. We asked what's so funny and he said, "This—it's a microcosm of the internet age." Whatever that means, you'll find all these (and more) on the universe's favorite website.

- List of active sumo wrestlers
- List of animals with fraudulent diplomas
- List of deaths by laughter
- List of Eiffel Tower replicas
- List of English words containing Q not followed by U
- List of entertainers who died while performing
- List of famous trees
- List of fictional colors
- List of films featuring giant monsters
- List of films that most frequently use the word "f***"
- List of frivolous political parties
- List of hats and headgear
- List of fictional pigs
- List of humorous units of measurement
- List of hypothetical solar system objects
- List of inventors killed by their own invention
- List of Kim Jong-Il's titles
- List of Las Vegas casinos that never opened
- List of lists of films
- List of lists of lists

- List of microorganisms tested in outer space
- List of missing landmarks in Spain
- List of nicknames used by George W. Bush
- List of people claimed to be Jesus
- List of people who died on the toilet
- List of people who lived at the airport
- List of people with reduplicated names
- List of premature obituaries
- List of school pranks
- List of serial killers by country
- List of sexually active popes
- List of silent musical compositions
- List of *Star Trek* races
- List of television series canceled after one episode
- List of television series canceled before airing an episode
- List of unexplained sounds
- List of UFO religions
- List of unsolved problems
- List of U.S. state dinosaurs
- List of wartime cross-dressers
- List of celebrities who own wineries and vineyards

Weird NBA record: In 2019 Klay Thompson of the Golden State Warriors scored 43 points and only dribbled the ball four times.

A VERY MUPPET SCANDAL

What goes on behind the scenes at the Jim Henson Company?
Turns out it's not all laughs and rainbow connections.

KERMIT THE FRAUD

Only three people have ever been the official puppeteers behind the most famous Muppet of them all, Kermit the Frog. The first was his creator, Jim Henson, from 1955 until Henson's death in 1990. The second: veteran Muppet operator Steve Whitmire. Personally selected by Henson's wife and son (Jane and Brian), Whitmire, whose most prominent role to that point was Rizzo the Rat, performed Kermit through multiple Muppet movies, TV series, commercials, and talk show appearances…until 2017, when Brian Henson abruptly fired him. Henson was cagey with reporters about his reasons, noting only that Whitmire had engaged in some "unprofessional" conduct dating back to the 1990s, suggesting that Whitmire acted as if he knew Kermit better than anyone. And he used that status as leverage to get more money from Henson and more control over the Muppet character. Brian Henson also didn't care for Whitmire's evolving interpretation of Kermit, saying that the character had "flattened out over time, and had become too square and not as vital as it should have been." For his part, Whitmire said he was punished for being too "outspoken about what's best for the Muppets." (The third puppeteer: Matt Vogel, who was the voice of Big Bird and Count von Count at the time he was promoted to take over Kermit.)

MURDERING *HAPPYTIME*

Sesame Street and the Muppets are inexorably linked. Jim Henson's company's creations, such as Big Bird, Cookie Monster, and Elmo, helped make the long-running children's educational series the cultural icon that it is. Those ties were tested in 2018 when the Sesame Workshop, producer of *Sesame Street*, sued the Jim Henson Company—specifically its HA! Henson Alternative division. Reason: in August 2018, HA! planned to release the first Muppet-based feature film in five years, an R-rated, extremely dark comedy called *The Happytime Murders*. (The plot: a Muppet detective teams up with a human detective, portrayed by Melissa McCarthy, to investigate the grisly murders and overall deviant behavior of the puppet cast of a *Sesame Street*–like show called *The Happytime Gang*.) Promotional materials, including posters and a trailer, used the tagline "No Sesame, All Street." Sesame filed suit, claiming the line would cause "irreparable harm" to *Sesame Street's* wholesome reputation and "defile" its brand. A judge threw out the case, and ruled that *Happytime* producers could continue to use the tagline.

Apollo 17 (1972) astronaut Harrison Schmitt had a nasty allergic reaction to moon dust.

JUST FRIENDS

For decades, the rumor has circulated that Bert and Ernie are more than just friends—that they're less of an *Odd Couple* than they are an actual couple. In the early 1990s, there was even an urban legend that claimed *Sesame Street* planned to kill off the characters because so many enraged parents had threatened to form a boycott of a show with openly gay characters. (It wasn't true.) Numerous representatives of the show have released statements over the years stating that Bert and Ernie aren't gay… or straight: "They're puppets," one statement drolly explained. But in 2018, former *Sesame Street* writer Mark Saltzman reawakened the controversy when he told the gay lifestyle blog *Queerty* that the puppet couple *are* gay. "When I was writing Bert and Ernie, they were," Saltzman said. He said he drew on his own long-term same-sex relationship to inform how sketches featuring the duo were crafted. After news spread online that a *Sesame Street* writer "confirmed" that Bert and Ernie were, indeed, in love, the Sesame Workshop had to release a statement. "Bert and Ernie are best friends," it read. "They were created to teach preschoolers that people can be good friends with those who are very different from themselves."

* * *

A RANDOM BIT OF FACTINESS

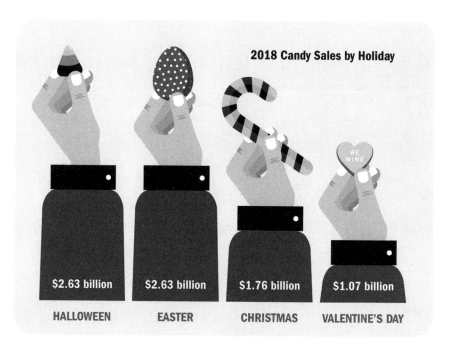

2018 Candy Sales by Holiday

| $2.63 billion | $2.63 billion | $1.76 billion | $1.07 billion |
| HALLOWEEN | EASTER | CHRISTMAS | VALENTINE'S DAY |

A ROOMBA WITH A POO

Have you ever seen the sci-fi anthology TV show Black Mirror? *It presents worst-case scenarios of modern technology. This true story could make the grossest* Black Mirror *episode of them all.*

THE POOPENING

One problem with a robot vacuum cleaner: it has no sense of smell. Otherwise it would know not to spread a pile of dog doo all over the house. Jesse Newton of Little Rock, Arkansas, learned that lesson the hard way in 2016. In the middle of the night, the family dog made a sizable "deposit" onto the living room floor. The family Roomba, meanwhile, was making its nightly rounds. Then, as Newton later wrote, the Roomba "spread the dog poop over every surface within its reach, resulting in a home that closely resembles a Jackson Pollock poop painting." The grossest part: "When your four-year-old gets up at 3 a.m. to crawl into your bed, you'll wonder why he smells like dog poop."

In Newton's Facebook account of his unfortunate event (which went viral), he warns other Roomba/dog owners: "Do not, under any circumstances, let your Roomba run over dog poop." Duly noted.

You can read his entire account online (it's hilarious). But be warned, it gets *really* gross when he tries to clean up the mess.

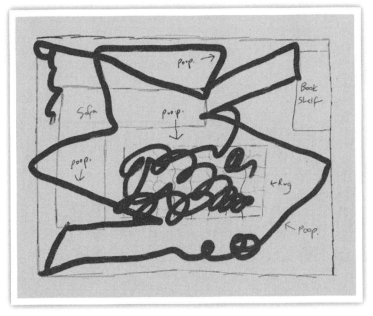

Here's Newton's drawing of the Roomba's "Pooptastrophe"

There's a person on the Queen of England's staff whose job it is to break in all of Her Majesty's new shoes.

WEIRD CANADA

O, Canada: where the mountains are capped with snow, the maple trees and beavers are abundant, and the news stories are really, really strange.

PURRLOINED

In the summer of 2017, a neighborhood in North Delta, British Columbia, was beset by a crime wave. The offense: laundry hanging out to dry on backyard clotheslines started disappearing. There was no rhyme or reason to it, with everything from shirts to socks to pants to underwear being stolen on a regular basis. The thefts continued until September 2018, when the culprit—or rather, the culprit's representative—came forward. Shawn Bell admitted that his cat, Bella, had been grabbing dangling clothes and bringing them home. "Last year I thought it was just a phase, and then she just ramped it up. Instead of bringing home one article a day, she was bringing home multiple," Bell told the CBC. "Last summer it wasn't that bad but now we're getting into the territory of people's full wardrobes." When it got out of hand, he went to the media, and then started posting photos of his cat's ill-gotten gains on the North Delta Community Corner Facebook page. "It's getting to be quite a big pile and I don't want to do other people's laundry," he said. (No word on why he waited more than a year to speak up.)

LEGAL ARRRRG-UMENTS

After the popularity of the *Pirates of the Caribbean* movies, a Halifax, Nova Scotia, man named Dwight Parker formed an entertainment troupe called Pirates of Halifax. Parker and his friends are "re-creationists" who dress up in pirate costumes and put on elaborate, swordfight-heavy shows at parks, events, and children's birthday parties. All was calm on the high seas until 2016, when the Pirates of Halifax forced Parker to walk the plank (i.e., they kicked him out), and so he formed a rival group…which he *also* called the Pirates of Halifax. While the two groups worked out some legalities—one owned the rights to "piratesofhalifax.com," but both used the name on social media and in promotional materials—neither had outright ownership of the name "Pirates of Halifax," so in 2018 they took the matter to a small-claims court. Winner: no one.

> **A TIP FROM UNCLE JOHN**
>
> Settling in Canada? According to Canada's immigration office, when you move into a new home, neighbors (or "neighbours") will probably show up with a gift to introduce themselves. Thereafter, if you see them around town, it's customary to say hello, but not to stop and have a conversation.

Adjudicator (the equivalent of a judge) Eric Slone ruled that the first group's various filings consisted of a legal partnership, but since it was never dissolved when Parker was kicked out, neither group has a legal claim on the name.

DON'T DRINK AND FARM

Police responding to a call about a drunk driver who is causing property damage is, unfortunately, not particularly unusual. But it is a bit odd if the driver's vehicle is a tractor and the location is a golf course. In July 2018, Royal Canadian Mounted Police responded to a call at Riverbank Golf & RV Park, near the eastern Alberta town of Wandering River. Park owner Derek Getty was in the clubhouse that evening when one of his customers reported seeing a man on a John Deere tractor "tearing it up" across a fairway. After Getty chased him for a while (on foot), the police arrived, caught the joyrider, Bobby Trefaneko, and charged him with a series of crimes. "What we like to remind motorists is that any sort of vehicle that has a motor, the same traffic laws apply," Constable Andrew Deme told reporters.

SACRE BLEU LANGUAGE

Canada is a bilingual country—federal signage must be displayed in both English and French, and there's a robust francophone broadcasting industry. The Canadian Broadcasting Standards Council determines what's appropriate for the airwaves no matter what language is being broadcast, and in November 2017, the panel decided that the F-word (not fart) was no longer profane…but *only* if it were used in its English form, on French-language programs. That means it can be used freely, any time of day. "Language is evolutionary and reflects current society," the CBSC said in its ruling, arguing that the English F-word was now "part of the common French spoken language" and did not carry the same "vulgar connotations" as when it's used in English.

A CALL FOR ORDER!

Former all-time *Jeopardy!* champion Ken Jennings is obviously a curious guy—if he wasn't, he wouldn't have acquired enough general knowledge to win 74 straight episodes of the popular show. In 2012 Jennings announced on social media that he'd been using Google Earth to work on a project: He had successfully located the world's largest "third-order island." What's that? It's an island located in a lake, which in turn is surrounded by another island, surrounded by another lake, which is on an island, inside an ocean. Jennings discovered a small, unnamed land mass (inside of a lake, et cetera, et cetera) on Victoria Island, located in the territory of Nunavut in the far north of Canada.

Rowan Atkinson, "Mr. Bean," has a master's degree in electrical engineering.

WORD ORIGINS

Ever wonder where words come from? Here are some interesting stories behind them.

RAISE

Meaning: To nurture and prepare a child for adulthood
Origin: "You can raise or rear a child. The word *raise* comes from the Old Norse term *reisa*, and *rear* is a native English word, but both are descended from the same Germanic ancestor, *raizjan*. Under certain conditions the Germanic *z* became *r* in the West Germanic languages, of which English is one. However, the original consonant (spelled *s*) remained in other Germanic languages, including Old Norse. Both *raise* and *rear* are related to *rise*. No words related to these three verbs have been found outside of Germanic." (From *Word Mysteries & Histories: From Quiche to Humble Pie*, by the editors of American Heritage Dictionaries)

DRUMSTICK

Meaning: The lower joint of the leg of a cooked chicken, turkey, or other fowl
Origin: "The drumstick of a turkey or other fowl is so called because it looks like a drumstick in shape. But the word is a euphemism of British origin, invented as a substitute for *leg*, which the Victorians found offensive enough to call a *limb*." (From *The Facts on File Encyclopedia of Word and Phrase Origins*, by Robert Hendrickson)

CAUCUS

Meaning: A meeting of supporters or members of a specific political party or movement
Origin: "*Caucus* entered English as a byproduct of the conspiratorial activities in Boston that helped ignite the American Revolution. John Adams wrote in his diary in 1763: 'This day learned that the Caucas Clubb meets at certain Times in the Garret of Tom Daws, the Adjutant of the Boston Regiment.' Of much debated origin, *caucus* had often been regarded as probably Algonquian [a family of North American native languages spoken from the Atlantic seaboard to the Great Plains]. But expert opinion currently holds it more likely to have come from Latin *caucus*, 'drinking vessel.'" (From *O Brave New Words! Native American Loanwords in Current English*, by Charles L. Cutler)

ROSEMARY

Meaning: An herb that comes from an aromatic evergreen shrub
Origin: "This shrub once had strong associations with weddings and was a symbol of fidelity in love. *Rosemary* is a lovely name, but the original Latin is even better: *ros*

The title Mahatma (as in Gandhi) is Sanskrit for "great-souled."

marinus, 'sea dew,' perhaps because it grew in coastal margins. That name was taken into English as *rosmarine* about the turn of the first millennium and survived until the 17th century. But well over a century before Shakespeare's day, people had taken this odd, little Latinate word and shaken it into something that looked more sensible, changing *ros* to *rose* and altering the ending, perhaps to refer to the Virgin Mary." (From *Ballyhoo Buckaroo and Spuds: Ingenious Tales of Words and Their Origins*, by Michael Quinion)

ACHE

Meaning: To feel pain in a particular part of the body
Origin: "The word *ache* is a good example of the way that English spelling and pronunciation have developed and in many cases have diverged from each other. The noun comes from Old English and used to be pronounced 'aitch' (like the letter H), whereas the verb was originally spelled *ake* and pronounced the way *ache* is today. Around 1700, people started pronouncing the noun like the verb (*ake*) used to be. The modern spelling is largely due to lexicographer Samuel Johnson, who mistakenly assumed that word came from Greek *akhos* 'pain.' Other pairs of words that have survived into modern English with *k*-for-the-verb and *ch*-for-the noun include *speak* and *speech* and *break* and *breach*." (From *Oxford Dictionary of Word Origins*, by Julia Cresswell)

TERRORIST

Meaning: A member of a clandestine organization aiming to coerce a government by acts of violence
Origin: "This term was originally applied (as an Anglicization of the French *terroriste*) to the Jacobins and their agents and partisans in the French Revolution, especially to those connected with the Revolutionary tribunals during the 'Reign of Terror'; and in the mid-19th century it was used to denote members of any of the extreme revolutionary societies in Russia." *Terrorist* entered English in the 1940s. (From *20th Century Words*, by John Ayto)

IDIOSYNCRASY

Meaning: A mode of behavior or way of thought peculiar to an individual
Origin: "The Greek root *idio* means 'of a particular person' or 'personal' and pops up in many other English words such as *idiom* ('one's own way of speaking') and *idiot* (originally 'common man'). The Greek root *synkrasis* meant 'a blending or mixture' or 'meshing.' Put all the pieces together, and we have *idiosyncrasy*, meaning 'an individual's mixture of personal characteristics.' Incidentally, *idiosyncrasy* is one of those rare English words whose modern sense corresponds almost precisely to the combined meanings of its ancient root. Language almost never operates in such an orderly fashion." (From *The Word Detective*, by Evan Morris)

The average automobile spends 95% of its useful life parked.

OLD-TIME RACISM

If you ever feel that someone is being too politically correct, take a look at these examples of subtle cultural racism that most people once considered "harmless."

SAMBO'S RESTAURANT

In the 1960s—at the height of the 20th century's civil rights movement—millions of Americans regularly ate at one of more than 1,000 locations of this family restaurant chain. Originally, it was named for the owners, Sam Battistone and Newell Bohnett, but the restaurants' theme and decor used images from an old children's book called *The Story of Little Black Sambo.* And although the word is traditionally a nasty slur against African Americans dating back to the 1850s, the book was about a boy from India—whose skin isn't brown, it's *black*-black. By the 1960s, customers started to complain that the paintings of a dark-skinned child that decorated the walls of Sambo's (taken from the book) were offensive, so restaurant execs changed the art so that Sambo would more closely follow *Indian* stereotypes—they lightened the mascot a few shades and gave him a jeweled turban.

Throughout the 1970s, many cities passed laws banning the use of the name Sambo's, forcing the company to change the names of multiple locations to the Jolly Tiger and, later, to No Place Like Sam's. There's only one Sambo's left, and it's in Santa Barbara, California.

DARKIE TOOTHPASTE

Beginning in 1933, the Hawley and Hazel Chemical Company distributed a brand of toothpaste called Darkie. The box features what's clearly supposed to be a minstrel show performer: a guy in blackface, a top hat...and flashing his shiny white teeth. It was sold with that name around the world for more than 50 years. In 1985 Colgate bought the company that manufactured Darkie and in 1989, responding to public pressure, changed the brand name to "Darlie"—a change small enough so that consumers could still identify the product, but big enough so that the name could no longer be identified as racist.

SIAMESE TWINS

It's hard to get people to stop calling things what they've always been called. For example, the medical syndrome once called leprosy is now properly referred to as Hansen's disease. Similarly, conjoined twins used to be called Siamese twins. That's because the first time most people heard about two babies born attached were Chang and Eng Bunker, two conjoined twins who became famous when they toured the United States in the 19th century as a "freak show" attraction. The Bunkers were

The 85 richest people on earth own about as much wealth as the 3.5 billion poorest.

Chinese, but born in Siam (now known as Thailand), so they were billed as "Siamese twins." Use of that term today is considered offensive to both people from Thailand as well as conjoined twins.

PICKANINNY PEPPERMINTS

Dating back to the 1700s, "Pickaninny" (from the Portuguese *pequenino*, "little") was a racial slur used to describe dark-skinned African children, particularly slave children. In 1899 the chocolate company Whitman's (which is still around today) debuted chocolate-covered Pickaninny Peppermints. The packages featured smiling black kids (one of whom is eating watermelon) and sold well with little backlash… until 1939, when NAACP lawyer and future Supreme Court justice Thurgood Marshall wrote a letter of complaint to Whitman's. Their response: "We feel that the term connotes a cute Negro child" and that to throw away all of the unused packaging "would be quite a hardship." But Marshall persisted and, four years later, Whitman's discontinued the product.

GHETTO BLASTER

Before everyone carried the entirety of recorded music around on their smartphones, one of the few ways to enjoy tunes on the go was with a portable stereo, colloquially referred to as a boombox because they were loud. Those things were mostly speaker, and required about 10 D-cell batteries to work. Introduced in the United States in the late 1970s, within a few years they found a market with urban youth, who could not only listen to them at home, but could carry them around on the subway and down the street, blasting tuneage for all the world to hear. They were a big part of hip-hop and urban African American youth culture, which led to the widespread, pejorative use of the phrase "ghetto blaster" to describe those portable stereos.

CHINESE CHERRY AND INJUN ORANGE

Introduced in 1927, Kool-Aid dominated the powdered drink market by the 1960s, by which time the brand was owned by the conglomerate General Foods. In 1964 Pillsbury tried to break into that market with a Kool-Aid knockoff called Funny Face. Just as Kool-Aid had a kid-friendly hook of a mascot—a sentient, man-sized pitcher of Kool-Aid—Funny Face brought its own flair. Each flavor had a memorable name with an anthropomorphized fruit pictured on the envelope. In addition to "Goofy Grape" and "Freckle-Face Strawberry," Funny Face was available in "Chinese Cherry" and "Injun Orange." The cherry character sported stereotypically slanted eyes and buck teeth, while the orange one wore a headdress and "war paint." Before the year was out, Pillsbury pulled those two flavors and replaced them with "Jolly Olly Orange" and "Choo Choo Cherry."

Roman emperor Caligula threatened death to anyone who mentioned…

PLAYING WITH POOP

Well, it seems the world has finally caught up with the Bathroom Readers' Institute. What's the latest poop in toys and games? Poop-themed toys and games. Here are some real ones. (Uncle John spotted them at the toy store when he was looking for the restroom.)

Toy: Sticky the Poo

Manufacturer: Hog Wild

Details: Can a game that combines darts with going to the bathroom be bad? This one is. It consists of a target that you hang on a wall directly in front of your toilet. Then sit down and throw the brown, google-eyed, plastic dart (shaped like a turd) at the target and try to score a bull's-eye. The manufacturer—educational toy seller Scholar's Choice—claims it helps kids develop "gross motor skills."

Toy: Flushin' Frenzy

Manufacturer: Mattel

Details: To play this game, kids first set up a small toilet replica consisting of a tank and a bowl. Players then take turns, rolling the dice (which is done by flushing the toilet, like a slot machine) to see how many times they have to push a toy plunger into the bowl. If you plunge and nothing happens, it's the next player's turn. If your plunging sends a brown plastic log ("Pooper") shooting up from out of the tank, all players try and grab it to earn tokens. Object of the game: catch the poop!

Toy: Don't Step In It!

Manufacturer: Hasbro

Details: This game replicates the experience of what it feels like to step in dog poop…barefoot. A Don't Step In It! box contains a long, green mat made to look like grass. Players then use the included Play-Doh-esque compound to mold little poop piles. One player then puts the poop on the mat while the other player puts on a blindfold and then walks on the poop-covered mat without shoes or socks. If they step on what's reportedly some very realistic-feeling fake poop, they lose.

Toy: Poo-Dough

Manufacturer: Skyrocket Toys

Details: How this toy company managed to avoid legal action from Hasbro, the venerable maker of Play-Doh, we do not know. Regardless, this poop-themed crafting kit comes with modeling clay in various shades of brown (and one yellow). Place your desired combination into the included mold, and extrude a four-inch segmented log that looks like it could have come from a human or a dog.

Toy: Flush Force

Manufacturer: Spin Master

Details: The Flush Force series is like a toilet-themed Pokémon—little monsters said to have come from the sewers. Looking kind of like animals who've been adversely affected by nuclear waste, the figurines come with slime-covered toilets, which they now call home. There are 150 characters (collect 'em all!) with names like Stink Eye and Hot Clog, Bile Burger, Log Jammer, Upchuck Duck, Brown Trout, and Dung Digger.

Toy: Doggie Doo

Manufacturer: Goliath Games

Details: Goliath claims that this toy "models responsibility in a fun (and gross!) way." How? It gets kids ready for what it's like to have a real dog by having to clean up the leavings of a toy dog (a google-eyed plastic Dachshund). Kids feed him plastic food pellets and then squeeze his leash…until either a fart noise or a pellet comes out the other end.

Toy: Fishing for Floaters

Manufacturer: Ales Toy

Details: This one supposedly helps kids learn hand-eye coordination—and maybe it does. But it's also just an excuse to fill the bathtub with (plastic) poop. Here's how the game is played: Put the coiled turds and brown logs (all with eyes glued on) into a filled-up tub or sink, and two players take turns trying to catch them with plastic fishing poles and nets. (Simple! Fun! Yuck!)

Toy: Toilet Trouble

Manufacturer: Hasbro

Details: Similar to Flushin' Frenzy, but it's a bit more of a visceral bathroom-emulating experience. Players take turns spinning a toilet paper roll to determine how many times they must flush the handle of a miniature tabletop toilet. Lucky players hear the flushing sound…and get off scot-free; unlucky ones get a spray of toilet water to the face.

Toy: Mr. Turd

Manufacturer: The Pet Turd

Details: It's a takeoff on the inexplicable 1970s Pet Rock fad, updated to reflect (and capitalize on) today's apparent obsession with plastic poop. Mr. Turd, billed as "the perfect family pet," comes packaged in a brown cardboard box, just like the original Pet Rocks, sitting atop a nest of comfortable hay. Mr. Turd himself is quite real-looking, a brown, coiled turd that fits right in the palm of one's hand. And also like the Pet Rock, Mr. Turd isn't a game, it doesn't "doo" anything—you just have it. (After you buy it.)

The & originated as a combination of the "e" and "t." *Et* is the Latin word for "and."

BEASTLY PLACES

If you love animals, you might want to consider moving to one of these cities.

- Buffalo, New York
- Turkey, Texas
- Duck, West Virginia
- Chicken, Alaska
- Alligator, Mississippi
- Sturgeon, Pennsylvania
- Badger, Minnesota
- New Falcon, Texas
- Wild Horse, Colorado
- Elk, Washington
- Anaconda, Montana
- Spider, Kentucky
- Grey Eagle, Minnesota
- Bumble Bee, Arizona
- Pigeon, Michigan
- Caribou, Maine
- Hoot Owl, Oklahoma
- Wildcat, Wyoming
- Salmon, Idaho
- White Swan, Washington
- Trout, Louisiana
- Bison, South Dakota
- Elephant, Pennsylvania
- Antelope, California
- Parrot, Georgia
- Blue Heron, Kentucky
- Flamingo, Florida
- Tiger, Washington

- Beaver, Alaska
- Carp, Nevada
- Dinosaur, Colorado
- Porcupine, South Dakota
- Rabbit Town, Maryland
- Whitefish, Michigan
- Fox, Alaska
- Pig, Kentucky
- Coyote, New Mexico
- Crab Orchard, Nebraska
- Marlin, Texas
- Goat Town, Georgia
- Lions, Louisiana
- Pelican, Louisiana
- Bear, Arizona
- Crane, Missouri
- Peacock, Michigan
- Mustang, Oklahoma
- Toad Suck, Arkansas
- Wolverine, Michigan
- Cougar, Washington
- Mastodon, Michigan
- Deer, Arkansas
- Moose, Wyoming
- Wolf, Wyoming
- Otter, Montana
- Partridge, Kansas
- Swanville, Minnesota

Average annual water bill for a golf course: $81,000.

STOLEN SCIENCE

A list of Nobel Prize winners in the sciences is a Who's Who of the men who've advanced their fields. Only problem: the men credited (and rewarded) for some of those advances may have leapfrogged over the women who actually made the discoveries.

LISE MEITNER

FIELD: Nuclear fission

STORY: In the 1930s, two scientists led a group at the Kaiser Wilhelm Institute in Berlin, Germany: Austrian physicist Lise Meitner and German chemist Otto Hahn. The two shared a lab for more than 30 years, and the work they did together changed history. Their findings were critical to the development of nuclear power (and atomic bombs). Though Meitner's Jewish ethnicity forced her to flee Nazi Germany in 1938, she continued to guide Hahn through correspondence (and the occasional secret meeting) as he performed experiments in the lab they'd once shared. When an experiment bombarding uranium with neutrons produced barium, Hahn couldn't figure out why. "Perhaps you can come up with some sort of fantastic explanation," Hahn wrote to Meitner. Meitner could, and did. She realized that the uranium had split into smaller elements, and the mass that it lost was converted to energy. She called the process "fission." Hahn published their findings...without listing Meitner as coauthor. The Nobel Prize for the discovery of nuclear fission was awarded in 1944.

And the award went to... Otto Hahn, despite the fact that renowned physicist Neils Bohr made the nomination, listing Meitner's name first and Hahn's second. Over the course of her career, Meitner received 48 nominations for Nobel Prizes. How many did she receive? Zero.

MARIETTA BLAU

FIELD: Particle physics

STORY: The field of particle physics wouldn't exist without the ability to investigate and record cosmic rays. The scientist who figured out how to do that, Marietta Blau, has been largely lost to history. Blau was born in 1894 to an upper-middle-class Austrian family and, as such, was given a university education. After earning her diploma in physics and mathematics from Vienna University, Dr. Blau joined the Vienna Institute for Radium Research as an unpaid staff member. When she applied for a paid position, she was rejected...but it wasn't because of her abilities. "You are a woman and a Jew," she was told, "and the two together are simply too much."

Plural of cul-de-sac: culs-de-sac.

In 1937 Blau and one of her students, Hertha Wambacher, became the first physicists to capture nuclear processes on film. They developed the use of film emulsions to track and identify particles from radioactive materials, accelerators, and cosmic rays. What happened next? Adolf Hitler. Germany annexed Austria in 1938, so Blau fled to Mexico. For the remainder of her career, she worked in relative obscurity, usually for little or no pay. In 1950 a sole winner was awarded the Nobel Prize in Physics for "developing the photographic method of studying nuclear processes."

And the award went to... Cecil Frank Powell. His work relied directly on Blau's research, methods, and discoveries. But he didn't give her any credit in his acceptance speech. Over the course of her career, Blau was nominated for five Nobel Prizes, one in chemistry and four in physics. Two of those nominations came from the physicist Erwin Schrödinger (of the cat-in-a-box fame). But despite being one of the most accomplished scientists of the 20th century, Blau never received a single Nobel Prize. When she died in 1970 in a Viennese hospital from a radiation-related illness, she had listed the concierge of her apartment building as her next of kin.

VERA RUBIN

FIELD: Dark matter

STORY: As recently as 50 years ago, the universe was thought to be made up of "normal matter": mainly atoms and subatomic particles with perhaps a bit of gas and dust. But something didn't quite add up. In the 1930s, Swiss astronomer Fritz Zwicky noted something he called "missing mass." He'd been observing the Coma Cluster of galaxies, 321 million light-years from Earth, and according to Zwicky's calculations, the cluster had to contain much more mass than was visible. If that wasn't so, instead of clustering around a central core, the galaxies would have spiraled off into open space. In the 1970s, American astrophysicist Vera Rubin worked with astronomer Kent Ford to examine how galaxies rotate. They concluded that nearly all spiral galaxies were spinning much too fast to be accounted for by the gravitational pull of "luminous matter"—that which can be seen through a telescope. There must be some giant invisible source of gravitational attraction. Though Zwicky first noted the "missing mass," Rubin and Ford's work provided conclusive evidence for the existence of dark matter. In 2011 a Nobel Prize in Physics was awarded for work related to the mysterious dark stuff of the cosmos.

And the award went to... Three men—Saul Perlmutter, Brian Schmidt, and Adam Reiss. They were awarded the prize for discovering "dark energy" from the observations of distant supernovas. But what about the woman who provided the evidence that 90 percent of the cosmos is made up of dark

> She waited more than 45 years for a Nobel Prize that never came.

The underground vault at Lego headquarters in Denmark contains nearly every Lego set ever made.

matter? Nothing. Vera Rubin waited more than 45 years for a Nobel Prize that never came. She died in 2016.

CHIEN-SHIUNG WU

FIELD: Nuclear physics

STORY: Theories are crucial to scientific advances, but without testing, they're just brain games. In the 1950s, Chinese physicists Tsung-Dao Lee and Chen-Ning Yang were attempting to understand how particles behaved, and they wondered whether decaying particles would obey the "law of conservation of parity." This law states that two physical systems that are mirror images should behave in identical ways. Lee and Yang thought that, under some conditions, the law might not hold. There was another physicist—a woman named Chien-Shiung Wu—who was working on the problem. Rather than just *think* about the idea, she tested it. Using cobalt-60, a radioactive form of the cobalt metal, she observed that in the presence of a strong magnetic field, the decaying particles showed a "handedness," a preferred direction of decay. The "Wu Experiment" overturned the law of conservation of parity, a law that had been accepted in theory for 30 years. The 1957 Nobel Prize was awarded for this discovery.

And the award went to... Tsung-Dao Lee and Chen-Ning Yang, without a single mention of the contributions of Chien-Shiung Wu. Later in life, she was an outspoken critic of the sexism that had kept her from being awarded a Nobel Prize: "I wonder whether the tiny atoms and nuclei, or the mathematical symbols, or the DNA molecules have any preference for either masculine or feminine treatment."

> **A TIP FROM UNCLE JOHN**
>
> Afraid of someone stealing your invention? According to *Forbes*, reveal as few details as possible about it to coworkers, friends, and clients. You can even employ a legally binding nondisclosure agreement. Then apply for a trademark, provisional patent, or copyright—whichever one applies. And at every step of the way, document your progress—a paper trail is tough to defeat.

* * *

MYTH-CONCEPTION

Myth: Cats were first domesticated by ancient Egyptians.

Fact: The first archaeological evidence of cats being selectively bred as pets goes back nearly 10,000 years to Neolithic paintings found in Cyprus, Greece. The Egyptians didn't start breeding cats for another 5,000 years...and because they worshipped the animals as gods, one could argue that it was the cats who domesticated them.

A statue of Nikola Tesla in Silicon Valley serves as a free Wi-Fi hotspot.

GUN GOOFS

A friendly reminder that a firearm is not a thing to be trifled with. The outcomes of these stories could have been a whole lot worse.

THE RIGHT TO BEAR ARMADILLOS

> In 2015 a Georgia man named Larry McElroy had an unwanted armadillo digging up his rural property, so he got out his 9-mm pistol, took aim, and fired. Predictably, the bullet bounced off the animal's armored shell. Unpredictably, the ricochet hit a fence, then went through the back door of McElroy's mother-in-law's trailer, and hit her square in the back (after passing through a recliner). Carol Johnson (the mother-in-law) suffered only minor injuries. The local sheriff's office offered this advice: "[If you're] going to shoot at varmints and whatnot, maybe use a shotgun."

> A Texas man also tried to shoot an armadillo in 2015. At around 3:00 a.m., he grabbed his .38 revolver, stormed outside, and fired three shots at the animal. One of the bullets bounced back and hit the man right in the face. The armadillo wandered away, and the man's shattered jaw had to be wired shut.

TEACHER, TEACH THYSELF

The lesson that day in March 2018 was gun safety. Dennis Alexander, a high school math teacher and reserve police officer in Seaside, California, told his students the first thing is to make sure the gun isn't loaded. But pointing it at the ceiling and pulling the trigger is probably *not* the best way to do that. Thinking the chamber was empty, that's what Alexander did. A mass of ceiling debris came down on the neck of a 17-year-old student. But the teen said he was okay, and no one else was hurt, so Alexander continued the lesson. He even let the kids hold the unloaded weapon and take selfies with it. It wasn't until after school, when the injured student arrived home with blood on his shirt and pieces of the ceiling (and possibly some bullet fragments) lodged in his neck, that the incident was reported to the police. Alexander was ultimately not charged with a crime, but he's no longer a teacher. Or a police officer.

DOOR PRIZE

"I blew my arm off," lamented a 68-year-old North Carolina man in a really depressing 911 call. Here's how he did it: When he stepped out of his back door to feed the squirrels, he triggered a trip wire, which set off a shotgun that shot him in the arm. The booby-trap was one of several he set up on his land to thwart (according to his warning sign out front) "all you crack heads, meth heads, heroin users, drug dealers, or anyone doing criminal activity!" An ambulance arrived and took him to the hospital. It's unclear from press reports if doctors were able to save his arm, or if the squirrels ever got fed.

GUN NUTS

> "Florida man sits on gun, accidentally shoots self in genitals," read the actual news headline. The Florida man was Cedrick Jelks. One morning in July 2017, he was getting into his car when he sat down…and the gun went off. He ran screaming into his girlfriend's bathroom, and she rushed him to the hospital. Emergency surgery was somewhat successful, but Jelks, 38, had other problems. Due to a 2004 conviction, he cannot legally possess a firearm. At last report, he was looking at a minimum of three years in prison.

> In November 2018, a man (unnamed in press reports) was shopping in the Buckeye, Arizona, Walmart when the semiautomatic handgun he keeps unholstered in his pants started to slip. As he tried to readjust the gun, it went off, sputtering a bunch of rounds into his manhood. According to the *Arizona Republic*, "Police found the man in the meat section of the Walmart with survivable injuries."

NOT MUCH OF A MULTITASKER

Rorn Sorn was in the men's room of a Florida strip club in 2017 when he tried to take a mean-looking selfie. But holding up his handgun while aiming his phone back at himself proved a bit too much to handle, and the gun fired. The bullet pierced the stall wall and went into the ladies' room, which (this being a strip club) was empty. In addition to the .40-caliber firearm, Sorn, 34, also had in his possession a gun magazine, some marijuana, and a container of Xanax pills. That, along with a rap sheet that included burglary and attempted murder, got him sentenced to six years in prison.

FLIPPING BUREAU OF INVESTIGATION

An FBI agent did a backflip and shot an innocent bystander. Ta-da! It happened in a Denver, Colorado, nightclub in July 2018. A 29-year-old off-duty agent named Chase Bishop (which sounds like it came from a TV writer) was "cutting it up" on the dance floor. When a crowd gathered around, cheering him on, he attempted the acrobatic dance move. Bad move. As soon as Agent Bishop's feet got over his head, his service weapon fell out of his pants and landed on the floor. He lunged to pick it up, and it fired a bullet into the left leg of Thomas Reddington, 24, who was sitting at a nearby table. "It's bizarre," Reddington told ABC News. "Beyond bizarre. It's beyond comprehension I think right now for me, just with all the factors involved." Agent Bishop (who was legally allowed to carry a concealed weapon) pled guilty to third-degree assault in order to avoid jail time. It's not known whether he's still employed by the FBI. As for Reddington, he's been left with a permanent injury to his leg, but he said he doesn't hold a grudge against Bishop: "I've done stupid things at bars to impress girls, too."

What's *cryptophasia*? The language twins invent to talk to each other.

DOGS AND CATS

Ever wonder what your furry friend is trying to tell you?

SNEEZING DOG: You're playing with your dog, or watching her play with another dog, when all of a sudden she starts sneezing. This isn't due to dust in the air, or an allergy. It's a behavioral signal that translates to: "This might look like fighting, but I just wanted to remind us both not to get carried away, because we're just playing."

TERRITORIAL CAT: Your cat roams all over the house, rubbing his face on curtains, chairs, table legs, your legs…pretty much everything. This behavior, called "bunting," is your cat's way of marking his territory. His scent glands are located around his chin, cheeks, and mouth. He leaves his barely detectable but unique odor on everything he rubs up against.

EYE OF THE DOG: Humans treat eye contact as a sign of respect when meeting others; dogs do not. When your dog sees a stranger (human or dog), he might turn his eyes or his entire head away. He's not being rude, or expressing distrust or disinterest. By *not* staring the stranger down, your dog is saying, "You aren't a threat to me, and I'm not a threat to you."

LAP CAT: Does your cat try to jump on your lap or your laptop every time you sit down to work? You may think she's seeking attention, but she isn't. This action is actually of great biological significance. Your cat's optimal body temperature is about 20 degrees higher than yours is, so when she's feeling chilly, she'll seek out the warmest place in the house…which is often you or your laptop.

YAWNING DOG: This is another case of people projecting their own behaviors onto their pets. Your dog *might* yawn when he's tired or bored (like you), but in times of stress—such as when he's being scolded, or he's at the vet—he's not being dismissive with his yawn. That quick gulp of air immediately helps to calm him down.

PROFESSOR CAT: Although cats have been domesticated for millennia, their instinct to hunt remains strong. Whether your outdoor cat plops a bird or a mouse on the porch, or your indoor cat presents you with a feathery cat toy, this isn't a "gift." Animal behavioral experts believe your cat is doing this to teach *you*. He doesn't see *you* hunting, so by presenting you with this dead prey, he's trying to show you how it's done.

Pseudis paradoxa, or the paradoxical frog, is four times larger as a newborn than it is as an adult.

THE SUPERHERO ORPHAN QUIZ

For superheroes, it's almost as much of a cliché as their selfless urges to fight for justice and save the day: It seems that every one of them is an orphan, scarred for life by their parents having died while they were so young. But can you match up the superhero (or supervillain) with the horrible way their parents croaked?

1. Batman

2. Spider-Man

3. Daredevil

4. Wolverine

5. Superman

6. Robin

7. Captain America

8. Jessica Jones

9. Catwoman

10. Green Hornet

11. Hawkeye

12. Iron Man

13. Elektra

14. Captain Marvel

a) Home planet exploded

b) Father died in prison

c) Killed by assassins

d) Killed in a grisly car accident

e) Killed in a car accident that spilled radioactive goo

f) Both killed during World War I

g) Killed by a mugger in the street

h) Killed in a plane crash

i) Killed by the Winter Soldier

j) Father killed by the Mob; mother joined a convent

k) Killed in a botched extortion attempt

l) Father killed by the hero in question; mother committed suicide

m) Suicide

n) Killed by their assistant during an archaeological dig

Answers:

1. g; **2.** h; **3.** j; **4.** l; **5.** a; **6.** k; **7.** f; **8.** e; **9.** m; **10.** b; **11.** d; **12.** i; **13.** c; **14.** n

Mamma mia! A single strand of spaghetti is called a spaghetto.

WE FORFEIT!

In modern professional baseball, forfeits are exceedingly rare. It's a sophisticated game where a lot of variables can be accounted for, so a team suddenly unable to play is an almost impossible prospect. Here are some of the few times it's happened.

BACKGROUND

In the Major League Baseball book of rules, a forfeit occurs when a team can no longer play, or the home team can no longer host a game in a reasonable, safe fashion. All statistics for hitting, pitching, and fielding are counted toward the players' and teams' totals, but the official score is listed as 9–0 (one run per inning of the game). The loss goes to the team that forfeited, and the win to the team that wasn't at fault.

WASHINGTON SENATORS vs. NEW YORK YANKEES

After the Washington Senators moved to Minnesota in 1961 (where they became the Twins), the American League expanded from eight to ten teams, and one of the new expansion teams was a new version of the Senators. The new Washington Senators lasted in D.C. until a planned move to Arlington, Texas, for the 1972 season and a team name change to the Texas Rangers. The Senators' final home game at RFK Stadium on September 30, 1971, was hardly a bon voyage party. Fans felt jilted by the move and got more and more upset as the game went on, even though the Senators led the Yankees 7–5 with one out in the top of the ninth. That meant the game was two outs from being over—without incident, unless you count the deafening boos—when fans ran out and started vandalizing the field. There was no chance of cooler heads prevailing and security putting an end to the melee. Reason: stadium guards, angry about losing their jobs, had left the stadium early in the game, allowing thousands of fans to overcrowd the stadium…without paying the price of admission. Umpires called the game, and the forfeit went to the Yankees.

CLEVELAND INDIANS vs. TEXAS RANGERS

On June 4, 1974, Cleveland Stadium held a promotion to get fans into seats: Ten Cent Beer Night. While those four words might seem synonymous with phrases like "really bad idea" and "the fans are going to wreck the place," the Indians had been holding similar promotions for years without anything going wrong. But in 1974, tensions against the visiting Texas Rangers were high following a bench-clearing brawl when the Indians had played at the Rangers' home field a week earlier. Fans came into Cleveland Stadium angry and looking to get drunk, which the ballpark obliged by offering 12-ounce servings of beer for a dime (regular price: 65 cents). There was

176 countries have fewer citizens than the city of Beijing, China (21.5 million).

no limit on the number of beers an individual could purchase, so the stadium quickly became a sea of angry drunks. It all culminated when Cleveland fans stormed the field and went after Rangers outfielder Jeff Burroughs. The field rush turned into a full-on riot, as fans threw objects (including seats they'd ripped out) at players from both teams, the umpires, and each other. The grounds—and fans—were in such a terrible state that game officials called a forfeit. The game was nearly over, too—the teams were tied at five, halfway through the ninth inning. (Texas officially got the win.)

BALTIMORE ORIOLES vs. TORONTO BLUE JAYS

Beyond riots and field rushes, forfeits can also come about as a result of relatively peaceful situations. On September 15, 1977, rain threatened a game at Toronto's Exhibition Stadium between the Blue Jays and the visiting Baltimore Orioles. Officials ordered the grounds crew to place a tarp over the two pitcher's mounds in the Blue Jays' bullpen, which sat in foul territory just by left field. The Blue Jays cruised to a 4–0 lead by the bottom of the fifth inning, which is when Orioles manager Earl Weaver told umpire Marty Springstead that he had a problem—those bullpen tarps were wet, and since it was just outside the field of play, one of his outfielders could feasibly slip or trip on it while trying to catch a fly ball. Weaver refused to send his players out onto the field until officials removed the wet tarps, and Springstead compromised, removing one tarp—the one closest to the foul line. That wasn't good enough for Weaver, who argued with Springstead for 20 minutes before returning to the dugout at an impasse. When the Orioles, per Weaver's direction, did not take the field, Springstead called the game a forfeit: the Blue Jays "won," 9–0.

LOS ANGELES DODGERS vs. ST. LOUIS CARDINALS

For decades, "Free Ball Night" has been a fun team promotion—paying customers receive a free baseball emblazoned with the team logo. Nowadays they're given out as fans leave the stadium, rather than when they arrive, specifically because of what happened at Dodger Stadium on August 10, 1995. That night, thousands of Dodgers fans had these hard projectiles in their hands when a game against the visiting Cardinals soured over some controversial calls. In the bottom of the ninth inning, the Dodgers sent batter Raul Mondesi to the plate, with the team down 2–1. He was called out on strikes, then argued the call with umpire Jim Quick, who ejected Mondesi from the game. That upset Dodgers manager Tommy Lasorda. He stormed out of the dugout to give Quick a piece of his mind. That, in turn, prompted Dodgers fans to protest, which they did by hurling their "Ball Night" balls onto the field, aiming for Cardinals players. The Cards immediately fled the field. When the balls stopped raining down, they returned to the field, only to have fans in the center field section start throwing balls at them again. Umpires had no choice but to call the game out of safety concerns, in favor of the Cardinals.

One of the first fictional "rich guy" characters to wear a monocle:
Mr. Barnacle in Charles Dickens's *Little Dorrit* (1857).

ALTERNATE TV GUIDE

*Some actors are so closely associated with a specific role or TV series
that it's hard to imagine he or she wasn't the first choice.
But it happens all the time.*

DAVID LETTERMAN as ANDY TRAVIS (*WKRP IN CINCINNATI*, 1978)

MTM is a TV production company co-founded by Mary Tyler Moore, and responsible for classic shows like *The Mary Tyler Moore Show* and *The Bob Newhart Show*, among others. In 1978 the company had two big shows in the pipeline for CBS: *Mary*, a variety show starring Moore, and *WKRP in Cincinnati*, a workplace sitcom set at a failing rock 'n' roll radio station. MTM had also just signed a quirky young comedian named David Letterman to a deal, and he was in demand throughout the company—he was *WKRP* creator Hugh Wilson's first choice to play the lead role of program director Andy Travis. But Moore's show took precedence, and the producers cast Letterman in its ensemble of sketch players (alongside a young Michael Keaton). *Mary* was ultimately canceled after three weeks, and *WKRP*, starring Gary Sandy as Andy—CBS executives' first choice for the part—ran for four years.

CONNIE BRITTON as OLIVIA POPE (*SCANDAL*, 2010)

After the success of her hospital drama *Grey's Anatomy*, ABC invited creator and producer Shonda Rhimes to pitch more shows. In 2010 they bought her idea for a political intrigue–heavy prime-time soap about a high-powered Washington, D.C., "fixer" who carries on a secret affair with the president. ABC's first choice for the lead role in *Scandal* was *Friday Night Lights* star Connie Britton. Rhimes shot it down—she insisted that the main character, Olivia Pope, had to be an African American woman. A number of actors tried out (including Taraji P. Henson of *Empire*), but Kerry Washington wound up with the career-making role.

ROBERT KLEIN as TRAPPER JOHN MCINTYRE (M*A*S*H, 1972)

Klein was one of the most popular and visible stand-up comedians of the 1970s, appearing on *The Tonight Show* dozens of times, selling millions of copies of his albums, and starring on the very first HBO comedy special in 1975. He probably wouldn't have done a lot of those things had he taken a big acting gig that he was offered in 1972: the role of Trapper John on the TV adaptation of M*A*S*H. Producers offered it to Wayne Rogers after Klein decided he wanted to focus on comedy, not acting. (And Wayne Rogers only took the part after refusing to audition for the other lead role, Hawkeye Pierce, which went to Alan Alda.)

📺 ED O'NEILL as AL SWEARENGEN (*DEADWOOD*, 2004)

O'Neill is the rare actor with significant roles on two long-running network sitcoms to his name: Al Bundy on *Married...with Children* and Jay Pritchett on *Modern Family*. He almost managed to nab a third iconic role in between those two: foul-mouthed, terrifying gold rush town brothel owner Al Swearengen on HBO's *Deadwood*. O'Neill claims that when the show was in preproduction, *Deadwood* creator David Milch called to tell him he'd written the part just for him. However, O'Neill was just about the only person Milch had told that news. After casting was underway, Milch informed HBO of his choice, which they rejected, fearing viewers would associate O'Neill with Al Bundy. They gave the role to British actor Ian McShane instead, who received an Emmy nomination and a Golden Globe Award for his performance.

📺 JOHN POSEY as DANNY TANNER (*FULL HOUSE*, 1987)

Posey is a veteran character actor, probably best known for recurring roles on MTV's *Teen Wolf* and ABC's *How to Get Away with Murder*. He almost starred on one of the most beloved sitcoms of all time. Actually, he *had* the part...and then lost it. In 1987 Posey played widowed father Danny Tanner in the pilot episode of *Full House*. It was his big break, only the second acting gig he'd ever landed, and one he got because the producers' first choices, comedians Bob Saget and Paul Reiser, had turned it down. So, when ABC picked up the show to series, Posey packed up his house in Atlanta and headed out to Los Angeles. Along the way, he checked in with his agent...who told him that Saget had changed his mind. Posey was out.

📺 HELEN HUNT as ALICIA FLORRICK (*THE GOOD WIFE*, 2009)

Julianna Margulies so ably played the role of wronged wife and powerful Chicago attorney Alicia Florrick on *The Good Wife* that she received four Emmy nominations and won twice. Coming off her role in *ER*, it may seem that the show was designed as a vehicle for her, but she was far down on the list of actors that producers considered. *Mad About You* star Helen Hunt turned it down because she was taking a break from acting, Ashley Judd said no because she wanted to stick to movies, and 1980s star Elisabeth Shue could've had a major comeback with the show, but she declined the chance to audition because she wanted to focus on her family.

* * *

SCI-FI TRIVIA QUIZ

Q: Who was the only actor to be "killed" by a Terminator, Predator, and Alien?

A: Bill Paxton. The late actor appeared in movies in the *Predator*, *Terminator*, and *Alien* franchises, and in each one, he met his end at the hand of the titular character.

"Crayola" comes from a combination of two French words that means "oily chalk."

THE SCUNTHORPE PROBLEM

America Online was once the world's largest internet provider. That's how millions of people all over the world were introduced to the internet. But not the people living in Scunthorpe, England...

GUILT BY ASSOCIATION

In the mid-1990s, the World Wide Web was still in its infancy, and the way that more than 20 million people took their first steps online was by subscribing to an internet service provider called America Online. But when Doug Blackie of Scunthorpe, England, tried to set up an AOL account, the company blocked his attempt. When he contacted the company to find out why, AOL explained that when Blackie entered his address during the registration process, the company's "profanity filter" flagged the town's name as an offensive word because it contained a string of four letters (beginning with the letter c) that the filter had interpreted as obscene. Because the company did not allow subscribers to enter obscene words as town names or anything else, Blackie—and everyone else in Scunthorpe who tried to open an AOL account—had effectively been locked out of the internet.

At first AOL instructed the townspeople to spell the name of the town as "Sconthorpe" when registering for an account. Then, after a considerable amount of bad press, it updated its profanity filter so that even people who spelled Scunthorpe correctly could get an account. The days when America Online dominated the internet are long gone, of course, but more than 20 years after Doug Blackie first tried to open an AOL account, the "Scunthorpe Problem," as it has become known, lives on—even in Scunthorpe, where Facebook banned online ads containing the name in 2016 because of "inappropriate language." The English towns of Clitheroe, Penistone, and Lightwater (it's a four-letter word starting with "t") haven't fared much better.

Here are a few more examples of a name being interpreted as more than just a name:

✳ SOCIALISM

No ideology is perfect, but socialism picked up a *new* shortcoming in 2003 when the erectile dysfunction drug Cialis hit the market. Cialis is often marketed using junk e-mail, and unfortunately, many e-mail filters have a hard time distinguishing between the ads and legitimate e-mails containing the words "socialist," "socialism," and even "specialist."

First female African American streetcar operator in San Francisco: Maya Angelou.

✳ TYSON GAY

The American Family Association, a conservative group, does not approve of using the word "gay" to mean "homosexual," so when they reprint Associated Press articles on their website, their software automatically changes every occurrence of the word "gay" to "homosexual." And when the AP ran a story on the American Olympic sprinter Tyson Gay, who was competing for a spot on the U.S. Olympic team in 2008, the website changed the headline to read, "Homosexual Eases into 100 Final at Olympic Trials." (Pro basketball player Rudy Gay didn't fare any better.) Similarly, websites that try to automatically replace "ass" with "butt" when reposting articles run into trouble when the stories contain words like "classical" ("clbuttical") and "assassinate" ("buttbuttinate").

✳ SUPER BOWL XXX

In 1996 search engines filtered out websites featuring that year's Super Bowl, because the Roman numerals for 30, XXX, can also refer to pornography.

✳ HISTORY

In 2010 Canada's National History Society had to change the name of its magazine to *Canada's History* after it had been published under its old name for 90 years. Reason: the journal's original name, the *Beaver*, kept getting blocked by e-mail and web search filters that mistook it for a porn magazine.

✳ NATALIE WEINER

When this New York sports reporter tried to register with MaxPreps, a website that covers high school athletics in August 2018, she got as far as entering her last name before she was blocked by an error message: "Offensive language discovered in the last name field." When she took a screenshot of the message and posted it on Twitter, the post went viral and attracted dozens of sympathetic responses from people with names like James Butts, Ben Schmuck, Gracie Shitara, and Richard Gaywood, who had similar tales of woe. "When I got my computer I had to set my last name as 'Spron' because Sporn contains offensive language," a man named Phillip Sporn wrote. "In high school I would tell substitute teachers that the 'S' is silent lol."

> **The post attracted dozens of sympathetic responses from people with names like James Butts, Ben Schmuck, Gracie Shitara, and Richard Gaywood.**

✳ GRADUATING SUMMA CUM LAUDE

When proud mom Cara Koscinski's son Jacob graduated from high school with a 4.79 GPA, she tried to order a cake for him at her local Publix supermarket.

The Irish brewer Guinness estimates that 93,000 liters of beer disappear into beards in the UK each year.

She wanted the words *Summa Cum Laude* written on the cake, but the store's website wouldn't let her enter the word *cum* into the system, so she left additional information in the "Special Instructions" field explaining that the expression means "with highest honors" in Latin. Publix delivered a cake that read "Congrats Jacob! Summa - - - Laude." "How utterly ridiculous. I will be speaking to a manager for a refund," Koscinski posted on Facebook. "Shame on you Publix for turning an innocent Latin phrase into a total embarrassment for having to explain to my son and others (including my 70 year old mother) about this joke of a cake. My son was humiliated!!! I seriously couldn't make this crap up!!!!"

✳ JENNIFER NULL
This Virginia woman's last name is also a programming instruction that means "empty name field," so frequently when she tries to enter "Null" into a name field, she gets blocked. As an example, for many years it was almost impossible for her to buy plane tickets online. "I feel like I still have to do things the old-fashioned way. On one hand it's frustrating for the times that we need it, but for the most part it's like a fun anecdote to tell people," she told the BBC in 2016.

✳ STEVE SUCONCOCK
No comment.

✳ LUC ANUS
In September 2018, this Belgian candidate for a council seat in the district of Lobbes was blocked from running campaign ads on Facebook on the grounds that his last name is "offensive and inappropriate." He changed his name to "Luc Anu" in the ads. The controversy generated publicity for his campaign, but he still lost in the end. (Get it? In the end!)

* * *

SURPRISE!
Peng Xiuhua was 101 years old when she was declared dead in 2013, following a fall in her home in China. Her two daughters, both in their 70s, bathed the old woman and helped the undertaker put on her funeral dress. As well-wishers were preparing to place Peng into her coffin, she suddenly sat up and asked why so many people were in her house. "I am a lucky woman," Peng later told reporters. "Not only did I get to see how many people care for me, but I also woke up before they took me to the crematorium."

Blood donors in Sweden receive a text when their blood gets used by a person in need.

MOUTHING OFF

TALK SILLY TO ME

Some random thoughts on silliness.

"If people did not sometimes do silly things, nothing intelligent would ever get done."
—Ludwig Wittgenstein

"Until you're ready to look foolish, you'll never have the possibility of being great."
—Cher

"Keep smiling. It makes people wonder what you've been up to."
—Anonymous

"Happiness makes up in height for what it lacks in length."
—Robert Frost

"A LAUGH IS A SMILE THAT BURSTS."
—Mary H. Waldrip

"Happiness is not a station to arrive at, but a manner of traveling."
—Margaret Lee Runbeck

"YOU ARE MUCH HAPPIER WHEN YOU ARE HAPPY THAN WHEN YOU AIN'T."
—Ogden Nash

"THE U.S. CONSTITUTION DOESN'T GUARANTEE HAPPINESS, ONLY THE PURSUIT OF IT. YOU HAVE TO CATCH UP TO IT YOURSELF."
—Benjamin Franklin

TURTLE TALES

Some random facts and stories about our favorite reptile.

LEGO TURTLE

In 2018 an eastern box turtle was taken to the Maryland Zoo with multiple fractures on its *plastron* (the bottom of the shell). Veterinarians used surgical wire to attach small metal plates to keep the shell together, but the turtle couldn't walk, and there's no "turtle wheelchair" they could order online. A friend of one of the vets happened to be a Lego aficionado, so a few weeks later, "The turtle received his very own multi-colored Lego brick wheelchair," said zoo vet Garrett Fraess. "The small Lego frame surrounds his shell and sits on four Lego wheels. Plumbers-putty attaches the device to the edges of the turtle's upper shell, which gets him off of the ground and allows his legs to be freed up so he can move." The box turtle really took to his new wheels. The vets are hoping that he'll walk on his own again one day.

ALIEN TURTLE

On a nighttime dive off the Solomon Islands in 2015, a marine biologist named David Gruber was filming the neon colors of biofluorescent coral reefs when, "Out of the blue, what almost looked like a bright red and green spaceship swam underneath my camera!" The "spaceship" turned out to be a hawksbill sea turtle, and Gruber's light beam made the patterns on its shell and head glow like a psychedelic black light poster. Because this phenomenon can only be seen at night under a special type of light, no one had ever witnessed it in sea turtles before. And while there are several other plants and animals that exhibit biofluorescence, like coral and eels, this is the first biofluorescent *reptile* ever witnessed. Gruber says it's unclear why these turtles fluoresce; it could be to blend in with the coral, or to put on an impressive display for a potential mate. More study is required. Meanwhile, the critically endangered hawksbill only stayed with the divers for a few minutes. "It's like he came and divulged his secret," said Gruber. And then he swam away.

BORED TURTLE

How's this for excitement? A British biologist named Anna Wilkinson studied red-footed tortoises to see if their yawns are contagious. But first, she had to teach a tortoise named Alexandra *how* to yawn. "We presented her with a red stimulus (a small square piece of paper) and rewarded her whenever she opened her mouth while the stimulus was present," said Wilkinson. "After she learned this we started to reward her

Hot water pours at a higher pitch than cold water does.

only when she opened it slightly wider and so on. Once she was opening her mouth the appropriate amount we then only rewarded her when she also tipped her head back. It took a long time!" Roughly six months, it turns out. Once her team got the tortoise to yawn on command, they wanted to find out if other tortoises would mimic that behavior. If so, it could help shed light on whether contagious human yawns are due to a physiological mechanism or merely a social response. So how did the turtles do? Not well. "The red-footed tortoise does not yawn in response to observing a conspecific yawn. This suggests that contagious yawning is not the result of a fixed action pattern but may involve more complex social processes." (In another study, Wilkinson taught her tortoise Moses how to navigate a maze faster than lab rats.)

HANDSY TURTLES

Neither mutants nor ninjas, some sea turtles have been observed using their front flippers to "karate-chop" prey. It was long assumed that sea turtles' flipperlike front legs are only used for swimming and digging. Researchers at the Monterey Bay Aquarium in California now say that sea turtles are quite dexterous. They can use their flippers to hold a slippery jellyfish for easier eating, to grasp onto delicate reefs while sucking out sponges, to roll scallops across the ocean floor, and to chop a jellyfish right down the middle. They even "lick their fingers" after eating. The big takeaway from the study is that the sea turtle is a lot smarter than previously thought. Unlike the elephant's agile trunk, sea turtle flippers haven't evolved to be able to perform so many specific tasks. It's the sea turtle's brain that has become more advanced. "We expect these things to happen with a highly intelligent, adaptive social animal," said lead researcher Kyle Van Houtan. "With sea turtles, it's different. They never meet their parents; they're never trained to forage by their mom."

TURTLE RECALL

"Several years ago, a client brought me a box turtle that had been hit by a car," said Shannon Moore, a veterinarian from Logan, Ohio. Her specialty is dogs and cats, and this turtle was in really bad shape. Unsure what else to do, she covered the shell with clear fiberglass. The turtle could walk, and seemed to be fine, so she let it go in the woods near her house. As time went by, however, Moore became more and more concerned about the turtle's condition. She found out that box turtles need to periodically shed, and the fiberglass might prevent that from happening. But all she could do was hope it was okay.

More than two years went by. Then, while walking on a hillside near her house, Moore saw a familiar orange-and-yellow pattern in the grass. It was the same turtle, and it seemed to be doing just fine. "It filled me with joy," she said.

Tsundoku is a Japanese word that means "to buy books but never read them."

COMICAL BEGINNINGS

The origins of some of our favorite characters from the funny pages.

Comic strip: *The Family Circus* (1960–present)

Story: There's the old adage that smart writers who want to get things done "write what they know," and cartoonist Bil Keane did just that with *The Family Circus*. In 1960 he started drawing a daily, single-panel sweet and sentimental strip based on his home life with his wife Thelma and their five children. He turned his five kids into four characters, combining sons Billy and Chris into "Billy," son Jeff into "Jeffy," baby P.J. into "P.J.," and daughter Gayle into "Dolly," which was Thelma Keane's nickname for all little girls. Like the real Keanes, the comic family lives in Scottsdale, Arizona, with a stay-at-home mom and a dad who works as a cartoonist. The strip still runs today—the real Jeff Keane took over after Bil Keane's death in 2011—but it's not the same as when it started. For its first few years, for example, the dad was named "Steve," not "Bil," and the strip was titled *The Family Circle* because it was encased in a black circle. It had to be changed after *Family Circle* magazine threatened to sue.

Comic strip: *Hagar the Horrible* (1974–present)

Story: In 1954 Dik Browne and Mort Walker created the family-oriented strip *Hi & Lois*, a spinoff of Walker's *Beetle Bailey*. (Lois Flagstaff and Beetle Bailey are brother and sister.) In 1973 Browne launched a new strip with a new collaborator: his teenage son, Chris. Dik Browne could be a bit of a grump, and when Chris and his brother, Chance, were little kids, they coined a nickname for Dad when he was in one of his moods: "Hagar the Terrible." The elder Browne thought that sounded like the name of a Viking, but he changed it to "Hagar the Horrible" for the sake of alliteration. The Browne-like Hagar—gruff and tough but ultimately kind and devoted to his family—isn't the only character in the strip based on a real person. Hagar's loyal, bumbling assistant Lucky Eddie is named for Browne's brother, Edmund Browne, who once dodged a falling piano on the streets of New York, only to fall into the path of a taxi…and emerge without a scratch. Dick Browne died in 1989, and Chris Browne has been in charge of Hagar ever since.

Comic strip: *Life in Hell* (1978–2012)

Story: In 1977 a 23-year-old aspiring cartoonist named Matt Groening left Portland, Oregon, to make it big in Los Angeles…and he hated it. He found it too hot and too crowded, and a series of low-paying jobs less than fulfilling. He channeled his resentment of LA into a self-published, underground comic book called *Life in Hell*. The main characters: an identical same-sex couple named Akbar and Jeff—who look like deformed Charlie Browns, because Groening had tried to draw Charlie Brown and failed—and a group of bunnies named Binky, Sheba, and Bongo. In these dark-humor comic books—which he sold for $2 each at a record store—Groening was able to keep the spirit of 1960s counterculture alive. Result: *Life in Hell* caught on fast. *Wet* magazine hired Groening to turn it into a comic strip in 1978. Then it jumped to alt-weekly newspapers such as *L.A. Reader* and *L.A. Weekly*. By 1986, *Life in Hell* could be found in hundreds of publications all over the country. That's when a television producer named James L. Brooks saw *Life in Hell* and liked it so much that he asked Groening to adapt it into animated shorts for Fox's *The Tracey Ullman Show*. Not wanting to lose the rights to his precious creation, Groening kept *Life in Hell* for himself and instead gave Fox a show about an oaf named Homer Simpson (which did pretty well, we're told). That show made Groening a rich man, but he still found time to draw *Life in Hell* until he ended the comic in 2012.

Comic strip: *The Boondocks* (1996–2006)

Story: *The Boondocks* was one of the most popular—and controversial—daily comic strips of the late 1990s and early 2000s. Created by Aaron McGruder, the strip follows the exploits of two African American kids representing two opposite sides of black culture: Huey is a black nationalist in the vein of his namesake, Black Panther founder Huey Newton; and Riley worships gangsta rappers. McGruder, who is African American himself, initially wanted *The Boondocks* to be an animated television series, but he figured he'd only get that opportunity if he were to adapt a successful comic strip. So that's what he did. The strip debuted in 1996 on a music site called *The Hitlist Online* before he moved it to *The Diamondback*, a student newspaper at the University of Maryland, where McGruder was majoring in African American Studies. Just two months later, national hip-hop magazine *The Source* picked it up, and within a year *The Boondocks* was on the comics page in 150 newspapers. But McGruder wanted more from his strip than fame and fortune, he wanted to address race relations and racial politics, and give a voice to African Americans in a place where they'd rarely been seen: on the funny pages. "It was me recognizing that there was this void in the cultural discourse," said McGruder. By the time he ended *The Boondocks* in 2006, it reached an estimated 300 million readers each week. (And it did become a TV show, airing on *Adult Swim* from 2005 to 2014.)

That bend in a flamingo's leg is its ankle, not its knee.

SMELLS LIKE CHEESE!

Gone are the days of simple lavender or honeysuckle. Candles have become big business, and now there's an aroma for everyone! (Although we're not sure exactly who would want some of these scents.)

Gasoline

Burrito

Corn Chips

Zoo

Body Odor

Car Exhaust

Nacho Cheese

Garlic

Dill Pickles

Chlorine

Skunk

Vomit

Urine

Urinal Cake

Fart

Turkey and Stuffing

Marshmallow Chicks

Schnitzel with Noodles

Resident Evil. (For burning while playing the zombie-killing video game *Resident Evil*. It smells like blood and sweat.)

Bavarian Pretzel

Riding Mower

Burning Books

Whiskers on Kittens

Snow Day

Wood Ash

New Mac

Old Books

Joe Biden. (Available in the former vice president's home state, at the Delaware History Museum.)

White Castle

Beard

Dentist Office Waiting Room

Frat House Basement

Hermit Crab

Sandcastles & Sunburn

Root Beer Float

Rome Burning

Locker Room

Fried Chicken

Calamine Lotion

Money

Pizza

Mountain Dew

Newsprint

Stripper

Barber Shop

Trash Compactor

Only two states allow ex-convicts to vote: Maine and Vermont.

NUDES AND PRUDES

Sometimes it seems like the world can be divided into two kinds of people—those who are offended by public nudity…and those who are offended by those who are offended by public nudity. Which side of the fence do you fall on?

NUDE It happened on a hot August night in 2018 in the town of Floyd, Virginia, after a contentious junior varsity softball game. Debbie McCulley, the wife of the losing coach, walked out to the pitcher's mound and, in what soon became known locally as "Moon Over Virginia," pulled down her pants with her right hand and exposed her right butt cheek. McCulley, 57, was cited for indecent exposure; she claimed that she showed some skin to create a distraction because she thought the other coach was "going to attack" her husband, but police couldn't confirm that. In the end, McCulley had to write a letter of apology and perform community service. And she's banned from all future Floyd County High School sporting events.

PRUDE The BBC's popular *Great British Bake Off* drew controversy in 2016 after network executives decided that a squirrel's not-very-private parts were too risqué for viewers. The "well-endowed squirrel," as the *Independent* described it, showed up for a long second during the opening credits (which often feature the wildlife around the baking tent). The following season, the BBC replaced the squirrel with a pheasant. And that, said the *Independent*, "has driven some Tweeters nuts." One tweeted, "What's with the pheasant? Bring back the bake-off squirrel!" Some even threatened to boycott *Bake Off* if they didn't. But the BBC kept the pheasant (and declined to comment about the squirrel), and the show still managed to bring in more than 10 million viewers.

NUDE In July 2018, famed American nude photographer Spencer Tunick wanted to do a photo shoot of 500 people on the roof of a Woolworths supermarket in Melbourne, Australia, but the store's managers denied him permission. It wasn't because they were prudes; they simply didn't want the shoot—scheduled for a Saturday—to disrupt business. So Tunick agreed to do it on a Monday, and it was a go. But there was another problem: It was cold! July is mid-winter in Australia, and afternoon temperatures were only in the 40s. Nevertheless, 500 models showed up for Tunick's photo shoot. Tunick told CNN that he was amazed he got permission from Woolworths at all: "It's very rare for a corporation to be part of something where the body is nude."

Truth in advertising: 19th-century English butchers marketed sausage as "Bags of Mystery."

PRUDE In 2015 Italian premier Matteo Renzi hosted an official state visit by the crown prince of Abu Dhabi, Mohammed bin Zayed bin Sultan Al Nahyan. In order to not offend the prince, whose culture is much less tolerant of public nudity than Italy's, Renzi made a slight alteration to a sculpture called *Gazing Ball*, by American artist Jeff Koons, which features a nude man holding up a globe. Renzi's alteration: he had his staff put a windbreaker on the statue to cover up its…manhood. (It's unclear from news reports whether the crown prince even noticed.)

> He had his staff put a windbreaker on the statue to cover up its… manhood.

NUDE "Walking around naked doesn't really fit in with normal society, but here on the island it feels right, it's like a uniform," said Masafumi Nagasaki, a Japanese man who spent 30 years living alone—and in the buff—on a small island at the end of an archipelago between Japan and Taiwan. He moved there in 1989, giving up city life for good. He wore clothes at first, at least when ships passed by. But then after a typhoon swept away all his worldly possessions, Nagasaki became known as the "Naked Hermit." He'd only get dressed for boat trips to a nearby island for rice cakes and supplies (he lived on a small monthly stipend provided by his family). Otherwise, it was just Nagasaki living naked in the bright sun. His wish was to die on the island, but in 2018 a passerby reported that he looked "sick and weak," so the Japanese government brought the Naked Hermit home. At last report, Nagasaki was trying to return to the island to die in peace…and in the buff.

PRUDE Jenica Igoe, 30, of the village of Red Hook, New York, likes to work in her garden topless. Not for any weird reason, she only does it when it's hot. No one in her multifamily building has ever complained, but police officers had previously requested she wear pasties over her nipples—even though, legally, she doesn't have to. Reason: It's not against the law in New York for women to be topless in public (the law was changed in 1992). Even so, Igoe always stayed in her yard, and always covered up the offending bits with pasties. That's how she was adorned on a warm afternoon in May 2018 when an unidentified woman drove by the house, snapped a photo of the topless gardener, and sent it to the police. A few minutes later, Officer Travis Sterritt of the Red Hook Police Department showed up and arrested Igoe for "public lewdness." A judge later dismissed the charges—because she didn't break any laws—but she sued the Village of Red Hook for violating her civil rights. The case is pending, but Igoe's lawyer offered some advice to the woman who called the cops: "The simple solution to that 'offense,' turn your attention back to the road you are driving on."

NUDE In 2018 Jen Seidel, a well-known body-paint artist from Baltimore, Maryland, decided to put her skills to the test. She hired a model to go on a Tinder date completely naked to see if the date would even notice. Seidel painted the model—named Joy—to look like she had on tight blue jeans and a floral top. She met the young man (whom she didn't know) at a shopping mall, and the rendezvous was secretly filmed. After he helped her remove her coat, he complimented her outfit and the two sat down for coffee. They really hit it off, and he seemed oblivious to the fact that she was naked, though he couldn't understand why so many people wanted to snap selfies with Joy. Finally, after the couple walked outside, Joy exclaimed, "Oh wait—it's raining!" That's when the young man asked, "Is that paint on you?" It was an awkward moment, but she said yes. "Maybe next time," he said sheepishly, "you can *not* have paint on you?"

PRUDE Royal Caribbean Cruise Lines got an earful from dozens of "concerned families" who got more than they bargained for on a 2018 cruise. Unbeknownst to them, the cruise ship was also hosting a conference for an Indian company, which bought 1,300 tickets for its employees…and brought in some family-unfriendly entertainment that featured scantily clad dancers and young women wearing little Playboy Bunny outfits. "It was crazy," one mother told Australia's *A Current Affair*, and added, "You know this is a family boat." The conference, which another passenger described as a "big bachelor party," spilled over onto the pool decks, the bars, and even the buffets. Many of the parents had to keep their kids inside their cabins for the remainder of the cruise. Afterward, Royal Caribbean apologized and gave all the embarrassed families a refund.

* * *

LIGERS AND TIGONS? OH, MY!

When a male lion mates with a female tiger, their offspring is called a *liger*. Oddly, the baby ultimately grows to be larger than either the parent lion or tiger. That's different from a *tigon*, the result of a male tiger breeding with a female lion. Adult tigons are smaller than lions or tigers.

Before he wrote the *Goosebumps* books, R. L. Stine wrote Bazooka Joe comics.

PLEASE USE OUR NEW NAME (SAME AS OUR OLD NAME)

A name is important, a symbol of one's cultural pride and history. When the names of places get changed because of external forces or internal politics, it can be offensive to the people who live there…and sometimes they get to change it back.

THEN…AND NOW: Cape Canaveral
IN BETWEEN: Cape Kennedy
STORY: In 1961 President John F. Kennedy publicly gave NASA a goal and the encouragement to meet that goal: land a man (an *American* man) on the Moon by the end of the decade. NASA did achieve the goal in 1969, but Kennedy, who was assassinated in November 1963, didn't live to see it happen. Shortly after Kennedy's death, his widow, Jacqueline Kennedy, suggested to the new president, Lyndon B. Johnson, that a good way to memorialize JFK would be to rename NASA's Launch Operations Center in Cape Canaveral, Florida, in his honor. Johnson went one better, renaming the entire area after the president. Less than a week after the assassination, on Thanksgiving 1963, Johnson announced that Cape Canaveral would be renamed Cape Kennedy. The Department of the Interior (which has to approve name changes) supported the change, but locals never much liked having the region renamed without their input. Ten years later, the Florida state legislature passed a law that renamed Cape Kennedy…Cape Canaveral.

THEN…AND NOW: Kingdom of Cambodia
IN BETWEEN: Kampuchea
STORY: After attaining independence from France in 1953, the Southeast Asian nation of Cambodia named itself the Kingdom of Cambodia. In 1970 General Lon Nol staged a military coup to oust Prince Norodom Sihanouk and renamed the country the Khmer Republic, after the name for the predominant ethnic group and language in the area. Pol Pot's communist group, the Khmer Rouge, defeated Lon Nol's army and took over in 1975. That began a reign of terror and isolationism, including a brutal genocide to rid the country of any outside or intellectual influence, and gave the Khmer Republic another new name: Democratic Kampuchea. *Kampuchea* is the Khmer word for Cambodia, but there was little democracy or rule "by the people" under Pol Pot. After an invasion by the Vietnamese overthrew Pol Pot in 1979, the name of the country was changed again, to the People's Republic of Kampuchea. The United

Nations took temporary control of the torn nation in 1989, and in 1993 the monarchy was restored. Prince Norodom Sihanouk returned (he became king), and the country's name reverted to the Kingdom of Cambodia.

THEN...AND NOW: Cabo Verde

IN BETWEEN: Cape Verde

> **A TIP FROM UNCLE JOHN**
>
> To legally change your name, you must have a valid reason. Examples: your given name is too cumbersome, or you're getting married. Invalid reasons: you're adopting a celebrity's moniker, or changing your name to avoid debts.

STORY: This is a tiny nation consisting of 10 small islands off the coast of western Africa, in the Atlantic Ocean. Only about half a million people live there now, but it was once a valuable stopover point between Africa and Europe for traders and shippers. The islands weren't even inhabited when they were discovered in the mid-1400s. Explorer Antonio de Noli, born in Genoa but sailing for the Portuguese, was the first to make landfall in 1456, and King Afonso V of Portugal made him governor. The collection of islands was named Cabo Verde, or "green cape," after another Portuguese-controlled landmark of the same name, a cape off the coast of Senegal. Over the centuries, "Cabo Verde" got translated into other languages, and became most commonly known as Cape Verde. By 2013 enough was enough, and the government of the country (it won its independence in 1975) told the United Nations that it was reverting to its official name of the Republic of Cabo Verde.

THEN...AND NOW: St. Petersburg

IN BETWEEN: Leningrad

STORY: In an effort to transform imperial Russia into a wealthy nation of high repute on par with the nations of western Europe, such as France, Austria, and the Netherlands, Russian czar Peter the Great took over the small village of Nyen in 1703, intending to make it the new national capital. By 1710 he'd moved his family and the federal government there, and had also given Nyen a new name: St. Petersburg, or rather, Sankt Pieter Burkh—essentially a Dutch name, reflecting Peter's reverence for the status of western Europe. (The czar technically named it after St. Peter, the apostle, but it was an open secret that he'd also named it after himself.) Two hundred years later, Germany and Russia found themselves rival combatants in World War I. The Russian government renamed the city Petrograd, which means "Peter's City" in Russian. Then in 1917 came the Bolshevik Revolution, which violently expelled Peter the Great's descendant, Czar Nicolas, from power. A new socialist government was organized by the leader of the Bolsheviks, and Russia became the Soviet Union. After Vladimir Lenin's death in 1924, the name of Petrograd was changed again, this time to Leningrad. The Soviet Union (and Soviet communism) collapsed in 1991, and in the first free elections that followed, Leningrad's citizens approved a referendum to change the name back to St. Petersburg.

BAD SPORTS NICKNAMES

Message to Jadeveon "Doo Doo" Clowney: Uncle John wants his nickname back.

"Famous" Jameis Winston: This Tampa Bay Buccaneers quarterback trademarked the nickname "Famous Jameis." However, he's arguably more famous for being charged with shoplifting and sexual assault than for his play on the football field.

Lester "the Molester" Hayes: In football, "bump-and-run coverage" is a tactic employed by a defender in which he uses his entire body—hands and all—to get in the receiver's way and disrupt his route (within the rules, of course). Hayes, who played with the Raiders from 1977 to 1986, got so… handsy with his bump-and-run coverage that his opponents gave him this disturbing nickname.

Fred "FredEx" Mitchell: The Philadelphia Eagles wide receiver gave himself this nickname because he was "always delivering" on the football field. But the nickname doesn't really reflect his mediocre four-year stint in the NFL. Other nicknames he gave himself: "Fast Freddie," "Sultan of Slot," "First Down Freddie," "the People's Champ," and "Hollywood."

Kevin "the Servant" Durant: This NBA superstar gave himself this nickname, which is a bit odd. Sure, he's a great passer, but he's best known for his dominant scoring ability. So why the

nickname? "I like to serve everybody: my teammates, ushers at the game, the fans."

Jadeveon "Doo Doo" Clowney: Clowney's mom says she gave her son the nickname when he was a toddler in the 1990s. It was inspired by a rap song by Luke Skyywalker called "I Wanna Rock (Doo Doo Brown)." But a childhood friend of Clowney's has another explanation: "When we were little, we were in the swimming pool, and he doo-dooed." Unfortunately for Clowney, the nickname stuck. Not so unfortunately, he was the first pick in the 2014 NFL Draft, and has since distinguished himself as one of football's best linebackers.

Harold "Baby Jordan" Miner: This NBA player won two slam-dunk contests. That's how he got his nickname—he reminded people of basketball's all-time greatest dunker, Michael Jordan. (The nickname was certainly not for Miner's paltry nine points per game over a four-year career.)

Adam "Big Donkey" Dunn: Nothing vulgar here. This Major League Baseball slugger—who's 6 feet, 6 inches and 285 pounds—hit a lot of home runs in his career, but the nickname comes from his tendency to strike out and the fact that he's not very fast.

A horse has 205 bones.

HERE LIES JOHN ADAMS

Here's the second part of our story about where America's Founding Fathers are buried. John Adams (1735–1826) was the second president of the United States. And like George Washington, his body lies in a different spot today than where it was originally interred. (Part I is on page 227.)

A MAN OF CONVICTION

"Jefferson lives." Those were the widely reported last words of John Adams, in honor of his friend and former political rival, Thomas Jefferson. The joke was on Adams, though, because Jefferson had died earlier that day—July 4, 1826—the 50th anniversary of the signing of the Declaration of Independence, on which the two had collaborated. (July 4 is kind of a made-up anniversary, which we'll talk more about in "Here Lies John Hancock.")

Unlike Jefferson, Adams was a church-going man. His father had wanted him to be a minister, but he became a lawyer instead. In 1765 Adams got swept up in politics after the British Parliament enacted the Stamp Act, which decreed that anything printed on paper—documents, books, playing cards, etc.—had to, by law, be printed on pre-stamped paper made in England. It couldn't be paid for with paper money made in the colonies; it had be purchased with British currency. Adams was one of the first men to call the Stamp Act "taxation without representation," and he said so in a speech in Boston. With that, he was a revolutionary.

LAWYERING UP

Adams successfully defended British soldiers after the Boston Massacre of 1770—a riot in which several colonists were shot dead by those soldiers. Although he was criticized for defending the British, he said he was more interested in getting to the truth than to giving in to "hysterics" of anti-British sentiment. Those who knew Adams knew he was a true patriot.

He went on to represent Massachusetts in the First Continental Congress, where he was one of the fiercest advocates for declaring independence from England. He helped draft the preamble to the document, and it was by his recommendation that George Washington was selected to head up the war effort. Adams later became vice president under Washington, and then narrowly beat Thomas Jefferson to become the second U.S. president (and the first to move into the newly constructed White House). In 1800, after a tumultuous term that saw the major political parties grow further apart, Jefferson narrowly beat Adams to become the nation's third president. By this time, the two had become bitter enemies.

John Wayne, who fought cancer several times in his life, coined the term "the Big C"...

A few months later, Adams's son Charles died unexpectedly, and all he wanted to do was retreat to his farm in Quincy and live out his days with his wife Abigail. She died in 1818, a few years after Jefferson and Adams reconciled.

LAID TO REST

John Adams took his last breath eight years later, just shy of his 91st birthday. He was buried next to Abigail in Hancock Cemetery, not far from Peacefield, the Adams family farm in Quincy. But he wouldn't stay there for long.

Plans were already underway for the construction of a new Greek Revival–style church across the road from the cemetery, on the grounds of "Ye Church of Braintry," a 200-year-old structure where Adams's Puritan ancestors first congregated in the 1630s. A man of considerable wealth, Adams put up most of the money for building the United First Parish Church himself, and most of the granite came from his own quarry. He hired one of Boston's best architects, Alexander Parris, to design it, and one of the best stonecutters, Abner Joy, to build it. The project reportedly cost $30,489 (about $775,000 today).

Two years after his death, John and Abigail were interred in a specially built crypt in the church's basement. Twenty years later, John Quincy Adams, who was president of the United States when his father died, was interred in the same crypt, along with his wife, Louisa.

THE CHURCH OF PRESIDENTS

United First Parish Church is located in Quincy Center (also designed by Parris), 11 miles south of Boston. Today, the church and cemetery are located in a bustling downtown area (on the same block as a Dunkin' Donuts and Liberty Tax Service). In the 1830s, Quincy was farmland and tree stands as far as the eye could see. Adams's "Stone Temple" towered over everything in sight. On top of the main building is a granite tower with a clockface on each of its four sides, and above that are eight granite pillars, topped by a Greek-inspired dome. Most impressive are the four huge pillars out front. They are 20 feet tall and weigh 25 tons each. They were so massive that they had to come from a deeper quarry than Adams's.

Among the presidents who have visited the "Church of Presidents" were William Howard Taft in 1910, Franklin D. Roosevelt (who drove past it in 1936), and Harry S. Truman, who gave a stump speech on the front steps in 1948 (only a week before the famous "Dewey Defeats Truman" headline). Rumor has it that Truman whacked his head against the low ceiling of the Adams crypt. Rumor also has it that he swore like a sailor.

> **Rumor has it that Truman whacked his head against the low ceiling of the Adams crypt.**

...as a euphemism for the disease because he hated saying "cancer."

THE GRAVESITE TODAY

In 1970 United First Parish Church was placed on the National Register of Historic Places. And it still has an active Unitarian Universalist congregation that runs an outreach program for the homeless in the same basement where two presidents are resting in peace. The Adams family crypt, however, isn't owned by the church but rather by a trust originally set up by John Adams himself. Tours are available. And there's a lot more to see here than a presidential tomb.

- The Adams Pew: Inside the main congregation hall, the ornate domed ceiling is decorated like a passion flower surrounded by lotuses. Row 54 has a small brass plate marked "Adams Pew," where several generations of his family have worshipped.

- Revere's Bell: The church bell was originally cast by noted silversmith and patriot Paul Revere. Ironically, the man who loudly alerted his compatriots that "the British are coming" made a bell that—it was later discovered—wasn't loud enough for everyone in Quincy to hear, so it was melted down and recast by another silversmith. (There are several other bells in New England made by Revere that are still in use today.)

- Hancock Cemetery: Located just across the street from the church, Hancock Cemetery is one of the oldest graveyards in the United States. It was named after a Founding Father's father, Reverend John Hancock, who was once the pastor of the old First Parish Church before it was rebuilt by Adams. Founded in 1640, the cemetery—the only thing that remains from the original settlement of Braintry—contains some of the oldest granite headstones in the New World.

Our next Founding Father, John Hancock, is buried on page 332…or is he?

* * *

OOPS!

Ben Belnap and his wife, Jackee, stashed all their extra cash in an envelope, trying to save enough to buy two tickets to a University of Utah football game. But in the fall of 2018, when Belnap went to retrieve the money—over $1,000 in small bills—the envelope was gone. After a frantic search, the Belnaps finally found the cash and the envelope…shredded to bits in the family shredder. The culprit: their two-year-old son. According to Belnap, he is "grounded from all fun."

Technically, if you put something off until the day after tomorrow, you're *perendinating*, not procrastinating.

ASK THE EXPERTS

*Everyone's got a question they'd like answered—basic stuff like
"Why is the sky blue?" Here are a few more questions, with
answers from the world's top trivia experts.*

TANKS A LOT

Q: *Do water towers actually hold water?*

A: "One might expect, in this modern age, that the water tower has run its course as a useful device and is now strictly ornamental. Most towns draw their water from wells, rivers, or lakes. Water towers draw water to serve as reservoirs that come in handy when water is in high demand (such as in the early morning, when people are getting ready for work and school) and the town's pump can't keep up by adding its supply to the flow. When demand drops, the globes fill back up.

"The higher the tower, the more water pressure builds up, and the farther and faster the pipes can deliver water to surrounding areas. This is one reason why water remains available during a power outage: The pumps are down, but water towers, which use gravity and water pressure as power, keep delivering (they contain about a day's worth). It is also why you often see water towers perched atop the highest point in the area or on the tops of buildings.

"So water towers still serve a purpose, though it might not be long before they recede into history. More and more cities are going to electric pump systems to deliver their water. And that's a real shame. How can you paint a titanic 'Look Up To Jesus' message (Gem, Indiana) on an electric pump?" (From *Why Do Men Leave the Seat Up? 150 Questions We Aren't Afraid to Answer,* by Apandisis Publishing)

DIY

Q: *Why aren't shoes laced up when you try them on in stores?*

A: "We learned how to tie our shoes when we were four. But no one ever taught us how to lace up a shoe from scratch. Our assumption was that this shoe store practice was simply to annoy and humiliate us, but indeed, the experts we consulted named four reasons for leaving shoelaces unlaced:

1. Lacing shoes is labor-intensive and can't be done by machine. Therefore, it would be an added expense.

2. Different customers have special preferences in lacing techniques.

Gerbils communicate by stomping their feet.

Shoe consultant and historian William Rossi told us that 'shoes are left unlaced to allow the buyer to choose his or her own lacing "style."'

3. It allows customers to try on shoes with easy entry. Some buyers interpret any difficulty in putting on a shoe as indicating that the shoe is too small.

4. Perhaps the most important consideration is psychological. Florsheim's N. B. Albert indicates that, subliminally, the unlaced shoe is 'brand new.' Stan Sterenberg, owner of Athlete's Foot store in New York City, reports that a few customers refuse to buy any shoes that are already laced. After all, who knows who's been trying on the shoes before you?" (From *What Are Hyenas Laughing at, Anyway?*, by David Feldman)

HERE COMES THE SUN

Q: *Do solar panels have to be so darn big? How come we can't harness the sun's energy in a material that's not so…cumbersome?*

A: "Today, most solar panels are made from silicon—a semiconducting material that absorbs solar radiation and converts it into electrons. To get a current, you need something called an *electrical junction*, which passes the electrons into a circuit. Now with a single junction you can only absorb the light from one part of the spectrum, so even the best laboratory solar cells made this way are only about 25 percent efficient. (That's why they have to be so large.) But there are some very high efficiency cells that get over 40 percent by using multiple electrical junctions, fed by multiple layers of semiconducting materials capturing light from different parts of the spectrum. These are complex structures built for powering satellites and they're expensive. But there's interest in using those in solar concentrators—you focus high concentrations of solar radiation on a small area and you can cut your costs because you're only using a small amount of material. We've all seen the panels bolted on to houses, but can you imagine buildings of the future where the building fabric itself is actually generating electricity?" (From *The Big Questions of Science: The Quest to Solve the Great Unknowns*, by Hayley Birch, Mun Keat Looi, and Colin Stuart)

THERE…

Q: *Why does the consistency of an egg change from liquid to more or less solid as it cooks?*

A: "The important change is in the arrangement of the protein molecules. A protein molecule is a long chain of smaller molecules, called amino acids. The amino acids are linked by strong bonds between atoms. Those chains are not likely to break while

10 names considered for Disney's seven dwarfs and rejected...

you're cooking an egg, but another change happens when you turn on the heat under a raw egg.

"In a raw egg each protein molecule is folded up into a compact ball. There are weak bonds between atoms that hold the protein molecule in its folded-up position. When you heat the egg, you increase the tiny random joggling motion of the molecules. In any material warmer than absolute zero, the atoms and molecules move around at random. Higher temperature means faster random motion. As the egg heats, the random motion gets fast enough to break the bonds that keep the proteins folded up. So the protein molecules unfold. The kind of weak bonding that once held the protein molecules in a folded position now works in another way. Here and there, a loose end of one protein molecule comes alongside a loose end of another. The loose proteins form a mesh, with water filling in the spaces within the mesh. As more protein molecules unfold and connect to each other, the mesh gets stronger. And the egg becomes more solid." (From *Why Socks Disappear in the Wash*, by Don Glass)

> ### A TIP FROM UNCLE JOHN
>
> Omelets are one of the more difficult ways to prepare eggs. (There's a reason proper omelet prep is traditionally one of the first things taught in culinary school.) Here's a cheat to making a better omelet. Crack two or three eggs into a resealable plastic bag, add fillings, shake it up, and place the closed bag into a pot of simmering water. Let it cook until the eggs solidify.

...AND BACK AGAIN

Q: *Can you unboil an egg?*

A: "Scientists might not have figured out how we can live on the Moon, but they have solved one of breakfast's most important mysteries. Yes, it is possible to unboil an egg—at least the white part of it.

"Eggs are protein-rich, and these proteins, like others, are made of amino acids—building blocks arranged in a specific way, giving the protein its unique shape and useful properties. When these proteins are subjected to an increase in temperature, the connections are disrupted, causing the protein to unravel and tangle. This is what causes an egg to go from clear to white when boiled.

"At the University of California, Irvine, research chemists added a urea substance to cooked egg whites. This waste product chewed away at the whites, returning the solid egg to a liquid. They then used a special vortex fluid device, which stressed the proteins back into their original formation. These scientists weren't trying to figure this out just for fun. Research into reversing or preventing the misfolding process caused when proteins are formed has lots of underlying implications for cutting the costs of food production and for cancer treatments, among other things." (From *Who Knew? Questions That Will Make You Think Again*, by Sarah Herman)

...Chesty, Tubby, Burpy, Deafy, Hickey, Wheezy, Jumpy, Gabby, Baldy, and Awful.

TRUCK SPILLED *WHAT?*

*On page 84, we told you about some messy and costly spills involving
trucks carrying food. Just in case you haven't had your fill,
here are some more. (You might want a bib.)*

SAUCES AND SIDES

If you think spaghetti sauce is hard to clean out of a plastic container, imagine cleaning hundreds of broken jars of the stuff off a grassy median. The sauce crash occurred at 3:00 a.m. on an Arkansas highway because the truck driver was "distracted by his GPS device" and left the road. Then he overcorrected, drove into the median, and rolled over. Out came the sauce. The driver was briefly trapped but didn't suffer any major injuries.

In March 2018, a truck full of frozen McDonald's french fries veered off an embankment and overturned in Irvine, California. Despite the severity of the crash, the driver (who may have fallen asleep) was uninjured. The same can't be said for the fries—not even ketchup could save them.

BEVERAGES

In 2008 a truck hauling hundreds of 12-packs of Keystone Light beer failed to negotiate a curve on I-70 in Colorado, and tipped over. According to Lisa Stigall of the Wheat Ridge Police Department, most of the beers were "uninjured," but there were thousands of cans spread over a wide area. It took dozens of people several hours to pick up all that beer (and judging from news photos, not all the beer picker-uppers worked for the Department of Transportation).

The Trans-Canada Highway was closed for 10 hours one night in 2014 after the driver of a wine truck crossed the median near Hope, British Columbia, and collided with a truck carrying pulp. Neither driver was injured, but thousands of bottles of wine exploded, creating a mess of wine, glass, and pulp that took workers an entire night to clean up.

A terrible accident occurred in 2018 when two tractor-trailers collided on I-40 in Arkansas. No one was seriously injured, but it looked really bad: one of the trucks burst into flames and sent a fireball into the sky. The other truck lost its entire load...of Fireball Whisky.

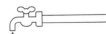

About 3% of Antarctic glacier "ice" is actually penguin urine.

It's simple physics: if a tanker hauling 30,000 pounds of milk veers to the right shoulder, then swerves left, and then swerves right again, the momentum of all that liquid will continue moving to the left. That's what happened on Highway 34 in Iowa in June 2018. Result: the tanker slid on its side for 200 yards, leaving a sea of spilt milk in its wake. (No crying was reported.)

DESSERT

May 15 is "National Chocolate Chip Cookie Day." Coincidentally, May 15, 2018, was also the day a cargo truck was speeding down Highway 17 in North Carolina when the back doors came open and 20 large tubs of raw chocolate chip cookie dough came rolling out. It didn't cause a wreck, but it did leave a sticky mess on the hot asphalt that took all day to remove.

Also in May 2018, 12 tons of liquid chocolate came gushing out of an overturned tanker in western Poland. By the time the truck was removed from the roadway, the chocolate had hardened in the midday sun. It was slicker than ice. Traffic was backed up both ways for several hours while workers used blasts of hot water to melt the chocolate, and bulldozers to scrape it up.

> By the time the truck was removed from the roadway, the chocolate had hardened in the midday sun.

Someone—it's unclear who—was hauling a load of cupcakes, cookies, and bread on I-95 through Palmyra, Maine, in November 2013, when the pastries fell out and blocked one entire lane. A moment later, a motorist, David Morrison, approached the scene in his Toyota minivan and slowed down. But the driver directly behind him, Jonathan Marquis in a Ford Explorer, couldn't stop in time. He collided with Morrison and his Explorer rolled over, sending Marquis to the hospital with cuts and bruises. Morrison was uninjured, but the two vehicles were a tangled mess. Officials were unable to track down whoever lost the baked goods. According to news reports, police believe "somebody was hauling a load of pastry either for use by a hunter as bear bait or by a farmer to feed pigs."

Now that you've had your fill of food truck disasters, set your GPS for page 426 to find out what happens when other things—cash, yard waste, missiles—end up all over the road.

The first alarm clock, invented in 1787 by a New Hampshire clockmaker who liked to get up early, could only be set to go off at 4 a.m.

LIMERICKS

Limericks, which have been around since the 1700s, are often rather bawdy. Here are a few cleaner ones, suitable for print.

If you catch a chinchilla in Chile
And cut off its beard, willy-nilly,
It can truly be said
That you prob'ly just made
A Chilean chinchilla's chin chilly.

There was a young schoolboy of Rye
Who was baked by mistake in a pie.
To his mother's disgust,
He emerged through the crust,
And exclaimed, with a yawn, "Where am I?"

An elderly man known as Keith
Mislaid his set of false teeth.
They'd been left on a chair,
He forgot they were there.
He sat down and got bitten beneath.

There was a young lady named Rose
Who had a large wart on her nose.
When she had it removed,
Her appearance improved,
But her glasses slipped down to her toes.

As for beauty, I am not a star,
There are others more pretty by far.
But my face, I don't mind it,
For I am behind it,
It's the people in front that I jar.

There was an old gal from El Paso
Who had such a beautiful ass-o.
It was not round and pink,
As you probably think,
But was gray, had long ears, and ate grass-o.

One Saturday morning at three
A cheese shop in old Gay Paree
Collapsed to the ground,
With a thunderous sound,
Leaving only a pile of de brie.

An ambitious young fellow named Matt
Tried to parachute using his hat.
The world looked so small
As he started to fall,
Then got bigger...and bigger...and SPLAT!

As I stared at a fly on the wall
I wondered, "Why does it not fall?
Because its feet stuck?
Or was it good luck?
Or does gravity miss things that small?"

There was an old man of Peru
Who dreamt he was eating his shoe.
He awoke in the night,
With a terrible fright,
And found it was perfectly true.

There once was a young man named Kyle,
Who worked at the circus a while.
He flew through the air,
With hardly a care,
And that's why Kyle lies in a pile.

I'm papering the walls in my loo
And frankly, I haven't a clue.
For the pattern's all wrong,
And the paper's too long,
And I'm stuck to the toilet with glue.

Déjà rêvé is like déjà vu, but it describes the feeling that you've experienced
a moment before in a dream.

DIDN'T THERE USED TO BE A HOBBY SHOP HERE?

*You used to see these shops and businesses in every town in the country.
Nowadays…not so much. Here are some establishments that
have virtually disappeared from the retail landscape.*

CAMERA STORES. These shops were once the go-to places for serious photographers to purchase camera bodies, lenses, filters, light meters, film, developing chemicals, and so on. The digital revolution cut into this business on two fronts: 1) point-and-shoot cameras—and later smartphones—gave novice shooters a much simpler option than bulky equipment. 2) Amazon and other online camera sellers started selling high-end camera gear at a lower cost than the stores could. It got to the point where photographers were going to camera stores to look at equipment…that they would later purchase online. By the 2010s, most of these camera stores were out of business.

PHOTO-DEVELOPING HUTS. If you took photos with a film camera, you had to go somewhere to get your film developed. Camera stores offered that service, and so did tiny drive-through film-developing kiosks, which offered one-day (or even one-hour) service—a big deal in the days before instant digital photography. It seems like every strip mall housed a Fotomat, or one of its competitors…but not since the mid-1990s.

VIDEO STORES. Shortly after VCRs appeared on the scene in the late 1970s, thousands of small "mom-and-pop" stores started cropping up to offer recent (and classic) movies to watch on cassette. It cost a couple of bucks to rent a movie for a day or two. Eventually, massive chains like Blockbuster Video moved in and soon dominated the market with a huge selection and inventory that drove most small, local shops out of business. At its peak, there were more than 9,000 Blockbusters in the United States. Today, thanks to online streaming video services like Netflix and Hulu, there's just one Blockbuster still standing (in Bend, Oregon). The other big chains, Hollywood Video and Movie Gallery, are long gone, too.

ARCADES. Since video games burst on the scene in the 1970s, kids and teenagers (and adults) have loved spending their time and money helping a pixelated character move on to the next level. Early technology wasn't very advanced; a massive cabinet was required to hold all the machinery necessary for Pac-Man to eat "pac-dots" and chase (or be chased by) ghosts. But as the technology improved, it also shrunk. After Atari

The Confederate States of America permitted slavery, but banned international slave trading.

popularized home console video gaming, Nintendo, Sega, Sony, and Microsoft came out with their own systems that allowed gamers to play better games without having to go to the noisy arcade down the street and endlessly pump quarters into the machines.

RECORD STORES. People just don't listen to music on "physical media" that much anymore. (Except Uncle John, who still plays 45s and 78s.) Over the past decade, compact disc sales have dropped by more than 80 percent. Now, instead of going to a store to get the hottest new LPs, eight-tracks, cassettes, or CDs, you just download songs to your iPhone or stream them via listening services like Apple Music and Spotify. Music stores couldn't take the hit, and they're a relic now. Even though vinyl LPs are making a comeback, big chains like Media Play, Hastings Entertainment, National Record Mart, Musicland, Sam Goody, and Tower Records, along with hundreds of mom-and-pops across the country, are now history.

VARIETY STORES. Before big-box stores like Target and Walmart moved into every region, Americans bought everything from greeting cards to vitamins to clothing to school supplies to lawn furniture at neighborhood variety stores. (Some even had lunch counters, offering sandwiches and hot dogs, back before the proliferation of fast-food restaurants.) Most towns had a local variety or general store, but from the 1880s to the 1960s, variety store chains like Woolworths and Newberry's dominated retail. The rise of big-box stores—essentially extra-large variety stores—killed this quaint slice of Americana. Woolworths and Newberry's started petering out in the 1970s, and by 2000 they were gone.

SPORTS CARD STORES. Baseball cards—little pieces of cardboard bearing a photo and statistics of athletes—started to become a mass-produced collectible for sports-crazed kids in the 1950s. Topps, Donruss, and Fleer were the big players, selling packs of 5 to 20 cards for anywhere from a nickel to 50 cents. Back then, the cards were sold in candy stores or variety stores. The whole thing blew up in the 1980s. "Premium" publishers like Upper Deck hit the market, as did artificial scarcity. Result: some cards were estimated to be worth hundreds of dollars. That transformed collecting baseball cards from a kids' hobby into financial speculation, as adults fought over supposedly rare cards they thought would someday fund their retirement. To meet growing demand, the card companies ramped up production…which made all cards less scarce. The bubble burst by 1993, rendering most cards virtually worthless. Then a baseball players' strike in 1994 left a bad taste in fans' mouths, and many kids eventually moved on to fads like POGs and Pokémon cards. In 1990 there were more than 10,000 baseball card shops in the United States. By 2015 only about 500 were left.

Beethoven never learned any math beyond basic addition.

UNCLE JOHN'S PAGE OF LISTS

Top random tidbits from our bottomless files.

22 Types of Disasters (according to the American Red Cross)

1. Chemical emergency
2. Drought
3. Earthquake
4. Fire
5. Flood
6. Flu
7. Food safety
8. Heat wave
9. Highway safety
10. Hurricane
11. Landslide
12. Nuclear explosion
13. Poisoning
14. Power outage
15. Terrorism
16. Thunderstorm
17. Tornado
18. Tsunami
19. Volcano
20. Water safety
21. Wildfire
22. Winter storm

10 Men Taylor Swift Wrote Songs About

1. Calvin Harris
2. Tom Hiddleston
3. Harry Styles
4. John Mayer
5. Jake Gyllenhaal
6. Taylor Lautner
7. Joe Jonas
8. Cory Monteith
9. Drew Hardwick
10. Tim McGraw

4 of the World's Oldest Trees

1. "Methuselah" (bristlecone pine, CA): 4,900 years old
2. "Gran Abuelo" (cypress, Chile): 3,000 years old
3. "Oliveira do Mouchão" (olive tree, Portugal): 3,350 years old
4. "The President" (giant sequoia, CA): 3,200 years old

5 Types of Insomnia

1. Acute insomnia (caused by stress; temporary)
2. Chronic insomnia (long-term pattern)
3. Comorbid insomnia (occurs with another condition)
4. Onset insomnia (difficulty falling asleep)
5. Maintenance insomnia (difficulty staying asleep)

5 Types of Nouns

1. Common noun (bathroom, plunger)
2. Concrete noun (rest area, urinal cake)
3. Proper noun (Uncle John, the Toilet Museum)
4. Abstract noun (stench, relief)
5. Collective noun (load of garbage, culture of bacteria)

On average, men get bored 26 minutes into a shopping trip.

THE SECRET LIVES OF GAME SHOW HOSTS

Game show hosts always seem so sunny and excited that it can be tough to imagine they're real people who have lives apart from the brightly lit sets. Boy, do they ever. Here's some behind-the-scenes trivia about those who ask questions and award fabulous prizes.

GENE RAYBURN In the 1970s, Rayburn presided over the intoxicated zaniness that passed for an episode of *Match Game*. One of the show's most frequent celebrity panelists (who had to answer fill-in-the-blank questions and try to match the contestants' answers) was former Broadway star Charles Nelson Reilly. Rayburn, who began his career as a radio announcer, was also a stage actor. In 1961 he replaced Dick Van Dyke as Albert in the original Broadway production of *Bye Bye Birdie*. His understudy: Charles Nelson Reilly.

BOB EUBANKS When he was a teenager in the 1950s, the future host of *The Newlywed Game* was one of best roller skaters in the world. He won several national competitions, and when it was rumored the International Olympic Committee would add roller skating to the 1958 summer games, he was a contender to join the U.S. Olympic team. The IOC didn't do it, and so Eubanks went into entertainment, first as a radio disc jockey, then as a concert producer (he produced the Beatles' 1964 and 1965 concerts at the Hollywood Bowl), and then as a game show host.

PAT SAJAK The longtime *Wheel of Fortune* host enlisted in the U.S. Army in 1968, during the Vietnam War. While stationed in Saigon, he was assigned a job as a disc jockey on Armed Services Radio. In December 1969, he was in a studio, making sure the feed of President Nixon's Christmas address broadcast smoothly. Then Nixon wrapped up, and went quiet. Thinking the address was over, Sajak played a record ("1,2,3 Red Light" by the 1910 Fruitgum Company). It wasn't over. Sajak heard Nixon start speaking again, to deliver an address specifically for military personnel in Vietnam…but by the time he could get Nixon's remarks on the air again, the president's speech was over.

CHUCK WOOLERY Long before he hosted *Wheel of Fortune* and *Love Connection*, Woolery formed and fronted a psychedelic pop band in the late 1960s called the Avant-Garde. Woolery never recorded an album with the band, only two singles. One of them, "Naturally Stoned," hit #40 on the pop chart in the summer of 1968.

BERT CONVY Convy was a Broadway actor (he was in the original productions of *Fiddler on the Roof* and *Cabaret*) who wound up hosting game shows in the 1970s and

Wide load: A blue whale can eat 500,000 calories in a single bite.

'80s, such as *Super Password*, *Tattletales*, and *Win, Lose or Draw*, but he had a wild path to television. He was a baseball player before he was an entertainer. At age 18, he signed with the Philadelphia Phillies and played in their farm system for two years. When that career fizzled out, he joined a singing group called the Cheers. They hit the top 10 in 1955 with the song "Black Denim Trousers and Motorcycle Boots."

GEOFF EDWARDS Edwards was a "have mic, will travel" kind of host, helming numerous game shows like *The New Treasure Hunt*, *Jackpot*, and *Play the Percentages*. In 1983 he hosted *Starcade*, a game show in which kids competed to see who could get the highest scores at various video games, a novelty at the time. Edwards took over for previous host Mark Richards, and didn't want to lose the gig, so he studied up on video games…and became a fan. He reportedly kept up with all the latest systems and games until his death in 2014. Another fact about Edwards: as a news reporter for a Los Angeles radio station, he was in the basement of the Dallas Police headquarters on November 24, 1963, and witnessed Jack Ruby shooting Lee Harvey Oswald.

MONTY HALL The host (and co-creator) of *Let's Make a Deal* studied chemistry and zoology at the University of Manitoba in the 1930s. The son of a Jewish butcher from Winnipeg, Hall (real name: Monte Halparin) decided to continue his studies by going to medical school so he could become a doctor. It was a surprise to him when he wasn't admitted. The reason: it was later revealed that some Canadian medical schools had secret quota systems in place to limit the number of Jewish students.

PETER MARSHALL Miss America pageant host Bert Parks hosted the pilot episode of *The Hollywood Squares* in 1965, but when NBC picked up the show, they couldn't afford to keep Parks on, so they actively sought out new talent. Peter Marshall, a character actor and comedian, auditioned because he needed the money—he didn't really want the gig and only took it because he heard that if he passed, the job would go to comic Dan Rowan (of *Rowan & Martin's Laugh-In*)…who happened to be Marshall's nemesis. Marshall ended up hosting the show for 15 years.

RICHARD DAWSON The most popular game show of the late 1970s and early '80s was *Family Feud*, hosted by gregarious, female-contestant-kissing Richard Dawson. In May 1981, a family called the Johnsons appeared on *Family Feud*, and during their episodes, Dawson heavily flirted with their grown daughter, Gretchen. After the Johnsons were eliminated, Dawson asked Gretchen if he could see her outside the show. She said sure, and gave him her phone number. For three days, Dawson called her repeatedly and got no response. He figured her phone number was a fake…but she'd actually just unplugged her phone while recovering from dental surgery. When they finally reconnected, Dawson invited her to his Los Angeles home, where he made her beef Wellington. They wed in 1991, and remained married until Dawson's death in 2012.

Only about 25 percent of the Sahara Desert is sandy; the rest is mostly gravel.

SIMPLE SCIENCE EXPERIMENTS

Here are three impressive demonstrations that, when mastered, look like magic.

GLOWING GOO

Objective: Create a glowing psychedelic substance that turns solid and then liquid again.

What You'll Need:

- Cornstarch or potato starch
- A large mixing bowl and stirring spoon
- Sugar-free tonic water
- A black light

What to Do:

1. Add ½ cup of starch to mixing bowl.

2. Slowly add about ½ cup tonic water while stirring (with a spoon or your finger).

3. Continue combining the starch and water until you have the right consistency. The ratio should be about 1:1. Your goal is to form a liquid that turns solid when you tap it or move it around.

4. Turn off all the lights except for the black light, and start playing with your goo. Swiftly form it into a solid ball in your hands, and the instant you stop moving, it will liquefy and fall back into the bowl.

5. When you're finished playing, slowly pour the goo in the sink along with a *lot* of water so it becomes diluted and doesn't clog the drain.

The Science Explained: You've just created a non-Newtonian fluid. A Newtonian fluid, first described by Sir Isaac Newton, has the same *viscosity*—the ease with which it flows—whether it's at rest or in movement. The most popular Newtonian fluid: water. The viscosity of a non-Newtonian fluid depends on the amount of force applied to its interconnected molecules. With your glowing goo, if force is applied quickly, the molecules don't have enough time to "get out of the way," and they remain bonded. But if the molecules are at rest, they don't offer much resistance and you can slip right through them. Not all non-Newtonian fluids act this way. Ketchup does the opposite: shake it and it liquefies; leave it be and it behaves like a solid. Another non-Newtonian fluid: Silly Putty. Apply a small amount of force and you can shape it;

Not a bunny: A baby rabbit is called a kitten.

apply a lot of force and it bounces (and then you have to find it).

This glowing goo experiment works the same with starch and regular water; it just doesn't glow. The tonic water makes it more fun because it includes *quinine,* a nontoxic substance that glows under a black light. Why use diet tonic water? There's no sticky sugar in it.

Bonus: Increase the amount of water and starch until you have enough to fill a wading pool. Slowly step in, and your foot will immediately sink to the bottom, but if you run across it really fast, you'll stay on the surface.

THE VANISHING TEST TUBE

Objective: Make a piece of glassware invisible.

What You'll Need:

- A large, transparent pitcher. Pyrex is preferred, but you can use any large vessel.
- A Pyrex test tube, or a smaller beaker made of Pyrex. (You may already have these—check your glass measuring cups. If they're Pyrex, then you can get started. You may even have a glass bowl made of Pyrex. Otherwise, you can find Pyrex beakers at any specialty kitchen store. But if you can get ahold of a Pyrex test tube, that gives this experiment the biggest "wow" factor.)
- 100% pure blended vegetable oil
- A small funnel (if necessary)

What to Do:

1. Fill the large pitcher about ⅔ to ¾ full with vegetable oil.
2. Place the smaller beaker or test tube inside it.
3. If the smaller Pyrex vessel is submerged completely, it will disappear. If you have a test tube, then use the funnel to pour oil into the test tube and watch it disappear!

The Science Explained: This experiment demonstrates an interesting property of refraction. You don't really "see" glass. When light rays travel through glass, because it's a different medium than air, the light rays change direction, distorting the appearance of objects on the other side. That's refraction. It's what makes your legs look really funny in a pool. The *refractive index* refers to the speed at which light rays bend. It just so happens that Pyrex glass and vegetable oil both have the same refractive index: 1.147. (Pyrex is the brand name of *borosilicate* glass, which is used for both laboratory glassware and kitchenware.) So when the light rays travel through the oil, and then through the oil-filled glass, they don't change speed or bend. Because there are no hard edges on the tube, it seems to vanish completely.

Most popular singer in Kenya: Kenny Rogers.

🧪 BENDING WATER

Objective: Use static electricity to alter the course of falling water.

What You'll Need:

- A plastic comb
- A sink

What to Do:

1. This experiment works best with low humidity, so don't do this with wet hair, or in a bathroom right after someone has taken a shower.

2. Turn on the sink so the water flows in a small but steady stream less than a centimeter wide.

3. Comb your hair for at least 10 seconds. (If you're Uncle John, you'll need to find an assistant with hair. Otherwise, rubbing a balloon on your bald head will work.)

4. Place the teeth of the comb (or the balloon) about an inch away from the faucet, and the stream of water will bend toward it. (If it doesn't, comb your hair some more, or reduce the flow from the faucet.)

The Science Explained: Static electricity is defined as "an electric charge that has accumulated on an object." The plastic comb is made of atoms that are surrounded by charged electrons. The act of combing disrupts the electrons in your hair, and they "jump" from the hair to the comb. The hair that lost the electrons now has a positive charge, whereas the comb that gained the electrons has a negative charge. Meanwhile, the stream of water has both positive and negative electrons, giving it a neutral charge. Just as it is with magnets, opposites attract. So when the negatively charged comb gets close enough to the water, the positive electrons in the water are attracted to the buildup of negative electrons, and that attraction pulls the entire stream of water toward the comb.

Bonus: Have you noticed that during some times of the year—usually in the fall—you get shocked a lot more by static electricity? That's because the relative humidity is low. As you walk around (especially if you shuffle your feet), you build up static electricity. With no moisture in the air to dissipate that charge, it keeps building and building until you touch a doorknob or a car latch...and then—ZAP!—you've been shocked by science!

*   *   *

"You cannot teach a man anything; you can only help him discover it in himself."

—Galileo

According to Toyota, the plural of Prius is Prii.

UNCLE JOHN'S STALL OF FAME

Uncle John is amazed—and pleased—by the unusual ways people get involved with bathrooms, toilets, toilet paper, and so on. That's why he created the "Stall of Fame."

HONOREE: Lisa Levy, a conceptual artist and comedian from Brooklyn, New York

NOTABLE ACHIEVEMENT: Speaking up by sitting down

TRUE STORY: "The Artist Is Present" was the name of a 2010 Museum of Modern Art performance piece by Marina Abramovic, in which the celebrated artist sat in a chair (wearing only a robe) and talked to patrons, who sat in a chair across from her. "Art" pieces like that have always made Lisa Levy roll her eyes (you, too?), so in 2016, she decided to make her own statement about the pretentiousness of modern art with "The Artist Is Humbly Present." For ten hours, the 59-year-old former advertising art director sat naked on a toilet in Brooklyn's Christopher Stout Gallery, where patrons sat on a toilet opposite her for a few minutes (fully clothed). "My idea," Levy explained to the *New York Daily News*, "is to re-create that experience [of Abramovic's piece], except that I'm in a completely vulnerable place instead of an elevated experience. It's a let's-have-fun kind of thing, free and comfortable." (And no, she said, she wouldn't be *using* the toilet during the performance.)

HONOREE: Bill Gates

NOTABLE ACHIEVEMENT: Putting poop on a podium

TRUE STORY: In November 2018, Gates took the stage at the Reinvented Toilet Expo in Beijing and held up a small jar. "You might guess what's in this beaker," he said. "And you'd be right—human feces." Just in case the audience wasn't grossed out enough, Gates went on to explain what might be contained in his jar of poo: "as many as 200 trillion rotavirus cells, 20 billion *Shigella* bacteria, and 100,000 parasitic worm eggs." The billionaire philanthropist further explained that these diseases kill hundreds of thousands of people every year, and a big reason is poor sanitation. In developed countries, wastewater goes to a treatment plant. But in less-developed countries, much of the waste—bacteria, parasites, and all—ends up in the drinking water. According to the World Health Organization, 2.3 billion people worldwide lack access to basic sanitation.

But new toilet technology might change that. How? By putting the treatment plant *inside* the toilet itself. That's the challenge Gates had given to the 20 companies and academic institutions that showed up at the Toilet Expo. As Gates put it, these

King Tut's parents were brother and sister.

new toilets will be "the most significant advance in sanitation in nearly 200 years." The Expo showed that the technology is in place to make an effective self-contained toilet, except that each one costs about $500. Gates told his audience that he wants that amount cut down by a factor of ten. And speaking of ten, that's how many minutes Gates stood at the podium with his jar of poo.

HONOREE: Mary Winchenbach, a 57-year-old entrepreneur from Somerville, Maine

NOTABLE ACHIEVEMENT: Turning crap into a thriving business

TRUE STORY: Winchenbach collects moose turds—plentiful in Maine—and transforms them into trinkets, figurines, and whatever else she can think of, even earrings. She calls her business Tirdy Works, and she's been selling the turds up and down the East Coast since the mid-2000s (she uses a secret process to dry and de-stink the turds). In 2018 Winchenbach brought her wares to a country fair, where they were such a big hit that news station WABI (Bangor, Maine) decided to send a reporter to Winchenbach's house to find out more about her. Result: a highly quotable interview. Here are a few excerpts:

- How lucrative is her business? "A moose craps out between two and 400 turds every time they take a crap, so I get five bucks a turd for these things, so I jump right up and down…when I see a turd, you know?"

- Where does she get her materials? "The turds are all local. I've found that when a moose takes a dump, you walk about 50 yards in any direction, and they take another dump."

- How does she come up with the names of her products? They're "everyday terms that people are used to hearing, so I just kind of try to combine the two to come up with something halfway decent that's funny. For example…instead of a cuckoo clock this is a Poo-poo Clock. We took them turds and we cram them in between the numbers, so there's one-turdy, two-turdy, three-turdy. Over here we make Fecal People. And depending upon the shape of them middle turds right there, we can do them with big boobs or guts or butts or long legs or short legs because there are no two turds that are ever alike."

- Then she asked the reporter, "Have you ever seen two turds that are alike?" and answered "no" herself before he had a chance to respond.

- Are her products available by mail? "Yes, I ship sh*t anywhere!"

HONOREE: Prince Harry

NOTABLE ACHIEVEMENT: Constructing a top toilet at the bottom of the world

TRUE STORY: The prince (technically, the Duke of Sussex) is an Apache helicopter pilot, a skilled outdoorsman, and, it turns out, one heck of a toilet maker. In 2013, while taking part in the South Pole Allied Challenge, a 200-mile expedition consisting of wounded veterans and celebrities, Harry put his unique skillset to use. According to actor Dominic West, "[Harry] seemed to specialize in building the latrines and he built these incredibly elaborate ones. He did one with castellated sides and a flag pole, a loo roll holder, and you're sitting there thinking, 'This is a real royal flush!'"

HONOREE: Mr. Sato

NOTABLE ACHIEVEMENT: Pampering his backside like a billionaire, and somehow making a news story out of it

TRUE STORY: A Japanese man referred to only as "Mr. Sato" told the Japanese-English site *Sora News 24* that he had recently come to a realization: He wasn't treating his bum with enough respect. "It's a little embarrassing," Mr. Sato told *Sora* reporter Katy Kelly, "but I've never once used luxury toilet paper. My butt has never felt the soft caress of that high-quality cloth, and why? Well, because I didn't know it existed."

> "I've never once used luxury toilet paper. My butt has never felt the soft caress of that high-quality cloth, and why? Well, because I didn't know it existed."

But once Mr. Sato found out that there was such a thing as luxury TP, he saved up his money and splurged on a 5,000-yen box of Hanebisho Luxury Japanese Classic Butterfly Design Toilet Paper (the same kind the Japanese imperial family uses). That works out to about $45…for a few rolls of TP. Kelly described Mr. Sato's "zenith of bottom-wiping" experience in great detail (minus the gross parts). "The paper itself is as soft as swans' down to the touch." Mr. Sato admitted he was hesitant to even use the TP after seeing how fancy it was, but he did anyway. So how was it? Kelly reported that it "was full-bodied and deliciously thick" and makes it feel as if you're being "caressed with silk."

HONOREE: Dennis Malone of Palm Springs, Florida

NOTABLE ACHIEVEMENT: Spreading one whale onto six rolls

TRUE STORY: A Florida artist named Dennis Malone spent several months carefully typing the entire manuscript of Herman Melville's novel *Moby-Dick* onto six rolls of toilet paper. (He even included the footnotes.) In 2018 the TP was given a spot in Orlando's "Odd Is Art" show, put on by the folks at *Ripley's Believe It or Not*. From their description: "The average person uses 8.6 sheets per trip—meaning Malone's novel should last nearly 350 reading sessions."

HONOREE: Harry Littlewood, 68, a retired engineer from Stockport, England

NOTABLE ACHIEVEMENT: Not letting a treasured artifact go to waste

TRUE STORY: Littlewood was saddened to learn that the Victorian-era cottage he lived in as a boy in the 1950s was going to be torn down in 2016 (to be replaced by a movie theater and shops). So he decided to give it a visit. When he got there, workers gave him a tour and showed him some of the "artifacts" they saved from the rubble, including three old copper-colored toilets. One of the toilets immediately called to the old man: "It was the one I used when I was a nipper 60-odd years ago," he told the *Manchester Evening News.* "I never thought I'd see it again." So he rushed over to the Stockport Council and asked if he could have his old commode. They agreed, and even presented it to him in a little ceremony. "I can't really use it as a fruit bowl," Littlewood said, "so I'll probably give it pride of place in the garden and use it as a planter. It brings back some memories."

HONOREE: Hasbro

NOTABLE ACHIEVEMENT: Doing for poop what Mr. Potato Head did for the potato

TRUE STORY: We described some clever poop-themed toys on page 245, but none of them match the genius and simplicity of the Play-Doh "Poop Troop" play set. Use the mold to sculpt your brown Play-Doh into a poo-shaped emoji. Then stick on the provided accessories (arms, eyes, lips, etc.) to create your own Poop Troopers. "Dropping now," said Hasbro on its Facebook page in 2018, "the Play-Doh Poop Troop play set. Create over 50 hilarious characters." Not everyone thinks this is a great idea. Case in point: below Hasbro's Facebook announcement, the commenter who got the most likes was Bonnie Elizabeth Price, who unequivocally asserted: "Nope. Children should not be taught that poop is a toy. Some of them already struggle with that concept anyway. #poopisntfingerpaint #kidsaregross"

* * *

HUH?

"People who didn't need people needed people around to know that they were the kind of people who didn't need people."

—Terry Pratchett

Warthogs have no warts. The "warts" on their faces are fat-filled bumps that provide padding during fights.

CELEBRITY SIBLINGS

Some well-known brothers and sisters are obviously related—the Wright brothers, the Marx brothers, the Olsen twins, the Pointer sisters, the Jonas brothers. Some others may be a little less obvious.

During the second season of *The Cosby Show*, star **Phylicia Ayers-Allen** (Clair Huxtable) married former NFL player and sportscaster Ahmad Rashad and took her husband's name. While they divorced in 2001, she still goes by Phylicia Rashad professionally. Her sister: dancer, choreographer, and director **Debbie Allen**, who starred in the hit 1980s movie (and TV show) *Fame*. She later served as producer-director of the *Cosby Show* spinoff *A Different World*.

❖

Donna de Varona was among the most talented and accomplished swimmers of all time. By the time she turned 13 in 1960, she'd already set the world record in the 400-meter individual medley and qualified for the U.S. Olympic team. In the 1964 Summer Olympics, she won the gold medal, beating the second-place finisher by six seconds in record-breaking time. She was named Most Outstanding Woman Athlete in the World that year, and moved into a career as a sportscaster for ABC's *Wide World of Sports*. In the 1980s, her younger sister, **Joanna Kerns**, starred on the hit family sitcom *Growing Pains* as mom Maggie Seaver. When that wrapped up, she went on to become a prolific director on television, directing episodes of *Grey's Anatomy*, *Scrubs*, *ER*, *Ghost Whisperer*, and many others.

❖

American author **Henry James** was among the most important authors of the late 18th century, bridging the gap between the stark realism of authors like Charles Dickens and more experimental modernists like James Joyce. His novels most often dealt with the differences between British high society and East Coast Americans. Among his works: *The Portrait of a Lady*, *Daisy Miller,*and *The Wings of the Dove*. His brother, **William James**, was also a writer, but of a different sort—he was an influential psychologist, credited with getting Americans to take the discipline seriously. His works, such as *The Principles of Psychology*, argued that psychological disorders could be addressed as a biological concern, and that the brain was different than the mind. He also wrote a number of philosophical works that formed the basis of the political theory of *pragmatism*, the pursuit of practical solutions.

One family produced two stars of classic TV shows. For a record 20 seasons—from 1955 to 1975—**James Arness** (born James Aurness) portrayed Marshal Matt Dillon on the Western *Gunsmoke*. In 1967 his brother, Peter Aurness, was cast as Jim Phelps on the TV spy show *Mission: Impossible* and in 1980 was given the role of Captain Clarence Oveur in the movie *Airplane!* But he never acted under his real name; he used the stage name **Peter Graves.**

◆◆◆

While not a household name, English actor and singer **Murray Head** is an icon of musical theater. He played the role of Judas on Andrew Lloyd Weber's 1970 concept album *Jesus Christ Superstar,* and sang lead on the top-20 hit "Superstar." He also sang on the very last hit song from a musical: "One Night in Bangkok," from the 1986 musical *Chess.* His brother, **Anthony Head**, is best known for two acting roles. In the early 1990s, he played half of a couple that slowly got together over a series of commercials for Taster's Choice coffee. And from 1997 to 2003, he starred as Rupert Giles on the TV series *Buffy the Vampire Slayer.*

◆◆◆

Steve Jobs is arguably the most famous American businessman in recent history. He co-founded Apple Computer in 1976, and with the Macintosh, helped make the personal computer a part of everyday life. Forced out of Apple in 1985, he returned in 1997 and changed technology again, introducing the iPod, iPhone, and iPad to the world. Jobs was raised by adoptive parents, but his birth parents later had another child, a daughter named Mona Jandali. Under the pen name **Mona Simpson**, she became a successful novelist. Her first, *Anywhere But Here,* was a best-seller in 1986, and in 1999 it was adapted into a movie starring Susan Sarandon and Natalie Portman. Jobs and Simpson didn't meet until 1982, when both were well into adulthood.

> **A TIP FROM UNCLE JOHN**
>
> In all likelihood, your relationship with your siblings will be the longest-lasting one in your lifetime—from birth until death. Parenting experts say that one way you can help forge a bond between your kids early on is to make them rely on and help each other. The older sibling can help younger ones get dressed, for example, while the little ones can help the bigger ones clean up their rooms.

*   *   *

Brothers and sisters are as close as hands and feet.

—**Vietnamese Proverb**

The French name for a French kiss is *galocher*. It means "to kiss with tongues."

SWEET TRIVIA

These individually wrapped candy facts are pretty tasty.

A lot of major candy bar brands were introduced by Chicago-based manufacturers, including Tootsie Roll, Baby Ruth, Butterfinger, Milky Way, 3 Musketeers, Oh Henry!, and Snickers. According to many food historians, trick-or-treating began in the Chicago area…with the encouragement of local candy companies.

Snickers bars were introduced in 1930. But when they were first sold in the UK, they were sold under the name Marathon. Reason: the manufacturer, Mars, Inc., didn't want people to associate Snickers with "knickers"—British slang for underwear.

Since the 1860s, American store shelves have seen about 40,000 different types of candy bars.

Chocolate wasn't terribly popular in the United States until the launch of the Hershey's chocolate bar in 1900. In 1893 company founder Milton Hershey went to the Chicago World's Fair and saw a German company manufacturing chocolate candy. He bought the demonstration equipment for a bargain price because the Germans didn't want to pay to ship it all back to Europe.

Heath Bars (chocolate-covered toffee) have an incredibly long shelf life—about a year. They're so durable that they were included in soldier ration packs during World War II. The manufacturer marketed it as a health food because it was made with "natural" ingredients (mostly sugar). An early slogan: "Heath for Better Health!"

Before he created the successful Reese's Peanut Butter Cups, which he named after himself, candymaker Harry Burnett Reese developed two products named after his children, the Lizzie Bar and the Johnny Bar. Both flopped.

What's the difference between a Hershey Bar and a Mr. Goodbar? Mr. Goodbar is a Hershey Bar with peanuts added. In 1995 Hershey changed the formula it had been using since 1925. The switch: more peanuts.

Malted milk shakes (milk, chocolate syrup, malt powder, and ice cream) became pretty popular in early 20th-century soda fountains. That's why the Milky Way was invented in 1923—it's supposed to taste like a chocolate malt (but be more portable).

In the 18 months after MTV's *16 and Pregnant* debuted in 2009, teen pregnancy rates dropped 5%.

🍫 The 5th Avenue bar—flaky, peanut butter–flavored wafers covered in chocolate (similar to a Butterfinger)—was created in 1936 by William Luden, the man behind Luden's Cough Drops.

🍫 "Junior Mints" is a play on *Junior Miss*, a hit Broadway play in the 1940s.

🍫 During the Great Depression, candymakers marketed their products as inexpensive meal replacements, giving their candy bars names like Chicken Dinner and Idaho Spud. Early Hershey's chocolate bar wrappers bore the slogan "More sustaining than meat."

🍫 According to the American Chemical Society, it would take 262 "fun size" Halloween candy bars to kill an adult. (But you'd probably throw it all up first.)

🍫 Hershey's Kisses were once called Silver Tops.

🍫 In tests using "licking machines," the manufacturer of Tootsie Pops determined that it took between 364 and 411 licks to reach the center. Human testers needed to take between 144 and 252 licks.

🍫 When Mars introduced a candy bar made of vanilla nougat with a dark chocolate coating in 1936, it was called Forever Yours. The bar was reintroduced in 1989 as Milky Way Midnight.

🍫 First product introduced by Brach's Candy: individually wrapped caramels (1904). They sold for 20 cents a pound.

🍫 Candy bars hold their shape and melt in your mouth, not in your hand thanks to the innovations of chocolatier Rodolphe Lindt. He added cocoa butter (a mixture of chocolate and butter) into chocolate.

🍫 In Japan, you have to be an adult to purchase a special flavor of Kit Kat: the sake variety. It contains sake powder that's 0.8 percent alcohol.

🍫 In 2009 Nestle introduced the Butterfinger Buzz, a candy bar fortified with 80 milligrams of caffeine—about the same as a very strong cup of coffee. It flopped.

🍫 Starburst was conceived by the Wrigley Company as a healthy candy. They're citrus flavored and contain vitamin C.

🍫 World's oldest candy bar: Joseph Fry's Chocolate Cream Bar, introduced and mass-produced in 1866. But Fry's bars weren't like today's candy bars because they were made with bittersweet chocolate. It wasn't until 1875 that Swiss chocolatier Daniel Peter added powdered milk made by his neighbor to create the creamier, sweeter chocolate we know today as milk chocolate. The neighbor's name: Henri Nestlé.

HEART OF SASS

The new wave/punk band Blondie made it big with 1978's "Heart of Glass." Lead singer Debbie Harry took some flak from punk rockers for doing a "disco song." Harry didn't care, and she refused to hold her tongue in interviews—making her an inspiration to aspiring rockers. Here's a bit of what she's had to say over the years.

Interviewer: "Do drugs make you happy?"

Harry: "Well, I think you'd have to be more specific about what drugs."

"How can one be a woman and not be a feminist?"

"I have a lot of regrets, but I'm not going to think of them."

"The only person I really believe in is me."

"I COULD BE A HOUSEWIFE...I GUESS I'VE VACUUMED A COUPLE OF TIMES."

"In music the only thing that changes is the technology."

"I'M A CULTURE VULTURE, AND I JUST WANT TO EXPERIENCE IT ALL."

"Being hot never hurts."

"The only place left for rock to go is toward more girl stars. There's nothing left for men to do. There's bound to be more male stars, but they can't express anything new."

TAKE ME OUT TO ASPARAGUS NIGHT

All summer long, minor league baseball teams across the country try to lure in fans with special promotions. Some get a lot more creative than giving away T-shirts and bobbleheads.

AWFUL NIGHT

The Altoona Curve hosts this annual event, the goal of which is to provide a laughably terrible night at the ballpark. One year the park announcer intentionally mispronounced all the players' names. In 2007 every fan got a free plastic spork with "Curve" written across the handle in black marker. In 2008 (Awful Night VI), they held a "Hot Coffee Chugging" contest.

A TRIBUTE TO BACON

The Richmond Flying Squirrels honored America's favorite salty meat product by selling bacon and bacon-wrapped snacks at the concession stands…and they brought in Kevin Bacon to throw out the first pitch. (It wasn't the actor Kevin Bacon—it was a Virginia police detective named Kevin Bacon.)

ASPARAGUS NIGHT

A large portion of the asparagus grown in the United States comes from the Stockton, California, area, and the Stockton Ports pay tribute to its local cash crop by having players wear special asparagus-themed jerseys and adding food items such as asparagus fries and asparagus hot dogs to its concessions menu. (The ballpark bathrooms probably smell *terrible*.)

FULL HOUSE NIGHT

The Frisco RoughRiders honored the late 1980s sitcom *Full House* in 2015. Cast member Dave Coulier (Joey Gladstone) threw out the first pitch and hosted a *Full House* cast member lookalike contest. After the game, the RoughRiders held a fireworks show set to the *Full House* theme song.

TED WILLIAMS POPSICLE NIGHT

Williams is best known for two things: His long Hall of Fame career with the Boston Red Sox, and for having his body cryogenically frozen after he died in 2002. In

"Umop apisdn" is "Upside down" spelled upside down.

honor of both of those accomplishments, the Bisbee-Douglas Copper Kings held this promotion in 2003…in which the first 500 fans got free popsicles.

GOOD GRIEF NIGHT

In 2016 the Lake County Captains wore yellow-and-black jerseys inspired by Charlie Brown's shirt. In the *Peanuts* comic strip, Charlie Brown's ball team always lost, but oddly enough, on Good Grief Night, the Captains won.

ORGAN DONOR NIGHT

As a public service, in 2011 the Memphis Redbirds encouraged fans to become organ donors. They did that by having their players wear "inside-out" jerseys—jerseys that were printed with what the inside of a body looks like.

FIELD OF DREAMS GAME

The Portland Sea Dogs build it…and the fans come. To celebrate the classic 1989 baseball movie *Field of Dreams*, once a year the team constructs a mini cornfield in the outfield, which players walk through to enter the ballpark.

ALTERNATIVE FACTS NIGHT

Echoing White House spokesperson Kellyanne Conway, the Erie SeaWolves argued that there's more than just "truth" and "fiction"—there are "alternative facts," too. In 2017 fans arriving at Alternative Facts Night received a replica of the SeaWolves' 2016 league championship ring. (They didn't actually win the title in 2016.)

* * *

A RANDOM BIT OF FACTINESS

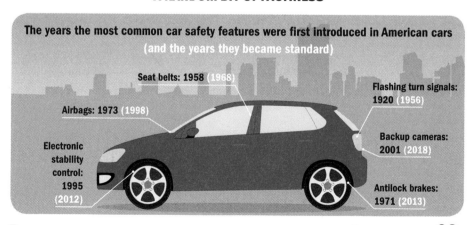

The years the most common car safety features were first introduced in American cars (and the years they became standard)

Seat belts: 1958 (1968)
Flashing turn signals: 1920 (1956)
Airbags: 1973 (1998)
Backup cameras: 2001 (2018)
Electronic stability control: 1995 (2012)
Antilock brakes: 1971 (2013)

More than 100 people born in Kentucky went on to become governors of other states.

NOW, *THAT'S* HOT (SAUCE)

The "heat" of a chili pepper is measured in Scoville units, and Tabasco's
signature classic red hot sauce registers at 2,000. Now compare that to
the following—some of the hottest hot sauces ever produced.

LETHAL INGESTION All the hot sauces on this list should be stored away from normal food items in your pantry, so a child or unassuming adult doesn't mistakenly drench their tacos with one of them. To make you aware of this danger, CaJohns Lethal Ingestion Hot Sauce comes in a faux medicine bottle that looks like something a nurse would inject a syringe into. The label helpfully instructs, "Use only prescribed dosage." It's not a joke: Made with Fatalii chilies, Red Savina chilies, and Bhut Jolokia chilies, Lethal Ingestion is advertised as the world's hottest hot sauce with no added extracts. That probably won't mean much when your mouth explodes from the heat, which tops the charts at around 1.1 million Scovilles.

THE HOTTEST SAUCE IN THE UNIVERSE, THE SECOND DIMENSION Psychedelic drugs can help you feel like space and time is in the fourth dimension, but one drop of this hot sauce will have you in the second dimension…by knocking you flat on the ground with its 3.5 million Scovilles. Made by Pepper Palace, each batch of The Hottest Sauce In The Universe is made with 40 pounds of ghost peppers. That's about 39.99 pounds more than anyone in their right mind should need to spice up a curry, but to each their own.

THE RAPTURE One drop of Torchbearer's The Rapture sauce will have you wishing for the apocalypse. It's billed as "THE HOTTEST NATURAL SAUCE IN THE WORLD!!!!" with 16 scorpion peppers per bottle (and four exclamation points). Just one scorpion pepper registers between 500,000 and 1.4 million Scovilles.

REAPER SQUEEZINS Hot sauce may be torture going in, but this brand advertises the less-than-enjoyable time you'll have getting it out of your body. The PuckerButt Pepper Company's Reaper Squeezins, which tops out at 2.2 million Scovilles, is made from founder Smokin' Ed Currie's signature Carolina Reaper peppers. If you want to grow your own batch, Smokin' Ed will sell you the seeds.

MAD DOG 357 GOLD Ashley Foods is known far and wide for their insanely hot hot sauces, none more so than their Mad Dog 357, which will make you regret putting even a single drop on your tongue. The sauce itself is 1 million Scovilles, but it's buttressed with "Scoville Plutonium Extract," which kicks it up to more than 10 million Scovilles. The extract comes in a solid form and needs to be heated before it can be served. Proceed at your own risk.

Technical name for cat lovers: *ailurophiles*.

SPICY BIOLOGY

Here's what happens to your body when you eat fiery food.

TONGUE LASHING Your body's entry point for food is the mouth, of course, where your tongue is the first line of defense. A multitude of flavors come through when spicy food hits your taste buds, and with them, an intense tingling, burning sensation that will (hopefully) subside in a few minutes. Your tongue is reacting to *capsaicin*, a molecule found in chili peppers that binds to receptors on your tongue; these receptors alert your brain that you're in severe pain. No permanent damage is done because spicy food doesn't cause any lasting effects to soft tissue.

THE HEAT IS ON A launch sequence has been activated. Now that your brain knows your mouth is dealing with capsaicin, it starts a process called *thermogenesis*, or "heat production." You body's internal core temperature rises slightly—just enough to cause sweating and a runny nose. This causes increased blood flow, dilating tiny blood vessels called capillaries. That, in turn, makes your face and neck turn red. But again, it's only temporary.

IF IT FEELS GOOD, DO IT Collectively, your symptoms represent a stress response. Your nervous system sends in the cavalry in the form of endorphins. Released into the bloodstream, these pain-alleviating chemicals work in part by numbing your nerves… including the nerves on your tongue. That's why eating spicy food is painful at first, but then becomes pleasurable—it's your brain kicking in the endorphins.

IT'S MOUTHWATERING In addition to blood and mucus running a bit more freely, capsaicin causes your salivary glands to ramp up production and wash away the spicy molecules.

THE PAIN LINGERS ON Capsaicin is hard to get rid of. When you swallow the spicy food, the capsaicin makes its way down your esophagus and into your stomach. Both organs are lined with receptors. The ones in your throat convey the same burning sensation as those in the mouth, which can give the false sensation of heartburn. After it reaches your stomach, the capsaicin can cause the muscle valve at the top to stay open for too long, which allows acid back up into your esophagus, causing real heartburn. If the capsaicin makes it into your small intestine, receptors respond by releasing a neurotransmitter that causes stomach cramps…and diarrhea.

Now that you know what happens when you overindulge, it should be easy to prevent the agony of spice-induced gastritis…until the next time you're tempted by tacos or vindaloo.

Nikola Tesla thought his brother Dane, who was killed by a kick from a horse, was smarter than he was.

1980s MOVIE TRIVIA

Put down the Rubik's Cube, don't worry where the beef went, and enjoy these facts about some Reagan-era classic films.

Die Hard (1988)

In one scene, John McClane (Bruce Willis) leaps into an elevator shaft and grabs onto a vent for dear life…after missing a *different* vent. That wasn't supposed to happen—Willis's stunt double (the guy we see performing the scene) really did miss his first mark, but producers liked it because it spoke to the plot of McClane being a regular guy in over his head foiling a terrorist plot, so they left it in the final cut of the movie.

Caddyshack (1980)

Would the fast and loose golf comedy still be such a classic had filmmakers landed all of their first choices for the roles? The main role of teen caddy Danny went to Michael O'Keefe, who edged out future Academy Award nominee Mickey Rourke. For the crass golfer Al Czervik, director Harold Ramis wanted comedian Don Rickles…until he saw Rodney Dangerfield on *The Tonight Show*. The part of Danny's love interest, Lacey Underall, went to Cindy Morgan, but only after producer Jon Peters unsuccessfully pursued Bo Derek, and Michelle Pfeiffer turned it down because she didn't want to do nudity.

Raiders of the Lost Ark (1981)

While filming on location in Tunisia, the entire cast and crew fell ill due to a nasty case of food poisoning. Well, *almost* the entire crew. Only director Steven Spielberg stayed upright and kept all of his fluids in his body—he hadn't eaten the catered food. Instead, he chose to live off of the crate of canned Spaghetti-O's he'd had shipped in.

Beetlejuice (1988)

Michael Keaton stars as the "ghost with the most" who helps a recently dead couple try to haunt their old home so the new tenants will leave. He wasn't director Tim Burton's first choice. Early in the production, when the script called for Beetlejuice to be a Middle Eastern man with a Las Vegas lounge singer sensibility, Burton tried to get consummate entertainer Sammy Davis Jr. for the role.

If you were to pour one inch of water over one acre of land, it would weigh about 113 tons.

Ghostbusters (1984)

Stars Dan Aykroyd and Harold Ramis wrote the role of the smarmy researcher (and ghostbuster) for John Belushi. But Belushi died of a drug overdose in 1982, and Bill Murray got the part instead. Nevertheless, Belushi does "appear" in the movie. Aykroyd and Ramis asked special effects wizard Steve Johnson to create the slob ghost, Slimer, in Belushi's image. Johnson later claimed that as he worked, the ghost of John Belushi appeared to him to act as a model for Slimer.

The Goonies (1985)

The blood on One-Eyed Willy's treasure map is real blood. Production designer J. Michael Riva didn't think it looked authentic enough without some blood drops, and since the prop department didn't have a shade of red he liked, he cut his own finger and dropped a few bits of his own blood onto the map.

Crocodile Dundee (1986)

Paul Hogan wrote and directed the movie about a fish-out-of-water Australian in New York City just for Australians, but it unexpectedly got attention overseas. When it was released in the United States, the film's distributors insisted on retitling it *"Crocodile" Dundee* (with quotation marks) because they were worried that Americans might think it was a movie about an actual crocodile.

Back to the Future (1985)

Sid Sheinberg, head of Universal Studios, didn't like the title—he thought that movies about "the future" were passé. His suggestion: *Spaceman from Pluto*. Shrewdly, producer Steven Spielberg sent Sheinberg a note, thanking him for the "joke memo." Rather than admit his idea had been serious, Sheinberg backed down.

Fatal Attraction (1987)

While filming the movie's extremely violent ending, in which Dan (Michael Douglas) fights off and kills his mistress-turned-stalker Alex (Glenn Close), Douglas threw Close into a mirror too hard. Close suffered severe cuts and a concussion, and during her hospitalization, she learned she was pregnant. She also had to be treated for eye and ear infections that developed after she was repeatedly held under water for her bathtub drowning sequence. (Her baby turned out fine.)

The Pentagon has its own Starbucks, but its official name is Store Number 1.

CRAPPY FACTS

Poop may be disgusting, but it's part of everyone's lives, so why not embrace it? Okay, maybe not embrace it—maybe just learn a little more about it. Here are some facts about a fascinating subject.

💩 Poop is referred to as "solid waste," but that's misleading, because it's actually about 75 percent water. The remainder is stuff like undigested food, fats, matter the body can't digest and, of course, bacteria.

💩 Sloths poop just once a week. They have to climb down from trees to do it, and it can be dangerous. More than half of all sloths are killed during their weekly "constitutional."

💩 Regular people: Studies show that about half of Americans move their bowels once per day. About two-thirds of those do it in the morning. (So if you're reading this right now, we hope you have a great day!)

💩 What's the Mariko Aoki phenomenon? The sudden urge to hit the restroom when you're inside of a bookstore. No, it's not because of the coffee you just grabbed at the nearby Starbucks. The theory is that the smell of paper and ink has a laxative effect in certain people (such as Mariko Aoki, the scientist who first wrote about the concept in 1985). It could also be why people like to read in the bathroom.

💩 Have you ever experienced *defecation syncope*? That means you pooped so hard you lost consciousness.

💩 The reason your poop is (usually) one shade of brown or another: bile. That's generated by the liver, which helps in the digestion of fat. The mixture of bile and fat is (usually) brown.

💩 A lot of people refer to poop (or the act of pooping) by an unprintable "S" word. That's derived from the Old English word *scitte*, which technically means "diarrhea."

💩 The Bill & Melinda Gates Foundation has helped fund the development of the Omni Processor, a machine that extracts the water from human fecal matter, and then purifies it.

💩 Among the impossible-to-process substances that appear in trace amounts in food: precious metals. The average person poops out about $13 worth of those valuable materials (mostly gold and silver) every year.

💩 Across all of the *Apollo* Moon missions, astronauts left 96 bags of poop on the Moon. (Neil Armstrong, the first man up there, personally left four.)

💩 What's *tinnuculite*? It's a substance that forms when a falcon—specifically, a European kestrel—flies over a burning coal fire and drops its poop into the flames.

In Mary Shelley's original novel, Dr. Frankenstein's monster is a vegetarian.

THE WORLD'S WORST BUSINESS DECISIONS

To succeed in business, you need to make the right choices. These companies did not.

FOX GIVES AWAY A GOLDEN GOOSE

The movie business was a lot different before *Star Wars* came along in 1977 and changed everything, so you can't fault Fox for not knowing that the film would spawn one of the biggest cultural phenomena of all time. But they truly blew it when they accepted George Lucas's offer to lower his directing fee in exchange for merchandising and sequel rights for *Star Wars*. This deal, which gave George Lucas monetary rights to the seemingly infinite volume of *Star Wars* merchandise sold over the years, was the single reason Lucas became a billionaire. And that was *before* Disney handed him $4.05 billion for the franchise in 2012. Lucas made so much money from merchandising rights that his five other *Star Wars* films, while distributed by Fox, were technically independent films since he financed them himself and maintained full creative control. (Ironically, as of 2019, Disney now owns both *Star Wars* and Fox.)

MOTOROLA ARRIVES LATE

In the mid-2000s, Motorola was on top of the cell phone world. Their popular, super-thin Razr held 22 percent of the market by itself. But they were slow to recognize the impact that the revolutionary Apple iPhone would have when it was released in 2007. And by the time they released their own touchscreen smartphone in 2009, it was too late. The company's shares had plummeted from its pre-iPhone high of $72 to just $12. In 2012 the mobile phone pioneer was bought by Google, only to be sold (again) to Lenovo in 2014.

ROSS PEROT BALKS...AND MISSES

The swaggering Texan businessman and would-be politician Ross Perot gives the impression that he made his fortune as an oilman, but the former IBM salesman was one of the first computer electronics billionaires. And he'd be even richer if he'd pulled the trigger on a deal to purchase Microsoft during its early days. In 1979 Perot entered negotiations with 23-year-old Bill Gates to acquire the $2 million company. But Perot, who wanted to acquire smaller computer companies to help out his

"Mushroom" and "cheese" are two types of screws.

Electronic Data Systems behemoth, balked at Gates's asking price of $40–60 million. Perot later said in a Gates biography that he blew his chance to "buy a ringside seat" and that he should've just said, "Now Bill, you set the price and I'll take it." Gates remembers it differently and has said that his price was closer to $15 million...and that he wasn't really interested in selling. When Steve Jobs was forced out of Apple in 1985, Perot didn't want to miss out on another Next Big Thing, so he invested $20 million in Jobs's next company, NeXT.

OPPORTUNITY KNOCKS; EXCITE DOESN'T ANSWER

During the internet's first boom, Yahoo's biggest competitor in the search engine business was Excite. It was such a threat that Yahoo considered buying it for around $5 billion in 1998. But it was a different near-acquisition that's given Excite executives headaches for decades. In 1999 the upstart search engine Google was steadily gaining users who liked its simple interface, but co-founders Sergey Brin and Larry Page, still grad students at Stanford, wanted to sell. They offered it to Excite for $1 million, but CEO George Bell turned them down. One of Excite's financial backers, Vonod Khosla, got them to *lower* their offer to $750,000, but in one of the dumbest business decisions of all time, when Excite was offered a chance to get the fastest and most accurate search engine technology that's ever existed, Bell turned down Brin and Page again. In a 2015 interview, Bell explained that Brin and Page had wanted them to "rip out all of the Excite search technology and replace it with Google"...which probably would have been a good idea. Google is currently worth about $730 billion.

KODAK SELF-DESTRUCTS

Kodak was once so dominant in amateur and professional photography that the term "Kodak moment," meaning the perfect moment to take a picture, became part of the English lexicon. But by 2012, the advent of digital photography had demolished Kodak's business, forcing the company into bankruptcy. And it was nobody's fault but Kodak's...considering the fact that they actually invented the digital camera. In 1975 a Kodak engineer named Steve Sasson developed the world's first electronic camera. But Kodak sat on it, afraid that it would cannibalize the company's financially successful film department. Kodak eventually debuted the DC40, one of the world's first consumer digital cameras, in 1995, but did little to market it compared to their other products. And that led to the company's brand becoming essentially unknown to anyone under 25 today. Kodak ended up being right: digital cameras did cannibalize their film department. But they had a two-decade head start to make sure it was an internal feast, not the death of the company.

A newborn baby octopus is about the size of a flea.

SLAVE STATES

The enslavement of African Americans in the American colonies and early United States went on for hundreds of years…and it took almost as long to eradicate it. Here's how every state eventually and finally ended slavery.

1780   On March 1, 1780, the Pennsylvania state legislature passes "An Act for the Gradual Abolition of Slavery." It bans the importation of slaves into Pennsylvania and holds that all children born in the state from that day forward are free, even if their parents are slaves. There is, however, a "grandfather clause" included, stating that slaves born *before* March 1, 1780, will remain slaves for life. (In 1847 the state legally emancipates all of the "grandfathered" slaves still living—approximately 100 people.)

1783   The Massachusetts Bay Colony has had a law on the books since 1630 protecting runaway slaves from being returned to their owners if they can prove they'd been abused. But the colony was also the first to explicitly *legalize* slavery in its 1641 charter, the Body of Liberties. Times and people change, and after a series of legal challenges, Massachusetts abolishes slavery—in theory—via a state supreme court decision on July 8. In ruling on a wrongful imprisonment suit brought by a former slave, the court holds that "All men are born free and equal." No laws are passed, but Massachusetts becomes a center of the abolitionist movement, and slaveholders are trusted to voluntarily stop using slaves, which they actually do. By 1790 the census lists Massachusetts's slave population as zero.

1783   New Hampshire will became a state in 1788, but the state constitution, written this year, contains a clause stating that "all men are born equal and independent," imbued with rights that included "enjoying and defending life and liberty." Slavery continues in the "Live Free or Die" state, but, as in Massachusetts, slave owners are expected to phase out the concept. The 1790 census notes 158 slaves. That drops to eight by 1800 and zero by 1810.

1784   Connecticut banned the importation of slaves into the state 10 years earlier. Those who remain in forced servitude must wait until the passage of a 1784 bill, which provides for their gradual emancipation. The law says that all slaves, as well as all children of African or mixed racial heritage born after March 1 of this year, can gain their freedom at age 25. (In 1797 the legislature amends the bill to reduce the age of freedom to 21.)

Only nation in the world named after a woman: Saint Lucia.

1784 | Rhode Island also passes a gradual emancipation law. Children of slaves born after March 1 are legally considered unpaid "apprentices," rather than slaves, and will get their freedom when they reach a certain age—18 for girls, 21 for boys.

1791 | Vermont becomes the 14th state in the Union, and the first state not to have been one of the original 13 colonies. Slavery isn't an issue for Vermont—it was an independent nation before joining the Union, and had banned slavery in 1777. That law remains in force when it becomes a state.

1799 | New York adopts Pennsylvania's "Act for the Gradual Abolition of Slavery." Like similar "gradual freedom laws," it grants emancipation at a future date for slaves born in 1799 or later—age 28 for males and age 25 for females. Those who were already slaves remain slaves. (However, in 1817 New York will enact a statute that frees all slaves born before the 1799 law.)

1803 | Ohio becomes a state, operating under a constitution that delegates wrote in 1802, which includes a clear and explicit prohibition of slavery.

1804 | New Jersey passes its own "Act for the Gradual Abolition of Slavery." Like its predecessors, it frees slaves when they hit a benchmark age (21 for women, 25 for men).

1820 | With a civil war over the issue of slavery looming—not to mention the power balance of slave states and free states—Congress passes the Compromise of 1820, commonly known as the Missouri Compromise. It admits Missouri into the Union as a slave state and Maine, formerly part of Massachusetts, as a free state. To further maintain the balance between north and south, the act bars slavery in the vast Louisiana Territory...above the 36° 30´ latitude line, which comprises the southern border of Missouri.

1820 | When Indiana got statehood in 1816, its constitution included a slavery ban, but numerous legal challenges to the ban were presented to courts. Sometimes the courts granted freedom to slaves—most of whom had been brought into Indiana from states where slavery was legal—sometimes they did not. In 1819 abolitionists challenged that inconsistency in an attempt to free a woman called Polly, slave to a Fort Wayne family and in servitude since before the passage of antislavery laws. In 1820 the Indiana Supreme Court rules that not only should Polly be freed under state law, but that *all* slaves in Indiana should be freed immediately.

1848	Illinois was granted statehood in 1818 and allowed slavery. In 1848 a state constitution is adopted, with a section in its "Declaration of Rights" banning forced servitude. But although slavery is banned, racism continues. In 1853 the legislature will pass the Illinois Black Code, an extremely restrictive set of laws for African Americans, including a measure that bars any person of color from staying in the state for more than 10 days.
1859	Kansas attempts to enter the Union as a free state, despite four years of violent confrontations between pro- and antislavery factions. Senators from Southern states delay voting on admitting a free Kansas into the nation until 1861.
1861	The Civil War is on, as South Carolina becomes the first of 11 slaveholding Southern states to secede from the United States. A few "border states" opt to stay with the Union, but to keep slavery. Those states: Delaware, Kentucky, Maryland, and Missouri.
1863	On January 1, President Abraham Lincoln signs the Emancipation Proclamation. It legally frees all slaves in 10 Southern slave states… although it doesn't do much good for slaves in the "rebel" states that are still under the control of the Confederacy. Any slaves in Union-controlled areas of the South, however, are immediately freed.
1863	On June 20, West Virginia secedes from Virginia. Most of the population in that region-turned-state are against slavery both in theory and practice. In the middle of the Civil War, West Virginia joins the Union, while Virginia continues to fight for the Confederacy.
1864	Maryland holds a referendum to determine whether or not it should free all of the slaves in the state. Emancipation wins, but just barely: 50.3 percent to 49.7 percent.
1865	The Thirteenth Amendment is added to the Constitution. It reads, in part: "Neither slavery nor involuntary servitude, except as a punishment for crime whereof the party shall have been duly convicted, shall exist within the United States, or any place subject to its jurisdiction." The act requires approval of both houses of Congress as well as that of three-fourths of state legislatures. Over the course of 1865, that 75 percent majority is reached: Illinois ratifies it first, followed by Rhode Island, Michigan, Maryland, New York, Pennsylvania, West Virginia, Missouri, Maine, Kansas, Massachusetts, Virginia, Ohio, Indiana, Nevada, Louisiana, Minnesota, Wisconsin, Vermont, Tennessee, Arkansas,

Good news: 40 percent of Americans say they poop every day.

Connecticut, New Hampshire, South Carolina, Alabama, North Carolina, and, putting it over the top on December 6, Georgia. Secretary of State William Seward certifies the vote 12 days later. After the three-fourths threshold is reached, Oregon, California, Florida, Iowa, and New Jersey all sign on by early 1866. That marks a definitive end to the Civil War, and the states that had seceded rejoin the Union after agreeing to abide by the Thirteenth Amendment.

1867 to 1976

With codification of a federal law outlining all aspects of slavery, any new states entering the Union after the Thirteenth Amendment's ratification date of 1865 are de facto free states. Between 1867 and 1959, 14 new states join the Union: Nebraska, Colorado, North Dakota, South Dakota, Montana, Washington, Idaho, Wyoming, Utah, Oklahoma, New Mexico, Arizona, Alaska, and Hawaii. However, even though slavery is illegal, several states will not ratify the Thirteenth Amendment until *long after* the end of the Civil War. Kentucky, for example, won't do it until 1976, just in time for America's bicentennial.

1870

The legal status of slavery in Texas shifted about as often as Texas switched allegiances in the 19th century. In 1829 Mexican president Vicente Ramon Guerrero Saldaña banned slavery throughout the country's territories, which included Texas. But when Texas won its independence in 1836 after the violent Texas Revolution, the Constitution of the Republic of Texas legalized slavery. The Lone Star State continued to use slaves when it was annexed as an American state in 1845, and sided with the Confederacy in the Civil War. Slavery only ends in Texas upon the federal enactment of the Thirteenth Amendment, which the state legislature won't approve until 1870.

2013

The last holdout: Mississippi, which finally got around to approving the antislavery amendment in 1995. (Yes, 1995.) However, that still didn't count. In 2013 a Mississippi resident named Ranjan Batra watches the film *Lincoln*, which details President Abraham Lincoln's drive to get the Thirteenth Amendment passed in the final months of his life. It inspires Batra to read up on the legal abolition of slavery, and he discovers that while his home state *said* it ratified that amendment, it hadn't legally taken effect because the state never sent documentation to the federal government. Batra alerts Mississippi's secretary of state, Delbert Housemann, who gets the paperwork in order and sends it to the Office of the Federal Register. Those officials certify the results, and so, on February 7, 2013, slavery officially becomes outlawed in all 50 states.

The term "EGOT," which refers to an actor winning an Emmy, Grammy, Oscar, and Tony Award...

HORSE GAITS

On page 215, we told you all about the different types of horse
races. Now let's learn about horse ambulation.

INTRODUCTION

Humans have different types of gaits—walking, jogging, skipping, running, prancing,
etc.—each one involving specific muscle usage, limb movement, and footfall patterns.
The same is true for horses. Their gaits are commonly divided into four basic types,
from slowest to fastest—walk, trot, canter, and gallop. There are a few more, as we'll
see below, and interestingly, not all horses can perform some of these extra gaits; the
ability to do so is actually genetically predisposed, and is an inherited skill. But first,
here are the four basic horse gaits.

WALK: This is a horse's slowest gait, averaging about 4 miles per hour. It's
characterized as a four-beat gait, meaning the hooves hit the ground one at a time, in a
regular one-two-three-four-one-two-three-four pattern. Also, a horse moves its head in
a combination of up-and-down and side-to-side motions as it walks, which is thought
to help maintain balance and assist in the alternating lifting of its front legs. Knowing
these natural movements and how to work with them are important skills in horse
riding. The "footfall order" is just what it sounds like: the order in which a horse's
hooves hit the ground. During a walking gait, it always starts with its right-rear foot
and goes: right-rear, right-front, left-rear, left-front.

TROT: A trot is a two-beat gait, meaning that during this gait, two of the horse's
hooves—one in the front and the opposite rear—hit the ground at the same time.
Then the other two do the same, creating an even one-two, one-two, one-two rhythm.
Trots can range from very slow to very fast, but average around 8 mph, and because it
is a very efficient gait, horses can maintain it for long periods of time. But it can also
be quite uncomfortable for riders, especially novices, because it jars the rider upward
every time the diagonal pair of hooves hit the ground. To compensate, the rider will
do what's called "posting," intermittently standing up and sitting down in the stirrups,
matching the up-and-down motion of the horse (which sounds simple but takes some
time to master). Posting is safer and more comfortable for both the horse and rider.

CANTER: Also called a "lope," a canter is a "three-beat" gait that averages between
10 and 17 mph. The sound of this gait is distinctive, with the three beats coming
in rapid succession, interrupted by a pause. (This creates the classic "ba-duh-dum…
ba-duh-dum…ba-duh-dum" running horse sound heard in countless Western movies.)
A canter is a smoother ride than a trot for riders, but one that can take years to master,
because of the complicated movements of the horse's body, along with the speed of

this gait. (Canter footfall order, starting with the right rear: right-rear, left-rear and right-front at the same time, then left-front. This is reversed when starting with the left-rear.)

GALLOP: The gallop is the fastest horse gait, averaging speeds of 25 to 30 mph. It is basically just a sped-up canter, but the additional effort causes the pattern of the horse's gait to change slightly. This makes the gallop a four-beat gait; all four hooves are regularly off the ground at once in the course of this gait. Riding a galloping horse also takes a long time to master, and because of the high speeds, it can be very dangerous. (Gallop footfall order: right-rear, left-rear, right-front, left-front—but really, really fast.)

GIDDYUP! (MORE HORSE GAITS)

JOG: A jog is basically just a slow trot, employing the same footfall pattern, but it's smoother than a trot. Credit for this gait usually goes to American ranchers in the Old West, who needed to cover great distances on their horses but wanted an easier ride than the jarring and bumpy traditional trot.

PACE: The pace gait is a two-beat gait, similar to the trot, but instead of two diagonal hooves moving forward and landing together, two lateral hooves—on the same side of the horse—move and land together. This same-side gait causes the body of a pacing horse to move from side to side as it runs, especially when pacing very fast, so many riders find this a difficult and uncomfortable gait for riding.

AMBLING GAITS

Ambling gaits describe several four-beat gaits that are similar to walking gaits, but they can range from slightly faster than a walk to slightly slower than a canter. As we mentioned earlier, not all horses can perform these. Those that can are known as "gaited horses." Here are some of the most popular.

The **Tennessee Walking Horse** is best known for its "running walk," a smooth gait similar to a normal walking gait, but the horse can reach speeds of up to 20 mph (with seemingly exaggerated head nods).

The **Icelandic Horse** performs a gait known as the *tölt*. This smooth, fast, and prancing gait can reach speeds of up to 20 mph.

The **American Saddlebred** is known for its racking gait, another very smooth and fast gait in which the horse's legs reach up before coming down to land in a prancing, almost forced style. Saddlebreds are also known for their versatility. With training, they can be used for competitive trail riding, endurance riding, dressage, and show jumping.

Other gaited breeds include the Boerperd (South Africa), the Peruvian Paso (Peru), the Mangalarga Marchador (Brazil), the Kathiawari (India), and the Messara, a horse found only on the island of Crete in Greece.

In the 1400s, the word *fizzle* meant to quietly release a fart.

MOUTHING OFF

THE MUSK OF ELON

Elon Musk (born 1971) is that eccentric tech genius who wants to make electric cars universal via his company Tesla Motors, and make space travel common via his company SpaceX. He says some pretty eccentric things, too.

"I need to find a girlfriend. That's why I need to carve out just a little more time. How much time does a woman want a week? Maybe 10 hours?"

"I've been to Disneyland, like, ten times. I'm getting really tired of Disneyland."

"We're trying to have the non-weird future get here as fast as possible."

"The rumor that I'm building a spaceship to get back to my home planet Mars is totally untrue."

"WHY SHOULD COMPANIES EXIST AT ALL?"

"If there was a way that I could not eat, so I could work more, I would not eat. I wish there was a way to get nutrients without sitting down for a meal."

"On one of the SpaceX flights, we had a secret payload: a wheel of cheese. We flew to orbit and brought it back, so it was the world's first 'space cheese.'"

"YOU CAN TELL IT'S REAL BECAUSE IT LOOKS SO FAKE."
—on SpaceX launch footage

"A ceiling is simply a floor from below."

"I would like to die on Mars. Just not on impact."

STICKS & SQUIGGLY LINES

Even if you've never invested in the stock market, you probably know some basic Wall Street words, such as "opening bell," "dividend," "portfolio," and other market lingo. Here are some colorful financial terms that you've probably never heard before.

Clowngrade. A portmanteau of "clown" and "downgrade." It's when an analyst downgrades the value of a stock for a silly reason, such as if they have a "bad feeling" about it.

Castles in the sky. It means "no solid foundation" and refers to when a company's stock value appears far too high in relation to earnings projections.

Don't catch a falling knife. An adage that means "don't buy a stock when its value is rapidly plummeting."

Pigs get slaughtered. Something traders say to warn investors against buying too much of a stock, no matter how good it looks, because it could kill you in the end.

Boredom trading. Trying to sell stocks at just a small profit on days when the markets are quiet and there isn't much movement.

Painting the tape. When a group of investors illegally moves a stock by having each individual trade their shares at the same time. (The "tape" refers to the stock ticker.)

Stick. When a stock rises in value by two sticks, it increases in value by two points.

Dead cat bounce. When a stock undergoes a temporary recovery in value after a prolonged decline, followed by a continued downward trend.

Pump and dump. When financial analysts encourage investors to buy a certain stock to artificially inflate its value…and then they sell their own shares, making a huge profit. (Technically, this is fraud, but it does happen.)

Squiggly lines. The trend lines on a chart tracking a stock's activity.

Mine and yours. Bandied about on the NYSE trading floor or at busy brokerages, "mine" is shorthand for buying a stock, and "yours" means to sell.

Fallen angels. High-grade bonds that have been downgraded to a junk bond by rating services such as Moody's or Standard & Poor.

Unicorn. A privately held company valued at $1 billion or more that's considering a move to the publicly traded sector with an IPO, or "initial public offering," of stock. (They're rare.)

Piker. A derisive term for a stock "expert" who clearly doesn't know what they're talking about and, as a result, makes very little money.

In seminary school, Martin Luther King Jr. got a C in public speaking.

TALK OF THE '10s

More word and phrase origins from the 2010s.

CLICKBAIT

Meaning: A linked image or headline on a web page, designed to entice—and often deceive—the reader into clicking on it

Story: From the same idea as "to bait a fishhook," this internet term started life as "linkbait" in the early 2000s. According to the website *Know Your Memes*, linkbait referred to "web content produced to encourage links from other websites for search engine optimization purposes." Riffing on that word, in 2006 a corporate systems advisor named Jay Geiger coined "clickbait" in a blog post, defining it as "any content or feature within a website that 'baits' a viewer to click" the mouse button. "Clickbait" made its way into *The Urban Dictionary* that year, and into *The Oxford English Dictionary* in 2014.

Backlash: The word "clickbait" sums up the more cynical aspects of the 2010s in that it describes something that looks flashy and promises a great reward, but ultimately falls short of what was expected. But the practice was so successful at generating ad revenue that it felt like clickbait articles had started to outnumber real ones.

Swooping in to help stem the tide is an organization called "Stop Clickbait," founded in 2016 by a Colorado college student named Daniel Tuttle. "We've reached a point where publishers are creating content for the sole purpose of bringing in clicks," he complained. So he and a team of volunteers click on clickbait stories and then navigate the host site's auto-play ads, pop-up windows, lists, surveys, and whatever other hoops they make you jump through to get to the payoff. Then they post the "spoilers" online as a public service for their 200,000 Facebook fans. Twitter users can submit their own spoilers with the hashtag #StopClickbait. Here are a few amusing examples:

Clickbait: "Find out what Prince George is Called at Preschool" (*People.com*)
Spoiler: "George."

Clickbait: "Dogs In Wheelchairs Gather Around Owner. But What They Do NEXT? This Is Incredible…" (*Liftable.com*)
Spoiler: "They chase a stick."

Clickbait: "He Thought It Was Bigfoot's Skull, But Then Experts Told Him THIS" (*Diply.com*)
Spoiler: "It's a rock."

Clickbait: "Man Swallowed a MicroSD Card and You Won't Believe What Happened Next!" (*The Verge.com*)
Spoiler: "He pooped it out."

Carrots and spinach have fewer nutrients in them than they did 40 years ago.

TWERK

Meaning: A racy dance in which the backside protrudes while shaking at a high rate of speed

Story: This quirky word has had quite a history in the English language. In 1820 a man named Charles Clairmont wrote in a letter to *Frankenstein* author Mary Shelley, "Really the Germans do allow themselves such twists & twirks of the pen, that it would puzzle any one." The word was used in the 1840s as "to move something slightly by twitching" (like a cat's tail), in the 1920s as a variant of "jerk," and in the 1940s to describe a bad situation that just got worse. And in 1993 New Orleans–based rapper DJ Jubilee wrote in his song "Jubilee All," "Shake baby, shake baby, shake, shake, shake. Twerk baby, twerk baby, twerk, twerk, twerk." The modern meaning came out of New Orleans's bounce music scene, and while the most common theory is that it's a combination of two words, exactly which two is unclear. It's either "twitch" and "jerk," or "twist" and "jerk," or it's a variation of "work," as in "footwork" or "work it." In New Orleans, where the dance originated, the going consensus is that it's a contraction of "to work," as in "t'work," or "t'werk," finally morphing into "twerk."

Backlash: However it shook into being, few people outside of America's "dirty south" ever heard the word until August 2013, when Miley Cyrus performed the raunchy dance on MTV's Video Music Awards. By a strange coincidence, the show aired the very same week that Oxford announced the addition of "twerk" to its online dictionary. The timing led some in the media to speculate, as *USA Today* did, "Did Miley Cyrus help 'twerk' land in the dictionary?" No, she didn't, said Oxford's Katherine Connor Martin, who assured outraged lexicographers that Oxford had been planning to add the word for several months. (And so far, it's only in the *Oxford Dictionary Online*, not the more hallowed *Oxford English Dictionary*.) Martin said that if you want to blame someone, blame the millions of people who made "twerk" Google's number-one "What is…" search that year. (It was runner-up for Oxford's Word of the Year, losing to "selfie.")

> "Did Miley Cyrus help 'twerk' land in the dictionary?" No, she didn't.

Bonus: *Twerk* wasn't the only word added to Oxford that ruffled language-lovers' feathers. Other controversial additions included *srsly*, *vom*, *apols*, and *squee*. (In case you require translating, they mean "seriously," "to vomit," "my apologies," and "an expression of great delight.")

But what word had the biggest impact on the 2010s?
To find out, go to page 467. #heres_a_clue

The shade "Indian yellow" was originally made from the urine of cows who ate a lot of mangoes.

THE END IS NEAR

A few tidbits about death to liven up your day. (Warning: a few of these are disturbing.)

CRY FOR ME: If you live in Ghana and you want people to know how beloved you were, then you'll want a lot of people crying loudly at your funeral. The louder, the better. In 2018 news outlets reported about a new service being offered in the African nation: professional mourners. The Kumasi Funeral Criers Association charges based on the size of the funeral, and will go to whatever lengths are necessary to make sure you get the send-off you deserve, including wailing, rolling on the floor, and vomiting.

GRAND THEFT CADAVER: In September 2018, a 40-year-old man identified in press reports as Annibal Saul N. was walking past a hospital in Mexico City when he noticed a large vehicle parked out front with the windows down and the keys in the ignition. Annibal decided to take it for a joyride. It's uncertain whether he was aware when he started driving that the dead body of an 80-year-old man was in the back awaiting transport to a funeral home. But he soon realized it. When police caught up to him, he was parked on the side of the highway, standing outside the vehicle.

BLUE MAN DOWN: In 2017 a train passenger in Dusseldorf, Germany, reported seeing a lifeless body. Rescuers were dispatched to search near the tracks for a "deceased bearded man in a blue coat and red trousers." When they found the man, it turned out to be…a Papa Smurf balloon. The police announced that despite being a bit "deflated," Papa Smurf would make a full recovery.

ON ICE: Police said there were no signs of foul play in the 2015 death of Arma Ann Roush, 75, of North Carolina. It's what happened afterward that was foul. Her daughter, Marcella Jean Lee, 56, didn't report the death. Instead, she put her mother's body in a freezer, taped it shut, and sold the appliance to a neighbor at a yard sale for $30. She told the neighbor that some people from her church would come by and pick up the freezer's contents, to be put into a "time capsule." After no one came for two weeks, the neighbor opened the freezer and made the grim discovery. Meanwhile, Lee had skipped town. Authorities captured her a year later; she got six months in prison.

FORMER TENANTS: Think your house may be haunted? Go to *DiedInHouse.com* to find out if anyone has ever died there…and if your house is "stigmatized." The website was created by a software engineer and landlord named Roy Condrey. He said the idea was born out of a cryptic text he received from one of his tenants saying, "Do you know that your house is haunted?" After searching and searching and finding no online database for residences where people had died, Condrey decided to create his own, using public records and internet searches. According to his estimates, more than 4.5 million American homes are stigmatized…maybe even yours.

Each main *Friends* cast member earns about $20 million in royalties each year.

WEIRD MUSICALS

If you think a Broadway show about singing cats or a rapping Alexander Hamilton is unusual, then have we got some musicals for you.

Show: *Octomom! The Musical* (2009)

Details: Nadya Suleman briefly became a tabloid celebrity and subject of fascination in January 2009, when she gave birth to only the second set of octuplets (eight babies) in American history. The media nicknamed her "Octo-mom," and less than six months later, a California artist named Chris Voltaire had written a musical about her. When it played in Los Angeles, Voltaire set aside an entire row of seats—14 of them— just in case the Suleman family showed up. (They didn't.)

Highlights: The show isn't about Suleman's life, says Voltaire, it's about Americans' insatiable appetite for scandals. That could explain why one of the characters in the cast is financial con man Bernie Madoff.

Show: *Urinetown* (2001)

Details: There's a musical for everyone, even bathroom lovers (like Uncle John). But *Urinetown* isn't a juvenile comedy—it's actually a rebuke of capitalism. It takes place in a small town where free, public bathrooms are outlawed, forcing the citizens to use pay toilets installed by a megacorporation called Urine Good Company. After it moved from Off-Broadway to Broadway in 2002, it won Tony Awards (really) for Best Book of a Musical (the script) and Best Score, along with a nomination for Best Musical.

Highlights: Despite the show's serious theme, the songs have titles like "It's a Privilege to Pee" and "I See a River."

Show: *Shinbone Alley* (1957)

Details: In the 1910s and 1920s, one of the most popular features in New York's *Evening Sun* newspaper were columnist Don Marquis's stories about a romantic cockroach named Archy and an alley cat named Mehitabel, illustrated by *Krazy Kat* cartoonist George Herriman. (The stories were supposedly written by Archy by jumping on the keys of an old typewriter, but because he couldn't hit two keys at once, the characters' names appeared as "archy and mehitabel.") In 1954 singer and Broadway star Carol Channing recorded two "archy and mehitabel" concept albums, which became the inspiration for the 1957 Broadway musical *Shinbone Alley*, featuring dialogue by future filmmaker (and *The Producers* mastermind) Mel Brooks.

Highlights: None. It closed after 49 performances.

Bananas naturally curve because they grow toward the sun.

Show: *Flahooley* (1951)

Details: This musical is set in the company town of Capsulanti—home to Bigelow, Inc., the world's biggest toy company—where its chief inventor, Sylvester, is about to introduce the company's biggest product yet: Flahooley, a doll that laughs and shakes. But those plans are thwarted when a delegation from Saudi Arabia begs for the company's help. Their lucrative oil production only occurs thanks to the help of a magical genie named Abou Ben Atom, who lives in a magic lamp. But the lamp is broken and the Arabians need Sylvester to fix it. (Guess how the genie is finally released: by a rub of the lamp with Flahooley's tiny plastic hand.) It closed on Broadway after 40 performances.

Highlights: The show's book and lyrics were written by *Wizard of Oz* lyricist E. Y. Harburg, who was run out of Hollywood in 1950 when he was blacklisted. He laced *Flahooley* with his rage and resentment over Communist-seeking Senator Joseph McCarthy and the political cronies Harburg thought were McCarthy's puppets. The show's opening song: "You Too Can Be a Puppet."

Show: *Hands on a Hardbody* (2012)

Details: It's a fairly common promotional event: A radio station will give away a car or truck to whichever contestant can hang around and keep one hand on the vehicle the longest. Pulitzer Prize–winning playwright Doug Wright (*I Am My Own Wife*) saw a 1997 documentary film called *Hands on a Hardbody* about the phenomenon of people standing around a truck, desperate to win it, and thought it would make an interesting Broadway musical. He teamed up with singer-songwriter Amanda Green (daughter of Tony and Academy Award–winning lyricist-playwright Adolph Green) and Trey Anastasio (of the rock band Phish) to write it. The plot: Two dozen characters sing songs about how they really need to win that truck, while also dancing and not letting go of that truck.

Highlights: It played on Broadway for less than a month but still managed to earn three Tony Award nominations, including Best Score.

* * *

GLUTEUS EXPELLIARMUS!

One of the most obscure details in J.K. Rowling's huge Harry Potter universe is a small collective of wizards and witches who hate to wear pants. They claim that magic's true source is a person's rear end, and that pants block the natural flow of that force. So they don't wear pants, and they call their belief "Fresh Air Refreshes Totally"…or F.A.R.T.

When Frisbee inventor Walter Frederick Morrison died, he was cremated and made into a Frisbee.

DO THE CHURCHILLIAN DRIFT

British prime minister Winston Churchill (1874–1965) was well-known for his wit and his wisdom, so it's no surprise that a lot of famous quotations are attributed to him. But there are also a lot of quotes that sound like Churchill could have said them…even though he didn't. It's a phenomenon sociologists call "Churchillian drift." Here are some of the wisest and most clever things Churchill never uttered.

"There's no such thing as a free lunch."

Churchill reportedly made this quip casually at a graduation ceremony, but if he did say it, he was paraphrasing Rudyard Kipling. The *Jungle Book* author used it in an essay in *American Notes* when talking about a unique bar in San Francisco that gave free salty food to customers as a way of encouraging them to buy more beer.

"If you're not a liberal when you're 25, you have no heart.
If you're not a conservative by the time you're 35, you have no brain."

Churchill reportedly became more liberal as he got older, so this wouldn't make much sense for him to say. Besides, it's actually derived from a quote in a book published in 1875 by French writer Jules Claretie.

"The only traditions of the Royal Navy are rum, sodomy, and the lash."

This tongue-in-cheek comment was made by Churchill's assistant, Anthony Montague-Browne…but Churchill remarked several times that he *wished* he'd said it.

"A lie gets halfway around the world before the truth has a chance to get its pants on."

Ironically, this quote about how incorrect information spreads…is often incorrectly attributed to Churchill. And before that, it was attributed to Mark Twain. But its real origin goes back to English minister Thomas Francklin, who wrote in 1787: "Falsehood will fly, as it were, on the wings of the wind, and carry its tales to every corner of the earth; whilst truth lags behind; her steps, though sure, are slow and solemn."

"There is no such thing as a good tax."

Churchill wasn't quite so black-and-white about taxation. In an address to the House of Commons in Parliament in 1906, he said, "Taxes are an evil—a necessary evil, but still an evil, and the fewer we have of them the better."

Antarctica's Horlick Mountains were named by Richard Byrd during his 1930s expedition…

"Never give up. Never, never, never give up!"
Close. He actually said "Never give in. Never, never, never, never, except to convictions of honor and good sense."

"A nation that fails to honor its heroes soon will have no heroes to honor."
It's a corruption of a line from *The Closing of the American Mind* by Allan Bloom, in which Bloom says the modern world has "no heroes to emulate."

"You have enemies? Good. That means you've stood up for something, sometime in your life."
Nope, not Churchill. The real source is Victor Hugo, author of *The Hunchback of Notre Dame*, who wrote something to that effect in his 1845 essay "Villemain": "You have enemies? Why, it is the story of every man who has done a great deed or created a new idea."

"Distrust first thoughts; they are usually honest."
Churchill did say it. He said it to Parliament in 1948…but it's only *part* of what he said—he preceded that phrase with "As the cynic has said."

"The destiny of a great nation has never yet been settled by the temporary condition of its technical apparatus."
Churchill did say it, but he was quoting Leon Trotsky.

Lady Astor: If I were married to you, I'd put poison in your coffee.
Churchill: If I were married to you, I'd drink it.
The exchange actually did take place, although it was between Lady Astor and British statesman F. E. Smith, 1st Earl of Birkenhead…and he was just repeating an old joke.

"I am a man of simple tastes. I am quite easily satisfied with the best of everything."
The Earl of Birkenhead strikes again: F. E. Smith said something very similar *about* Churchill: "Mr. Churchill is easily satisfied with the best."

A TIP FROM UNCLE JOHN
If you're researching something online, here's a tip: don't believe everything you read. The entirety of human knowledge seems to be available at your fingertips on the internet…but there's also a lot of myth-information out there—some of which was put there intentionally to deceive you. So how do you know what's true? When you come across an interesting fact, seek out its source—a trustworthy site will provide links. Then verify that information. You can probably believe it if, say, it came from a direct interview or appeared in a reference book. Interviews offer first-hand verification; reference books can be trusted because publishers hire fact-checkers to ensure whatever they publish is legitimate.

…after his chief sponsor, the Horlick's Malted Milk Company.

THE 29ERS

This amazing tale is equal parts sad and uplifting…and a tad bit freaky.

"MOMMY! MOM! MOM! I MET ROD CAREW TODAY!"

Ever since he could remember, 11-year-old Konrad Reuland wanted to become a pro athlete just like his idol, Rod Carew, one of the best hitters in the history of baseball. So when the little boy got to meet the Hall-of-Famer at his elementary school, it was the best day of his life. Another great day came nearly a decade later in 2011 when Reuland—now a 6-foot-5, 260-pound football tight end—was signed by the San Francisco 49ers.

Described by friends as an "Ivan Drago lookalike with a big heart" (Drago was the imposing Russian boxer from *Rocky IV*), Reuland's NFL career was off to a great start…until he injured his knee in 2013. The next few years were frustrating, as he was traded from team to team, rarely making the starting roster, all the while training as hard as he could to get back in the game. That's what he was doing—working out—on November 28, 2016, when he heard a "click" in his head and felt a sharp pain behind his left eye. At the hospital, doctors confirmed the worst: it was a brain aneurysm. A few days later, while lying in his hospital bed, Reuland sent this text to his mother, Mary: "I'm about to kick this thing's butt, with the help of God. He has something big in store for me." A few minutes later, Reuland had a second, even larger, aneurysm. After 17 hours of surgery, he was placed on life support. Mary stayed by his side for days, frequently putting her ear on her son's chest to listen to his beating heart.

OLD FRIENDS

Rod Carew wasn't doing well, either. After suffering a massive heart attack in 2015, he was told he'd need a new heart and kidney. If he didn't get them, the doctors said, he would be dead within a few years. By December 2017, the 71-year-old's condition had worsened, and no matching donors had been found. He and his wife Rhonda were losing hope.

On December 12, Konrad Reuland died. He had checked the "Organ Donor" box on his driver's license, so you can guess what happened: His liver went to a man in his 50s, his right kidney went to a woman in her 60s, and his heart and left kidney went to his childhood hero, Rod Carew—who happened to have the same blood type as Reuland and lived only 12 miles away in Los Angeles.

The coincidences don't end there: A year earlier, Rod and his wife Rhonda started a heart disease awareness campaign called The Heart of 29 (Carew's jersey number), and he ended up with the heart of a 29-year-old. "You never know," he joked after the transplant surgery, "it could be time for a comeback." And when the Carews and Reulands finally met in the spring of 2018, Rod let Mary put her ear on his chest and listen to her son's beating heart.

A sloth has more bones in its neck than a giraffe does.

MXC: THE DOMED CITY OF TOMORROW

Sci-fi movies and books of the 20th century frequently presented our future as a world in which the magic of everyday science would make our lives calm and easy. Here's the story of how some people in Minnesota tried to make that idealistic vision a reality.

HAUS OF LEARNING

Athelstan Spilhaus fit the classic definition of a *polymath:* an extremely intelligent person adept at numerous disparate disciplines. Educated at MIT, he'd had experience in (or written about) cartography, meteorology, mechanical engineering, urban planning, and oceanography. He was also a dean of the University of Minnesota, where one of his chief accomplishments was the creation of the Sea Grant College Program, creating a network of member universities that would share research about the oceans and Great Lakes. Beyond academia, Spilhaus had an eye for popular science: he designed the "Science Expo" pavilion at the 1962 Seattle World's Fair, a gig he got because of his futurist comic strip.

Yes, he also wrote a comic strip. *Our New Age* ran from 1957 to 1973, appearing in more than 100 newspapers nationwide at its peak. Each week Spilhaus wrote about different themes, detailing in vague but optimistic terms how science, technology, and engineering could be used to solve all of humanity's ills to create a progressive, worldwide utopia. When Spilhaus met John F. Kennedy in the run-up to the 1962 World's Fair, the president told him, "The only science I ever learned was from your comic strip in the *Boston Globe.*"

COMICAL BEGINNINGS

One of the biggest problems Spilhaus saw for the future was one a lot of people were worried about in the 1960s: overpopulation. "Too many students for the schools, too much sludge for the sewers, too many cars for the highways, too many sick for the hospitals, too much crime for the police, too many commuters for the transport system. Too many fumes for the atmosphere to bear, too many chemicals for the water to carry," Spilhaus wrote in a 1967 proposal for construction of a utopian city.

> **Too much sludge for the sewers, too many cars for the highways, too many sick for the hospitals, too much crime for the police.**

The inspiration for that proposal—to build an actual prototype for a city of the future—was "Experimental City," an edition of his *Our New Age* comic strip. Some

Technically speaking, bananas are berries. So are eggplants.

of the text in the proposal is very close to what appeared in his strip. ("Cities are now springing up all over the world without proper planning—with the result that air, land and water are polluted, traffic and sewers are congested, and schools overflow.") But Spilhaus wasn't just complaining—he had a solution. Over images of shiny towers and transport tubes, Spilhaus waxed about factories "grouped to reuse their residues and waters," that "luxurious mass transportation could make automobiles unnecessary," and how "homes, factories, and churches may be wired for closed circuit T.V., so that entertainment, news, and education may be piped anywhere!"

TOMORROW'S CITY, TODAY

Spilhaus cited early 1960s reports projecting that the U.S. population could explode to 400 million by the year 2000. Rather than expand population centers outward into endless suburbs, Spilhaus believed that urban planners should just build brand-new, ground-up, prefabricated cities, each of which could accommodate a population of 250,000. And he had the design for those cities—the one from his comic strip.

Assisting Spilhaus in his drive to build a sample version of his future city was fellow Minnesotan (and futurist) Otto Silha, publisher of the *Minneapolis Star Tribune*. In 1966 Silha agreed to use his media contacts and influence to launch a public-relations campaign that would draw interest and funding to the project, which they gave the accurate-but-uninspiring name of "Minnesota Experimental City," or MXC for short.

ALL ABOARD

Among the luminaries who signed on to serve on the steering committee: James Cain, a Mayo Clinic physician and President Lyndon B. Johnson's personal doctor; civil rights leader Muriel Snowden; economist Walter Heller; National Urban League director Whitney Young; and engineer Buckminster Fuller, at the time known for his own utopian proposal—a plan to ensconce Manhattan under a domed roof.

But Silha's biggest "get" was former Minnesota senator and then–vice president Hubert Humphrey. Humphrey secured $250,000 in federal funds to get the Minnesota Experimental City project up and running—a drop in the bucket, considering that Spilhaus estimated it would cost around $10 billion ($75 billion in today's money). But it was still a decent amount of seed money and, more important, it represented federal government support for the project. (And there would probably be a lot more federal money to come, if Humphrey were to win his 1968 presidential bid.) Besides, there was plenty of money coming in from sponsors like Boeing, Ford, Honeywell, and 3M, which was also on board to open a manufacturing facility inside MXC.

Actor George Lazenby added a bunch of fake movies to his résumé to land the part of James Bond in the 1969 film *On Her Majesty's Secret Service*.

A SPEC-TACLE

Here's how Spilhaus, Silha, Fuller, and associates envisioned their city of tomorrow:

- It would sit on a plot of 60,000 acres (about 94 square miles), which is roughly the size of Boston.
- One quarter of the property would be paved and hold buildings. The rest would be reserved for parks, green spaces, and the farms that would be used to grow the city's entire food supply.
- There would be no schools. Spilhaus, while himself formally educated, advocated a vague idea of education called "lifelong learning," a combination of everyone informally educating everyone else, while also taking classes at an on-site branch of the University of Minnesota remotely, from home computer/TV terminals.
- Those computer/TV terminals would also be used to buy all household goods remotely.
- Homes and businesses would use completely waterless toilets.
- All wastewater would be recycled and used for crop irrigation.
- Spilhaus thought existing cities were far too car-centric, utilizing huge amounts of valuable space for roads and parking lots. His solution: ban traditional, gas-powered cars inside the city limits because they pollute the air. Residents could drive *out* of the city with those cars, but once they arrived at the MXC, they'd be shut off and parked on a guided rail system that moved the car around the city like a combination gondola and moving sidewalk. All vehicle parking would be underground.
- There would be a system of moving sidewalks, or "people movers," that wrapped around the city.
- Waste would be recycled in an underground processing plant.
- The city would have its own electricity supply…generated by the nuclear reactor located right in the middle of town.
- None of that air pollution outside the city would matter much to MXC… because the entire city would be covered by one of Buckminster Fuller's geodesic domes to allow for optimal climate control.
- Estimated opening day: sometime in 1984.

THANKS, BUT NO THANKS

Spilhaus lost patience when, a year after he filed his proposal, construction still hadn't begun. So, in 1968, he stepped down as co-chairman of the Minnesota Experimental City. But Silha and the rest of the steering committee continued,

Cambridge University researchers invented the webcam to keep an eye on how much coffee was left in the office coffee pot.

ignoring all the problems and choosing instead to focus on finding the right location for the project. The board convinced the Minnesota legislature that they had a good idea going, and got them to create the Minnesota Experimental City Authority, tasked with locating a site so that construction could start by 1973.

> **Locals were adamantly opposed, both to the massive construction project and to the eminent domain land grab.**

Very quickly, the MXCA identified the "perfect" spot: swampland in central Minnesota near the sparsely populated town of Swatara. Locals were adamantly opposed, both to the disruption caused by such a massive construction project and to the eminent domain land grab that would be necessary to accommodate a 60,000-acre city. Grant Merritt, head of the Minnesota Pollution Control Agency, an environmental group that believed industrialization was already ruining the planet, led the opposition. In 1972 Merritt led a small group of protestors on a 160-mile march from Swatara to the capitol building in St. Paul to demonstrate their dissent. Spilhaus dismissed the group as "uninformed" and prone to "nonsense emotionalism."

CITY IN RUINS

The strong local opposition, along with Humphrey's loss to Richard Nixon in the 1968 election (which meant he would no longer have the political clout needed to secure government support), ultimately doomed the Minnesota Experimental City. The Minnesota Experimental City Authority's funding was pulled in 1973, and the planning committee disbanded. Any hopes of reviving the project got pushed to the side during America's economic problems of the early 1970s, including gas and oil shortages, and skyrocketing interest rates.

But what really killed the MXC was its utter lack of a plan. Sure, Spilhaus had a vision, and he hired some of the top minds in the world to help him brainstorm, but ultimately, all of the board's plans were hollow because they had no idea how to execute the project. For example, Spilhaus and company never hired an architect to design any of the housing, a vital component of a plan that was supposed to accomodate 250,000 people. Other elements of the project were so future-forward that they hadn't even been invented yet, notably Spilhaus's idea of remote learning at in-home computer terminals, which predated the rise of today's internet by a good 35 years.

While his ideas were exciting, Spilhaus was just in way over his head in turning his comic-strip utopia into a real utopia in the wilds of Minnesota. Oddly, he never quite realized that. Shortly before he died in 1998, he revived his "Experimental City" idea, but this time he suggested that engineers build it in an even more difficult, expensive, and—probably—technologically impossible location: underwater.

Rise and shine: When ants wake up, they stretch.

THE MYSTERY OF THE CRYSTAL SKULL, PART II

Just like their on-screen counterpart, real-life crystal skulls are shrouded in mystery and controversy—none more so than the Mitchell-Hedges crystal skull. (Part I is on page 199.)

THE PLOT THICKENS

Anna Mitchell-Hedges maintained until her 100th year that it was she who found the crystal skull in Belize on her 17th birthday in 1924. Or maybe it was 1926. In most versions, it was "on top of a pyramid," but other times it was "under a collapsed altar inside a temple." Her accounts changed over the years—even contradicting her father, who once wrote that he found the skull "in the 1930s." There's a lot about Anna's versions of events that haven't added up over the years. That's a habit she picked up from her father.

STORY TIME

Just who was this F. A. Mitchell-Hedges, anyway? His given name was Frederick Albert, but he went by Mike. Born in London in 1882, the self-described "adventurer, traveler, and writer" spoke in a thick British accent and always had a pipe in his mouth. He was rumored to be one of the inspirations for Indiana Jones, but George Lucas, who created the character, has never confirmed that. Mitchell-Hedges's 1954 autobiography, *Danger My Ally*, doesn't even mention the word "archaeologist." In that book and others (with titles like *Battles with Giant Fish*), and on his popular New York–based radio show in the 1930s (with jungle drums beating in the background), Mitchell-Hedges would dramatically detail his harrowing "true stories" of fighting off scary savages, wrestling sea monsters, and discovering the "cradle of civilization" in Nicaragua. Listeners had no way of knowing whether his stories were real, but it was all very entertaining. And just as outlandish as his exploits were the famous friends he claimed he'd made along the way.

After leaving England at 18 (he didn't want to be a banker like his father), Mitchell-Hedges ended up in New York, where he worked as a stockbroker by day and a high-stakes poker player at night. It was during this time that he may (or may not) have shared a room with noted Marxist Leon Trotsky. He later wrote that Britain's MI6 wanted him to spy on the Russian revolutionary, but he declined (Trotsky always paid his rent on time, he said).

In 1913, when Mitchell-Hedges was in Mexico looking for work, he told of being captured by the revolutionary general Pancho Villa, who accused him of being a spy. Standing in front of a firing squad, the adventurer claimed he was able to save himself by singing an "off-key rendition of 'God Save the King.'" Villa took Mitchell-Hedges under his wing and made him a spy. That's when the Englishman said he first developed an interest in archaeology. He came to believe that there must be some link between the lost city of Atlantis and the ancient Maya, and he started funding expeditions to discover that link.

It was a few years later, in 1917, when Mitchell-Hedges was in Canada, that a good friend of his died, leaving behind a 10-year-old orphan named Anna. He "informally" adopted her. (But even that story has been disputed; some suspect that F. A. Mitchell-Hedges was Anna's biological father.)

DANGER HIS ALLY

Piecing together Mitchell-Hedges's story doesn't get any easier after reading *Danger My Ally*. The thing he's most known for only gets one paragraph in the entire manuscript. Next to a page-size photo of the "sinister Skull of Doom" he writes that it...

> ...is made of pure rock crystal and according to scientists it must have taken 150 years, generation after generation working all days of their lives, patiently rubbing down with sand an immense block of rock crystal until the perfect Skull emerged. It is at least 3,600 years old and according to legend was used by the High Priest of the Maya when performing esoteric rites. It is said that when he willed death with the help of the skull, death invariably followed. It has been described as the embodiment of all evil. I do not wish to try and explain this phenomena. How it came into my possession I have reason for not revealing.

Five years later, Mitchell-Hedges died, leaving no more clues behind. And in subsequent printings of *Danger My Ally*, all mentions of the crystal skull were removed. In fact, the only source for Anna's version of events was Anna herself. Her father wrote a lot about his time in Central America, and he described the artifacts he found there in great detail...with the curious exception of the crystal skull. What was he hiding?

ITEM NO. 54

When actual scientists and historians attempt to trace the story of the crystal skull, the first verifiable account of the rock's association with the Mitchell-Hedges family doesn't come until October 15, 1943, when item no. 54 was put on the auction block at Sotheby's in London. Here's the listing:

> A Superb Life-Size Crystal Carving of a Human Skull, the lower jaw separate, the details are correctly rendered and the carver has given the orbits, zygomatic arches and mastoid processes the similitude of their natural forms, glabellar-occipital.

Technical name for stomach rumbling: *borborygmus*.

A receipt reveals that F. A. Mitchell-Hedges purchased the skull at that auction for £400 (roughly $5,000 in today's money) from a London antique dealer named Sydney Burney. That would explain why Mitchell-Hedges never mentioned finding the skull on his 1930s radio show—he hadn't even bought it yet.

Anna Mitchell-Hedges didn't deny that her father had purchased the skull at that auction, but she said he was buying it *back*. She claimed that years earlier, when her father needed funds to finance an expedition, he gave the skull to Burney, a childhood friend, as collateral for a loan. Instead of giving it back, however, Burney (or his son) tried to sell it to the highest bidder. When Mitchell-Hedges got wind of it, he "was so furious that for a while he was unable to speak." He called the auction house and told them to call off the sale; they refused, so he went there and bought it back himself. That was Anna's story, and she stuck to it.

CASTING DOUBT

Of the numerous scholars, scientists, and skeptics who question the veracity of Mitchell-Hedges's claims about the skull, the most vocal is Joe Nickell, a senior research fellow with the Committee for the Scientific Investigation of Claims of the Paranormal. "It's clear her father bought it off a collector," he wrote in the 1988 book *Secrets of the Supernatural*. Nickell points to a letter that Sydney Burney had written a decade prior to that auction: "The rock-crystal skull was for several years in the possession of the collector from whom I bought it, and he in his turn had it from an Englishman in whose collection it had been also for several years." The only actual "evidence" that F. A. Mitchell-Hedges had the skull prior to that auction was a 1999 report by a British inn owner who said the explorer and his daughter had the skull with them when they stayed there in the early 1930s.

After all the conflicting origin stories, it becomes more and more difficult to say for certain that the crystal skull is genuine, but that hasn't stopped true believers from saying it is. "While its history may be somewhat controversial," says the website CrystalSkulls.com, "the fact remains that the Mitchell-Hedges Crystal Skull is a true so called 'out-of-place-artifact'—meaning that despite the most evolved research, including extensive laboratory examination by Silicon Valley's Hewlett-Packard, no one has been able to prove it is a hoax."

> **A TIP FROM UNCLE JOHN**
>
> According to the Archaeological Institute of America, if you find an artifact in your backyard, try not to move it. If you have to, take photos of it first, and then call your state's archaeology office (every state has one) and they will send someone to authenticate it.

The end? Not really. To hear what modern science has to say about the Mitchell-Hedges crystal skull—and what it's been up to in recent years—fund an expedition over to page 436.

Mozart had a childhood phobia of trumpets.

HERE LIES JOHN HANCOCK

*John Hancock's audacious autograph on the Declaration of Independence led
to the phrase "put your John Hancock here" when signing a document. Now
let's find out where they put the real John Hancock, along with a few other
Founding Fathers…and Mother Goose. Here's the third part of our story about
where America's Founding Fathers are buried. (Part II is on page 274.)*

WAYWARD SON

Here's a trick question: Which Founding Father is buried at Hancock Cemetery?
Answer: None of them. Even though Hancock Cemetery was named after his father,
Reverend Colonel John Hancock Jr., John Hancock III (1737–93) never had much of
an attachment to his birthplace of Braintree, Massachusetts. Hancock was only seven
when the reverend died, so he was raised by his rich uncle in nearby Boston, where he
later attended Harvard College and then took over his uncle's mercantile business.

When relations with King George III started breaking down in the 1760s, most
of Boston's elite sided with the British. But Hancock, along with his friend, fellow
Bostonian Samuel Adams, joined the fight for independence. In 1774, with Adams's
help, Hancock became president of the Massachusetts Provisional Congress, and
soon after became president of the First and Second Continental Congresses—the
legislative body that declared the colonies' independence from England.

As president of the Continental Congress, Hancock was the first person to sign
the Declaration of Independence. As he inked his fancy, six-square-inch signature, he
proclaimed to everyone in the room, "There, I guess King George will be able to read
that!" (Sounds of laughter.)

MYTH-MAKERS

That anecdote fits right in with Hancock's reputation for flaunting his wealth and
always speaking his mind. But did he really say that? No one knows what he said on
July 4. Or maybe it was the 2nd, or the 6th…or maybe August? Most of these tales-
turned-school-lessons (like George Washington's cherry tree and Abe Lincoln's log
cabin) weren't even written down until decades after the subjects had died.

The Declaration of Independence wasn't signed by 59 patriots on July 4, 1776,
but that's how it's been portrayed in countless history books and paintings. Congress
actually voted for Independence on July 2 (that's the date many of the Founding
Fathers thought should be a holiday). The final draft wasn't approved until July 4,
which is when the broadsheet was sent to the printer. That's why it says on top, "IN
CONGRESS, July 4, 1776." Only a few men were on hand to sign it; the first was John

Hancock, and his words were not recorded. (We still find it humorous that in King George's diary, he noted that "nothing important" happened on July 4, 1776.) It wasn't until August that most of the other signers put their John Hancocks on the document. (Hancock may or may not have said his famous quote *that* day.)

And while we're at it, July 4, 1776, isn't really the nation's birthday: the Declaration of Independence was just that, a declaration stating that the colonies were breaking away from England. The nation wasn't "founded" until the U.S. Constitution was ratified on June 21, 1788. None of this diminishes Hancock's role as a Founding Father, nor would it be the last tall tale associated with him.

LAID TO REST

In 1780 Hancock was elected the first governor of Massachusetts and served in the position on and off for the next 10 years. By the early 1790s, he was more figurehead than governor, and his health was failing fast. He'd had severe gout—a painful arthritic condition—since he was 36. He was only in his mid-50s, but he looked and felt like a much older man. He succumbed to the disease in October 1793, becoming one of the first of the signers to die. His body was kept in Hancock Manor (on Beacon Hill in Boston) for a week.

Samuel Adams took over as governor and declared Hancock's funeral a state holiday. The largest crowd that had ever gathered in Boston up to that point—20,000 people—paid their respects as Hancock's body was taken through the city from the State House to Granary Burying Ground. His lead coffin was placed inside a tomb along a long brick wall. A white marble slab with his name on it was attached to the wall.

Why the Old Granary? Anybody who was anybody in Boston was interred there. In addition to Hancock, you can also visit the markers of Samuel Adams, Paul Revere, Robert Treat Pine (another signer), Benjamin Franklin's parents (but not Franklin himself), five colonists who were killed in the Boston Massacre, and Mary "Mother" Goose (not the original Mother Goose herself, but the mother-in-law of a publisher of Mother Goose books). Also buried there is Samuel Sewall, one of the judges during the Salem witch hunts of the 1690s. Sewall later wrote an "article of penitence," begging forgiveness for his part in the hysteria.

TWO FEET UNDER

Unlike typical graveyards, burying grounds are just what they sound like. A single grave or tomb can contain several people, even from different families. And not all these graves were given proper markers. Boston's third-oldest cemetery (after the first two filled up), the Old Granary was established next to a grain storage building in the 1660s on what was basically swampland. Because of the area's low water table, the graves had to be quite shallow—most are less than two feet belowground. It wasn't uncommon after heavy rainfall for bones to find their way to the surface. (As recently as 2009, an unfortunate tourist fell through the dirt and landed waist-deep into a previously unknown crypt.)

By the time Hancock was laid to rest there in 1793, the burying ground was already overcrowded. Over the next century, as the city of Boston rose up around it, the Old Granary went through several renovations. Graves were rearranged and rows were straightened to make room for sidewalks. Unless a family could afford to replace their crumbing headstone, whoever was buried beneath it would be lost to history. Out of the estimated 5,000 to 8,000 people who were buried at the Old Granary, less than a third of them were even given proper gravestones in the first place.

THE DUSTBIN OF HISTORY

Though a household name today, John Hancock was largely forgotten after his death. That was pretty much the case for every Founding Father whose name wasn't George Washington. Admiration for Washington, the Revolutionary War hero and nation's first president—even by his sworn enemies—was almost universal. In the 1800s, as the only man equally admired in the North and the South, he came to embody *all* the Founding Fathers. Because John Hancock's fame faded so quickly after his passing, no care was taken to preserve his legacy. In 1809 John Adams lamented that both Hancock and Samuel Adams had been "buried in oblivion." By 1863 Hancock wasn't even famous enough for his house on Beacon Street to be saved.

PUBLIC RELATIONS DISASTER

Then came the centennial. Observance of the nation's 100th anniversary in 1876 sparked a renewed interest in all of the Founding Fathers. And Boston, a city that played a large role in the country's formation, saw a huge jump in tourism. That created a problem at the Old Granary. Over the next two decades, as historical plaques and markers honoring Boston's forgotten heroes started popping up all over the city, no one knew exactly where Hancock's body was.

Not helping matters was an 1886 account by a local historian named Edwin M. Bacon. In *Bacon's Dictionary of Boston*, he wrote that, back in the 1860s, when construction workers were building a new basement in a building on neighboring Park Street, they removed a high wall across the street to let more light in:

> In tearing down the old wall, the tomb of John Hancock must have been broken into, as the wall formed one side of it, so there is no proof that even his body remains there. The body was inclosed in a lead coffin: who knows but this may have been converted into water pipes, or used up in various plumbing operations?

It takes 27 hours to change the oil on a Bugatti Veyron sports car—and costs $21,000.

If Bacon's account is true, then it's most likely that the workers threw all of the human remains—including Hancock's—in the trash.

And that's not Bacon's only Hancock tale. He also wrote that not long after Hancock was laid to rest, grave robbers dug up the Founding Father and tried to pry the expensive rings off his fingers, but they were so bloated by rigor mortis (the fingers, not the robbers) that the rings wouldn't budge. So the robbers removed Hancock's hands instead. If this did indeed happen, then Bacon was the first to write about it...80 years later.

THERE HE IS!
True or not, stories like that only added to the Founding Fathers' lore, and as Hancock was finally starting to get the credit he deserved, it would be advantageous for Old Granary officials to determine where he was. In early 1895, plans were announced for a new monument to be erected at his grave site. That August, the *Boston Globe* reported that workers renovating the site had located Hancock's intact coffin, and it would be securely reburied underneath a massive granite obelisk in the Old Granary. The monument went up quickly, but other than that one newspaper article, there is no record of Hancock's body ever being found. The only way to know for sure if he's actually buried there would be to exhume the grave and look for a skeleton (with or without any hands), and there are no plans for that to happen.

THE OBELISK
If you'd like to see Hancock's grave, it's not hard to miss. Like his famous signature, the stone monument—with a flattering portrait of the statesman etched into its side—dwarfs all the other markers around it. In fact, it's the third-largest obelisk in the entire burying ground. And even though it wasn't erected until a century after he died, it's a good bet that Hancock would be impressed. (Of course, he would also be impressed by the 790-foot John Hancock Tower, which has been Boston's tallest building since the bicentennial.)

There are several other graves surrounding Hancock's (which you have to stand on when looking at his obelisk). One of the markers is for Hancock's wife, Dorothy, who died 37 years after him. Another nearby headstone marks the grave of...

FRANK
Servant to
John Hancock Esqr.
lied interr'd here
who died 23d Jan
1771

The Toll House Inn, where chocolate chip cookies were invented, burned down in 1984. Today a Wendy's fast-food restaurant sits on the spot.

As a testament to Hancock's wealth and power, Frank is one of the few African Americans ever interred in the Old Granary. Another was Crispus Attucks, a runaway slave who was the first African American killed in the Revolutionary War.

HERE LIES LONGFELLOW

John Hancock isn't even the most visited grave at the Old Granary. That accolade goes to Paul Revere (1735–1818), the silversmith who, in 1775, rode his horse all over Massachusetts in a single night and warned his compatriots that the British were coming. That's according to Henry Wadsworth Longfellow's 1861 poem "Paul Revere's Ride"…which altered some key details. For one, it didn't take one rider one night but several riders several days to spread the news of the impending British invasion. Because Longfellow's story happens to be the most popular one, that's how most people think it happened. The poet wasn't trying to give a history lesson, though, he was creating a fictionalized account of history to serve his own purpose—a warning against the impending Civil War.

Thanks to scores of historians over the centuries who have studied that fateful ride, what we do know is that if Paul Revere—along with fellow patriots William Dawes, Samuel Prescott, and others whose names are lost to history—hadn't warned John Hancock and Samuel Adams about the impending invasion, the wanted men would probably have been captured and hanged for treason. However, it did take a bit of prodding by Revere when Hancock refused to retreat. "If I had my musket," said Hancock, "I would never turn my back on these troops." But Revere did convince him to leave, and two years later, John Hancock signed the Declaration of Independence.

THE OLD GRANARY TODAY

The Beantown Pub, located across from the Old Granary on Tremont Street, is probably the only place you can drink a Sam Adams Lager while looking out at the grave of Samuel Adams. His marker is a large rock, about four feet high, with a green plaque that dates to 1898 (nearly a century after his death). Located steps away from a subway station, the Old Granary receives about 3,000 visitors every day. It's one of the most popular spots on the Freedom Trail, which consists of 16 historical sites between Boston Common and the Bunker Hill Monument.

Can't make it to the Old Granary yourself? You can visit it virtually on Google Earth, where you can see markers on the graves of John Hancock, Samuel Adams, and Paul Revere…whose remains may or may not be with their headstones.

Our tour of the Founding Fathers' final resting places takes us next to Philadelphia, where the Liberty Bell isn't the only famous piece of history with a crack in it. Off to page 387.

A blue whale's tongue is bigger than a rhinoceros.

ASK THE EXPERTS

*Still more questions about the world we live in, with
answers from the world's top trivia experts.*

WHITE WASH

Q: *Why is toilet paper white?*

A: "One of the primary reasons toilet paper is white is the same reason most toilets are: white toilet paper looks cleaner than the natural brownish color the paper is before it's bleached. If toilet paper was the original brown hue, on a purely aesthetic level, would you use it? Or, perhaps more aptly, would you prefer it over the white variety? The consensus among toilet paper makers, like Kimberly-Clark, who rang in on this issue, is that people consistently choose the white. One can only assume they've done extensive marketing studies to back that notion up, but even without access to those studies, it makes intuitive sense.

"That said, there are other factors at play. For starters, white isn't just an aesthetic choice, the white color of toilet paper is usually achieved by bleaching the paper, and this can make the paper much softer. The bleaching process removes lignin, a polymer in wood that makes the tree more rigid. Besides the added softness, removing lignin adds a shelf-life to the paper. If you've ever seen an old newspaper, you may notice that the paper starts to yellow as it ages; this yellowing is due to the presence of lignin in the newspaper. Obviously toilet paper that yellows over time, especially unevenly, isn't going to fly off the shelves.

"So that's partially why many toilet paper manufacturers bleach the toilet paper in the first place, but why don't they still color it in many countries? The primary reason here probably has more to do with the extra cost. To make up for this, they'd need to charge a little more for the dyed version. If this would have the potential to increase sales, they'd no doubt start making colored toilet paper tomorrow." (From "Why Is Toilet Paper Always White?" by Karl Smallwood for TodayIFoundOut.com)

TELL ME MORE ABOUT MY EYES

Q: *Why do blue eyes seem to be so much bluer than other eyes seem to be the color they are?*

A: "Brown eyes get their color from melanin, the same pigment that colors your skin. But blue eyes don't have any blue pigment in them. Blue eyes get their color the same way water and the sky get their blue color. They scatter light so that more blue light reflects back out.

"The colored part of the eye is called the iris. It's a structure that contains muscle and other kinds of cells. You can see the iris in action when it squeezes or relaxes to let in more or less light through the pupil. The iris is made up of two layers. For almost everyone—even people with blue eyes—the back layer (called the pigment epithelium) has brown pigment in it.

"The front layer of the iris (called the stroma) is made up of overlapping fibers and cells. For people with brown eyes, some of the cells also have brown pigment in them. If there is no pigment at all in this front layer, the fibers scatter and absorb some of the longer wavelengths of light that come in. More blue light gets back out and the eyes appear to be blue." (From "Your Blue Eyes Aren't Really Blue," by Dan T. Gudgel, American Academy of Ophthalmology)

TOILET-TRON 2000

Q: *Why do so many scientific words end in "tron"?*

A: "If you grew up in the 1980s, chances are you'll remember riding the Gravitron at the local fair, or struggling to get past level one of the video game Robotron. That would be after you got up early to watch Voltron on the eponymous TV series, and rushed out to see Disney's 1982 film *Tron*.

"The suffix *-tron*, along with *-matic* and *-stat*, are what Stanford University historian Robert Proctor calls 'embodied symbols.' Like the heraldic shields of ancient knights, these morphemes were painted onto the names of scientific technologies to proclaim one's history and achievements to friends and enemies alike. *Stat* signaled something measurable, while *matic* advertised free labor; but *tron*, above all, indicated control. The suffix emblazoned the banners of nuclear physics' Cosmotron, modern biology's Climatron, and early AI's perceptron—displaying to all our mastery over matter, life, and information. By the turn of the millennium, though, most of that was gone. True, Sony's jumbotron still helps to broadcast presidential addresses and rock concerts, but today it's all too easy to forget the technological promise that *tron* contains, and hear only its kitschy and cartoonish overtones.

"In contemporary usage the term springs from ancient Greek, with the invention of the first vacuum tube or 'kenotron' around 1904; its creator came up with the name by combining the Greek words for 'empty' (*keno*) and 'tool' (*tron*). Subsequently, the radiotron, thyratron, klystron, and rhumbatron went on to become vital components of the radio industry in the 1930s, while the resonant cavity magnetron was at the heart of every radar set in the Second World War. Don't be deceived, though: These components bear scant relationship to elementary particles such as the electron, neutron, and positron, all of which really end in the suffix *-on*." (From "A Tale of 'Trons': The Suffix That Tells the Story of Modern Science" by David Munns for *Aeon* magazine)

In India, Spider-Man's alter ego Peter Parker is known as Pavitr Prabhakar.

GOOD BOOKS, BAD MISTAKES

Even the best editors can miss a typo now and then, and that includes the folks who worked on these famous books. (Please don't hold it agenst them—it could happin to ennyone.)

- An editor at Merriam-Webster noticed in 1939 that there was a word in the *Webster's New International Dictionary, Second Edition* that had no etymology… and that nobody on staff had ever actually heard of. That word: *dord*, supposedly from the worlds of physics and chemistry, and meaning "density." An internal investigation revealed that the word had been submitted for addition to the dictionary back in 1931 by Webster's chemistry editor, Austin Patterson. He'd intended to add "D or d" to the dictionary, referring to acceptable abbreviations of density. Patterson tended to make his letters a little too close together, and another editor read "D or d" as "dord."

- Jeni Wright's 2007 cookbook *The Pasta Bible* included recipes for all kinds of Italian-inspired noodle dishes. The entry for "Spelt tagliatelle with sardines & prosciutto" was a bit confusing for home cooks. Publisher JG Press later blamed an overly aggressive automatic spellchecker for why the ingredient list included "salt and freshly ground black people."

- William Shakespeare introduced a lot of words to the English language—*eyeball, manager,* and *swagger,* to name just a few—as well as names. "Jessica" first appears in *The Merchant of Venice* and "Imogen" comes from *Cymbeline.* But that one was a mistake. The play is based on historical events, and includes a character Shakespeare called Innogen. In the first printings of his plays—and all of them after—the "nn" in the name looked like an "m" and entered the language as Imogen.

- Spellcheckers and editors are more likely to catch misspelled words than they are to catch homonyms—words that sound alike but are spelled differently. Think "fair" vs. "fare," or "sea" vs. "see," or "fleas" vs. "flees." The first two additions (sorry, editions) of Pearl S. Buck's Pulitzer Prize–winning 1931 novel *The Good Earth* fell victim to that problem. On page 100, Buck describes a wall lined with crudely crafted huts. "It stretched out long and grey and very high, and against the base the small mat sheds clung like flees to a dog's back."

- Robert A. Heinlein's 1961 novel *Stranger in a Strange Land* is a landmark work of science fiction, which is probably why no editor had dared change a word of the manuscript even after this error was discovered. Alice Douglas is a major character in the book...or, as she's called from time to time in the novel, Agnes.

- Mark Twain's *The Adventures of Huckleberry Finn* could lay claim to the title of "Great American Novel," or at least "first Great American Novel," a best-seller and instant classic when it hit bookshelves in 1885. It's a bit difficult to read at times, as Twain wrote large portions of the book phonetically, imitating dialects spoken in the South and Midwest. But there's one odd use of English that was entirely unintentional. A character says, "I took the bag and ripped a hole in the bottom of it with the was." What's a "was"? Twain accidentally wrote "saw" backward.

- The very first Harry Potter book was published in 1997 in the UK under the title *Harry Potter and the Philosopher's Stone.* (It was changed to *Sorcerer's Stone* for the American edition.) There's a lot of "world building" in the book, establishing the rules and details of author J. K. Rowling's universe of wizards and witches. When Harry first learns he's a wizard and prepares to ship off to Hogwarts for training, he has to make a stop for magical school supplies. His list of requirements in the first edition of the book contains a mistake. It says he needs "1 wand, 1 cauldron, 1 telescope, 1 set brass scales, and 1 wand."

- Karen Harper specializes in historical romance fiction, and strives for accuracy, which means she probably didn't mean to refer to Chinese food appetizers in her 2010 Tudor–era novel *The Queen's Governess.* When describing Kat Ashley, a lady-in-waiting awoken by criminals in the night, Harper wrote, "In the weak light of dawn, I tugged on the gown and sleeves I'd discarded like a wonton last night to fall into John's arms."

- Sir Isaac Newton's *Principia* (1687) was the scientist and mathematician's crowning achievement, and created the foundation of modern science.

Apparently nobody noticed Newton's error for more than 300 years.

(Newton describes such important concepts as the laws of motion and the law of universal gravitation.) His proof of how the world literally goes 'round comes in the form of extensive mathematical equations, and, amazingly, one of his calculations was wrong. (The solution gave him "11" instead of the correct "10.5"—close, but close doesn't count in high-level math.) More amazingly, apparently nobody noticed Newton's error for more than 300 years. In 1987, 23-year-old University of Chicago physics student Robert Garisto figured it out.

Rebecca, a raccoon, was supposed to be served at Thanksgiving dinner at the White House in 1926...

WHERE THE STARS GO

Those Hollywood celebrities—they're just like us! (By which we mean they get themselves into embarrassing situations with toilets, restrooms, urinals, and the like.)

MAGNUM, PEE? AYE!

Even Tom Hanks, the world's most likable movie star, can embarrass himself once in a while. In a 2013 interview, he recounted a moment he wished he could take back. At the 1998 Academy Awards, when nature called, he responded with a trip to the men's room. "I found myself in the bathroom in a stall, next to Tom Selleck," Hanks said, referring to the former star of *Magnum, P.I.*, who was there in support of Oscar nominee Joan Cusack, his co-star in *In & Out*. "So I leaned over and I said, 'Looks like we're a couple of peeing Toms.'" Hanks thought Selleck would find his wordplay (and his violation of the unspoken "code of silence" of men's bathrooms) hilarious. He didn't. "His angry silence is something I'll never forget."

MATERIALLY EXTREME

In 2008 Madonna's concert tour took her to the Palais Nikaia, a concert hall in Nice, France. Apparently the Material Girl expects backstage areas to be as clean as possible, but she went the extra mile to make sure that it was *very* spotless. A person who worked at the hall revealed to the gossip magazine *In Touch Weekly* that, prior to her arrival for the performance, Madonna had a crew remove all of the toilets, sinks, and showers, scrub them thoroughly, and then reinstall them at the Palais Nikaia.

NO ONE POOPS LIKE GASTON

Before he became an action movie star and the guy who played Wolverine in the *X-Men* movies, Hugh Jackman was primarily a star of stage musical productions. In 1996 he starred as the villainous Gaston in an Australian production of Disney's *Beauty and the Beast.* The rigors of performing left him unhealthy, and he suffered from headaches and dehydration. Then one show day, he got diarrhea, too. He thought he'd passed a little gas while talking to reporters before the show, only to realize that he'd passed, well, more than that. Jackman threw out his underwear and had to rush on stage. He went "commando" for his performance that night, but his body kept sabotaging itself, well into his first musical number. "Literally I'm picking up Belle, and as I pick her up, I stopped singing and right in that moment I realized the muscles you need to release in order to sing are the ones you don't want to release if you need to go," he said on *The Rachael Ray Show.*

...but First Lady Grace Coolidge decided to keep her as a pet instead.

STARTED AT THE BOTTOM

While touring Europe in March 2014, singer Drake treated himself and his entourage to a night on the town in a Glasgow, Scotland, nightclub called Cirque. Big stars often request a private room for their party, but Drake's management also wanted exclusive use of the closest bathrooms, "and that happened to be the female one," Cirque manager Mark Loney told reporters. The club agreed, so as soon as the star arrived, club staff cleared women out of the bathroom…even while they were still using it. "I don't care who Drake is, or his toilet requirements, but it's a basic right to be able to use the women's toilets," one woman said. "We were told that we could use the men's. That's disgusting."

AN EVEN WORSE BRAND OF MCCARTHYISM

Before she was an actor and co-host of *The View*, Jenny McCarthy got her big break as a *Playboy* centerfold. The job requires lots of public appearances and "meet-and-greets." One of those sessions is one she'll never forget. "I once had really bad diarrhea at a *Playboy* autograph signing," McCarthy said. "I was squeezed into a tight red dress, dripping in sweat, and knew something was not right." She held it in as she posed with fan after fan, but after what seemed like an eternity, she'd had enough…and she didn't make it to the restroom. "I was like, 'Oh no, the demon is about to be unleashed,'" McCarthy recalls. "And it was unleashed for about 20 guys to witness."

NOT THINKING OUT LOUD

British singer-songwriter Ed Sheeran is known for his sensitive, heartfelt songs about love and romance, such as "Shape of You," "Perfect," and "Thinking Out Loud." He recently admitted that while playing in front of a receptive audience (he wouldn't say where), he felt some gas build up in his undercarriage. He was playing with a band behind him, so he wasn't worried about the noise factor and he let it rip. Big mistake: It wasn't a fart, but rather its, um, gift-bearing cousin, the "shart" (figure it out). "It was midway through a performance, and I was really lively, and then halfway through I was like, all right," Sheeran said. "I'm just gonna stand still for the rest of this performance and hope it's over soon and then go home and throw these trousers out."

* * *

A WORD ORIGIN

People in the Middle Ages were so afraid of one particularly large forest mammal that they wouldn't even say its name. In fact, if it had a name, it's been lost to history. Instead, the animal was referred to as *bera*, which in Old English meant "the brown one." It's from this that we get the modern word *bear*.

Automaker Ferruccio Lamborghini hated the clutch on his Ferrari. That's what prompted him to start his own car company.

DEATH BY TOILET: TV AND MOVIE EDITION

A lot of famous people have died in the bathroom—most notably Elvis Presley in 1977. No one is immune to the deadly dangers of the john...not even fictional characters.

Character: Donald Gennaro (Martin Ferrero)

Movie: *Jurassic Park* (1993)

R.I.P.: Dinosaurs rip a lot of people to shreds in Steven Spielberg's classic adaptation of Michael Crichton's science-run-amok novel, but none more violently than Donald Gennaro, the park's milquetoast lawyer. He tries to escape an angry (and hungry) Tyrannosaurus rex by hiding in an outhouse, but that thin wood isn't enough to protect him. "Nature finds a way," to quote *Jurassic Park.* The T. rex breaks right through the privy walls and tears the lawyer to bits.

Character: Vincent Vega (John Travolta)

Movie: *Pulp Fiction* (1994)

R.I.P.: After two decades of successful movie roles, Travolta received his second Oscar nomination for his work in Quentin Tarantino's crime saga. Over the course of three intersecting stories, audiences get to know (and like) Vincent, who is a hit man and a heroin addict. He takes his boss's wife, Mia (Uma Thurman), out to dinner and dancing at a 1950s-themed restaurant, then he goes back on duty and is ordered to kill a double-crossing boxer named Butch (Bruce Willis). While waiting for Butch at his apartment, Vincent answers the call of nature. Butch comes home, finds a gun he doesn't recognize, and, after barging in on Vincent in the bathroom, fills him full of lead.

Character: Tywin Lannister (Charles Dance)

Television series: *Game of Thrones* (2014)

R.I.P.: Both in George R. R. Martin's *A Song of Ice and Fire* series and the popular HBO series based on those books, ruling patriarch Tywin Lannister gets what's coming to him for his years of ruthless scheming and treating his adult children badly. After trying to pin a murder on his son Tyrion (Peter Dinklage), one night he gets up to use his primitive bathroom chambers. While he's sitting there using the facilities, Tyrion shoots him with a crossbow.

Seven percent of Americans believe chocolate milk comes from brown cows.

Character: Philip Hardin (J. Downing)
Movie: *Ghoulies II* (1987)

R.I.P.: There are four *Ghoulies* movies and they're all rip-offs of the more popular (and bigger-budgeted) *Gremlins* movies. Like *Gremlins*, they're about nasty little green creatures that can kill. The poster for the first film depicts one jumping out of a toilet alongside the tagline "They'll get you in the end!" (Get it?) The first *Ghoulies* movie didn't actually feature a scene where a Ghoulie emerged from a commode, but producers liked the poster so much that they had filmmakers shoot a scene where that happened. In *Ghoulies II*, an evil businessman named Philip Hardin uses a public restroom, which is where the Ghoulies get him "in the end."

Character: Georgia Lass (Ellen Muth)
Television series: *Dead Like Me* (2003)

R.I.P.: The cult Showtime dramedy was about a group of "reapers"—ghosts who wander about Seattle, tasked with killing people whose numbers are up. In the first episode, the show's protagonist, 18-year-old Georgia, or "George" as she's known, dies and becomes a reaper. She's not in a bathroom when the moment comes. During her first day working as a temp at an office job, she's sitting outside on her lunch break when a toilet seat falls all the way from the *Mir* space station, through the atmosphere, and bonks her right on the head, killing her. For months, her fellow reapers call her by the nickname "Toilet Seat Girl."

* * *

THANKS, MARILYN

Before Marilyn Monroe was a movie star, she was an up-and-coming singer. One of her biggest influences: Ella Fitzgerald. Years later, in the mid-1950s, when Monroe was at the top of her fame, she heard that Fitzgerald wasn't allowed to play a posh Hollywood club simply because she was black. So here's what happened, as recounted years later by Fitzgerald: "I owe Marilyn Monroe a real debt. She personally called the club owner and told him she wanted me booked immediately, and if he would do it, she would take a front table every night. She told him—and it was true, due to her superstar status—that the press would go wild. The owner said yes, and Marilyn was there, front table, every night. The press went overboard. After that, I never had to play a small jazz club again. She was an unusual woman—a little ahead of her time. And she didn't know it."

A *pteronophobe* is someone terrified of being tickled by feathers.

COPS SAY THE DARNDEST THINGS

These are the stories of the men and women of law enforcement, and the strange utterances they find themselves uttering.

STUNNING

Quote: "No one wants to tase anyone, much less an 87-year-old woman."

Who Said It: Police Chief Josh Etheridge of Chatsworth, Georgia

Story: In August 2018, police received a 911 call from a Boys and Girls Club staffer reporting that an old woman was on club grounds and refused to leave, and she was holding a knife. Chief Etheridge and another officer responded to the call and confronted the woman. Not taking any chances, the two cops drew their guns and ordered the octogenarian—Martha Al-Bishara—to drop her weapon. But Al-Bishara, who stands about 5 feet tall and speaks no English, didn't understand the severity of the situation. She was smiling as she explained that she was cutting dandelions (to use in a traditional Middle Eastern dish), and walked closer so she could show them her kitchen knife. But there was a downslope behind the officers, which gave Al-Bishara the high ground. Seeing no other option, the cops tased her. Then they took her to the hospital, where she was charged with criminal trespassing and obstructing an officer.

Outcome: After a public outcry, Etheridge insisted that there was no other option: "It was the lowest use of force we could have used to simply stop that threat at the time." He pledged to conduct an internal use-of-force review. No word on whether the charges were dropped, but the family was clearly upset: "What happened to Mayberry?" lamented her grandson, speaking about the idyllic Southern town from *The Andy Griffith Show.* "Would you ever see Andy Griffith tase an 87-year-old woman?"

QUIET TIME

Quote: "In retrospect, while there is legal precedent for gagging a defendant to keep order in a court, I apologize for taking that action last week."

Who Said It: Judge John Russo of Cleveland, Ohio

Story: Russo's controversial "gag order" occurred in the summer of 2018 during the sentencing hearing of Franklyn Williams, who'd been convicted of several crimes, including robbery and kidnapping. Williams, 32, didn't think his lawyers were doing a good job, so he kept talking over them, and even over Judge Russo, who told the defendant to "zip it" numerous times. But Williams would not zip it. So the judge ordered five deputies to hold Williams and duct-tape his mouth shut. Then Russo sentenced Williams to 24 years in prison. Afterward, as Williams was being escorted out of the courtroom, he yelled, "Freedom of speech! Duct tape! Hash tag!"

Outcome: Judge Russo initially defended his actions, but after complaints from civil rights organizations, and the threat of a lawsuit from the ACLU, he apologized (while still defending his actions). Russo was removed from the case, and a new judge was brought in to sentence Williams.

CRUDE RENDERING

Quote: "We released all of those details...in the hope that someone recognizes the suspect. This was not done in jest."

Said by: A police spokesperson in Lancaster, Pennsylvania

The Story: The cops actually posted this witness-created police sketch in a Facebook post. And it really does look like a joke. But the picture actually helped lead to a suspect's capture. After a man stole some cash from a vendor at a farm stand, an eyewitness (quickly) drew the likeness. Without much else to go on, the cops posted the picture.

Almost immediately, the mocking began: "That guy does look pretty sketchy," wrote one commenter. Another suggested that he needs a *"Where's Waldo* striped hat."

Outcome: Despite the mocking—and an admission from the police that the drawing was "amateurish and cartoonish"—it reminded one investigator of a man he'd had run-ins with before: Hung Phuoc Nguyen (who, despite the name, doesn't appear Asian). The officer placed Nguyen's mug shot among others, and the witness pointed him out. (Amazingly, the suspect really does look like the sketch.) "We appreciate their effort and continued cooperation," said Sergeant William Hickey of the witnesses who came forward. "People like that make our job easier...and more enjoyable."

Honey turns green under a blacklight.

SNOWPACK TO THE FUTURE

Note: "Vous avez fait notre soirée." ("You made our night.")

Who Wrote It: Two unidentified police officers in Montreal, Quebec

Story: During a snowstorm one night in early 2018, a DeLorean DMC-12 (like the one from *Back to the Future*) was illegally parked on a Montreal street. It appeared to be completely covered with snow; only a windshield wiper was visible. A patrol car stopped behind it, and an officer got out and started writing a ticket. Then he hesitated. Another cop showed up and the *two* of them walked around the car a few times, carefully inspecting it.

Outcome: Instead of ticketing the car, they left the note saying "You made our night" under the wiper and left. Soon thereafter, a photo of the first cop inspecting the DeLorean went viral on the internet. Why? Turns out, it wasn't a car at all—it was a full-size snow sculpture of a DeLorean, carved as a prank by a local designer named Simon Laprise. Earlier that day, he was inspired by a pile of snow that the plows had left behind, and decided to make it his next art piece. "To me," he later explained to *Vice* magazine, "snow is a great free material to sculpt anything out of." For the final touch, Laprise added a windshield wiper where a real one would go (he found it nearby on the ground), making it look just like a car that was covered in snow. Although Laprise wasn't there when the cops showed up, he was delighted to receive their note.

* * *

WHAT TO NAME THE BABY

A baby cow is a calf, and a baby pig is a piglet. Here's what you call the young of other animals.

- Turkey: *poult*
- Fox: *kit*
- Swan: *cygnet*
- Eagle: *eaglet*
- Rooster: *cockrell*
- Platypus: *puggle*
- Eel: *elver*
- Hare: *leveret*
- Llama: *cria*
- Squid: *paralarva*
- Spider: *spiderling*
- Sea urchin: *pluteus*
- Porcupine: *porcupette*
- Rat: *pinkie*
- Guinea fowl: *keet*
- Mosquito: *wriggler*
- Jellyfish: *ephyna*
- Hog: *shoat*
- Hawk: *eyas*
- Skunk: *kitten*
- Salmon: *parr*
- Pike: *pickerel*
- Elephant seal: *weaner*
- Ape: *baby*

The Vatican City's ATMs are the only ones in the world that speak Latin.

THE SINISTER WORLD OF CYBERCRIME, PART II

Tech columnist Kevin Roose describes today's world as "a time when everything from refrigerators to baby monitors is networked, internet-connected, and vulnerable to attack." Does that make you nervous? It should.
(Part I of our survey of cybercrime is on page 187.)

RISE OF THE MACHINES

Proving that life imitates art, many households now utilize *Star Trek*–like technology called Internet of Things (IoT), a network of devices that can be operated remotely. Now you can activate your coffeemaker, lock your front door, or command your "smart speakers" (Amazon Echo, Google Assistant, etc.) to play your favorite songs, all from a distance. The possibilities are impressive…but also terrifying. As malware expert David Balaban puts it, "We are all lucky enough to live a world full of interconnected devices, which is very cool because it's so easy to keep remote things at your fingertips wherever you are. The flip side: anything connected to the Internet is potentially vulnerable." Most IoT manufacturers focus on convenience, not security, and that makes sense, because most consumers don't want to enter a complex password every time they adjust the thermostat or turn on a light, and who'd want to hack those things, anyway? Spoiler: Cybercriminals would.

When you turn on an unsecured IoT gadget (and many of them are), tech-savvy criminals could tap into it, steal your Wi-Fi password, and then intercept data transmitted on your network. Samsung's smart refrigerator, for example, displays users' Gmail calendars on its door—but a flaw made it possible for outsiders to steal the users' Gmail login credentials. Even easier: *anyone* can access your appliance using its default name and password if you didn't bother to change them (who does?). Rutgers student Paras Jha and two cohorts took advantage of this in 2016, when they wrote software that seized control of 200,000 IoT devices and created the first IoT *botnet*—a collection of computers controlled remotely without the owners' knowledge. By directing their army of unlikely soldiers (thermostats, refrigerators, and home surveillance cameras) to overload servers, Jha and friends conducted at least four massive attacks on the college's computer network. (One of them was done specifically to delay Jha's calculus exam.) And before he was caught, Jha released the code for his software, called Mirai. That spawned several copycat botnets, which caused widespread damage to other major computer networks across the country.

Whoa! The average U.S. high school senior spends nine hours a day on "screen time."

WHO'S DRIVING THE CAR?

IoT properties are now common in critical electronics from cars to cardiac devices, which if hacked could have serious consequences. In 2016 Chinese security researchers demonstrated one potential danger when they took control of a moving car—from 12 miles away. The car was a Tesla Model S, but the researchers from Keen Security Lab say the hack would work on other Tesla models, too. By commandeering the car's network of computers (which is built into all modern vehicles), the team could remotely operate all of its electronic features. Whether the car was parked or driving, they could apply the brakes, unlock the doors, open the trunk, turn on the wipers, and change the seat adjustments. All the hackers needed was to: 1) connect the car to a Wi-Fi hotspot that they set up, and 2) turn on the car's web browser. Although Tesla eliminated this vulnerability, experts worry that cybercriminals will find new ways to crash cars, sabotage heart monitors, and generally wreak havoc using IoT devices.

UNFREE AS A JAILBIRD

According to *Infosecurity* magazine, nine out of ten cybercrime victims suffer financial harm. But some, like Los Angeles resident Gerber Guzman, suffer an even worse fate: Their freedom is imperiled. About 14 percent of identity fraud victims are falsely implicated in crimes when the thief provides *their* identification to police when caught. Around 2008, Guzman experienced this nightmare when officers arrested him for a crime he didn't commit. They believed he was a drug offender who had skipped court.

Details of how the cybercriminal obtained Guzman's data are hazy. Perhaps he stole it online and created an ID with his own photo. Or maybe he wasn't even a hacker, because criminals can just buy personal information on the black market or on the dark web. In 2015 reporters for the online news site Quartz found more than 600 seller offers for "fullz" (a full data set, including the victim's name, address, birth date, Social Security number, and possibly credit card information). On average, each fullz sold for only $21.35.

But however Guzman's thief acquired the data, he was walking around free while Guzman was locked up in jail. Not surprisingly, the cops paid no attention to Guzman's claims of innocence, which sounded exactly like those of everyone else who's in jail. He pleaded for days…then a week…then another week…until— finally—U.S. marshals compared his fingerprints to those of the drug offender who had used his identity. They didn't match, so after 16 days in jail, Guzman was set free. But the story wasn't over.

After his release, authorities assured Guzman that his case record would be corrected. Except…six years later, when Guzman was pulled over during a traffic stop, police said he had an outstanding warrant in New York for drug crimes, and took him

A record 4,239 guns were seized at U.S. airports in 2018. (86% were loaded.)

to jail. He was separated from his two children and his wife, who was eight months pregnant. Guzman's wife, Yanira Hernandez, explained everything to the DEA, but nothing happened. Desperate, Hernandez turned to the news media for help. In an interview with KCBS in Los Angeles, Hernandez lamented, "They know it's not him, but they still have him in there, and that's what's heartbreaking." Ultimately, KCBS was able to help get Guzman out…but only after he'd spent 12 days in jail.

CYBER PEEPING TOMS

You've probably seen it in suspense movies or TV shows: Computer hackers remotely activate someone's computer webcam so they can spy on their victim. Secretly, they watch, snap photos, or record video of whatever appears in the webcam's field of view, which for many people includes their bedroom. Called *camfecting*, this spying is devastating to victims. If they're lucky, the hacker is just a creepy stalker. If not, it's a creepy stalker who blackmails them with photos of them undressing (or worse) which is known as *sextortion*, and it's more common than you think. In Britain, the number of webcam blackmails rose from nine in 2011 to nearly a thousand in 2016. And that's only the ones that were reported.

In 2013 Cassidy Wolf, a model and winner of the Miss California Teen beauty pageant, was terrorized by a hacker who spied on her for a year before threatening to post photos of her if she didn't comply with his demands. His demand: that she create a sex video for him. Taking a risk, she decided to ignore his threats and reported him to the police. Eventually, authorities identified him as 19-year-old computer science student Jared Abrahams. Through malware known as "creepware," he had tapped into the webcams of more than 100 women and underage girls. He served 18 months in prison while Wolf, now Miss Teen USA 2013, toured schools to warn about sextortion.

How did Abrahams install the creepware? He sent out phishing messages—so called because they're designed to bait and hook you like a fish. Once unsuspecting victims click on the link provided, they download malware that lets hackers access their computers. Or maybe someone physically installs it on their devices. That's what happened to ten women who asked a friendly University of Florida student to repair their computers. When he fixed the machines, he planted spy software that automatically opened as soon as the webcams detected movement. As if that violation of their privacy wasn't bad enough, he

A TIP FROM UNCLE JOHN

You can't rely on your webcam's light to come on when it's recording. Hackers can disable the light. Your best bet is to cover the webcam when you're not using it. Famously, Mark Zuckerberg, former FBI director James Comey, and Pope Francis all place tape over their webcams…but a hacker can still listen through the microphone.

used video he'd taken of one woman as a marketing tool to sell his program to other hackers. And after a stint in jail…he started a marketing business.

YOU DON'T HAVE TO PUT ON THE RED LIGHT

There's a scene in the 1995 cult classic *Hackers* in which tech-savvy teens break into New York City's traffic control system and cause citywide gridlock. That really happened during a Los Angeles rush hour in August 2006. At four of the city's busiest intersections, drivers were stuck for what must have seemed like forever. Red lights were unusually long; green lights were very short. Traffic jams plagued Los Angeles International Airport, Studio City, and other crowded destinations for four days. But unlike in *Hackers*, the perpetrators weren't pesky teens—they were city traffic engineers. Angry over a pay dispute, Kartik Patel and Gabriel Murillo stole a supervisor's credentials, logged into the system, and reengineered the lights. To further jam things up, they changed the access codes so that managers couldn't reset the lights. Besides frustrating commuters, the stunt threatened public safety. City workers have to be able to manage traffic lights to help first responders get to a crime scene, but for days they lost that ability. It could've been worse, though. If the engineers had been able to disable the lights, they might've caused deadly crashes instead of just making everyone want to take a long drive off a short pier.

Jump-drive to page 440 for the most destructive cybercrimes.

*   *   *

A RANDOM BIT OF FACTINESS

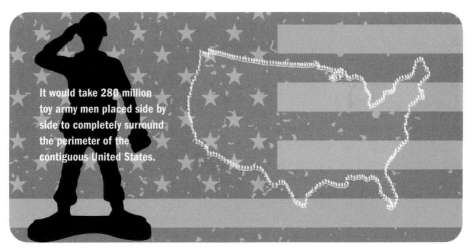

It would take 280 million toy army men placed side by side to completely surround the perimeter of the contiguous United States.

Queen drummer Roger Taylor has a four-octave vocal range, just like Queen singer Freddie Mercury.

COLORFUL PHRASE ORIGINS

What's blue, black, pink, brown, green, red, and read all over? This article!

OUT OF THE BLUE

MEANING: Without warning, all of a sudden

SAMPLE SENTENCE: *"Susie was at dinner with Tad, and she proposed to him out of the blue!"*

ORIGIN: Not surprisingly, this phrase originated with the idea of something suddenly appearing from the sky, which explains the variation "out of the clear blue sky." The original version was "a bolt out of the blue." It refers to a lightning bolt—which would indeed be unexpected if it appeared out of a blue sky. The longer version of this phrase showed up around the 1830s; the shortened version came—not quite out of the blue—about 40 years later.

JET-BLACK

MEANING: Intensely black in color; glossy black

SAMPLE SENTENCE: *"Cathy's jet-black Corvette was a beauty—until that garbage truck hit it."*

ORIGIN: A lesser-known meaning of the word *jet* is "a semiprecious gemstone related to coal." Unlike most gems, though, jet isn't a mineral. It comes from organic matter—compressed, decayed wood. Revered for its dark, black sheen, jet has been mined for jewelry since ancient times. The earliest known use of "jet" in reference to its color goes back to the Dark Ages (no pun intended). In the 1425 epic poem *Troy*, English monk John Lydgate describes the ebony tree as "blak as is get," which in modern English means "black as jet."

TICKLED PINK

MEANING: Very pleased, delighted

SAMPLE SENTENCE: *"Shirley was tickled pink when Edna invited her to the motorcycle race."*

ORIGIN: This phrase comes from the idea of being "tickled," as in "pleasantly surprised" (rather than physically tickled by someone's fingers), and it dates to at least the early 17th century. The meaning of the phrase—so pleased as to give off a glow—dates to the turn of the 20th century, and its exact origin is unknown. Its earliest known use was in 1910: The *Daily Review*, a newspaper in Decatur, Illinois, reported that Grover Lowdermilk, a recently traded Major League Baseball player, "was tickled pink over Kinsella's move in buying him from St. Louis."

Don't eat a polar bear liver — it contains so much vitamin A that it can kill you.

BLUE BLOOD

MEANING: Someone of noble or aristocratic birth, or just an upper-class family or person

SAMPLE SENTENCE: *"All that old blue blood does is sit on his sofa and binge-watch Blue Bloods."*

ORIGIN: To get to the bloody truth of this phrase origin, we have to go to Spain in the eighth century, when the Iberian Peninsula was conquered by the Moors—Muslims from North Africa. For the next 700 years or so, the peninsula was in a state of almost constant warfare between various Moorish and European Christian forces.

> Why blue? Historians believe it was simply a way for Spanish royalty to highlight their lighter skin tone.

During one such conflict, members of royal families in the kingdom of Castile, in the north of modern-day Spain, started to refer to themselves as *sangre azul*, or "blue blood." The implication was that their blood was "pure" because, according to them, their ancestors had not intermingled with the Moors. Why blue? Historians believe it was simply a way for Spanish royalty to highlight their lighter skin tone—which shows the blue vein lines under the skin more clearly than darker skin does—as a way of proving that they did not have Moorish blood. The phrase evolved to its more general meaning by the early 19th century.

CAUGHT RED-HANDED

MEANING: To be seen or apprehended during the act of committing a crime or other wrongdoing

SAMPLE SENTENCE: *"Gordon was caught red-handed when the sausage fell out of his trousers."*

ORIGIN: "Caught red-handed" has its roots in 15th-century Scotland, when nefarious types were said to be caught "red hand" or "redhand." Most likely, it was a reference to someone having actual blood on their hands after a murder or violent assault. The phrase first showed up in print in Scottish author Sir Walter Scott's 1819 novel *Ivanhoe*, which includes this account of the capture of an outlaw in a forest: "I did but tie one fellow, who was taken red-handed and in the fact, to the horns of a wild stag, which gored him to death in five minutes."

GREEN AROUND THE GILLS

MEANING: Sick or sickly looking; nauseous

SAMPLE SENTENCE: *"Thom looked a little green around the gills after his first boat ride."*

ORIGIN: Although it first appeared in the mid-19th century, "green around the gills"

came into popular usage after 1900. The color green has been associated with sickness and nausea since ancient Greek times. Why "around the gills"? Some etymologists have traced it back to fisherman's slang as a way to describe landlubbers who easily get seasick. And a fish's gills, while normally red, can turn green when the fish is sick.

Bonus: This phrase has some lesser-known variations, some going even farther back in time. In the 17th century, one who was "rosy about the gills" was said to be in good health and cheerful; in the 1620's, English philosopher Sir Francis Bacon described "redness about the cheeks and gills" as an unseemly symptom of anger; in the early 20th century, to be "blue about the gills" signified sickness or nausea…but also sadness.

BROWNIE POINTS

MEANING: An imaginary form of credit one receives for doing something useful or nice

SAMPLE SENTENCE: *"I sure did earn a bunch of brownie points for detailing my dad's truck."*

ORIGIN: This is one of those phrases that doesn't have a clear origin, but the possibilities are equally fascinating:

- Many people assume this phrase came from the Brownies, the Girl Scouts organization for younger girls, who earn points for doing certain deeds and tasks. Although the phrase is associated with the Brownies today, there's no indication the organization directly inspired it.

- Brownie points could come from a discipline system developed for railway workers in the late 19th century by George Ransom Brown, the superintendent of New York State's Fall Brook Railroad Company. Good behavior earned merit points, which came to be known as "brownie points."

- According to the *Oxford English Dictionary*, the phrase "probably" originated from "brown-nose." That phrase, in turn, started as 1940s military slang "from the implication that servility is tantamount to having one's nose in the anus of the person from whom advancement is sought." (That's a whole different kind of brownie right there.)

* * *

"Don't use words too big for the subject. Don't say 'infinitely' when you mean 'very'; otherwise you'll have no word left when you want to talk about something really infinite."

—**C.S. Lewis**

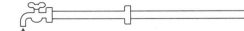

It's against tradition for Queen Elizabeth II to sit on any throne but her own, real or fictional…

MIRACLE IN THE CHANNEL

Remember 2009's "Miracle on the Hudson," when a commercial airliner had to make an emergency landing in New York's Hudson River? The passengers and crew of the plane were saved thanks to the fact that everyone remained calm and they had a smart, savvy captain. Here's the story of a similar plane crash that happened in the English Channel, way back in the 1920s, at the dawn of commercial aviation.

UP, UP, AND AWAY

One afternoon in October 1926, ten passengers—six male and four female—boarded an airplane in Croydon, South London, on a flight bound for Paris. At the time, the airline industry was still in its infancy, and the airline, Imperial Airways, was not quite two years old. In that short span of time, Imperial had flown 25,000 passengers more than two million miles all over the far-flung British Empire, with only one fatal plane crash—an impressive safety record in those early days of commercial aviation.

The plane on this flight was a twin-engine Handley Page Type W, which though a fairly sturdy and reliable aircraft in its day, would be considered a shockingly primitive aircraft by today's standards. For one thing, it was a biplane made not of aluminum but of wood, canvas, and wire. And though the ten passengers sat in a tiny enclosed cabin, the pilot, Fredrick Dismore, and his mechanic, Charles Pearson, sat in an open cockpit, exposed to the elements. (One modern touch: the Handley Page was the first airliner designed with an onboard lavatory.)

THAT SINKING FEELING

The flight began normally enough, but about an hour and fifteen minutes into the flight, the plane lost power in the starboard (right) engine as it was crossing over the English Channel. Perhaps because the plane was fully loaded with fuel, passengers, luggage, and sacks of mail, the plane's remaining working engine wasn't powerful enough to keep the plane in the air. It began losing altitude. Unable to restart the engine, Captain Dismore realized he was going to have to ditch the aircraft in the English Channel. "And to make matters worse," he later recalled, "there was not a boat in sight."

Dismore began making distress calls on the radio and kept at it for as long as the plane remained airborne. "I knew that once the airplane touched the water the wireless [radio] would be put out of action," he said. While he sent out one mayday call after another, mechanic Charles Pearson went back into the passenger cabin and started passing out life preservers to the passengers. "There was no panic of any kind, but we all realized we were in great peril," a passenger named Bertram Cook said later.

SPLASH!

The plane remained airborne for another four minutes before splashing down about nine miles off the coast of France. "The sea came nearer and nearer. The airplane was going at about forty miles an hour, and I knew that everything depended on landing in such a way that the machine would not be overturned. It was touch and go, but the sea was calm, and I was just able to land absolutely flat," Captain Dismore told the *Daily Express* newspaper.

Thanks to a combination of luck and Dismore's skill, the plane did not break apart when it hit the water, nor did it roll or flip over. It was intact, upright, and afloat…for now. Perhaps one benefit of being made largely of wood and canvas was that it floated better than it might have if it had been made of metal. Captain Dismore estimated it might remain afloat for as long as an hour, but no longer.

LET 'ER RIP

Bertram Cook was seated in the rear of the cabin, and after the plane hit the water he saw a notice on the ceiling that read "In Case of Emergency, Pull the Ring." He pulled the ring, and "the canvas of the roof came apart," he later recalled, creating an opening and giving him a means of exiting the cabin. He clambered out of the airplane, then helped two female passengers climb out onto the tail of the aircraft after him. As he did, he saw passengers in the front of the cabin climbing out of a window onto the wings.

Once everyone was safely out of the aircraft, there was nothing to do but wait… and hope to be rescued before the plane sank. Amazingly, considering the plight they were in, the passengers did not panic, as passenger Virginia Bonney, 21, later recounted in a letter home to her fiancé, Joe Jeffrey. "Joe, you never saw such a calm lot of people. No one screamed or even talked loud—maybe I did. I don't know. I was so dazed I really thought I was dreaming."

The engines were the heaviest part of the aircraft, and as the plane took on water it began sinking by the nose. As it did, Captain Dismore ordered the people sitting on the wings to move back toward the tail in an attempt to keep the plane level for as long as possible. "The men formed a sort of chain and hauled as many of the women as they could to the best position on top of the tail," he told the *Daily Express*.

DEFLATED

By now the passengers had their life vests on, but they were an inflatable type—and in this era, long before mandatory preflight safety demonstrations, no one had told the passengers how to inflate their vests. "The worst thing in the affair was the life belts. No one knew how to use them," Bonney wrote to her fiancé. "They were no more use

The oldest surviving ice cream recipe dates to 1665. The ice cream was flavored with mace and orange flower water.

than a canvas jacket. Here we were all hanging on the tail of a sinking airplane—all of us in heavy coats, and no air in our life preservers. It was about fifteen minutes before we could get anyone to tell us how to blow them up."

Fortunately, those 15 minutes were about all it took for a fishing boat named the *Invicta* to steam to the rescue. Dismore was wrong when he said that he thought there were no boats in the area: The *Invicta* and a few others were nearby, and they saw the plane crash into the sea several miles from where they were fishing. As soon as it did, the skipper of the *Invicta*, Tom Marshall, cut loose his fishing nets (losing the value of the nets and the catch) and steamed at full speed toward the downed plane. By the time he arrived those 15 minutes later, the plane had taken on so much water that some of the passengers were standing in it up to their waists. "In another five minutes," he remembered, "I think we would have been too late."

A second fishing boat, the *Jessica*, arrived soon afterward, and together the two crews loaded the plane's survivors on board. The boats had been fishing a few miles off the French coast, but rather than drop the passengers off in a French port, they were kind enough to take them all the way back to Folkestone, a port town on the southern coast of England. "Those fishermen were splendid, Joe," Bonney wrote to her fiancé. "They took their own clothes off their backs and wrapped us in them. They only make 2 pounds a week and they lost 400 pounds by cutting their nets to come to us."

ROUGH SAILING

But for Bonney and other survivors who were prone to seasickness, the trip back to Folkestone was nearly as harrowing as the crash itself. "We were three hours on that boat, and sick!" Bonney told her fiancé. "I was so cold I had to go down in the cabin and be sick. I couldn't stand it on deck. It was awfully funny: Five of us huddled in there, taking turns throwing up on the floor, sometimes several of us going at once."

On the way to Folkestone, the *Invicta* met up with a British Admiralty tugboat that had a radio aboard; it sent word to shore that everyone aboard the flight had been saved. (This was the first news that Imperial Airways received since Captain Dismore's distress calls ended abruptly when the plane hit the water, causing the airline's managers to fear that the plane and everyone aboard had been lost.) By the time the boat arrived in port, quite a crowd had gathered at the pier to celebrate the survivors' good fortune. Cozy hotel rooms awaited, complete with warm baths that were already being drawn. "Everyone was nice to us," Bonney wrote to her fiancé. "Except the reporters who literally tried to bribe the chambermaid to let them in our room with her key so they could take pictures of us—this after they had been told we had no clothes—only borrowed nightgowns. When we got to London we were besieged by them—we felt so important!"

In the next 10 million years or so, Neptune's moon Triton will get too close to the planet, split apart, and form a set of rings around Neptune.

DOWN SHE GOES

Other boats that arrived at the site of the crash tried to keep the downed plane afloat long enough to tow it back to port, but their efforts were unsuccessful, and the plane sank to the bottom of the English Channel. (The boats did manage to retrieve two sacks of Royal Mail airmail before the plane sank: after the letters were dried out, the letters whose addresses were still legible after soaking in seawater were sent on to their destinations.) Because the plane was not recovered, the cause of the engine failure was never determined. Imperial Airways lost its plane, but its record of no fatalities and no injuries remained intact: Most of the survivors escaped with only cuts and bruises. The most serious injury was suffered by mechanic Charles Pearson, who inhaled some exhaust fumes after he grabbed onto the plane's exhaust pipe and it broke off in his hand.

There was one casualty, however: a passenger's Pomeranian dog, which was somehow lost at sea before the fishing boats arrived. "We did not see what happened," one unnamed female passenger told the *Daily Express*. "The dog was quite safe one moment, and the next thing we noticed that it had vanished."

AND THEY LIVED HAPPILY EVER AFTER

"I still can't believe it was possible to be so lucky," Bonney wrote. "None of us, down in our hearts, thought we had a chance till we saw those fishing boats coming toward us. Why there happened to be a boat in that very part of the Channel and why they happened to see us go down is so remarkable it's hard to believe."

Virginia Bonney and Joe Jeffrey, 1926

(Virginia Bonney was reunited with Joe Jeffrey, and in June 1927 they were married. She lived to the age of 88 and passed away in 1993. The story, her letters, and the newspaper clippings describing the rescue come to Uncle John's Bathroom Reader *courtesy of her son, David L. K. Jeffrey. Thank you, David!)*

The division symbol ÷ has a name—it's called an *obelus*.

RANDOM ORIGINS

Once again, the BRI asks—and answers—the question:
Where does all this stuff come from?

GLITTER

Have humans always enjoyed shiny objects? There's archaeological evidence that 30,000 years ago, prehistoric people added flakes of mica to their cave paintings to make them sparkle. In the late 19th and early 20th centuries, ground glass—a byproduct from the German crystal glass industry—became the glitter material of choice. In the early 1930s, however, World War II was ramping up and Germany ended all glass glitter exports to focus its industrial capabilities on making war machinery. Suddenly, the world needed an alternative source of glitter. Enter a New Jersey machinist named Henry Ruschmann. He came up with a better, cheaper glitter in 1934…although that was not his intention. He was trying to devise a way to compress and compact garbage in garbage dumps. One day he tried smashing scrap plastic and found that instead of flattening, it broke into teeny-tiny little pieces…and they were shiny, too. So, with a landfill's worth of plastic ready to recycle, Ruschmann formed Meadowbrook Inventions, which remains the world's top glitter maker today.

THE ICE CREAM MAN

When they hear the tinny sounds of "The Entertainer," "Pop Goes the Weasel," or "Turkey in the Straw" wafting through the hot summer air, kids follow the music, carrying handfuls of quarters and shouting, "Ice cream man! Ice cream man!" The kids' older relatives might refer to him as "the Good Humor Man," and that's how this hot-weather tradition began. After Iowa ice cream parlor owner Christian Nelson made bars of chocolate-covered ice cream—thus inventing the Eskimo Pie—in 1919, Youngstown, Ohio, parlor operator Harry Burt stole the idea. Burt figured out how to make his own ice cream bars, with the added innovation of putting his bar on a wooden stick to make it more convenient to eat and less messy. Realizing he'd just made ice cream portable, he hired a fleet of 12 food vending trucks, outfitted them with freezers, and had drivers canvass the city, selling "Good Humor Ice Cream Suckers" while alerting consumers to their presence by ringing bells. Lots of ice cream parlors shut down during the Great Depression, but ice cream sold from trucks was a relatively cheap treat. (A Good Humor bar cost a nickel.) As car culture developed and the suburbs exploded in the 1950s, Good Humor followed, and local dairies around the country hired their own trucks and drivers to sell ice cream bars, ice cream sandwiches, and ice pops. That lasted until the 1970s, when rising gas prices hit the

Now you know: The shark fin's visible above the water is its dorsal fin.

ice cream man hard. In 1978 Good Humor sold off its fleet of around 1,000 trucks and concentrated on selling their products in supermarkets. Today the few ice cream trucks that remain are independently owned, and Good Humor, Klondike, and Popsicle are all owned by Unilever.

SILLY STRING

Silly String is a can of weird-smelling, nontoxic foam that comes out as soft, squishy plastic string...and it's a lot of fun to spray all over your friends. It was never intended to be a party favor—it was supposed to be a medical product. In 1972 inventor Leonard Fish and chemist Robert Cox were trying to create a liquid in an aerosol spray that, when exposed to air, turned into a foaming, hardening substance that could be used as a cast (to set a broken bone) in an emergency situation. The formula they devised worked, but while figuring out exactly what kind of nozzle to use—they tested more than 40—Fish discovered one that turned the liquid into a ropey substance...and which shot it all the way across a room. Fish decided the product might be more marketable as a toy than instant-cast. They altered the formula so that it was less sticky and added colors to make it bright and attractive to kids. They knew nothing about toy marketing, so they took it to Wham-O (producers of the Frisbee and Slip-N-Slide). Fish demonstrated the product, spraying it all over an executive...and they were thrown out. The next day, that same executive asked for 24 cans of the product for marketing tests. The tests were successful, and a few weeks later Wham-O bought the rights to produce what they first called "Squibbly," but ended up being called Silly String.

SUSHI GRASS

If you've ever dined out in a Japanese restaurant, then you've probably encountered this odd, nonedible garnish on your plate of sushi or chicken teriyaki: a thin piece of green plastic approximating a tuft of grass. In the traditional Japanese lunch called bento, a rectangular box is filled with half a dozen or more individual food items, such as tempura shrimp, edamame (steamed soybeans), rice, and fish or meat. To keep the tastes—and, more importantly, smells—separate, lunch-packers separated the foods with *haran,* the leaf of an orchid or lily. Over the decades, that gave way to *baran,* bamboo leaves, which are much more plentiful and much less expensive. Even more inexpensive: PET plastic. But that's just one reason chefs switched to "sushi grass," as it's now known. The sushi grass is just as effective at keeping flavors separate as an organic leaf would be. Plus, it's antimicrobial (making it more sanitary than real leaves) and it's shelf-stable (meaning it will never go bad).

Near miss: The Cleveland Cavaliers were almost named the Cleveland Presidents.

MOUTHING OFF

HOW DO I LOOK?

Unhappy with your appearance? Join the club.

"My face looks like a wedding cake left out in the rain."
—W. H. Auden

"I KNOW WHAT I LOOK LIKE: A WEIRD, SAD CLOWN PUPPET. I'M FINE WITH THAT."
—Rainn Wilson

"I JUST DO ART BECAUSE I'M UGLY AND THERE'S NOTHING ELSE FOR ME TO DO."
—Andy Warhol

"I was so ugly my mother used to feed me with a slingshot."
—Rodney Dangerfield

"Whenever I wear something expensive it looks stolen."
—Billy Connolly

"Actually, the reason I look like this is because my father was from Sweden and my mother was Elton John."
—Jim Gaffigan

"ALL BABIES LOOK LIKE ME. BUT THEN, I LOOK LIKE ALL BABIES."
—Winston Churchill

"I look like a duck. It's the way my mouth curls up, or my nose tilts up. I should have played Howard the Duck."
—Michelle Pfeiffer

SING, BATTER BATTER

The only thing more American than baseball? Goofy songs about the national pastime.

Song: "Go Joe Charboneau" (1980)

Artist: Section 36

Story: When the Chicago Cubs won their first World Series in more than a century in 2016, it made the Cleveland Indians the team that had gone the longest without winning it all, having last been champs in 1948. In 1980 fans thought a rookie named Joe Charboneau could be the guy to turn it all around, with a debut season in which he hit .289 with 23 home runs and 87 RBIs. He was also a real character who did crazy things (by 1980 standards), like dyeing his hair weird colors and drinking beer through his nose using a straw while sitting in the dugout (okay, that's still crazy). He didn't turn it around for Cleveland. In fact, he was out of baseball by 1984. But that was enough time to inspire a Cleveland band called Section 36 to record "Go Joe Charboneau," which became a hit on local radio.

Sample lyrics: "Who's the one to keep our hopes alive? / Go Joe Charboneau. / Straight from the 7th to the pennant drive?/ Go Joe Charboneau."

Song: "Joltin' Joe DiMaggio" (1941)

Artist: Les Brown and his Orchestra

Story: Already one of the most popular and best players in baseball, Joe DiMaggio did something on the field in 1941 that nobody else did before or since: he got a hit in a whopping 56 straight games. Following the progress of "Joltin' Joe" became a national obsession (and a nice distraction from the escalating World War II in Europe). Les Brown and his Orchestra, one of the most popular big bands of the day, got in on the action with a song celebrating the man who would one day marry Marilyn Monroe.

Sample Lyrics: "He started baseball's famous streak / That's got us all aglow / He's just a man and not a freak / Joltin' Joe DiMaggio"

Song: "Charlie Hustle" (1979)

Artist: Pamela Neal

Story: By the end of the 1970s, Pete Rose had helped guide his hometown Cincinnati Reds to four World Series appearances. And "Charlie Hustle," as Rose was known, became one of the league's all-time best hitters, with a record 4,256 career hits (but a lifelong ban from baseball for gambling on the sport). In 1979 two things happened: 1) Rose shockingly left Cincinnati for the Philadelphia Phillies, and 2) a little-known, breathy singer named Pamela Neal recorded "Charlie Hustle" in his honor. It's a disco song—nearly seven minutes long—and it was a total flop...but Rose got a cut of what little profits there were.

Sample lyrics: "Look at him run / while everybody walks / son of a gun, Charlie Hustle"

Song: "Fat Is In" (1985)

Artist: Terry Forster and the Lovehandles

Story: Relief pitcher Terry Forster enjoyed a good run in the major leagues in the 1970s and 1980s, racking up a career ERA of 3.23 and accumulating 127 saves. During that time, he had difficulty keeping his weight down, topping out at 270 pounds when he played for the Atlanta Braves in 1985. David Letterman noticed, and one night on *Late Night with David Letterman*, he called Forster a "tub of goo." (The next night, Letterman apologized.) Forster took it in stride and good humor, going on *Late Night* with candy falling out of his pockets and doing a cooking demo (he made tacos). Forster also capitalized on his brush with non-baseball fame by recording a song called "Fat Is In." Parodying two pop-culture phenomena of the time—singer Chaka Khan and rap group the Fat Boys—Forster begins the song with a send-up of the "Chaka Khan / Chaka Khan" rap from her "I Feel for You," before rhyming his way through lyrics about how it's cool to be heavy.

Sample lyrics: "Fat is in / stuff your face and don't be thin / double chins are tons of fun / on the beach you block the sun"

Song: "Vida Blue" (1971)

Artist: Albert Jones

Story: When you think of 1970s baseball, with its loud uniforms, elaborate mustaches, and huge Afro hairdos, you're probably picturing Vida Blue. The pitcher won more than 200 games over a long career (he retired in 1986), but he was at his absolute peak in the early 1970s. In 1971 he went 24–8 with a 1.82 earned run average for the Oakland A's, earning him both the Cy Young and Most Valuable Player Awards. That inspired soul singer Albert Jones to write and record this jubilant (and funky) song about Blue, which sounds like James Brown discovered baseball.

Sample lyrics: "Baseball is still our national game, but the last few years were kinda tame / Now they're buzzin' from town to town, 'cause ain't no hitter put Vida down"

Antarctica was originally called Australia, until the other Australia adopted that name, leaving the icy continent nameless from 1824 to 1890.

Song: "Talkin' Baseball" (1981)

Artist: Terry Cashman

Story: Cashman was a semipro baseball player for a farm team of the Detroit Tigers in the late 1950s; part of the 1960s folk-pop trio Cashman, Pistilli, and West in the late 1960s; and produced hit records for Jim Croce in the 1970s. But his most lasting success was with "Talkin' Baseball." Inspired by a picture he saw of Willie Mays, Duke Snider, Mickey Mantle, and Joe DiMaggio, he wrote this name-dropping ode to 1950s baseball. Cashman released it in 1981 and it became a hit—possibly because a strike had shortened the baseball season, and bitter fans looked fondly to the sport's past. Over the next few years, Cashman recorded versions of the song for several MLB teams, substituting in the names of local legends for all-time greats from the '50s.

Sample lyrics: "They knew 'em all from Boston to Dubuque / Especially Willie, Mickey, and the Duke"

Song: "The First Baseball Game" (1961)

Artist: Nat King Cole

Story: Cole, an accomplished jazz pianist who became an even more successful crooner, made classics out of romantic songs like "Unforgettable," "Mona Lisa," and "The Christmas Song." But he recorded a variety of tunes, and on this one, he created something that's both funny (mildly) and wholesome: a story-song set thousands of years ago in which figures from the Bible play ball. It was the equivalent of a fun sermon set to music, and it failed to crack the pop charts.

Sample lyrics: "And the angel that day, made a double play / That's when Adam and Eve were thrown out."

* * *

THEY'VE GOT HIS NUMBER

Emile Ratelband of the Netherlands was born on March 11, 1949. In 2018 he filed a lawsuit against the Dutch government to legally advance his birthday by 20 years, to March 11, 1969. Why? He wanted to meet more single women on the internet, and believed that listing his biological age of 69 was preventing that from happening. "You can change your name. You can change your gender. Why not your age? Nowhere are you so discriminated against as with your age," he told reporters, adding that he was discriminated against when he was looking for work opportunities, too. "When I'm 69, I am limited. If I'm 49, then I can buy a new house, drive a different car. I can take up more work." A few weeks later, a judge threw out the case.

Volleyball was originally called "mintonette."

THE LIFE AND TIMES OF GRIZZLY ADAMS

What comes to mind when you hear the name "Grizzly Adams"? If you're like us, you probably think of the lead character in the 1970s TV show The Life and Times of Grizzly Adams, *not the real person on whom the TV character was based. Well, here's the story of the original—John Adams (1812–1860), a larger-than-life character who had the rare ability to bond with one of the forest's fiercest predators: the grizzly bear.*

BACKGROUND

In the Old West, most men didn't stand out—there were cowboys, miners, farmers, storekeepers, bartenders, and fancy business types. But John "Grizzly" Adams was one of a kind. Here he is described by his biographer:

> Adams...was a man a little over medium size, muscular and wiry, with sharp features and penetrating eyes. He was apparently about fifty years of age; but his hair was very gray and his beard very white. He was dressed in coat and pantaloons of buckskin, fringed at the edges and along the seams of arms and legs. On his head he wore a cap of deerskin, ornamented with a fox-tail, and on his feet buckskin moccasins.

During the California gold rush of the 1850s, from Santa Fe to the Oregon Territory, stories were told of this wild man who dressed like an Indian, and rode around on the back of a 600-pound grizzly bear called Lady Washington, with two younger grizzlies and a host of other wild animals in tow. In Adams's time, he was just as famous as other frontiersmen, like Davy Crockett and Daniel Boone. And he was tougher than either of those "greenhorns." From the look of Adams, you'd think he was raised in the woods. Not quite.

THE ADAMS FAMILY

Born John Adams in 1812 in Medway, Massachusetts, to Eleazer and Sibel Adams, he was related to the famous New England Adamses—a family that had produced two presidents, John Adams and John Quincy Adams, as well as Revolutionary War hero (and beer brewer) Samuel Adams. Not a kid who took to school, when Adams was 14 he got a job as a cobbler (shoemaker) at his father's shop in Boston, where he learned how to tan hides and make leather. At 21, he headed for the wilds of Maine, where he learned how to hunt, trap, and survive in the wilderness. Before long, he landed a job as a wrangler for a traveling show of exotic animals. In what would become a recurring theme throughout his life, Adams's natural ease with big predators led to overconfidence. He got the first of many hard lessons during a training session when a Bengal tiger turned on him and mauled him. Adams barely escaped with his life.

GO WEST, YOUNG MAN

After spending the next few months in Boston recovering from severe spinal injuries, Adams went back to work with his father. Within a few years, he had his own family to take care of—his wife, Cylena, and their three children, Arabella, Arathusa, and Seymour. When the California gold rush began, Adams and his father hatched a plan to turn their combined life savings—about $6,500—into shoes and other garments to sell to miners and prospectors in St. Louis. Those plans went up in flames—literally— in the St. Louis Wharf Fire of 1849. The Adamses lost everything, and Eleazer committed suicide. Broke and destitute, John Adams decided to follow the thousands of other gold-seekers to California. He promised Cylena he would send money home when he could, and that he would return a rich man.

The journey west was rough. Adams nearly died from illness twice along the way, and he was still suffering from back pain. By the time he arrived in California in 1852, he was only in his late 30s, but he was already sporting wild hair and a gray beard.

INTO THE WOODS

Adams tried his hand at ranching and gold mining, both of which were disastrous. He was swindled out of his sluice-mining claim by an unscrupulous partner, and then bank creditors foreclosed on his 160-acre ranch outside Stockton. So, he later explained, "I abandoned all my schemes for the accumulation of wealth, turned my back upon the society of my fellows, and took the road toward the wildest and most unfrequented parts of the Sierra Nevada, resolved thenceforth to make the wilderness my home, and the wild beasts my companions."

> "I abandoned all my schemes for the accumulation of wealth, turned my back upon the society of my fellows, and took the road toward the wildest and most unfrequented parts of the Sierra Nevada."

Adams drove his oxen cart into the mountains and settled not far from where Yosemite National Park is today. Back then, it was Indian country. While most white men of his time bragged about taking in the $5 bounty for every Indian they killed, Adams befriended the Miwok tribe. He shot deer for them, and in return they helped him build his cabin and stables. The Indians also provided Adams with the buckskin outfit he'd wear for the rest of his days.

It was around this time that he began referring to himself as James Capen Adams (possibly to avoid creditors). That was his brother's name, but John Adams assumed it as his own. Most people just called him Adams, though, or "the wild Yankee." He was known to take in any stranger at his cabin (when he was there), but he often said he preferred the company of Indians over white men, and animals over people in general.

BEAR AND MAN

The concept of animal rights is a very recent one, and much of what Adams did may seem cruel when viewed through a modern lens—and illegal. He captured hundreds of wild animals and sold them to zoological societies and private collectors. He killed thousands more for meat and clothing. Adams and other trappers like him sold grizzlies to animal shows, where they were forced to fight each other or bulls. But in Adams's defense, he never killed for sport, and he trapped more animals alive than probably anyone else in his time.

And he wouldn't have become as famous as he did if it had been any other animal, but the California grizzly bear (*Ursus arctos californicus*) was the most feared beast in the forest. Fiercer and nearly twice as large as comparatively docile black bears, they attacked (and ate) livestock, so when Europeans encountered grizzlies, they killed them on sight.

Adams, however, revered the grizzly: "There is a vastness in his strength, which makes him a fit companion for the monster trees and giant rocks of the Sierra and places him, if not the first, at least in the first rank of all quadrupeds." But even in his reverence, he never thought to protect the species. Once numbering in the tens of thousands, the California grizzly bear survived alongside native peoples for millennia. Only 75 years after the gold rush began, the California grizzly was declared extinct in 1922. Montana and Washington are the only states in the contiguous United States that have a wild grizzly population today.

MAN AND BEAR

Adams learned how to trap grizzlies in 1854, when he spent two years (the best of his life, he said) leading numerous hunting and trapping expeditions throughout the West. He constructed large cages out of timber, and baited them with fresh meat. When the bear took the bait, a trapdoor fell and caged it. That's how Adams brought in the largest grizzly ever captured alive. Weighing more than 1,500 pounds, he named the beast Samson and added it to his growing menagerie. Another method he used to capture grizzly cubs was to kill their mother. That's how he got his favorite bear, Lady Washington, who became his closest companion. "From that day to this," he later wrote, "she has always been with me and often shared the dangers and privations; born my burdens and partaken of my meals." (Sorry, Cylena.)

Adams soon collected more grizzlies—including General Fremont, Happy Joe, and Benjamin Franklin. Tamed at only a year old, Ben was Adams's most docile bear, but he was fiercely protective of his owner. One day in 1855, while Adams and Ben were in the Sierras, a mama grizzly charged at them. Adams couldn't raise his shotgun in time,

Could you tell? Skittles candies have different scents but identical flavors.

and the grizzly walloped him in the head, tearing off part of his scalp. Then she sunk her teeth into his neck and was about to finish him off when Ben bit the larger bear's haunch. That distracted her long enough for Adams to scramble up a tree. He shot the grizzly dead, but not before she bit out one of Ben's eyes and trampled him. Even though Adams and Ben both survived, neither would ever fully heal from their wounds.

THE CITY BY THE BAY

In addition to the numerous grizzly attacks, Adams was mauled by a wolf (which took a chunk of his arm) and trampled by a buffalo (which nearly suffocated him). He needed to find a safer line of work. So in 1856, he and his wild animals (and his dog, Rambler) settled in San Francisco, where he opened the Mountaineering Museum in a basement on Park Street. For the next four years, Adams was a San Francisco fixture. He could often be seen walking through town with one of his grizzly bears; he'd leave it tied outside a restaurant while he dined inside.

Admission to see the animals in the museum was a quarter. With his whip always in his hand, Adams would bark commands at his bears, make them do tricks, wrestle them, and tell action-packed accounts of their captures. Most of the grizzlies were chained to the stone floor (except for Samson, who was so powerful that he had to be restrained in an iron cage). Adams's overconfidence continued to be a problem; he was regularly swatted, bitten, and kicked—and on at least two occasions his head wound was reopened, revealing on his forehead a silver dollar–sized hole that exposed his brain.

One day in 1857, a young reporter named Theodore Hittell approached Adams and asked if he could interview him for the San Francisco *Bulletin*. That started a friendship that would lead to a widely read series of newspaper articles and a biography. And as Adams's popularity grew, so did the show. He soon had to move his newly named Pacific Museum to a new building.

ADAMS'S ARK

By 1859 ticket sales weren't bringing in enough money to feed six grizzly bears and dozens more hungry animals every day. Once again, creditors were closing in. So the "Barnum of the Pacific," as the newspapers were calling him, decided to leave town and take his show back East, where he would work for the real P. T. Barnum, reconnect with his estranged family, and then take his show to Europe. That was the plan, anyway. Adams sold a half-interest in the museum to cover the cost to get all his animals home. Then he loaded them all onto a clipper ship (the transcontinental railroad hadn't been completed yet) and sailed south around the tip of South America and then north to New York City.

In addition to Samson, Lady Washington, and General Fremont, Adams brought seven other grizzlies and, according to the *Daily Evening Bulletin*, "black and brown and

Op-ed means "opposite editorial" not "opinion editorial."

cinnamon bears…elk, deer, buffalo, coyote, and many birds, including the California condor, various eagles, pelicans, and other species of the feathered tribe." The arduous 100-day journey took a further toll on Adams's health. Not surprisingly, he reopened his head wound during one of his "demonstrations" on the ship's deck.

ON BROADWAY

Adams has the distinction of being the first national celebrity to come from the recently founded state of California. He arrived in New York City in early 1860 and went straight to Barnum's office to sign a contract. Concerned about his star attraction's health, Barnum sent Adams to his personal physician, who basically told him two things: 1) it was a miracle Adams was alive, and 2) his head wound would never heal. Adams's wife Cylena traveled down from Massachusetts to help care for him while he prepared for the new show, and they hired a doctor to dress the head wound daily.

> During one performance, General Fremont took a chunk out of Adams's arm to the horror of the audience.

On opening day in the spring of 1860, Adams and three of his grizzlies paraded down Broadway behind a marching band to the big tent where his "California Menagerie" was housed. Over the next few months, thousands of people, most of whom had only heard stories about grizzly bears, showed up to see Adams make them do tricks and wrestle with them. During one performance, General Fremont took a chunk out of Adams's arm to the horror of the audience. (His dog Rambler saved his life.) At another show, a black bear bit Adams's leg and flung him several feet across the floor. At another show, a monkey jumped onto Adams's shoulder and bit his head wound.

Though it was obvious he should have quit immediately, Adams made a deal with Barnum that if he could do the show for ten more weeks, Barnum would pay him $500. And Adams did last those ten weeks…barely. By the time the engagement was over, he couldn't even walk. With his contract completed, Adams sold his animals to Barnum and moved back home with his wife. Two days later, he turned 48; three days after that, he died in his bed. Adams was buried in the family plot in Charlton, Massachusetts. His gravestone was paid for by Barnum.

THE SHOW MUST GO ON

Most of what you just read is true. It's tough to know for sure, because the primary sources for historians are Hittell's 1860 biography, *The Adventures of James Capen Adams, Mountaineer and Grizzly Bear Hunter of California* (which didn't even get his name right), and the writings of known embellisher P. T. Barnum. But when it comes to Adams, any of these stories *could* be true, which is why he became as famous he did. It's also why Barnum wasn't ready to let his star attraction go. Barnum took the California Menagerie around the world, hiring actors to portray Adams for the next 30 years.

Most prominent feature on the Louisiana state flag: A pelican feeding her young.

After that, Adams's popularity waned, and wouldn't rebound until the late 20th century, when he was portrayed on the big screen by famed director John Huston in the 1972 film *The Life and Times of Judge Roy Bean*. He appeared on the small screen five years later, in the TV show *The Life and Times of Grizzly Adams*, portrayed by a California animal wrangler named Dan Haggerty.

A WILD LEGACY

As for the dozens of wild animals that Adams "tamed," many of them ended up in zoos on both coasts, with a few of their descendants living well into the 20th century. And despite some embellishing, Adams's observations of the now-extinct California grizzly—an animal he knew more about than anyone else—have been invaluable for naturalists who study bears. In 1953 lawmakers in Sacramento gave the California grizzly the posthumous honor of being designated the official state land animal (as evidenced by all the high school teams and landmarks called the Grizzlies). There was a petition in 2014 to reintroduce the grizzly to California, but the U.S. Fish and Wildlife Service rejected it. Reason: it would be nearly impossible for a predator that requires such a large ecosystem to live in a state populated by 40 million people.

One final legacy: Thedore Hittell's biography about Grizzly Adams was illustrated with wood carvings by one of California's first celebrated artists, Charles Nahl. Unlike most wildlife illustrators of the time, who used taxidermied animals for reference (such as John James Audubon, who killed thousands of birds in order to draw them), Nahl preferred live subjects. His 1855 portrait of Adams's largest grizzly, Samson, was later used for the California state flag. Here's Samson:

> **A TIP FROM UNCLE JOHN**
>
> A bear can and will attack if it feels threatened or thinks you're food. If you hike on marked trails, you'll probably never encounter one, but if you do, stand still, and wave your arms slowly. That will let the bear know that you're people, not lunch. (It also makes you look bigger and, thus, more imposing.) Remain calm, and do not make any sudden movements or sounds that could agitate the bear. Then back away slowly.

What happened when Grizzly Adams returned to American pop culture in the form of Dan Haggerty? To find out, turn to page 485.

Fingerprints are unique. Heel prints aren't.

1990s MOVIE TRIVIA... AS IF!

The decade that gave us the phrase "talk to the hand" also gave us quite an array of memorable films. Here are some hella-cool facts about some of our favorites.

Ghost (1990)

Producers suggested to director Jerry Zucker that he cast Patrick Swayze in the role of Sam, the ghost who watches over his former wife (Demi Moore). Zucker said no. Why? He'd seen some of Swayze's other movies, like *Dirty Dancing* and *Road House*, and hated them. But producers let Swayze audition anyway, and his performance was so heartfelt that it made Zucker cry. Despite barely getting the part, Swayze refused to do the movie if Zucker didn't cast Whoopi Goldberg as Oda Mae Brown. They wanted someone else, but she and Swayze were a package deal. She got the part...and won an Oscar for it.

The Addams Family (1991)

A lot of old TV shows were adapted into movies in the 1990s, such as *The Flintstones, Maverick,* and *The Beverly Hillbillies.* The trend started with a big-screen version of the *Addams Family* TV show. It came about when Twentieth Century Fox executive Scott Rudin happened to hear a friend's kid singing the show's famous theme song during a car ride, prompting a singalong. The next day, Rudin proposed the idea of an *Addams Family* film to his colleagues. Good idea: it turned out to be one of the top-grossing movies of the year.

Wayne's World (1992)

The film takes place in the Chicago suburbs, but co-writer Mike Myers inserted a lot of his native Canada into the movie. For example, Wayne, Garth, and their metalhead friends hang out at Stan Mikita's Donuts. Mikita was a local legend for the NHL's Chicago Blackhawks, but the donut shop is an Americanized parody of a Canadian institution: Tim Hortons, a north-of-the-border chain co-founded by hockey star Tim Horton.

Martha Stewart dated Anthony Hopkins...until his work as Hannibal Lecter scared her.

Tommy Boy (1995)

One of the Chris Farley/David Spade buddy comedy's most famous moments is "Fat Guy in a Little Coat," wherein the large Tommy (Farley) dances around in Richard's (Spade's) blazer, which is much too small for him, while singing "Fat guy in a little coat." It wasn't in the script. It's a bit that Farley used to do to annoy Spade—with his jeans jacket—when they were cast members on *Saturday Night Live*.

The Shawshank Redemption (1994)

This prison drama that always seems to be on TV is based on the Stephen King novella *Rita Hayworth and the Shawshank Redemption*. When the film went into production with that title, director Frank Darabont received dozens of headshots from actresses clamoring to play Rita Hayworth. Only problem: Hayworth isn't in the story; she "appears" in the film, but only as an image on a poster. The title was shortened, partly to end the confusion, but also because producers feared the full title was too long to fit on movie theater marquees. That irked co-star Morgan Freeman, who felt that they'd cut the title in half…and kept the wrong half. "Don't choose *Shawshank Redemption*," he complained to Darabont, "when you've got Rita Hayworth!" Freeman thought the hard-to-say "Shawshank" would turn moviegoers off. He was wrong.

Clueless (1995)

The film that introduced the phrase "As if!" into 1990s culture is an adaptation of the 1815 Jane Austen novel *Emma*. It follows the same plot of an overly confident rich socialite trying to navigate through her teen years. Austen's goal with her main character, Emma, was to create "a heroine whom no one but myself will much like," which is a good description of Cher, the role that made Alicia Silverstone a star.

Toy Story (1995)

The movie's protagonist was originally going to be an antique drummer toy named Tinny (who made his debut in director John Lasseter's 1988 short film *Tin Toy*). Plot: Tinny gets left behind at a rest area, befriends a ventriloquist dummy, and the two try to find their way home. But the producers thought a drummer toy would be too old-fashioned for modern audiences, so the character was recast as an astronaut, first named Lunar Larry, and later renamed Buzz Lightyear. The ventriloquist dummy was deemed too creepy and ended up as a cowboy ragdoll named Sheriff Woody Pride.

Iceland has never won a medal in the Winter Olympics.

THE FILTHIEST ARTICLE IN THE BOOK

People have this notion that a toilet seat is really filthy. Makes sense—after all, it is the point of direct skin contact with the place where we deposit human waste. (Many people used to believe—incorrectly—that they could catch diseases from using a public toilet.) But it turns out that a toilet seat is a lot cleaner than some things you come into contact with all the time...with your hands.

PHONES

Smartphones are pretty much attached to most people's hands these days, and we carry them everywhere while we go about our daily business. But unless you wash your hands every time before you pick up your phone, you're transferring the germs you've picked up throughout the day to your phone the moment you touch it. According to a study by the University of Arizona, the average smartphone carries 10 times as much bacteria as a toilet seat.

CUTTING BOARDS

You've probably got a well-used wood block that you use to slice chicken or beef for dinner. Every time your knife touches the surface, it makes grooves in the wood. That's a prime breeding ground for the germs (a lot of them fecal bacteria) that live on raw meat. The average cutting board contains 200 times as much bacteria as a toilet seat.

PET FOOD DISHES

The plates and bowls that the humans in your house use typically get washed after every meal. But your dog's or cat's dish probably goes a while between cleanings. The germs from your mouth get onto your forks and bowls, and your pet's germs live on their bowls. There's about nine times as much bacteria on a dog bowl as there is on a toilet seat (although some dogs lick both).

COMPUTER KEYBOARDS

Our advice: consider using hand sanitizer before you use your computer. All the stuff that gets on your hands during the day rests right on your keyboard the second you sit down to work. According to a British study, those keys are home to five times more bacteria than could be found on a toilet seat.

Why do chocolate bars melt so much easier than chocolate chips?
The bars contain more cocoa butter.

MAGAZINES AT THE DOCTOR'S OFFICE

Why would you touch something that's been handled by dozens of people over many weeks—people that are very likely sick—and that *never* gets cleaned? (Who cleans glossy paper?) Flu viruses, for example, can survive on that magazine for as long as 18 hours. That's about the same amount of time that *E. coli* can hang out.

AIRPORT SECURITY BINS

They're reused over and over again, and even if airport security wanted to, there's very little time to clean them out between uses. But those bins, where everybody puts their stuff before they get on a flight—stuff that's been touched and handled by thousands of people—spread germs. A 2018 British study found that half of airport security bins carried germs that could make you contract the flu or a cold.

CARPETS

Household dust and dirt is loaded with dead skin cells. You shed about 1.5 million of them per hour, and also drop tiny bits of food, not to mention the pet dander, pollen, and other impurities that make their way into your home. Bacteria will happily eat all of that…and then breed. The average square inch of carpet is home to around 200,000 bacteria (such as salmonella and *E. coli*), which is 700 times as many as the ones that live on a toilet seat.

A TIP FROM UNCLE JOHN

You might use a sponge to wash dishes or clean your kitchen countertops. But all that dirt and gunk you removed from plates and surfaces just transferred to the sponge, which means you've got to clean the sponge, too…unless you want germs and bacteria to grow and fester. Here's an easy way to clean a sponge. Get it soaking wet and put it in the microwave for two minutes on the highest setting. Studies show the cooking and steaming incapacitates more than 99 percent of bacteria and viruses within.

* * *

WHAT'S IN A NAME?

In the early 1980s, Henry Harrod ran a small restaurant in the tiny town (population: 2,000) of Otorohanga, New Zealand, called, logically, Harrods. But in 1986, Mohamed Al Fayed, who owned Harrod's department store in London, caught wind of it, and threatened to sue Henry Harrod. In defense of their fellow citizen, nearly every business in the town of Otorohanga changed its name to Harrods. Then the town went even further—it changed its name from Otorohanga to Harrodsville. The London media picked up on the story, and Al Fayed was so thoroughly mocked in the press and on television that he dropped his suit. Harrodsville changed its name back to Otorohanga, and the businesses resumed their old names. (And Harrods stayed Harrods.)

Earth's atmosphere contains more water than all the world's rivers combined.

THE COUNTRY MUSIC GEOGRAPHY QUIZ

Country music is an American original, and its songs have always focused on the towns, cities, and states of the U.S. of A. Can you name the places that complete these famous country song titles? (Answers are on page 501.)

1. "_____ Lineman" (Glen Campbell)

2. "_____ by Morning" (George Strait)

3. "The Devil Went Down to _____" (Charlie Daniels Band)

4. "_____" (Marty Robbins)

5. "_____" (Johnny Cash and June Carter)

6. "Okie from _____" (Merle Haggard)

7. "You're the Reason God Made _____" (David Frizzell and Shelly West)

8. "By the Time I Get to _____" (Glen Campbell)

9. "Does _____ Ever Cross Your Mind?" (George Strait)

10. "Streets of _____" (Dwight Yoakam and Buck Owens)

11. "_____ Sugar Babe" (Johnny Cash)

12. "Midnight in _____" (Alan Jackson)

13. "Take Me Back to _____" (Bob Wills)

14. "Blue Moon of _____" (Elvis Presley)

15. "All My Exes Live in _____" (George Strait)

16. "_____ or Leave It" (Dixie Chicks)

17. "God Blessed _____" (Little Texas)

18. "South of _____" (Brooks & Dunn)

19. "_____ Girl" (Faith Hill)

20. "_____ Lovin' Man" (Johnny Cash)

21. "I Can Still Make _____" (George Strait)

Morgan Freeman owns a 124-acre wild bee sanctuary in Mississippi.

MYTHS FROM DOWN ON THE FARM

For huge parts of America, farming is still a way of life. It's so ingrained in our culture that there are lots of things we think are true about farm animals and crops. It turns out a lot of that stuff isn't true.

Myth: Dairy and beef cows eat grains and grass.
Fact: They do if they're "free range" livestock, but the milk and meat end up costing more, because feed made from grains and grass is relatively expensive and it takes a lot to feed a large animal like a cow. Commercial dairy and beef cattle eat a carefully devised concoction of hay, grain, proteins (soybean meal, which is low-cost and effective), extra vitamins, and something called *silage*—a nutritionally dense, partially fermented mixture of vegetables and grains. Some big dairies (and beef cattle operations) might supplement that with whatever they can get on the cheap, such as unsold cookies and candy, or even sawdust.

Myth: Chickens are stupid.
Fact: They're not quite birdbrained. Studies show that chickens scored almost as high as primates on intelligence tests. For example, they seem to understand their coop's "pecking order," and, if given a choice between an immediate food reward and waiting for a better one later on, they'll wait. Chickens are also capable of more than 20 different vocalizations, each with a different meaning.

Myth: Organically raised crops are free of pesticides.
Fact: Organic crops are still crops, and they're subject to being devastated by germs, bugs, and birds. Organic farmers can't risk letting their fields be destroyed, so they still get a little help from pesticides—organic, caustic chemical–free pesticides that have been certified organic by the USDA, but pesticides nonetheless. The most common: Bt (*Bacillus thuringiensis*), an insect-killing protein found in soil bacteria. And vitamin D3 is an especially effective rodent killer.

Myth: Goats will eat anything, even tin cans.

Fact: That's why farms have traditionally kept goats around in the first place—they'll devour a lot of farm waste, such as the inedible parts of crops. There's also the notion that goats will eat *anything*, even inedible stuff like tin cans, newspapers, or clothing. But they're not really eating. They're "browsers" (not "grazers"), which means they'll put something in their mouth if they think there's food on it or in it…and then spit out the item if they can't actually eat it.

Myth: Brown eggs are more nutritious than white eggs.

Fact: The brown ones tend to cost a little more than white ones, leading to the idea that the higher price tag has something to do with higher quality, or more vitamin-based bang for the buck. The color of the shell actually tends to reflect the size of the chicken that laid the egg—bigger breeds make brown eggs, and since they're larger, they require more feed (hence the higher cost).

* * *

ANOTHER MYTH-CONCEPTION

Myth: TV's first interracial kiss was between Captain Kirk and Lieutenant Uhura on *Star Trek* in 1968.

Fact: It wasn't even the first interracial kiss on *Star Trek*. The kiss in question occurred in the episode "Plato's Stepchildren." A hostile alien uses telepathy to force Kirk (William Shatner) and Uhura (Nichelle Nichols) to lock lips. As *Star Trek* grew in popularity over the next few decades, biographies of the show—and even the actors themselves—started bragging that the kiss was a television first (though Shatner denied their lips touched), and that it had a huge impact on society during the turbulent civil rights years. In truth, the kiss didn't make a lot of news at the time (though NBC initially balked at airing it). Because it took place at the end of an episode in *Trek*'s low-rated third season, not that many people even saw it. Besides, a lot of interracial kisses had occurred on TV before that. For example: Lloyd Bridges kissed Nobu McCarthy on *Sea Hunt* in 1959; Robert Culp kissed France Nuyen on *I Spy* in 1966; Robert Conrad kissed Pilar Seurat on *The Wild Wild West* in 1966, Sammy Davis Jr. kissed Nancy Sinatra on *Movin' with Nancy* in 1967, and William Shatner kissed France Nuyen on another *Star Trek* episode that had aired earlier in 1968.

When you cup your hands to form a bowl, that's called a *gowpen*.

THE DEATH OF SATURDAY MORNING CARTOONS

*If you grew up in North America in the past few decades, then you
probably spent your Saturday mornings watching cartoons on TV.
Today's kids don't get to engage in that ritual...and here's why.*

HEY, KIDS!

For decades, Saturday mornings were a time-honored tradition for millions of children.
They'd rise at 7:00 a.m. or so, pour themselves a big bowl of sugar-coated cereal, and
plop down in front of the TV for several hours to watch nonstop cartoons on the
three (and later, four) broadcast television channels. Why Saturday morning? Well,
they were cartoons, and kids have always loved cartoons, but that was the *only* time
the networks put aside just for that age group—showcasing hours of programs like *The
Smurfs, The Bugs Bunny and Tweety Show, Scooby-Doo, Roger Ramjet, Muppet Babies,
What's New, Mr. Magoo?, The Care Bears, Fat Albert and the Cosby Kids, Atom Ant,
Heathcliff and Dingbat, King Leonardo and his Short Subjects, Laff-A-Lympics, Super
Friends, Dungeons and Dragons*, and whatever else was on.

    Viewership for Saturday morning cartoons peaked in the 1970s and '80s, and then
started to dwindle...until the programming block disappeared from all the big networks
entirely in the 2010s. What caused the demise of Saturday morning cartoons?

WON'T SOMEBODY THINK OF THE CHILDREN?

Almost since the widespread adoption of television in the 1950s, parents and
educators worried about the effect that watching television (and absorbing ads) was
having on children. Peggy Charren formed a watchdog group in 1968 called Action
for Children's Television, which pressured the industry to provide educational TV
for children. The group gained national prominence in the 1980s, when kid-targeted
programming consisted primarily of shows like *G.I. Joe, Transformers*, and *My Little
Pony*—cartoons produced to sell toy lines, with ad space sold to toy makers, fast-food
restaurants, and cereal manufacturers.

    There were educational programs on the air, but both ACT and FCC chairman
Mark Fowler noticed that the TV networks were trying to bury them. In 1981,
for example, ABC canceled its long-running weekend series *Animals, Animals,
Animals*, and CBS shortened *Captain Kangaroo* from an hour daily broadcast to a
half-hour, and then moved it to Saturday. Wholesome content for children was

Lucky devil! In 2000 the president of Zimbabwe won the Zimbabwe lottery.

being replaced by the superficial, commercial-driven programming the networks put up on Saturday mornings.

It became such a part of the public conversation—and with ACT's heavy lobbying of lawmakers—that in 1990 Congress passed the Children's Television Act. Going into effect on October 1, 1991, it mandated that ad time during children's programming be limited to five minutes per half hour, and it banned ads for tie-in products on related shows. In other words, networks couldn't advertise He-Man toys during airings of *He-Man and the Masters of the Universe*. So not only were there three fewer minutes of advertising every half-hour (which translates to millions in lost revenue), ad time couldn't be used to advertise the products that companies most wanted to advertise to their captive audience of children.

Further changes to the law in 1995 required TV stations to broadcast three hours of child-oriented "educational/informational" programming per week. Because Saturday morning was becoming a little less lucrative (and that was where the kid stuff was already located), the networks used that slot for their government-ordered "E/I" shows. That alone cut out three potential cartoon hours for each TV channel, replacing them with shows like *Jack Hanna's Animal Adventures*.

PRETTY SMURFING EXPENSIVE

However, by the time the networks started abiding by the law and airing fewer cartoons, the writing was on the wall. As early as 1988, NBC was looking into eliminating Saturday morning cartoons. Its biggest hit at the time was *The Smurfs*. Although it looks cheap and choppy by today's animation standards, one episode of the adventures of the little blue creatures cost $300,000 to produce. NBC entertainment president Brandon Tartikoff wondered if that was still worth it, since ratings for the network's entire Saturday morning lineup were slipping. Some internal network research showed that it would be much cheaper for the network to air three hours of a newsmagazine, such as a Saturday extension of *The Today Show*.

So, in 1992, that's what NBC did. The cartoons from 7:00 to 10:00 a.m. were gone, replaced by *Today*. From 10:00 to noon they aired barely educational, teen-oriented shows like *Saved by the Bell*.

PLAY BALL

NBC also figured that fans of sports, which had long dominated TV on weekend afternoons, would watch their teams play, even if games aired on Saturday morning. (Before that, college football games traditionally started after noon, but they'd preempted TV cartoons on the West Coast for years, which is three hours behind the East Coast.)

> Wholesome content for children was being replaced by the superficial, commercial-driven programming the networks put up on Saturday mornings.

How about yours? The average U.S. household uses about 100,000 gallons of water each year.

So, in 1991, NBC made a plan that would signal the final death blow to its kid-friendly lineup: It signed a long-term deal to air Notre Dame football games on Saturdays. The Peacock network paid a whopping $1 million per game...which was *still* cheaper than producing six hours of cartoons. Besides, NBC could charge more for advertising during higher-rated football games than lower-rated cartoons, and without the advertising time and content restrictions placed on cartoons.

CHANGING CHANNELS

Other networks continued to air cartoons, making them with their own in-house production facilities or contracting the rights for producing individual shows to independent TV producers. In the early 2000s, ABC and CBS realized that they could still air cartoons but do it for a lot cheaper by airing kids' programming from their corporate siblings. ABC was owned by Disney, so its Saturday morning lineup was bussed over from the Disney Channel. CBS gave its Saturday mornings over to programming it leased from Nickelodeon, which, at the time, was owned by Viacom, just like CBS. That agreement ran out in 2006.

Fox held out until 2008 when it got rid of its Fox Kids lineup in favor of *Weekend Marketplace*, which is a fancy title for a block of infomercials. By that time there was a fifth (if smaller) broadcast network—the CW—and by 2014 it was the only remaining network with its own Saturday morning cartoons, a block of programs called Vortex. That year, though, it ended, and was replaced with easier-to-run educational/informational content: animal shows and travelogues called *One Magnificent Morning*.

CARTOONS EVERYWHERE

Not one of the TV networks would have killed off Saturday morning cartoons if Saturday morning cartoons had continued to pull in tens of millions of young viewers every week. They would have just dealt with the government restrictions and kept at it. But they didn't. Ratings had started slipping way back in the late 1980s, thanks to two major developments in the TV landscape: syndicated children's programming and cable.

What became of those thinly veiled (and very effective) toy ads, such as *Transformers* and *Thundercats?* They were sold to local stations for use in after-school time slots. Disney was particularly successful with a two-hour block called *The Disney Afternoon*, which ran on independent TV stations in the late afternoon from 1990 to 1999 and featured hits like *DuckTales, Darkwing Duck*, and *Goof Troop*. But more than just a couple of hours a day came from niche-based cable TV stations. Suddenly, instead of having to wait until Saturday, kids had all-day channels like Nickelodeon and Cartoon Network to provide nearly endless streams of cartoons. And a few years after that, they got YouTube, then Netflix, then Hulu...

Why was Disney's *Moana* renamed *Vaiana* in Italy? Moana is the name of an Italian adult film star.

SATURDAY MORNING'S GREATEST HITS

And by "greatest" we mean "weirdest." How many of these cartoons do you remember?

Meatballs & Spaghetti (1982) The title characters are a husband-and-wife musical act who tour the country in their RV along with their dog, who is also their drummer.

ProStars (1991) This sports-themed superhero show featured NBA star Michael Jordan (superpower: genius), MLB and NFL star Bo Jackson (superpower: strength), and NHL star Wayne Gretzky, whose superpower seems to be that he's always hungry.

Inch High Private Eye (1973) He's a hard-boiled gumshoe—the kind you'd find in an old crime novel. But he's only an inch tall. Tagging along to help him solve cases are his niece Lori, a dog named Braveheart, and the Hushmobile, a car so silent it can sneak up on criminals. (Quiet cars were science fiction in the 1970s.)

Wheelie and the Chopper Bunch (1974) Thirty years before Pixar's *Cars*, Wheelie is a Volkswagen Beetle that battles evil motorcycles in the Chopper Bunch. Viewers complained about the cartoon's excessive violence, and it was canceled after 13 episodes.

The Robonic Stooges (1978) The Three Stooges move into cartoon-land as bumbling, crime-fighting robots.

Saturday Supercade (1983) CBS jumps in on the video games fad with cartoons featuring such video arcade stars as Frogger, Donkey Kong, and Q*bert.

Yo Yogi! (1991) Yogi Bear gets a '90s makeover. He and his pal Boo-Boo wear neon clothes and skateboard around Jellystone Mall.

The Space Kidettes (1966) Child astronauts Scooter, Snoopy, Countdown, and Jenny blast off on outer-space adventures to look for treasure…while trying to avoid the evil space pirate Captain Skyhook.

Camp Candy (1989) Kids attend a summer camp that's owned and operated by movie star John Candy.

The Gary Coleman Show (1982) At the height of his popularity on *Diff'rent Strokes*, Coleman voiced a cartoon character named Andy, an angel-in-training sent to Earth to help kids.

Devlin (1974) Cashing in on the popularity of daredevil motorcycle jumper Evel Knievel, this dramatic cartoon features stuntman Ernie Devlin, who uses his stunts to help people. (In one episode, Devlin jumps his bike onto an island where some Boy Scouts are trapped, thus saving them…somehow.)

As much as 10 percent of a can of asparagus may be comprised of asparagus beetles or their egg sacs.

UNCLE JOHN'S PAGE OF LISTS

Top random tidbits from our bottomless files.

14 "Intimate" Couples Who Starred in a Movie Together

1. Reese Witherspoon and Ryan Phillippe: *Cruel Intentions*

2. Winona Ryder and Johnny Depp: *Edward Scissorhands*

3. Humphrey Bogart and Lauren Bacall: *The Big Sleep*

4. Elizabeth Taylor and Richard Burton: *Cleopatra*

5. Ben Affleck and Jennifer Lopez: *Gigli*

6. Angelina Jolie and Brad Pitt: *Mr. and Mrs. Smith*

7. Robert Pattinson and Kristen Stewart: *Twilight*

8. Annette Bening and Warren Beatty: *Bugsy*

9. Burt Reynolds and Sally Field: *Smokey and the Bandit*

10. Tom Cruise and Nicole Kidman: *Far and Away* and *Eyes Wide Shut*

11. Jim Carrey and Renee Zellweger: *Me, Myself & Irene*

12. Michael Douglas and Catherine Zeta-Jones: *Traffic*

13. Cameron Diaz and Matt Dillon: *There's Something About Mary*

14. Sylvester Stallone and Brigitte Nielsen: *Cobra*

8 World Cup Winners

1. Brazil (5 wins)

2. Germany/ West Germany (4)

3. Italy (4)

4. Argentina (2)

5. Uruguay (2)

6. France (2)

7. Spain (1)

8. England (1)

9 Names with Greek Origins

1. Alexander

2. Chloe

3. Christopher

4. Jason

5. Luke

6. Melissa

7. Nicholas

8. Peter

9. Sophia

5 Insured Celeb Body Parts

1. Tom Jones's chest hair: $7 mil

2. Daniel Craig's body: $9.5 mil

3. America Ferrera's smile: $10 million

4. Jennifer Lopez's butt: $27 million

5. David Beckham's legs: $195 million

The Reuters news service once relayed financial news via pigeons.

HOW TO DO CIVIL WAR-ERA AMPUTATION SURGERY

Some of the most haunting images of the Civil War are of fallen soldiers undergoing leg amputations in field hospitals. Doctors had little to work with—saws, scalpels, and old rags… and no antiseptics. So let's pretend you're a time traveler going back to be a Civil War surgeon (or "operator" as they were called). Here's your game plan.

WHAT YOU'LL NEED

- A soldier with a bullet wound
- A flat surface (upon which the soldier may lay)
- A cloth
- Bowl full of cold water
- Surgical probe (optional)
- Chloroform
- Scalpel
- Bonesaw
- Silk, cotton, or horsehair threads
- Needle
- Isinglass plaster (a gelatinous preparation made from fish bladders)
- Bandages

HOW TO DO IT

1. Perform triage. Briefly examine (with your eyes—time is of the essence) the soldiers whose cries of pain and pain-induced delirium fill the crude field hospital tent. Using what little energy you have left after performing somewhere around 50 surgeries in the last 12 hours, determine which patient is most likely to die soonest. Does he have an injury to the head, stomach, or chest? These are the soldiers most likely to die, so move them off to one side and let them die because they can't be saved.

2. Now, find the person who needs treatment due to a bullet wound in an extremity—the farther from the torso it is, the more likely it is that he can be saved. (Not the leg, but his life.

Although he'll still probably die of sepsis in a few months.) Operate on *this* person.

3. Wash out the inside and outside of the wound with a cloth. Don't worry about germs—germ theory is still considered cutting-edge nonsense from Europe. Simply take a rag, any rag, be it covered in soldier blood or not, and rinse it in a bowl of cold, likely bloody water, and dig around inside of the wound, wiping off the blood so you know what you're working with.

4. Probe the wound, with either a surgical probe or, because it's highly unlikely that you even have one of those, your finger. (Didn't have time to wash your hands? Oh well.) Dig around

What's an *oubliette*? A prison cell entered from the ceiling.

and remove any stray bits of uniform cloth, bone, gristle, and, finally, the bullet. If it's one of those gigantic, bone-splitting, muscle-flaying .58-caliber Minié bullets used in the Civil War, there's nothing you can do to treat the tremendous damage to the body. Diagnosis: *immediate* amputation.

5. Administer the Civil War–era's most common form of anesthesia: chloroform. Knock the patient right on out with it because they are not going to want to be awake for what comes next. Also, they won't kick and scream to resist the horrific surgery you're about to perform.

6. As soon as the soldier has passed out from a combination of pain and chloroform, take a scalpel (that you've "cleaned" by rinsing off the last guy's blood in cold water) and make a cut on the leg above the bullet wound. Keep cutting (or sawing—that scalpel is probably pretty dull) through every layer of the skin, and keep cutting through any and all muscles until you get all the way down to the bone.

7. Now, do that on the other side of the leg, cutting through skin and muscle so that the bone is all the way exposed on *two* sides.

8. Here's the part that earned Civil War army surgeons the nickname "Sawbones." Take your bonesaw, and at the cut you've already started with the scalpel, just saw through the bone. Just go back and forth, back and forth as you would if you were cutting down a tree. Keep going until you've completely severed the bone.

9. Throw the bloody, severed leg (or arm) onto the pile with the others, over in the corner of the tent, near the poor fellows who you decided aren't going to pull through.

10. But wait—you're not done yet! There's far more to a leg (or arm) than just skin, muscle, and bone. There are also many arteries, and they're all *full* of blood. The operation just severed them, and the patient will immediately bleed out and die if you don't do something. So tie them off, using threads made of silk, cotton, or horsehair.

11. Without any random blood spraying all over your face, you can get back to work on that amputated bone...or what's left of it. Using a scraping tool, scrape the ends of the bone until they're smooth, not unlike using sandpaper on wood. This will decrease discomfort for the solider later on—he's not going to want a sharp edge of a bone poking out through his skin.

12. Take the flaps of skin surrounding the amputation, pull them together, and with the needle and thread, close the incision. (Don't forget to leave a small drainage hole!)

13. Cover the stump with several applications of isinglass plaster to form a protective seal. Thoroughly wrap in bandages.

14. Move on to the next patient. Repeat steps 1 through 13.

In the local language, the name Astana—the capital city of Kazakhstan—means "the capital."

STRUCK BY LIGHTNING!

Lightning, as the 1982 Marcia Griffiths song "Electric Boogie" said, "It's electric! (Boogie woogie woogie.)" It's also frightening, sudden, potentially deadly, and very weird—as these people can attest.

SECOND SIGHT

In 1971 Edwin Robinson of Falmouth, Maine, got into a truck accident while driving over an ice-covered overpass. His injuries left him blind, but he adjusted to his new life, learning exactly how many steps it was from the bedroom to the kitchen and from the bathroom to the porch, and how many steps led down to the cellar. He went about his business for nine years, until one day in June 1980, when, while tending to his pet chicken in the backyard during a storm, he walked under a tree, and WHAM! he was struck by lightning. It knocked him to the ground, face first. After passing out for a few minutes, he staggered back into his house, and then took a short nap. When he woke up, he could see again. And not only could he see again, he had excellent vision: 20/25 in one eye, and 20/20 in the other.

> He walked under a tree, and WHAM!

THE PRICE OF GAS IS SHOCKING

In April 2015, lightning struck the sign at a Speedway gas station in Trotwood, Ohio. It was the type of sign that has an electronic display to let customers know current gas prices. But when lightning hit the sign, it scrambled the numbers. Result: regular gas, which cost $2.24 per gallon before the lightning strike, suddenly cost $9.94. (The staff honored the pre-lightning price.)

AN ELECTRIC CONNECTION

One night in 2009, Jens Gottlieb, 36, and his girlfriend Lisa Gruhn, 28, pulled off the A44 motorway in North-Rhine Westphalia, Germany, and into a gas station parking lot. But they didn't need gas—they were feeling romantic and craved an "intimate" encounter. So they parked, exited their cramped car, and headed for some nearby woods. Behind some trees and bushes, away from prying eyes, the couple disrobed, and, well, did what people in love do. And they were so focused on what they were doing that they didn't notice (or care about) the rumbling thunder and flashes of lightning that lit up the sky. That changed, however, when a bolt of lightning struck the ground a few feet away from them. They jumped up and ran, naked, out of the bushes and into the parking lot. Another driver noticed them and called police, who reunited the couple with their clothes and escorted them home.

If McDonald's were a country, it would have the 68th-biggest economy in the world.

THANKS, GRANDMA!

In 2009, 14-year-old Sophie Frost and her boyfriend were walking near their school in England one day when it started to rain, so they took shelter under a tree. Bad idea: Sophie was struck directly by lightning. The good news: it hit her right in the iPod she had in her pocket. Doctors say the music player and the headphone wire diverted the 300,000 volts of electricity contained in the lightning bolt away from her vital organs. She sustained burns to her chest and legs, but survived and was relatively unscathed. Frost hadn't bothered to put down her iPod during the storm because she was so excited to have it—her grandmother had given it to her as a gift only four days earlier.

> **A TIP FROM UNCLE JOHN**
>
> Ninety percent of people who get hit by lightning survive, but many are severely affected, suffering eye problems, brain injuries, heart attacks, and lifelong seizures. Obvious tip: stay inside during lightning storms. But if you can't do that, avoid poles, trees, and open fields. Then run for cover. The best protection: inside a fully constructed building, or a vehicle with a metal roof.

SHINE ON

In movies and books, getting struck by lightning can be seen as a sign from the universe (or from God) that a character ought to stop whatever it is they're doing… because the cosmos disapproves. In 1986 Jennifer Mann, a 15-year-old from Midland Park, New Jersey, was wiling away a rainy day by reading Stephen King's supernatural horror novel *The Shining* while sitting on her bed in her room. It must have felt pretty spooky then, when a lightning bolt came in through the window and hit her where she sat. It lit the bed on fire (which the girl's father put out with an extinguisher), but apart from ringing ears—and being totally creeped out—she was fine.

GOOD NEWS, BAD NEWS

A Croatian man named Zoran Jurkovic was riding his bicycle home from work in July 2016, pedaling and listening to the portable radio clipped to his belt via headphones. As he rode, a thunderstorm broke out. Jurkovic pedaled faster, trying to find shelter before the storm got too dicey. No such luck…and he was struck by lightning. Fortunately, he was wearing his rubber work boots, which stopped the electricity from flowing all the way through his body and into the ground. But the charge had to exit *somewhere*, so it did…through his penis. Doctors say the electricity traveled along his headphone cord, through the radio that was on his belt, out his private parts. While that was undoubtedly painful (ouch!), it prevented the lightning from traveling through—and probably stopping—Jurkovic's heart.

Sasquatch comes from *se'sxac*, a word in the Salish tribe's language that means "wild men."

HERE LIES BENJAMIN FRANKLIN

As you may recall from our visit to John Hancock's grave (page 332), he's buried in the Old Granary. In 1830 some Bostonians tried to change its name to Franklin Cemetery, in honor of Boston-born Benjamin Franklin. They might have gotten their wish if Franklin had actually been buried at the Old Granary. Here's part III of our story about the Founding Fathers' graves.

RENAISSANCE MAN

Benjamin Franklin (1706–90) began his career as a humble printer, but he accomplished a lot more in his 84 years—including cowriting and signing the Declaration of Independence, discovering new properties of electricity (via the famous lightning experiment with the kite and the key), and publishing several influential works (most notably *Poor Richard's Almanack*). Franklin also invented the first library where books could be checked out, the volunteer fire station, the lightning rod, swimming fins, bifocals, the Franklin stove, the "long arm" (for retrieving books from a high shelf), the glass armonica, and, surprisingly, crowdsourcing.

Unlike most of the Founding Fathers, who were just reaching middle age when the American Revolution began, Franklin was already an old man. And he was already one of the most famous people in the Western world. As his end was approaching, it was a big deal to Philadelphians that he be laid to rest there. True, he was born in Boston, and even though he ran away as a young man and settled in Philadelphia, he still had ties to Beantown—including a spot in the Franklin family plot at the Old Granary if he wanted one. But there wasn't much to debate; Franklin had decided decades earlier that he would spend eternity with his wife and children in his adopted hometown of Philadelphia.

A STATE FUNERAL FOR A COMMON MAN

After a long illness, Franklin succumbed to empyema on April 17, 1790, and the world mourned. Count Mirabeau of the French National Assembly said, "He was able to restrain thunderbolts and tyrants." Back in Philadelphia, more than 20,000 people attended Franklin's funeral (the city's population at the time was 28,000). Sixty years earlier, he'd written his own epitaph:

> The Body of B. Franklin, Printer; like the Cover of an old Book, Its Contents torn out, And stript of its Lettering and Gilding, Lies here, Food for Worms. But the Work shall not be wholly lost; For it will, as he believ'd, appear once more, In a new & more perfect Edition, Corrected and amended By the Author

Place on earth farthest from any sea: the Eurasian Pole of Inaccessibility (northern China).

But as Franklin grew older and wiser, his last wishes became more modest. Where most other Founding Fathers wanted massive obelisks to mark their graves, Franklin's will stipulated that he be buried under a flat marble ledger tablet "6 feet long, 4 feet wide, plain, with only a small moulding round the upper edge." He wanted his marker to say only "Benjamin Franklin, Printer."

LAID TO REST

After his coffin was carried from the State House to Christ Church (where George Washington worshipped while in Philadelphia), Franklin was buried in the church's adjacent burial ground beneath a 1,000-pound stone slab, inscribed with the words "Benjamin and Deborah Franklin – 1790." Deborah had died 25 years earlier. Their son Francis, who died of smallpox at age four, was also buried there. Their daughter Sarah would complete the quartet in 1808.

The Christ Church Burial Ground was established in 1719, but it's only in the last century or so that graveyards have become tourist attractions, which is why few people visited Franklin's grave for the first 70 years after his death. Another reason: there was a tall stone wall separating his slab from the sidewalk. In the mid-1800s, Philadelphia's leaders decided to capitalize on Franklin's fame by tearing down the wall and replacing it with a steel fence, so that people walking along Arch Street could view his grave site.

The Christ Church Preservation Trust was set up in 1858 to raise the money for the project. To make Franklin's slab more visible, workers lifted it out of the ground and raised it up a few feet. The plan worked. Ever since the steel fence went in, millions of people have paid homage to the man who coined the phrase "a penny saved is a penny earned" by throwing pennies onto his grave. (Uncle John's note: If you'd like to pay homage to the actual coiner of that phrase, you'd have better luck visiting the grave of George Herbert at St. Andrew's Church in Bemerton, Wiltshire, England; in his 1633 book *Outlandish Proverbs*, Herbert wrote, "A penny spar'd is twice got.")

WWW.GOFUNDME.COM/SAVEBENFRANKLIN

Have you ever heard the phrase "nibbled to death by ducks"? That's what was happening to the Franklin family's marble slab, only instead of ducks it was pennies. The Preservation Trust, which is still active today, wishes people would throw hundred-dollar bills instead (also known as "Benjamins"). That would cause far less damage and help pay for the costly work required to seal the huge crack that stretches from one end of the rock to the other. The pennies didn't cause the crack—blame that on the improper setting of the stone when it was raised in 1858—but the pennies were slowly eroding the stone, one pockmark at a time. And the crack was getting a little wider each year.

"For a long time, people wanted to do a big restoration of the old marker," said Marco Federico, who oversaw the team that restored the grave site in 2017.

Odds of survival if you stow away in the wheel well of a jet airplane: 1 in 4.

"They basically wanted to toss the old stone and put in some glorious, grandiose monument, which [Franklin] never wanted. His will is very specific." But even a "simple" restoration was estimated at more than $80,000. The trust was able to secure most of the money from universities and historical societies, but they were still $10,000 short. So in 2016, the trust set up a "Save Ben Franklin" GoFundMe page in order to raise the rest of the money.

> They were still $10,000 short. Then Jon Bon Jovi swooped in to save the day.

The campaign stalled at a few thousand dollars. Then Jon Bon Jovi swooped in to save the day. After hearing about the fund-raiser, he and his wife, Dorothea, pitched in $5,000. "It was kind of funny," observed Christ Church project overseer John Hopkins. "I joked when we received the news, that we were 'halfway there, living on a prayer,' and then he kind of put us over the top." (That's a reference to Bon Jovi's 1986 hit song.) Then more people and more groups, including the Philadelphia Eagles, made donations, and the work began.

HISTORY UNDER FIRE

"Most people probably won't even notice we did anything," explained Federico, whose team carefully lifted the stone off the ground, sealed the crack, and filled in all the penny-caused pockmarks. The crack is still visible, though. Like the famous crack in the Liberty Bell, it has also been preserved as part of its story.

An odd thing happened during the restoration. The area had been sealed off, the fence was covered up, and signs were erected telling people *not* to throw pennies. Hopkins was at the site, being interviewed by *Hidden City Philadelphia*, and just as he was saying, "It's a tradition, it's hard to change, but we can try to alter the culture of it," a barrage of pennies flew over the fence and pelted him. "It's disrespectful," he growled. "These [tour] groups come by, they tell them to throw the pennies, and they walk on. They don't talk about the most important American to ever live!"

YE OLDE GO FUND ME

Not seriously injured by the penny attack, Hopkins added that he is grateful for one thing: "The beauty of the GoFundMe was the donations from regular citizens. Ben Franklin was a man of the people, and he was a fund-raiser in his time. He probably would have invented GoFundMe if he was alive." In a way, he did. In Colonial times, if money was needed for a project, it always came from the top down (like King Ferdinand funding Columbus's voyage to America). But Franklin, who believed in democracy, realized that if you can't get one king to give a whole lot of money, you can get a whole lot of people to donate one pence each. During his lifetime, Franklin organized several successful fund-raising campaigns. That's how he helped set up the first subscription library and the first volunteer fire department, and when Christ

Age group that gets the most colds: kindergartners, with about 12 a year.

Church's steeple needed to be replaced in the 1750s, Franklin helped manage a lottery to raise the money for it. He wasn't much of a churchgoer himself, so why would he be so interested in building a tall steeple? Hopkins believes that Franklin had an ulterior motive "to do some experimenting with the electricity and the height of the building." (Franklin later decided to do the experiment with a kite instead.)

In May 2017, Franklin's grave site reopened to the public. That day was the culmination of a lot of restoration work that took place at the site in the early 21st century. Twelve years earlier, on the statesman's 300th birthday in 2005, a new brick path had been installed around the grave. And a plaque was set into the bricks with several quotations about the patriot, in *Poor Richard's Almanack* style:

The Last Resting Place of Benjamin Franklin

"Venerated for Benevolence, Admired for Talents, Esteemed for Patriotism, Beloved for Philanthropy."
—WASHINGTON

"The Sage Whom Two Worlds Claimed as Their Own."
–MIRABEAU

"He Tore from the Skies the Lightning and From Tyrants the Sceptre."
–TURGOT

THE GRAVEYARD TODAY

Franklin isn't the only Founding Father you can find at the Christ Church Burial Ground. Five of the 1,400 graves include signers of the Declaration of Independence. In addition to Franklin, there's Joseph Hewes, Francis Hopkinson, George Ross, and Dr. Benjamin Rush. There's also a monument to Commodore Uriah P. Levy, the man who saved Thomas Jefferson's final resting place from ruin.

The Burial Ground is located at the intersection of 5th and Arch in Old City Philadelphia. It receives about 100,000 visitors annually and offers guided tours, but it's closed during the winter months, so check before you go. Or, you can always view Franklin's grave from the sidewalk through the fence. And while the trust always welcomes donations, when you're visiting Franklin's slab, they'd rather you throw praise than pennies.

Our next Founding Father, Alexander Hamilton, is buried a few blocks away from where his titular hip-hop Broadway musical opened to rave reviews in 2016. That story is on page 429.

Technical name for nose-picking: *rhinotillexis*.

BE A HOUSEHOLD MacGYVER

The TV character MacGyver famously uses everyday objects to escape dangerous situations—like a paper clip to diffuse a bomb, or wineglasses to play the notes to open a vault. Here are some clever tricks (or life hacks) to help you get out of some slightly more mundane situations.

Oh no! The blades of my ceiling fan haven't been dusted for years, and I have a tall person coming to visit. I need a way to dust it fast without getting the dust all over the house!

MacGyver: Place an old pillowcase over one of the blades and slowly wipe off the dust. Take the pillowcase outside and shake it out. Repeat for each blade.

Oh no! I've been in a fender-bender, and it will cost a fortune to pull this dent out!

MacGyver: Get a plunger, wet the rim, and plunge it like you would a clogged toilet. You just might get that dent out for a lot cheaper.

Oh no! The little pull-tab on my zipper just broke off!

MacGyver: Get a paper clip and thread it through the little hole where the puller was, and then you can zip again. (And get me another paper clip, so I can diffuse this bomb.)

Oh no! I want to play my band's new demo on my phone, but the tiny speaker isn't loud enough for everyone to hear and be impressed by it!

MacGyver: Get a large glass—like a pint glass—and place your phone inside it. The glass will amplify the sound considerably.

Oh no! I have to weed an area full of jagged rocks, but I have no kneepads. (I'm a computer geek, Jim, not a gardener!)

MacGyver: If you're really a computer geek, get two old mouse pads and some duct tape, and voilà! You have kneepads!

Oh no! My face feels really dry and I'm all out of moisturizer!

MacGyver: Make a face wrap by mashing up a banana and spreading it on your face. You'll be moisturized in minutes, and the fruit's vitamins and antioxidants can help reduce puffiness and redness.

Oh no! I was screwing in a light bulb, and it broke! Now I can't grab it and unscrew it!

MacGyver: Get a potato (or a similar fruit or vegetable) and press it firmly against the assembly. You should be able to grab the base enough to unscrew the threads.

Oh no! I'm trying to paint my windowsills, but I'm getting paint on the outside of the paint can every time I wipe off the brush after dipping it in the paint.

MacGyver: Get a rubber band large enough to go around the entire paint can from top to bottom. Now, when you refill the brush, wipe off the excess paint on the rubber band rather than on the edge of the can, and the drips will fall back into the can.

Oh no! I'm trying to wrap these presents, but I have so many rolls of ribbon that I can't keep track of them all!

MacGyver: Get a shoebox and cut a hole in the center of each of the short sides. Then fashion a dowel out of a long stick (like a ruler) to make a convenient ribbon dispenser.

Oh no! My half-eaten containers of ice cream get little ice crystals all over the surface, so I have to eat the whole thing at once.

MacGyver: First, put down the spoon. Then secure the top of the container with plastic wrap, and put the lid on. That'll keep your ice cream fresh and crystal-free.

* * *

A PHARMA FLOP

In 2006 the FDA approved Exubera, an insulin delivery system for diabetics, made by drug giant Pfizer. The drug was marketed as a game-changing alternative to the multiple insulin injections that diabetics had to take each day; the company estimated that by 2010, it would be making $1.5 billion annually on it. Exubera allowed insulin to be inhaled through the nose. But unlike the small inhalers used by asthmatics, the Exubera device was large and clunky—about the size of a can of Pringles. One other problem: Pfizer didn't account for the fact that taking injections was no longer a big deal for diabetics, because insulin syringes had become super-fine and very short, meaning most users could barely feel them. One more problem: many diabetics were already using pain-free insulin delivery methods, such as insulin pens and insulin pumps. Result: just two years after Exubera became available, it had captured a grand total of 1 percent of the market.

Best-selling book in Japan in 1985: a *Super Mario Bros.* strategy guide.

WHERE WERE YOU IN '62?

Here's a look at what the world was like in 1962…when the world still had to wait 26 long years for Uncle John's Bathroom Reader *to be invented.*

MAJOR EVENTS

- On February 20, astronaut John Glenn is launched into space and becomes the first American to orbit the Earth via the *Friendship 7* capsule.
- The Space Needle, the centerpiece of the Seattle World's Fair, opens on April 21.
- Spider-Man debuts in the August edition of Marvel Comics' *Amazing Fantasy.*
- Riots and protests break out at the University of Mississippi in September, as an African American student named James Meredith tries to enroll in classes. President John F. Kennedy sends in federal troops to ensure Meredith's safety.
- The Cold War nearly ends in a deadly conflict with the 13-day Cuban Missile Crisis, which starts on October 16 after American spy planes discover Soviet missiles in Cuba; the United States blockaded the island nation, leading the Soviet Union to threaten war before ultimately agreeing to remove its missiles.
- In a speech at Rice University on September 12, President Kennedy challenges the nation to send a man to the Moon by the end of the decade.

MOST ADMIRED

John F. Kennedy and Jacqueline Kennedy are voted the most admired man and woman in a Gallup poll. That's the first time that respondents named both the American president and the sitting First Lady.

BIGGEST BOX OFFICE HITS

1. *Lawrence of Arabia,* an epic about British military figure T. E. Lawrence
2. *The Longest Day,* a war film about D-Day, which starred many of the most popular actors in Hollywood, from John Wayne to Red Buttons to Henry Fonda to Rod Steiger
3. *In Search of the Castaways,* a Disney high seas adventure starring Hayley Mills and Maurice Chevalier
4. *That Touch of Mink,* a romantic comedy starring Cary Grant and Doris Day
5. *The Music Man,* the film adaptation of the hit Broadway musical

Lawrence of Arabia wins seven Oscars at the Academy Awards, including Best Picture, Best Director for David Lean, and Best Musical Score…but Peter O'Toole loses Best Actor to Gregory Peck in *To Kill a Mockingbird.*

DEATHS

- January 26: Mob boss Lucky Luciano, 64
- June 1: Adolf Eichmann, 56, Nazi leader and architect of the Holocaust (he is tried and hanged for his crimes)
- July 6: American novelist William Faulkner (*The Sound and the Fury*), 64
- August 5: Marilyn Monroe, 36
- September 3: Modernist poet E. E. Cummings, 67
- November 7: Eleanor Roosevelt, 78, United Nations ambassador, activist, and former First Lady

MUSIC

According to *Billboard*, these are the top five hit songs of the year:

1. "Stranger on the Shore" by Acker Bilk (a clarinet-based instrumental)
2. "I Can't Stop Loving You" by Ray Charles
3. "Mashed Potato Time" by Dee Dee Sharp
4. "Roses Are Red (My Love)" by Bobby Vinton
5. "The Stripper" by David Rose

NOW AVAILABLE IN STORES

- Lemonheads candy, Planters Dry Roasted Peanuts, Kellogg's Froot Loops, and Diet Dr Pepper (actually called Dietetic Dr Pepper)
- Fisher-Price introduces the Chatter Telephone in 1962, the classic toddler pull toy consisting of a smiling rotary telephone. It will be Fisher-Price's best-selling toy until 1980.

WHAT THINGS COST

A new home (on average): $12,550	A daily newspaper: 10¢
A new refrigerator: $500	A stamp to mail a letter: 4¢
A color television: $400	Eggs: 32¢ a dozen
A new car: about $2,900	A loaf of bread: 20¢
Gasoline: 27¢ a gallon	Ground beef: 40¢ a pound
An LP record album: $3	Sugar: 89¢ for a 10-pound bag
A 45 rpm record: $1	Bacon: 69¢ a pound
A movie ticket: 50¢	Coffee: 85¢ a pound
Popcorn at the movies: 20¢	A candy bar or pack of gum: 5¢

How are you going to pay for all that? The average American household earns about $6,000 a year. (The minimum wage is $1.25 an hour.)

A good gig if you can get it: "Wealth therapists" help rich people deal with the guilt and isolation that comes from having lots of money.

SPORTS

- The seventh annual FIFA World Cup of soccer takes place in Chile. Brazil wins its third global championship.
- The first Super Bowl and the merger of the American and National Football Leagues are years off, but there are still two end-of-the-year football championships. In the AFL title game, the Dallas Texans defeat the Houston Oilers; in the NFL, the Green Bay Packers prevail over the New York Giants.
- In Major League Baseball, the National League expands for the first time in more than 60 years, going from eight teams to ten with the addition of the New York Mets (following the Giants' move to San Francisco) and the Houston Colt .45s (later renamed the Astros).
- In basketball, NBA superstar Wilt Chamberlain achieves something not replicated since. On March 2, he scores 100 points in a game. His Philadelphia Warriors defeated the New York Knicks 169–147.
- Boxer Sonny Liston becomes the world heavyweight champion after knocking out Floyd Patterson. Liston gets the job done just two minutes and six seconds into the match, one of the quickest knockouts ever.
- Australian tennis player Rod Laver does what only one other player (Don Budge, 1938) had done to that point: win all four major singles titles—the Australian Open, French Open, U.S. Open, and Wimbledon—in a single calendar year.
- Under the tutelage of coach Punch Imlach, the Toronto Maple Leafs win their first of three straight Stanley Cups. They'd win once more in the '60s, in 1967… and, as of 2018, they have yet to win one since.

TELEVISION

- ABC becomes the third of the "big three" TV networks to introduce color programming on September 23, when it broadcasts the first episode of *The Jetsons*. (The futuristic show will be canceled at the end of the 1962–63 season.)
- NBC's *The Tonight Show* has been the dominant late-night show since 1954. Steve Allen hosted until 1957, when Jack Paar took over, but the show takes a giant leap toward legendary status on October 1, when comedian and game show host Johnny Carson takes over. *The Tonight Show Starring Johnny Carson* will run for 30 years and vanquish all competitors along the way, including Dick Cavett, Merv Griffin, Joey Bishop, Joan Rivers, and Pat Sajak.
- CBS's fall lineup includes a goofy sitcom about a bunch of yokels who strike oil and use the money to move to Beverly (Hills, that is). *The Beverly Hillbillies* gets panned by critics…but instantly becomes the #1 show on TV.

All German animal shelters are no-kill shelters.

DUMB CROOKS

More proof that crime doesn't pay.

IF AT FIRST YOU SUCCEED, TRY AGAIN AND FAIL

Two shoplifters nabbed thousands of dollars' worth of electronics from a Seattle Costco in 2018. But several employees saw their faces, ensuring that the thieves would be easily recognized if they came back. They came back. Employees stealthily watched as the two young men shoplifted $2,200 worth of electronics. By the time they ran out through the emergency exit (the same place they'd escaped the previous time), several officers were waiting for them.

IF AT FIRST YOU FAIL, TRY AND FAIL AGAIN

One night in November 2017, several people witnessed a man trying to break into cars in a Trinity Oaks, Florida, neighborhood. All the cars were locked, though, so the man went away empty-handed. On the off chance that the thief might be dumb enough to return to the scene of his failed crime, deputies parked an unmarked squad car on the street and waited inside. Later that evening, the door opened and in popped Stephen Titland, 49, the same man from the previous night. He was immediately arrested.

HALL'S BIG HAUL

In 2017 William Jason Hall, 38, entered a Lakeland, Florida, 7-Eleven and—when he thought no one was looking—stuffed a quart of motor oil down his comically oversized pants. Then he stuffed in another quart, then another, and another, until he had 15 quarts of oil in his pants. (He'd tied them at the bottom so nothing would fall out.) Then Hall sauntered on over to a rack of DVDs and casually knocked it onto the floor. Oops. He picked them up, stacked them nicely, and then stuffed 30 DVDs into his pants. "Then he waddles like a duck out of the store," said the Polk County Sheriff's Facebook page. He waddled right past Detective Phil Ryan, who was sitting in an unmarked car and had watched the entire episode transpire. "I don't think so," said Ryan as he escorted Hall back into the 7-Eleven, where he removed all 15 quarts of oil and 30 DVDs and put them back. (Even if Ryan hadn't been there, Hall was clearly visible on the CCTV footage.) Hall was arrested, but what happened to his contraband is somewhat controversial. As one Facebook commenter queried,

> Then he stuffed in another quart, then another, and another, until he had 15 quarts of oil in his pants.

Hollywood lore: Andre the Giant let out a 16-second fart on the set of *The Princess Bride*.

"Am I the only one that is grossed out by the fact that they put them back on the shelf after being in his nasty a$$ pants? Yuck."

DUMB CROOK, MEET DUMB LUCK

In June 2018, Flora Lunsford, a 58-year-old waitress from Pine Bluff, Arkansas, was getting gas when her purse was stolen from her car. No one got a good look at the crooks (it was a two-man job), and security footage wasn't clear enough to positively ID them, so all Lunsford could do was report her credit cards stolen and get back to her life. Two days later, one of the thieves—Shamon West—walked into the diner where Lunsford worked, which is just down the road from the gas station. West, 21, ordered a bunch of food, scarfed it down, and then tried to pay Lunsford with her own credit card. "Where's the rest of my stuff?" she asked. He wouldn't tell her, but he did tell the police after they showed up a few minutes later and arrested him. Here's the dumb part: Lunsford's driver's license was in her wallet, right next to her credit card, and it has her picture on it. One look at it and West would have known to eat elsewhere. Lunsford was shaken by the entire ordeal…except for the driver's license goof. "That part," she says, "is funny."

THWARTED BY PHYSICS

Picture a man with a brick. He throws the brick at a window. The brick bounces off the window and hits him in the head, knocking him out. You don't have to picture it in your head—you can watch the viral video (recorded by CCTV in Maryland in 2018) on the internet. Just type in "burglar throws brick into window, hits himself in head." But don't confuse that one with "bungling car thief throws brick at window, knocks himself out." That video (also very funny) was recorded in Ireland in 2015. A guy spends half an hour throwing rocks at a car's windows; then he throws a brick at it, which bounces back and knocks him out. And don't confuse *that* one with "dumb burglar knocks his buddy out with a brick," recorded in China in 2010. A robber throws a brick at a window (which doesn't break), and as he's stepping aside to avoid the rebound, another robber throws another brick, which hits *him* in the head, knocking him out. And don't confuse *that* one with our all-time favorite, "robber knocks buddy and himself out with a brick," from 2007. It's incredible: First, a robber throws a brick that bounces back and knocks out his accomplice, then he throws a *second* brick and knocks himself out. (Maybe crooks should steer clear of bricks.)

* * *

"Stupidity without malice isn't horrible; some people can't help it."
—**Ricky Gervais**

The most commonly used pope names: John (21), Benedict (17), Gregory (16), and Clement (14).

MOUTHING OFF

ON IRONY

Our handy dictionary defines irony as 1) "an incongruity between the actual result of a sequence of events and the normal or expected result"; and 2) "an event or result marked by such incongruity." So that clears it up, right? Hardly. Here are some thoughts on what irony is…and what it isn't.

"IRONY IS INHERENTLY CONFUSING. NOT ONLY ARE ITS DEFINITIONS CONFUSING, IT IS CONFUSING BY DEFINITION."
—Jennifer Thompson

"From even the greatest of horrors, irony is seldom absent."
—H. P. Lovecraft

" Irony is really only hypocrisy with style. "
—Barbara Everett

"When irony first makes itself known in a young man's life, it can be like his first experience of getting drunk; he has met with a powerful thing which he does not know how to handle."
—Robertson Davies

"Irony is the hygiene of the mind."
—Elizabeth Bibesco

"Irony deals with opposites; it has nothing to do with coincidence."
—George Carlin

"The presence of irony does not necessarily mean that the earnestness is excluded. Only assistant professors assume that."
—Søren Kierkegaard

"Ironic philosophies produce passionate works."
—Albert Camus

"A vast percentage of the human race is literally not wired neurologically to get irony. More than half of humanity takes life at face value, which is to me terrifying."
—Douglas Coupland

"IRONY IS WASTED ON THE STUPID."
—Oscar Wilde

"Irony regards every simple truth as a challenge."
—Mason Cooley

"If a person who indulges in gluttony is a glutton, and a person who commits a felony is a felon, then God is an iron."
—Spider Robinson

"The great thing about irony is that it splits things apart, gets up above them so we can see the flaws and hypocrisies and duplicates."
—David Foster Wallace

"Irony is Fate's most common figure of speech."
—Trevanian, *Shibumi*

"Irony is an insult conveyed in the form of a compliment."
—Edwin Percy Whipple

"It is the oldest ironies that are still the most satisfying: Man, when preparing for bloody war, will orate loudly and most eloquently in the name of peace."
—Alan Moore, *Watchmen*

"The struggle for a free intelligence has always been a struggle between the ironic and the literal mind."
—Christopher Hitchens

"Irony is the form of paradox. Paradox is what is good and great at the same time."
—Karl Wilhelm Friedrich Schlegel

GHOST STORIES

*It was a dark and stormy night. Uncle John was in the "reading room"
when a disembodied voice suddenly whispered into his ear, "You don't
have to believe in ghosts to be entertained by ghost stories."*

A PAIR OF JACKS

Amanda Teague, a 45-year-old single mother of five from Northern Ireland, told this
odd love story to *People* magazine in 2014. She was lying in bed one night when the
ghost of an 18th-century Haitian pirate appeared and introduced himself as Jack—
which is quite a coincidence, because Teague performs as a professional Captain Jack
Sparrow impersonator herself. Over the next few months, Teague and the ghost pirate
got to know each other. He told her he'd been left at the altar and that he was later
executed for thievery; she told him about her life impersonating Johnny Depp's *Pirates
of the Caribbean* character. Then it got even weirder as the two developed...feelings
for each other. Before long, Teague was on a boat in international waters getting
married to Jack. A medium was brought along to say "I do" for the ghost pirate, and
Teague (dressed as herself, not as Depp) placed a ring on a candle in place of Jack's
finger. Sadly, in 2018, she told the *Irish Times* that she and Jack had gotten divorced.
She wouldn't say why, only warning others, "Be VERY careful when dabbling in
spirituality, it's not something to mess with."

NOT-SO-MERRY PRANKSTERS

"A Pervy Ghost's Stealing My Knickers!" reported the *Mirror* in 2014. But it was no
laughing matter for the woman who had her knickers stolen, Pauline Hickson. And the
activity went way beyond that: "One day me and my sister came back from the shops and
the kitchen looked like someone had wiped it down with dirt and then freeze-dried it." At
first Hickson, 58, thought her sister was pranking her, but as the strange activity increased,
she started to suspect her friends, all of whom vehemently denied having anything to
do with it. "I didn't believe anyone and I started to lose people from my life," Hickson
lamented. "I would spend all day just wandering around the streets, trying to stay out of
the house." It got so bad that she moved from Hull (in northern England) to a flat in
Cambridge, about 150 miles southeast. Then the activity not only continued, she says, it
increased: Her clothes went missing—especially, for some strange reason, her underwear.
The shower would turn on in the middle of the night. And then she'd wake up to find
dishes all over the kitchen floor and scratches on the wall. At this point Hickson was
convinced that *several* ghosts were tormenting her. Even though she moved seven times
in two years—sometimes living in hostels—she couldn't seem to shake them.

Not knowing what else to do, she hired paranormal investigator Steve Kneeshaw. He performed a "hypno-exorcism," which is just what it sounds like: he hypnotized Hickson and then performed an exorcism, which concluded with a "blast of cold air" that carried the apparitions of "a large, old man and a 14-year-old boy" out of Hickson's life for good. (It's unclear how he knew the younger ghost's age.) Hickson doesn't care how old the ghosts are or were—she's just glad they're gone. "It was like I was dead inside, but now, my eyes are sparkling, my spirit is back, I look around and all I see is color."

HIGH SPIRITS

In August 2018, a budtender named Andy Gomez was working at Five Zero Trees, a marijuana dispensary in Oregon City, Oregon, when, "I kind of felt like someone was standing next to me," he told Portland's KGW8 News, "like somebody was right here." Just then a glass jar fell off the counter and landed on the floor. A bit freaked out, Gomez checked the pot shop's surveillance footage, and it very clearly showed the jar sliding off the counter…all by itself. "It's like, what's going to happen next?" Gomez asked no one in particular. But that wasn't the only strange occurrence. On another day, at another counter, surveillance footage showed some pens rearranging themselves in a cup. "Those are state-certified videos," asserted general manager Samantha Davidson, adding that it's actually illegal to doctor them. Did some prankster break the law? Davidson believes the activity is caused by the ghost of a pharmacist who dispensed medicine in that same building a century ago. "I just hope that the pharmacist is happy we're here." She thinks he's "organizing the counter." At the conclusion of the story, one of the local newscasters offered up a different theory: "Maybe the ghost just wanted to roll up a big fatty."

THE SCREAMING GHOSTS OF CLIFTON HALL

After investing in nursing homes and running a hotel in Dubai, by the time Anwar Rashid was 32 years old, he was a millionaire. In 2007 he moved his young family into Clifton Hall, a 900-year-old mansion in Nottinghamshire, England. On the first night, they heard mysterious knocking sounds and then a disembodied voice asking, "Hello, is anyone there?" Over the next few months, Rashid said that more strange things occurred—screams in the night, ghostly children watching TV, and other stereotypical haunted manifestations. Rashid did some research and discovered that Clifton Hall has had a sordid history: a "woman in white" jumped from one of the upstairs windows to her death, and the tunnels underneath the house were once used for satanic rituals.

Rashid called in the Ashfield Paranormal Investigation Network. The lead investigator, an active-duty police officer named Lee Roberts, said it was "the only place where I've ever really been scared, even in the light. It's just got a really eerie

A comet has an atmosphere, and it's called a "coma."

feeling about it." The team said they saw the apparition of a boy, but they were unable to rid the mansion of ghosts.

The final straw came when Rashid discovered spots of blood on his baby's quilt. The next day, only eight months after moving in, the Rashids moved out. "Clifton Hall is a beautiful property—I fell for its beauty," he told the *Telegraph*. "But behind the facade it is haunted. We were like the family in *The Others*. The ghosts didn't want us to be there."

Update: A few months after Rashid's ghost story made national news, he filed for bankruptcy, and then the truth came out. Turns out he isn't worth nearly as much as he said he was, and he'd been accused of scamming people in the past. It now seems likely that he made up the entire haunting thing because he had a case of buyer's remorse.

THE HAUNTED DVD

One day in 2009, a movie studio executive was given a DVD of a new low-budget horror movie to see if he'd be interested in distributing it to theaters. He watched the video at home that night and it reportedly "scared the hell out of him." Even scarier, right after the movie ended, he discovered the door to his room was locked from the outside, and he had to call a locksmith to get out. The executive was so convinced the DVD was haunted that he had to get it out of his house. He brought it to the studio the next day in a trash bag. In the end, he did decide to distribute and market the film. Good idea. It was the found-footage ghost story *Paranormal Activity*. Made for only $15,000, it went on to become one of the most profitable movies of all time. And the DreamWorks executive who to this day is still convinced that his DVD was haunted: Steven Spielberg.

BOO-NUS FACT

A study performed at Wright State University in Ohio in 2003 looked at 100 homes that were "psychologically impacted" (it's tough for actual scientists to use the word "haunted"). Their results were a bit spooky: It will take twice as long to sell a haunted house as it will to sell a non-haunted house and, on average, it will sell for about 2.4 percent less.

* * *

"I believe in everything until it's disproved. So I believe in fairies, myths, dragons. It all exists, even if it's in your mind. Who's to say that dreams and nightmares aren't as real as the here and now?"

—John Lennon

Unicorns are mentioned in the Bible nine times.

THE AMERICAN LOTTERY

Ever been in a convenience store and wondered why there are so many lottery games? Bank a Million, Megabucks, Cash4Life, SuperCash!, Lucky Dog, Jumbo Bucks, Gopher 5, Wild Money, Triple Twist, Monopoly, Lucky for Life, Rolling Cash, Money Bags, and, of course, Powerball ...and that's just a drop in the bucket. Where'd they all come from? It turns out that the lottery has quite a long history in North America. Here's the story of how we got lotto fever.

1612–1616
The Virginia Company of London holds a series of lotteries to raise funds to pay for ships to bring a new round of settlers to the Jamestown Colony in the New World. The prize: 4,000 crowns—about $180,000 in today's money. The lottery brings in the equivalent of about $10 million.

1630s–1740s
Many of America's earliest—and still most prestigious—colleges and universities pay for construction with lotteries. Among them: Harvard, the College of William and Mary, Yale, and Princeton.

1740s–1760s
In the New World, lotteries become a common way to raise funds to build everything from churches to roads to schools.

1768
George Washington, by this time a political and social figure in Virginia, spearheads a lottery to build a road across the Alleghany Mountains. It fails to generate the necessary funds.

1776
The First Continental Congress, America's self-appointed colonial government, founds a lottery to pay for the enormous expense of the Revolutionary War. The colonists have to find other means (such as the assistance of France) when the lottery fails. It's the first lottery in the colonies to pay out not in British money but in the brand-new Continental currency. Its value fluctuated a great deal, and wasn't terribly stable (nor was the government that backed it), so few people were willing to purchase tickets.

1819
Congress creates a National Lottery to fund a Washington, D.C., beautification initiative. It never pays out due to rampant corruption among the city government officials charged with running the program.

1821
In the Supreme Court case *Cohens v. Virginia*, two Virginia brothers who ran various financial businesses were arrested and convicted of violating a state law that prohibited the sale of out-of-state and national lottery tickets. The court rules to uphold the conviction.

Makes sense: There's a "sequel" to the card game Uno called Dos.

1826	In the months before his death, Thomas Jefferson receives permission from the State of Virginia to hold a private lottery to pay off his huge personal debt. It's held after his death and, because of lingering anti-lottery sentiment among the public, doesn't raise nearly enough money to cover Jefferson's bills.
1860	The crookedness of state and national lotteries leads almost every state (except for Delaware, Missouri, and Kentucky) to ban them by this time. In their absence, secret, illegal lotteries develop, with tickets sold and shipped around the country. Most of them never pay out.
1868	The Louisiana State Lottery Company, operating illegally for years, receives a 25-year charter to go legit. Within a few years, it's shut down again when it's revealed that the state legislature only approved the charter due to widespread bribery from a New York–based criminal syndicate.
1890	After several states try lotteries again, widespread corruption leads the federal government to ban by-mail lotteries.
1895	Invoking the Commerce Clause of the U.S. Constitution, Congress de facto bans all lotteries, as the law doesn't allow for the shipment of lottery tickets across state lines. The government begins an aggressive decades-long campaign to shut down illegal lotteries until they almost entirely disappear.
1934	The scandals of the 1800s long forgotten, the first modern-day, government-run and regulated lottery in the United States debuts in the territory of Puerto Rico.
1964	The New Hampshire Sweepstakes becomes the first highly regulated lottery in the United States proper. To cut down on cheating and fixing, the results involve two separate number drawings and correctly guessing the results of a horse race.
1966–1975	The New Hampshire Sweepstakes operates without incident and raises so much money for the government that neighboring states launch their own gaming systems. New York's begins in 1967, New Jersey's begins in 1970, and by 1975, 10 more states have created lotteries.
1973	Scientific Games Corporation is founded, and uses algorithms to produce secure "instant win" or "scratch-off" lottery games. The first one will be launched in 1974 by the Massachusetts Lottery.
1975	The New Jersey Lottery becomes the first organization in the United States to use a computerized system for picking numbers.

Monty Python member Michael Palin was president of the Royal Geographical Society from 2009 to 2012.

1980	Congress considers—and rejects—a national lottery run by the federal government.
1982	Computerized lottery terminals, built by a company called GTECH, hit grocery and convenience stores. These machines also introduce the "quick pick" in which lottery numbers are randomly selected by a computer, as opposed to chosen by the player.
1985	The first multistate lottery debuts. Tri-State Megabucks tickets are available for sale in Maine, New Hampshire, and Vermont.
1986	The lottery tech company Scientific Games introduces touch-screen, self-service lottery kiosks. First to use them: the Iowa Lottery.
1987	The Multi-State Lottery Association forms. Five states (and Washington, D.C.) combine their lottery resources to make much larger jackpots for a new game called Lotto America.
1992	Lotto America, by now comprising 15 states, changes its name to Powerball. (Today, 44 states and territories participate.)
1996	Another huge, multistate lottery, the Big Game, starts up, offering multimillion-dollar prizes in Georgia, Illinois, Maryland, Michigan, Virginia, and Massachusetts.
2002	The Big Game changes its name to Mega Millions. At the time, 10 states participated. Today, 44 states, the District of Columbia, and the U.S. Virgin Islands do.
2011	The Iowa Lottery introduces the first lottery smartphone app, allowing players to check to see if their numbers won or lost.
2012	Why go inside? The Minnesota Lottery makes it even easier to buy lottery tickets, allowing the installation of self-service sales terminals at gas pumps and ATMs.
2013	The Georgia Lottery introduces Keno…played over the internet.
2016	Powerball reaches $1.58 billion on January 13, 2016, the first ever jackpot worth more than a billion dollars. It's won by three people, one each in California, Florida, and Tennessee.

What's next? Digital technology is changing so fast that it's hard to predict. Smartphone apps that can buy instant lottery tickets? Virtual reality lotteries? All we can say is, "Alexa, buy me a lottery ticket."

More good news: Germs can travel through up to 10 layers of toilet paper.

WHY IS A RAVEN LIKE A WRITING DESK?

Is there an answer to Lewis Carroll's unanswerable riddle in his classic 1865 novel, Alice's Adventures in Wonderland? And if there is an answer to the raven riddle, and it's nonsense, does it still matter?

CHAPTER 7: A MAD TEA PARTY

"There was a table set out under a tree in front of the house, and the March Hare and the Hatter were having tea at it: a Dormouse was sitting between them, fast asleep, and the other two were using it as a cushion, resting their elbows on it, and talking over its head. 'Very uncomfortable for the Dormouse,' thought Alice; 'only, as it's asleep, I suppose it doesn't mind.'

"The table was a large one, but the three were all crowded together at one corner of it: 'No room! No room!' they cried out when they saw Alice coming. 'There's *plenty* of room!' said Alice indignantly, and she sat down in a large arm-chair at one end of the table."

It is then that the Mad Hatter asks Alice the infamous riddle: "Why is a raven like a writing desk?" After considerable hemming and hawing (and realizing she doesn't know much about ravens or writing desks), Alice finally gives up and asks the Mad Hatter the answer. "I haven't the slightest idea," he says.

Neither, it turns out, did Lewis Carroll (real name: Charles Dodgson). Had he known how incredibly popular his book would become, maybe he would have given the riddle a little more thought. Much to his delight, *Alice* was an instant hit, selling out its entire print run in a short time. (Even the notoriously stodgy Queen Victoria said she was amused.) And the more copies that sold, the more readers wanted to know: why *is* a raven like a writing desk? Despite Carroll insisting over and over (and over) that the Mad Hatter's riddle has no answer, his fans continued to pester him for it.

GO ASK ALICE

This went on for 30 years. Then, in the foreword to the 1896 edition of *Alice*, Carroll offered this explanation: "I may as well put on record here what seems to be a fairly appropriate answer, viz: 'Because it can produce few notes, tho they are very flat; and it is nevar put with the wrong end in front!' This, however, is merely an afterthought; the Riddle, as originally invented, had no answer at all."

That's what Carroll originally turned in to his publisher. He deliberately misspelled the word *never* as "nevar"—which is *raven* spelled backward. Whatever joke or clue

Processed cheese is 49 percent cheese—the rest is additives and filler.

he meant by the misspelling was lost when a dutiful copyeditor "corrected" the word to *never*. Carroll died soon after, *nevar* having gotten the chance to correct his incorrection…not that it would have mattered.

Despite the author's insistence that the nonsensical riddle has no answer—scholars, writers, and casual *Alice* fans alike have spent the last 150-odd years trying to eke some sort of meaning out of it. One popular theory is that Carroll wrote *Alice* at a pub called Ravensworth Arms, so perhaps the Ravensworth *was* his writing desk. Another intriguing theory: Carroll was interested in the occult, so maybe the answer is that both ravens and writing desks can help one commune with the dead. Could that be what horror author Stephen King had in mind when he was writing his 1977 novel *The Shining*? In one passage, the hotel's evil spirits torment a little boy by asking him: "Why is a raven like a writing desk? The higher the fewer, of course! Have another cup of tea!"

GUESSING GAME

Dozens more possibilities have been put forth over the years in articles, essays, and even magazine contests. Here are some intriguing attempts to answer the riddle: why is a raven like a writing desk?

- "Both have quills dipped in ink."
- "Because it slopes with a flap."
- "Because one has flapping fits and the other fitting flaps."
- "The notes for which they are noted are not noted for being musical notes."
- "Because one is a crow with a bill, while the other is a bureau with a quill!"
- "A raven eats worms; a writing desk is worm-eaten."
- "Because they are both used to carri–on de–composition."

- "Because it bodes ill for owed bills."
- "Because one is good for writing books, and the other better for biting rooks."
- "Because a writing desk is a rest for pens, and a raven is a pest for wrens."
- "Because you cannot ride either of them like a bicycle."
- "Because Poe wrote on both." (Edgar Allan Poe's most famous poem is "The Raven.")
- "There is a 'b' in both and an 'n' in neither."

CURIOUSER AND CURIOUSER

That last answer was provided by *Brave New World* author Aldous Huxley in 1928, and it makes about as much sense as any of the others. Perhaps it was Alice herself who had the most fitting response to the Mad Hatter…and to Carroll: "I think you might do something better with the time than wasting it in asking riddles that have no answers."

Why? Why? The inability to pronounce "r" sounds is called…"rhotacism."

JURASSIC PARK, STARRING JIM CARREY

Some roles are so closely associated with a specific actor that it's hard to imagine he or she wasn't the first choice. But it happens all the time. Can you imagine, for example…

🎬 JACK NICHOLSON AS ROY NEARY

(CLOSE ENCOUNTERS OF THE THIRD KIND, 1977)

While Steven Spielberg was in preproduction on *Close Encounters*, every so often someone would knock on his office door and say something like, "Nicholson is too crazy," or "Pacino has no sense of humor." That someone was Richard Dreyfuss, who'd had his eye on Spielberg's alien movie ever since the two had discussed it while filming *Jaws* in 1975. Spielberg's first choice to play Roy, an Indiana utility worker who sees a UFO, was Hollywood's reigning "King of Cool" Steve McQueen, but he turned it down because he couldn't cry on cue (a trait he thought was necessary for the character). Jack Nicholson was nearly cast, but he couldn't commit to a long shoot. Spielberg also considered Al Pacino, Dustin Hoffman, James Caan, and Gene Hackman. But Dreyfuss's door-knocking campaign paid off, and he got the part.

🎬 MARK WAHLBERG AND ANNE HATHAWAY AS PAT and TIFFANY

(SILVER LININGS PLAYBOOK, 2012)

Writer-director David O. Russell originally had Vince Vaughn and Zooey Deschanel in mind for this romance about mental illness and positivity. But Russell was having so much trouble adapting Matthew Quick's 2008 novel that he put it aside and made *The Fighter* with Mark Wahlberg, which was a big hit with audiences and critics. So, when Russell returned to *Playbook*, he had his pick of A-listers to choose from, and cast Wahlberg along with Anne Hathaway.

Not long after, Hathaway abruptly left the project due to "scheduling conflicts with *The Dark Knight Rises*"…or so it was reported in the press. Neither Hathaway nor Russell has given any details on what actually went down (there were rumors of creative differences), but Hathaway's departure opened up a role that several other leading ladies had been coveting—including Elizabeth Banks, Kirsten Dunst, Angelina Jolie, Blake Lively, Rooney Mara, and Rachel McAdams. But the part went to 21-year-old newcomer Jennifer Lawrence. "She shares with the character a degree of confidence and a degree of directness about her," explained Russell, "that is really refreshing and unencumbered by preciousness or neuroticism."

Before he made cookies, Famous Amos was a talent agent who signed Simon and Garfunkel.

But there was a problem: Lawrence still had to finish filming *Hunger Games*, and Wahlberg had already signed on to star in the crime drama *Broken City*, so he had to leave before filming could begin. At that point, Russell already had someone else in mind to play Pat: Bradley Cooper. The following year at the Academy Awards, Lawrence took home the Best Actress Oscar for *Silver Linings Playbook*, and Hathaway won Best Supporting Actress for *Les Misérables*. Wahlberg's cop movie flopped.

🎞 JENNIFER LAWRENCE AS ALICE

(*ALICE IN WONDERLAND*, 2010)

"The only time I've ever been truly devastated by losing an audition," admitted Lawrence, "was Tim Burton's *Alice in Wonderland*." When she read for the part in 2008, she wasn't a big star yet, and she couldn't really do a British accent, so she didn't get it. (Not long after, Lawrence auditioned for the lead in *Winter's Bone*, which she did get.) Mia Wasikowska, the Australian actor who Burton did cast as Alice, wasn't his first choice. Burton's first choice: Frances Bean Cobain (daughter of Courtney Love and Kurt Cobain). But Cobain was only 17 years old—and she'd never acted—so she chose to go to college instead. Anne Hathaway was offered the part of Alice at one point, but she thought it was too similar to other roles she'd played, so Burton cast her as the White Queen. Amanda Seyfried and Lindsay Lohan were reportedly interested in Alice, too, but they all lost out to Wasikowska, whom Burton chose for her "gravity." *Winter's Bone* made Lawrence a star, and *Alice* made a billion dollars, so it worked out pretty well for everyone involved.

🎞 WESLEY SNIPES AS T'CHALLA

(*BLACK PANTHER*, 2018)

Thanks to standout performances in *Major League*, *Passenger 57*, *Demolition Man*, and *White Men Can't Jump*, Snipes was one of Hollywood's most bankable stars in the 1990s. And he wanted his next movie role to be the comic book superhero T'Challa, the Black Panther. Snipes assured the folks at Marvel Comics, which was close to bankruptcy and desperate for a hit film, that *Black Panther* would be huge. Columbia Pictures green-lit the project and brought in John Singleton (*Boyz n the Hood*) to direct, but Singleton wanted the movie to take place in the United States during the civil rights movement, whereas Snipes wanted it set in the futuristic African city of Wakanda, which would have cost a lot more money. That disagreement, and others, put *Black Panther* in "development hell." So Snipes found another superhero to play: Blade the vampire-hunter.

Blade (1998) was Marvel's first big-screen hit, and marked the beginning of its reign on Hollywood. Feeling empowered, Snipes wanted to return to *Black Panther*. "But ultimately," he told the *Hollywood Reporter* in 2018, "we couldn't find the right combination of script and director and at the time, the technology wasn't there to do what they had already created in the comic book." (His Black Panther suit was going to be a "leotard with cat ears.") By the time the Marvel Cinematic Universe got around to introducing Black Panther in 2016, Snipes had aged out of the role. But he says he's very supportive of Chadwick Boseman's take on the character and Marvel's depiction of Wakanda, which is pretty close to what Snipes had envisioned 25 years earlier.

🎬 JAMES STEWART AND BARBARA STANWYCK AS NORMAN AND ETHEL

(*ON GOLDEN POND*, 1981)

Ernest Thompson's play about a cantankerous "old poop" and the wife who puts up with him was so well received when it premiered off-Broadway in 1979 that it was only a matter of time before some Hollywood big shot scooped up the rights. That big shot was nearly James Stewart, who at 70 years old really needed a hit after his 1978 flop *The Magic of Lassie*. But the *It's a Wonderful Life* actor wasn't fast enough, and Jane Fonda bought the rights so she could star in *On Golden Pond* with her father, Henry Fonda…who happened to be Stewart's best friend. Katharine Hepburn was cast to play wife Ethel, but she broke her arm playing tennis a few weeks prior to filming. Just in case Hepburn wasn't able to heal in time, Barbara Stanwyck (who'd been in three previous films with Henry Fonda in the 1930s and '40s) was called in to replace her. After a pep talk from Fonda, Hepburn showed up on day one with a very sore arm (and was reportedly upset that a scene in which she picks up a boat with that sore arm was cut from the film).

On Golden Pond was the second-highest-grossing film of 1981 (after *Raiders of the Lost Ark*). Hepburn and Fonda, who'd never met prior to that fateful pep talk, won that year's Oscars for Best Actor and Best Actress. And Henry and Jane Fonda became the first (and so far only) father-daughter acting team to be nominated for Oscars. As for Stewart, he took a break from acting and invested his *Lassie* money in "real estate, oil wells, and a charter-plane company." (He became a multimillionaire.)

🎬 WILL SMITH AND BEYONCÉ AS JACKSON AND ALLY

(*A STAR IS BORN*, 2018)

Previous versions of *A Star Is Born* had left some pretty big shoes to fill: Janet Gaynor, Judy Garland, and Barbra Streisand as the up-and-coming performer; and Fredric March, James Mason, and Kris Kristofferson as the aging alcoholic who falls in love with her. So it was big news in 2002 when Warner Bros. announced that Joel Schumacher would direct Will Smith as the aging alcoholic (Smith also considered playing the up-and-comer) and Alicia Keys as the singer. But Keys turned it down because her agent thought that a singer playing a singer wouldn't be challenging enough. Jennifer Lopez was close to taking the part, but then, as often happens, the project fizzled due to scheduling conflicts.

Dinosaurs roamed the earth for about 800 times as long as humans have been around.

A *Star Is Born* picked up steam again in 2010 when Nick Cassavetes was hired to direct Will Smith and Beyoncé. Then Smith left (it's unclear why) and Russell Crowe was brought in, and then Cassavetes was out (also unclear why) and Clint Eastwood took over to pilot the film. Eastwood's first choice for the male lead: Leonardo DiCaprio, who considered it but decided instead to do Quentin Tarantino's *Django Unchained*. Also considered were Eddie Murphy, Robert Downey Jr., Christian Bale, and Jon Hamm. Next glitch: Beyoncé got pregnant in 2012, further delaying the project. Two singers were considered to replace her—Esperanza Spalding and Rihanna. There was still no male lead, so Eastwood looked at Tom Cruise (who showed off his singing chops in *Rock of Ages*), Eminem, Hugh Jackman, and Johnny Depp.

The first piece finally fell into place in 2015 when Bradley Cooper landed the part of Jackson. Then Warner Bros. decided to mold Cooper as a leading man/director à la Ben Affleck, so all of a sudden Eastwood was out and Cooper was given the helm. Next glitch: by that time, Beyoncé was the biggest star in the world and Warner Bros. could no longer afford her. But the producers already had someone else in mind for the role of Ally: Lady Gaga. The studio heads weren't convinced that Gaga—known for her over-the-top stage performances—could play a humble young singer. "It wasn't unanimous until we did the screen test," said producer Bill Gerber, "and when they saw it, it took them seconds to say yes." All that waiting was worth it, as *A Star Is Born* was a critical and box office success, and left even bigger shoes to fill for the next *Star* reboot.

🎬 SIMON PEGG AS SCOTT LANG

(*ANT-MAN*, 2015)

British writer-director Edgar Wright had wanted to bring Marvel's littlest Avenger to the big screen since 2003, when he was making *Shaun of the Dead*. Wright spent much of the next decade developing *Ant-Man*, and rumors were swirling that he'd be making it with his longtime collaborator, Simon Pegg. After years of speculation, in 2013 Pegg officially took himself out of the running, for two reasons: "[Wright] has to spread his wings as a director and be seen not to just come with me as a package," and "Ant-Man…has to be a lot younger than me. If Edgar asked me, I'd think about it. But as his friend and his lawyer, I would advise strongly against asking me." (His lawyer?)

Wright didn't ask Pegg. He considered Ewan McGregor, who's never showed much interest in playing a superhero, and Adrien Brody, who was reportedly very interested. But in the end, Wright didn't want a typical Hollywood hunk; he wanted an "everyman" comic actor. It came down to Joseph-Gordon Levitt, who'd previously turned down *Guardians of the Galaxy*, and Paul Rudd, best known for his comedic turns in *Anchorman* and *40-Year-Old Virgin*. When Rudd got the part, his nine-year-old son said, "Wow, I can't wait to see how stupid that'll be." (Also, Rudd was 44 when he was cast, a year older than Pegg.)

Wright, however, was losing passion for the project, especially after Disney bought Marvel and started making changes to his script. They wanted to include other superheroes, but Wright wanted it to be a stand-alone film. They wanted it to have a Hollywood feel, whereas Wright wanted to use his trademark quick-editing style. By that point, Wright felt like a "director-for-hire" and reluctantly abandoned the movie he'd been working on for ten years. (Wright's next film: *Baby Driver*.) Adam McKay, who'd worked with Rudd on *Anchorman*, was offered the job, but declined out of respect for Wright. At the last minute, the job went to longtime Marvel fan Peyton Reed, who'd directed Jim Carrey in *Yes Man*. Reed kept much of Wright's script and all of Wright's major casting choices, but he made it the typical Marvel film that Disney wanted. Has Wright ever seen *Ant-Man*? "No," he said in 2017, "It would kind of be like asking me, 'Do you want to watch your ex-girlfriend have sex?'"

🎬 JIM CARREY as DR. IAN MALCOLM
(*JURASSIC PARK*, 1993)

When *Jurassic Park*'s casting director Janet Hirshenson read Michael Crichton's dinosaur novel, she envisioned Jeff Goldblum as Dr. Malcolm, the snarky mathematician. But director Steven Spielberg wanted to look at a range of actors, so he also screen-tested Ted Danson, Michael Keaton, Johnny Depp, Steve Guttenberg, Michael J. Fox, Bruce Campbell, and Jim Carrey. It was down to Goldblum and Carrey, whom Hirshenson said "did terrific, but I think pretty quickly we all loved the idea of Jeff." Merely getting a part doesn't mean it'll end up on the screen, though. Just before filming, Spielberg told Goldblum that they were thinking of writing Malcolm out of the movie. Most of his lines would be given to Sam Neil's character. Goldblum argued that the Malcolm character was pivotal, and Spielberg ultimately decided to leave him in.

EXTRAS

- **Bette Midler's** biggest career mistake: "There was *Sister Act,* which was written for me, but I said: 'My fans don't want to see me in a wimple.' I don't know where I got that from. Why would I say such a thing? So Whoopi [Goldberg] did it instead and, of course, she made a fortune. I also didn't do *Misery* and Kathy Bates won an Oscar for it. That's not to say I would have. It was so violent and I had no relation to it. I was afraid."

- **Nicolas Cage** said the biggest roles he ever turned down were Aragorn in *The Lord of the Rings* and Neo in *The Matrix*. But he's glad he said no. Why? "I get to enjoy those movies as an audience member, because I don't watch my own movies."

RANDOM FIRSTS: 1927

Uncle John jumped into his patented Wayback Machine, spun the dial to a random year, and landed in the roaring '20s—1927, to be exact. That's the bee's knees!

January 7: The first official transatlantic telephone call is made between Walter S. Gifford, president of the American Telephone & Telegraph Co. (AT&T), in New York City, and Sir Evelyn Murray, the UK's Secretary of the Post Office, in London. The call lasts 4 minutes and 29 seconds. (It's the first *official* call because, a day earlier, two technicians had made the first *actual* call to prepare for this one. The American remarked, "Distance doesn't mean anything anymore. We are on the verge of a very high-speed world.")

January 15: The first sports broadcast takes place on BBC Radio. Former rugby star Teddy Wakelam gives a live account of a match in which England bests Wales 11 to 9.

March 11: The first armored truck robbery occurs near Pittsburgh, Pennsylvania. The Flatheads Gang blows up the truck and absconds with the cash. Gang leader Paul Jaworski will go to the electric chair two years later.

April 6: Pilot License No. 1—the first private pilot's license ever issued in the United States—goes to William P. MacCracken Jr., Assistant Secretary of Commerce for Aeronautics, and a former World War I flight instructor.

April 14: A Volvo Ö V4—an elegant, two-door convertible with a dark blue body and black fender wings—drives out of a factory in Gothenburg, Sweden. It's the first Volvo automobile ever produced.

May 20–21: Charles Lindbergh makes the first solo, nonstop transatlantic flight from Roosevelt Field, in Long Island, New York, to Le Bourget airport, just outside Paris, in his single-engine monoplane, the *Spirit of St. Louis*. A month later, four million New Yorkers will honor him with a ticker-tape parade.

June 1: *The Tower Treasure*, the first Hardy Boys mystery novel, is published. It's the first of 58 Hardy Boys books released between 1927 and 1979. (The books were written by several authors, all under the pseudonym of Franklin W. Dixon.)

September 7: In his San Francisco lab, American inventor Philo Farnsworth uses an "image dissector camera tube" to transmit the first image (a straight line) onto a picture screen. Broadcast television is born.

October 4: Using jackhammers and dynamite, workers begin carving into a granite rock face in the Black Hills mountain range near Keystone, South

Dakota. When completed in 1941, the sculpture of four presidents will be known as Mount Rushmore.

November 13: At 12:01 a.m., the first cars enter the Holland Tunnel (underneath the Hudson River) linking New Jersey and New York City. The tunnel had officially opened the day before, but only for foot traffic. About 20,000 people took the opportunity to walk the 1.6 miles through the longest underwater tunnel in the world.

December 2: The first Ford Model A automobile rolls off the line at the Ford factory in Detroit, Michigan. At the wheel is Henry Ford's son, Edsel. The "modern" Model A replaces the successful but outdated Model T, introduced in 1908. More than 4.3 million Model A's will be made before it's taken out of production in 1931.

December 3: *Putting Pants on Philip*, the first (Stan) Laurel and (Oliver) Hardy film, is released.

Bonus: The first Pez candies are produced in Vienna, Austria, by Eduard Haas in 1927, but the exact date is unknown. (The candy came in a small tin; the iconic Pez dispensers won't be introduced until 1949.)

* * *

A RANDOM BIT OF FACTINESS

Most Visited Amusement Parks in the World (2018)

Walt Disney World 20.4 million

Disneyland 18.2 million

Tokyo Disneyland 16.6 million

Universal Studios Japan 13.9 million

Year the world's population reached two billion: 1927.

THE CURSE OF GILES COREY

Giles Corey was a central figure in the Salem witch trials of 1692 (and a character in Arthur Miller's 1953 play about the trials, The Crucible). Corey got caught up in the mass hysteria of accusing people of witchcraft, and he paid for it with his life. But according to local lore...Corey had his revenge.

BEWITCHED, BOTHERED, AND BEWILDERED

In the spring of 1692, a handful of girls in Salem, Massachusetts, started acting strangely, falling into convulsive fits and screaming jags. During one of these episodes, the girls claimed to be possessed by the devil...and then they accused several Salem women of being witches, in cahoots with Satan. As absurd as this sounds, the local government and church officials believed the girls were telling the truth—it *would* explain their odd behavior—and also, they weren't far removed from the strict, God-fearing Puritans who'd settled the area about 60 years earlier.

That began one of the darker events in American history: the Salem witch trials. Over the course of 1692, more than 200 men, women, and children were accused of witchcraft. Many, obviously unable to prove that they were *not* witches, were convicted and executed. Nineteen people—most of them women—were hanged on Gallows Hill.

Before they could be prosecuted in the formal Court of Oyer and Terminer, the accused had to endure a brutal public "examination" before local magistrates— essentially a trial before the trial where the so-called witches had to answer for themselves. A local man, an 80-year-old farmer named Giles Corey, attended some of those examinations, watching judges and ministers berate young women who were accused by other young women of using evil magic.

A RANDOM BIT OF FACTINESS

It wasn't just humans who were tried for witchcraft in Salem. Seventeenth-century conventional wisdom held that witches kept an animal "familiar" (a supernatural spirit in the guise of an animal) to help them carry out their evil deeds. Result: dogs and cats were accused of witchcraft, and a few were even executed for it. One of the first women accused was a slave named Tituba, who admitted to using dark magic against two cats that had threatened her. In another case, two dogs were put down for suspicion of witchcraft, although one was found not-guilty after its death.

PERHAPS THERE'S A MORE REASONABLE EXPLANATION

Corey's wife, Martha, also attended the examinations…until she started to feel that it was all nonsense. She urged her husband to stop supporting the tribunals and reportedly tried to get him to stop attending them by hiding his horse's saddle. But in the hysterical environment of Salem at the time, all of that behavior looked suspicious—the only reason Martha Corey would be against the witch trials is if she *herself* were a witch. On March 21, 1692, Martha Corey was arrested by the sheriff of Salem on suspicion of witchcraft. Two days later, Giles Corey testified *against* her at an examination—his wife being a witch would explain why their ox suddenly got sick, or why he'd spotted her silently praying in front of the fire at night. (She must have been praying to Satan.)

Then, on April 18, 1692, the man who had pinpointed supposed witchery in his own wife was himself accused of witchcraft by five local women. *Now* he started to believe that all this witchcraft stuff was a sham. During Corey's examination, his hands were tied to prevent him from doing any witchcraft inside the courtroom, but he refused to give any more evidence of his wife's "evil" ways or admit to any wrongdoing of his own. Corey failed the examination, and his case advanced to a full trial that September. He pleaded not guilty to all charges but used a defense tactic called "standing mute"—he remained silent at every question from prosecutors and judges. That stopped the trial dead in its tracks.

BOARD 'EM

Under the English law that governed the colonies in 1692, the court was forced to respond to a prisoner who stood mute with *peine forte et dure*, "strong and harsh punishment." Corey's punishment: Sheriff George Corwin ordered him tortured. On September 17, 1692, the defendant was marched to an empty field next to the Salem jail, stripped of his clothes, and laid out on the ground. Authorities then placed a board on Corey, and on top of that board, heavy stones. Over the course of three days, they added more and more stones, increasing the crushing weight on Corey. When given the chance to make the pain go away, either by owning up to his "crimes" or agreeing to stop standing mute, Corey replied, "More weight!" On September 19, Corey died. (Cause of death: "Crushed by heavy stones.")

Before his execution, Corey prepared for the future. Knowing he'd either be killed for standing mute, or, if he went to trial, railroaded into a conviction for witchcraft and hanged, he deeded his land to his adult children. Under the law at the time, the sheriff could seize the property of anyone with a conviction, but Corey's canny arrangement got around that. Nevertheless, after Corey was executed by the colonial government

Popes can't be organ donors because "their bodies belong to the Church."

(as was Martha Corey), Sheriff Corwin extorted payment from Corey's children, threatening to seize the family's estate if they didn't pay him 11 pounds and six shillings. They paid up, having to sell their livestock and most of their possessions to do so.

I CURSE YOU!

But did Corey actually get the upper hand over the cruel sheriff who tortured and killed him, and then extorted his children? In addition to cries of "More weight!" as he lay under heavy rocks, some say Corey also shouted, "Damn you! I curse you and Salem!" in the direction of Sheriff Corwin. No one knows if that's true, but here's one thing that is known: In 1696 Corwin dropped dead of a heart attack.

Nearly 300 years later, in 1978, Essex County sheriff Robert Cahill suffered a heart attack *and* a stroke. He survived, but doctors were unable to determine the cause of his ailments. Greatly weakened by his health problems, Cahill retired and focused his energies on becoming a local historian. In the course of his research, he learned that every sheriff after Corwin had an office in the Salem jail, which overlooked the spot where Corey was crushed to death. He also discovered that every man who served as sheriff after Corwin either died in office or had to retire early because of heart- or blood-related issues. Apparently Corey hadn't cursed one sheriff of Essex County... he'd cursed *all of them*.

THERE'S A NEW SHERIFF IN TOWN

Despite Cahill's claims, Salem's death records from the 1700s and early 1800s are spotty at best. But there are a number of confirmed early exits for the sheriffs. In 1919 Sheriff Samuel A. Johnson died in office. So did Sheriff Arthur Wells in 1932, and his son, Sheriff Earl Wells, in 1964. Cahill's successor, Charles Reardon, seemingly beat the curse...because the sheriff's physical office was moved to a new prison in nearby Middleton. But in 1996 Reardon had to resign from office after pleading guilty to corruption charges.

According to local folklore, not only did Corey curse Salem, but his spirit still hangs around to make sure his words took effect. Over the years, there have been numerous eyewitness accounts of an elderly man wandering around the Howard Street Cemetery, Corey's "resting" place. Several people claimed to have seen him in 1914... right after a fire destroyed dozens of buildings in Salem. And that fire started very near Gallows Hill...the place where Martha Corey was hanged for witchcraft in 1692.

* * *

"It's easier to love humanity as a whole than to love one's neighbor." —**Eric Hoffer**

First hip-hop song to win the Best Original Song Oscar: Eminem's "Lose Yourself" from *8 Mile* (2003).

MMMM...GUEST STARS

*"Special guest stars" have always been a part of TV sitcoms. But no show
has ever had the volume or variety of famous guests as* The Simpsons *has.
Here's nearly every famous person who's ever visited Springfield (so far).*

MUSICIANS

- Michael Jackson
- Aerosmith
- Ringo Starr
- George Harrison
- Paul McCartney
- Linda McCartney
- Tony Bennett
- Sting
- Tom Jones
- Linda Ronstadt
- Barry White
- David Crosby
- Red Hot Chili Peppers
- The Ramones
- James Brown
- Robert Goulet
- James Taylor
- Tito Puente
- Paul Anka
- Smashing Pumpkins
- Trombone Shorty
- Plácido Domingo

- The Who
- The Moody Blues
- Cypress Hill
- Sonic Youth
- Peter Frampton
- U2
- Cyndi Lauper
- Dolly Parton
- Elton John
- The B-52s
- NRBQ
- Mick Jagger and Keith Richards
- Britney Spears
- BTO
- Kid Rock
- Willie Nelson
- 'N Sync
- REM
- Phish
- Lenny Kravitz
- Elvis Costello
- Alison Krauss and Union Station

- Brian Setzer
- "Weird Al" Yankovic
- Tom Petty
- The Baha Men
- Blink-182
- David Byrne
- Jackson Browne
- 50 Cent
- Metallica
- The White Stripes
- Sir Mix-a-lot
- Ludacris
- Lionel Richie
- The Dixie Chicks
- Fall Out Boy
- Chris Martin
- Clarence Clemmons
- Yael Naim
- The Who
- Katy Perry
- Lady Gaga
- Hank Williams Jr.

- OK Go
- Bob Boilen
- Joe C.
- Donald Fagan
- Common
- RZA
- Snoop Dogg
- Yo-Yo Ma
- Sammy Hagar
- Pharrell Williams
- Johnny Mathis
- Marvin Hamlisch
- The Decemberists
- Max Weinberg
- Sonny Rollins
- Justin Bieber
- Sigur Rós
- Little Richard
- Ted Nugent
- Eartha Kitt
- Rob Halford
- Glen Hansard and Marketa Irglova

COMEDIANS

- Steve Allen
- Bob Hope
- Jay Leno
- Bob Newhart
- Johnny Carson

- Conan O'Brien
- Mel Brooks
- Janeane Garofalo
- Bobcat Goldthwait
- Steven Wright

- Penn & Teller
- Jeff Ross
- Ellen DeGeneres
- Jon Lovitz
- Marc Maron

- Rob Reiner
- Sarah Silverman
- Tom Arnold
- Bruce Vilanch
- Andy Dick

After he was assassinated, John F. Kennedy's brain was stored in the
National Archives...until it disappeared in 1966.

- Jon Stewart
- Denis Leary
- Smothers Brothers

- Russell Brand
- Dick Cavett
- David Letterman

- Ricky Gervais
- Cheech and Chong
- Ricky Jay

- Judd Apatow
- Nathan Fielder
- Drew Carey

ATHLETES

- Magic Johnson
- Wade Boggs
- Jose Canseco
- Roger Clemens
- Ken Griffey Jr.
- Don Mattingly
- Steve Sax
- Mike Scioscia
- Ozzie Smith
- Darryl Strawberry
- Lisa Leslie
- Joe Frazier
- Gerry Cooney
- Johnny Unitas

- Tom Kite
- Bret Hart
- Joe Namath
- Mike Tyson
- Rosey Grier
- Troy Aikman
- Dan Marino
- Mark McGwire
- Andre Agassi
- Pete Sampras
- Venus Williams
- Serena Williams
- Larry Holmes
- Tony Hawk

- Oscar De La Hoya
- Tom Brady
- Warren Sapp
- LeBron James
- Yao Ming
- Michelle Kwan
- Randy Johnson
- Sal Bando
- Gene Tenace
- Elvis Stojko
- Cristiano Ronaldo
- Lance Armstrong
- Peyton Manning
- Eli Manning

- Kareem Abdul-Jabbar
- Dennis Rodman
- Terry Bradshaw
- Danica Patrick
- Shaquille O'Neal
- Matt Leinart
- Wayne Gretzky
- Charles Barkley
- Steph Curry
- Edwin Moses
- Jeff Gordon
- Chuck Liddell
- Joe Montana

ACTORS

- James Earl Jones
- George Takei
- Neil Patrick Harris
- Adam West
- Burt Ward
- Elizabeth Taylor
- Richard Dean Anderson
- Leonard Nimoy
- Brooke Shields
- Bette Midler
- Luke Perry
- Ernest Borgnine
- James Woods
- Meryl Streep
- Dennis Franz
- Mickey Rooney
- Suzanne Somers

- Mary-Kate and Ashley Olsen
- Tim Conway
- Alec Baldwin
- Kim Basinger
- Ron Howard
- Mark Hamill
- Mel Gibson
- Lucy Lawless
- Butch Patrick
- Betty White
- Paul Newman
- Jay North
- Gary Coleman
- Richard Gere
- Carmen Electra
- Andrew Rannells
- Daniel Radcliffe

- Michael Chiklis
- Leslie Mann
- Paul Rudd
- Seth Rogen
- Channing Tatum
- Ian McKellen
- Mr. T
- Isabel Sanford
- Nichelle Nichols
- James Caan
- Halle Berry
- Kevin Dillon
- Gal Gadot
- Tracy Morgan
- David Copperfield
- Emily Deschanel
- Billy Boyd

- Cat Deeley
- Treat Williams
- Susan Sarandon
- David Hyde Pierce
- Bob Denver
- Ed Begley Jr.
- Elliott Gould
- Gary Busey
- Jason Bateman
- Jennifer Garner
- Jennifer Tilly
- John C. Reilly
- John Lithgow
- Melanie Griffith
- Robert Wagner
- William H. Macy

First live-streaming presidential inauguration: Bill Clinton's in 1997.

NEWSMAKERS AND PUBLIC FIGURES

- Evan Marriott
- Buzz Aldrin
- Stephen Jay Gould
- Elon Musk
- Rupert Murdoch
- Tony Blair
- Rudolph Giuliani
- Mark Cuban
- Adam Silver
- Jeff Bezos
- Mark Zuckerberg
- Julian Assange
- Ted Sarandos
- Magnus Carlsen
- Ken Jennings
- Richard Branson
- Janet Reno
- Bill de Blasio

BROADCASTERS AND HOSTS

- Larry King
- Chick Hearn
- Dr. Joyce Brothers
- Jack LaLanne
- Dr. Demento
- Roy Firestone
- James Lipton
- Regis Philbin and Kathie Lee Gifford
- Jerry Springer
- John Madden
- Pat Summerall
- Pat O'Brien
- Nancy O'Dell
- Charlie Rose
- Casey Kasem
- Dr. Phil
- Keith Olbermann
- Dan Rather
- Kurt Loder
- Chris Hansen
- Terry Gross
- Huell Howser
- Bob Costas
- Marv Albert
- Ira Glass
- Dick Clark
- Michael Buffer
- Ed McMahon
- Leeza Gibbons
- The *American Idol* judging panel
- Don Pardo
- Jamie Hyneman and Adam Savage
- Alex Trebek
- Suze Orman
- Robert Siegel
- Rachel Maddow
- Anderson Cooper
- Carl Kasell
- Peter Sagal

CELEBRITY CHEFS

- Alton Brown
- Wolfgang Puck
- Tom Colicchio
- Gordon Ramsay
- Mario Batali
- Anthony Bourdain

WRITERS, ARTISTS, AND CREATORS

- Stephen King
- Amy Tan
- John Updike
- Stan Lee
- Robert Pinsky
- Helen Fielding
- J. K. Rowling
- Thomas Pynchon
- Tom Clancy
- Tom Wolfe
- Gore Vidal
- Michael Chabon
- Frank Gehry
- Jonathan Franzen
- James Patterson
- Stephen Sondheim
- Alan Moore
- Art Spiegelman
- Dan Clowes
- Neil Gaiman
- Nick Park
- Jim Jarmusch
- Will Shortz
- Merl Reagle
- Mitch Albom
- Gary Larson
- Marjane Satrapi
- Shepard Fairey
- Ken Burns
- Michael Moore
- George Plimpton
- David Mamet
- Martha Stewart
- Hugh Hefner
- Jasper Johns
- Robert Evans
- Alison Bechdel
- Roz Chast
- Dan Harmon
- Norman Lear
- John Baldessari
- Pendleton Ward
- Doris Kearns Goodwin
- Theo Jansen
- Joyce Carol Oates
- Robert McKee
- Richard Dawkins
- Harlan Ellison
- Neil deGrasse Tyson
- Stephen Hawking
- Matt Groening

Andy Warhol always wore the same brand of green underwear.

A PORTABLE HISTORY

Everyone recognizes a portable toilet when they see one, but you never knew much about them…until now.

The technical name for this convenience is "portable toilet." While they're commonly known as "Porta Potties," that's not a generic term—it's a trademarked brand name.

How they work: Human waste (and toilet paper) doesn't get flushed, it stays right where it landed, in a holding bin. There's an "output" slot on the outside to which the sanitation company—the firm that rents out and maintains the portable toilets—attaches a large hose. Using technology similar to that of a vacuum cleaner, they suck the mess into a large tank on a truck. With the portable toilet now empty, they refill the holding bin with bacteria-and-odor-fighting chemicals, then drive their truckload to a special sanitary cleaning facility that treats the waste.

Largest bank of portable toilets in the United States: Nearly 5,000 were ordered to accommodate attendees of President Barack Obama's first inauguration in 2009.

Cost to rent one? On average: $75 to $100 a day. (Though for longer periods, the price comes down significantly—roughly $300 a month.)

The average portable toilet holds 60 to 70 gallons of waste before it's too full to use.

Most people *really* hate using them. A poll by a portable toilet manufacturer found that 95 percent of women and 93 percent of men either lay toilet paper over the seat…or "hover" above it.

The portable toilet's distinctive smell is technically "cherry." It's the easiest and cheapest "flavor" of deodorizer available, so most companies go with that one. ("Bubble gum" is a distant second.)

That's a lot of butts: The average portable toilet lasts for about 10 years. They're made of high-density polyethylene—plastic—which doesn't rot and isn't porous, meaning germs don't stick around.

It seems like there's never enough of them at outdoor events, but portable toilet companies have some formulas they follow. The rule of thumb for outdoor concerts and festivals is one toilet per 60 people. For marathons, it's one toilet for every 10 participants—competitive runners drink a lot of water (and pee a lot more), and can't stand around waiting.

Largest bank of portable toilets in the world: About 8,000 were needed for the religious pilgrims who visited German-born Pope Benedict's open-air mass in Munich in 2006.

Good news? Every day you produce enough saliva to fill a wine bottle.

EVEN GANDHI HATED OHIO STATE!

Every week in the fall, ESPN sends its College GameDay crew to broadcast a football game from a major college campus. Students and fans clamor to appear on TV behind the hosts, and they achieve this by displaying colorful homemade signs with clever messages…like these.

I TRIED TO CHANGE MY PASSWORD TO "NAVY" BUT GMAIL SAID IT WAS "TOO WEAK"

DEAR MOM AND DAD, NO MATTER WHAT HAPPENS TODAY, TUITION IS DUE ON MONDAY

THE 3RD GRADE IS TOUGHER THAN THE ACC

EVEN LEBRON LEFT OHIO

RUSSIA HACKED THE RANKINGS

IF YOU CAN READ THIS SIGN YOU ARE CLEARLY NOT AN ALABAMA FAN

THE LAST TIME OLE MISS WON THE SEC JFK WAS PRESIDENT

THE ALPHABET HAS MORE W'S THAN TEXAS

Don't mess with Texas: In 2010 the City of Houston banned inflatable tube men…

THIS SIGN HAS WON AS MANY NATIONAL CHAMPIONSHIPS AS OREGON

I DON'T ALWAYS TALK TO AUBURN GRADS...BUT WHEN I DO I ORDER FRIES

VILLANOVA LOOKED @ THE ECLIPSE WITHOUT GLASSES

WHO CARES ABOUT FOOTBALL, BRING HOCKEY BACK!

EVEN GANDHI HATED OHIO STATE!

AT LEAST WISCONSIN DOESN'T HAVE DETROIT

WHY DOESN'T ARMY FOOTBALL HAVE ITS OWN WEBSITE? THEY COULDN'T STRING TOGETHER 3 "W'S."

EVEN FORREST GUMP GOT INTO ALABAMA

I SKIPPED MY COURT DATE FOR THIS

...and other "attention getting devices" used by businesses to attract customers.

STUNTS GONE WRONG

Performing movie stunts is one of the most dangerous professions in the United States, with a fatality rate of 2.5 per 1,000 injured. A lot of time and careful preparation go into executing a stunt, and nearly all go as planned. Here are a few that resulted in fatalities.

xXx (2002)

Stuntman: Harry O'Connor

Story: O'Connor was a former Navy SEAL who became a well-known California stuntman. While doubling for star Vin Diesel in a chase scene for the extreme-sports action film, O'Connor was paragliding on the Vltava River in Prague, Czech Republic. Pulled along by a speedboat, he was supposed to slide down the long line and pass under a bridge, missing it by inches. O'Connor, 45, had successfully performed the stunt once already, but they decided to do one more take. Something went wrong, and he crashed into the bridge, breaking his neck. He died on the spot. "Stuntmen know they are in danger," said director Rob Cohen. "They make their living through danger. Most of the time, it's all right. Sometimes, unfortunately, it isn't."

DEADPOOL 2 (2018)

Stuntwoman: Joi "SJ" Harris

Story: Harris was an experienced motorcycle rider who was working on her first film as a stuntwoman when tragedy struck. On the Vancouver set of *Deadpool 2*, Harris was doubling for Zazie Beetz for a scene in which her character, Domino, is riding her motorbike down the street. She was supposed to go only 10 miles per hour, but for some unknown reason, Harris sped through the stop mark and accelerated to 50 mph. She hit a curb and was thrown through the plate-glass window of a nearby building. Because Domino wasn't wearing a helmet in the scene, neither was Harris. She died at the scene.

TOP GUN (1986)

Stuntman: Art Scholl

Story: A big reason this movie about elite U.S. Navy fighter pilots was such a hit (other than Tom Cruise) was for its impressive array of aerial stunts. With over 30 years of stunt pilot experience, Art Scholl was among the best in the business. But something went wrong while he was performing what's called a flat spin. That's when the plane seems to be spinning out of control; it takes a skilled pilot to regain control. "I've got a problem here," said Scholl, on his radio. "I have a real problem." Those were his last recorded words before the aircraft crashed into the Pacific Ocean off the coast of San Diego. The cause of the accident was never determined, and neither Scholl's body nor the plane were ever recovered.

Monkeys floss.

FOR YOUR EYES ONLY (1981)
Stuntman: Paolo Rigoni
Story: The 12th entry in the James Bond franchise features one of the most thrilling chase scenes in movie history. A motorcycle rider chases Bond, who is skiing down a bobsled track right in the middle of a race. On the last take, a bobsled overturned and one of the riders—23-year-old Rigoni—was trapped beneath it. He didn't survive. Surprisingly, although several other stunt performers have suffered serious injuries, this is the only fatality in 26 Bond films.

VAMPIRE IN BROOKLYN (1995)
Stuntwoman: Sonja Davis
Story: Davis was doubling for Angela Bassett in this Wes Craven/Eddie Murphy horror flop. In what should have been a routine stunt, Davis, hanging from a building, was going to fall 42 feet onto a large airbag. Her family was visiting the set that day, and they all watched. "Are you sure?" they heard her ask, presumably to the director. Those were her last words. Davis fell onto the airbag as planned, but it had too much air in it, causing her to bounce off into another building headfirst, which caused massive head trauma that led to her death days later. Davis's mother, Wanda Sapp, sued Paramount for $10 million for failing to provide the proper safety equipment.

COMES A HORSEMAN (1978)
Stuntman: Jim Sheppard
Story: This Western drama is notable for having a stuntman-turned-actor, Richard Farnsworth, receive an Oscar nomination for Best Supporting Actor. It's also notable for the tragedy that occurred on location in Colorado. Jim Sheppard was doubling for Jason Robards's character, who gets dragged by a horse to his death. The horse was supposed to run straight through the middle of a wide gate, but it veered to the side… and Sheppard's head hit a fence post. He was airlifted to a hospital in Cañon City, where he later died from his injuries. Filming on the movie was completed the next day.

THE EXPENDABLES 2 (2012)
Stuntman: Kun Liu
Story: This trilogy features 1980s action stars attempting to relive their glory years. The second unit (without any of the main actors present) was shooting a scene in Bulgaria. Stuntmen Kun Liu and Nuo Sun were both on an inflatable boat when an explosion killed Kun, who was only 26. Nuo was critically injured but survived. After the accident, a Bulgarian newspaper reported that the two stuntmen were the doubles for stars Sylvester Stallone and Jet Li, but that turned out to be false. Kun's family later filed a wrongful death lawsuit, claiming the filmmakers "recklessly organized" the stunt.

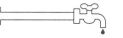

First person asked to join the cast of *Saturday Night Live* in 1975: Gilda Radner.

TRUCK SPILLED *WHAT?*

On page 280, we told you about some messy truck spills of the edible kind. What the following accounts lack in grossness… they make up for in weirdness.

MONEY

 Imagine you're driving down the highway and suddenly it starts raining $20 bills. That actually happened in May 2018 on I-70 in Indianapolis when the back door of a Brinks armored truck came open. "I was in shock at first," one motorist, Jazmyne Cooper, told *Inside Edition*. Although she was "very tempted," she didn't help herself to any of the cash. But several other people did, including a school bus driver who slammed on the brakes, jumped out, grabbed a pile of cash, and drove away. It's uncertain how much money left the scene, but the Brinks truck was carrying around $600,000. As one police officer said, "Some people should have enough to buy a car."

 Eight million dimes—total: $800,000—ended up on I-15 in Nevada after a semi left the road, hit the guardrail, and overturned. Because the crash occurred at 3:30 a.m., there wasn't a mad scramble to steal the loose coins. Even if there had been, the Nevada Highway Patrol quickly cordoned off the area as if it were a crime scene, and stood guard while workers picked up eight…million…dimes.

 In 2010, on a busy freeway in Foggia, Italy, an armored truck burst a tire, sideswiped a car, and then crashed into a barrier. The trailer burst open, and 2 million euros' worth of 1- and 2-euro coins poured out. "It was a real free-for-all," said one eyewitness. "People were running across the lanes to reach the coins. I am amazed no one was killed." By the time it was all cleaned up, at least 50,000 euros ($70,000) had been stolen. The worst part, according to a police officer: "Two drivers in the truck and two in a car were hurt, but no one was bothered about them."

WEAPONS

 Here's something you don't see every day: a Tomahawk cruise missile in the middle of the highway…in the Bronx. In 2006 a flatbed truck hauling the 20-foot long, 3,000-pound missile was on its way from Rhode Island to Virginia when it broke down on I-95 in New York City and was rear-ended by another truck, knocking the missile onto the highway. (Fortunately, there was no warhead on the missile.)

Communism pays: The London cemetery that is home to Karl Marx's grave charges an admission fee to visit his grave.

In July 2008, a semi left Minot Air Force Base in North Dakota carrying a booster rocket for a Minuteman III intercontinental ballistic missile. Not long into the trip, the truck left the road, and tipped over in a ditch. When military crews arrived to clean up the wreck, they were faced with a huge problem: Together, the truck and the rocket weighed 37 tons. Result: armed guards patrolled the crash site for an entire week until a crane arrived to remove the rocket. The mishap reportedly cost the military $5.6 million. Good thing the rocket wasn't armed—the accident occurred within the capital city of Bismarck (pop. 60,000). The cause of the crash? According to the U.S. Air Force, the driver became distracted by a large insect that flew in a window and landed on his back.

> **Armed guards patrolled the crash site for an entire week.**

INDUSTRIAL SUPPLIES

 A flatbed truck was hauling a large piece of "industrial construction equipment" in September 2017 on New York's Major Deegan Expressway when the equipment tumbled off its trailer. In the next lane was a charter bus carrying 20 people…and there was no time for the driver to swerve out of the way. The bus hit the equipment head-on, smashing the front window and mangling the front end. People, purses, and phones went flying as the bus came to an abrupt stop. None of the passengers were seriously injured, but they were all stranded on the side of the highway for half an hour until another bus arrived to rescue them.

In 2012 CTV News reported that a pickup truck lost "several industrial-sized buckets of white paint" on Canada's Halifax Harbour Bridge. The paint ended up splattered over 100 yards of the roadway. Cleanup crews arrived quickly, but not fast enough to prevent hundreds of vehicles from driving through the spill. Perhaps the worst affected by the white paint was the driver of a black convertible BMW. "I expect he'll be calling somebody," said Steve Snider of the Harbour Bridge Commission, who advised anyone with paint on their cars—or themselves—to call. (The driver's insurance company paid to clean up the mess.)

 Truck driver Robert Herman picked up a load of 2-pound steel "grinding balls" (total weight: 44,000 pounds) in Seattle in 2018, and was supposed to haul them 800 miles to Salt Lake City. However, only two miles into the journey, as Herman was driving up a steep hill in a neighborhood, the trailer door came open. The result looked like something out of a screwball comedy. "I'm looking back and I see all these balls rolling down the street," he said. No one was hurt, but several cars and probably one or two garden gnomes were damaged. Herman was issued a ticket. He promised to "check the load better" next time.

Testarossa means "redhead" in Italian, and a Ferrari Testarossa is named for its engine's cylinder heads, which are painted red.

WOOD AND EARTH

 It was a Texas-sized game of "pick-up sticks" on a Houston freeway after a lumber truck lost its load of two-by-fours in October 2018. Thousands of them went flying all over the place—one even pierced the windshield of a passing pickup truck. Bad news: six vehicles were involved in the crash. Good news: no one was seriously injured. Bad news: the wreck occurred at the beginning of the evening rush hour. Traffic stayed at a standstill well into the night as crews feverishly worked to pick up all those sticks.

 In 2017, on a rainy day on California's Highway 101, a driver lost control of a garbage truck hauling yard waste on a curve, and took out about 100 feet of the center divider before the truck landed on its side on the left shoulder. And then, only five minutes later, on the same stretch of road, "The same kind of truck, same company, loses control and overturns onto the *right* shoulder," said CHP Officer Jon Sloat. That's two trucks from one company, only five minutes apart, together covering the road with tons of leaves, grass, and branches onto both sides of the highway. The cause of the accident, according to the California Highway Patrol: they were driving too fast.

* * *

BLUES MUSICIANS HAVE THE BEST NICKNAMES

- Baby Tate
- Backwards Sam Firk
- Barbecue Bob
- Barrelhouse Chuck
- Johnny "Big Moose" Walker
- Otis "Big Smokey" Smothers
- Blind Lemon Jefferson
- Kenny "Blues Boss" Wayne
- Bumble Bee Slim
- Catfish Keith
- Cow Cow Davenport
- Furry Lewis
- Clarence "Gatemouth" Brown
- H-Bomb Ferguson
- Hip Linkchain
- Hollywood Fats
- Ironing Board Sam
- Johnny Drummer
- Laughing Charley
- Lazy Lester
- Mr. Blues
- Peg Leg Sam
- Piano Red
- Huey "Piano" Smith
- Pinetop Perkins
- Popa Chubby
- Rabbit Brown
- Seasick Steve
- Smoky Babe
- T-Model Ford
- Washboard Willie
- Paul "Wine" Jones

How to tell the Olsen twins apart: Ashley is shorter than Mary-Kate, and has a freckle above her lip.

HERE LIES ALEXANDER HAMILTON

If we'd written about Alexander Hamilton's grave site before mid-2015, this article would be a page or two shorter. But because one man was inspired by a history book, a whole new chapter has begun for a previously unsung Founding Father.

TRINITY CHURCHYARD

In 1804 Aaron Burr shot and killed Alexander Hamilton. In 2015 Lin-Manuel Miranda brought him back to life. But the story of Hamilton's final resting place begins in the 1660s when Dutch settlers in New Amsterdam started burying their dead on a small plot of land next to what is now Wall Street in Lower Manhattan. In 1697 the parish of Trinity Church built the first of three churches that have stood in that spot. The most recent is a Gothic building with a tall steeple completed in 1846. Once the nation's tallest building, the church is now dwarfed by skyscrapers. The graveyard's most famous occupant, Alexander Hamilton, rented pew number 92 at Trinity Church, even though he wasn't much of a churchgoer himself.

SELF-MADE MAN

What sets Hamilton apart from most of the other Founding Fathers is that he didn't come from a prominent family. So, unlike Washington, Jefferson, and Adams, his surname got him nowhere. Openly called a "bastard" by his contemporaries, Hamilton was born out of wedlock in 1757 in the Caribbean and was an orphan by age 11. As a teenager, he taught himself to read while working random jobs in St. Croix. He so impressed his elders that they paid for his secondary education in New York City. Hamilton arrived there in 1774 to attend King's College (now Columbia University), and was on a path to become a lawyer or a banker when he took up the fight against King George III and joined the militia. The young soldier worked his way up to become General George Washington's chief military aide during the Revolutionary War. A natural-born leader, Hamilton was later put in charge of the new Continental Army.

ON THE MONEY

One reason Hamilton's contributions aren't more widely known is that they dealt mostly with unglamorous pursuits, such as banking and deficits and economics. But his part in the founding of the United States was huge: he coauthored the "Federalist Papers," which led to the creation and then ratification of the U.S. Constitution (Hamilton was the only New Yorker to sign it). His input led to an independent judiciary, a professional

Cities with the most overall team sports titles: New York, Boston, Chicago, Montreal.

army, and an economy driven by industry and innovation. He later served as Secretary of the Treasury (America's first) under Washington, where he was the architect of the nation's banking and financial systems. As if that weren't enough, Hamilton also founded the U.S. Coast Guard and the *New York Post*. Also, unlike many of the other Founding Fathers who owned slaves, Hamilton was a staunch abolitionist who truly believed that all men are created equal. His most lasting legacy, however, is that his economic policies helped turn 13 weak colonies bankrupted by war into a strong United States. That legacy earned Hamilton a spot on the $10 bill…which used to be the main reason people even knew his name. That, and how he was killed.

I CHALLENGE YOU TO A DUEL!

> As a man who demanded satisfaction, Alexander Hamilton had a penchant for dueling.

As a man who demanded satisfaction, Alexander Hamilton had a penchant for dueling (an upper-class method of solving disagreements, in which two rivals face each other and fire their pistols at the same time). And he wasn't the most disciplined of the Founding Fathers. Any presidential aspirations Hamilton may have had were quashed in 1795 when, while serving in President Washington's cabinet, his extramarital affair with a woman named Maria Reynolds went public. He resigned and went home to New York to mend things with his wife, Eliza. He started practicing law and had a bunch of kids, but he couldn't keep himself out of trouble.

Hamilton had been in a few duels before, though none had led to a shot being fired—duels were more of a way for him to make a point. And that may be what he was up to in 1804, when he relentlessly taunted his political rival, Vice President Aaron Burr, whom Hamilton publicly called "unprincipaled, both as a public and private man." After successfully preventing Burr from first becoming U.S. president and then New York governor, Hamilton published an open letter full of vague insults (vague because he knew his lack of specifics would anger Burr) that ended with, "I trust upon more reflection you will see the matter in the same light with me. If not, I can only regret the circumstances and must abide the consequences."

There were consequences. As expected, Burr challenged Hamilton to a duel. At dawn on July 11, 1804, across the Hudson River in Weehawken, New Jersey, the two men faced off and fired their weapons. Hamilton's bullet hit a tree branch 12 feet above the ground. Burr's bullet tore through Hamilton's gut.

LAST RITES

Barely clinging to life, Hamilton was taken by boat back to Manhattan and placed in the upstairs bedroom of a friend's mansion. Knowing his end was near, Hamilton called for the Reverend Benjamin Moore, the rector of Trinity Episcopal Church, to give him communion, but Moore refused. Dueling, though technically legal at the time, was

Hawaiian Punch was first marketed as an ice cream topping.

frowned upon, so Moore (the future bishop of New York) didn't want it to appear as if the church approved of it. Besides, although Eliza was the devout Christian, Hamilton wasn't even a regular churchgoer.

Hamilton called for another reverend, who also refused (wrong denomination), so Hamilton called Moore back in and literally begged him for communion. With the reverend at his bedside, Hamilton professed his love of God and insisted that he'd never intended to shoot Burr, and that he forgave him for shooting him. (Some historians have speculated Hamilton told all this to the reverend in order to kill Burr's political career, which, true or not, is what happened.) Then he told the reverend that, if he were to recover, "I would employ all your influence in society to discountenance this barbarous custom." With Eliza and several of Hamilton's friends also putting pressure on Moore, he finally relented and gave the dying man communion. "I remained with him until 2 o'clock this afternoon," Moore wrote, "when death closed the awful scene—he expired without a struggle, and almost without a groan."

LAID TO REST

Hamilton's funeral was the largest that had ever taken place in New York City up to that point. Thousands of mourners paid their respects as his body was taken from Jane Street to Trinity Church. Even though Hamilton didn't attend the church regularly, he had a lot of ties to it. In the past, he'd offered the clergy his legal services, and as a young soldier-in-training, he'd performed drills in the churchyard. And several family members were already interred there, most recently Hamilton's son Philip. (Ironically, three years earlier, Philip was killed in a duel—against someone who insulted his father—in the same spot where his father would be killed three years later.) After Hamilton was eulogized by the governor of New York, he was laid to rest beneath a large white obelisk surrounded by four urns, at the edge of the graveyard next to an iron fence looking over Rector Street. His epitaph reads:

The PATRIOT of incorruptible INTEGRITY.

The SOLDIER of approved VALOUR

The STATESMAN of consummate WISDOM.

Whose TALENTS and VIRTUES will be admired

Long after this MARBLE shall have mouldered into DUST.

A WITNESS TO HISTORY

There have actually been three churches built on the site of Trinity Church. The first one, built in 1698, burned down during the Revolutionary War in the Great New York City Fire of 1776. The second, completed in 1790, was where George Washington and other Founding Fathers worshipped when New York was the nation's capital. In the winter of 1838, the 200-foot-tall church was heavily damaged by snow and had to be torn down. The third church, completed in 1846, was well within the debris field when the World Trade Center was destroyed in the terrorist attacks of September 11, 2001. The church was saved by a 70-year-old sycamore tree, which didn't survive. Today, an iron casting of the tree's roots are on display in the churchyard.

Looking up from Hamilton's grave site, the Freedom Tower looms overhead. Across Rector Street is an outlet shoe store. And all around you are hundreds of weather-beaten tombstones, some from as far back as the 1680s. At the base of Hamilton's grave, you're likely to find flowers, wreaths, and lots of coins—which makes a lot of sense for the man who established the U.S. Mint. The grave site was rededicated in 2014, and in 2018 the church underwent extensive renovations, making it more accessible to visitors. These days, there's almost always someone at the grave (when the churchyard is open). But until a few years ago, the most likely people you'd see there were Wall Street brokers taking their lunch break. Then a hip-hop musical turned it into the most visited graveyard in New York.

> **A TIP FROM UNCLE JOHN**
>
> Thinking of writing your own hit musical, like *Hamilton*? First, study the form by watching or listening to as many musicals as possible. You'll notice that they all have a similar structure, namely that songs aren't merely songs—they advance the action of the play, particularly the big emotional moments. Some experts say that the best way to start, after determining what your subject and story will be, is to figure out the emotional core of the play—what it's about, emotionally speaking. Knowing that can help you figure out the big moments best expressed through song, and you can plan your script around those.

WHO TELLS YOUR STORY?

Before *Hamilton* the musical, there was *Hamilton* the 2004 biography, written by Brooklyn-born journalist Ron Chernow. Chernow's sympathetic portrayal of Hamilton struck a chord that previous biographies hadn't. One reviewer described it as a "popular biography that should also delight scholars"; it spent three months on the *New York Times* best-seller list. And unlike Henry Wadsworth Longfellow's historically inaccurate poem that greatly embellished Paul Revere's midnight ride, Chernow tried to tell who Hamilton really was. "He had always been portrayed as this ferocious snob, the stooge of the plutocrats," said Chernow. "For most Americans, there was a feeling that he was a second- or third-rate founder. And yet the more that I read about his achievements, they were so monumental that I decided that they needed to be up there with those of George Washington, Thomas Jefferson, Benjamin Franklin et al."

And so did a rising Broadway playwright named Lin-Manuel Miranda, who read Chernow's book while vacationing in Mexico. Inspired, Miranda decided to

What's the difference between Broadway and Off-Broadway theaters?
Seats: Broadway theaters...

turn Hamilton's life into a hip-hop musical with minorities portraying the Founding Fathers, and he hired Chernow as a consultant, telling him, "I want historians to take this seriously"…not an easy task when a black Thomas Jefferson is rapping about meeting lots of ladies in Paris. But it worked.

Hamilton: An American Musical (starring Miranda as Alexander Hamilton) opened on Broadway—about six miles north of the Trinity Church graveyard—in August 2015. It became an instant phenomenon. Hamilton's grave site even gets mentioned in the musical's closing number, "Who Lives, Who Dies, Who Tells Your Story."

Before *Hamilton*, Hamilton's grave site seldom drew a crowd, except for yearly memorials on his birth and death dates. Thanks to the play, people now come every day. It's become something of a pilgrimage for fans to see the show and then pay their respects. "For years," said Rand Scholet, president of the Alexander Hamilton Awareness Society, "huge numbers of people have visited Washington's Mount Vernon, Jefferson's Monticello. Now Hamilton is getting his due."

HERSTORY

Located in the grass a few feet away from Hamilton's obelisk is an unassuming granite slab bearing the inscription:

E L I Z A

DAUGHTER OF

PHILIP SCHUYLER

WIDOW OF

ALEXANDER HAMILTON

INTERRED HERE

For 50 years after her husband's death, Eliza never remarried, and she visited his grave site often. Because she's a main character in both the book and the musical, her grave site now receives as many (some days more) gifts than her husband's. Largely forgotten until *Hamilton*, Eliza (or Betsey, as she was also called) is now being celebrated for, among other things, advocating for the building of the Washington Monument. She was on hand for the laying of the obelisk's cornerstone on July 4, 1848.

Hamilton fans even ask to see the grave of Eliza's sister, Angelica Schuyler Church, who had a brief flirtation with Alexander. Her remains are located inside a vault marked "Winchester."

A SINGULAR SENSATION

In April 2016, after *Hamilton* cleaned up at the Tony Awards and established itself as one of the most successful Broadway musicals of all time, a tourist snapped a photo that made headlines around the country. This one is from the *Hollywood Reporter:* "Lin-Manuel Miranda Pays Respects at Alexander Hamilton's Grave." (The fact that this photo was actually newsworthy is the kind of thing that pleases historians.) The musical was so influential, in fact, that it helped keep Alexander Hamilton's portrait on the $10 bill. He was initially going to be replaced by a woman, but in 2016 *Hamilton* fans helped convince the U.S. Treasury Department to instead replace Andrew Jackson on the $20 bill with abolitionist Harriet Tubman.

Why has it taken so long for Hamilton to get his due? As Chernow explains, it's because of who originally told the Founding Father's story: "Hamilton's political enemies were John Adams, Thomas Jefferson, James Madison, James Monroe—I just named presidents two, three, four, and five—and if history is written by the victors, history had very much been written by Alexander Hamilton's enemies."

THE CHURCHYARD TODAY

If you're looking for a quiet graveyard, Trinity Church is not for you. The cacophony of car horns, squeaking breaks, and sirens can make it difficult to imagine what it was like in colonial days when horse carriages clopped up and down Wall Street, and the church steeple was the tallest thing around. The churchyard is the oldest of three cemeteries in Manhattan run by Trinity Church. The other two are Trinity Church Cemetery and Mausoleum in Upper Manhattan, and the Churchyard of St. Paul's Chapel, which is still active today. A tour of all three cemeteries will take you to the graves of such luminaries as steamboat inventor Robert Fulton (1765–1815), whose monument is right next to Hamilton's, and colonial American printer William Bradford (1660–1752). At the Trinity Church Cemetery and Mausoleum, located on Riverside Drive overlooking the Hudson River, the most famous grave belongs to John Jacob Astor (1763–1848), a business magnate whose family was known as the "landlords of New York," and his son, millionaire John Jacob Astor IV, who died on the *Titanic.*

Bonus: In 1801 a New York sea captain named Robert Richard Randall left detailed plans in his will to create what would become the young nation's first retirement home on Staten Island. Until it closed in 1978, thousands of old sailors lived at Sailors' Snug Harbor, and most of them were buried there. (The cemetery made grim news in 2018 when more than 100 tombstones were discovered in a basement. They'd been taken there decades earlier to protect them from vandals, but now no one knows where the graves they belong to are.) The lawyer who drafted Randall's will: Alexander Hamilton.

Our final installment—on page 491—takes you to Monticello, the home of one of Hamilton's most bitter enemies.

Alan Stillman started TGI Fridays so he could meet the flight attendants and models that lived in his neighborhood.

THE BOOK OF NEIL

British author Neil Gaiman is known for his fantasy novels (Good Omens), spooky stories (Coraline), and comic books (The Sandman). He's also very quotable.

"The world always seems brighter when you've just made something that wasn't there before."

"The imagination is a muscle. If it is not exercised, it atrophies."

"I lost some time once. It's always in the last place you look for it."

"Life is always going to be stranger than fiction, because fiction has to be convincing, and life doesn't."

"Life is life, and it is infinitely better than the alternative, or so we presume, for nobody returns to dispute it."

"WHATEVER YOU HAVE TO SAY, MEAN IT."

"It is difficult to kill an idea because ideas are invisible and contagious, and they move fast."

"I've never known anyone who was what he or she seemed...or at least, was *only* what he or she seemed."

"You get ideas from daydreaming. You get ideas from being bored. You get ideas all the time. The only difference between writers and other people is we notice when we're doing it."

THE MYSTERY OF THE CRYSTAL SKULL, PART III

When last we visited the convoluted capers of the crystalline cranium, the occultists continued to cling to the conclusion that this cheeky chunk of quartz is indeed a magical Mayan remnant. (Part II is on page 329.)

THE LAB CRUSADE

"[The skull] is not powerful, not scary, and not at all what it purports to be." That's the conclusion of Jane MacLaren Walsh, an anthropologist at the Smithsonian Museum of Natural History in Washington, D.C. She's been studying Mesoamerican cultures and artifacts since the early 1990s. In November 2007, after Anna Mitchell-Hedges died, Walsh was finally able to get a good look at the purported "pre-Columbian artifact" (thanks to a loan from skull-keeper Bill Homann). Working with the British Museum, Walsh and her fellow scientists threw everything they had at the Mitchell-Hedges skull: electron microscopy, X-ray crystallography, computerized tomography, ultraviolet light, and more—including poring through everything they could find that was said or written by F. A. and Anna Mitchell-Hedges. After all was said and done, the scientists determined that the Mitchell-Hedges crystal skull "was probably made in Europe in the 20th century."

Walsh's findings are similar to those made five years earlier by Professor Ian Freestone of Cardiff University in Wales, who studied another crystal skull, supposedly Aztec in origin, that was sold to the British Museum in 1897. His analysis concluded that that skull was "probably made in 19th century Europe from a lump of poor quality Brazilian crystal."

MYTHS & FINDINGS

Now that the scientists, historians, and theists have had ample opportunity to study the skull, here's some of what they've found out.

Myth: The Mitchell-Hedges crystal skull was polished by hand using sand.
Findings: It was made by modern jeweler's equipment. The obsidian tools the Mayans used to make much of their artwork would have left marks in the quartz crystal that could be detected by a microscope, as virtually every other Mesoamerican artifact does. Tests have shown that the skull was made using a "wheeled instrument" that bore the "tell-tale signature of a metal tool augmented by diamond."

In 1985 Michigan declared Aretha Franklin's voice a state "natural resource."

Myth: The Mitchell-Hedges skull is unique.
Findings: According to Walsh, it's "a veritable copy of the British Museum skull, with stylistic and technical flourishes that only an accomplished faker would devise." The only difference between the two is that the eyes and teeth of the Mitchell-Hedges skull are more detailed.

Myth: The skull's ambient surface temperature is a constant 70° Fahrenheit, proving that it has some kind of internal power source.
Findings: It behaves no differently than any other chunk of quartz. Frank Dorland disproved that rumor at Hewlett-Packard back in 1970, but it still persists today.

Myth: The crystal skull is modeled after an ancient Mesoamerican person (or god).
Findings: A forensic artist named Gloria Nusse made a facial reconstruction based on the skull's features and concluded that the model was most likely a "young European woman."

Myth: The crystal skull is the product of "five generations of skilled craftsmen" and is "impossible to replicate, even with modern machinery."
Findings: *National Geographic* hired a crystal artist named Barry Liu to make an exact replica of the Mitchell-Hedges skull. He did it in eight days.

Myth: Ancient Mayans and Aztecs worshipped crystal skulls.
Findings: They didn't. In his book *Dream Catchers: How Mainstream America Discovered Native Spirituality*, historian Philip Jenkins writes that crystal skulls weren't really a thing until 19th-century Europe; they are merely "products of a generation of creative spiritual entrepreneurs." Skeptic Joe Nickell puts it even more bluntly: "The chief power of the skulls seems to be that of attracting the credulous, including some with fantasy-prone personalities, and transporting them to a mystical realm from which they return with addled senses. It seems likely that further revelations about the crystal skulls will best come, not from channeling sessions, but from science and scholarship."

WHAT HAPPENED AT LUBAANTUN

Perhaps the tallest tale of all is that Anna Mitchell-Hedges found the skull while on an expedition with her father to British Honduras (now Belize) in 1924. She said she could prove she was there because, when she returned to Lubaantun in 1989, some of the Mayans recognized her. What other proof does she have? None. "All my father's papers," she told a reporter in 1983, "were lost in Hatteras during a cyclone—photographs and all."

That doesn't explain why none of the other members of F. A. Mitchell-Hedges's Central American expeditions ever mentioned him finding the crystal skull, or why none of them could verify that Anna was ever there with him. The existing photographs (the ones that didn't get lost in a cyclone) don't show the skull or Anna.

According to the *Skeptical Inquirer*, an archaeologist named Dr. John Morris went to Belize to try and retrace Anna's steps, but he "couldn't find any of the tunnels or passages she described." So why make up such a fantastical account? Because the real origin of the crystal skull is a lot less glamorous.

THE REAL ORIGIN

In late 19th-century Europe, Mesoamerican artifacts were all the rage. Wealthy adventurers—the same types who went on African safaris to bring home big game treasures—funded expensive editions, where they basically pilfered sacred sites for trinkets and artifacts that they sold for a tidy profit to museums and collectors. It was such a booming business that Mexican—and later European—jewelers started making and selling fake ancient artifacts. Even then, these fakes riled science-minded archaeologists such as the Smithsonian's William Henry Holmes, who wrote as early as 1886 that it is easy for "a native artisan to imitate any of the older forms of ware [ceramics]; and there is no doubt that in many cases he has done so for the purpose of deceiving."

Despite archaeologists' warnings, newly made crystal skulls were readily passed off as ancient Mayan and Aztec in origin, even though they bore little resemblance to real artifacts made by those cultures. But most collectors didn't know that. As far as they were concerned, they had in their possession an impressive conversation piece that "the natives believe hold magical powers." According to anthropologist Jane MacLaren Walsh, "The first generation of fakes were made in Mexico…between 1856 and 1880. This 24-year period may represent the output of a single artisan, or perhaps a single workshop." Then European fakers got in on the act. One of these skulls was put on display at the British Museum in 1898. Sometime in the 1920s or '30s, a German jeweler—most likely in the town of Idar-Oberstein, which is known for its stunning quartz artworks—made a copy of that skull. The forged artifact then changed hands a few times before F. A. Mitchell-Hedges purchased it in London in 1943.

CRYSTAL CLEAR

Just because the crystal skull isn't a magical object brought to Atlantis by aliens doesn't mean it's not an amazing piece of craftsmanship. Even skeptics marvel at it. Here are some of its stats:

- **Material:** The Mitchell-Hedges crystal skull was made from a single block of clear quartz "rock crystal." The lower jaw, which is detached, was made from the same block.

- **Age:** It's most likely less than a century old. Unfortunately, as the British Museum explains, "Contrary to popular belief, there are no satisfactory scientific techniques which can be used to accurately establish when a stone object was carved."

- **Weight:** 11 pounds, 7 ounces. (A real human skull weighs about two pounds.)

- **Dimensions:** 7 inches long, 5 inches wide, and 5 inches high. The skull is anatomically accurate, but smaller than that of an adult.

- **Value:** It's difficult to come up with a dollar amount—there isn't really a going price for, as Joe Nickell described it, "an ancient artifact that's not really ancient but still has some interesting history." F. A. Mitchell-Hedges paid about the equivalent of $5,000 in today's money for it. An appraisal in the 1970s—when it was still thought to be a genuine ancient Mayan artifact—valued it at $500,000. But after Anna Mitchell-Hedges died in 2007, the skull was appraised for a paltry $3,000. If it were to actually go on the auction block, its status as the most famous crystal skull in the world *could* spark a competitive bidding war, but another auction doesn't seem to be the fate of this crystal skull.

DON'T STOP BELIEVING

Those who truly believe in the "mystical properties" of crystal skulls are unlikely to be dissuaded by scientific evidence. The going argument among the faithful is that the reason the Mitchell-Hedges crystal skull doesn't look like anything else the Mayans or Aztecs made is because it was made by even more ancient peoples, using alien technology too advanced for modern scientists to understand. According to author and "Crystal Skull Explorer" Joshua Shapiro, who claims to have searched Central and South America for the rest of the fabled 13, "The crystal skulls, in my opinion, are the ancient computers which have stored special and important wisdom and knowledge that humanity can access to help us create a peaceful world."

And even though Bill Homann made the skull available for scientific study, he says he still believes in its power, and he still honors the woman who entrusted it to him. According to Crystalskulls.com, Homann is "carrying out the wishes of Anna Mitchell-Hedges as he travels around the world making the famous crystal skull available directly to the public, instead of having it reside behind glass in a museum." There hasn't been much news about the skull in the last few years, but we did find this October 2017 Facebook announcement for a one-day event in Bellingham, Washington:

> **NEWS FLASH:** This is your special opportunity to have one of the most amazing experiences you may ever know, to encounter the most famous skull in the world, known as the Mitchell-Hedges Crystal Skull and the guardian Bill Homann. Could this skull be the lost skull of Atlantis?
>
> **PRIVATE VIEWING SESSIONS:** 10:30 a.m. to 2:30 p.m. — $25 for 15 minutes.

Makeup maker Max Factor's real name: Maksymilian Faktorowicz.

THE SINISTER WORLD OF CYBERCRIME, PART III

In the final installment of our cybercrime series, we offer some light reading on cyberterrorism and cyberwarfare, which sound implausible…but are actually more likely threats than you think. (Part II of the story is on page 348.)

WEAPONS OF MASS DISRUPTION

It may sound like the stuff of Hollywood movies, but some cybercrimes actually *can* endanger entire cities or even nations. It's called cyberterrorism, politically motivated computer attacks intended to cause fear or disruption. Former telecommunications executive John Mariotti warns about this kind of cyberattack: "We worried for decades about WMDs—weapons of mass destruction. Now it is time to worry about a new kind of WMDs—weapons of mass disruption." In May 2017, cyberterrorists launched a malicious *ransomware* program called Wanna Decryptor, or WannaCry, which caused a global crisis for four days. By some estimates, it infected 400,000 computers, holding their data hostage and demanding ransom from each user before access to their data would be restored. Victims were suddenly greeted with the message: "Ooops, your files have been encrypted!" along with information on how to pay the ransom ($300 in the cryptocurrency Bitcoin) and two heart-pounding countdowns (three days until the ransom doubles and seven days until the data is permanently deleted).

Not only did the malware sabotage personal computers, it also infected corporate computers that controlled systems in hospitals, airports, factories, and more. Flights were canceled, emergency rooms turned away ambulances, FedEx halted shipping, and manufacturing plants were shut down. Britain's medical centers were especially hard-hit: 37 hospitals were incapacitated, including some that took themselves offline to avoid being attacked by WannaCry. In China, gas stations and at least one police department were unable to provide services. According to Interpol, it was the biggest ransomware attack ever. From lost revenue to lost data, it caused $4 billion in damage, and it was still infecting computers in 2018.

How did WannaCry cause such pandemonium?

- Unlike most ransomware, which starts with phishing e-mails, WannaCry scanned computers for vulnerabilities, specifically exploiting flaws in Microsoft Windows operating systems older than Windows 10.
- If it detected a weakness, it forced the computer to run the ransomware, which encrypted files and demanded the ransom.

The robot WALL-E from *WALL-E* was named after Walter Elias Disney.

- WannaCry is a worm, which means that it travels automatically to other computers on the network without needing people's help to spread it.
- The malware took advantage of the fact that many computer users don't back up their data. According to the security software company Barkly, only 42 percent of ransomware victims fully recover their files.
- Evidence suggests that the attackers' main goal was to cause chaos, not to make money. As the cybersecurity company Symantec notes, the payment collection system they designed was oddly primitive. There was no way to easily see which victims had paid, nor did there seem to be an automated process to decrypt files—it required the hackers to decrypt them manually. Less than 1 percent of victims paid the ransom.
- The worm exploited known vulnerabilities in Microsoft systems that would've been fixed if Windows users had simply clicked "download update now" instead of closing the annoying pop-up reminders.

Here's the kicker: The cyberterrorist attack was made possible by…the National Security Agency (NSA). To spy on terrorists, agents had been developing hacking tools—which were stolen by hackers and leaked online a few weeks earlier. Although the designers of WannaCry haven't been caught, U.S. authorities blame a group linked to North Korea. Tech reporter Brian Fung sums up the disaster: "The story of Wanna Decryptor, ultimately, is the story of nearly all weapons technology: Eventually, it will get out. And it will fall into the wrong hands."

HACKERS WIELD ALL THE POWER

Though WannaCry didn't cause permanent physical damage, for years U.S. officials have warned that cyberterrorists might launch a more harmful attack. Especially vulnerable are smart cities, which rely on computers to collect data to run services and infrastructure. According to Peter J. Beshar, a lawyer who counsels on cyberthreats, "As we move closer to a world of smart cities, driverless cars and a connected everything, the potential for crippling physical attacks only increases." The U.S. power grid would be the most probable target, according to cybersecurity professionals. Most likely, the attackers would shut down power for a few hours. If they somehow managed to sabotage power grids for weeks or months—which experts say would be difficult, but not impossible—widespread panic would ensue, because hospitals, transportation, food, and nearly all other services are dependent on electricity.

Alarmingly, in March 2018, the FBI and the Department of Homeland Security reported that a cyberattack on power plants was no longer hypothetical; hackers had already breached our infrastructure. The Russian government, they charged, had penetrated the systems of American nuclear generators, aviation companies, water

Studies show: Whenever you hear a "Man walks into a bar" joke,
you likely always picture the same bar.

facilities, and—where it found the most success—power plants. Over a two-year campaign, hackers used a multipronged approach:

- The perpetrators obtained employees' login credentials through *spear phishing*—e-mails targeted to people who are likely to be fooled because the message comes from someone they know. Example: you get an e-mail from your manager asking you to fill out a self-review so you can get a raise. You open the attachment, naturally, and hackers gain entry to your computer. (More bad news: there's no raise.)
- The cyber intruders also created *watering holes*—an attack strategy that targets trusted industry websites, including infrastructure trade journals. By altering the websites' code, the hackers captured usernames and passwords of frequent visitors to those sites.
- Armed with stolen credentials, the Russian hackers logged into energy companies, set up local administrator accounts, and installed programs on the networks that recorded confidential information. For example, they observed how power is generated and took screenshots of a power grid's control panels to determine what switches to flip.

RED ALERT!
The news that Russian criminals had achieved operational access to U.S. infrastructure, meaning they had the ability to shut off circuit breakers, sent shock waves across the country. Although cyber intruders had sabotaged power grids in Ukraine, they'd never been known to infiltrate American power companies. It's also notable that U.S. intelligence blamed Russia's government, not just rogue hackers. What's even more stunning about the power the hackers wielded is that they haven't done anything with it—they haven't caused blackouts or mass hysteria…but maybe they're just awaiting further orders.

HIGHLY SPECIALIZED CYBERWARFARE
Imagine that the Russian government did sabotage U.S. infrastructure. That would be considered cyberwarfare, in which a country or international organization launches a cyberattack on another country. It could cause damage or even deaths, and most worryingly, cyberwarfare could trigger a war with real military strikes. Neither the United States nor Russia would risk it…right?

Apparently, the United States took that gamble when it (allegedly) partnered with Israel to develop the world's first cyberweapon, which was launched at Iran in 2009. Many nations were concerned that Iran was developing nuclear weapons, so a sophisticated worm called Stuxnet was designed to target that nation's nuclear facilities. Although the worm spread to computers worldwide, it acted only on those that controlled

specific sites in Iran, eventually infiltrating the nation's largest nuclear facility, located near Natanz. That in itself is remarkable because the highly secure facility is air-gapped, meaning its computers are completely isolated from the internet and considered unhackable. In 2014 the *New York Times* reported that NSA agents can tap into air-gapped computers using a transmitter planted on the computer, radio frequency signals, and a cell phone—from up to eight miles away. In this case, though, experts decided the worm was probably carried in on a USB stick by an employee, either knowingly or unwittingly, and physically transferred from one station to another.

Once installed, Stuxnet seized control of centrifuges that enrich uranium for use in nuclear reactors or bombs. The program then caused some of the delicate centrifuges to accelerate so fast and for so long that they broke, without setting off safety warnings. In all, the malware destroyed nearly 1,000 centrifuges, which was 20 percent of the country's stock, according to the *New York Times*.

Liam O'Murchu, director of the Security Technology and Response group at Symantec, examined Stuxnet and described it as "by far the most complex piece of code that we've looked at—in a completely different league from anything we'd ever seen before." It's also the first malware that caused physical damage, ushering in a new era in which governments can strike another country without risking a single human life (unless there's retaliation).

So, who was responsible? The U.S. government refuses to discuss its possible involvement. When asked about Stuxnet, former CIA and NSA chief Michael Hayden responded, "I don't know, and if I did, I wouldn't talk about it anyway."

Music to their ears: A scientist who witnessed a Stuxnet attack claims that infected computers played rock music (which is banned in Iran) at full volume. The song they played: AC/DC's "Thunderstruck."

WEAPONIZED SOCIAL NETWORKING

Perhaps the most menacing cyberwarfare weapons are the most subtle: Russia's highly personalized social engineering attacks. Social engineering manipulates people into disclosing information or behaving in a way they normally wouldn't. During a panel discussion at the Future in Review conference in 2017, Ukrainian politician Dmytro Shymkiv revealed how Russians allegedly use social engineering on his country's government officials. First, researchers scour their targets' social media accounts to identify what they like, what links they click on, and how susceptible they are to suggestion. With this data, the attackers create a detailed psychological profile of their mark. Then psychiatrists and neurologists design a campaign to influence each targeted victim. By directing specific content at social media users and their friends, the attackers can shape the marks' opinions. Shymkiv acknowledged that the strategy seems far-fetched: "People say, 'Well, that's a science fiction.' It's not."

Apparently, Russia has aimed this digital weapon at the U.S. government. In 2017 U.S. counterintelligence officials discovered that Russian hackers sent malware to more than 10,000 Department of Defense (DOD) workers via Twitter. They wrote individualized messages tailored to the employees' interests, including links to open attachments or "to learn more." If the marks clicked on the link (and it's unclear whether any did), hackers would then be able to take control of their devices and Twitter accounts. The discovery prompted fears that Russians could distribute false information from official DOD accounts, which could have disastrous effects during a crisis.

Besides spreading malware, Russians distribute fake news, targeting journalists, commentators, or other prominent people likely to help spread their propaganda, according to officials. And unlike malware, these attacks are almost undetectable. Americans were shocked when intelligence agencies reported that Russian president Vladimir Putin used social media to try to sway their opinions about candidates before the 2016 U.S. presidential election. Though the Department of Justice can't (or won't) say whether Putin's actions directly affected the election's outcome, in 2018 it indicted 13 Russians for election interference.

Given all this, it's difficult not to wonder how a country so unlike our own can understand Americans' social lives well enough to conduct these pointed attacks. Here's an answer from Kevin Mitnick, computer hacker and author of *The Art of Deception*: "Why are social engineering attacks so successful? It isn't because people are stupid or lack common sense. But we, as human beings, are all vulnerable to being deceived because people can misplace their trust if manipulated in certain ways." In other words, we shouldn't beat ourselves up for being gullible…but we shouldn't click on links without knowing where they lead and we shouldn't use "password" as a password.

* * *

A RANDOM BIT OF FACTINESS

How many peanuts does it take to make a standard 12-ounce jar of peanut butter?

CREAMY 540

CRUNCHY 540

…But creamy outsells crunchy by a 4-to-1 margin

In 2014 *The Wolf of Wall Street* broke the record for most uses of the F-word in…

LOST VERSES

Like any other kind of artist, songwriters have to go through an artistic process to get their work just right. Sometimes they write a whole verse, and decide to chuck it before they record the tune.

Song: "Daniel" (1973)
Artist: Elton John

Story: It's one of John's most memorable—and most cryptic—songs, about someone named Daniel, who runs away to Spain to escape "the pain of the scars that won't heal." But who is Daniel, and what is the nature of his relationship to the song's narrator? John sings "Daniel, my brother," so he could be a sibling, a friend, or a lover. And what event has so shaken him that he has to move far, far away? Years after the song was released, lyricist Bernie Taupin explained that Daniel is, in fact, the narrator's older brother, and that he's blind (hint: "your eyes have died"), due to an injury he received in the Vietnam War. There's another, unpublished verse, in which Daniel goes home to Texas, where he is treated like a hero for his wartime service, but he soon tires of the hero worship and decides to leave the country.

Song: "Glory Days" (1984)
Artist: Bruce Springsteen

Story: One of many hits off the *Born in the USA* album, "Glory Days" is about living in the past, when who you were was more satisfying than who you are today. In the first verse, the narrator meets an old high school friend who was a star baseball player back in the day, but now all he has are his "glory days." In the second verse, he remembers the prettiest girl from high school, who's now a divorced, lonely mother. Springsteen wrote another verse—about the narrator's father, who got fired after working for 20 years on a Ford factory assembly line. He, too, likes to remember his glory days...even though he never really had any. Springsteen thought it was too bleak and didn't fit the rest of the song, so he edited it out.

Song: "Hallelujah" (1984)
Artist: Leonard Cohen

Story: This haunting ballad is one of the most-covered songs in pop music. Hit versions recorded by John Cale, Jeff Buckley, Rufus Wainwright, k. d. lang, and several *American Idol* contestants, to name just a few. (It even popped up in *Shrek* in 2001.) It was originally written and performed by Canadian singer-songwriter Leonard Cohen for his 1984 album *Various Positions*, and quickly became one of his signature tunes. Music critics still struggle to figure out what the song means, apart from being about mental and emotional anguish, and Cohen himself (who died in 2016) never made it clear. In fact, he reportedly wrote as many as 80 different verses for the song. When performing the song live, he'd often switch out one of the verses for a new one that nobody had ever heard before. Has anyone ever seen the "full" version of "Hallelujah"? Probably only John Cale. When he covered the song in 1991, he persuaded Cohen to fax him all of the verses, from which he chose the ones he wanted to use.

Song: "The Big Rock Candy Mountain" (1928)

Artist: Harry McClintock (and Pete Seeger, Burl Ives, Bing Crosby, and many others)

Story: This classic children's song, revived and made famous (again) by the 2000 movie *O Brother, Where Art Thou?*, didn't just have a lost verse—it got an entire makeover. The version we know today tells of a magical place, a mountain made of candy, and where "little streams of lemonade come a-tricklin' down the rocks." What a wonderful place! Sure, if you're hearing the cleaned-up version of the song. The original, adapted from older folk songs by Harry McClintock, was a "hobo's fantasy"…and very much a product of the Great Depression. There are no "peppermint trees" the way McClintock sang it; there are "cigarette trees." And the "lakes of gold and silver" were originally "stew and whiskey." Years later, when McClintock tried to prove in a copyright lawsuit that he was the true writer, he revealed the lyrics of the lost last verse… which are too disturbing to print here. (A young boy follows a hobo to the Big Rock Candy Mountain, where the other hoboes want to do bad things to him.) The judge didn't buy it. Result: McClintock lost his copyright, and the song became public domain.

> **A TIP FROM UNCLE JOHN**
>
> Writing song lyrics is really about editing. Few songwriters come up with entire songs, with perfect rhymes and rhythms that say exactly what they want to say, on the first draft. Best way to start: get all your ideas on paper. What do you want the song to be about, what story do you want to tell? Then, organize those concepts. Here's a classic technique: First, introduce the listener to the story or the "world" of your song. Second, add perspective by telling them how you feel about it. Third, how do you want to leave the listener—hopeful, sad, desolate? What you've just done has given you a rough outline of your song's first, second, and third verses.

Eggplants contain nicotine…but you'd have to eat 20 pounds to get one cigarette's worth.

LOCAL HEROES

Now for some true stories that will restore your faith in humanity,
brought to you by the kindness of strangers.

CLEAN-UP IN AISLE 7

Marianne LaPlante and her 94-year-old mother were shopping at a Howell, New Jersey, grocery store in 2018 when LaPlante suddenly felt ill. She tried to steady herself on her shopping cart, but lost consciousness and fell headfirst onto the floor. Blood pooled around her head, and she started having convulsions. No one knew what to do. Suddenly, a middle-aged woman rushed in and told another customer to keep pressure on the head wound while she checked LaPlante's vital signs. Then LaPlante stopped breathing. The stranger administered CPR until paramedics arrived, while her daughter comforted LaPlante's elderly mother. LaPlante survived. When she later came to at the hospital, no one there knew who the stranger was, so she posted this Facebook status:

> "I would like to thank the woman who resuscitated me at Aldi's yesterday afternoon. You may have well saved my life. Also, thank you to the woman who held my 94-year-old Mom and said prayers with her while waiting for the ambulance. You may never see this post or know my gratitude to the both of you, but I will forever think of the two women who jumped into my life and made it possible for me to see a new day. There is still great good in this world."

The post went viral and a State of New Jersey Facebook page shared it, which is where Lisa Manoy saw it. The former nurse had been shopping with her daughter Lindsay that day when she stepped in and saved LaPlante's life. (Manoy had actually tried to contact LaPlante at the hospital but couldn't due to privacy laws.) At last report, the two women have become close friends. "We were meant to cross paths," Manoy said.

BATTLE BUDDIES

Rabbi Michael Harari, a U.S. Army chaplain serving on a base near Tacoma, Washington, was driving to the airport in August 2018 when he saw a man standing on a highway overpass. Fearing that something was wrong, Harari turned off at the next exit and drove back to the man, who was still there, on the other side of the guard rail. The loud traffic made it hard to hear, so Harari asked the man to come a bit closer so they could talk. "He wasn't so coherent," Harari later told reporters, but he'd managed to get him far enough away from the edge, so that "physically I would be able to restrain him if I needed to." He didn't need to. Upon learning that the man was a veteran, Harari told him he was an army chaplain, and that it's his job to talk to struggling soldiers just like him. That did the trick, and Harari was able to talk the man down and get him help. "We all have to look out for each other, not only here on-post but also off-post," Harari said after receiving an Army Commendation Medal for his heroics, adding, "We have to be everyone's battle buddy."

TONGUE-TIED

"It wasn't the first time I have done that, it's something like the fourth time," soccer player Francis Kone said somewhat nonchalantly, adding, "twice in Africa, once in Thailand." Kone wasn't talking about scoring a winning goal—he was talking about saving other players' lives. In his most recent save in February 2017, the Ivory Coast–born striker was playing in a Czech First League game when his teammate, running in front of him, collided with the opposing goalkeeper, Martin Bekovec. The next thing Kone knew, Berkovic was flat on his back, unconscious, and choking on his tongue. Without hesitation, Kone lunged to the ground and reached into Bekovic's mouth. He kept the man's airway open until the medics arrived to take Bekovic to the hospital, where he made a full recovery. Without Kone's quick thinking, Bekovec could have choked to death right there on the field. "I'm always checking the players," said Kone, "to make sure they have not swallowed their tongue."

PAY THE PIPELINE

In December 2015, professional surfer Evan Geiselman, 22, was surfing the famed Pipeline in Oahu, Hawaii, when a massive wave crashed down on top of him like a ton of bricks. His lungs filled up with seawater and his head slammed into a reef, knocking him out in the heavy surf. Andre Botha, a world champion bodyboarder, was watching closely when Geiselman went under. "A bit of time passed and I was still expecting him to come up," Botha told *FreeSurf* magazine. "At one point it clicked that he wasn't going to." So Botha, 34, swam over to the "impact zone" and, after getting slammed by a huge wave, was able to find Geiselman. He was "just limp, dark purple, and foamy at the mouth," said Botha. "Eyes were rolled back, and honestly I thought he was dead at that point." Botha blew a big breath straight into Geiselman's mouth, and a whoosh of water spouted out…but Geiselman was still unconscious. Another huge wave crashed down, and then another. Botha was able to keep them both alive until other surfers and lifeguards could get them to the beach. Back on shore, medics gave the injured surfer mouth-to-mouth resuscitation while his fellow surfers yelled, "Come on, Evan! You got this, Evan, you got this!" A moment later, Geiselman started coughing. He was rushed to the hospital, where he made a full recovery (although it took a while). "People are calling me the hero," said Botha, "but I think Evan is just as much a hero. He's such a warrior to survive something like that."

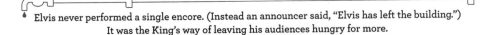

Elvis never performed a single encore. (Instead an announcer said, "Elvis has left the building.") It was the King's way of leaving his audiences hungry for more.

EXODUS

It looked like there would be no escape from Paradise as a wildfire roared through the northern California mountain town in November 2018. It wasn't just one fire, "it was coming down in 1,000 places," Kevin McKay told CNN. The Camp Fire wiped most of Paradise off the map, including McKay's house. Thankfully his family was able to evacuate on one of the few roads out of town. But McKay, a 41-year-old bus driver with only a few months' experience, chose to stay behind after receiving an emergency call that there were people stranded at Ponderosa Elementary School. He rushed over there and loaded 22 students and two teachers onto his bus. By the time they got to their only escape route, traffic was barely moving and the fires had blacked out the sun. It got even more terrifying when smoke started filling up the bus. The two teachers on board—Abbie Davis, 29, and Mary Ludwig, 50—kept the kids calm while also "trying to keep each other from crying," Ludwig later told CBS News. The smoke was getting thicker, and there was only one gallon of water on the bus. Then McKay had an idea. He took off his shirt, and the teachers tore it into smaller pieces, which the kids dipped in the water to use as moist rags. It actually helped keep smoke out of their lungs…but they still had a long way to go. At one point, they contemplated getting out and making a run for it, but conditions were even worse outside the bus, so they all rode it out together. Five hours and 30 miles later, the "bus driver from heaven" (as headlines read) had finally gotten everyone to safety. The Camp Fire was the deadliest wildfire in the history of California, taking 76 lives that day, but if not for the level-headed thinking of a bus driver and two teachers, it probably would have been even worse. When a reporter referred to McKay as a hero, he pointed out who the real heroes were: "Our firemen were going the opposite direction we were. And that's pretty awesome."

> By the time they got to their only escape route, traffic was barely moving and the fires had blacked out the sun.

PAY IT BACKWARD

"This random act of kindness was directed at me on this day for a purpose," read an anonymous letter sent to the *Durham Region* in Ontario in November 2017. The writer said that, a few months earlier, on a really bad morning, he or she had come to the decision that they would commit suicide that night. While tying up loose ends, they stopped at a Tim Hortons drive-through for a coffee and a muffin. At the pay window, the cashier said the previous driver had already paid for their breakfast. Not only that, but he'd instructed the cashier to tell the breakfast beneficiary to "have a great day in case you're not already having one."

The letter writer was floored: "I wondered why someone would buy coffee for a stranger for no reason. Why me? Why today?" Believing it was a sign, "I decided at that moment to change my plans for the day and do something nice for someone. I ended up helping a neighbor take groceries out of her car and into the house." After that, the person started doing good deeds for strangers every day. The letter concluded: "To the nice man in the SUV, thank you from the bottom of my heart, and know your kind gesture has truly saved a life."

Update: The breakfast benefactor's identity was later revealed as a local man named Glen Oliver. Every time he goes to Tim Hortons for a "medium dark roast with a little bit of milk," he also pays the tab for whoever is in line behind him…along with wishing them a nice day. "It's the least I can do for people, you know?" Oliver told *Global News*. "It's like holding the door."

LADY IN THE WATER

"I dread to think what would have happened had I not driven past her that afternoon," wrote Jo Stewart-Smith in the *Guardian* in 2017. The documentary filmmaker was recounting a harrowing incident that happened to her four years earlier. She was driving through the English countryside when she saw a woman slumped over in her car on the shoulder, not far from Stewart-Smith's sprawling farm. She pulled over and slowly walked back to the car. The woman was sitting up, but she was acting oddly, at one point saying, "I've stopped listening to music in peace."

"I'm calling help," Stewart-Smith told her, but the woman insisted she was feeling better. So, reluctantly, Stewart-Smith went home. Unable to "shake the feeling that something was wrong," she drove back later that day; the car was still there, with the engine running, but the woman was nowhere to be seen. So she called the police, and a search party was formed. "We wanted to help," she wrote, "but were told we could contaminate the search." By midnight, Stewart-Smith and her husband were getting frustrated by the lack of progress. They told an officer—yet again—that because it was their land that the woman was lost on, they knew where all the obstacles and cattle were (there were fears of a stampede). Finally, two officers agreed to go out with the spouses. "About ten minutes after we set off," Stewart-Smith wrote, "I saw what looked like a lumpen pile of fat, white sausages in our pond. I knew immediately it was the woman. I plunged in. She was lying on her back, her hair flowing in the reeds, like Ophelia." She was alive…barely. At the hospital, doctors treated her for a brain bleed—that was the cause of her strange behavior. The doctors told Stewart-Smith that without her intervention, the woman would have only lasted another 30 minutes.

WHAT A CATCH!

Byron Campbell of Dallas, Texas, was driving home on the day before Thanksgiving in 2018 when he saw smoke billowing out of an apartment building. He pulled over,

jumped out, ran into the building, and started knocking on doors as he yelled, "Fire! Fire! Get out!" Before long, the smoke and flames forced him back outside. But there were still people trapped on the third floor, including Shuntara Thomas and her one-year-old daughter, and firefighters hadn't arrived yet. "Drop your baby!" Campbell yelled up to her, "Just trust me—I got her, I got her." With the flames blocking her exit, Thomas had no choice: She dropped her crying baby daughter from her third-story window, and Campbell made a perfect catch. Then he handed the baby to a woman and helped save more people. Thanks to Campbell's and others' quick thinking, no one was injured in the fire, and six people made it down safely from third-floor windows, including one very fortunate little girl. When Thomas told her story to KDFW News, she could still barely believe what happened: "Throwing my baby out to a complete stranger that I didn't know…and without him my child's life would not have been saved."

OUT IN THE COLD

The Maple Heights (Ohio) Police Department posted a special Christmas message in 2018, praising two young men named Rayfield Hallman and Steven W. Wood. On the cold night of December 23, they were out driving when they noticed a small child all alone on a sidewalk. They almost kept going but decided to stop. Good thing, too. The kid's mother was slumped over on the walk in front of her house, which was locked. The men called 911 and put the little girl and her pet poodle in the car to warm up, while they waited with the woman until help arrived. She was treated for a seizure at the hospital. The cops wrote: "Rayfield and Steven's decision to show concern… probably saved not only the woman's life, but possibly saved the life of her 3-year-old daughter, who was outside in the night cold (36 degrees). I'm sure that other people drove past and decided not to do anything." The two heroes were given a "heart-felt thank you" from the police department, as well as two Mr. Chicken gift cards.

NEARLY CROAKED

One of the more interesting days on the job for Australian reptile wrangler Jamie Chapel took place in June 2018 when "I was called to relocate a common tree snake from an elderly lady's pot plants." When Chapel got to the snake, it had a "lump" inside it…which it then regurgitated. Out popped a mucus-covered frog that Chapel described as "limp, lifeless, and looking dead." He went to set it aside so he could concentrate on the snake, but then the frog had a "very tiny movement of its leg." All of a sudden the snake became secondary. "I decided to clean it up [the frog] and start CPR to see if I could revive it." Chapel kept up the tiny chest compressions until the frog finally regained consciousness. He took the frog home, dressed its bite wounds, and nursed it back to health. A week later, he told Australia's ABC network, "He's really done well. He's putting on a little bit of weight now." Chapel named the frog Lucky.

Fun fight fact: According to Welsh folklore, fairies rode corgi dogs into battle.

MOUTHING OFF

OM NOM NOM

As George Bernard Shaw observed, "There is no love sincerer than the love of food." (Some of these people may need to get a room.)

"Nothing like mashed potatoes when you're feeling blue. Nothing like getting into bed with a bowl of hot mashed potatoes already loaded with butter, and methodically adding a thin, cold slice of butter to every forkful."
—Nora Ephron

"ICE CREAM IS EXQUISITE. WHAT A PITY IT ISN'T ILLEGAL."
—Voltaire

"*Everything you see I owe to spaghetti.*"
—Sophia Loren

"The best comfort food will always be greens, cornbread, and fried chicken."
—Maya Angelou

"We must have a pie. Stress cannot exist in the presence of a pie."
—David Mamet

"When one has tasted watermelon he knows what the angels eat."
—Mark Twain

"All you need is love. But a little chocolate now and then doesn't hurt."
—Charles M. Schulz

"It's difficult to think anything but pleasant thoughts while eating a homegrown tomato."
—Lewis Grizzard

"Chowder breathes reassurance. It steams consolation."
—Clementine Paddleford

"TOO FEW PEOPLE UNDERSTAND A REALLY GOOD SANDWICH."
—James Beard

"The noblest of all dogs is the hot dog: it feeds the hand that bites it."
—Laurence J. Peter

"My idea of heaven is a great big baked potato and someone to share it with."
—Oprah Winfrey

"IF PROPERLY DRIED AND TRIMMED, NEW YORK-STYLE PIZZA COULD BE USED TO MAKE A BOX FOR CHICAGO-STYLE PIZZA."
—Nick Offerman

"Life expectancy would grow by leaps and bounds if green vegetables smelled as good as bacon."
—Doug Larson

"My biggest thing is banana pudding, but it's the devil! So no one is allowed to bring it into my house. Because I can't control myself. So why put it in my domain?"
—Jennifer Hudson

"Hot dogs and Red Vines and potato chips and French fries are my favorite foods."
—Betty White

"There's no better feeling in the world than a warm pizza box in your lap."
—Kevin James

A.T. THE ARTIFICIAL-TERRESTRIAL

Steven Spielberg could have directed the first Harry Potter movie in 1999, and he actually might have…if Stanley Kubrick hadn't died. Here's the story of an odd friendship and the odd—and some say classic—movie that came out of it.

INITIAL MEETING

After Stanley Kubrick read "Supertoys Last All Summer Long" in the late 1970s, he decided that the short story about a robot boy yearning for his human mother's love would be the basis of his next movie. He hired Brian Aldiss, the author of the story, to start working on a screenplay and then started developing the project, but it didn't get very far. The technology required to make a convincing robot boy—as well as several other robots in various states of disrepair—just wasn't there yet.

Then, in 1982, Kubrick saw Steven Spielberg's blockbuster *E.T. The Extra-terrestrial*, about a boy who befriends a lost alien. Inspired, Kubrick decided to call his movie *A.I. Artificial Intelligence*. He was taken by Spielberg's ability to make a high-tech sci-fi film grounded in emotion and realism—so taken that, in 1985, he called Spielberg and asked him to direct the movie. Spielberg was, as he later described it, "in shock." Flattered that one of his heroes would offer him the job, he was actually intimidated by Kubrick, who was 18 years his senior. Spielberg said no, telling Kubrick, "This is a great story for *you*." The *E.T.* director, who has been described as "a regular guy with the brain of a genius," famously never refers to himself as an artist. "Stanley Kubrick," he always insisted, "is an artist."

If it seems odd that these two filmmakers admired each other, it is. "A huge gap separated their styles and sensibilities," noted *The A.V. Club*. "There's Kubrick's philosophical *2001: A Space Odyssey* on one hand and Spielberg's emotional *Close Encounters of the Third Kind* on the other. Were one forced to choose between them, it would be a choice between a detached analyst of the human condition and a humanist." Or, as Kubrick's brother-in-law and executive producer, Jan Harlan, put it, "They are both great writers but they have different handwriting."

LONG-DISTANCE RELATIONSHIP

One of the main reasons Spielberg got into filmmaking in the first place was because he was so mesmerized by Kubrick's 1964 political satire, *Dr. Strangelove: Or How I Learned to Stop Worrying and Love the Bomb*. It wasn't until 1979, when Spielberg himself was a successful director, having already made *Jaws* and *Close Encounters*, that

The Ethiopian calendar is seven years behind the rest of the world's, and consists of 12 months of 30 days, plus one made up of five days.

he summoned up the courage to call Kubrick and tell him he was a fan. Spielberg was delighted to learn the feeling was mutual. Although the two directors rarely saw each other in person (Kubrick was quite the recluse, preferring to stay sequestered on his English estate when he wasn't working on closed movie sets), they wrote letters back and forth and spent long hours on the phone talking about all things filmmaking. Well, one of them did. "I'd tell Stanley everything I was doing," Spielberg later told the *L.A. Times*, "and Stanley would never tell me anything he was doing. Stanley was a benevolent inquisitor. He'd absolutely pump you dry of any knowledge you might have that he might find compelling." Including Spielberg's directing techniques: "Gee," Kubrick once asked Spielberg, "how did you get that kid to cry that way? Did you have to threaten to kill his dog?" Like an apprentice wanting his mentor's approval, Spielberg sent Kubrick a cut of every film he made before it was released, hoping for some constructive criticism. He usually just got accolades. And as much as Spielberg was tempted to direct *A.I.*, he didn't think their styles would combine into anything successful.

> "Gee," Kubrick once asked Spielberg, "how did you get that kid to cry that way? Did you have to threaten to kill his dog?"

STOPS AND STARTS

Kubrick's *A.I.* troubles went beyond Spielberg's refusal to direct: the screenplay wasn't coming together either. Brian Aldiss, who wrote the source material, thought the movie should be dark like *Dr. Strangelove*; Kubrick wanted it to be more like a "futuristic Pinocchio" in which the robot boy wanted to become a real boy. Aldiss wasn't buying it. (Kubrick had similar creative differences with Stephen King while making *The Shining*.) Unable to come to an agreement, Kubrick fired Aldiss in 1989. Then he hired a few other writers who had similar issues, but he did manage to get a 90-page treatment from English sci-fi author Ian Watson. It wasn't complete, but it was enough to start shooting with…if they'd had something to shoot. Unfortunately, the visual effects technology of the early 1990s still wasn't advanced enough to make a convincing robot. That's right—Kubrick wanted the star of *A.I.* to be not an actor but a remote-controlled robotic boy. (A running joke was that it took the notorious perfectionist so long to make his movies that a real boy would age too much during filming.)

More than ten years after coming up with the idea, Kubrick's movie wasn't any closer to getting made. And it was mostly Steven Spielberg's fault.

INTERTWINED ODYSSEYS

Spielberg had a profound impact on Kubrick's career:

- Kubrick didn't know what to do with "Supertoys" until *E.T.* inspired him to call it *A.I.*

- Kubrick was preparing to make a Holocaust film, *Aryan Papers*, but abandoned the project after he saw Spielberg's 1993 film *Schindler's List*. (Kubrick's *Full Metal Jacket* had come out a year after Oliver Stone's similar take on the Vietnam War, *Platoon*, and Kubrick didn't want to be seen as a Johnny-come-lately yet again.)
- Kubrick started to work on a screenplay for a World War II movie...until he learned Spielberg was doing *Saving Private Ryan*.

But it was Spielberg's CGI-dinosaur extravaganza, *Jurassic Park*, that had the most impact on the *A.I.* project. After seeing it, Kubrick was blown away, and even more convinced that *A.I.* had to be directed by Steven Spielberg. So he invited the younger director to his estate in England, where Kubrick delivered his best pitch yet: "The title card will read great! It'll say, 'A Stanley Kubrick production of a Steven Spielberg film.' Don't you think people will come to see that?" Spielberg's answer was still no, and he later explained, "I thought this was one of the most commercial stories that Stanley had ever developed for him to direct, and I didn't want Stanley to be robbed. Stanley wanted a hit! But he wasn't willing to compromise his art for one." And neither was Spielberg.

ILL EFFECTS

Now on a Pinocchio-like quest himself to make *A.I.* into a real movie, Kubrick hired the visual effects team from *Jurassic Park*, including Oscar winner Dennis Muren, who helped bring the metallic Terminator to life in *Terminator 2: Judgment Day*. But even Muren couldn't bring Kubrick's robot boy to life. As executive producer Jan Harlan recalled, "We tried to construct a little boy with a movable rubber face to see whether we could make it look appealing. But it was a total failure, it looked awful." So Kubrick decided to go with a young actor, and tested Joseph Mazzello, who played the little brother in *Jurassic Park*. The project was finally starting to come together, but Kubrick *still* didn't want to direct it.

He called Spielberg in 1995 and asked him once more to helm *A.I.*, but Spielberg had (conveniently) already started working on *Saving Private Ryan*. So Kubrick moved on to another film he'd been trying to make since the 1970s called *Eyes Wide Shut* (it took him so long because he couldn't think of an ending). *Eyes Wide Shut*, Kubrick's first film in 12 years, was released in 1999, and with that hurdle finally behind him, Hollywood was buzzing with the prospect of Stanley Kubrick once and for all making *A.I. Artificial Intelligence*.

And then he died.

WHEN STEVEN MET HARRY

Kubrick's sudden death from a heart attack at age 70 sent shock waves throughout show business, and it appeared as if his long-gestating tale about a robot boy would

Worth the wait? Demodex are mites that live on your face.
They don't have anuses, and don't evacuate their bowels until they die.

never get made. At the same time, fresh off the success of *Saving Private Ryan*, Spielberg was looking for his next project when Warner Bros. hired him to helm *Harry Potter and the Sorcerer's Stone*. But Spielberg was reluctant from the start (although his own children were thrilled with the idea). He knew it would be a huge film—thanks to the unparalleled popularity of J. K. Rowling's books—regardless of who directed it. "It would be like shooting ducks in a barrel," he said. And Spielberg did spend a few months developing *Potter*, but he actually thought it would work better as an animated film starring Haley Joel Osment as the voice of Harry. Warner Bros. execs disagreed; they wanted a live-action film, which slowed Spielberg's involvement with the project.

Then in late 1999, Christiane Kubrick (Stanley Kubrick's widow) called Spielberg and said that it was her husband's lifelong dream to see *A.I.* become a reality, and the only way that would happen is if Steven Spielberg directed it. Otherwise, the movie would be shelved for good.

Spielberg finally said yes.

WORKING IN THE SHADOWS
Despite all the work Kubrick had put into developing *A.I.* over 20-plus years, when Spielberg finally took over, there wasn't a lot to work with, just some storyboards, a few CGI tests, and an incomplete screenplay. Spielberg hadn't written a screenplay alone since 1978's *Close Encounters*, usually preferring to collaborate on his stories, but this project was different. He had to do it alone. "I was like an archeologist," he recalled, "picking up the pieces of a civilization, putting Stanley's picture back together again." Every moment that he worked on that film, "I felt like I was being coached by a ghost."

After Spielberg finished Ian Watson's screenplay, filming on *A.I.* began in August 2000. Spielberg was so intent on following in the reclusive director's footprints that he kept a closed set just like Kubrick did. Spielberg rarely worked with storyboards (still images that lay out scenes in advance of shooting), but in this case, he used the storyboards that Kubrick had commissioned from acclaimed sci-fi artist Chris "Fangorn" Baker. (The giant "open-mouth tunnels" on the bridge to Rouge City come straight from Baker's imagination.) One thing that Spielberg didn't do that Kubrick did: work very slowly (or torment his actors...but that's another story).

After filming wrapped a few months later, Spielberg worked on *A.I.*'s postproduction while also working on *Minority Report*, which was admittedly taxing. But he had the biggest names in the visual effects world—Dennis Muren and Stan Winston—on hand to finally bring Kubrick's vision to the big screen.

STEVELY KUBERG
After several months of building excitement—and curiosity—*A.I. Artificial Intelligence* opened on June 29, 2001. The critical reviews were mostly positive, and the box office

First president to sit for a three-dimensional portrait: Barack Obama.

was predictably high for a Spielberg summer tent-pole film, bringing in nearly $30 million on its opening weekend (although *Harry Potter* would pull in three times that amount a few months later).

But from the day of its release, *A.I.* has been a polarizing movie. The film's most loyal fans seem to be Kubrick's friends and family, who all agree the auteur would have loved it. Producer Bonnie Curtis called it a "Stevely Kuberg" film: "Every word, every thing you see has both of them in it." Even Brian Aldiss, who hadn't worked on the project in more than a decade, liked the film, although he did admit, "There are flaws in it." He was especially bothered by the new ending. (Minor spoilers ahead.) The movie is broken up into three parts: family gets a robot boy, robot boy gets lost in a strange city, and ... that's all you need to know. Suffice it to say, the third act took the movie in a much different direction, which a lot of people—especially Kubrick fans—called "saccharine."

ROLE REVERSAL

Here's the ironic twist, as Spielberg is always quick to point out: "It was Stanley who did the sweetest parts of *A.I.*, not me." Those "sweetest parts" mostly come at the beginning and end. And they were mostly Kubrick. It was Spielberg who darkened up the middle section that most people assumed was Kubrick's doing, including keeping a robot gigolo character from the source material (although Spielberg did omit the robot sex scene that Watson had written in). And it was Kubrick, not Spielberg, who added the plot point that the robot, David, wants to find the "Blue Fairy so she will turn me into a real boy" (not what you'd expect from the man who directed *A Clockwork Orange*). Most people assumed it was Spielberg who tapped Robin Williams to play a cartoon version of Einstein called "Dr. Know," but that was also Kubrick's idea.

"[A.I.] shows a side of Stanley that people haven't seen before," Spielberg told his biographer, "which was a very deeply emotional and lonely side." So it could be said that *A.I.*'s unevenness is the result of two filmmakers trying to cop each other's styles within the same film.

PARTING GIFTS

Spielberg had another goal with *A.I.*: drop clever references to Kubrick's other films. Our favorite: in the scene where the robot David (played quite convincingly by Haley Joel Osment) is stuffing spinach into his mouth, the father (Sam Robards) says, "Stop, Dave, please stop." That's what the HAL 9000 computer (Douglas Rain) said to Commander Dave Bowman (Keir Dullea) in Kubrick's 1968 masterpiece *2001: A Space Odyssey*...the film that inspired Spielberg to make *Close Encounters of the Third Kind* (which has a lot of Pinocchio references).

Technically speaking, birds can't pee, because they don't have urethras.
(They pee and poop at the same time.)

BAD CANADIAN TV

If you think America has created the worst TV shows of all time, you could be right. (Remember Manimal?*) Not so fast, says Canada. Here are some contenders from the Great White North.*

THEY'RE PLAYING OUR SONG (1975) Each episode featured a few famous Canadian guest stars, who would talk about their favorite songs, and then guest musicians would play them. Only problem: it was meant to celebrate Canadian culture, but the songs were almost always from the United States. Example: Montreal Expos star Gary Carter requested "California Dreamin'" by José Feliciano.

WHAT ON EARTH (1971) Five panelists—generally non-TV people like museum curators and art historians—took turns handling and then guessing what a strange found or historical object might be. Sometimes it was a mummy ear, or an ancient tool.

OOOPS! (1970) It was a game show on which contestants had to get the audience to laugh. If they failed, they lost points. The players were kids, but they didn't have to come up with their own jokes—they told corny quips sent in by kids watching at home. For some reason, the series employed a duck theme, with host Harry Brown referring to himself as "the Great Drake" and comedian John O'Leary interrupting the game to give a "Weather for Ducks" report loaded with puns like "Duck pond's still frozen, but watch out for quacks in the ice."

UP CANADA (1974) This confusing series was one part *60 Minutes*, with investigative reporters heading to far-flung locales to delve into news and human-interest stories. It was also one part *Saturday Night Live*, in that the show included comedy sketches produced to *look like* news reports. The only way to tell the difference: the jokes in the fake news bits were terrible. (One segment was about a philandering member of Parliament who hailed from a town called Nookie-in-the-Islands.)

UNCLE ED'S PARTY (1952) Singer Ed McMurdy hosted this bizarre children's show from a ramshackle house (the only way in was through a coal chute) that was inhabited by a taxidermied talking moose head and a ghost who sat in a rocking chair and delivered aphorisms.

SOME OF MY BEST FRIENDS ARE MEN (1975) This public-affairs discussion program focused on the burgeoning feminist movement. In addition to the straight-laced talk between host and panelists, contributor Florynce Kennedy added rude Andy Rooney–style commentaries, and comedian Dave Broadfoot starred in short sketches where he'd demonstrate typical male chauvinist behavior…and be punished with a pie to the face.

Channing Tatum's first on-screen role: a shirtless bartender in a Ricky Martin video ("She Bangs," 2000).

TALES OF THE RIVERBANK (1960)

A kids' show about a wacky group of animal friends in a small Canadian town, including Hammy Hamster, a rat named Roddy, and a guinea pig inventor named Guinea Pig who spoke in a W. C. Fields imitation. And it wasn't a cartoon. Producers used real hamsters, rats, and guinea pigs dressed in costumes and pushed them around a tiny set while off-screen actors dubbed their voices.

EYE BET (1972)

Contestants had to remember tiny details of the film clip they just watched to win prizes like toasters and blenders. The show was canceled when movie studios realized it was using old movie footage without permission and without paying for it.

ROCKET ROBIN HOOD (1967)

The CBC spent $1.5 million ($11 million in today's money) to bring this to the air—the first animated series in color to ever be produced in Canada. All that money went to telling a futuristic version of…Robin Hood. Taking place in "the astonishing year 3000" in Sherwood Forest—which now occupies an asteroid hurtling through space—Rocket Robin Hood does battle with the evil Sheriff of N.O.T.T. (National Outerspace Terrestrial Territories) with weapons like an atomic vacuum cleaner and a jet-powered Sphinx.

PET PEEVES (1986)

Host Harvey Atkin asked celebrity guests and people on the street what little things in life annoyed them most. And that was pretty much the whole show.

THE RAES (1978)

Robbie and Cherrill Rae were a real husband-and-wife disco act who scored just three hits (in Canada) in the late 1970s, including a thumping version of Doris Day's "Que Sera Sera." That was enough to land them their own disco-themed variety show. They did their own songs, plus covers of other disco songs, such as the Village People's "In the Navy." But the true centerpiece of the show: the reading of the weekly numbers in Canada's Lucky Seven lottery. The show ended in 1980, and the Raes divorced in 1982, citing the stress of making the show as a factor.

PITFALL (1981)

In this game show hosted by Alex Trebek (he's Canadian) a few years before he took over *Jeopardy!*, contestants answered questions to navigate a set stuffed with metal junk, pipes, and machinery. If they got a question wrong, they were sent to a pit full of steam, and the only escape was to answer another question correctly.

NICKNAMES OF FAME (1961)

People were called up from the studio audience to team up with the show's panelists to guess the mystery guest's nickname.

HEY, TAXI (1972)

A strange sitcom about a college student (whose name is never given) who wins a Vancouver taxicab license in a game of Scrabble. The show then features the driver bumming around Vancouver, interacting with colorful locals of different nationalities all played by the same actor. Canadian TV critic Kaspars Dzeguze said that *Hey, Taxi* was "as low as television can get."

SIGNED, SEALED & DELIVERED

July 4, 1776, is best known as the date the Declaration of Independence was adopted, but the founding fathers did something else that day: They appointed a committee to design a "Great Seal of the United States." A simple job, maybe, but the project dragged on for years.

THE A TEAM

After the Second Constitutional Congress ratified the Declaration of Independence, they assigned a committee of three people with the task of coming up with "a seal for the United States of America"—a national emblem or coat of arms for the new country. In the 1700s, when countries signed treaties and other agreements, they did so by stamping the official documents with their state seals. Now that the United States had declared itself to be an independent nation, it was going to need a state seal too. And fast.

ROUND ONE

The three people chosen to design the new seal were three of the men most responsible for writing the Declaration of Independence: Thomas Jefferson, John Adams, and Benjamin Franklin. But they turned out to be better with words than they were with symbols and imagery. After considering numerous biblical and classical themes and failing to come up with something on their own, they enlisted the aid of a Swiss-born artist named Pierre Eugène du Simitière.

Du Simitière sketched a rough design (shown left) that featured two human figures: an allegorical female representing Liberty and a male representing an American soldier. These figures stood on either side of a large shield, the center of which featured symbols for six countries that large numbers of European Americans hailed from: England, Scotland, Ireland, France, Germany, and Holland.

Most human beings will see more of the surface of the Moon than they ever will of Earth.

Surrounding the six national symbols were emblems displaying the initials of the 13 colonies, and floating above the shield was an "Eye of Providence in a radiant Triangle whose Glory extends over the Shield and beyond the Figures."

A motto on a scroll at the bottom of the scene read: E Pluribus Unum ("From Many, One," a reference to the 13 colonies that had joined together to form the Union).

ROUND TWO

Du Simitière's design was submitted to the Continental Congress in August 1776. They were not impressed. Rather than approve it, Congress sat on it until 1780, when it handed off du Simitière's design and other materials to a new committee and asked them to try again. This second committee passed the buck to Francis Hopkinson, the designer of the first American flag. Hopkinson developed du Simitière's design further, adding 13 red and white diagonal stripes to the shield, and replacing the Eye of Providence with 13 six-pointed stars surrounded by clouds. He moved the male figure to the left and the female figure to the right, and put an olive branch in her left hand, symbolizing peace. Hopkinson also replaced E Pluribus Unum with Bello vel pace paratus, which means "prepared in war or peace," and circled the design with the words "THE GREAT SEAL OF THE UNITED STATES OF AMERICA."

ROUND THREE

The Continental Congress must not have liked that design either, because in 1782 it appointed a third committee to revise the work of the first two committees. The third committee relied on the artistic talents of a Philadelphia attorney named William Barton, who came up with his own version of the seal. His design kept the male and female figures with the shield between them, but this time the female (moved back to the left of the shield) represented the "Genius of America." Her olive branch was replaced by a dove perched on her right hand. Barton also added a small white

eagle atop the shield, holding a sword in its right talon and an American flag in its left, with an upper motto that read *In Vindiciam Libertatis* ("In Defense of Liberty") and a lower one that read *Virtus Sola Invicta* ("Only Virtue Unconquered").

Barton also proposed a design for the back of the seal that included an unfinished pyramid with 13 rows of stone, topped by the Eye of Providence that had been proposed by the first committee, and featuring the motto *Deo Favente* ("With God's Favor") and *Perennis* ("Everlasting").

ROUND FOUR

The Continental Congress didn't think much of Barton's proposals either, so in June 1782 it took all the work that had been done by the three committees and dumped it in the lap of the Secretary of the Continental Congress, Charles Thomson. He didn't have an artistic background, so rather than try and create something entirely new, he just picked the elements that he liked from each of the previous designs and used them to create his own design.

He removed the male and female figures, reduced the size of the shield, and greatly enlarged Barton's eagle so that it was big enough to support the shield on its breast. Over the eagle's head was a constellation of six-pointed stars surrounded by clouds and rays of light. In its left talon the eagle clutched 13 arrows, symbolizing war; in its right talon it clutched an olive branch, symbolizing peace. In its beak it held a banner bearing the motto from the first design, *E Pluribus Unum*.

For the reverse side of the seal, Thomson stuck with the unfinished pyramid and the Eye of Providence, but changed Barton's mottos to *Annuit Coeptis* ("He Has Favored Our Undertakings") and *Novus Ordo Seclorum* ("New Order of the Ages").

Thomson gave his ideas back to Barton for fine-tuning. Barton simplified the design and altered a few details, pointing the eagle's wingtips upward and replacing the chevrons on Thomson's shield with vertical stripes.

Then he presented the design to the Continental Congress on June 20, 1782. At last! The Congress

Leeches were once used to treat nymphomania.

finally had a design it liked, and it approved it that same day. The first seal was created later that same year. And though the unfinished pyramid design was approved for the reverse side, it was never actually made into a physical seal that could be applied to treaties. One of the very rare times it has ever been used for anything was in 1935, when President Franklin D. Roosevelt ordered both the front and the back of the Great Seal to be placed on the back of the $1 bill. It has been there ever since.

The Great Seal was first used on September 16, 1782, to sign a document authorizing General George Washington to negotiate an exchange of Revolutionary War prisoners with the British. It remained in regular use for another 59 years. By then it was pretty worn, and like an old coin, some of the details from the seal's metal die, used to stamp or impress the image of the seal onto documents, had gotten kind of fuzzy. So in 1841 a new die was commissioned. It's believed that the engraver of the new die simply copied the details from the old, worn die, rather than base his design on the 1782 legislation that established the details of the design of the seal, because

that legislation specified that the eagle's left talon should hold 13 arrows. In the new seal, the eagle holds only six. The new design also used five-pointed stars in the constellation over the eagle's head. The old seal had six-pointed stars. Because of these discrepancies, the 1841 seal has become known as "the illegal seal," even though the treaties and other documents that the seal was affixed to were just as legal as they would have been if the design had followed the letter of the law.

NIP AND TUCK

The next die, engraved in 1877, copied the design of the 1841 die. It wasn't until 1881, when the 100th anniversary of the first seal was approaching, that the State Department decided to have the design of the seal updated to bring it back into compliance with the 1782 specifications. It took until 1884 for the U.S. Congress to appropriate $1,000 to pay for the work, after which the New York jeweler Tiffany & Co. was commissioned to update the design. Their head designer, James Horton Whitehouse, came up with the design for the 1885 seal.

If this seal looks familiar, that's because very few changes have been made to the design since then. When the 1885 die was ready to be replaced in 1903, the commission went to a Philadelphia firm called Bailey Banks & Biddle, but rather than let the firm's engraver, Max Zeitler, have a free hand with the look of the new die, he was instructed to produce a "facsimile" of the 1885 seal. So Zeitler produced what is essentially the same design, but brought out in finer, sharper detail (pictured).

The seal that's in use today is still based on Zeitler's 1903 design, and it's unlikely to change anytime soon. In 1986 the Bureau of Engraving and Printing made a "master die" based on the 1903 design. In the future when the metal dies used to emboss treaties and other documents wear out, new dies will be made from this master die.

SOMETHING BORROWED, SOMETHING BLUE

What is believed to be the first official use of the Great Seal as a symbol of the presidency came in April 1877, when President Rutherford B. Hayes used an image of an eagle grasping at arrows and olive leaves on invitations to his first state dinner, given in honor of a visiting Russian grand duke. In 1902 President Theodore Roosevelt ordered that a version of the official seal be installed in the floor of the White House's Entrance Hall; the designer of that image, a French-American sculptor named Philip Martiny, added the words

THE SEAL of the PRESIDENT of the UNITED STATES

around the edge of the circle. (Another change: the eagle's head is turned to its left, facing the talon that held the arrows of war, instead of to the right, where the olive branch of peace was held.) That eagle remained in place on the floor of the Entrance Hall until Harry S. Truman became president in 1945. Truman didn't like the idea of visitors to the White House walking all over the seal, so when he ordered his own extensive renovations to the White House in 1948, he had the seal removed from the floor and installed over the doorway of the Diplomatic Reception Room, where people could admire it but not step on it.

Berkshire, Buckinghamshire, Essex, Hertfordshire, Kent, Surrey, and Sussex
are considered the "home counties" of England because they all surround London.

Truman was the first president to codify the design of the presidential seal, in his Executive Order 9646. Before the executive order, presidents used (or didn't use) the official state seal as the presidential seal however they wished. In his executive order, Truman made a few changes to the presidential seal. He dictated that, as had always been the case with the Great Seal of the United States used by the State Department, the eagle on the presidential seal should have its head turned to its right, facing the olive branch of peace.

Truman also ordered that the presidential seal should be set on a dark blue background and be encircled by 48 stars, representing the 48 states in the Union. (He also considered adding a bolt of lightning issuing from the arrowheads, to represent the new power of the atomic bomb. The "importance of the new atomic bomb is so tremendous that [Truman felt that] some symbolic reference to it should be incorporated into the flag," Clark Clifford, a military aide, noted at the time. But Truman changed his mind and the idea was dropped.) The only changes to the presidential seal since then came in 1959 and 1960, when a 49th and then a 50th star were added to the seal to represent the admission of the states of Alaska and Hawaii to the Union.

* * *

"I am a firm believer in the people. If given the truth, they can be depended upon to meet any national crisis. The great point is to bring them the real facts."

—Abraham Lincoln

Octopuses can't be inoculated against disease.

#TALKOFTHETEENS_ HASHTAGS

On page 317, we shared the stories behind some of the most ubiquitous words and phrases of the 2010s. As we were finishing up, we realized we almost forgot one of the most ubiquitous: "hashtag." The story of this little symbol turned out to be so big that we had to give it its own article. #origins #technology #popculture #bathroomreading #arewedoingthisright

HASHTAGS 101

When Baby Boomers, Gen Xers, and Gen Yers look at this thing— # —the phrase that springs to mind is probably "number sign" or "pound sign." But for most Millennials and anyone born after 2000, the only thing this symbol has ever been is a hashtag. And it seems that the younger you are, the more natural the concept of hashtagging is. So for you older non-tech types out there, here's how it works: the practice of "hashtagging" is typing a number sign, followed by a word or phrase, on social media websites like Twitter, Facebook, Pinterest, and Instagram. Once you type it, the word or phrase (the hashtag) becomes blue, turning it into a hyperlink. Now, the post or tweet that it's attached to is instantly accessible to anyone else who views that same hashtag. Structurally, a hashtag can consist of only letters, numbers, or underscores (no other symbols or spaces).

Let's say you post a photo of a toilet and then caption it, "Look at my awesome toilet!" No matter what social media site you're on, if that's all there is to your post, then only your "friends" (people you're connected to) can see it. But if you add the hashtag #toilet after the post, then any of the other millions of people on that site who are interested in toilets can find your toilet pic. The more relevant hashtags you add (#awesome #porcelain #sitting_pretty), the more chances for people to see it. Also referred to as "keywording," this is just one of the hashtag's many functions. You can use them to add commentary or self-deprecating humor to your posts (such as #isanyonereallyreadingthis), for advertising campaigns, and to follow developing news stories.

But how did the number sign come to be called a hashtag?

SYMBOLIC ORIGINS

The number sign (#) and the British pound sign (£) have had an intertwining history. For example, the number sign is also called a pound sign, but that refers to the weight measurement, not British currency. Both symbols, however, come from the Latin *libra pondo* ("pound weight"), which was shortened to this: ℔. The horizontal line was

Florida's Kingsley Lake, a former sinkhole, is the most circular natural lake in the world.

added to clarify that it's the letter l and not the number 1. And over time, as written shorthand developed, the symbol eventually transformed into this: #. It's unclear exactly when that happened, but by the time typewriters became available in the 19th century, they all included the #. Since then, the symbol has served many purposes: it is most commonly used to indicate numbers and weights; in musical notation, it indicates a sharp; in copyediting, it means to add a space; and if you're notating a chess match, a # means "checkmate."

In the 1960s, the symbol changed yet again when technicians at Bell Labs placed it below the number 9 on the first telephones with touch-tone keypads. They called the thing an "octatherp" or "octothorpe" (the stories vary), claiming it was a combination of the ancient Greek *octo* and the Old Norse *thorpe*, meaning "eight villages." That's what we reported in 2001 in our *Supremely Satisfying Bathroom Reader*, but later research revealed that the Bell techs may have named the word after famed Native American athlete Jim Thorpe. Or maybe it came from James Oglethorpe, the British general who founded the state of Georgia.

Whatever the true origin, it doesn't matter because "octothorpe" never caught on as a name for the symbol—which has also been called a crunch, diamond, grid, mesh, thud, thump, splat, tic-tac-toe, pig-pen, crosshatch, and hash mark. And if you phone businesses in some Asian countries, you may hear, "Please enter your phone number followed by the hex key."

COMMON KNOWLEDGE

The # symbol moved from analog to digital in the 1980s when it started showing up in early text-messaging IRC (Internet Relay Chat) networks to label groups. So in August 2007, it wasn't a huge leap for a San Francisco typographer named Chris Messina to type, "How do you feel about using # (pound) for groups. As in #barcamp [msg]?" Messina was on Twitter, which was barely a year old. And #barcamp is now considered the world's first hashtag. Here's the tweet:

Chris Messina
@chrismessina

how do you feel about using # (pound) for groups. As in #barcamp [msg]?

♡ 10.4K   11:25 AM - Aug 23, 2007

◯ 5,208 people are talking about this   >

Nintendo translates to "leave luck to heaven."

Messina, who also had a hand in developing Google and Uber, was proposing using a hyperlinked word to connect online users who were discussing the same topic. "At the time," he later recalled, "we were thinking Twitter needs some kind of group organizing framework." Messina said he chose the number sign mainly because it was easy to access on his Nokia phone. (In those days, phones didn't have QWERTY keyboards, so texting was a more painstaking process on the numbers keypad.)

Two days later, a fellow techie named Stowe Boyd elaborated on Messina's idea in a blog post he called "Hash Tags = Twitter Groupings," writing, "I support the hash tag convention." And that marked the first use of the term "hashtag." Boyd was drawing from yet another name for the # symbol, a hash mark. The "hash" part is British (short for "cross-hatch"), which most likely came from the stripes on 1910s military jackets, but it's unclear exactly when the word became associated with the symbol. Regardless, Boyd's term "hashtag" had a lot going for it from the start: it's short, fun to say, and nothing had ever been called that before.

TRENDING TOPIC

Messina brought the hashtag concept to Twitter executives, explaining that it might help "organize tweets so you know what to pay attention to and what to ignore." But other Twitter users were slow to embrace it, as were the higher-ups at the company. "They didn't like it," Messina told the *New Statesman* in 2014. "They said it was 'for nerds' and would likely never catch on."

The hashtag got a huge boost in October 2007 when a wildfire broke out near San Diego, California. Messina noticed that several people were tweeting about the fire, and suggested to one of them that he follow each tweet with #sandiegofire. Soon others were using the same hashtag, and Messina realized that a lot of people around the world wanted to be able to participate in conversations like these, and using hashtags was a simple way to achieve that goal.

Still, for the next couple of years, hashtags were mostly viewed as something that only tech geeks used. But Messina kept pushing the idea, and in 2009 Twitter started automatically linking anything that began with a hashtag. "The more companies they acquired that supported hashtags," he said, "the more inevitable it became that Twitter would need to officially support them." A year later, the company added hashtag-generated "trending topics" to its home page, and the word went mainstream. In January 2011, Audi released the first hashtag campaign in a Super Bowl commercial. Two Super Bowls later, half of the commercials featured hashtags.

JOIN THE CONVERSATION

In 2012 the American Dialect Society voted "hashtag" Word of the Year, explaining that it had become "a ubiquitous phenomenon in online talk…creating instant social trends, spreading bite-sized viral messages on topics ranging from politics to pop culture." Merriam-Webster added the word to its dictionary in 2014. By that time, all the other major social media outlets had installed a hashtag feature. Result: if you want to build a huge following on photo-sharing sites like Instagram and Pinterest, you have to master the use of hashtags. In fact, some users prefer to follow hashtags and not people. Hashtag use became so rampant, in fact, that social media sites now enforce a strict no-more-than-30-hashtags-per-post limit.

Now that the internet has been taken over by #s, their impact is being felt all over the real world. Some examples:

#breaking_news: Place a hashtag in front of an unfolding event like #puertorico or #bostonmarathon and your post becomes the leading news source. This feature has made Twitter a competitor to 24-hour cable news networks—routinely beating them to breaking news stories and allowing unfiltered, on-the-ground information to get out to the public. As a result, more and more journalists have turned to Twitter as a source.

#activism: Put a hashtag in front of an idea, and it can help launch an entire social movement. Examples: #Bahrain (the hashtag that launched the #ArabSpring), #TaxedEnoughAlready (the hashtag that launched the Tea Party), as well as #OccupyWallStreet, #BlackLivesMatter, and #MeToo. In 2014 hashtags helped the #IceBucketChallenge (a summer trend that saw people pour ice water on themselves) raise more than $115 million for ALS research, which actually led to the discovery of a previously unknown gene that causes the neurodegenerative disease.

#advertising: Creative uses of hashtagging have become crucial tools for businesses both big and small to increase fans and awareness. One of the earliest successes was the NBA's decision in 2012 to allow fans to vote for their All-Star Game picks using the hashtag #NBAVOTE along with the player's name and/or Twitter handle. Marketers love these types of campaigns because they get the customers to do the advertising for them. For example, in 2015 Disney (in conjunction with the Make-A-Wish Foundation) kicked off its five-year-long #ShareYourEars campaign, inviting Twitter's 330 million users to post a selfie wearing Mickey Mouse ears and then tag it #ShareYourEars. The tweeters got to feel like they were part of something bigger, Make-A-Wish made tens of millions of dollars, and Disney increased their brand awareness (as if they needed it).

#education: If it's been a few years since you were in school, you'd be amazed at the ways hashtags are being incorporated into assignments and curriculums. For example, teachers who want to join a "Personal Learning Network" will read this

Every time he plays President Donald Trump on *Saturday Night Live,* Alec Baldwin gets $1,400.

on the "Getting Smart" home page: "When used properly, education hashtags can help you take part in important conversations and make valuable connections whether you're a teacher, principal, or superintendent. Some hashtags are genuinely helpful when you are trying to search for important things like #GOPDebate or #NationalCatDay, while some of them are #completelymadeupandridiculous."

#completelymadeupandridiculous: Uncle John's favorite use of the symbol, not surprisingly, is the wordplay game "Hashtag Wars," popularized by the Comedy Central game show @*Midnight* (2013–17), in which comedians had to come up with witty puns based on hashtag challenges. The game outlasted the show, and is still played online today. (We can't mention this game and then not give an example. The hashtag challenge #AddStarWarsImproveAMovie inspired such entries as *A Death Star is Born*, *The Hills Have Jedis*, *R2-D2 Mighty Ducks*, *The Sith Sense*, and *Cool Hand Luke Skywalker*.)

> **A TIP FROM UNCLE JOHN**
>
> People with huge followings on social media tend to use a lot of hashtags. You may think that seems annoying, or that the poster is "fishing" for attention by casting a wide net with hashtags...and you're right. Using that many hashtags will attract many more eyeballs. But how many is too many and how few is too few? According to the social media marketing experts at TrackMaven, the perfect number is nine. Posts with exactly nine hashtags receive more "engagement" (meaning views, reposts, likes, and comments) than posts with more or fewer.

When the hashtag turned 10 years old in 2017, *Wired* magazine summed up its impact: "Sure, it can indicate where you're posting from (#OvalOffice) or what you're posting about (#FakeNews), but the hashtag has also shaped elections, launched social movements, and transcended its meaning as a mere keystroke to become a defining symbol of the digital age."

#BACKLASH

These days, it seems, nothing can get *this* popular and not have its share of "haters" (another term from the 2010s), especially after the term "hashtag" made the jump from cyberspace to real life. Take the 2013 Grammy Awards—host LL Cool J was either trying to sound hip, or he was making fun of the word, when he said to the crowd, "I've been backstage reading all your tweets about hashtag Grammys. We're going to see hashtag Carrie Underwood, hashtag Jack White, hashtag Kelly Clarkson, hashtag Bruno Mars, and hashtag Sting." And among Millennials and members of Generation Z, it's not uncommon for an awkward silence to be broken with the statement, "Hashtag awkward!" Another one you might hear is "hashtag winning."

But for some reason, hearing the word uttered in the real world really riles some folks. Case in point: A 2017 comment thread on the website Mumsnet that was titled "To not understand what someone means when they say 'hashtag'?" There was post after post (59 in all) of bewildered moms trying to explain to each other what "hashtag" means. Many of the posts read like this one: "It's nonsense. It makes no sense, which is why you do not understand it! # is a reference to Twitter, but people seem to think it is cool to say it in [real life] when it should be left on Twitter."

A 2011 *Gizmodo* article called "How the Hashtag Is Ruining the English Language" was even harsher: "Hashtags at their best stand in as what linguists call 'paralanguage,' like shoulder shrugs and intonations. That's fine. But at their most annoying, the colloquial hashtag has burst out of its use as a sorting tool and become a linguistic tumor—a tic more irritating than any banal link or lazy image meme."

HASHTAGS FOR ALL

Like all elements of a living language, hashtags have proven their versatility and ability to adapt to whatever users want them to be—not unlike the # symbol from which they came. So don't expect hashtagging to fade out like other 2010s fads (remember Gangnam Style?). "Nowadays," wrote the entrepreneur website Seed Spot, "Hashtags are more than a #throwbackthursday or #mancrushmonday. They are the lifeline of social media, connecting followers with causes and increasing donation power. Hashtags give a voice to those without a pedestal, unify complete strangers, and can generate unstoppable momentum."

And it's important to note that "Open Source" advocate Chris Messina never copyrighted his idea because he believes hashtagging should be a tool that any user on any social media site can use…for free. "The hashtag was not created for Twitter," he is quick to remind people. "The hashtag was created for the internet." And he's especially proud of where it came from: "Of all the possible symbols I could have chosen, I think the octothorpe was the best one. As a typography lover, I do like the look of the symbol. It's one of the more dense characters, so you can see it from a distance or at a glance—it's hard to miss!" #he_aint_kidding

*   *   *

PERFECT FOR THE ZOMBIE APOCALYPSE

A firearms manufacturer in Kentucky has figured out a way to weaponize the chainsaw. They developed a Chainsaw Bayonet, which is exactly what it sounds like: a small, fully powered chainsaw that attaches to the end of an AR-15 semiautomatic rifle.

What happens at the Eiffel Tower each night at 1 a.m.? They turn off the lights.

UNCLE JOHN'S STALL OF SHAME

Not everyone who makes it into the Stall of Fame is there for a good reason. That's why Uncle John created the "Stall of Shame."

DUBIOUS ACHIEVERS: Random drug-test takers in Jacksonville, Florida

CLAIM TO FAME: Desecrating a microwave oven

True Story: Word on the street is that if you want to pass a drug test, warm up your urine sample. (There is considerable debate as to whether this is true). True or not, it was bad news for Parul Patel, who owns a convenience store near a drug-testing clinic in Jacksonville. "Every day," she complained to the *Orlando Sentinel* in 2018, "random people walk in off the street, microwave their urine containers, then leave." She tried telling them to stop, but most of them did it anyway. One woman even got belligerent and argued that she should be able to put her pee in the microwave because there's no sign telling her not to.

Outcome: Patel put up a sign telling people not to put their pee in the microwave.

DUBIOUS ACHIEVER: Joseph Stalin, dictator of the Soviet Union from 1923 to 1953

CLAIM TO FAME: Stealing the poop of his political enemies

True Story: In 1949 Chinese chairman Mao Zedong spent ten days in Moscow to work out a partnership with Stalin. Unbeknownst to Mao, the toilet in his guest room wasn't connected to the sewer line; instead, Mao's leavings were rerouted to a special box. The poop was delivered to a secret laboratory, where scientists analyzed its chemical makeup. To what end? So they could create a psychological profile of Chairman Mao. According to a former Soviet agent named Igor Atamanenko, who exposed the top-secret program in 2016, "If the scientists detected high levels of amino acid Tryptophan, they concluded that person was calm and approachable." Mao's poop had low levels of potassium, which was seen as "a sign of a nervous disposition and someone with insomnia." Atamanenko said that Mao knew something was up because he felt more like Stalin's prisoner than a guest. Convinced that his room was bugged (it probably was), at one point Mao yelled, "I am here to do more than eat and sh*t!"

Outcome: According to BBC News, "Once Mao's stools had been scrutinized and studied, Stalin reportedly poo-poo-ed the idea of signing an agreement with him." Stalin analyzed several other world leaders' feces before he died in 1954. Then the program was flushed.

If they sense they're being watched, squirrels will pretend to hide nuts to throw off interlopers.

DUBIOUS ACHIEVER: Jillian Mai Thi Epperly, an entrepreneur from Canton, Ohio

CLAIM TO FAME: Using quack medicine to create a "Poop Cult"

True Story: Epperly sells a book online called *The Jilly Juice Protocol: Exposing the Lies Candida Weaponized Fungus Mainstreaming Mutancy*. Readers learn the recipe and protocol for Jilly Juice, a drink that causes explosive bouts of diarrhea. Epperly refers to these bouts as "waterfalls." What's the difference? "Diarrhea," she told the *Daily Mail* in 2018, "is when you poison the body," whereas waterfalls heal the body by ridding it of "cancer-causing candida." She has also claimed that Jilly Juice can "reverse 100 percent of health problems," including "regrow lost limbs, cure autism, and turn gay people straight." Epperly has amassed more than 60,000 Facebook followers—referred to by some in the press as the "Poop Cult." She's even pitched her book on *Dr. Phil.*

Everything was right as rain for Epperly until 2018, when the U.S. Federal Trade Commission (FTC) told her to put a plug in her outlandish claims—after a man with stage four pancreatic cancer became emaciated and died after drinking nothing but Jilly Juice for a month. The FTC warned Epperly that because she provides no scientific evidence to back up her claims, she is "in violation of regulations on false advertising of unproven health benefits."

Outcome: Last time we checked, Epperly was still selling the book. But she told the *Daily Mail* that she "can't be held accountable" for what happens to her followers. "Out of like 60,000 people that took my juice, how many people have died? It's not fair to hold me to that kind of standard." Yet Epperly has muddled up the language on her website to avoid litigation. Interested in enjoying your own...waterfalls? Jilly Juice's ingredients are "fermented cabbage, water, and Himalayan sea salt." Drink a gallon a day.

DUBIOUS ACHIEVER: Transport Canada

CLAIM TO FAME: Giving a lady the runaround after she got dumped on

True Story: In May 2018, Sue Allan took her son out to lunch near Kelowna International Airport in British Columbia. It was a nice day, so she opened the car's sunroof...which turned out to be a bad idea. While stopped at a red light, "The 'sky poop' started falling," she recounted to the *Salmon Arm Observer*. "It got all over my car, it got all over me and my son. It smelt horrific." Right after the onslaught, Allan saw a plane overhead. Then her son vomited. They drove straight to a car wash and sprayed themselves off, and soon realized that the car would need to be professionally cleaned. Worse yet, her eyes started itching, so she went to the doctor the next day and found out she had conjunctivitis (pink eye) in both eyes.

> "It got all over my car, it got all over me and my son. It smelt horrific."

Beep-beep! A coyote can actually run faster than a roadrunner.

Allan looked to Transport Canada for an explanation, an apology, and compensation for car-cleaning bills. But after several phone calls, all she had were conflicting explanations, no apology, and no compensation. "First I was told that there were three planes that flew over that area at that time, then I was told that there was one plane, and now all of a sudden no plane flew over the area at that time." They also told her that it's unlikely that a pilot dumped the plane's sewage on purpose; rather, some of it leaked and froze onto the fuselage, and then, as the plane neared the ground, melted and splattered all over Allan's car. She also discovered that this was the 18th report of an unfortunate shower near that airport in the past month.

Outcome: After receiving no help from the authorities, Allan told her story to the press. When asked to comment, a Transport Canada spokesperson said, "We are aware of the incident you describe and are looking into it."

DUBIOUS ACHIEVER: "Parrotheads," aka Jimmy Buffett fans
CLAIM TO FAME: Turning a parking lot into a hazardous waste area

True Story: Every August, the Xfinity Center in Mansfield, Massachusetts, hosts Jimmy Buffett and the Coral Reefer Band. Thousands of Parrotheads roll in—donning their customary leis, loud sunglasses, and tacky hats—for a night of cheeseburgers in paradise (that's a Jimmy Buffett song). Before the show, there's always a big party in the parking lot. And instead of waiting in long lines for the portable toilets, some resourceful Parrotheads have taken to bringing their own makeshift loos: most commonly a five-gallon bucket with a lid. Then they leave the full buckets in the parking lot after the show. According to Mansfield police chief Ronald Sellon, this problem is unique to Jimmy Buffett concerts. In 2015 nearly 100 Parrotheads were told to put away their buckets and use the commodes. "It's unsanitary and just disrespectful," complained Chief Sellon.

Outcome: Prior to each year's show, the Mansfield PD issues a friendly reminder to Parrotheads to use the "actual, health-code-compliant toilets that aren't attached to the bumper of a pickup truck"…but the conflict continues.

DUBIOUS ACHIEVER: Lamarr Chambers, a 24-year-old suspected drug dealer from London, England
CLAIM TO FAME: Putting his bowels through hell for a month and a half

True Story: On January 17, 2018, Essex police arrested Chambers on suspicion of selling drugs. But where were they? The cops thought he swallowed them, so they took Chambers to jail and waited for nature to take its course. He didn't poop on the first day or the second, and thus began #PooWatch. As days passed and the drugs didn't, the police tweeted about the suspect's (lack of) progress. Some examples:

Official state sport of Maryland: jousting.

- *Day 3:* Male has now been in police custody for the past 50 hrs and will remain until he passes said items. #PooWatch
- *Day 8:* Suspect has now been with us for an entire week and not been to the toilet once! Back to court tomorrow to request further detention until items are recovered. #PooWatch
- *Day 19:* We still have no movement, male doesn't seem to understand that eventually he will need/have to go. #PooWatch

Chambers received daily doctor visits, and occasionally ate some fruit and nut bars, but his bathroom strike kept going and going. After a while, the cops even got tired of updating #PooWatch: "We will make one final announcement when he does what he needs to do." Meanwhile, Chambers's lawyer demanded his client be released so he could go on his own, telling BBC News that Chambers is "in an arena of risk of death."

Outcome: Nothing came out. On March 5, 2018—after 47 days—Chambers was released…and was taken straight to the hospital. The drug charges didn't stick.

DUBIOUS ACHIEVER: J. B. Pritzker, an Illinois gubernatorial candidate in 2018
CLAIM TO FAME: Using toilets to get out of paying taxes

True Story: With only a month to go in the governor's race, the billionaire Democrat's chances were tainted after a document was leaked from the Cook County Inspector General's office. It seems that back in 2007, Pritzker and his wife (heirs to the Hyatt Hotels fortune) had purchased a second mansion next to their mansion on Astor Street in Chicago. Then they didn't live in it. Not wanting to pay high property taxes on an empty house, in 2015 the Pritzkers found a loophole: They had a plumber disconnect all the toilets, which technically made the mansion "uninhabitable," thus lowering its value from $6.3 million to a paltry $1.1 million…and lowering the property taxes considerably. (And after the tax assessment was made, the toilets were hooked back up.) Once the scandal became public, the incumbent Republican candidate, Governor Bruce Rauner, released a political ad calling Pritzker the "Porcelain Prince of Tax Avoidance." Pritzker called the leak a political ploy, but he admitted to disconnecting the toilets, while maintaining that he "didn't break any rules." And he did agree to pay back $330,000 in back taxes.

Outcome: The Porcelain Prince of Tax Avoidance unseated his opponent.

* * *

"I've been rich and I've been poor; rich is better."
—**Sophie Tucker**

A comet's tail always points away from the sun.

A HISTORY OF PTSD

Here's the fascinating history of what our great-grandparents called "shell shock."

BACKGROUND

Post-traumatic stress disorder is a condition usually associated with men and women of the military who have lived through intense combat situations. But the condition, marked by flashbacks, intrusive negative thoughts, depressive behavior, and anxiety, affects more than just soldiers. Any sort of trauma—a violent attack, a stressful period, or a major hardship—can have long-lasting effects on the brain (and a person's life). Around 4 percent of American men and 10 percent of American women may receive a PTSD diagnosis at some time in their lives…and those are just the ones who've been diagnosed. The true number of sufferers may be much higher. Consisting of a suite of different symptoms, PTSD has proved tricky for doctors to fully define. It's actually taken hundreds of years for us to understand—and provide proper, effective care for—the condition commonly referred to as PTSD.

490 B.C. In writing about the Battle of Marathon, ancient Greek historian Herodotus describes the plight of Epizelus, an Athenian soldier who suddenly goes blind (and remains so for life) "without blow of sword or dart" after he witnesses a "gigantic warrior" from the other side kill an Athenian in front of him. A physical result of experiencing a traumatic event, this is the first historical mention of what would later be called post-traumatic stress.

A.D. 1190s In the *Itinerarium Peregrinorum et Gesta Regis Ricardi*, an account of the Third Crusade (1187–1192) recorded immediately after soldiers returned from the Middle East, the writer notes that the men "survived unharmed, but their hearts were pierced by swords of sorrows from different sorts of suffering."

1350 A French knight named Geoffroi de Charny writes *The Book of Chivalry*, a guidebook for fellow knights. It includes fair warning of what a knight in battle may suffer, including the horrors of killing and having to kill. He also writes of battles *after* the battles: "When they would be secure from danger, they will be beset by great terrors," implying that a warrior may suffer psychological effects after the fact.

1761 Austrian doctor Josef Leopold writes about a condition common among veterans of wars that he calls *nostalgia*. Far different from the definition of

Only baseball player named MVP in both the National and the American League: Frank Robinson.

what we'd call nostalgia today (an aching for a time or experience of long ago), Leopold reports that those soldiers who'd endured traumatic combat reported sadness, anxiety, sleep problems, and homesickness. Soldiers aren't treated for nostalgia in any meaningful way.

1860s During the Civil War, American doctor Jacob Mendez Da Costa studies soldiers experiencing anxiety issues. Because they also experience elevated pulse and difficulty breathing (anxiety often manifests physically as well as psychologically), Da Costa concludes that there's something wrong with the veterans' hearts and diagnoses them with "Da Costa's syndrome," also known as "soldier's heart." Chalking it up to overstimulation of the heart and nervous system brought on by active duty, the doctor and his contemporaries prescribe a few days of bed rest and regular doses of foxglove (*Digitalis*). After that, they are returned to the front.

1866 Meanwhile, doctors and scientists in Europe don't realize it, but they are studying the same things as Da Costa. Research there holds that PTSD can result from any traumatic life event, not just combat. In 1866 British surgeon John Eric Erichsen publishes his study *On Railway and Other Injuries of the Nervous System*. It explores the phenomenon of "railway spine," a commonly diagnosed condition among people who'd been in train accidents. For example, author Charles Dickens survived a railway mishap in 1865, and reported experiencing anxiety, difficulty sleeping, and nightmares thereafter.

1887 Doctors recognize that suffering from anxiety, nightmares, sadness, and other symptoms may not be a temporary condition that occurs right after a trauma. French doctor Jean-Martin Charcot publishes a study concluding that "hysterical attacks" could occur months or even years after the triggering event.

1890s The rise of psychotherapy and "talking cures" for psychological disorders, credited to Sigmund Freud, is first used to treat patients suffering from both soldier's heart and railway spine.

1915 Thanks to research in the years after the Civil War, "soldier's heart" is a bit better understood, and is widely referred to—particularly among World War I troops—as "shell shock." Thought to be a reaction to the experience of being near (or the target of) exploding artillery shells, troops exhibit symptoms such as panic attacks, anxiety, and depression. Doctors don't believe it is a psychological condition, but rather a neurological one. The prevailing science is that shell shock is the manifestation of a physical brain injury sustained in combat. Just as in the Civil War, treatment consists of a few days of R&R before returning to battle. That's in the United States; in Europe, military doctors utilize electroshock therapy and hypnosis to treat what they call "war neuroses."

1941 to 1945 During World War II, American soldiers fighting in Europe and Japan face extra-long tours of duty, leading to physical and emotional exhaustion. Military doctors diagnose them with what they are now calling "battle fatigue" or combat stress reaction (CSR). About half of all military discharges in World War II are due to CSR, and are routinely treated with rest.

1945 Every major war seemingly brings with it a reexamination (and better understanding) of the effects of combat on those who fight, and World War II is no exception. In one of the mainstream media's first mentions of what we now call PTSD, *Life* magazine runs a photo of a painting called "Marines Call It That 2,000 Yard Stare," by artist Tom Lea. It depicts a Marine at the Battle of Peleliu. He appears despondent and distant, and gazing off into the long distance. That alerts American civilians that their troops may not come home the same as they remember them. (It's also the origin of the phrase "the 2,000-yard stare," sometimes called "the 1,000-yard stare.")

1952 The American Psychiatric Association publishes the *Diagnostic and Statistical Manual of Mental Disorders* (DSM), a standardized guide for recognizing and diagnosing every known mental disorder. Among its listings is a condition called "gross stress reaction," which refers to a disorder in which people live relatively normal lives but continue to suffer psychological effects of a trauma, such as combat, a natural disaster, or a violent crime. While that opens up the definition of the disorder to include traumas other than combat, the DSM also holds that gross stress reaction generally resolves itself after six months. If the patient still suffers nightmares, flashbacks, and anxiety, the DSM recommends that doctors look for another condition to diagnose.

1968 In the first revision of the DSM, titled the *DSM-II*, gross stress reaction is eliminated in favor of "adjustment reaction to adult life." Similar to previous diagnoses, such as CSR and shell shock, it recognizes certain symptoms (anxiety, sleep trouble) but limits its definition of trauma and post-event trauma to just three very specific situations: unwanted pregnancy with suicidal thoughts, military combat resulting in fear, and Ganser syndrome, which is a condition in which prisoners on death row are so distraught about their impending execution that they can't process or answer questions correctly.

1974 Psychologist Ann Wolbert Burgess and sociologist Lynda Lytle Holmstrom write about a disorder they call "rape trauma syndrome." The researchers conclude that women who have suffered a sexual assault endure the same kinds of stress responses as soldiers in combat.

1980 After widespread research on Vietnam War veterans who served in the 1960s and 1970s—and factoring in studies like the one by Burgess and Holmstrom—the American Psychiatric Association adds post-traumatic stress disorder to the newly issued *DSM-III*. It creates a definitive, recognized link between the trauma of war and a struggle to adjust to post-service civilian life.

1989 Congress creates the National Center for PTSD. Administered by the Department of Veterans Affairs (VA), it becomes the leading researcher and treatment facility for the condition.

2013 Reflecting ongoing research at the VA and other facilities, the *DSM-5* is published, and no longer classifies PTSD as an anxiety disorder. As PTSD is more specifically associated with "mood states" such as depression and reckless behavior, the APA now considers it a "trauma and stressor-related disorder." The *DSM-5* also lists four types of "official" PTSD symptoms: intrusion, or reliving the traumatic event (nightmares, flashbacks); eschewing situations that remind the patient of the traumatic event (a veteran avoiding fireworks); negative changes in beliefs and feelings (long confused with clinical depression); and feelings of being "charged up" (often confused with anxiety). PTSD is diagnosed if all four symptoms are present, last for a month or longer, and adversely affect the patient's daily life and relationships.

A better understanding of PTSD means better treatments for PTSD. Psychologists around the world now treat it with counseling, medication, cognitive behavioral therapy (a therapy that focuses on changing the patient's thought patterns), and eye movement desensitization and reprocessing (EMDR), a nontraditional therapy in which the patient's eye movements are used to control distressing memories of traumatic events. Confronting past trauma in a safe, controlled environment (a doctor's office) typically has three aims: to alleviate symptoms, teach coping skills, and restore the patient's self-esteem. But like most mental illnesses, there is no blanket cure for the condition...yet.

Not all at once: The average American spends a total of two weeks each year sitting on a toilet.

CREEPY STORIES

When real life feels more like an episode of The Twilight Zone.

THE HAUNTING OF IPSWICH

It was a dreary January day in the English town of Ipswich in 2018 when the strange music first appeared: A recording of a young child warbled out over the countryside, slowly singing, "It's raaaining…it's pooouring…the ollld man is snoooring…" The nursery rhyme brought several people outside, but no one knew where it was coming from. Then it stopped. "It sounded like something from a horror movie," a frightened mom told the *Ipswich Star*. That was just the beginning. The song played again several times over the next few months, but there was no pattern, and it always stopped before anyone could trace its source. It was driving the townsfolk crazy. Finally, on a chilly September evening, the disembodied voice sang its song, and town workers on high alert tracked it down to its source—a nearby business park. The next day, the apologetic business park owner issued a statement: "The sound is only supposed to act as a deterrent for opportunistic thieves that come onto our property, and it's designed only to be heard by people on our private land, but it looks like we've had it turned up too loudly." And it only went off when the business park was empty, which is why no one there was aware of the havoc it was wreaking upon the town. Here's the creepiest part of all: The music was being triggered by motion sensors, which were being triggered by spiders crawling across the lenses of the park's surveillance cameras.

SILENT TREATMENT

Born in Yemen in 1963, identical twins June and Jennifer Gibbons moved to Wales when they were babies. As the only black kids at their Welsh school, the sisters were relentlessly teased and bullied. Their coping mechanism: silence. They rarely spoke to anyone except each other, and only in their own secret language. Shutting out the rest of the world, the teens took to writing strange crime novels with such titles as *Pepsi-Cola Addict* and *Discomania*. Then they turned to actual crime. A spree of arson and theft landed the 18-year-olds in Broadmoor, a high-security psychiatric hospital in England. Toward the end of their 12-year stay, the "silent twins," as they were known, decided that one of them had to die. "This sister of mine," wrote June in her diary, "a dark shadow robbing me of sunlight, is my one and only torment." During an interview with their biographer, Jennifer said, "I'm going to die. We've decided." On the day of their release in 1993, it happened—Jennifer suffered a massive heart attack and died on her sister's shoulder. No official cause of death was ever found, but June was convinced that her sister willed herself to die. "I'm free at last, liberated," she wrote.

The Otis Spunkmeyer cookie company's name draws inspiration
from 1970s NFL player Otis Sistrunk and popcorn magnate Orville Redenbacher.

"Jennifer has given up her life for me." As of last report, June was "living quietly and independently near her parents in West Wales."

UNSEEN FORCES

In 2018 Erica Glaze of Houston, Texas, was out shopping when she received an alert from her alarm company: someone or something had set off three alarms in different areas of her house. She rushed home and found shattered glass all over her dining room. Curiously, no doors were open and nothing was missing. But the glass top of her new $2,000 dining room table had exploded into a thousand pieces. There was nothing on the table heavy enough to make the glass buckle, much less shatter it with enough force to trigger alarms all over the house. "Normally, if something is going to break from weight, it caves in," Glaze told KHOU News. "This exploded externally. There was force behind it." It's a good thing the family wasn't home—their baby's chair and toys are kept right next to the table. Glaze later discovered that several other glass tables—all made by the same manufacturer—had met similar ends. (The high-end furniture company had no comment for the press.) The Glazes were given a new table from the furniture store…by a different manufacturer.

SITTING IN TRAFFIC

On a rainy Sunday in Aberdeen, Scotland, in 2018, a mysterious man placed a large red chair in the middle of a busy intersection and then sat down. A local woman named Bernadine Magee posted a photo of the sitting man, which went viral. The *Scottish Sun* asked her to describe the odd scene, and she was obviously still trying to process it herself:

> "It's not often you see someone sitting on a red leather chair in the middle of the road. We thought it was quite funny. It was just him sitting in the middle of the road and we were beeping at him. He was just sitting there on the chair in the middle of the road with his eyes closed taking no notice of anybody. He never smiled, never moved, he just sat there. I've never seen anything like that before. He was just sitting there chilled out. We beeped our horn and he never opened his eyes, never looked around, nothing. The cars were having to drive around him. If somebody had come along in a big lorry he might have been in danger. A lorry could have hit him. But he was just in the middle of the road. He was sitting there for ages. We were stuck at the traffic lights and he was still sitting there. I just started laughing. I thought it was hilarious. I was like, 'Talk about chilling on a Sunday afternoon!' "

That wasn't even her full statement. When Magee returned to the intersection later that night, the red chair was on the sidewalk and the mysterious sitter was gone.

In 1912 a Paris orphanage held a raffle in which the prizes were babies.

WORD ASSOCIATION QUOTATIONS

*Here's a game our resident quote monkey made up to keep himself amused:
He started with a quotation about a bathroom, and then found
another quote based on something from the end of that quote,
and so on, and so on, until he found his way back to the
bathroom. Let's see how many quotes it took him!*

> "Always go to the bathroom when you have a chance."
> **—King George V**

> "Chance is a word void of sense; nothing can exist without a cause."
> **—Voltaire**

> "The complexities of cause and effect defy analysis."
> **—Douglas Adams**

> "Analysis does not transform consciousness."
> **—Jiddu Krishnamurti**

> "Consciousness is only possible through change; change is only possible through movement."
> **—Aldous Huxley**

> "'Movement is life'; and it is well to be able to forget the past, and kill the present by continual change."
> **—Jules Verne**

> "They must often change, who would be constant in happiness or wisdom."
> **—Confucius**

> "Happiness has to do with your mindset, not with outside circumstance."
> **—Steve Maraboli**

> "Circumstances define us; they force us onto one road or another, and then they punish us for it."
> **—Ivan Turgenev**

> "You will not be punished for your anger, you will be punished by your anger."
> **—Buddha**

Estimate: In the U.S., 1 million dogs are listed as the primary beneficiary in their owners' wills.

> "Pent-up anger is oftentimes more destructive than a good quarrel."
> **—Kilroy J. Oldster**

> "We make out of the quarrel with others, rhetoric, but of the quarrel with ourselves, poetry."
> **—William Butler Yeats**

> "Poetry might be defined as the clear expression of mixed feelings."
> **—W. H. Auden**

> "Feelings come and go like clouds in a windy sky. Conscious breathing is my anchor."
> **—Thich Nhat Hanh**

> "All you need is one safe anchor to keep you grounded when the rest of your life spins out of control."
> **—Katie Kacvinsky**

> "The control of information is something the elite always does, particularly in a despotic form of government."
> **—Tom Clancy**

> "Government's first duty is to protect the people, not run their lives."
> **—Ronald Reagan**

> "Our lives begin to end the day we become silent about things that matter."
> **—Martin Luther King Jr.**

> "Matter, that thing the most solid and the well-known, which you are holding in your hands and which makes up your body, is now known to be mostly empty space."
> **—Jeanette Winterson**

> "I see nothing in space as promising as the view from a Ferris wheel."
> **—E. B. White**

> "The worst wheel of the cart makes the most noise."
> **—Benjamin Franklin**

> "Ten people who speak make more noise than ten thousand who are silent."
> **—Napoleon Bonaparte**

> "Without silence, there cannot be any real appreciation in life."
> **—Deepak Chopra**

> "Life is like a movie—since there aren't any commercial breaks, you have to get up and go to the bathroom in the middle of it."
> **—Garry Trudeau**

The U.S. Congress recognizes Colon, Michigan, as the "magic capital of the world."

THE LIFE AND TIMES OF GRIZZLY ADAMS, PART II

You have probably heard of the legendary mountain man we told you about in part one of this tale. But there's much more of the story to tell—the story of the classic 1970s TV show and the mountain man who portrayed him. (Part I of the story is on page 365.)

BACKGROUND

"They call me Mad Jack, and if there is anybody in these mountains that knows the real story about James Adams, that'd be me. So I'm putting it down in writing just how it happened in hopes of setting the record straight."

If you're of a certain age (old), then that introduction should sound familiar. It was the opening narration from *The Life and Times of Grizzly Adams*, a one-hour drama that aired on NBC on Wednesday nights in 1978 and 1979. But the show didn't really "set the record straight." That would have been a pretty bad idea for a family show, because the real Adams was a mountain man who killed thousands of wild animals. The TV Grizzly Adams was much kinder and gentler. A lot of that had to with the sensibilities of the 1970s, and a lot of it had to do with the man they hired to portray Adams.

MUSCLE MAN

If anyone was born to play Grizzly Adams, it was Dan Haggerty. As a teenager in the 1950s, he worked at his family's wild animal attraction in Pound, Wisconsin, where he learned, among other things, how to train bears to do tricks. Like Adams, he had a favorite bear that followed him around. Also like Adams, he left home to make it big in California. His mom had wanted him to be a priest. Instead, he went to live with his dad, a movie technician, in Hollywood.

Young Haggerty grew into a tall man with broad shoulders, a barrel chest, and sandy-blond hair. His good looks and powerful physique landed him small roles in 1964's *Muscle Beach Party* (starring Frankie Avalon and Annette Funicello) and 1965's *Girl Happy* (starring Elvis Presley). Acting didn't come as easy, though, and he wasn't getting any good parts, so he supplemented his income wrangling wild animals for various Disney productions and TV shows. An avid motorcycle rider, Haggerty also worked on the bikes, including the ones that Peter Fonda and Jack Nicholson rode, in 1969's *Easy Rider*, and he plays a hippie in the film. Because, as Haggerty often joked, "actors don't like animals leaping on them," he also found steady work as a stuntman. That's what he was doing in 1974 when he was plucked to play Grizzly Adams. But this was a much different Adams than the real-life character, and a much different time.

Camels were used as pack animals in Nevada until 1870.

BACK TO NATURE

After 150 years of rapid growth and industrialization, by 1970 the United States was a polluted mess. A river caught fire in Cleveland, and a blanket of brown smog was smothering Los Angeles. It got so bad that President Richard Nixon created the U.S. Environmental Protection Agency. With that, the modern environmentalism movement was born. This "back to nature" fad led to popular frontier shows like *The Waltons* (1971–81) and *Little House on the Prairie* (1974–83). Hoping to cash in, in 1972 an up-and-coming TV writer and producer named Charles E. Sellier wrote a novel called *The Life and Times of Grizzly Adams*. Despite the subtitle's claim that it was "the true story of a man exiled in the wilderness who learns how to survive," Sellier had no intentions of telling Adams's true story. His was a sanitized, made-for-TV version that left out all the gory details. Two examples: the real Adams was a failed rancher and failed miner who fled to the woods in part to escape his unpaid debts; Sellier's Adams was a gentle farmer who was wrongly accused of murder. The real Adams captured his grizzly cub by killing its mother; Sellier's Adams rescued an orphaned cub from a cliff.

THE MOVIE

> He noticed a burly stuntman with a big beard who was chasing a tiger across a frozen lake and said, "Now that's Grizzly Adams!"

As soon as the book was published, Sellier started shopping it to movie studios. He partnered with Patrick Frawley at Sunn Classic Pictures, and they started filming the movie. But the actor they'd hired to play Adams wasn't working out. Most of the footage was unusable, and the project stalled. Then, while Frawley was looking at some daily footage from another movie they were making called *The Snow Tigers*, he noticed a burly stuntman with a big beard who was chasing a tiger across a frozen lake and said, "Now *that's* Grizzly Adams!" Frawley asked his secretary, Diane, "Do you know that guy?"

"Yes," she said. "That's my husband."

Haggerty enthusiastically accepted the role, and they scrapped the existing footage—which had cost $500,000—and used the $185,000 they had left in the budget to film *The Life and Times of Grizzly Adams* in the mountains outside of Park City, Utah.

The movie opens with Haggerty as Adams heading off into the wilderness, where he finds a grizzly cub he names Ben and befriends an Indian named Nakoma. If you're a fan of the TV show, watching the movie can be a bit disconcerting because Haggerty's voice was deemed too "California surfer" by Frawley, and was overdubbed by another actor who doesn't sound like Haggerty. Nevertheless, the movie outperformed everyone's expectations, making $45 million domestically and another $20 million overseas. It was the seventh highest-grossing film of 1974—coming in just behind *The Godfather Part II*—and is still one of the most profitable independent films ever made.

Yams are more closely related to lilies than they are to sweet potatoes.

When NBC aired the movie in 1976, it drew a huge 45 percent market share. NBC brass wanted a Grizzly Adams TV show, and they wanted Haggerty to play him. For Haggerty, it was a dream come true.

A WILD DR. DOOLITTLE

As one of the characters, Mad Jack, describes Adams at the beginning of each episode, "He had a special kind of way with animals. They'd just come right up to him like he was a natural part of the wilderness." Haggerty fit that bill perfectly. He was just as comfortable with his wild co-stars as he was with the mountains of Utah where they filmed *The Life and Times of Grizzly Adams* (or Arizona or New Mexico when the weather didn't cooperate). Unlike the real Grizzly Adams, who killed untold numbers of wild animals, this Adams wouldn't even eat an animal, much less kill one. "Calm your bones, Ben," Adams says as the bear pokes his nose into a satchel. "We've got to save these berries for Jack's special blueberry pie. First, the berries go into the fillin', and then the pies will be fillin' you. Doesn't that sound like a dandy idea?" Ben growls in agreement.

Ben was played by a 600-pound female Kodiak bear (a subspecies of the grizzly from Alaska) named Boz (short for Bozo). Haggerty and Boz formed an instant bond, and they remained friends until her death in 1999. Also living at Adams's cabin are two skunks named Mary Lou and Daniel, a raccoon named Joshua, and a hawk named Hawk. He talks to them like they're human and, like a western Dr. Doolittle, instinctively knows what they're trying to tell him.

SUPPORTING PLAYERS

Mad Jack, a roving trader who narrates the show, bears a closer resemblance to the real John Adams, right down to his long white beard, buckskins, and fur cap. Played by veteran character actor Denver Pyle (Uncle Jesse on *The Dukes of Hazzard*), he often got the laugh lines, especially when bickering with his pack mule, Number 7: "You'd better stop bein' so ornery, Number 7, or I'm gonna have to go and find me a Number 8!"

Nakoma, a member of an unnamed Indian tribe, is Adams's "blood brother." He was played by a stuntman named Don Shanks, who is of Cherokee and Illini descent. During a time when most Native Americans on-screen were either savages or sidekicks, Nakoma was portrayed so realistically that he spoke his own language.

Typical storylines revolved around Adams and his friends helping strangers—a girl lost in the forest, a runaway slave, a down-on-his luck hot-air balloonist. In one episode, Adams saves the life of a young "greenhorn from back East" who turns out to be Teddy Roosevelt. In one of the more dramatic storylines, Ben is accused of stealing fish from the chief of Nakoma's tribe. Can Adams save his grizzly bear while honoring the ways of the Indians?

Wil Wheaton (Wesley on *Star Trek: The Next Generation*) auditioned for the role of Ralphie in *A Christmas Story*.

PEOPLE'S CHOICE

The Life and Times of Grizzly Adams premiered in January 1977 up against ratings juggernauts *Good Times* and *The Bionic Woman*. It performed strongly, bringing in an impressive 32 percent market share. Critics weren't too impressed with Haggerty's acting—which did improve somewhat as the show progressed—but viewers loved his "Aw, shucks" demeanor and strong moral compass (two qualities that helped President Jimmy Carter get elected in 1976 after the messiness of the Nixon/Ford years). Haggerty won the People's Choice Award for Favorite Male Performer in a New Program that year, and (along with Boz/Ben) he became the first person featured on the cover of *TV Guide* twice in six months. Grizzly Adams took his rightful place on school lunch boxes alongside *Star Wars* and *Happy Days*. Part of the show's appeal, said Haggerty at the time, was that it's "a change for viewers who are sick of screaming brakes, cars exploding, and fight scenes. Pretty scenery and a couple of guys traipsing through the woods is a relief."

In season two, Haggerty wanted Adams to get a wife, but his request was denied. The network told him more women would tune in if they thought Adams was an eligible bachelor. Then, for reasons that are still not known, NBC canceled the show, even though it was still bringing in viewers. Haggerty only got to play the character two more times in TV movies, concluding with 1982's *The Capture of Grizzly Adams*. If Haggerty had his way, he'd have played Adams for the rest of his life, but that's not how it worked out.

PEAKS AND VALLEYS

Like Adams, Haggerty was in his mid-30s when he became famous. And, like Adams, he called that time the best two years of his life. But unlike Adams, Haggerty became less famous when he emerged from the wilderness. The only money he made from the show was his weekly salary. He didn't reap any of the considerable merchandising or rerun profits, and went back to being a struggling actor. (Charles Sellier trademarked the Grizzly Adams brand name and made a fortune off it in merchandising.) In the early 1980s, Haggerty paid the bills by directing animals on movie sets and guest-starring on shows like *CHiPs*, *Charlie's Angels*, and *The Love Boat*. He hit rock bottom in 1985 when he was arrested in Los Angeles for selling cocaine to undercover cops, and served 90 days in jail. Haggerty became friends with the two officers who ran the sting, though, and tried to maintain a positive outlook after he served his time, saying, "The system's been good to me."

Maybe...but adversity was never far off. In 1987 he was in a serious motorcycle accident. While he was recovering, he was charged with tax evasion. Then in 1991, he was in an even worse motorcycle accident, which left him in a coma and required 18 surgeries to heal. (In 2008 his second wife was killed in a similar bike accident.)

First ever submarine: the *Drebbel I* in 1620. It was an enclosed rowboat.

THE IRONY AGE

Though he tried, Haggerty was never able to rekindle the Adams flame, probably because the world had simply moved on. The 1980s brought Ronald Reagan, who famously said, "A tree is a tree, how many more do you need to look at?" And while shows like *Little House* and *The Waltons* did manage to retain a spot in the cultural zeitgeist, for the most part popular entertainment was getting edgier and more cynical. By the 1990s, "Grizzly Adams" had become fully transformed from "patron saint of the animals" to the go-to joke about any man with a burly beard, as evidenced in *Happy Gilmore, 30 Rock, Veep, Family Guy*, and countless more movies and TV shows.

> By the 1990s, "Grizzly Adams" had become fully transformed from "patron saint of the animals" to the go-to joke about any man with a burly beard.

Unfortunately for Haggerty, whose acting range was limited, that led to a lot of "stunt-casting" in low-budget movies. He shows up in forgettable roles in a number of forgettable movies—as a "loose-cannon mall Santa" in the schlocky horror flick *Elves*, as a repo man in the action yarn *Repo Drake*, as an ex-con who gives Rob Schneider horrible advice in the raunchy comedy *Big Stan*, as a biker in *Dead in 5 Heartbeats*, and as a lumberjack in *Axe Giant: The Wrath of Paul Bunyan*. Haggerty's final performance, as Captain in *The Untold Story*, premiered in 2019, three years after he died.

But none of Haggerty's acting parts earned him enough to feed all his wild animals and his family at his sprawling ranch in Malibu Canyon. So later in his life, he supplemented his income with convention appearances and—in true Grizzly Adams fashion—he managed a company that sold log cabins. He also opened a restaurant where he sold his own brand of Cajun barbecue sauce, he sold the only surviving original motorcycle from *Easy Rider*, and he appeared on a late-night infomercial for hair transplants.

But the thing Haggerty wanted most—a Grizzly Adams revival—never happened. He was diagnosed with spinal cancer in August 2015. His daughter started a GoFundMe campaign to raise the $100,000 required for treatment, but it barely brought in $10,000. Once among the most popular TV stars in America, Dan Haggerty died with little fanfare in January 2016 at the age of 73.

MIXED MESSAGES

Watching *The Life and Times of Grizzly Adams* today is like watching an idealized version of the 1850s as told by an idealized version of the 1970s. On one hand, the storylines revolved around tolerance, racial harmony, pacifism, and environmentalism. On the other hand, impressionable little kids got to watch a nice man hand-feed wild animals, which we now know is harmful to wildlife. Even worse, kids saw Adams walk right up to large predators and talk to them as if they were human. When Haggerty

Hugh "Wolverine" Jackman holds the record for playing the same superhero in the most movies: 11.

was later asked about the dangers of his chosen profession, he offered this advice: "Working with a bear, it's like being married. It has its moments. But anything with teeth and claws, be careful."

To see the worst-case scenario of how this mindset can play out, watch the 2005 documentary *Grizzly Man*, about Timothy Treadwell, described by one critic as a "New Age Grizzly Adams with a video camera." Treadwell's attempts to make friends with— and humanize—the grizzly bears in the wilds of Alaska ended up getting him and his girlfriend killed.

THE RETURN OF GRIZZLY ADAMS?

Who knows if *The Life and Times of Grizzly Adams* TV show will see a resurgence in popularity, or if the character will ever be rebooted for modern audiences? That's happened for other shows of the era, such as *Battlestar Galactica* and *Hawaii 5-0*. By the time you're reading this, Adams may already be back. For now, though, the series is available on DVD. So if you want to be transported back to a simpler time, make yourself some flapjacks and gather your family 'round, because Mad Jack sure has a whopper of a tale to tell ya.

Bonus: If someone tries to tell you that Dan Haggerty was the only actor to lose his star on the Hollywood Walk of Fame because of his 1985 cocaine arrest, it's just an urban legend. It came about because of a typo on *Don* Haggerty's star. Don played a lot of cowboys in the 1950s and '60s, but his name was misprinted as "Dan." The name was changed from Dan to Don shortly after Haggerty's arrest, leading to the rumors. In 1994 Dan Haggerty did get a much-deserved star on the Hollywood Walk of Fame.

* * *

A RANDOM BIT OF FACTINESS

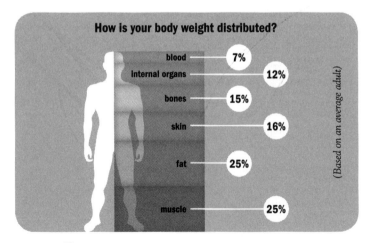

How is your body weight distributed?

blood — 7%

internal organs — 12%

bones — 15%

skin — 16%

fat — 25%

muscle — 25%

(Based on an average adult)

The wooliest sheep on record held 90 pounds of wool.

HERE LIES
THOMAS JEFFERSON

As we learned in the previous installment of "Finding the Founding Fathers" (page 429), the reason Alexander Hamilton wasn't better known (until the musical) was because "his history had very much been written by his enemies." One of those "enemies," Thomas Jefferson, wasn't going to let anyone but himself tell his story…but that's not how it worked out.

THE PROMISE
In Virginia's Blue Ridge Mountains, about 100 miles southwest of Washington, D.C., there's a clearing near the top of a forested hill where a large oak tree once stood. In the 1760s, two college students who'd been best friends since they were children spent many an hour studying together under that tree. They cherished each other and that spot so much that they made a pact: whichever one died first, he would bury the other one under that tree. Today, that spot is known as the Monticello Graveyard.

Compared to the other Founding Fathers' graveyards, this one has the most complicated and at times ugliest history—and it's still unfolding today. But it's impossible to tell the story of the graveyard without telling the story of Monticello.

NATURE BOY
Of all the words used to describe Thomas Jefferson—revolutionary, statesman, writer, architect, inventor—at heart he was a farmer. His agrarian upbringing (his father was a farmer) helped form his belief in a small federal government that gave more rights to the states and to landowners like himself. While serving as the nation's first secretary of state, under President George Washington, Jefferson clashed with Secretary of the Treasury Alexander Hamilton, who, like the president, wanted a strong federal government. It drove a wedge between Washington and Jefferson that would never be resolved. Jefferson's decades-long feud with John Adams, however, did get resolved late in their lives, and the two Founding Fathers famously died on the same day: July 4, 1826—50 years after the Declaration of Independence was signed.

LITTLE MOUNTAIN
Born on April 13, 1743, Jefferson was the third of ten children. After his father died, Thomas, still just a teenager, inherited the family plantation—a 1,000-acre tract of land on rolling green hills overlooking Charlottesville, Virginia—that the family had acquired in 1735. Jefferson called the estate Monticello, an Italian word that translates to "hillock" or "little mountain."

Inspired by Italian Renaissance architect Andrea Palladio, Jefferson started

1970s music artists The Captain and Tennille weren't married when their record label told the world they were (so they got married).

designing his dream home in 1770. He hired the best builders from Charlottesville and used slaves to level the top of a hill and start construction on what would eventually become a 43-room brick mansion with a domed roof and pillared front entry. Because it wasn't completed until 1809, the final year of Jefferson's presidency, historians have called Monticello his "architectural autobiography." (Having trouble picturing this "neoclassical masterpiece in the Palladian style"? Take a look at a nickel—Jefferson's profile is on one side; Monticello is on the other.)

The 1760s and early 1770s were Jefferson's best years, when he and his young wife, Martha Wayles Skelton, started a family. A lawyer by day—he mostly represented slaves suing for their freedom—Jefferson spent his evenings playing music in the parlor (he on violin, Martha on piano). But tragedy was never far off in colonial times, and in 1773, he returned home from a trip to learn that his best friend, Dabney Carr—the one he'd made the burial pact with—had come down with a sudden illness and died. Grief-stricken, Jefferson paid to have his friend's body disinterred from a churchyard and buried under that oak tree. Carr became the Monticello Graveyard's first inhabitant.

RELEASE THE PRISONER

Jefferson took over Carr's legislative seat in the Virginia House of Burgesses, kicking off one of the most celebrated political careers in world history. Just three years later, the rising star would be chosen to pen the first draft of the Declaration of Independence, which included the revolutionary concept that "all men are created equal." Jefferson's checkered history as a slave owner aside, that phrase has been called "the most potent and consequential words in American history."

Now one of the most famous people in the fledgling nation, Jefferson was elected governor of Virginia in 1779. Three years later, his beloved wife Martha, a diabetic, died at 33, a few months after bearing her sixth child in ten years. Thomas never recovered from the heartbreak and, per her request, never remarried, though it's believed that he had a 40-year affair with a slave named Sally Hemings.

After resigning from George Washington's cabinet over political differences (and never speaking to him again), Jefferson was later elected the third U.S. president. His first term brought about the Louisiana Purchase, which doubled the size of the United States. His second term was marred by a failed embargo of British ships that nearly tanked the American economy. In December 1807, Jefferson announced that he would not seek a third term. The day before his successor, James Madison, took office, Jefferson compared his exit from public life to being "a prisoner, released from his chains."

DEFICIT SPENDING

After retiring to Monticello, Jefferson spent much of his time with his daughter Martha, one of only two of his and Martha's children who made it to adulthood. As old age set in, Jefferson kept himself busy inventing things, buying books, writing

You can bring your horse into the Fountain Inn in South Dakota...if it's wearing pants.

letters, buying books, tending to his farms, buying books, entertaining visitors (which he grew tired of), buying books, founding and designing the University of Virginia, buying books, and then selling 6,700 of those books to the Library of Congress to get out of the huge debt he'd acquired after buying so many books. (Not to mention all the money he'd spent remodeling his house over and over, and his failed horticultural projects, including the gardens at Monticello and five other farms in Virginia.) Congress paid Jefferson $23,950 for his book collection, which came at a crucial time because British troops had burned the library's previous collection in the War of 1812.

> **Jefferson was 83 years old and $100,000 in debt—more than $2.5 million in today's money.**

But it wasn't enough. In 1826 Jefferson was 83 years old and $100,000 in debt—more than $2.5 million in today's money. Slowly succumbing to rheumatoid arthritis and various urinary disorders, Jefferson woke up on July 4, 1826, and asked, "Is it the Fourth?" He died a few hours later. Martha had died 44 years earlier, and she was waiting for him in the Monticello Graveyard.

BLUEPRINTS FOR ETERNITY

The day after Jefferson died, he was given a simple funeral with few in attendance (by his own request). At 5:00 that afternoon, with rain falling, he became the family graveyard's 13th inhabitant. But he had no grave marker. Unlike most of the other Founding Fathers, who left behind detailed instructions for their interments, Jefferson was a bit more…scattered. After he was dead and buried, his daughter was going through his bedroom and found "on the torn back of an old letter" some scribbled notes that included his epitaph, along with a crude sketch of his obelisk with little squiggles where the words should go. He began with a philosophical question:

Could the dead feel any interest in monuments or other remembrances of them, when, as Anacreon says,

Oligê de keisometha Konis,
osteôn lythentôn,

the following would be to my manes the most gratifying: on the grave a plain die or cube of three feet without any mouldings, surmounted by an obelisk of six feet height, each of a single stone; on the faces of the obelisk the following inscription, & not a word more:

Here was buried
Thomas Jefferson
Author of the Declaration of American Independence
of the Statute of Virginia for religious freedom
& Father of the University of Virginia

Nutella was invented during WWII—an Italian pastry maker mixed in hazelnuts to make a chocolate ration go farther.

because by these, as testimonials that I have lived, I wish most to be remembered. [It is] to be of the coarse stone of which my columns are made, that no one might be tempted hereafter to destroy it for the value of the materials . . . On the die of the obelisk might be engraved:

Born April 2, 1743 O.S.

Died ___

It's interesting that of the three things Jefferson wished to be remembered for, being president of the United States wasn't one of them. Two other points about his note:

- The verse is by the ancient Greek poet Anacreon, known for his drinking songs and hymns. The full stanza translates to:

> My soul to festive feelings true;
> One pang of envy never knew;
> And little has it learn'd to dread
> The gall that Envy's tongue can shed.

- The "O.S." refers to the Old Style Julian calendar that was in use until Jefferson was a boy. The British added 11 days to their calendar to join the rest of Europe, which was already following the newer Gregorian calendar. So even though the birth date on Jefferson's epitaph is April 2, his birthday is celebrated on April 13.

EVERYTHING MUST GO

Installing Jefferson's obelisk wasn't the family's first priority. If his daughter and her husband couldn't raise enough money to pay off the old man's debts, they'd have to sell Monticello. First to go were Jefferson's 140 slaves, who were sold at public auctions, as were most of Jefferson's possessions and artworks (only his bust of Voltaire remained). In accordance with Jefferson's will, Sally Hemings's children were freed.

By 1831, with all hopes of keeping Monticello in the family dashed, whatever remained was sold off to the highest bidders. Martha and her children moved to Edgehill, her husband Thomas Randolph's estate.

The only part of Monticello that the family didn't have to sell was the graveyard. Jefferson was concerned that if he lost his estate before he died, he would have no place to be buried. So he left the graveyard—and only the graveyard—to the Randolphs. It took Martha seven years to raise the funds for her father's obelisk, which was placed in the graveyard in 1833. It was made by two of Monticello's master carpenters, John M. Perry and James Dinsmore; they tried to follow Jefferson's instructions as best they could. But the epitaph couldn't be carved into the coarse stone that Jefferson had asked for, so it was inscribed onto a marble plaque that was attached to the marker.

Dirtiest place in a bathroom: the floor.

As Jefferson had predicted, trespassers soon started removing chunks from the obelisk, but not for the raw materials—they wanted souvenirs. Before long, the hard edges had been rounded, prematurely aging the rock. Both Thomas and Martha Randolph were dead by 1836, and the care of the graveyard went to their son Jeff Randolph. But he didn't spend much time tending to the cemetery, nor did the man who bought Monticello, and it fell into disrepair.

CHANGING HANDS

The man who purchased Monticello from Jefferson's estate was James Barclay, a 24-year-old Charlottesville druggist whom Martha had referred to as a "madman." Barclay paid $7,500 ($200,000 today) for the 500 acres that remained (out of 5,000). The Jeffersons wanted $20,000, but it was a tough sell. Not only was it located well out of town up a windy wagon road on top of a mountain, but as *Smithsonian* magazine described the main house, such "iconoclastic Jeffersonian details as narrow staircases and ill-defined bedrooms struck some well-heeled Virginia couples as the enemy of gracious living."

Barclay didn't care about preserving the history of the house or the graveyard, and he didn't like the former president or his politics. After tearing out most of the poplar trees and gardens that Jefferson had so lovingly tended, Barclay put in a grove of mulberry trees and tried to turn Monticello into a silkworm farm. His plan failed, and he put the land up for auction in 1833, after owning it for only three years. All it would take was for one more unscrupulous buyer to erase Monticello from history.

THE COMMODORE

Luckily, Jefferson had some friends in high places, including one he'd never met, a retired U.S. Navy commodore named Uriah Phillips Levy. A century earlier, Levy's Jewish ancestors had escaped religious persecution in the Old World and settled in the Georgia colony. Now a wealthy real estate developer, Levy credited his own prosperity to Jefferson's struggle for religious freedom—including his rise to become the U.S. Navy's first Jewish commodore after making a name for himself in the War of 1812.

Levy wanted to fund construction of a life-size bronze statue of Jefferson inside the U.S. Capitol. He was in France in 1833, where he visited the Marquis de Lafayette, a 75-year-old Frenchman who'd been Jefferson's close friend and compatriot in the Revolutionary War. Lafayette agreed to donate his portrait of Jefferson to the sculptor, and asked Levy what had become of "the most beautiful house in America." Levy said he had never been to Monticello, but that he would check on it as soon as he was able.

MONEY PIT

A year later, Uriah Levy's bronze Jefferson statue was put on display in the U.S. Capitol rotunda, where it still is today (two floors above George Washington's empty tomb). In 1836 Levy (whose other claim to fame was his successful campaign to end flogging as a punishment in the navy) set his sights on buying Monticello. Barclay had already sold off a lot of the land, and various disputes and lawsuits delayed the sale for another two years. When Levy finally took over ownership—for $2,700—the land was overgrown and the house was falling apart. But Levy didn't care. "My heart leaped," he reportedly told friends. Now considered one of America's first historical preservationists, Levy began the arduous task of restoring Monticello. One of the first things he did was to take the plaque bearing Jefferson's epitaph into the house before someone stole it. Trespassers were helping themselves to Jefferson's obelisk chunk by chunk.

In 1838 Colonel Jeff Randolph (Jefferson's grandson) took possession of the plaque and put up a nine-foot-tall brick wall around the graveyard. He left a gap in the wall next to Jefferson's obelisk so people could view it through an iron fence. After Jefferson's daughter, Martha, died that same year, Colonel Randolph buried her in the grave next to Jefferson's mother's. Randolph's wall did little to deter the vandals, though, and by the time the Civil War rolled around, Monticello Graveyard was in near ruins. Here's a description from an 1861 article in the *Charleston Mercury*:

> You climb, and climb, and climb...until you unexpectedly emerge in a small clearing around which a somewhat dilapidated, square brick wall runs. The iron gate is open, and as you enter, the eye glancing over a dozen or more marble slabs and head-stones rests on a granite pyramid, supported by a block of the same material, rudely hewn and blackened with age, which you know at once to be Jefferson's tomb.

'TIL THE COWS COME HOME

Back at the house, Commodore Levy had been making progress in his restoration, but he was slowed by old age and mired in a struggle with his heirs over who would inherit the estate. In his will, Levy bequeathed Monticello to "the people of the United States for the sole purpose of establishing an agricultural school." But while his children were fighting over who'd get the land, the Civil War broke out and the Confederate government seized control of Monticello—which was in Virginia, a Southern slave state—and put it up for sale.

Confederate colonel Benjamin Franklin Ficklin paid $80,500 in Confederate money for the property. (Prior to the war, Ficklin helped start the Pony Express, a mail service that greatly sped up transcontinental communication.) During the Civil War, he used the house as a convalescent home for wounded rebel soldiers. In the wintertime, it was used to keep cattle warm, and the upstairs bedrooms of Monticello were used to store grain. An 1864 *New York Times* article decried, "Shame! Shame upon our thoughtless countrymen. Why should they be so disrespectful to the

Civil War general Robert E. Lee traveled with a pet chicken, Nellie.
It laid the eggs he ate for breakfast.

sepulcher of the great patriot of the Revolution?" (After the war, Ficklin was arrested for assassinating President Abraham Lincoln—and later freed after the capture of John Wilkes Booth.)

NOBODY HOME

The Confederacy's defeat put the ownership of Monticello into question, and several of Levy's heirs tried to claim it as theirs. As the legal battles dragged on, no one lived at Monticello for the next 17 years. And it showed. "The windows are broken," Congressman Augustus Albert Hardenbergh (D-NJ) lamented to Congress after visiting the estate in 1878. "The room in which Jefferson died is darkened; all around it are the evidences of desolation and decay." He proposed that the federal government claim ownership of the estate. But then, in 1879, another congressman, Jefferson Monroe Levy (D-NY)—Uriah's nephew—bought out the rest of his family and took sole ownership. He paid $10,000, the equivalent of $240,000 today. And he would end up living at Monticello longer than Thomas Jefferson did.

> ### A TIP FROM UNCLE JOHN
>
> Are you planning to renovate your old house? You don't have to do what Thomas Jefferson did and spend several decades and most of your fortune to do it. According to *Mother Nature Network*, one way to save on home renovations is to make what's old new again. For example, instead of spending thousands on brand-new furniture, go to thrift stores and yard sales and buy beat-up old couches and chairs. Then spend a few hundred to have them refurbished and reupholstered. Another tip: If your home's hardwood floors are scratched or faded, it's less expensive to restore the hardwood than to replace it. And "original hardwood floors" will increase your home's resale value.

Levy made it clear from the get-go that he had no intention of selling Monticello, and he continued his late uncle's mission to restore it. Within a decade, the estate was looking much more like its former self. And Congress tried once again to buy it. The answer was still no. Levy was using Monticello as a summer home, and when he was home, he charged a 50¢ entrance fee to anyone who wanted to view the house. (He reportedly gave the money to Charlottesville charities.)

When Congress was unable to obtain Monticello, it set its sights on the graveyard. The plan: turn it into a national monument. Jefferson's heirs, which now exceeded 50, weren't interested. Nor was Levy. He owned the land surrounding the cemetery, and although he allowed visitors into Monticello, the graveyard was off limits to all but the Jeffersons.

THE OBELISK GOES SOUTH

But even though it couldn't own Jefferson's grave site, in 1878 Congress passed a resolution to pay for the restoration of the crumbling obelisk, along with a stronger wall to protect the graveyard. Unfortunately, the coarse stone monument was in such poor condition that it couldn't be repaired, so Congress reallocated the funds to replace it with a brand-new monument that was built exactly to Jefferson's specifications (right down to the "O.S."). One difference: the replacement obelisk is nearly twice as tall.

As for the old one, Jefferson's heirs gave it to the University of Missouri in 1883, along with the original plaque. It's not exactly clear why the gravestone ended up there, but it does make sense in one way, because the University of Missouri was the first college to be founded in the states that President Jefferson had acquired in the Louisiana Purchase. The obelisk and plaque were initially put on display on campus, but time was taking its toll on them, so they spent most of their 130 years at the university in a storage room. By 2013 they were so in danger of crumbling away into nothing that the Smithsonian Institution offered—at no cost to the school—to restore the headstone and plaque. The project took two years of painstaking work to complete. Today, the plaque is once again firmly attached to the obelisk, which you can find on campus in the Jefferson Garden.

EMINENT DOMAIN

In 1912 Maud Wilson Littleton, the wife of New York congressman Martin Littleton, had dinner at Monticello and was aghast to discover that the pictures on the walls were of the Levy family. "I did not get the feeling," she later wrote, "of being in the house Thomas Jefferson built and loved and made sacred." Littleton, or "the Lady of Monticello" as the newspapers called her, mounted a massive public campaign to wrestle Monticello away from the Levy family. It was a campaign that had, as the *Washington Post* described it, "a strong subtext of anti-Semitism." Referring to Levy as "greedy and unpatriotic," Littleton published pamphlets that accused the owners of letting Monticello "fall into ruin" (a lie that she later recanted).

Jefferson Levy countered that he was indeed caring for Thomas Jefferson's legacy, a big part of which was honoring the rights of landowners. The three-term congressman wasn't about to let the government take it from his family by eminent domain. At a contentious congressional hearing, Littleton testified that Uriah Levy's will bequeathed Monticello "to the people of the United States." She displayed photographs of the overgrown graveyard and said the Jefferson family rarely ever visited it. (The Jeffersons were firmly on the side of Levy.)

Levy's colleague, Senator Albert Cummins of Iowa, was on Littleton's side, and issued this threat: "When we build a railroad, if we find it necessary to take a man's property, we can take it by condemnation proceedings. And if the government of the United States wants Monticello, it can take it."

A joint resolution to take Monticello by eminent domain barely failed, and Levy had won round one. "When the White House is for sale," he said, "then I will consider an offer for Monticello." But Littleton didn't let up. She set up "campaign

Pringles flavors available outside the U.S.: blueberry hazelnut, prawn, and turkey.

headquarters" in New York City, and enlisted some big names to her cause, including President Woodrow Wilson.

As the years wore on, Levy eased up on his stance—and even considered an offer to turn Monticello into a presidential retreat, like Camp David in Maryland. Then World War I put everything on hold. By the end of the war, Levy's fortune was dwindling, and he offered up Monticello for $500,000, half of its estimated worth. A year before his death in 1923, Levy sold Monticello to a newly formed nonprofit group, the Thomas Jefferson Foundation. Sixty years later in 1985, a ceremony was held there honoring the Levy family, without whom Monticello might not have survived the 19th century.

THE GRAVE SITE TODAY

The work that the Levys had done on the house was admirable, but it would take a lot more to restore it to its condition of 1809. Today, a century after taking over Monticello, the Thomas Jefferson Foundation reports that more than 440,000 people visit every year, quite a feat considering the historic landmark's remote location. (George Washington's Mount Vernon, in the suburbs of D.C., gets more than a million visitors a year.)

From the visitor center, just a short drive up a windy road out of Charlottesville, you can take a shuttle bus the rest of the way to Monticello, or you can walk (it's half a mile). From the top of the mountain, you can look out on rolling green hills that look much as they did when Monticello was being built. A short walk from the house takes you to the base of stone steps that lead up to an iron gate with a placard that says, "This Graveyard Plot is the Private Property of Thomas Jefferson's Descendants."

You can't get close enough to touch the headstone, but you can toss a nickel through the gate. On the base of the platform, directly beneath Jefferson's epitaph, is an inscription for his daughter Martha. Also buried in the plot are Jefferson's wife Martha, another daughter, and his son-in-law. The 0.75-acre graveyard now contains more than 225 people, and three to four more are interred there each year. They're either related to Jefferson, or to someone with a connection to the family. (Several descendants of Jefferson's friend Dabney Carr are buried there.) But there is one group of people who cannot be buried at Monticello, though they're trying to change that.

THE RETURN OF SALLY HEMINGS

In 1998 the scientific journal *Nature* published the results of DNA tests that concluded there is a "high probability" that Thomas Jefferson was "the father of Eston Hemings, and that he was likely the father of all six of Sally Hemings's children listed in Monticello records." But there's also a slight chance the father was Thomas Jefferson's younger brother, Randolph. That's one of the reasons the Monticello Association, a group of Jefferson's descendants that maintains the graveyard, won't allow any of Sally Hemings's descendants to be buried there. The other reason is that they don't believe Thomas Jefferson would have done something like that. In 2002 they released a statement:

> The Monticello Association's 67-5 decision not to admit the Hemings was not based on race, as some have asserted. It would have been shockingly out of character for Jefferson to have sexually exploited a 13- or 14-year-old child whom he owned and to conduct such a relationship under the eyes of his daughters and his 11 grandchildren. In his Notes on the State of Virginia, he singled out for particular criticism the sexual exploitation of slave women, which he described as "unremitting despotism" by the master and "degrading submissions" by the victim. He condemned in particular the effect of such behavior on the master's children.

The Monticello Association has proposed building a second cemetery at Monticello for the Hemings family. But the Thomas Jefferson Foundation, Inc., which has been in charge of the rest of the property since 1923, has accepted the results of the DNA test. After a 25-year campaign, in 2018 the Sally Hemings exhibit opened at Monticello in the room where she and her brother most likely lived. For more than a century prior to that, it was used as a bathroom.

Another group called the Thomas Jefferson Heritage Society actively disputes the DNA test results, and claims that the Monticello Society has bowed to "political correctness" by including the Hemings exhibit.

CHANGING TIMES

In February 2019, a Caucasian man named Lucian Truscott and an African American man named Shannon Lanier appeared together on CBS *This Morning*. Both men are direct descendants of Thomas Jefferson, the former from Jefferson's marriage to Martha, the latter from Jefferson's 40-year relationship with Sally Hemings. "I don't want to be buried there," said Lanier, "but I should have a right to be buried there." He said he's pleased that Truscott and some other descendants of Martha Jefferson have welcomed Sally's family. The two sides "have been loving and knowing each other… as cousins." But he said there's still work to be done. "When we get to a point where… the sons of former slaves and the sons of former slave owners can sit down at the table of brotherhood and reconciliation, and be buried together, then times have changed." As it stands today, however, the graveyard is off-limits to them. The location of Sally's grave is unknown, which is the case for just about all of the 600 slaves who lived at Monticello while Jefferson was alive.

The fact that the Hemings story is still making headlines is yet another indication that the Founding Fathers' stories are still unfolding. And those stories probably won't be over as long as the country they founded survives. At that point, the only evidence that they ever existed in the first place may be their tombstones.

No one has ever won the video game *Missile Command*. It's impossible: the creator was inspired by Cold War–era "Mutually Assured Destruction."

ANSWERS

TRIVIA NIGHT (Answers for page 163)

1. There are no words that rhyme with *panther, purple, wolf, twelfth,* and *toilet.*

2. Necco Wafers. When Admiral Robert Byrd led an expedition to Antarctica in the 1930s, he brought 2.5 tons of Necco Wafers because they wouldn't spoil during the long journey. The New England Confectionery Company that made the wafers declared bankruptcy in 2018.

3. The U.S. Air Force. Originally called the Army Air Corps, it was part of the U.S. Army until shortly after World War II.

4. The hyoid is the only bone that isn't connected to any other bone. It anchors the tongue above the larynx. If a forensic investigator determines that this bone has been broken, the cause of death is most likely strangulation.

5. Michael and Jessica were the most popular baby names in the 1980s and 1990s, and then Jacob and Emily took over in the 2000s.

6. Professional wrestling. Born Peter Hernandez in 1985, when Mars was two, his father thought he looked like Bruno Sammartino (1935–2018), heavyweight champion of the WWF (World Wrestling Federation) in the 1960s and '70s. Since 2002, the organization has been called WWE (World Wrestling Entertainment, Inc.).

7. A farrier puts horseshoes onto horses.

8. The golden idol that Indiana Jones steals from a South American temple at the beginning of 1981's *Raiders of the Lost Ark.* It's based on a real artifact supposedly depicting the Aztec goddess Tlazolteotl during childbirth.

9. California, with approximately 4.7 million pickup trucks. Texas has 4.2 million.

10. Indonesia. This archipelago made up of more than 17,000 islands has a population of 261 million, making it the world's third largest democracy.

11. Pink. Albinism—the absence of any pigmentation or coloration—can affect mammals, birds, reptiles, amphibians, and fish. In all cases, their eyes are pink.

12. "I'm a Believer," written by Neil Diamond and sung by Micky Dolenz, was released in 1966 and became the best-selling single of 1967. That's the year "Daydream Believer," written by John Stewart of the Kingston Trio and sung by Davy Jones, became the Monkees' last #1 hit.

13. Nicki Minaj and Mariah Carey. Carey gave Minaj a career boost by letting her sing a verse on a remix of her hit song, "Up Out My Face," in 2010, but their relationship would soon erode.

14. Dom Perignon (1638–1715), a Benedictine monk from Hautvillers in northern France.

15. Uranus.

16. The Hague. According to the country's constitution, the actual capital of the Netherlands is Amsterdam.

17. Hummus. Dating back as far as the 13th century, hummus is short for *hummus bi tahina,* an Arabic dish meaning "chickpeas with tahini."

18. There are three teaspoons in a tablespoon.

THE TV DETECTIVE WITH SOMETHING EXTRA (Answers for page 172)

1. e; **2.** f; **3.** b; **4.** i; **5.** c; **6.** l; **7.** q; **8.** g; **9.** a; **10.** n; **11.** s; **12.** d; **13.** m; **14.** r; **15.** t; **16.** j; **17.** o; **18.** h; **19.** k; **20.** p

SEMORDNILAP! (Answers for page 222)

1. Dennis, sinned
2. Drawer, reward
3. Dog, god
4. Faced, decaf
5. Live, evil
6. Spools, sloops
7. Sleep, peels
8. Ward, draw
9. Room, moor
10. Naps, span
11. Pals, slap
12. Bonk, knob
13. Stressed, desserts
14. Warts, straw
15. Mined, denim
16. Snoops, spoons
17. Bats, stab
18. Time, emit
19. Wonk, know
20. But, tub
21. Tug, gut
22. Top, pot

THE COUNTRY MUSIC GEOGRAPHY QUIZ (Answers for page 375)

1. Wichita
2. Amarillo
3. Georgia
4. El Paso
5. Jackson
6. Muskogee
7. Oklahoma
8. Phoenix
9. Fort Worth
10. Bakersfield
11. Chattanooga
12. Montgomery
13. Tulsa
14. Kentucky
15. Texas
16. Lubbock
17. Texas
18. Santa Fe
19. Mississippi
20. Arkansas
21. Cheyenne

When young, it's a luffa and you can eat it. When old, it's a loofah and you scrub with it.

We are pleased to offer over 135 e-book versions of Portable Press titles—some currently available only in digital format! Visit *www.portablepress.com* to collect them all!

A blue whale's heart beats about 8 times a minute.

The last U.S. Navy battleship, the *Missouri*, was decommissioned in 1992.

THE LAST PAGE

FELLOW BATHROOM READERS:

The fight for good bathroom reading should never be taken loosely—we must do our duty and sit firmly for what we believe in, even while the rest of the world is taking potshots at us.

We'll be brief. Now that we've proven we're not simply a flush-in-the-pan, we invite you to take the plunge: Sit Down and Be Counted! To find out what the BRI is up to, visit us at *www.portablepress.com* and take a peek!

GET CONNECTED

Find us online to sign up for our email list, enter exciting giveaways, hear about new releases, and more!

🌐 Website: www.portablepress.com

f Facebook: www.facebook.com/portablepress

Ⓟ Pinterest: www.pinterest.com/portablepress

🐦 Twitter: @Portablepress

Well, we're out of space, and when you've gotta go, you've gotta go. Tanks for all your support. Hope to hear from you soon.

Meanwhile, remember…

Keep on flushin'!

If you feel like you need to go number two but then nothing comes out, that's called *tenesmus*.

"All truths are easy to understand once they are discovered; the point is to discover them." —Galileo

—Marlo Thomas. "The truth is what is, not what should be. What sh

Sometimes he will even tell the truth." —Patrick Murray. "Facts don't care a

is a revolutionary act." —George Orwell. "Delete the adjectives and y

—Uncle John. "Truth is such a rare thing, it is delightful to tell it." —Emily Dickinson. " Humor is al

"All we want are the facts, ma'am." —Sgt. Joe Friday. "The truth...is a beautiful an

"Whoever undertakes to set himself up as a judge of Truth and Knowledge i

how come no one has their hair done in the library?" —Lily Tomlin. "

hide." —Ice Cube. "Truth is like the sun. You can shut it out for a time, but it ain'

to prove anything that's even remotely true." —Homer Simpso

"Never face facts; if you do, you'll never get up in the morning." —

a dirty lie." —Lenny Bruce. "A lawyer will do anything to win a case. Sometin

—Ben Shapiro. "In an age of universal deceit, telling the truth is a revolution

—Harper Lee. "If the truth is buried, be the shovel." —Uncle John. "Tr

truth. Ever heard a joke about a father-in-law?" —Dick Clark. "All we want are the fa

therefore be treated with great caution." —J. K. Rowling. "Whoever undertake

of the gods." —Albert Einstein. "If truth is beauty, how come no one he

When the truth comes around, all the lies have to run and hide." —Ice Cube. "

"Facts are meaningless. You could use facts to prove anythi

once they are discovered; the point is to discover them." —Galileo Galilei. "Never face facts; if

is what is, not what should be. What should be is a dirty lie." —Lenn

truth." —Patrick Murray. "Facts don't care about your feelings." —Ben S

—George Orwell. "Delete the adjectives and you'll have the facts." —

thing, it is delightful to tell it." —Emily Dickinson. " Humor is always based on a modicum of truth

—Sgt. Joe Friday. "The truth...is a beautiful and terrible thing, and should th

himself up as a judge of Truth and Knowledge is shipwrecked by the laug

their hair done in the library?" —Lily Tomlin. "Truth is the ultimate

"Truth is like the sun. You can shut it out for a time, but it ain't goin' away." —Elvis

that's even remotely true." —Homer Simpson. "All truths are easy to unders

do, you'll never get up in the morning." —Marlo Thomas. "The trut

"A lawyer will do anything to win a case. Sometimes he will even tell the tru

age of universal deceit, telling the truth is a revolutionary act." —George